Design and Analysis Methods for Fish Survival Experiments Based on Release-Recapture

Kenneth P. Burnham

Department of Statistics
North Carolina State University, Raleigh, North Carolina 27695

David R. Anderson

Colorado Cooperative Fish and Wildlife Research Unit
Colorado State University, Fort Collins, Colorado 80523

Gary C. White

Department of Fishery and Wildlife Biology
Colorado State University, Fort Collins, Colorado 80523

Cavell Brownie and **Kenneth H. Pollock**

Department of Statistics
North Carolina State University, Raleigh, North Carolina 27695

American Fisheries Society Monograph 5
ISSN 0362-1715

Bethesda, Maryland
1987

Publication and Funding of this Monograph
were made possible by a grant from

Chelan County Public Utility District

Wenatchee, Washington   98801

American Fisheries Society Monographs: ISSN 0362-1715
Library of Congress Catalog Card Number: 87-070785
ISBN 0-913235-41-5

Contents

CONTENTS

CONTENTS

CONTENTS

CONTENTS

CONTENTS

CONTENTS

Preface

This monograph presents design and analysis methods for a large class of survival experiments based on release-recapture of marked populations. We developed the underlying theory primarily to address fishery issues involving spillways, hydroelectric turbines, bypass systems, and related structures on the Columbia River in the northwestern United States. Many other applications exist, however. Treatment might include dosing of lead or various pesticides to determine the chronic effect of a contaminant on survival. The general theory is for the analysis of multiple interrelated release-recapture data sets; the methods presented herein apply to any experiments involving treatment and control groups of marked animals.

During the past 20 to 25 years, much literature has appeared on the estimation of population parameters based on capture-recapture sampling. One branch of the literature includes bird-banding and fish-tagging studies where the data are from a single, terminal, harvest-related recovery, as synthesized by Brownie et al. (1985). During the same time period, other literature appeared on studies dealing with multiple recaptures of marked animals, often referred to as capture-recapture sampling for open populations, or "Jolly-Seber models" after two of the leading contributors. Seber (1982) reviewed this literature. The links between these two major developments were outlined by Brownie et al. (1985) and Brownie and Pollock (1985).

A general theory for ecological experiments and studies in which marked animals are used relies on both of the above bodies of literature plus other developments (e.g., White et al. 1982). Overall, this subject and the literature on which it is based are fairly complex and diverse. Until recently, the separate approaches and models were developed in isolation, usually using different literature, notation, and context. In the past 10 years a coalescing of this work has led to the recognition that most "capture-recapture" models are special cases of a more general theory. Today, the entire area of capture-recapture is being unified under one umbrella of theory, which provides the context for the developments we present here.

As an example of progress in the theory and computation for capture-recapture sampling, one might consider the analysis done by Hammersley (1953), who presented a method for estimating the death rate in open-population models and applied it to data on the alpine swift *Apus melba* banded in Switzerland during 1920-1950. His estimation method involved a 28 x 28 matrix and a complex iterative process. Minor iterative cycles were embedded in major cycles and were done on a desk calculator. Approximately six major cycles were required for the swift data, and each required about 10 days of hand computation. The inversion of the matrix required about 4 hours of SEAC computer time (at the U.S. National Bureau of Standards). Hammersley estimated that this inversion could have been done in "about 2 months" on a desk calculator. In summary, Hammersley's method required about

100 person-days of computation on desk calculators of the day for this large data set.

Biologists now enjoy the sophisticated formalism of the Jolly-Seber model and the many extensions and restrictions that have been published in the past 21 years. The Jolly-Seber method itself also benefited from the work of Hammersley (see Cormack 1968). Many Jolly-Seber models have parameter estimators in closed form, and estimates can be computed in a few minutes on a calculator if the data are summarized in a suitable form. Monte Carlo studies have investigated the small-sample properties of the Jolly-Seber class of models, and much is now known about the analysis theory of capture-recapture sampling data. The improved models and theory are accompanied by tremendous advances in computer technology. Commonly available desktop computers now can fully analyze the alpine swift data in about 20 seconds of computer time.

Program RELEASE, which can be run on IBM-compatible microcomputers, was developed to allow biologists to focus on design, data collection, analysis, and inference, rather than on computational details. This software is powerful and easy to use, but it can be misused if the material in this monograph is not understood. To avoid potential misuse, we encourage understanding and careful consideration of the material in this monograph (the Reader's Guide in Section 1.1.5 should prove useful). We hope readers will examine the theory and examples to gain familiarity with the basis of the methods presented. Practice running program RELEASE with example data sets would be helpful in understanding some of the issues covered. Readers are encouraged to compare theory and application and gain familiarity with the Monte Carlo features of the software.

Additional research and applications should be stimulated by this monograph. Biologists and statisticians need to work together more closely to ensure that additional well-designed, empirical studies result. We hope to see the various research findings published in refereed, primary journals. The lack of publication in primary journals has been a problem in the past (e.g., Fletcher 1985), as much of the fisheries research on the Columbia River has appeared in the gray literature.

The material in this monograph can be understood by persons with two or three upper division courses in statistics and some elementary computer skills. The less background one has in these subjects, the more one may have to struggle. The main prerequisites are an interest in the topic, an interest in science and experimentation, and a curiosity about sound and thorough inference procedures.

We express our sincere thanks to the Chelan County Public Utility District, Wenatchee, Washington, for funding the research that led to the publication of this monograph. The District was both unselfish and extremely farsighted in allocating funds to develop rigorous design and analysis methods for this class of experiments.

Part 1. Introduction

1.1. Introduction

In this monograph we present the statistical theory and its application for experiments to estimate survival probabilities (rates) of fish passing through hydroelectric dams and spillways in the Columbia River in the northwestern United States. The application of the methods developed here is more general, however, as it includes experiments to estimate survival of fish as they pass over spillways or through bypass systems and several dams. Additionally, this class of experiments includes studies on many vertebrate populations in which marked animals in control and treatment (dosage) groups are compared. We do not concentrate on these extensions, for they are special cases of the general methodology presented here, but we will illustrate them with some examples.

Fish release programs designed to estimate survival rates have been conducted on the Columbia River for several decades. In the associated literature and reports, little statistical formalism underlies the design or analysis of these research programs. Development of sampling (i.e., statistical) models should be an intrinsic part of knowledge acquisition, opinion, and belief formation (Hacking 1965; Kempthorne and Folks 1971).

1.1.1. Simple Example

A hypothetical example will illustrate a simple survival study and introduce the (often) more complex experiments to be addressed later. Consider a team of fisheries biologists concerned with the survival of young steelhead *Salmo gairdneri* as they pass through turbines in a hydroelectric dam on a large river. As has been the practice for many years, large numbers of hatchery-reared fish are marked and about half are released (releases = R) above the dam into the turbine intakes (let this number be R_{t1}) while the other half are released below the dam in the tailrace area (let this number be R_{c1}). The marks are different for the two groups: t = treatment and c = control. The releases are made at dam 1, and some fish are recaptured at three downstream dams (dams 2, 3, and 4). Let m_{ti} and m_{ci} be the number of treatment and control fish, respectively, recaptured at downstream dam i ($i = 2, 3, 4$). These data can be represented symbolically and numerically as:

Treatment group	Released at dam 1	Recaptured at		
		dam 2	dam 3	dam 4
t	$R_{t1} = 10{,}000$	$m_{t2} = 390$	$m_{t3} = 480$	$m_{t4} = 83$
c	$R_{c1} = 9{,}000$	$m_{c2} = 412$	$m_{c3} = 530$	$m_{c4} = 83.$

For simplicity, we assume that once a fish is captured at one of the three downstream dams, it is removed from the study and not rereleased. The recapture data thus come from a sample of the marked cohorts initially released.

How can we then estimate the survival rate (S) through the turbine from data such as these? The ratio of the two recapture rates at the first downstream dam is an estimate of the survival rate:

$$(m_{t2}/R_{t1})/(m_{c2}/R_{c1}) = (390/10{,}000)/(412/9{,}000) = 0.852.$$

Assuming passage through the turbine has no effect on downstream fish behavior, this estimator is essentially unbiased but it is inefficient because it does not use all the data relevant to estimation of the survival parameters. Likewise, the separate estimators, based only on data from dams 3 or 4,

$$(m_{t3}/R_{t1})/(m_{c3}/R_{c1}) = (480/10{,}000)/(530/9{,}000) = 0.815$$

and

$$(m_{t4}/R_{t1})/(m_{c4}/R_{c1}) = (83/10{,}000)/(83/9{,}000) = 0.900 \, ,$$

are poor for the same reason. One might try to pool the data, by weighting each of these three estimators, to get an improved estimator of survival. Equal weights might be desirable; however, one could weight the three estimates by the total number of fish captured, or by the number of treatment or control fish captured. Other ways of pooling data are also possible.

Without a formal theory underlying this class of studies, it is impossible to proceed in a rigorous manner. Lacking the necessary basis of a stochastic theoretical model, it is equally difficult to estimate the theoretical precision associated with estimates of survival rate. A proper estimator of the sampling variance is important as a measure of an estimator's precision or repeatability. A number of assumptions must be made in studies of this type, and these assumptions must be stated clearly because they form the basis for a model. Goodness-of-fit tests must be derived in an effort to assess the validity of the assumptions. Finally, one must know the degree to which an estimator of survival rate is sensitive to the partial failure of particular assumptions.

Because intuition was of little help in deriving an estimator and its sampling variance in the simple example, a rigorous approach is required for the more complex cases encountered in real life. These cases include studies in which (1) fish captured at downstream dams are released alive for potential second or third captures, (2) more than one treatment is involved (e.g., three release groups), (3) fish are released with unique tag numbers instead of simple batch marks, (4) fish size is used as a covariate, (5) several replicate releases (lots) are involved, and (6) survival is estimated for several dams and reservoirs in a long reach of the river. We attempt here to establish the analysis and inference theory for this general class of experiments.

This class of experiments is inherently difficult to treat. Unlike more standard experiments (e.g., agricultural field trials), these survival experiments allow less control by the investigators because fish are highly mobile animals whose behavior is poorly understood. Further, the use of sampling methods to reobserve the marked animals imposes substantial complexities. Important assumptions are required, and statistical tests must be made to assess carefully the validity of these assumptions. The fundamental concepts and analysis methods applied here are not trivial.

1.1.2. Historical Note

As our methodological research progressed, we found much existing theory in the scientific literature related directly to the estimation and testing of concern here. Existing theory falls under two broad categories. The first category is band or tag recovery studies, such as the one outlined in Section 1.1.1, where known releases of fish are followed by the removal of recaptured fish from the population upon first capture. The theory for this class of studies dates back to the early 1970s (Seber 1970; Robson and Youngs, unpublished report, 1971) (but see also Seber 1962); much of it was synthesized and extended by the two editions of the handbook of Brownie et al. (1978, 1985). Second, part of the existing theory for the so-called Jolly-Seber model (Jolly 1965; Seber 1965, 1982) was found to be relevant for the problems presented herein in which fish captured at downstream dams are released alive for possible subsequent recapture. In the context of this work, however, we cannot estimate population size or numbers of new recruits (which is possible under the Jolly-Seber framework: e.g., Hightower and Gilbert 1984) because it requires data on, and additional assumptions about, the unmarked members of the population. Brownie et al. (1985) summarized the large literature on Jolly-Seber models. Our primary focus is survival probability within the context of a treatment. We present a series of models, hypothesis tests, and sampling protocols that allow a treatment survival rate to be estimated and evaluated.

These two broad approaches to sampling marked populations are closely related. We have exploited this relationship in the present work, while extending the methodology to enable experiments on marked populations that lead to the assessment of a treatment survival rate. Technical discussions of these relationships were given by Brownie and Robson (1983), Brownie and Pollock (1985), and Brownie et al. (1985:170-175).

Many persons think of the field of statistics in terms of simple t and chi-square tests, analysis of variance, regression, and other such methods. In fact, the field is far broader than is suggested by the data analysis methods taught in beginning statistics courses. The field of statistics is not so much a branch of mathematics as it is an area of science concerned with the development of a practical theory of information (White et al. 1982:14). Statistics is primarily concerned with efficient methods of collecting data and establishing rigorous foundations for deriving efficient methods of making inductive inferences from sample data, and it is an integral part of the *scientific method*.

The conclusions drawn from sample data are intended to apply beyond the specific study or experiment. Biologists wish to make generalizations – "inductive inferences" – from a specific study to the population that was sampled. A theorem in logic states that there is uncertainty in inductive inference and that perfect generalizations therefore cannot be made about a population from studying only the sample. However, the degree of uncertainty can be measured if the experiment was performed in accordance with certain scientific principles (Mood et al. 1974). A critical function of the science of statistics is to provide a formalism for making inductive inferences and for measuring their degree of uncertainty (Ostle 1963).

1.1.3. Objectives

The present work is the culmination of several initial objectives. Our overall objective is to present a comprehensive statistical theory to support survival experiments that rely on recapture data collected after release of marked individuals. By an experiment, we explicitly mean at least two treatment levels, i.e., releases of "treatment" and "control" groups (the individuals are marked to reflect what group they are in), with the purpose of comparing results across treatment levels. The methodology developed here addresses both batch and unique marks, more than one treatment, and several other extensions. A series of experimental protocols is defined and maximum-likelihood estimators of parameters are given for each situation. Sampling variances and covariances are given as measures of precision and interdependency, respectively, for parameter estimators.

A second objective deals with hypothesis tests involving various models and assumptions about certain parameters. The interpretation of the test results allows the selection of a proper model for a particular experiment.

In principle, the theory is not complex, but computational details are tedious. Thus, a third objective is to demonstrate the ability of our interactive data analysis computer program RELEASE, which allows biologists to concentrate on the interpretation of experimental results rather than on computational matters. In addition, we wanted to produce a comprehensive monograph giving the relevant background, theory, and application in a way that would be useful to biologists conducting survival experiments. Our monograph illustrates the broad applicability of the underlying theory beyond studies of fish survival and provides an opportunity to illustrate the methods with output from program RELEASE.

Another important objective is to illustrate the performance of the various procedures with sample sizes and recovery rates typically encountered in practice. Therefore, Monte Carlo studies were performed to evaluate bias, confidence interval coverage, robustness, and power of tests. Capabilities for further Monte Carlo studies are incorporated into program RELEASE, allowing the user to study a particular situation.

Our final objective is to outline the design and sample-size requirements for release-recapture survival experiments. In particular, we consider the need for replication in survival studies and provide ways to treat these data in the analysis.

1.1.4. Reader's Guide

We believe everyone should read Part 1 because Part 1 provides background and the notation required for understanding the parts that follow. Persons with good statistical skills could bypass Chapter 1.2 on Statistical Concepts. The concepts in Part 1 are kept at a fairly elementary level, with the exception of Chapter 1.5. We recommend the use of program RELEASE as a learning tool. The data given in Chapter 1.3 are used in many places throughout the monograph. Interpretation of the program output enhances the rate of understanding, especially in becoming familiar with the different models and protocols.

Chapter 2.1 in Part 2 contains difficult material. However, we urge the reader to gain some insight into the concepts given. Chapters 2.2., 2.3, 2.4, and 2.5 are parallel in that they cover the four major sampling protocols. Each of these four chapters contains examples to aid in understanding the analysis theory presented; however, an understanding of Part 1 is assumed. The material in Part 2 deals with experiments involving one treatment and one control. We urge all readers to read at least Chapters 2.1, 2.2, and 2.4. Parts 1 and 2 of this work are written in the context of fish experiments and studies involving large hydroelectric dams. Other parts are less specific, to allow the reader to think more generally about experimental animals and sampling sites or occasions rather than only about fish and dams.

Part 3 is optional reading for biologists, unless their interest lies in more elaborate experiments involving two or more treatments and single or multiple control groups. Understanding Parts 1 and 2 is required to understand Part 3. In contrast, statisticians may want to scan the general theory presented in Part 3 before examining the various special cases given in later chapters.

The subject of replication in Part 4 is essential reading for all user groups. In particular, those considering the design of experiments should understand the need for replication. Biologists may want to postpone reading Part 5, but statisticians probably will want to consider this material in detail.

Part 6 relates to experimental design, and anyone contemplating this problem should find useful suggestions here. However, we caution the reader that only statistical features are stressed in Part 6; biological aspects of these experiments are not provided.

In Part 7, we examine some case studies in an attempt to provide insight into the generality of the methods developed here, and extend the coverage to other vertebrates. We urge all readers to study these examples.

Part 8 is for readers who have a good understanding of the preceding material. Part 8 is not meant to be complete; it is only a brief introduction to some of the extensions that are possible to develop.

Anyone expecting to make intensive use of computer program RELEASE should read Part 9. RELEASE is relatively easy to use if one follows the details given there. Most users will find the interactive features of RELEASE self-explanatory. We urge readers to use this program to work examples as they read Part 2. Finally, we have provided a Glossary of the notation we use.

We wish we could refer biologists to only one short section that would allow a quick understanding of the material presented here. Unfortunately, the subject is large, comprehensive, and complex. At the minimum, we believe most biologists should read most of Parts 1, 2, 4, and 9. We would hope statisticians would focus on Parts 3, 5, and 6, and develop additional theory (e.g., as indicated in Part 8) as well as explore properties of procedures developed using RELEASE.

1.2. Statistical concepts

1.2.1. Maximum Likelihood Theory

Fisher (1922, 1925) presented the method of maximum likelihood as an omnibus procedure for estimating parameters from sample data. Extensions of this method have produced a well-known, powerful means to derive point estimators and estimators of sampling variances and covariances. Likelihood theory allows one to assess the fit of the data to the model, and to test a variety of hypotheses (Mood et al. 1974; Lehmann 1983; Berger and Wolpert 1984). Parameter estimators, and likelihood-based inference in general, have excellent properties such as little or no bias and maximum efficiency. Likelihood methods have been the mainstay of most capture-recapture theory developed over the past 35 years (see Seber 1982), and we use them extensively in this monograph.

Data discussed in the present work are usually modeled as a sample from a multinomial distribution. The multinomial distribution is useful for discrete, mutually exclusive outcomes. The outcomes of each throw of a die ("trial") can be labeled 1, 2, 3, 4, 5, and 6, only one of which is possible. If n throws are made, frequencies of the six possible outcomes can be denoted as $n_1, n_2, ..., n_6$. Given that the n throws of the die are independent, the joint probability distribution (Pr) of the observed data is multinomial:

$$\Pr\{n_1, ..., n_6\} = \frac{n!}{\displaystyle\prod_{i=1}^{6}(n_i)!} \left[\prod_{i=1}^{6}(p_i)^{n_i}\right] ;$$

p_i = probability of the ith outcome, i = 1, ..., 6. The probabilities must satisfy the constraints $0 \le p_i \le 1$ for all i, and $p_1 + \cdots + p_6 = 1$. If the die is fair, each p_i is known to be one-sixth. In general, models contain parameters that are unknown; we wish to find estimators of these parameters that have "good" properties. The estimators are functions of the observed sample data and can be derived from the likelihood function L, which is the probability of the observed data viewed as a function of the parameters. The likelihood function for the die trials is

$$L(p_1, ..., p_6 \mid n_1, ..., n_6) = \frac{n!}{\displaystyle\prod_{i=1}^{6}(n_i)!} \left[\prod_{i=1}^{6}(p_i)^{n_i}\right]$$

and is read "the likelihood of the unknown parameters p_i given the observed (sample) data n_i."

The objective is to find the vector of parameter values that maximizes the likelihood function. That is, parameter values are selected to make the sample data seem "most likely." A simple graph of the likelihood can illustrate the concept; however, the above likelihood function cannot be graphed because it has five dimensions (only five because $p_1 + \cdots + p_6$ = 1). Therefore, let us consider a special case where only one unknown parameter exists. We consider a series of simple penny-flipping trials of an unfair penny. The likelihood function L is

$$L(p \mid n_h, n_t) = \frac{n!}{(n_h)!(n_t)!} p^{n_h}(1-p)^{n_t} .$$

Here p is the unknown probability of a "head" and n_h and n_t are the number of heads and tails, respectively, observed from n flips ($n = n_h + n_t$) and $1 - p$ is the probability of a "tail."

If a penny is flipped 16 times and 11 heads and five tails are observed, the likelihood shown in Figure 1.1 is a simple plot of the function $L(p \mid 11, 5)$ versus p where $0 < p < 1$. The likelihood function changes for different sample outcomes n_h and n_t. This change is illustrated in Figure 1.2 for the result of 80 flips (n_h = 55 and n_t = 25).

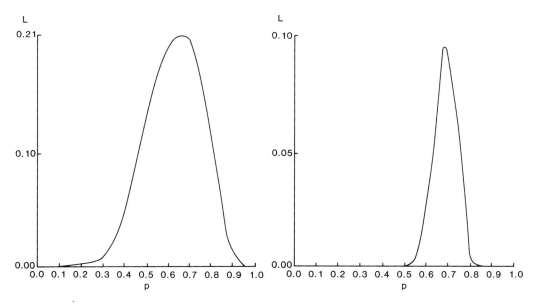

Figure 1.1. – Likelihood function for
a penny-flipping study where 11 heads
and five tails were observed in 16 flips.

Figure 1.2. – Likelihood function for
a penny-flipping study where 55 heads
and 25 tails were observed in 80 flips.

The graphs show that some candidate values of the unknown parameter p are "relatively unlikely" (i.e., those with small values of L) given the data observed. This phenomenon is more obvious as sample size increases because more information becomes available. For example, it appears that the penny is indeed unfair (the true p is probably not one-half). In fact, one might speculate that a likely value for the parameter p might be about 0.7 because the maximum value of the likelihood function corresponds to p at about 0.7.

The following extended example considers a likelihood function involving two unknown parameters. Consider the previous example of released fish. For simplicity, it is assumed that the marked fish were recaptured only at downstream dam 2 (a common situation). The data available for consideration are then

Group	Released	Recaptured
t	10,000	390
c	9,000	412.

The likelihood involves two estimable parameters, S, the survival rate of fish through (or over) the dam, and p_2 – the sampling rate at dam 2 (in this simple example it is assumed that $p_{t2} = p_{c2}$), given that the fish were alive just below the first dam (where controls were released).

Assumptions must always be made in any model. In this model, we assume independent fates of all fish, which allows us to write separate probability models for the treatment and control groups and to assume that the binomial model holds. We also assume that recapture of fish is like the penny-flipping situation with parameter Sp_2 (the probability of surviving the treatment, getting to dam 2, and being recovered) for the treatment group and p_2 for the control group. Finally, we assume that the effect of the treatment is negligible below dam 1. These assumptions allow us to write the two following probability models,

$$\Pr\{m_t \mid R_t\} = K_t (Sp_2)^{m_t} (1 - Sp_2)^{R_t - m_t}, \text{ and}$$

$$\Pr\{m_c \mid R_c\} = K_c (p_2)^{m_c} (1 - p_2)^{R_c - m_c};$$

$$K_t = \frac{(R_t)!}{(m_t)!(R_t - m_t)!} \ ; \ K_c = \frac{(R_c)!}{(m_c)!(R_c - m_c)!} \ .$$

In this example, one would take

$$\Pr\{m_c = 412 \mid R_c = 9{,}000\} = \frac{9{,}000!}{(412!)(8{,}588!)} (p_2)^{412} (1 - p_2)^{8{,}588} \ .$$

The product of these expressions yields the likelihood function for this simple experiment (terms are rearranged below):

$$L(S, p_2 \mid R_t, R_c, m_t, m_c) = (K_1 K_2)(Sp_2)^{m_t} (p_2)^{m_c} (1 - Sp_2)^{R_t - m_t} (1 - p_2)^{R_c - m_c} \ .$$

Four terms involving parameters appear in the likelihood because we must account for all fish both recovered and unrecovered from each of the two release groups. The expression on the left is read "the likelihood of the unknown parameters S and p_2, given the number of fish released in each group (R_t and R_c) and the number recovered at dam 2 (m_t and m_c), is equal to." Figure 1.3 provides a two-dimensional graph of the likelihood

$$L(S, p_2 \mid \text{data}) = K(Sp_2)^{390} (p_2)^{412} (1 - Sp_2)^{9{,}610} (1 - p_2)^{8{,}588} \ ;$$

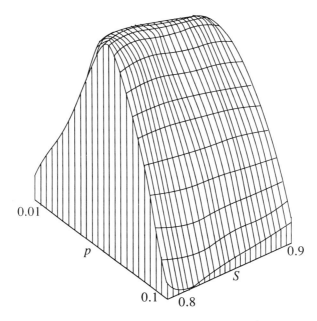

Figure 1.3. – Likelihood function for a simple survival experiment in which treatment and control fish are released at dam 1 and recaptured only at dam 2. Note that many values of the capture probability (p_2) and the treatment survival rate (S) are relatively unlikely.

$$K = K_1 K_2 = \left[\frac{10,000!}{390! \; (9,610)!} \right] \left[\frac{9,000!}{412! \; (8,588)!} \right].$$

The expression for K contains no unknown parameters and can therefore be ignored in terms of deriving estimators of parameters (however, K is useful in deriving tests of assumptions). The relative shape of the likelihood function is, of course, identical whether K is included or not.

Figure 1.3 also shows that most possible combinations of the parameters S and p_2 are unlikely for the data observed.

1.2.1.1. Point estimation. – The likelihood principle (Edwards 1972) states that the likelihood function contains all the information in the sample data and is the basis for deriving estimators of parameters and tests of assumptions. Estimators of parameters under the method of maximum likelihood (ML) are the values that maximize the likelihood. The ML procedure is conceptually appealing and has many optimal statistical properties, at least for large samples (Wilks 1962; Rao 1973; Mood et al. 1974) when the assumed model is true: little or no bias and 100% efficiency. In particular, the ML method provides estimators that are asymptotically normal, efficient, and unbiased.

The ML procedure is easy to apply in many situations. Consider a likelihood involving only one unknown parameter θ, $L(\theta|\text{data})$. If L is unimodal, its maximum occurs where the derivative (slope) with respect to θ is zero:

$$\frac{\partial L(\theta \mid \text{data})}{\partial \theta} = 0.$$

In practice, if the derivatives are to be found and the likelihood equations solved analytically, it is easier to work with the natural logarithm of the likelihood function, the log-likelihood, denoted as $\ln L(\theta \mid \text{data})$. Logarithms change the likelihood function from a product of terms to a sum of terms, and thus allows differentiation on a term-by-term basis. For the penny-flipping trials mentioned previously, the log-likelihood function (omitting the constant binomial coefficient) is

$$\ln L(p \mid \text{data}) = n_h \ln(p) + n_t \ln(1-p)$$

(in this case the generic parameter θ is denoted p as before). The partial derivative of $\ln L$ with respect to the unknown parameter p is

$$\frac{\partial[\ln L(p \mid \text{data})]}{\partial p} = \frac{n_h}{p} - \frac{n_t}{1-p} = 0.$$

The maximum likelihood estimator (MLE) of p is found by solving the likelihood equation for p. The resulting estimator is traditionally denoted as $\hat{p}$; in general, hats ("^") are used to distinguish estimators from parameters:

$$\hat{p} = n_h/(n_h + n_t), \text{ or } \hat{p} = n_h/n.$$

For the data observed, $n_h = 55$ and $n_t = 25$,

$$\hat{p} = 55/(55 + 25) = 0.69.$$

The example above provides an estimator said to be in "closed form," meaning that the likelihood equation(s) can be solved analytically for the parameter(s) of interest. If the likelihood equations are "open," i.e., cannot be solved algebraically, ML estimates can be derived by a variety of numerical methods on a digital computer, which performs an "intelligent search" for the parameter values that maximize the likelihood function. When values that simultaneously maximize L are found, they are taken as the MLEs.

In practical applications, one is interested in simultaneously deriving ML estimates of several parameters, say θ_1, θ_2, and θ_3. If these parameters are denoted as θ, a column vector containing $\hat{\theta}_1$, $\hat{\theta}_2$, and $\hat{\theta}_3$, the MLEs can be found by solving the system of three likelihood equations,

$$\frac{\partial \ln L\,(\theta \mid \text{data})}{\partial \theta_i} = 0, \quad i = 1, 2, 3.$$

Although the notation and algebra may not appear simple, the underlying concept of ML is both simple and intuitively appealing. If the likelihood equations can be solved analytically, ML estimates can be computed using a calculator. In the present work, we present closed-form estimators of parameters for most of the models under the various protocols. The computer program RELEASE computes ML estimates for an array of specific models to be introduced in Part 2.

Given a set of data and a formal statistical model (i.e., a likelihood function), one can find a reduction of the data. Thus, a smaller set of statistics, which contains all the information in the sample data, can be used instead of the raw data for all statistical estimation purposes. This reduction leads to the concept of sufficient statistics. A sufficient statistic is one containing all the necessary information about the sample. A sufficient statistic that cannot be reduced further is a minimal sufficient statistic (MSS) (see Hogg and Craig 1970; Huzurbazar 1976; Lehmann 1983).

Minimal sufficient statistics are important for a number of statistical reasons (see Mood et al. 1974). If an estimator is not based on the MSS, it is not fully efficient. If an MSS exists, the ML method can be used to find it. MLEs are functions of the MSS. In addition, test derivation often depends on the MSS. The MSS will be identified for the various models in later chapters.

1.2.1.2. Estimation of sampling variances and covariances. – A sampling variance is associated with each estimator and a sampling covariance is associated with each pair of estimators. The sampling variance is a measure of the precision or repeatability of the estimator and is usually a function of sample size and some of the unknown parameters. Sampling covariances measure the degree to which two particular estimators are dependent because they were computed from the same sample data. Often, these quantities are displayed in a *variance-covariance matrix,* usually denoted Σ:

$$\Sigma = \begin{bmatrix} \text{var}(\theta_1) & \text{cov}(\theta_1, \theta_2) & \text{cov}(\theta_1, \theta_3) & \cdots & \text{cov}(\theta_1, \theta_n) \\ \text{cov}(\theta_2, \theta_1) & \text{var}(\theta_2) & \text{cov}(\theta_2, \theta_3) & \cdots & \text{cov}(\theta_2, \theta_n) \\ \text{cov}(\theta_3, \theta_1) & \text{cov}(\theta_3, \theta_2) & \text{var}(\theta_3) & \cdots & \text{cov}(\theta_3, \theta_n) \\ \cdot & \cdot & \cdot & \cdot & \cdot \\ \cdot & \cdot & \cdot & \cdot & \cdot \\ \cdot & \cdot & \cdot & \cdot & \cdot \\ \text{cov}(\theta_n, \theta_1) & \text{cov}(\theta_n, \theta_2) & \text{cov}(\theta_n, \theta_3) & \cdots & \text{var}(\theta_n) \end{bmatrix}$$

The variances appear on the main diagonal and the covariances are symmetrical about the diagonal: i.e., $\text{cov}(\theta_i, \theta_j) = \text{cov}(\theta_j, \theta_i)$ for all i and j. Often, it is convenient to consider the variance of the ith estimator [$\text{var}(\theta_i)$] as the $\text{cov}(\theta_i, \theta_i)$, referring to a covariance matrix. For any actual study, one will have only estimates of the variance and covariances, and $\hat{\Sigma}$ usually is obtained by substituting estimates for parameter values. Conceptually, the sampling variance is related directly to the curvature of the likelihood function at its maximum. A comparison of Figures 1.1 versus 1.2 suggests that more is known from the large sample shown in Figure 1.2 than from the smaller one. Values at some distance from the ML estimate are relatively "unlikely," and this concept is measured by the sampling variance.

If the likelihood function contains only one parameter, the sampling variance estimator can be derived as the negative inverse of the second partial derivative of the log-likelihood function, evaluated at the ML estimate. In the previously described penny-flipping example,

$$\text{var}(\hat{p}) = -\left[E\left(\frac{\partial^2 \ln L(p \mid \text{data})}{\partial p^2} \right) \right]^{-1},$$

which is estimated by

$$\hat{\text{var}}(\hat{p}) = \left[-\left(\frac{\partial^2 \ln L(p \mid \text{data})}{\partial p^2} \right) \right]^{-1}_{p = \hat{p}}.$$

The procedure yields, for example, the often-used estimator of the variance of a binomial proportion,

$$\hat{\text{var}}(\hat{p}) = \frac{\hat{p}(1 - \hat{p})}{n}, \quad n = n_h + n_t.$$

If the likelihood contains more than one unknown parameter, the sampling variances and covariances can be estimated from the negative of the matrix of mixed second-order partial derivatives of the log-likelihood function. The resulting matrix, expressed as expected partial derivatives, is called the information matrix. Because the information matrix is a function of the parameters, it is denoted here as $I(\underline{\theta})$. Specifically, the (ij)th element of $I(\underline{\theta})$ is given by

$$-E\left[\frac{\partial^2 \ln L\left(\underline{\theta}\mid \text{data}\right)}{(\partial\theta_i)(\partial\theta_j)}\right],$$

the quantity evaluated at the true parameter value, $\underline{\theta}$.

If the elements of the information matrix are evaluated at the ML estimates, then the estimated variance-covariance matrix is

$$\hat{\Sigma} = [I(\hat{\underline{\theta}})]^{-1}.$$

Most numerical methods use a matrix of mixed second partial derivatives (the Hessian matrix) to find the maximum of the likelihood function and, therefore, the ML estimates $\hat{\theta}$. In this case, $\hat{\Sigma}$ can be estimated with $I(\hat{\theta})$ from the final iteration in the numerical procedure (see Kale 1962).

The delta method (Seber 1982:7-8) provides an omnibus procedure for approximating estimates of sampling variances and covariances. The method gives valid large-sample (i.e., asymptotic) estimates of variances and covariances and produces results asymptotically equivalent to the information matrix approach. We use this method at many points in the monograph. In addition, we encourage the use of empirical estimates of sampling variances in an effort to relax the assumptions made in some models and to allow for heterogeneity in the survival and recapture probabilities of individual fish (details on this subject are given in Part 4).

We chose the ML method for our development of statistical theory because it is an excellent omnibus approach (within a frequentist inference approach) and is particularly well suited for models based on the multinomial distribution (a member of the exponential family of distributions). Estimation methods are then based on a general stochastic model for the sampling distribution of the data. MLEs are asymptotically unbiased, fully efficient, and normally distributed. Some estimators have a "small-sample" bias and RELEASE allows bias adjustments to the exact MLEs to be made as an option.

1.2.1.3. Method of expectation. – A critical step in many statistical analysis problems is to specify one or more plausible sampling models for the data. Conceptually, these sampling models take the form of probability distributions; hence, the essence of the model is a mathematical statement. Symbolically the statement is

$$\Pr\{\text{data}\,|\,\text{parameters}\},$$

or

$$\Pr\{X_1, ..., X_n\,|\,\theta_1, ..., \theta_a\}.$$

As introduced above, once one has actually observed specific values of the variables, then one can convert the probability model to a likelihood in terms of the parameters and derive ML estimates. Rather than do this process on a case-by-case basis, mathematical statisticians have investigated short-cut ways to derive the ML estimates, $\hat{\theta}_1, ..., \hat{\theta}_a$. In particular, when the $\hat{\theta}_i$ exist in closed form, they can often be found by simple methods. We make extensive use of these more sophisticated methods here; we do not, in fact, find it necessary to write out the full likelihood for our recapture models, take partial derivatives, and solve the resultant equations.

The first, and most important, step in an analysis of a statistical model is to use the likelihood to identify the MSS under that model. There is much theory about finding the MSS (e.g., Lehmann 1983). The MSS will take the form of some l functions of the data, $T_i(X_1, ..., X_n)$, $i = 1, ..., l$. For example, in many situations the mean, $\overline{X}$, is one component of the MSS. In the capture-recapture models considered here, the MSS always turns out to be various sums of recapture counts. The dimension of the MSS is l.

Two situations distinguish themselves: (1) the dimension of the MSS is the same as the number of parameters (i.e., $l = a$), or (2) there are more MSS components than parameters ($l > a$). (The case of $l < a$ can occur, in which case not all a parameters can be estimated.) Once the MSS is known, the next step is to find its probability distribution (if possible), or at least find the expected values, variances, and covariances of the MSS. Let

$$E(T_i) = g_i(\theta_1, ..., \theta_a)\,, \quad i = 1, ..., l$$

be these expected values. In the full-rank case of $l = a$, the ML estimators of the θ_i can be found by solving the a equations that result from equating the observed values of T_i to the expected values:

$$T_i = g_i(\theta_1, ..., \theta_a)\,, \quad i = 1, ..., a.$$

Most of the models considered in detail in this monograph are full rank and the "method of expectation" is how we found the ML estimates. Davidson and Solomon (1974) provided insights on the justification of this procedure. Also, Appendix B of Brownie et al. (1985) gives some more technical details of this approach.

When the model is not full rank, but rather has $l > a$ (fewer parameters than MSS elements), iterative numerical methods are usually needed to find the MLE; i.e., closed-form solutions do not usually exist. Many models worth using or trying in capture-recapture are not full rank. (Those models can be analyzed using a combination of programs RELEASE and

SURVIV.) Appendix B in Brownie et al. (1985) gives some details of numerical procedures of parameter estimation with nonfull-rank models.

Whether the ML estimator $\hat{\theta}$ is obtained from closed-form formulae or numerically, it still has a variance-covariance matrix that can be estimated. Theoretically, those variances and covariances are defined in terms of second derivatives of the likelihood function. However, they need not always be found that way; there are short cuts to finding variances just as there are short cuts to finding the ML estimators. We have used those short cuts here. In the full-rank case, all one needs is the expectations and variances and covariances of the MSS. Then the link provided by

$$E(T_i) = g_i(\underline{\theta}) , \quad i = 1, ..., a$$

allows one to derive both $\hat{\theta}$ and the variance-covariance matrix of $\hat{\theta}$. Consequently, again we derived our results without having to take first and second partials of the likelihood. Note, however, results we present on the various models considered could have been derived by taking partials of likelihoods; it is just that there are easier, advanced methods available.

Finally, we again note that the key to these derivations of estimators (and tests) is identification of the MSS under any model and model sequence, and then the determination of the sampling distribution of that MSS.

1.2.1.4. Hypothesis testing. – Tests of various hypotheses are important in capture-recapture sampling and experimentation. Cormack (1968) stated, "In all cases every iota of information, both biological and statistical, must be gathered to check and countercheck the unavoidable assumptions." Much of the hypothesis testing herein relates to tests of underlying model assumptions or to selection of an appropriate model. Hypothesis tests, in the context here, fall into two broad classes: goodness of fit tests and between-model tests. The difference is illustrated by considering the null (H_0) and alternative (H_A) hypotheses for each type of test.

The null hypothesis for a goodness of fit test is that the model fits the data; the alternative hypothesis is that the model does not fit the data. The alternative is broad and not specific. We can expect the power of this test to be lower (often much lower) than the between-model test due to the generality of the alternative.

Between-model tests deal with a comparison of two specific models, e.g., model A and model B, wherein model A is a special case because it is a reduced parameter version of model B. The test evaluates model B as an alternative to model A (the null hypothesis). Specifically, the null hypothesis is that model A fits as well as model B; the alternative hypothesis is that model B fits the data better than model A.

Both tests involve a statement about one or more parameters in the model. Information regarding the validity of the null hypothesis is based on the value of a test statistic calculated from the experimental data. Most of the test statistics here are distributed approximately as chi-square under the null hypothesis. The approximation to the chi-square distribution improves as sample size increases. Figure 1.4 presents the chi-square distributions for 1, 3, 10, and 25 degrees of freedom (df). The probability of a test statistic being as large as that observed under H_0 (i.e., computed from the data) can be found from the chi-square distribution. Generally, if a test statistic is improbable (e.g., $P = 0.002$), the null hypothesis is rejected. Improbable values ($\alpha \leq 0.05$) of the chi-square distribution are shown in the shaded areas of Figure 1.4. Conversely, if the test statistic is probable under the null hypothesis (e.g., $P = 0.45$), there is no reason to reject the null hypothesis.

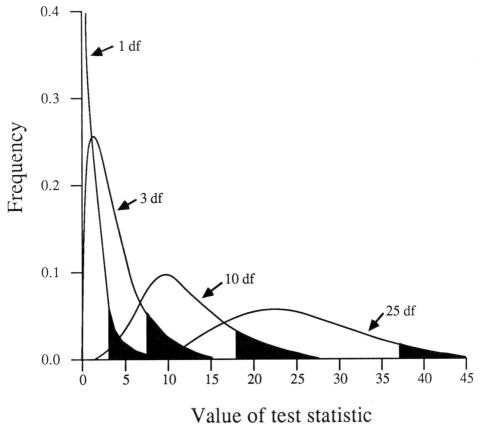

Value of test statistic

Figure 1.4. – The chi-square distributions for 1, 3, 10, and 25 df. In each case, the 0.05 rejection region is shown as a shaded area. Nearly all test statistics presented in this monograph are distributed asymptotically as chi-square. Program RELEASE computes the exact significance level numerically, making tables or arbitrary rejection levels unnecessary (from White et al. 1982).

As an example, consider the null hypothesis (H_0: $p = 0.5$) that a penny is "fair" (on the average 50% of the tosses will be heads and 50% will be tails). The alternative hypothesis (H_A: $p \neq 0.5$) is that the penny is "unfair." The results of a set of 1,000 trials might be that 506 tosses are heads and 494 tosses are tails. Intuitively, one might accept the null hypothesis that the penny is fair because the observed values are close to 50:50. Statistical hypothesis testing allows this intuition to be quantified and formalized. In this example, $\chi^2 = 0.1$ with 1 df. Figure 1.4 shows that this small value is likely if the null hypothesis is true. If, however, 55 heads are observed in 80 flips, $\chi^2 = 56$ with 1 df. The probability of a value this large, if the null hypothesis is true, is essentially zero and we conclude that the penny is unfair. Quantification allows statistical inferences to be made in complex situations where intuition is of little value.

Most of the tests presented in this monograph are in the form of contingency tables. The subject of contingency tables is covered in most statistical texts on elementary testing methods; we provide only a brief review here. Consider n randomly selected items classified according to two different criteria. The results could be tabulated by rows for one criterion and by columns for the second criterion in a contingency table:

n_{11}	n_{12}	n_{13}	$\cdots$	n_{1c}	$n_{1.}$
n_{21}	n_{22}	n_{23}	$\cdots$	n_{2c}	$n_{2.}$
n_{31}	n_{32}	n_{33}	$\cdots$	n_{3c}	$n_{3.}$
$\cdot$	$\cdot$	$\cdot$		$\cdot$	$\cdot$
$\cdot$	$\cdot$	$\cdot$		$\cdot$	$\cdot$
$\cdot$	$\cdot$	$\cdot$		$\cdot$	$\cdot$
n_{r1}	n_{r2}	n_{r3}	$\cdots$	n_{rc}	$n_{r.}$
$n_{.1}$	$n_{.2}$	$n_{.3}$	$\cdots$	$n_{.c}$	n

This $r \times c$ table contains the observed data for each cell. If n is large, a good approximation is to compute the test statistic

$$\chi^2 = \sum_{i=1}^{r} \sum_{j=1}^{c} (n_{ij} - E_{ij})^2 / E_{ij} \, ;$$

n_{ij} = the observed number in the (ij)th cell;
E_{ij} = the estimated expected number in the (ij)th cell under the null hypothesis.

The null hypothesis is one of homogeneity. The estimated expected value for n_{ij} under this null hypothesis is then

$$E_{ij} = \frac{n_{i.}n_{.j}}{n} \; ;$$

$n_{i.}$ = the total of row i, $n_{i.} = n_{i1} + \cdots + n_{ic}$;
$n_{.j}$ = the total in column j, $n_{.j} = n_{1j} + \cdots + n_{rj}$.

Note also that $n \equiv n_{..} = \Sigma \Sigma n_{ij}$. The degrees of freedom for these contingency tables are $(r - 1)(c - 1)$ (Ostle 1963; Snedecor and Cochran 1967).

We present many tests that are computed from a series of (conditionally) independent 2×2 tables. Standard statistical texts provide shortcut formulae for the computation of the test statistic from such tables with only two columns and two rows. A convenient computational method for a 2×2 table of the form

a	b	(a + b)
c	d	(c + d)
(a + c)	(b + d)	n

is

$$\chi^2 = \frac{n(ad - bc)^2}{(a + c)(b + d)(a + b)(c + d)} \; .$$

Such 2×2 tables have only 1 df (i.e., $[2-1][2-1] = 1$). By way of interpretation of this test, it is just testing that the expected proportions $a/(a + b)$ and $c/(c + d)$ are the same.

If some expected values (E_{ij}) are small (e.g., <2), the approximation of the test statistic to the chi-square distribution may be poor. This approximation can be improved by pooling cells by row or by column. Each cell pooled results in a loss of 1 df. When recapture data are sparse, rows and columns are often pooled to the extent that only a single 2×2 table remains.

Here we present material to provide biologists with some insight into how certain tests are derived using a simple example. No effort is made to provide the theory for the procedures outlined. The example is taken from Section 1.2.1: 10,000 treatment and 9,000 control fish were released at dam 1 and 390 treatment and 412 control fish were recaptured. The probability models for these two cohorts, presented earlier, are

$$\Pr\{m_t \mid R_t\} = K_t (Sp_2)^{m_t} (1 - Sp_2)^{R_t - m_t} \; , \text{ and}$$

$$\Pr\{m_c \mid R_c\} = K_c (p_2)^{m_c} (1 - p_2)^{R_c - m_c} \; ;$$

$$K_t = \begin{pmatrix} R_t \\ m_t \end{pmatrix} = \frac{(R_t)!}{(m_t)! \, (R_t - m_t)!} \; ;$$

$$K_c = \begin{pmatrix} R_c \\ m_c \end{pmatrix} = \frac{(R_c)!}{(m_c)! \, (R_c - m_c)!} \; .$$

Interest is in the hypotheses

H_0: The survival and capture rates for the two cohorts are equal (i.e., $S = 1$; no treatment effect) versus

H_A: The survival and capture rates for the two cohorts are different (i.e., $S \neq 1$; a treatment effect or $p_{t2} \neq p_{c2}$).

Under H_A, the MSS for the treatment cohort is $\text{MSS}_t = m_t$ and the MSS for the control cohort is $\text{MSS}_c = m_c$. Under the null hypothesis the MSS is $\text{MSS}_0 = m_t + m_c$.

A test of H_0 can be derived from the residual distribution of the data, conditional on the MSS, given H_0 is true. Symbolically, the distribution is

$$\text{Pr}_{H_0} \left\{ \text{MSS}_t, \text{MSS}_c \mid \text{MSS}_0 \right\} = \frac{\begin{pmatrix} R_t \\ m_t \end{pmatrix} \begin{pmatrix} R_c \\ m_c \end{pmatrix}}{\begin{pmatrix} R_t + R_c \\ m_t + m_c \end{pmatrix}} \; .$$

This type of test was used in similar contexts by Robson and Youngs (unpublished report, 1971), Brownie and Robson (1976), and Pollock et al. (1985). Moreover, this type of test is known to be optimal from the general theory of hypothesis testing (Lehmann 1959). When we define

$$K_0 = \begin{pmatrix} R_t + R_c \\ m_t + m_c \end{pmatrix},$$

the distribution is

$$\text{Pr}_{H_0} \left\{ \text{MSS}_t, \text{MSS}_c \mid \text{MSS}_0 \right\} = \frac{K_t \, K_c}{K_0} \; .$$

The distribution is hypergeometric, allowing a 2×2 contingency table and a chi-square test with 1 df to be derived. The table is

$$\begin{array}{|cc|} \hline m_t & R_t - m_t \\ m_c & R_c - m_c \\ \hline \end{array}$$

Columns of the contingency table represent "recaptured" versus "not recaptured" for each of the two groups. The values for the example provide the following table

$$\begin{array}{|cc|} \hline 390 & 10{,}000 - 390 \\ 412 & 9{,}000 - 412 \\ \hline \end{array}$$

Heuristically, this test is comparing the two estimated proportions

$$\hat{Sp}_2 = \frac{390}{10{,}000}$$

and

$$\hat{p}_2 = \frac{412}{9{,}000} .$$

The above contingency table results in $\chi^2 = 5.38$, 1 df, and $P \leq 0.02$; thus, we conclude that the treatment has affected survival of the treatment group or that the capture rates of the treatment and control groups were unequal.

Many between-model tests are made in later chapters. Testing between two models represents a way to test a complex hypothesis. In general, such tests can be derived as likelihood ratio tests, in which one model is a special case (i.e., reduced number of parameters) of the other model. As an example, let

$L(\underline{\theta}_1)$ = a likelihood function with n parameters (e.g., $\phi_1, \phi_2, ..., \phi_6, p_2), ..., p_6$, where $n = 11$);

$L(\underline{\theta}_0)$ = a likelihood function with fewer parameters, $m < n$ (e.g., $\phi_1, ..., \phi_6, p$, where $m = 7$).

The likelihood $L(\underline{\theta}_0)$ corresponds to the null hypothesis that the parameter p is constant (i.e., $p_2 = p_3 = \cdots = p_6 = p$). The alternative hypothesis is that the parameter p varies. Both hypotheses allow for variation in the parameter ϕ. A test of the null hypothesis is based on

$$\chi^2_{(n-m)} \doteq -2 \ln\left[\frac{L(\theta_0)}{L(\theta_1)}\right]$$

where both likelihoods are evaluated at their MLE values. The test is asymptotically chi-square distributed with $n - m$ df. A significantly large test statistic is taken as evidence that the null hypothesis is false (e.g., that the parameter p is not constant, as in the example above). Further information on likelihood ratio tests was given by Lehmann (1959) and Hogg and Craig (1970).

The contingency table procedure often results in a test that is equivalent to a likelihood ratio test, if no pooling is necessary because expected values are small. The contingency table approach outlined is preferable to the likelihood ratio test because data can be pooled easily if the expected values are small. Consideration of the partitioned test statistics is possible when data from more than two dams are available, thus a finer interpretation of the hypothesis test is allowed (however, the example used here cannot be partitioned). This general approach is used to derive most of the tests here.

In the case of a full-rank MSS for both the null hypothesis and alternative hypothesis models, the contingency table tests can often be found, and are then to be preferred. When the MSS are not full rank, one must usually rely on the likelihood ratio test procedure. The likelihood ratio test is an omnibus procedure justified by large-sample theory, we use it especially in the case of nonfull-rank models. However, for the most part, we were able to find the simpler contingency table tests of hypotheses that go with the full-rank models presented here.

1.2.2. Components of Variance

A conceptually difficult, but important, issue deals with components of variation in sampling and experimentation. A review of these concepts is presented here; more information can be found in White et al. (1982) and in many statistical texts. The two main classes of variation are population and sampling variation. For the moment, we concentrate on the meaning of these terms rather than on how they might be computed or estimated.

1.2.2.1. Spatial and temporal variation. – Variation in biological population parameters occurs commonly. A biological parameter (θ) is likely to vary over space and time (e.g., because of environmental factors), and may also vary among individuals. If the parameter is annual survival, it varies by species and age and perhaps by subpopulation. Survival probabilities may also vary among individuals from the same subpopulation, age, sex, size, and so forth. It is immaterial, for the moment, whether the value of the parameter over time, space, species, or subpopulation is known, but any population parameter may vary. In general, we denote this population variance as σ^2:

$$\sigma^2 = \frac{1}{N} \sum_{i=1}^{N} (\theta_i - \overline{\theta})^2$$

for N values of θ, θ_1, ..., θ_N corresponding to N different populations; no sampling variation is involved here. If N is large and a sample of n populations has been taken, then (for known θ_i) the estimator of σ^2 is

$$\hat{\sigma}^2 = \sum_{i=1}^{n} (\theta_i - \overline{\theta})^2 / (n - 1).$$

As an example of population variation, consider the number of bluegills *Lepomis macrochirus* in a small pond. A complete census on 10 June each year for 7 years provides the exact annual population size (by definition, this is a parameter). It would be unusual if the true number of fish was the same each of the 7 years. Thus, the population parameters vary. This population variation is conceptually measured as σ^2 and might, in this case, be termed temporal variation. The researcher or manager has no direct control over σ^2 (except, perhaps, by redefining the population itself or by some perturbation); it is a characteristic of the population.

Population variation might also occur spatially. For example, true population sizes are likely to differ among ponds of similar size and type. Spatial variation among population parameters is to be expected.

1.2.2.2. Sampling variation. – Sampling variation occurs because only partial information about the population normally is available. Exactly which members of a population fall into the sample is a result of a stochastic process, if the sampling process is unbiased toward particular members of that population. These processes are fundamentally unpredictable, as is the specific outcome of a flip of a penny.

Sampling variance is a measure of precision or repeatability of a result based on sample data; it is the measure of uncertainty. In general, sampling variance will be relatively small if each sample contains a large fraction of a population and relatively large if each sample contains few members of the population. The precision of results from a properly designed study can be estimated from information collected as part of that study.

Sampling variance of an estimator, $\hat{\theta}$, is denoted var($\hat{\theta}$). Technically, one should write var($\hat{\theta} \mid \theta$) because this measure of variation is conditional on the true (unknown) value of θ. Generally, one has only an estimate of the variance $\hat{\text{var}}(\hat{\theta})$. Unlike the population variance, the experimenter has considerable control over the magnitude of the sampling variance by virtue of the study design. The most obvious way to decrease the uncertainty of the sampling process, and decrease the variance, is to increase the size of the sample or the proportion of the total population sampled. Other common ways to decrease the sampling variance include stratification of the population or use of a better estimation method. The standard error (se), an alternative measure of an estimator's variability, is related to the variance by

$$\text{var}(\hat{\theta}) = [\text{se}(\hat{\theta})]^2 .$$

The terms "high precision" and "unbiasedness" represent indices of high accuracy. One can strive for this accuracy by careful attention in the design of surveys and experiments and in the use of good analytical methods. Consider a lake inhabited by lake trout *Salvelinus namaycush* susceptible to parasitism by sea lampreys *Petromyzon marinus*. An investigator wants to estimate the proportion (p) of these fish bearing at least one lamprey. An initial estimate, $\hat{p}_1 = 0.19$, is computed from the first sample (considered here as one unit of effort). Immediately, three additional samples are drawn and $\hat{p}_2 = 0.12, \hat{p}_3 = 0.18$, and $\hat{p}_4 = 0.27$. The variation among these estimates $\hat{p}_i$ is sampling variation, as the parameter p has not changed. In the example, the precision or repeatability for one unit of effort is only fair. However, if unit cost is low, sufficient sampling will lead to reliable results.

Finally, we consider an example where both population and sampling variation occur. Assume that the lake is surveyed once each year to estimate the proportion of lake trout bearing one or more sea lamprey. The data for 5 years are as follows:

Year	Unknown parameter	Estimate	Standard error
1	$p_1 = 0.13$	$\hat{p}_1 = 0.19$	$\hat{se}(\hat{p}_1) = 0.042$
2	$p_2 = 0.17$	$\hat{p}_2 = 0.12$	$\hat{se}(\hat{p}_2) = 0.034$
3	$p_3 = 0.16$	$\hat{p}_3 = 0.20$	$\hat{se}(\hat{p}_3) = 0.043$
4	$p_4 = 0.13$	$\hat{p}_4 = 0.18$	$\hat{se}(\hat{p}_4) = 0.035$
5	$p_5 = 0.16$	$\hat{p}_5 = 0.11$	$\hat{se}(\hat{p}_5) = 0.039$
$\bar{x}$	$\bar{p} = 0.15$	$\hat{\bar{p}} = 0.16$	$\hat{se}(\hat{\bar{p}}) = 0.017$

Here, $\hat{se}(\hat{\bar{p}}) = 0.017$ includes only the sampling variation. This $\hat{se}(\hat{\bar{p}})$ is the square root of the estimated theoretical $\hat{var}(\hat{\bar{p}})$;

$$\hat{var}(\hat{\bar{p}}) = \frac{1}{5^2} \sum_{i=1}^{k} \left(\hat{se}(\hat{p}_i) \right)^2 .$$

In contrast, if an average $(\hat{\bar{p}})$ is computed from these five estimates, the empirical variance of $\hat{\bar{p}}$ is

$$\hat{var}(\hat{\bar{p}}) = \frac{1}{5} \left[\frac{\sum_{i=1}^{5} (\hat{p}_i - \hat{\bar{p}})^2}{4} \right] = \frac{(0.041833)^2}{5} = (0.0187)^2 .$$

This $\hat{\text{var}}(\bar{p})$ includes both population (temporal) variation among the true p_i (σ^2) and conditional sampling variation of the $\hat{p}_i$ [var($\hat{p}_i$)]. Temporal population variation results from changes in the true proportion from year to year. Sampling variation occurs because only a sample of fish was examined, not the entire population. Often, one wishes to estimate σ^2, the variance among the true parameter values. This subject is discussed in Part 4. For now, the reader need only be aware of the distinction between these two types of variation.

1.3. Release-Recapture Protocols and Data

1.3.1. Introduction

The formal basis for the development of a statistical theory to underly survival experiments is the extensive literature on capture-recapture sampling (see Seber 1982, 1986 and Brownie et al. 1985 for recent reviews). This literature deals almost entirely with the estimation of population parameters (e.g., population size, survival rate, or number of births by time, sex, age-class, or geographic area) or the testing of various hypotheses concerning model assumptions. The theory presented herein extends capture-recapture methodology into survival experiments to assess the effect of a treatment on survival rate. The basis for such assessments is a control group of marked animals which enables the treatment-control comparisons that are standard experimental concepts of long standing.

We present extensive consideration of experiments with a treatment and a single control in Part 2. We consider extensions to multiple treatment and control groups in Part 3, which is more abbreviated, as it concentrates on presenting theory. Assume that a known number of fish in each of two groups is marked and released at dam 1. The first group is marked to denote that they are in the treatment group ($t = t$reatment), while the fish in the second group constitute the control group ($c = c$ontrol). The known numbers marked and released are denoted as R_{t1} and R_{c1} for treatment and control fish, respectively ($R = R$eleased), at dam 1. Throughout this monograph, we use a capital R to denote the number of fish released. We use an initial subscript to denote treatment or control as well as further subscripts to denote the specific release and recapture site (see Glossary).

The treatment may be the passage of the fish over a spillway, through a turbine or bypass system, or around a deflecting screen or barrier. Because survival of fish through various types of hydroelectric turbines is of concern, we use this as a primary example. Assume that a known number of marked fish (R_{t1}) is designated to receive the treatment and is released above dam 1 directly into a turbine intake. Simultaneously, a known number of control fish (R_{c1}) is released immediately below the dam near the end of the draft tube (see Figure 1.5).

As both groups move downstream, they are sampled at one or more downstream dams or other sampling sites. The only difference between the two groups is that some fish in the treatment group may have been killed while passing through the turbine and other parts of the dam structure.

Fish often are given only a batch mark, which is enough to allow their treatment or control status to be recognized when they are recaptured at sampling sites downstream. For example, all the treatment fish (R_{t1}) could be branded with a "T" and all the control fish (R_{c1}) with a "C" (or any other two marks that can be distinguished clearly).

Alternatively, fish may be marked with a unique tag or number. New technology may make this approach more feasible in the future (e.g., passive integrated transponder [PIT] tags). New types of tags are just starting to be evaluated (Prentice and Park 1984, 1985). We will assume here that tags are not lost and that marks remain readable.

A common example of unique marks is the individually numbered bird bands issued by the U.S. Fish and Wildlife Service. The use of unique marks has many advantages in that the

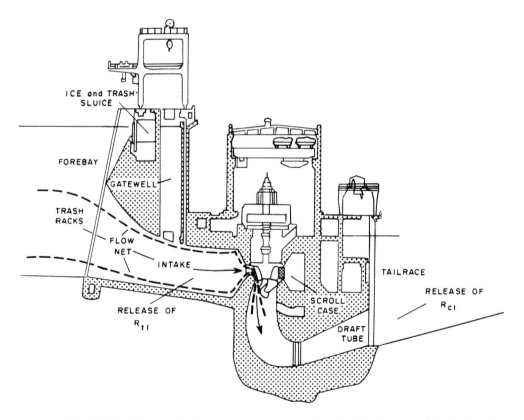

Figure 1.5. − Idealized diagram of a dam, some of its components, and points of release of the treatment and control fish. (Redrawn from Olson and Kaczynski, unpublished report, 1980.)

specific capture history and movements of each fish or other animal can be tabulated and analyzed. In the final assessment, the primary disadvantage is cost. These issues relating to uniqueness of marks will be covered in more detail in the material that follows.

The structure of the release-recapture data can be seen by considering only the control fish released below dam 1 (R_{c1}). If we consider only the first recapture for each fish (regardless of where this might occur), the recapture data have a multinomial sampling distribution if independent fates can be assumed. Thus, a fish released can be first recaptured at only one of the downstream dams (dams 2, ..., k), or it may never be recaptured. These outcomes are mutually exclusive and exhaustive.

Now consider the subset of the R_{c1} fish that are first recaptured at dam 2. We use m_{c12} to denote this number of fish; "m" is used because these recaptures are of marked fish. Three outcomes are possible:

(1) All m_{c12} fish survive recapture and handling and are rereleased at dam 2 as a subset called R_{c2}.

(2) Some fish are accidentally killed or injured or are removed deliberately; the remaining fish are rereleased and called R_{c2}.

(3) The number of m_{c12} fish recaptured that survive is added to a known number of new fish (to be initially released at dam 2) and the entire release is called R_{c2}.

The first two cases (1 and 2) are perhaps the most common in survival experiments; i.e., an initial release at dam 1 followed by the potential recapture and rerelease of the same fish at several downstream sites. In some studies (case 3), new fish are also released at the downstream capture sites along with the recaptured fish.

The term "losses on capture" is used in the literature (Jolly 1965) to describe fish killed accidentally or removed intentionally during recapture and handling. The important point is that the number of fish released or rereleased is known. In the above example, the releases at dam 2 (R_{c2}) could be

(1) less than the m_{c12} captures at dam 2 due to some losses on capture;

(2) equal to m_{c12} if no losses on capture occur;

(3) larger than m_{c12} due to the release of new fish along with "old" fish already in the experiment; or

(4) zero, because all fish were intentionally removed or accidentally killed.

In case 4 (above), only data on first captures are available. This situation is relatively simple and is examined in Chapter 2.2.

The sequence of possible recaptures of each fish leads us to consider the concept of a capture history for each fish used in the study. The capture history of a fish is a succinct way of tabulating the dams at which it was recaptured and possibly rereleased. Capture histories are denoted as a series of ones (= captured or recaptured) and zeros (not captured or recaptured). For example, the string of six values, {100101}, represents the capture history of a fish initially released at dam 1 and recaptured at dams 4 and 6. In general, if there are k release-recapture dams, the capture history consists of k-ordered ones and zeros. The ith digit represents what happened to the fish at the ith dam.

1.3.2. Capture Histories and Data Arrays

Statistical methods for the estimation of unknown parameters or the testing of hypotheses are based on the capture histories of marked fish. Practicalities aside, the most informative experiment is provided by an adequately replicated experiment involving the release of large samples of uniquely marked fish recaptured at a high rate at several downstream dams. Although this experiment may be the ideal, experimentation can be conducted under a host of other conditions. First, we must introduce several levels of data summarization.

1.3.2.1. CH matrix. – The capture history (CH) matrix provides specific capture histories (e.g., {110001}, or {101011}) as rows, along with the number of fish, by treatment group, having that capture history. Consider a particular row of a CH matrix as an example:

$$\{1011101\} \quad 37 \quad 43,$$

which represents the results for a particular capture history over seven dams. The interpretation is that, of all treatment and control fish initially released at dam 1, 37 treatment and 43 control fish were recaptured and rereleased at dams 3, 4, 5, and 7 (and these fish were not captured at dams 2 or 6).

Because the CH matrix is a concise summary of the basic data it is important that the reader become familiar with it. A minus sign indicates fish lost on capture or deliberately removed. For example,

$$\{1011101\} \quad -4 \quad -3$$

is similar to the previous example, but signifies that there were four treatment and three control fish with this capture history that were removed at dam 7. Therefore, 37 and 43 fish were recaptured and rereleased alive in addition to four and three fish that were recaptured but removed (e.g., they died accidentally, were seriously injured, or were intentionally removed).

In general, we recommend the use of the CH matrix as a starting point in the analysis. Program RELEASE can compute useful summaries of the data from the CH matrix.

A detailed example of a CH matrix is shown in Table 1.1. We make extensive use of this general numerical example.

Table 1.1. – The capture history (CH) matrix for the example data set. The numbers of fish either recaptured and rereleased or recaptured and removed are shown for each capture history by treatment (*t*) and control (*c*) groups.

Capture history	Number recaptured	
	t	*c*
100000	25925	24605
100001	563	605
100001	-27	-36
100010	508	522
100010	-23	-25
100011	17	23
100011	-1	-1
100100	1500	1678
100100	-81	-57
100101	45	48
100101	-3	-1
100110	37	44
100110	-2	-2
100111	1	2
101000	193	207
101000	-14	-10
101001	5	9
101010	7	4
101100	16	14
101100	-1	-1
101101	1	1
101110	1	1
110000	872	935
110000	-29	-33
110001	26	28
110001	-1	-1
110010	16	18
110010	-1	-1
110100	67	68
110100	-3	-4
110101	1	2
110110	2	1
111000	10	12
111001	0	1
111100	1	0

These data are from a hypothetical study of turbine survival where fish are released at dam 1 and recaptured at five downstream dams. We assume that 30,000 treatment fish are released into a turbine intake of the dam (R_{t1} = 30,000) and 29,000 control fish are released simultaneously immediately below the dam (R_{c1} = 29,000); see Figure 1.5. These data are useful for illustrating analyses because they were generated from known parameter values that we pre-selected. We took the treatment survival rate of fish passing through the turbine and structure of the dam to be 0.9 (S = 0.9), which means there is a 0.9 probability of a treatment fish surviving from the mouth of the turbine intake to the point of release of the control fish just below the dam. This subject is discussed in Chapter 1.5.

We assume that each fish was given a unique tag or mark. Losses on capture were small, averaging about 3.5% of the fish recaptured at each of the five downstream dams. The survival rates (ϕ_i) of fish between dams and recapture rates (p_i) are shown in Figure 1.6.

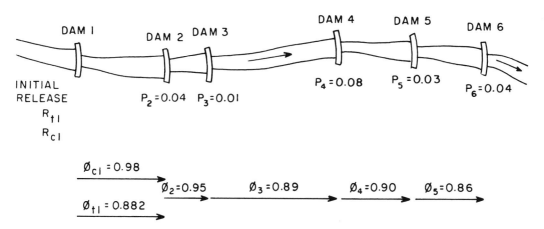

Figure 1.6. – Parameters used in the general numerical example. Because the recapture rates in this example are equal for treatment and control fish, the t or c subscripts are not used (i.e., $p_{c2} = p_{t2} = p_2$). Similarly, the dam-to-dam survival rates for treatment and control fish after the first survival rates are not subscripted for treatment group. The survival from dam 1 to dam 2 differs by treatment and control.

The release and recapture data are shown symbolically in Figure 1.7 and given numerically in Table 1.2. This example is simple but includes some ideal assumptions. These assumptions are relaxed in Part 2, but it is important to understand the formulation of the problem before various extensions and special cases are considered.

The recapture rates ($p_{t\,i}$ and $p_{c\,i}$) represent the probability of a fish being recaptured at dam i, given that the live fish reaches the ith dam. The recapture rates used in the example are small, averaging only about 4%. Although this recapture rate is typical for many studies that have been conducted on the Columbia River, it would be better if these rates were higher because precision and test power would be improved.

The survival rates $\phi_{t\,i}$ and $\phi_{c\,i}$ represent the probability of a fish in one of these two groups surviving from dam i to dam $i + 1$. We chose these parameters to be fairly high (0.86-0.98 for control fish); however, the total survival between dams 1 and 6 for control fish is 0.641 (the product of ϕ_{c1}, ϕ_{c2}, ϕ_{c3}, ϕ_{c4}, and ϕ_{c5}: $\prod_{i=1}^{5}\phi_{ci}$). The parameter representing the treatment effect is the survival rate S. In this simple example, $S = \phi_{t1}/\phi_{c1} = 0.90$. The estimation of the treatment effect S under different models and sampling protocols represents the focus of this monograph.

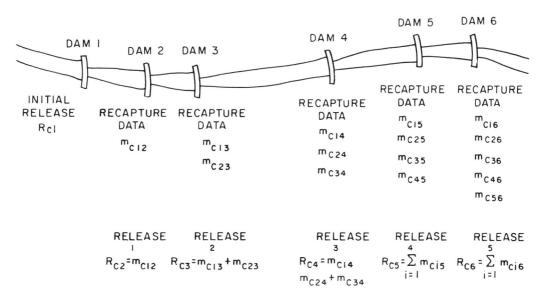

Figure 1.7. – Notation for the recapture and release or rerelease data for the control group in the general numerical example. In the figure, no losses on capture are assumed. If such losses occur, they are not included in the total to be rereleased ($R_{c\,i}$).

Table 1.2. – Survival and recapture probabilities for the general numerical example. Treatment and control fish are assumed to have been released at dam 1 and potentially recaptured and rereleased at dams 2-6.

Dam i	Recapture probabilities $p_{ti} = p_{ci}$	Survival probabilities[a] ϕ_{ci}		ϕ_{ti}
1		0.98	$\neq$	0.88
2	0.04	0.95	=	0.95
3	0.01	0.89	=	0.89
4	0.08	0.90	=	0.90
5	0.03	0.86	=	0.86
6	0.04			

[a] $S = \phi_{t1}/\phi_{c1} = 0.9$.

Examination of Table 1.1 shows that, of the initial releases, 25,925 treatment and 24,605 control fish were never recaptured at any of the five downstream dams (see row one of the CH matrix); 563 treatment and 605 control fish were recaptured and rereleased only at dam 6 (capture history {100001} in row two), and an additional 27 treatment and 36 control fish were recaptured only at dam 6 and lost on capture. The fish lost on capture are denoted with a minus sign because they were not rereleased. The interpretation of the rest of the CH matrix is similar.

1.3.2.2. Full m-array. – The CH matrix is a compact way to present the basic data from any survival experiment in which marked animals are released and recaptured. All estimation methods and tests can be based on the information contained in the CH matrix. However, the CH matrix can be summarized in what we call the full *m*-array as an equivalent representation of the data. The full *m*-array contains every iota of information from the experiment, but is more easily interpreted than the CH matrix because it is directly related in format to our statistical modeling of release-recapture data and to the computational procedures for some hypothesis tests.

For each treatment or control group in the study, there is a separate full *m*-array. The recapture data are represented as m_{vij}, the number of first recaptures, on occasion j from releases on occasion i ($i < j$), by group (v). The data are represented in a full *m*-array in terms of releases and first recaptures after release. Moreover, the releases R_{vi} and recaptures m_{vij} are partitioned by capture history h (at release time i) into all possible subcohorts. Thus, an example of one line of this full *m*-array is of the form

$$h = \{101\} \quad R_{t3h}, m_{t34h}, m_{t35h}, ..., m_{t3kh}.$$

We find that it is useful to append the values r_{vih} and $R_{vih} - r_{vih}$ (total fish ever recaptured from those released and those never seen again) onto the above line.

There will be $k - 1$ major portions (row groupings) of the array ($k - 1$ releases; releases at dam k are irrelevant). Within the ith portion (releases at dam i), the number of subcohorts is variable, as it depends on the number of previous capture occasions. Table 1.3 shows the full m-array for the treatment group data of the numerical example, e.g., for $h = \{101\}$, R_{t3h} = 224. The corresponding recaptures at dams 4, 5, and 6 are m_{t34h} = 19, m_{t35h} = 7, and m_{t36h} = 5, respectively. A fish recaptured n times will be represented in n different rows of the full m-array.

A detailed example will make the full m-array more clear. Consider the recapture data on treatment fish at dam 3 in Table 1.3, especially the shaded area. Of the 30,000 fish initially released at dam 1, 238 were first recaptured at dam 3 (their capture history is {101}). Of the 238 recaptured fish, 14 were lost on capture leaving 224 fish available to be rereleased. In addition, 1,029 fish were captured at dam 2 and, of these, 1,000 were released (29 were lost on capture). Of these 1,000 fish released at dam 2, 11 were recaptured at dam 3 and all were rereleased (no fish were lost on capture). These 11 fish have capture history {111}, as they were released at dam 1, captured and rereleased at dam 2, and then captured and rereleased at dam 3. Therefore, 235 fish were released at dam 3 (224 plus 11 = 235). In order to retain all the information in the CH matrix, the full m-array must also present losses on capture (shown in parentheses). The reader is encouraged to work through the meaning of the full m-array, as it is used frequently in material that follows.

Program RELEASE computes the full m-array as an option, if $k \leq 9$, from the CH matrix. Figure 1.6 presents material that aids in the interpretation of Table 1.4 for the control group.

1.3.2.3. Reduced m-array. – A summarization of the data from a survival experiment is the reduced m-array, which combines data over subcohorts within cohorts. The reduced m-array allows the biologist to view critical summary data in a simple format. Capture-recapture data are usually published in the literature in what we call the reduced m-array (see, for example, the data presented by Jolly 1965).

The reduced m-array contains all the information needed for estimation of the ϕ_i and p_i parameters under the usual Jolly-Seber assumptions, but lacks some important information required for components of the full testing procedure. Nonetheless, the reduced m-array is a valuable summary of the data, and extensive use is made of such summaries in this monograph. Program RELEASE allows the user to input the data as either a CH matrix or a reduced m-array.

Table 1.3. – Release-recapture data generated for the treatment group used in the general numerical example. The full m-array is given for the complete capture history protocol. Losses on capture are in parentheses and capture histories, up to and including dam i, are shown in braces (e.g., {1011} represents a fish initially released at dam 1 and recaptured at dams 3 and 4). Information on the number of fish released or rereleased appears to the left of the line and the number of first recaptures to the right.

	Release-recapture data (R_{tih} and m_{tijh})						Total recaptured r_{tih}	Never recaptured $R_{tih} - r_{tih}$
Release	1	2	3	4	5	6		
Initial release {1}	30,000	1,029(29)	238(14)[a]	1,669(81)	549(23)	590(27)	4,075	25,925
Rereleases at dam 2	{11}	1,000	11(0)	73(3)	17(1)	27(1)	128	872
Rereleases at dam 3		{101}	224	19(1)	7(0)	5(0)	31	193
		{111}	11	1(0)	0(0)	0(0)	1	10
Rereleases at dam 4			{1001}	1,588	40(2)	48(3)	88	1,500
			{1101}	70	2(0)	1(0)	3	67
			{1011}	18	1(0)	1(0)	2	16
			{1111}	1	0(0)	0(0)	0	1
Rereleases at dam 5				{10001}	526	18(1)	18	508
				{11001}	16	0(0)	0	16
				{10101}	7	0(0)	0	7
				{10011}	38	1(0)	1	37
				{11011}	2	0(0)	0	2
				{10111}	1	0(0)	0	1

[a]The shaded area represents the numbers captured, lost on capture, and rereleased. For example, 224 fish were released at dam 3 from the 238 caught; 14 were losses on capture.

Table 1.4. – Release-recapture data generated for the control group used in the general numerical example. The full m-array is given for the complete capture history protocol. Losses on capture are in parentheses and capture histories, up to and including dam i, are shown in braces. Information on the number of fish released or rereleased appears to the left of the line and the number of first recaptures is to the right.

| Release | Release-recapture data ($R_{c\,ih}$ and $m_{c\,ijh}$) | | | | | | Total recaptured $r_{c\,ih}$ | Never recaptured $R_{c\,ih} - r_{c\,ih}$ |
	1	2	3	4	5	6		
Initial release {1}	29,000	1,104(33)	247(10)	1,832(57)	571(25)	641(36)	4,395	24,605
Rereleases at dam 2	{11}	1,071	13(0)	75(4)	19(1)	29(1)	136	935
Rereleases at dam 3		{101}	237	17(1)	4(0)	9(0)	30	207
		{111}	13	0(0)	0(0)	1(0)	1	12
Rereleases at dam 4			{1001}	1775	48(2)	49(1)	97	1,678
			{1101}	71	1(0)	2(0)	3	68
			{1011}	16	1(0)	1(0)	2	14
Rereleases at dam 5				{10001}	546	24(1)	24	522
				{11001}	18	0(0)	0	18
				{10101}	4	0(0)	0	4
				{10011}	46	2(0)	2	44
				{11011}	1	0(0)	0	1
				{10111}	1	0(0)	0	1

Tables 1.5 and 1.6 show reduced m-arrays for treatment and control fish, respectively, for the general numerical example. Also shown in these tables are row totals r_i, column totals m_j, and a statistic z_j (z_j = the number of fish captured above and below, but not at, dam j). Of course, the specific notation includes t and c in the subscripts to denote group. The m_{vj}, z_{vj}, and r_{vi} for $v = t$ or c are not necessary aspects of the m-array; however, it is useful to show them there (they are redundant, given the R_{vi} and m_{vij} information).

Whereas the full m-array presents R_{vih} and m_{vijh}, the reduced m-array presents only the sums $R_{vi} \equiv R_{vi.} = \sum_h R_{vih}$ and $m_{vij} \equiv m_{vij.} = \sum_h m_{vijh}$ for $v = t$ or c. For example, in Table 1.5,

$$R_{t3} = 235 = 224 + 11 = R_{t3,\{101\}} + R_{t3,\{111\}},$$

and

$$m_{t34} = 19 + 1 = m_{t34,\{101\}} + m_{t34,\{111\}}.$$

Losses on capture may conveniently be shown in parentheses but are not necessary; we omit them from Tables 1.5-1.6.

1.3.3. Four Major Protocols

A technical team planning an experiment to estimate survival due to some treatment (e.g., passage over a spillway) must choose the basic experimental approach to be used in the field. We have identified four broad alternatives and have termed them "protocols." Each protocol is discussed in terms of the type of marking and recapture method and amount of information on the specific capture history of individual fish. We will make extensive use of the general numerical example introduced in Section 1.3.2 to aid in understanding these important concepts.

Table 1.5. – Reduced release-recapture data and summary statistics for the treatment group. Shown are the totals, by release occasion, over subcohorts. This table is the reduced m-array and is a condensation of the information given in Table 1.3.

Dam i	Releases R_{ti}	Treatment recapture data at dam j, m_{tij}					r_{ti}
		$j = 2$	3	4	5	6	
1	30,000	1,029	238	1,669	549[a]	590	4,075
2	1,000		11	73	17	27	128
3	235			20	7	5	32
4	1,677				43	50	93
5	590					19	19
Totals	m_{tj}	1,029	249	1,762	616	691	4,347
	z_{tj}	3,046	2,925	1,195	672	0	

[a]The sum of elements in the shaded area is $m_{t5} = 616$.

Table 1.6. – Reduced release-recapture data and summary statistics for the control group. Shown are the totals, by release occasion, over subcohorts. This table is the reduced m-array and is a condensation of the information given in Table 1.4.

Dam i	Releases R_{d}	Control recapture data, m_{dj}					r_{ci}
		$j = 2$	3	4	5	6	
1	29,000	1,104	247	1,832	571	641[a]	4,395
2	1,071		13	75	19	29	136
3	250			17	4	10	31
4	1,862				50	52	102
5	616					26	26
Totals	m_{cj}	1,104	260	1,924	644	758	4,690
	z_{cj}	3,291	3,167	1,274	732	0	

[a]The sum of elements in the shaded area is $z_{\mathrm{c3}} = 3,167$.

1.3.3.1. First capture history protocol. – Under the first capture history protocol, marked fish are released at dam 1 and are removed upon first recapture. Removal can be physical, or another mark or fin clip can be added (and the fish then released) that allows future recaptures to be ignored. Thus, removal data are multinomial, as each fish can be recaptured independently only at a single downstream dam (i.e., at one of dams 2, 3, ..., k) or "never."

Only batch marks are required to distinguish the two releases (e.g., the R_{t1} and R_{c1} fish must have different batch marks). First capture history protocol data can be summarized as a CH matrix. Table 1.7 provides an example of a study involving six dams ($k = 6$).

Table 1.7. – Capture history matrix for the general numerical example under the first capture history protocol. Negative values indicate that fish were removed upon recapture.

Capture history	Dam of recapture j	Number recaptured	
		t	c
110000	2	-1,029	-1,104
101000	3	-238	-247
100100	4	-1,669	-1,832
100010	5	-549	-571
100001	6	-590	-641
100000	never	25,925	24,605

The CH matrix shows that most fish were released and never recaptured; see capture history $h = \{100000\}$. The minus sign preceding the numbers recaptured in the treatment and control groups denotes the fish that were removed. All fish recaptured were removed; none were rereleased. All the data representations (the CH matrix, full and reduced m-arrays) are essentially equivalent. Only data on first recaptures (that are then removed) are available for analysis. Fish recaptured at the last dam (6 in this example, k in general) need not be removed as no further sampling will be conducted downstream.

The reduced m-array is a more convenient summary of data under this simple protocol (Table 1.8). Note that these data include only the first row of Tables 1.3 and 1.5 for the treatment group and Tables 1.4 and 1.6 for the control group because fish are not rereleased after capture.

The first capture history protocol allows only the treatment survival rate S to be estimated as an individual parameter. (Products of the other parameters [i.e., the ϕ_i and p_i] are estimable.) Limited tests of important assumptions are possible. Overall, the first capture history protocol is simple and useful if the effect of the treatment is acute, and if proper replication is included in the experimental design (see Part 4 for a discussion of replication).

1.3.3.2. Unknown capture history protocol. – In most fish survival experiments conducted in the Columbia River to date, capture histories of individual fish are unknown. Fish are given a batch mark, but the fish are not removed upon recapture; rather they are rereleased. Therefore, a particular fish may be released and recaptured two or more times, but one has no way of knowing its capture history. The resulting recapture data are not multinomial, and information needed to complete the CH matrix is not available with this protocol. The unknown capture history protocol, consequently, has several disadvantages, especially as the recapture probabilities (p_i) increase. The data are not amenable to any exact statistical analysis. However, when capture probabilities are low, the unknown capture history protocol is a potential alternative if there is sufficient empirical replication.

Unknown capture history data include the total number of fish, by treatment and control group, recaptured at dam j (i.e., $m_{tj} \equiv m_{t.j}$ and $m_{cj} \equiv m_{c.j}$, $j = 2, ..., 6$ in the general numerical example). The data are a pooling of recaptures over different capture histories; thus, some important summary statistics cannot be computed (e.g., r_{v1}, the total number of distinct fish

Table 1.8. – Data from the general numerical example under the first capture history protocol for treatment and control groups. The m-array is reduced to a single row for each group because no recaptured fish are rereleased; instead they are removed.

Group	Releases R_{v1}	Number recaptured and removed at dam j, m_{vij}				
		$j = 2$	3	4	5	6
t	30,000	1,029	238	1,669	549	590
c	29,000	1,104	247	1,832	571	641

recaptured from the initial release). Table 1.9 shows the data that would result from the general numerical example if this protocol had been used. The recapture data shown for this protocol are merely column totals from Tables 1.5 and 1.6 for treatment and control fish, respectively. The availability only of totals represents a loss of information and prevents an exact statistical analysis.

1.3.3.3. Complete capture history protocol. – In the complete capture history protocol, each fish bears a unique mark. The use of unique marks allows the capture history of each fish to be known and used in the analysis. Fewer assumptions are required, additional statistical tests about assumptions can be made, and flexibility in the estimation of parameters is increased. The use of unique marks will become increasingly feasible as new technologies develop.

We believe that the complete capture history protocol is often superior to the other three protocols because it provides more tests of key assumptions and provides flexibility in the analysis. This protocol should be given full consideration in the design of future studies. The data derived from all other protocols are special cases of this general approach. The advantages of the complete capture history protocol increase as the recapture rates at downstream dams increase. The CH matrix for the complete capture history protocol is given in Table 1.1, including the fish lost on capture. The full m-arrays are shown in Tables 1.3 and 1.4, and the reduced m-arrays in Tables 1.5 and 1.6.

1.3.3.4. Partial capture history protocol. – Under the partial capture history protocol we consider two useful methods that have many advantages in the field and produce adequate data for statistical analysis. A limitation of this protocol is that the application of a second batch mark is required, and it is crucial that this handling not affect survival. The partial capture history protocol involves the use of site-specific marks at one or more downstream dams (i.e., 2, ..., k-1) in conjunction with "removal" after the maximum number of marks are applied. The use of site-specific marks differs from use of unique marks on fish initially released at dam 1. We develop only two possible partial capture history protocols: scheme A and scheme B.

Table 1.9. – Data from the general numerical example under the unknown capture history protocol for treatment and control groups. Capture histories are pooled and necessitate approximate analysis methods. Losses on capture are shown in parentheses.

Group	Releases $R_{\cdot 1}$	Number recaptured at dam j				
		$j = 2$	3	4	5	6
t	30,000	1,029(33)	249(14)	1,762(85)	616(26)	691(32)
c	29,000	1,104(33)	260(10)	1,924(62)	644(28)	758(39)

In scheme A, treatment and control fish are batch-marked and then released at dam 1, as in the first and unknown capture history protocols. However, upon first recapture, each fish is given a second mark that is specific to that particular dam. If a fish is recaptured a second time, it is removed (either physically removed or a fin is clipped or a third mark is added to indicate its removal). A possible capture history with scheme A is {1001010}, which indicates a fish marked initially at dam 1, recaptured (and released) at dam 4 after being given an additional mark specific to dam 4, and recaptured and removed at dam 6 (and therefore unavailable for recapture at dam 7). Thus, only partial capture histories are available under this protocol (data cannot be gathered on fish recaptured more than twice).

Data under scheme A contain much of the information available from data under the complete capture history protocol, especially if capture probabilities are low. Marking equipment must be available at each downstream dam, but simple batch marks can be used.

The CH matrix for the general numerical example under scheme A is shown in Table 1.10, including fish lost on capture. Note that, unlike the CH matrix for complete capture his-

Table 1.10. – CH matrix for the general numerical example under the partial capture history protocol, scheme A.

Capture history	Number recaptured	
	t	c
100000	25,925	24,605
100001	563	605
100001	-27	-36
100010	508	522
100010	-23	-25
100011	-18	-24
100100	1,500	1,678
100100	-81	-57
100101	-48	-49
100110	-40	-48
101000	193	207
101000	-14	-10
101001	-5	-9
101010	-7	-4
101100	-19	-17
110000	872	935
110000	-29	-33
110001	-27	-29
110010	-17	-19
110100	-73	-75
111000	-11	-13

histories, no fish under scheme A are recaptured more than twice (i.e., there are no more than three ones in a capture history h: a row of the CH matrix). The m-arrays are shown in Table 1.11. For scheme A, the full and reduced m-arrays are identical, i.e., all releases at a given dam have the same capture history to that point, so there are no subcohorts based on capture histories.

In scheme B, it is assumed that treatment and control fish with distinguishing batch marks are simultaneously released at dam 1. All fish recaptured at the second dam (dam 2) are given a second mark to indicate that they were recaptured and then rereleased. However, all fish recaptured at dams 3, 4, ..., k are removed from the population. This scheme requires additional marking at only one downstream dam (dam 2). In this respect, scheme B is logistically better than scheme A, but the resulting data contain less information than those collected in scheme A. The CH matrix for scheme B is shown in Table 1.12, and the reduced m-arrays are shown in Table 1.13. The data are mostly removals and, therefore, similar to the data from the first capture history protocol (see Table 1.8).

Although some information is lost, we believe scheme B represents an excellent protocol that should be considered further in the design of future experiments. A disadvantage is the potential effect of handling and marking on subsequent survival. Scheme B represents a logistically reasonable protocol and scheme A is a statistically reasonable protocol.

Table 1.11. – The m-array for the general numerical example under the partial capture history protocol, scheme A.

			Number recaptured at dam j, m_{vij}				
Group	i	Releases R_{vi}	j = 2	3	4	5	6
t	1	30,000	1,029	238	1,669	549	590
	2	1,000		11	73	17	27
	3	224			19	7	5
	4	1,588				40	48
	5	526					18
c	1	29,000	1,104	247	1,832	571	641
	2	2,071		13	75	19	29
	3	237			17	4	9
	4	1,775				48	49
	5	546					24

Table 1.12. – The CH matrix for the general numerical example under the partial capture history protocol, scheme B.

Capture history	Number recaptured	
	t	c
100000	25,925	24,605
100001	-590	-641
100010	-549	-571
100100	-1,669	-1,832
101000	-238	-247
110000	872	935
110000	-29	-33
110001	-27	-29
110010	-17	-19
110100	-73	-75
111000	-11	-13

Table 1.13. – The m-array for the general numerical example under the partial capture history protocol, scheme B.

Group	i	Releases R_i	Number recaptured at dam j, $m_{\tau ij}$				
			$j = 2$	3	4	5	6
t	1	30,000	1,029	238	1,669	549	590
	2	1,000		11	73	17	27
c	1	29,000	1,104	247	1,832	571	641
	2	1,071		13	75	19	29

1.4. Release-Recapture Modeling Concepts, Notation, and Assumptions

In Chapter 1.3 we introduced some of the concepts regarding release-recapture, including ways to display the data and different study protocols (which produce different amounts of data). Here we elaborate on the subject by considering concepts essential to the modeling of such data. We also present an overview of the necessary notation required to represent symbolically the data and probability models for the data. Finally, we introduce the philosophy that guides our data modeling and analysis efforts for this class of fish survival experiments. We assume that the complete capture history protocol is the starting point because it is the most general data collection and modeling case; all other protocols should be viewed as special cases of the complete capture history protocol.

1.4.1. Introduction to Release-Recapture Concepts

Release-recapture is used widely to study animal survival processes. In fisheries, it is used more often to estimate population sizes. A cohort of R_1 marked animals is released and then a subsequent sampling process is used to catch (sample) the marked survivors. These survivors may be rereleased at the site (or time) of capture. Consequently, in typical capture-recapture studies (e.g., Jolly 1965), an individual can be captured at several sites. Such multiple recaptures lead to the idea of a capture history, which we introduced in Section 1.3.2. Although capture histories provide a convenient way to record data and enter it for computer analysis, they are not convenient for modeling though they have been so used. Capture histories have been used as the basis of models and subsequent data analysis in the log-linear approach (e.g., Cormack 1979, 1981). Crosbie and Manly (1985) also provided an analysis method based on the capture history representation. We base our models on an alternative conceptualization of the process, as presented by Brownie et al. (1985:170-175).

The first key concept is that one should model the recapture process and then analyze the recapture data, conditional on the known number of releases at each release site (or time). A probability model for the data may then depend on capture history at the time of release. In principle, the released fish at any recapture dam can represent a mix of "new" and recaptured fish. The critical question is whether or not such a mixed cohort meets the assumptions needed for a meaningful data analysis.

The second key concept is that release and recapture are paired; this concept is the essence of release-recapture. Each release of a fish is an experiment in itself. Assume a fish is released at dam 1 and recaptured at dam 3 (but not seen at dam 2). One now knows that the fish survived between dams 1 and 3. The rerelease of the fish at dam 3 starts another survival trial. One conditions (principle 1) on that release and again waits to see if that fish is recaptured.

Consider the capture history $h = \{101011\}$ for a study with six dams. An equivalent representation for this capture history follows.

Release occasion i	First recapture after release time i				
	2	3	4	5	6
1 (released)	0	1			
2					
3 (released)			0	1	
4					
5 (released)					1

This type of representation of data leads to the *m*-array.

The second concept states that the model is concerned *only* with the *first* recapture after any release. The data are represented as a series of linked release-recaptures. Conditioning on release and then modeling first-only recaptures are the keys to simplified modeling of release-recapture data. Throughout this monograph, recapture (or capture) of marked fish refers to the first recapture after a release. In this manner, releases and subsequent recaptures are uniquely paired (unless the fish is never observed again). Under the unknown capture history protocol, this pairing still exists in principle, but information about it is not available.

The recognition of different levels of data leads to additional terminology. The "cohort" is the focus of building either single or multiple release-recapture data sets. A cohort is a known number of animals released at a given site (or time). Given such a definition of a cohort, then, each animal in a cohort is either recaptured once or never observed again. Upon (first) recapture, if the animal is (re)released, it automatically becomes a member of a different study cohort.

The subcohort is a partition of a cohort. Suppose 500 fish are recaptured at dam 3 and 480 are released as cohort 3, $R_3 = 480$ (20 were lost on capture). Those fish can have one of two possible capture histories when they are released at dam 3:

h	R_{3h}
101	460
111	20
Total	480 .

The numbers of fish released with each capture history are defined as a subcohort of R_3. Therefore, in this example, cohort 3 has two subcohorts of sizes 460 and 20.

It is possible to define subcohorts on another basis, such as a fish's sex or size. The reason for distinguishing subcohorts within a cohort is that the subcohort data are useful for tests of assumptions. One can test that the capture and survival rates are not affected by the factors (especially capture history) defining subcohorts.

A data set is a collection of cohorts (releases) and the subsequent (first) recapture data from each cohort. Much of the capture-recapture literature deals with the analysis of only one data set. However, many important questions that can be investigated by release-recapture require collecting at least two related data sets (e.g., treatment-control, male-female, age-classes, or different locations; see Manly 1985 for numerous specific examples). Thus, one must be able to cope with the analyses of multiple, related release-recapture data consisting of the following levels:

(1) V release-recapture data sets (groups), e.g., $V = 2$ for t and c;

(2) $k - 1$ cohorts within each data set (for k dams);

(3) subcohorts within each cohort;

(4) first recaptures from each subcohort.

(Again, we note that some of these features vanish under protocols other than the complete capture history protocol.)

One final point regarding concepts: a capture history compiled at time of release is defined only with respect to the previous capture sites. Confusion can be avoided and simpler notation can be used when this is understood. Thus, if h represents a capture history at site i, then h has exactly i components, each component being either a zero or a one.

1.4.2. Release-Recapture Notation

We have already introduced most of our notation. We now present it in greater detail. Its comprehension should be facilitated if the previous ideas are kept in mind.

1.4.2.1. Notation for data. – Notation for data must allow one to distinguish levels of data: data sets (groups), cohorts, subcohorts, and first recaptures given releases. The following symbols are fundamental (see also the Glossary for notation):

k The number of release-recapture sites or times;

R_i Known number released at dam i, $i = 1, ..., k - 1$;

m_{ij} The number of fish recaptured (for the first time) at site j from the cohort released at site i, $j = i + 1, ..., k$.

These basic symbols must be elaborated upon to allow for subcohorts and multiple data groups. Elaboration is in the form of additional subscripts – v for data groups and h for subcohorts:

R_{vih} is the number of released animals in group v and subcohort h at site i.

m_{vijh} is the corresponding number of recaptures at site j for R_{vih}.

When only one data set is involved, the subscript v can be dropped. Thus, R_{ih} and m_{ijh} can arise. When results are pooled over all subcohorts, the h is dropped and R_{vi} and m_{vij} are used. We sometimes replace a subscript with a dot (.) to denote summation (i.e., "pooling") over that subscript. Thus, $R_{vi.}$ is equivalent to R_{vi}, although we prefer the simpler notation of R_{vi} in this situation.

The subscripts always appear in the same order: data group v, release site i, recapture site j, and subcohort h. However, all four subscript levels do not always occur (e.g., R never has subscript j). Various subscripts tend especially to be omitted in summary statistics.

In addition to R_i and m_{ij} (or R_{vih} and m_{vijh}), several summary statistics (i.e., of the m_{ij}) are commonly used. These statistics are sums of the recaptures (i.e., of the m_{ij}).

r_i The total number of the R_i that are recaptured again; a row total, $r_i = \sum\limits_j m_{ij}$.

m_j The total number of marked animals caught at site j; a column total, $m_j = \sum\limits_i m_{ij}$.

T_j The total number of captures at sites j, $j+1$, ..., k from releases in cohorts R_1, ..., R_{j-1} (hence released prior to site j).

z_j The total number of captures at sites $j+1$, ..., k from releases in cohorts R_1, ..., R_{j-1}.

Many variations of these summary statistics can occur. In particular, these are r_{tih}, r_{cih} (in the case of treatment and control groups and recaptures by subcohort), and r_{ih} (one group only). The quantities m_{vj}, T_{vj}, and z_{vj} also arise, along with $m_{.j}$, $T_{.j}$, and $z_{.j}$ (where summation is over groups). Because there are too many combinations to define explicitly, we imposed a logic on our notation in regard to the order and meaning of subscripts.

Summary statistics can be computed as various totals of the basic data: m_{vijh}; $v = 1$, ..., V; $i = 1$, ..., $k - 1$; $j = i + 1$, ..., k; and $h = 1$, ..., H_{vi}. The symbol H_{vi} represents the number of subcohorts in cohort i, data group v. For example,

$$
\begin{cases}
z_j = \sum\limits_{i=1}^{j-1} \sum\limits_{n=j+1}^{k} m_{in} , & j = 2, ..., k - 1 ; \\[2em]
z_k \equiv 0 ;
\end{cases}
$$

$$T_j = m_j + z_j ;$$

$$T_{j+1} = z_j + r_j .$$

Although there are many other relationships, the reader need not learn them. Program RELEASE computes the necessary summary statistics.

We selected our basic notation to be as consistent as possible with that used in the general capture-recapture literature, e.g., that used by Seber (1982). Our results are applicable to the analysis of Jolly-Seber data with respect to inferences about survival rates. The full analysis of Jolly-Seber data involves estimation of population size, which requires capturing unmarked animals and marking and releasing them. The extra notation needed is primarily u_i, the number of unmarked animals caught at site (or time) i; the notation u_{vi}, and possibly u_{vih}, could also be used. We do not use "u" in our notation, thereby making it available for use in extensions of results to the general open population capture-recapture situation (see, e.g., Chapter 8.3).

Table 1.14. – Symbolic form of the full m-array representation of a single release-recapture data set (see Table 1.3 for an example).

		Release-recapture data at dam j				Total recaptured	Never recaptured
		1	2	3	4	5		
$h = \{1\}$	R_{1h}	m_{12h}	m_{13h}	m_{14h}	m_{15h}	r_{1h}	$R_{1h} - r_{1h}$
	$h = \{11\}$	R_{2h}	m_{23h}	m_{24h}	m_{25h}	r_{2h}	$R_{2h} - r_{2h}$
		$h = \{111\}$	R_{3h}	m_{34h}	m_{35h}	r_{3h}	$R_{3h} - r_{3h}$
		$h = \{101\}$	R_{3h}	m_{34h}	m_{35h}	r_{3h}	$R_{3h} - r_{3h}$
			$h = \{1111\}$	R_{4h}	m_{45h}	r_{4h}	$R_{4h} - r_{4h}$
			$h = \{1011\}$	R_{4h}	m_{45h}	r_{4h}	$R_{4h} - r_{4h}$
			$h = \{1101\}$	R_{4h}	m_{45h}	r_{4h}	$R_{4h} - r_{4h}$
			$h = \{1001\}$	R_{4h}	m_{45h}	r_{4h}	$R_{4h} - r_{4h}$

Tabular forms for presenting data are given in Section 1.3.2. These forms (e.g., Tables 1.3 and 1.5) are directly related to our notation. There is a full m-array for each treatment group. This full m-array presents the data at the level of subcohorts, i.e., the R_{vih} and subsequent m_{vijh}. This form is shown in Table 1.14. Pooling over subcohorts within each cohort gives the data in the reduced m-array, which we usually merely refer to as the m-array (see Table 1.15). That data representation is the most common one used in capture-recapture studies; however, its use results in a loss of all the information (for testing assumptions) that is contained in the subcohort data.

Table 1.15. – Symbolic form of the reduced m-array representation of a single release-recapture data set (see Table 1.5 for an example).

Releases at dam i	Recapture data at dam j				Total recaptured
	2	3	4	5	
R_1	m_{12}	m_{13}	m_{14}	m_{15}	r_1
R_2		m_{23}	m_{24}	m_{25}	r_2
R_3			m_{34}	m_{35}	r_3
R_4				m_{45}	r_4
Summary	m_2	m_3	m_4	m_5	
statistics	z_2	z_3	z_4	z_5	

1.4.2.2. Notation for parameters. – Only two types of parameters are used in release-recapture models: survival rates and capture probabilities. The generic symbols for dam-to-dam survival rate and capture probability at a given dam are ϕ and p, respectively. Also, $1 - \phi$ represents mortality rate and $q = 1 - p$ = probability an animal is not captured. Precise definitions follow:

ϕ_i the conditional probability of a fish surviving from release at site i to site $i + 1$; and

p_i the conditional probability of a fish being captured at site i given that it is alive at (i.e., arrives alive at) site i.

Note the conditional nature of both parameters. Survival, ϕ_i, applies only to fish alive at site i. Also, ϕ_i is unrelated to whether or not the fish was captured at sites i or $i + 1$. Hence, survival and capture processes are evaluated as separate parameters.

The subscripts on these parameters can be expanded in accordance with conventions discussed previously. For example, we also have

ϕ_{vi}, p_{vi} when survival and capture rates vary by data group (e.g., $v = t$ or c).

ϕ_i represents a common survival rate from site i to $i + 1$ for all treatment groups (i.e., $\phi_{vi} = \phi_i$, for all v).

Similarly, we use p_i when the parameters p_{vi} do not vary by treatment v. The use of ϕ_i or p_i is equivalent to $\phi_{.i}$ or $p_{.i}$, except that the latter notation is used only rarely.

Survival and capture probability parameters often enter the models as complicated functions. Therefore, we define other parameters as functions of ϕ_i and p_i; in particular,

$$\lambda_i = \phi_i(p_{i+1} + q_{i+1}\lambda_{i+1}) , \quad i = 1, ..., k - 1 ,$$

$$\lambda_k = 0 \text{ (by definition)} ,$$

and

$$\tau_i = \frac{p_i}{p_i + q_i\lambda_i} , \quad i = 2, ..., k - 1 .$$

We note that λ_i = the probability that a fish released at dam i will be recaptured; thus, $E(r_i | R_i) = R_i\lambda_i$. Also, τ_i is the proportion of fish captured at dam i of those released prior to dam i and captured at dams i, $i + 1$, ..., k. Thus, $\tau_i = E\left(\dfrac{m_i}{T_i}\right)$.

The focus of this monograph is on the estimation of treatment effect S. Often, $S = \phi_{t1}/\phi_{c1}$ and, if the treatment has a detrimental effect on survival, $S < 1$ and can be considered as a probability. In other cases the treatment may enhance survival and, therefore, $S > 1$. If the effect of the treatment extends downstream to dam 3, then $S = (\phi_{t1}\phi_{t2})/(\phi_{c1}\phi_{c2})$.

The treatment effect can be partitioned under some sampling protocols. For example, $S_1 = \phi_{t1}/\phi_{c1}$ and $S_2 = \phi_{t2}/\phi_{c2}$; thus, the overall treatment effect is $S = S_1 S_2$. Other specific definitions of S are possible depending on the application and postulated effect of the treatment on the marked population. The important point is that S is a general measure of a treatment effect.

1.4.3. Release-Recapture Models

1.4.3.1. Modeling approach. – There are two conceptual aspects to the models used here: (1) the structure of the expected number of recaptures given the known releases, and (2) the specification of the nature of the random variation of the recaptures given their expected values. The structural aspects of the expectations are usually readily comprehended; however, a complete model is necessary for purposes of sound scientific inference. The complete model is a specification of the probability distribution of the recaptures m_{ij} given releases R_i.

Numerous modeling approaches have been used as a basis for the analysis of capture data (e.g., Cormack 1979). Conditional on the releases R_i and, given some specific assumptions, the recaptures $m_{i,i+1}, ..., m_{ik}$ are multinomial random variables. Multinomial models provide the most convenient approach when the emphasis is on estimating survival rates. Also, multinomial models provide a relatively easy and unified framework for theory development (e.g., Brownie et al. 1985:170-175; Burnham, unpublished report, 1987).

The most critical aspect of modeling release-recapture data is the specification of the expected values of the recaptures m_{ij} given the releases. Symbolically, this expectation is

$$E(m_{ij} \mid R_i) = R_i \pi_{ij}.$$

Thus, $\pi_{ij} = E(m_{ij} \mid R_i)/R_i, j=i + 1, ..., k$ is the probability that a fish released at site i will be recaptured at site j. By virtue of our definition of a recapture as meaning the first recapture after release, a fish released at site i is either recaptured at exactly one downstream site (site i + 1, or i + 2, ..., or k) or it is never observed again. We let $\lambda_i = \pi_{i,i+1} + \pi_{i,i+2} + ... + \pi_{ik}$; then $1 - \lambda_i = \text{Pr}\{$a fish released at site i is never observed again$\}$. Thus, after release at site i, the fish experiences exactly one of $k - i + 1$ mutually exclusive fates. Given the assumptions of statistical independence for the fates of released fish and that the same parameters π_{ij} apply to every fish, then the m_{ij} given R_i are multinomial random variables. The general mathematical form of the multinomial probability distribution for these recapture data is

$$\text{Pr}\{m_{i,i+1}, ..., m_{ik} \mid R_i\} = \begin{pmatrix} R_i \\ m_{i,i+1} \cdots m_{ik} \; R_i - r_i \end{pmatrix} \left[\prod_{j=i+1}^{k} (\pi_{ij})^{m_{ij}} \right] (1 - \lambda_i)^{R_i - r_i}.$$

Multinomial models are completely specified by giving (hypothesizing) the expected values of the m_{ij} given the releases R_i. Thus, by adopting this framework, we reduce the modeling to specification of the π_{ij}.

1.4.3.2. Model structures. – By model structure, we mean the expressions for the π_{ij} in terms of survival (ϕ) and capture (p) probabilities. The estimators of the survival and capture rates are determined by the model structure. The multinomial sampling distribution component of the models really only determines (theoretical) sampling variances and covariances. If sampling variances are obtained from replicate releases, the only critical part of the model is the structure assumed for the $\pi_{ij} = E(m_{ij} \mid R_i)/R_i$.

A convenient initial model structure to consider is that of assuming parameters to be time-specific only. Then, for example,

$$\pi_{i,i+1} = (\phi_i p_{i+1}) \; ;$$

$$\pi_{i,i+2} = (\phi_i q_{i+1})(\phi_{i+1} p_{i+2}) \; ;$$

$$\pi_{i,i+3} = (\phi_i q_{i+1})(\phi_{i+1} q_{i+2})(\phi_{i+2} p_{i+3}) \; .$$

Consider the interpretation of $\pi_{i,i+2}$, which is the probability that a fish released at site i will not be caught at site $i + 1$ but will be caught at site $i + 2$. The probability of survival from site i to $i + 1$ is ϕ_i, while $q_{i+1} = 1 - p_{i+1}$ is the probability that the fish is not caught at site $i + 1$ given that it survives to site $i + 1$. Next, the fish must survive from site $i + 1$ to $i + 2$ (probability = ϕ_{i+1}) and then be caught (probability = p_{i+2}). It is worth noting that presence in the released cohort is represented by the product $(\phi_i q_{i+1})$, whereas removal from the released cohort is represented by the product $(\phi_i p_{i+1})$. All the release-recapture models used here have this basic structure: the π_{ij} are products of $(\phi_n q_{n+1})$ terms, $n = i, \ldots, j - 2$, and a final $(\phi_{j-1} p_j)$ term. What distinguishes different models is how these survival and capture probability parameters depend on treatment and release or recapture site.

Table 1.15 shows the symbolic form of the reduced m-array for a single release-recapture data set. Any model for such data can be represented by an analogous table giving the $E(m_{ij} \mid R_i) = R_i \pi_{ij}$ (or giving just the π_{ij}). For example, Table 1.16 gives the basic model structure used as our starting point. This model is essentially the Jolly-Seber model (Jolly 1965; Seber 1965). The parentheses enclosing pairs of ϕq or ϕp are shown only to emphasize the way survival from site i to $i + 1$ and being captured or not captured at site $i + 1$ always appear together in the model structure. Seber (1982) used the symbols α_i and β_i to denote the products $\phi_i q_{i+1}$ and $\phi_i p_{i+1}$, respectively.

Table 1.16. – The Jolly-Seber (time-specific parameters) model structure for the symbolic data of Table 1.15.

Releases at dam i	Expected number of recaptures, $E(m_{ij} \mid R_i)$, at dam j			
	$j = 2$	3	4	5
R_1	$R_1(\phi_1 p_2)$	$R_1(\phi_1 q_2)(\phi_2 p_3)$	$R_1(\phi_1 q_2)(\phi_2 q_3)(\phi_3 p_4)$	$R_1(\phi_1 q_2)(\phi_2 q_3)(\phi_3 q_4)(\phi_4 p_5)$
R_2		$R_2(\phi_2 p_3)$	$R_2(\phi_2 q_3)(\phi_3 p_4)$	$R_2(\phi_2 q_3)(\phi_3 q_4)(\phi_4 p_5)$
R_3			$R_3(\phi_3 p_4)$	$R_3(\phi_3 q_4)(\phi_4 p_5)$
R_4				$R_4(\phi_4 p_5)$

1.4.4. Assumptions

The numerous assumptions involved in making inferences from release-recapture data vary in their importance and in terms of what the investigator can do to satisfy them. We next present the necessary assumptions by type of assumption, and order most-to-least important within type of assumption.

Assumptions 1-6 relate to study planning, field procedures, and generality of the desired inferences.

(1)   The test fish used are representative of the population of fish about which one seeks mortality information.

(2)   Test conditions are representative of the conditions of interest.

(3)   Treatment and control fish are biologically identical prior to release at dam 1. A strong version of assumption 3 is that initial handling, marking, and holding do not affect survival rate.

(4)   The numbers of fish released are exactly known.

(5)   Marking (tagging) is accurate; there are no mark (tag) losses and no misread marks (tags).

(6)   All releases and recaptures occur in brief time-intervals, and recaptured fish are released immediately.

Assumptions 7-8 relate to the stochastic component of the models.

(7)   The fate of each individual fish, after any known release, is independent of the fate of any other fish.

(8)   With multiple lots (or other replication), the data are statistically independent over lots.

Assumptions 9-12 relate to model structure.

(9)   Statistical analyses of the data are based on the correct model.

(10)   Treatment and control fish move downstream together.

(11)   Captured fish that are rereleased have the same subsequent survival and capture rates as fish alive at that site which were not caught, i.e., capture and rerelease do not affect their subsequent survival or recapture.

(12)   All fish (in the study) of an identifiable class (e.g., treatment or control, or size, or replicate) have the same survival and capture probabilities; this is an assumption of parameter homogeneity.

It is difficult to specify a set of assumptions that suffice to cover all the protocols and intended inferences presented here. In particular, stronger assumptions are required for estimation of the absolute survival rates ϕ than for the treatment effect $S = \phi_t/\phi_c$. Note particularly that a multiplicative bias that equally affects $\hat{\phi}_t$ and $\hat{\phi}_c$ has no effect on S. We next discuss the role of assumptions from this dual perspective.

No amount or sophistication of data analysis can salvage valid results from an invalid design. Also, statistical inferences cannot validly extend beyond the scope of the design. Assumptions 1 and 2 relate to this point; they are virtually self-evident, but worth bearing in mind. For example, if one wants to know something about a species of fish, then that species should be used as the test fish. Other factors to consider include genetic strain, size, general condition, and so forth. Test conditions (flow, turbine type, power settings, dam design) are also relevant. These types of studies are usually limited to one dam, and often one turbine, at a time. There is little or no random selection of test conditions, nor can there be. That does not affect models or analyses presented here. Assumptions 1 and 2 really just specify the limits of valid statistical inferences regarding fish survival rates and treatment effects. Inferences about salmon or conditions other than the test conditions must be justified on other than statistical grounds.

Assumptions 3, 4, and 5, and to some extent assumption 6, can be influenced by the investigator by the use of careful field procedures. Our reading of the fisheries literature shows that fisheries scientists are well aware of these assumptions; and that these scientists are able to do an excellent job of meeting assumptions 3-6, to the extent they can be met.

For the purposes of making inferences about treatment effect(s), a weak version of assumption 3 suffices: comparability of treatment and control fish when initially released. At this level assumption 3 is met, basically, by random assignment of fish to treatment groups and lots, and identical handling procedures for all treatment groups (often just treatment and control fish). Handling may affect the fish and their survival rates ϕ. If absolute survival rates are a study objective, a strengthened assumption 3 is needed: fish preparation and holding procedures do not affect survival rates. Potentially, assumptions 1 and 3 overlap. The common point being made is that S, or ϕ, is assumed to be the same for the released and wild fish. If the experimental fish are not representative a priori, this assumption fails.

It is critical to know the numbers of live, healthy fish released (assumption 4). Due to handling mortality or natural mortality, the release number R may be less than the number marked and placed in holding facilities. Accurate marking is also critical. Marks must not be lost or become unreadable. Assumption 5 points out that recapture data must be recorded accurately. This assumption is required to obtain unbiased estimates of absolute survival rates ϕ and capture rates p. However, $\hat{S}$ remains unbiased if the rates of tag loss (including, e.g., unreadable freeze-brands) are equal for treatment and control groups.

Assumption 6 relates to fish being recaptured over several days or weeks. In capture-recapture one should release all fish at a given dam (or occasion) simultaneously. Similarly, all recaptures at a given dam (or occasion) should occur simultaneously. When these conditions are met, all fish have been exposed to mortality risks for the same time interval, and the assumption of homogeneous survival and capture rates, by treatment group, is tenable. This assumption may fail when, for example, some control fish move from dam 1 to dam 2 in 1 week and others take 2 weeks. If survival rates depend only on distance moved, this movement time differential is not a problem; if survival rates depend strongly on elapsed time (as well as, or rather than, distance moved), however, then ϕ (absolute survival rate) is affected. At dam 1, fish should be released as quickly as possible. After the initial release the only control the investigator has is the spatial allocation of recapture effort. In terms of meeting assumption 6, it is best to concentrate recapture effort at dam 2, rather than farther downriver.

Assumption 6 can be weakened for purposes of estimating treatment effects; it suffices to have the same time distribution of recaptures and rereleases for all treatment groups (assumption 10). Thus, inferences about S require assumption 10 but not assumption 6.

Although much of the literature on the type of large-scale experiments we are addressing is unpublished, a number of reports nonetheless provide excellent information on, and examples of, careful field procedures. Useful studies include the following: Cramer and Oligher (1964), Semple (unpublished report, 1979), Olson and Kaczynski (unpublished report, 1980), Turbak et al. (unpublished report, 1981), and McKenzie et al. (unpublished report, 1984).

There is little the investigator can do about assumptions 7 and 8. Assumption 7 implies assumption 8, but not vice versa. Assumption 7 is needed to justify the multinomial probability models used herein. Assumption 8 suffices to justify the empirical estimators of variance in Part 4. Failure of assumption 7 has no serious effects on bias of any estimators but can seriously affect variances. Fish fates are expected to be independent. Independence fails if clusters of fish stay together and react together. This positive dependence effectively reduces actual sample sizes and increases actual variances (as compared to theoretical variances). We doubt that assumptions 7 or, especially, 8 are seriously violated.

Failure of assumptions 9, 10, 11, and 12 can seriously affect estimates of parameters. We focus here on these assumptions because they can be investigated by data analysis. Assumption 9 is general but worth stating because it is the essence of all statistical inference: the assumed statistical model is correct. By statistical model, we mean both the structural and stochastic components. Assumption 7 (independence) and assumption 12 (homogeneity) imply the multinomial model of recaptures given releases. Assumption 12 by itself implies the structural component of the models we use.

Assumption 10 can be examined on the basis of records of recaptures by day at any dam. If the time distribution of captures is the same for treatment and control fish, the results of the experiment are more likely to be valid. Differential movement of treatment and control fish need not invalidate results, although it may require a more complex model for data analysis. If any differential migration is a result of treatment, it is probably unavoidable. It is important to conduct the study so that the design and field procedures do not lead to such differences in movement between treatment versus control fish.

Assumption 11 relates to, among other things, handling mortality (e.g., Arnason and Mills, in press) and behavioral response to capture (Nichols et al. 1984). If capture and handling cause mortality, they will bias estimates of ϕ (and possibly S). In general, capture and release at dam i could affect the next recapture. If only capture probabilities are affected, generalized models can allow adjustment for this effect (e.g., Nichols et al. 1984). However, if assumption 11 is violated, it is most likely the survival rate after release that is affected. There is no analytic way to compensate for a handling effect on survival rate S and still use all the data for the types of experiments considered here. The solution to the problem, at least with respect to estimating S, is to use the first capture history protocol.

Assumption 12 is violated if fish used in the study vary a priori with respect to survival and capture rates. Such heterogeneity in parameter values is likely to happen to some extent. For example, fish size may influence survival ϕ and treatment effect S. If variation in fish size is modest, such heterogeneity causes no problems. That is, the analysis methods have some robustness to heterogeneity (see Nichols et al. 1982; Pollock and Raveling 1982). Studies should be designed to ensure that assumption 12 is true; the investigator should consider stratifying by fish size or eliminating extremes of fish size and using one strain (source) of fish for the entire study, or at least stratifying treatment and control lots by strain. Heterogeneity can result in actual variances exceeding estimated theoretical variances.

1.4.5. Data Analysis Philosophy

Our specification of assumption 9 as simply "the correct model is used" is motivated by our modeling and data analysis philosophy: start with a model sufficiently general so that it is likely to be true for any given experiment of the type of experiments being considered. That umbrella model is expected to be too general. Consequently, one then selects as part of the data analysis process a suitable special case of the general model that best fits one's specific experiment.

Historically, the approach to capture-recapture data analysis was to assume a specific model and use it, often with no testing of assumptions about model fit. Then one's assumptions about the model could be stated as specific assumptions about survival rates and capture probabilities. For the methods presented here, we assume that the Jolly-Seber model applies to each treatment group. This assumption simply means that for all treatment groups, survival and capture are assumed to be time-specific only, with no age, capture history, or handling effects. More general models are available; however, we do not believe they are useful for the analysis of this class of fisheries experiments where no new (previously unmarked) fish are released at dams 2, ..., k. Although this absence of any new releases simplifies the problem, it also restricts one's ability to use models more general than Jolly-Seber.

The assumption that parameters within a treatment group are time-specific is probably reasonable, especially if there is some stratification or control of fish size. Capture history could, in principle, influence parameters; however, testing could detect this effect. If such a capture history effect is found, it can be adjusted for analytically (i.e., by modeling and data analysis). The one effect that cannot be detected or adjusted for is a release (i.e., handling) effect at dams 2, ..., $k - 1$. That problem, however, is not circumvented by starting with an umbrella model more general than Jolly-Seber (see Chapter 3.8).

Two important aspects of our data analysis philosophy are as follows:

(1) Assumptions need to be stated explicitly, and tested, insofar as possible. The goodness of fit of the Jolly-Seber model can be tested thoroughly (Pollock et al. 1985). Overall goodness of fit tests can, and should, be partitioned into informative subcomponents. This partitioning is analogous to single-degree-of-freedom contrasts in the analysis of variance. It is important to do a series of such tests focused on specific alternatives because the omnibus (unpartitioned) goodness of fit test has low power.

(2) The analysis of release-recapture data should be thought of as model fitting, in the sense of seeking a "good" model for the data. With knowledge of the ecology of the species of interest as a starting point, one uses a combination of goodness of fit testing and testing between alternative models to search for the most parsimonious model (fewest parameters) that statistically fits the data and makes good ecological sense.

To facilitate this model selection process, we present (in Chapter 2.1) a menu of models of increasing generality and several data collection protocols. Thus, one can search for a model that fits the data. It is not possible to present analytic results for all possible models or model sequences. Thus, it may be necessary to use a model not included here; generally, that will require numerical analysis in which a combination of programs RELEASE and SURVIV is used.

Our focus here is on determining the extent and nature of the treatment effect on survival rates. The extensive testing and model selection, in terms of other parameters (e.g., p, τ, or λ), are essential to determine the extent and magnitude of the treatment effect and the best way to estimate that effect.

Finally, when a model is selected to fit the data from a given experiment, the investigator must remember that it is just a model. That model is not reality; rather it merely provides the best representation of the data at hand. These data may not be refined enough to demonstrate, at statistically significant levels, minor treatment effects. For example, the major effect may be found in $S_1 = \phi_{t1}/\phi_{c1}$; however, $S_2 = \phi_{t2}/\phi_{c2}$ may also be slightly different from one, but this effect may be too small to detect with the available data. One would then select a model wherein $\phi_{t2} = \phi_{c2}$ (thus, $S_2 = 1$) as the best model to describe the given data. As such, it summarizes the statistically significant information in the data and tells what statistical inferences the data justify, not necessarily what reality is.

1.5. Treatment-Control Mortality Concepts

1.5.1. Introduction

The objective of the experiments considered here is to make inferences about the mortality caused by one or more treatments. In particular, we concentrate on mortality at hydroelectric dams caused, for example, by spillways, bypass systems, turbines, or various deflecting screens. This type of mortality is mostly a sudden, "acute," form of treatment effect. However, there are other studies where treatment mortality may occur over a long period of time, for example, when treatment is a mildly toxic substance. In this latter case the treatment effect is referred to as "chronic." Both types of effects sometimes occur: sudden, direct treatment mortality is followed by chronic effects. Also, in principle, it is possible that a treatment is intended to enhance survival rates. This chapter explores these and other mortality concepts, and considers what mortality or survival effects can be estimated and tested for in release-recapture studies.

The complicating factor is the presence of "natural" mortality, which can occur in the treatment releases prior to recapture. The presence of natural mortality necessitates controls. However, using controls does not entirely solve the problems that arise when the treatment effect is partially or totally chronic and natural mortality forces are also present. Conceptually, one would like to estimate "total treatment mortality" (TTM), the total mortality caused by the treatment over a given period of time. Total treatment mortality is difficult to conceptualize and impossible to estimate without bias (independent of the level of natural mortality) unless the treatment mortality is of the acute type.

Further complications arise if the study occurs over any time period long enough to allow possible compensatory population mortality processes. No attempt is made in the methods here to allow for such a problem. We simply note that it is an important consideration in long-term studies of chronic effects.

In general, a treatment effect may be manifested in ways other than a differential survival rate of treatment animals; however, the only effects detectable from classical release-recapture data are altered survival rates (hence mortality effects) or effects on capture probabilities. We regard the latter as nuisance effects because capture probabilities are not fundamental population dynamics parameters. In the actual data analysis the investigator must be concerned with separating any treatment effects on capture probabilities from effects on survival rates. However, in this chapter our considerations are restricted to mortality effects.

Acute or chronic effects are general terms used to describe a treatment effect. When we deal with mortality as the effect, we use the terms direct mortality (an acute effect) or indirect mortality (a result of a chronic effect). Treatment effects are, of necessity, defined only with respect to a control.

1.5.2. Direct versus Indirect Mortality Effects

Direct mortality is effectively instantaneous. Fish either survive the turbine passage relatively unharmed, are killed outright (from a direct hit by a blade), or are fatally injured (e.g., by pressure-caused internal injuries). If a fish is fatally injured after passage through a turbine, its ultimate death is here considered a direct mortality even if it lives for a short time after exiting the turbine housing. All direct mortality occurs upstream from dam 2 (the first recapture site). The important point here is that the actual cause of direct mortality is the turbine, not a cause that operates on both treatment and control fish (e.g., predation or disease).

In contrast, indirect mortality would be revealed by a higher mortality rate in treatment fish than in controls between dams 2 and 3, 3 and 4, and so forth. Moreover, the proximate cause of that mortality would be natural. Basically, an indirect (possibly chronic) mortality effect means that treatment animals are more susceptible than control animals to natural mortality forces (mortality forces other than the treatment). This enhanced susceptibility may last indefinitely. For such indirect mortality, competing risk theory must be used to separate the treatment effect from the control level of natural mortality risk.

Table 1.17 gives a numerical illustration of one aspect of these mortality concepts. For the purposes of this example, some extended notation is needed. For treatment individuals, let $\phi_{t1} = \phi'_{t0} \phi'_{t1}$, where $1 - \phi'_{t0}$ is direct treatment mortality. Conditional on fish not experiencing direct mortality, ϕ'_{t1} is the survival rate to recapture site (or time) 2. By definition, $\phi'_{c0} \equiv 1$, hence, $\phi'_{c1} \equiv \phi_{c1}$. Capture methods allow us to estimate, at best, only ϕ_{t1} and ϕ_{c1}; for some protocols, only their ratio $S = \phi_{t1}/\phi_{c1}$ is estimable. In the case of turbine mortality, ϕ'_{t0} is survival through the turbine, and ϕ'_{t1} is the survival of treatment fish between the point where controls are released and dam 2. If all treatment mortality is direct, $\phi'_{t1} = \phi_{c1}$, and $S = \phi_{t1}/\phi_{c1} = \phi'_{t0}$. However, in general, $S = (\phi'_{t0}\phi'_{t1})/\phi_{c1}$, which has the interpretation

$$S = \frac{\text{Pr}_t(\text{survives turbine})\text{Pr}_t(\text{survives to dam 2} \mid \text{survives turbine})}{\text{Pr}_c(\text{survives to dam 2})}.$$

The treatment mortality is well-defined and estimable when it is entirely a direct effect. In the example of this case in Table 1.17, $\phi_{t1} = \phi'_{t0}\phi'_{t1} = (0.9)(0.9)$, and $\phi_{c1} = \phi'_{t1} = 0.9$, thus,

$$1 - S = 1 - \frac{\phi_{t1}}{\phi_{c1}} = 1 - \frac{0.81}{0.90}$$

$$= 1 - 0.9$$

$$= 0.1 = 1 - \phi'_{t0}.$$

Scenarios that include indirect effects are less well-defined. One possibility is to have

$$S = \frac{\phi_{ti}}{\phi_{ci}}$$

be constant (this situation will not occur in turbine studies). The indirect-only case in Table 1.17 has ϕ_{ti}/ϕ_{ci}, $i = 1, ..., 5$ as 1, 0.99, 0.97, 0.94, and 0.90, respectively. Table 1.17 also shows some mixed cases. Case 1 has the following estimable ratios ϕ_{ti}/ϕ_{ci}, $i = 1, 2, 3, 4, 5$: 0.81, 0.94, 0.97, 0.99, 1. For mixed-effects case 2, the estimable survival effects are 0.97, 0.95, 0.93, 0.92, 0.90.

1.5.3. Total Treatment Mortality

Generally, in Part 1, we have avoided examining subjects in detail (leaving that to later parts). However, because we do not return elsewhere to mortality concepts, we present the mathematical formulae here. This material is necessary only if one wants a thorough understanding of the limitations of release-recapture experiments in terms of which components of treatment mortality are estimable.

The methodology used here is basically derived from the competing risk theory of survival processes, which is a coherent mathematical theory of survival (or mortality) processes wherein the individuals are subject to several distinct forces of mortality. Much literature exists on competing risk theory (see David and Moeschberger 1978 and Kalbfleisch

Table 1.17. – Numerical illustration of treatment mortality concepts for cases of direct, indirect, and mixed mortality; note that $\phi_1 = \phi'_0 \phi'_1$. Survival rates ϕ_i are between release and recapture sites (and thus are estimable under certain protocols). Treatment occurs at release site 1; ϕ'_0 is the direct effect.

Survival rate	Control survival rate	Possible treatment survival rate			
		Direct only	Mixed case 1	Mixed case 2	Indirect only
ϕ'_0	1.00	0.90	0.900	0.980	1.000
ϕ'_1	0.90	0.90	0.810	0.880	0.900
$\phi_1 = \phi'_0 \phi'_1$	0.90	0.81	0.729	0.873	0.900
ϕ_2	0.85	0.85	0.800	0.807	0.842
ϕ_3	0.95	0.95	0.922	0.888	0.922
ϕ_4	0.78	0.78	0.772	0.718	0.733
ϕ_5	0.93	0.93	0.930	0.837	0.837

and Prentice 1980; also, Anderson and Burnham 1976 provided an ecological application of competing risk theory, and Fletcher 1985 used a competing-risks approach in an analysis of fisheries diversion experiments).

Definitions of some notation used here follow.

$\phi_t(0, d)$ — the survival rate of treatment fish from the release point to downstream distance d (results here are also interpretable with d as time).

$\phi_c(\varepsilon, d)$ — the survival rate of control fish from their release point (ε) to downstream distance (location) d; for convenience, define $\phi_c(0,\varepsilon) = 1$.

$h_t(x)$ — the instantaneous mortality rate (as a function of location, x) for the treatment fish.

$h_c(x)$ — the instantaneous mortality rate for the control fish.

$\Delta(x) = h_t(x) - h_c(x)$ — the instantaneous treatment mortality effect; this is a fundamental way of conceptualizing the effect of the treatment.

It is assumed that controls are released just downstream from dam 1 at location ε. By defining $\phi_c(0,\varepsilon) = 1$, the notation $\phi_c(0,d)$ becomes equivalent to $\phi_c(\varepsilon,d)$. Direct and indirect instantaneous treatment mortality effects are represented, respectively, as $\Delta(x) = h_t(x)$ for $0 \leq x \leq \varepsilon$ and $\Delta(x) = h_t(x) - h_c(x)$, $\varepsilon < x$.

Finite survival rates can be expressed in terms of the above instantaneous rates:

$$\phi_t(0, d) = \phi_t(0, \varepsilon)\, (e^{-\int_\varepsilon^d \Delta(y)dy})\phi_c(\varepsilon, d) \; ;$$

$$\phi_c(\varepsilon, d) = e^{-\int_\varepsilon^d h_c(y)dy} \; .$$

The objective here is to express mortality in the treatment cohort as the sum of two parts – mortality that is attributed to the treatment, and mortality that is natural ("natural" mortality being defined here as mortality from any risk factor affecting the controls):

$$1 - \phi_t(0, d) = 1 - e^{-\int_0^d h_t(y)dy} = TM(0, d) + NM(0, d),$$

where

$$TM(0, d) = \int_0^d \Delta(x)e^{-\int_0^x [\Delta(y) + h_c(y)]dy}dx,$$

$$NM(0, d) = \int_0^d h_c(x)e^{-\int_0^x [\Delta(y) + h_c(y)]dy}dx.$$

Here, *TM* denotes treatment mortality and *NM* denotes natural mortality. The quantity denoted $TM(0, d)$ is the total mortality over the distance interval 0 to d, that is validly attributed to ("caused" by) the treatment. This $TM(0, d)$ appears to be complex, and it cannot, in general, be simplified. Worse yet, it cannot be estimated without bias except in special cases.

Let there be a short interval $(0, \varepsilon)$ wherein all direct mortality occurs (or is caused). The turbine experiments fit this model. Then $TM(0, d)$ can be partitioned into direct and indirect treatment mortality, assuming that no indirect treatment mortality occurs in 0 to ε. The result is

$$TM(0, d) = 1 - \phi_t(0, \varepsilon) + \phi_t(0, \varepsilon) \int_\varepsilon^d \Delta(x) \, e^{-\int_\varepsilon^x [\Delta(y) + h_c(y)] dy} dx.$$

Thus, $TM(0, d)$ is expressed as equal to direct treatment mortality $1 - \phi_t(0, \varepsilon)$ plus indirect treatment mortality over the distance (or time) ε to d.

If treatment effect eventually wears off entirely (as regards mortality), one can conceptualize a distance $d*$ beyond which $\Delta(d) = 0$. If the notation is extended for finite survival rates, $\phi_t(d*, d) = \phi_c(d*, d)$ for all $d > d*$. Conversely, $\phi_t(0, d) < \phi_c(0, d)$ for all $d < d*$ (in turbine mortality experiments we expect $\phi_t < \phi_c$). If the treatment mortality effect never entirely vanishes, we take $d*$ as infinity. The total treatment mortality (TTM) can now be defined as $TM(0, d*)$. Eventually all the treatment animals die; TTM is the proportion of that 100% mortality that may validly be attributed to the treatment.

Inasmuch as TTM is an unambiguous measure of treatment effect, we would like to be able to estimate it. This estimation can be done without bias only when $d* = \varepsilon$, that is, when all the treatment mortality is direct. Then $\phi_{t1} = \phi_t(0, \varepsilon)\phi_{c1}$, so that the parameter we denote as $S = \phi_{t1}/\phi_{c1}$ satisfies TTM = 1 - S only in this special case. In general, for results over $(0, d)$

$$S = \phi_t(0, \varepsilon) \, e^{-\int_\varepsilon^d \Delta(y) dy} ,$$

whereas

$$1 - TM = \phi_t(0, \varepsilon) \left[1 - \int_\varepsilon^d \Delta(x) \, e^{-\int_\varepsilon^x [\Delta(y) + h_c(y)] dy} dx \right].$$

Finally, from

$$1 - e^{-\int_\varepsilon^d \Delta(x) dy} = \int_\varepsilon^d \Delta(x) e^{-\int_\varepsilon^x \Delta(y) dy} dx \geq \int_\varepsilon^d \Delta(x) e^{-\int_\varepsilon^x [\Delta(y) + h_c(y)] dy} dx ,$$

we derive

$$1 - S \geq TM ;$$

hence, for $d \geq d_*$, $1 - S \geq TTM$, with equality if and only if $d_* = \varepsilon$.

We add some interpretation of the above. If d_* lies above the first recapture dam, information on the treatment effect, in regard to survival, is entirely contained in ϕ_{t1} and ϕ_{c1}, and their ratio is one valid measure of the treatment effect. If, however, there are indirect effects, $1 - S$ exceeds the total mortality that should be attributed to the treatment effect. For fish passing through turbines, most of the effect will be direct mortality, and any indirect effects are likely to disappear at or before the next downstream dam. Consequently, for turbine (or bypass or spillway) experiments, the interpretation of $1 - (\phi_{t1}/\phi_{c1})$ as TTM should be a reasonable approximation.

The various equations above provide a basis for investigating the matter further. One can specify forms for $h_c(y)$ and $h_t(y)$, or $\Delta(y)$, and the value of d_* and numerically compute S, TTM, and $NM(0, d_*)$. This computation allows comparison of $1 - S$ with TTM over a wide range of conditions. We consider here a simple case which gives analytic formulae. Assume that $h_c(y) = h_c$ is constant over ε to d_* and then replace $\Delta(y)$ over this interval by its average value (say $\overline{\Delta}$) and hence define $\gamma = \overline{\Delta}/h_c$. For $d \geq d_*$, this case leads to the formula

$$\frac{1 - TTM}{\phi_t(0, \varepsilon)} = 1 - \frac{\gamma}{1 + \gamma}\left[1 - \left(\frac{S}{\phi_t(0, \varepsilon)}\right)^{\frac{1+\gamma}{\gamma}}\right]$$

and

$$S = \phi_t(0, \varepsilon)e^{-(d-\varepsilon)\overline{\Delta}},$$

or equivalently for S,

$$S = \phi_t(0, \varepsilon)[\phi_c(0, d)]^\gamma,$$

where $1 - \phi_c(0,d)$ is control mortality.

The reader can compute results with these formula for $d \geq d_*$ (modifications are needed to examine results over $d < d_*$). We have calculated representative results. For example, if direct treatment mortality is 0.1 [$\phi_t(0, \varepsilon) = 0.9$], control mortality is 0.15 [i.e., $\phi_c(0\ d) = 0.85$], and indirect treatment mortality is 0.02, then TTM = 0.12, and $1 - S = 0.12167$. Consideration of the theory here and extensive tabulation of results with the above simple formulae lead to some general conclusions:

(1) As d increases (beyond d_*), the error in using $1 - S$ to estimate TTM increases (when natural mortality is occurring in the river reach d_* to d). Consequently, recapturing should occur as close to d_* as possible.

(2) For fixed $d > d_*$, as the control mortality increases [$\phi_c(0, d)$ decreasing], $1 - S$ becomes a progressively poorer approximation of TTM.

(3) If control mortality (over 0 to d) is <0.15, the ratio $(1 - S)$/TTM is generally <1.1 irrespective of how much of TTM is direct mortality. In fact, if there is direct mortality, $(1 - S)$/TTM is likely to be <1.05.

(4) If most treatment mortality is direct ($\geq$ 70% TTM), the ratio $(1 - S)$/TTM appears to be approximately 1.05 at any level of control mortality or TTM.

For turbine mortality studies at hydroelectric dams, we believe that $1 - S$ is a good approximation of TTM. Viewed alternatively, the fact that $1 - S$ may not exactly equal TTM is of negligible concern in such large-scale studies compared with the size of $se(\hat{S})$ and the many practical problems that constitute possible sources of serious bias in $\hat{S}$.

1.5.4. Problems with Defining a Treatment Effect on Survival

In this section we pursue further the question of what reasonably constitutes the measurable treatment effect in release-resampling experiments. At best, we can only estimate separate survivals ϕ_{ti} and ϕ_{ci} between recapture dams $i = 1, ..., k - 2$. Thus, we can estimate quantities like $\phi_{c1} - \phi_{t1}$ or ϕ_{t1}/ϕ_{c1} as our measures (indices) of treatment effect. If there is indirect mortality, we cannot separate it from direct mortality. It is, however, possible to test for the existence and extent of the treatment effect under the complete capture history protocol or under the scheme A partial capture history protocol.

In Section 1.5.3 we showed that $1 - S$ is often a good approximation of TTM; if there is no indirect mortality, S is the best measure of the treatment effect. The primary alternative to S is the difference $\phi_c - \phi_t$. This difference is affected by the choice of d, whereas the ratio of ϕ_t/ϕ_c stabilizes as d increases. To clarify this point, we expand our notation and show the dependence of S on distance: $S(0, d) = \phi_t(0, d)/\phi_c(0, d)$. Of course, we can estimate this ratio at distances $d_2, ..., d_{k-2}$ corresponding to recapture dams (but only for certain protocols). As d increases toward d_*, $S(0, d)$ changes; however, for all $d > d_*$, $\phi_t(0, d)/\phi_c(0, d) = S(0, d_*)$. This stabilization of $S(0, d)$ contrasts with the difference $\phi_c(0, d) - \phi_t(0, d)$, which goes to zero as d increases; it is a valid measure of effect, and many of the tests presented here are actually based on the difference. However, one should be aware of the contrasting properties of the ratio versus the difference of survival rates.

A further reason for our emphasis on S as the measure of treatment effect is that only the ratio S is estimable as a convenient measure of treatment effect for the first capture history and unknown capture history protocols. Only for complete capture history and partial capture history protocols can one separately estimate, at least, ϕ_{t1} and ϕ_{c1}.

Although we have focused here on studies of fish passing through hydroelectric dams, the nature of the treatment effect could be quite different in other treatment-control release-recapture (or capture-recapture) studies. The anticipated pattern of mortality in any study significantly affects the types of models and the strategy of testing one should use. We have concentrated here on effects that are anticipated to be initially large and then vanish. Hence, we assume most of the effect is an acute, initial mortality. If any indirect effects vanish by or before dam 2 (thus, $d_* \leq d_2$), one can characterize the treatment effect with the single parameter $S(0, d_*)$ and estimate this parameter with the equation $S = \phi_{t1}/\phi_{c1}$. If an indirect effect persists beyond dam 2, then one needs to extend our characterization of the "treatment effect."

The preferred approach would be to compare the entire set of survival curves for treatment versus control cohorts. Thus, one compares $\phi_t(0, d)$ to $\phi_c(0, d)$ as functions of $d > 0$. The comparison(s) might be reduced to looking at functions of these, such as average life time (after release). Such simple comparisons are not possible with release-recapture data because only the discrete survival rates ϕ_{ti}, ϕ_{ci}, $i = 1, ..., k - 2$ can be estimated. Also, these estimators are subject to substantial sampling variances and covariances.

In this monograph, we emphasize intensive testing for differences between these survivals to identify the extent and size of the treatment effect. These "generic" tests can be improved if one has prior knowledge (or beliefs) about the treatment effects. In particular, if effects are chronic with no direct effect, one should consider imposing a parametric model on ϕ. The survival curve might be exponential, Weibull, or logistic; e.g., $\phi(0,d) = \exp[-(d/\alpha)^\beta]$. One then must assess the fit of this model (separately for treatment and control); if it is satisfactory, the treatment effect is reflected by differences in the parameters α and β between treatments and controls.

In studies with long-term chronic effects, one hopes that the effect is monotonic because it is then not difficult to hypothesize a useful parameter to reflect the treatment effect. Monotonic means that $\Delta(d)$ never changes sign. In this case some weighted combination of the ϕ_is should be considered as the basis of an efficient test for treatment effect. For example,

$$\overline{\phi} = \sum_{i=1}^{k-2} \left(\frac{d_i + d_{i+1}}{2} \right) \phi(d_i, d_{i+1})$$

or

$$\overline{\phi} = \sum_{i=1}^{k-2} i \, \phi(d_i, d_{i+1}),$$

where d_i is the time (or location) of the ith release-recapture with respect to $d_1 = 0$, and $\phi(d_i, d_{i+1}) \equiv \phi_i$ for treatment or control. One then gets the estimate of $\overline{\phi}$ for both treatments and controls and tests for a significant difference.

It is clear to us that chronic treatment effects substantially increase difficulties associated with capture studies. Problems worsen as more of the TTM becomes indirect and as the time duration of the study lengthens (i.e., years rather than weeks or months). In fact, simple capture-recapture studies are not suitable as a basis for a serious study of long-term chronic mortality effects. As just one illustration of difficulties, we note the following, using the equations at the end of Section 1.5.3. Let the control mortality be 0.7 and the TTM be 0.3, with no direct mortality. Then, for $d > d_*$ where $\phi_t = \phi_t(0, d)$ and $\phi_c = \phi_c(0, d)$, $1 - S = 0.48$. In this situation, tests for a treatment effect will be powerful, but there is no way to obtain a reliable estimate of TTM without some type of additional information.

Part 2. Protocols for Studies with a Control and One Treatment

Material in Part 2 presents the theory and application for experiments with single treatment and control groups (i.e., $v = t$ and c). An array of tests are given to assess model assumptions under each of the sampling protocols. The estimation theory for each of the five protocols follows. Data for the general numerical example (provided in Chapter 1.3) are used to illustrate the computations. Other points are illustrated using the output from program RELEASE.

2.1. Models, Hypotheses, and Tests: An Overview

2.1.1. Overview of Hypothesis Tests

The strategy we recommend in analysis of release-recapture data is to select the most biologically reasonable, parsimonious, statistical model for the data. This is a generally accepted basis for a good model (see McCullagh and Nelder 1983). Inferences about treatment effects and other parameters are then based on that model. The set of reasonable models to consider is determined by a priori reasoning (logic) based on the nature of the study. In ecological studies, however, logic alone is usually insufficient to specify a single (unique) model as *the* model for the data. Instead, statistical hypothesis tests must be used to determine if a model fits the data and to determine the simplest model, from an a priori sequence of models, that is most appropriate for the data.

Three major tests are used in this process: TEST 1, TEST 2, and TEST 3. Table 2.1 summarizes some aspects of these tests. If sample sizes are large enough, each test statistic is distributed as a chi-square statistic. Each test is computed as a series of independent, chi-square test statistics which, added together, give the overall test; however, the separate test components are often of more interest than their sums.

TEST 1, as an overall test, tests the null hypothesis, H_0, "there is no treatment effect," versus the alternative, H_A, "there is a treatment effect." Treatment effects are defined in terms of differences in the parameters ϕ_i and p_i between treatment and control groups. TEST 1 is computed on the basis of summary statistics from each treatment group.

TESTs 2 and 3 are goodness of fit tests applicable to an individual set of release-recapture data. If there is only one group of releases (e.g., only controls, or only turbine fish, or fish of only one age or sex group), TESTs 2 and 3 are still computable; however, TEST 1 does not exist unless there are two or more treatment groups. The sum of TESTs 2 and 3 is the fully efficient goodness of fit test for Jolly-Seber capture-recapture data.

Table 2.1. – Summary of three types of statistical tests for the four capture history protocols and associated models.

TEST 1 Summary statistics from the experimental groups are used to test for overall treatment effects. TEST 1 is computed as a series of contingency table tests that allow detailed interpretation of the results. Tests of this form have roots in the publications by Brownie and Robson (1976) and Pollock (1981a). Details of this test are given in Table 2.3.

H_0: All parameters ϕ_i and p_i are the same across treatment groups.
H_A: At least some parameters differ between or among groups.

TEST 2 Summary statistics from a single treatment group are used to test for goodness of fit of the model to the data. TEST 2 is conducted separately for each group and is computed as a series of tests that allow a detailed interpretation of the results. There are many ways to compute this test sequence; we use contingency tables. This test can be most directly traced back to Robson and Youngs (unpublished report, 1971), but it also appears in papers by Seber (1970), Brownie and Robson (1976), Brownie et al. (1978, 1985), Balser (1984), and Pollock et al. (1985). Details of this test are given in Table 2.4.

H_0: The parameters ϕ_i and p_i are specific to sampling occasions or sampling sites within each group.
H_A: The model does not fit the data. There may be a wide variety of reasons for this, including tagging effects and differential behavior.

TEST 3 Data from the full m-array for a single group are used to test for parameters that are specific to individual capture histories. TEST 3 is potentially computed as a large series of contingency tables; however, a great deal of pooling is usually required for most data sets. This test was developed by Pollock et al. (1985). Details of this test are given in Table 2.5.

H_0: The parameters ϕ_i and p_i do not depend on the capture histories of fish released on any release occasion.
H_A: Some of the parameters ϕ_i and p_i are dependent on the capture histories of fish in a given release; this implies that the corresponding subcohorts among which capture and survival rates differ should not be pooled (Table 1.3 indicates the nature of those subcohorts).

In following sections we elaborate on these tests, outlining their components, how they are computed under any given protocol, and some idea of their meaning. Under the complete capture history protocol, all components of TESTs 1, 2, and 3 can be computed. Under the first capture history protocol, TESTs 2 and 3 do not exist (i.e., cannot be computed) and some components of TEST 1 cannot be computed.

The material presented in Part 2 is complex and extensive. It is difficult to understand fully the various separate ideas until one comprehends the "big picture." Yet, that comprehension requires starting somewhere to learn the various separate components of models, protocols, hypotheses, tests, and estimators. Consequently, readers may find it useful to refer back to Chapter 2.1 as they study the rest of Part 2.

2.1.2. Sequence of Treatment Effects Corresponding to TEST 1

For any study of turbine mortality involving a treatment and control group and k release-recapture dams, the same types of parameters underlie the sample data: $\phi_{v1}, \phi_{v2}, ...,$ $\phi_{v,k-1}$ and $p_{v2}, ..., p_{v,k-1}, p_{vk}$, for $v = t$ or c. Only the data collection protocols and the number (k) of dams involved may vary. These two factors (i.e., the actual data taken) determine the survival and capture probabilities that that can be estimated, and the statistical tests that can be computed.

In any experiment, one wants to test for the nature and extent of treatment effects. When passage through a dam structure is the treatment, one wants to test hypotheses about equality of treatment and survival rates in the controls. It is also necessary to test for differences in capture probabilities (e.g., does $p_{t2} = p_{c2}$) to reach valid conclusions about effects on survival rates. Because of the spatial ordering of survival rates and recapture sites, there is a logical sequence of hypotheses to test concerning possible treatment effects. Table 2.2 is a representation of the corresponding sequence of possible hypotheses about how the treatment affects the parameters.

Table 2.2. – A summary is shown of specific hypotheses that are relevant to determining the extent of the treatment effect and thereby to selecting an appropriate model. Notation: E means that the parameter is assumed to be equal for t and c; D means that the parameter is allowed to differ for t and c.

Dam $j = 1\rightarrow$		2	$\rightarrow$	3	$\rightarrow$	4	$\rightarrow$	$k-1\rightarrow$	k
Model	ϕ_1	p_2	ϕ_2	p_3	ϕ_3	p_4	$\rightarrow$	p_{k-1}	$\phi_{k-1}p_k$
H_0	E	E	E	E	E	E	$\rightarrow$	E	E
$H_{1\phi}$	D	E	E	E	E	E	$\rightarrow$	E	E
H_{2p}	D	D	E	E	E	E	$\rightarrow$	E	E
$H_{2\phi}$	D	D	D	E	E	E	$\rightarrow$	E	E
H_{3p}	D	D	D	D	E	E	$\rightarrow$	E	E
$H_{3\phi}$	D	D	D	D	D	E	$\rightarrow$	E	E
.	.	.	.	.	.	.		.	.
.	.	.	.	.	.	.		.	.
.	.	.	.	.	.	.		.	.
$H_{k-1,p}$	D	D	D	D	D	D	$\rightarrow$	D	E
$H_{k-1,\phi}$	D	D	D	D	D	D	$\rightarrow$	D	D

The simplest model (i.e., statistical) hypothesis, denoted H_0, specifies that there are no treatment effects; thus, all survival and capture parameters are equal (E) between treatment and control groups. For hypothesis $H_{1\phi}$, only ϕ_{t1} and ϕ_{c1} differ (D); no other parameters are affected by treatment. In most turbine studies, it has been implicitly assumed that $H_{1\phi}$ applied, but this hypothesis has rarely been tested because the data that would allow such a test have not been collected. Hypothesis H_{2p} means the underlying parameters

$$\phi_{t1}, \phi_{c1} \text{ may be different, and}$$

$$p_{t2}, p_{c2} \text{ may be different,}$$

while

$$\phi_2, \phi_3, ..., \phi_{k-1}$$

and

$$p_3, ..., p_{k-1}, p_k$$

are the same for treatment and control.

Hypothesis $H_{k-1,\phi}$ represents the case where a treatment effect (on survival, capture, or both rates) persists at least to dam k. We choose to denote the final hypothesis in the sequence this way even though ϕ_{k-1} and p_k are not separately estimable under any sampling protocol. Thus, technically, we should write $H_{k-1,\theta}$ and define $\theta = \phi_{k-1}p_k$. Instead, we adopt the convention that under $H_{k-1,\phi}$ one must interpret ϕ_{k-1} as meaning the product $\phi_{k-1}p_k$. Under $H_{k-1,\phi}$ all identifiable parameters are allowed to be different between treatment and control groups.

TEST 1 is conveniently computed as a sequence of simple chi-square tests. Components of TEST 1 are named in Table 2.3 and related hypotheses are given in Table 2.2.

The interpretation of the individual components in TEST 1 could differ from that given here. Other sequences of hypotheses describe possible treatment effects. For example, one might have one or more survival rates differ by treatment but have all capture rates equal; thus, the most general model would be

$$\phi_{ti} \neq \phi_{ci}; \quad i = 1, ..., k-1 ,$$

$$p_{ti} = p_{ci}, \quad i = 2, ..., k .$$

The same sequence of tests could be carried out, but the corresponding H_0 and H_A would have a different interpretation. There are no simple closed-form tests or estimators for this model. Efficient inference methods for hypotheses such as those above must be based on numerical optimization procedures (using, e.g., program SURVIV, White 1983). In other contexts, such as testing data sets for male versus female (Brownie et al. 1985, Chapter 5), the separate components of TEST 1 are not of individual interest.

Table 2.2 presents hypotheses about the survival and capture parameters. These hypotheses by themselves do not specify a "model." A model here means a sampling distribution for actual data. Consequently, a model incorporates aspects of both the sampling protocol and a hypothesis about the underlying parameters. All tests of hypotheses take the form of

Table 2.3. – Explanation of TEST 1: its components, their identification, hypotheses tested, and computability of components by capture history (CH) protocol. The index v ranges over treatment groups, e.g., $v = t$ and c for treatment and control groups, respectively. There are $2k - 3$ test components ($k \geq 2$).

Component code	Summary statistics used	Hypothesis Null	Hypothesis Alternative	Complete CH	Partial CH Scheme A	Partial CH Scheme B[a]	First CH[b]	Unk. CH[c]
TEST 1.R1	R_{v1},r_{v1}	H_0	$H_{1\phi}$	Yes	Yes	Yes	Yes	Yes
TEST 1.T2	T_{v2},m_{v2}	$H_{1\phi}$	H_{2p}	Yes	Yes	Yes	Yes	Yes
TEST 1.R2	R_{v2},r_{v2}	H_{2p}	$H_{2\phi}$	Yes	Yes	Yes	No	No
TEST 1.T3	T_{v3},m_{v3}	$H_{2\phi}$	H_{3p}	Yes	Yes	Yes	Yes	Yes
TEST 1.R3	R_{v3},r_{v3}	H_{3p}	$H_{3\phi}$	Yes	Yes	No	No	No
.	.	.	.	.	.	.	.	.
.	.	.	.	.	.	.	.	.
TEST 1.Ti	T_{vi},m_{vi}	$H_{i-1,\phi}$	H_{ip}	Yes	Yes	Yes	Yes	Yes
TEST 1.Ri	R_{vi},r_{vi}	H_{ip}	$H_{i\phi}$	Yes	Yes	No	No	No
.	.	.	.	.	.	.	.	.
.	.	.	.	.	.	.	.	.
TEST 1.Tk - 1	$T_{v,k-1},m_{v,k-1}$	$H_{k-2,\phi}$	$H_{k-1,p}$	Yes	Yes	Yes	Yes	Yes
TEST 1.Rk - 1	$R_{v,k-1},r_{v,k-1}$	$H_{k-1,p}$	$H_{k-1,\phi}$	Yes	Yes	No	No	No

[a]For partial capture history scheme B, all TESTs 1.Ti are computable, however, only 1.$R1$ and 1.$R2$ are computable of the 1.Ri series; also, the exact meanings of the null and alternative hypotheses change when some components of TEST 1 drop out.

[b]For the first capture history protocol, the computable components are 1.$R1$ and 1.Ti, $i = 2, ..., k - 1$.

[c]For the unknown capture history protocol, the computable components are 1.$R1$ and 1.Ti, $i = 2, ..., k - 1$; also, these tests (hence, all of TEST 1) are only approximations under the unknown capture history protocol.

comparing two models: the sampling model under the null hypothesis versus that under the alternative hypothesis. Not all hypotheses in Table 2.2 are testable under all protocols, as shown in Table 2.3.

The simulated treatment-control data summarized in Tables 1.5 and 1.6 are used to illustrate TEST 1. Only the summary statistics R_{vi}, r_{vi}, $i = 1, ..., k - 1$ and m_{vi}, z_{vi}, $i = 2, ..., k - 1$ are used in TEST 1. Test components are based on the following tables:

TEST $1.Ri, i = 1, ..., k - 1$ TEST $1.Ti, i = 2, ..., k - 1$

		totals
r_{ti}	$R_{ti} - r_{ti}$	R_{ti}
r_{ci}	$R_{ci} - r_{ci}$	R_{ci}

		totals
m_{ti}	z_{ti}	T_{ti}
m_{ci}	z_{ci}	T_{ci}

For this example, one can easily construct these 2×2 contingency tables with the data from Tables 1.5 and 1.6:

TEST   TEST

$1.R1$

4,395	24,605
4,075	25,925

$1.T2$

1,104	3,291
1,029	3,046

$1.R2$

136	935
128	872

$1.T3$

260	3,167
249	2,925

$1.R3$

31	219
32	203

$1.T4$

1,924	1,274
1,762	1,195

$1.R4$

102	1,760
93	1,584

$1.T5$

644	732
616	672

$1.R5$

26	590
19	571

The chi-square test statistics and the overall TEST 1 results, in appropriate order, are

TEST	Hypothesis Null	Alternative	χ^2	df	P
1.R1	H_0	$H_{1\phi}$	29.63	1	0.000
1.T2	$H_{1\phi}$	H_{2p}	0.02	1	0.887
1.R2	H_{2p}	$H_{2\phi}$	0.01	1	0.920
1.T3	$H_{2\phi}$	H_{3p}	0.15	1	0.699
1.R3	H_{3p}	$H_{3\phi}$	0.16	1	0.689
1.T4	$H_{3\phi}$	H_{4p}	0.21	1	0.647
1.R4	H_{4p}	$H_{4\phi}$	0.01	1	0.920
1.T5	$H_{4\phi}$	H_{5p}	0.28	1	0.600
1.R5	H_{5p}	$H_{5\phi}$	0.84	1	0.359
TEST 1	H_0	$H_{5\phi}$	31.31	9	<0.001

If the individual hypotheses in this sequence make biological sense, this sequential testing is valuable. (This example is discussed further in Chapter 2.4.)

The proportion of R_{vi} fish released at site i that are ever recovered is r_{vi}/R_{vi}. TEST 1.Ri tests the equality of the expected proportion recaptured for treatment and control. That is, TEST 1.Ri compares

$$\frac{r_{ti}}{R_{ti}} \text{ and } \frac{r_{ci}}{R_{ci}}$$

to see if they are so different that one should believe different survival or capture rates are applicable to the treatment and control fish after their release at site i.

TEST 1.Ti is also comparing two proportions, namely

$$\frac{m_{ti}}{T_{ti}} \text{ and } \frac{m_{ci}}{T_{ci}}.$$

The totals T_{vi} are the numbers of fish known to be alive, at risk of capture, at site i. Of the total T_{vi}, m_{vi} is the number of fish actually caught at site i. If treatment and control fish have the same survival and capture rates at, and after, site i, then these proportions should not differ significantly. Conversely, rejection with TEST 1.Ti means there is some treatment effect evident at or after site i.

2.1.3. Goodness of Fit Testing Within a Treatment Group

2.1.3.1. TEST 1. – TEST 1 is computed across the different treatment groups. It is also possible to compute separately, for each group, a goodness of fit test to the general assumption of site- (time-) specific parameters. Examples of the types of factors that cause TESTs 2 and 3 to reject are heterogeneity of parameters over fish (caused, e.g., by fish size), failure of the assumption of independent fish fates, and behavioral response to capture and subsequent release (in some types of studies). Goodness of fit is especially critical in studies where new animals are released at each site or time. In such studies, new releases might be different from previously marked animals. This situation is not encountered commonly in fish-turbine survival experiments, but is relevant in studies in which simultaneous estimation of mortality rates at several dams is attempted (i.e., system-wide studies).

2.1.3.2. TEST 2. – TEST 2 is based on the m-array and is computed as a series of linked contingency tables. Table 2.4 gives the names of the separate components of TEST 2 and some information about each component. Program RELEASE computes these tests and labels them by the names listed in Table 2.4. Data required for TESTs 2 and 3 are not available (i.e., do not exist) under the first capture history and unknown capture history protocols. Under the partial capture history protocol scheme B, only TEST 2.$C2$ exists. TEST 2.$C2$ is the usual chi-square test of homogeneity based on the following $2 \times k - 2$ table:

m_{13}	m_{14}	$\cdots$	m_{1k}
m_{23}	m_{24}	$\cdots$	m_{2k}

Table 2.4. – Explanation of TEST 2: its components, their identification, hypotheses tested, and computability of components by capture history (CH) protocol. TEST 2 is computed separately for each data group; the data used are elements of the m-array (the m_{vij}). There are $k - 3$ test components ($k \geq 4$).

TEST	Summary statistics used	Null hypothesis	Complete CH	Partial CH scheme A	Partial CH scheme B	First CH	Unk. CH
TEST 2.$C2$	$m_{v13}, ..., m_{v1k}$ $m_{v23}, ..., m_{v2k}$	Parameters (ϕ, p) are the same for cohort 2 as for survivors at site 2 of cohort 1.	Yes	Yes	Yes	No	No
TEST 2.$C3$	$m_{vi4}, ..., m_{vik}$ $i = 1,2,3$	Parameters (ϕ, p) are the same for cohort 3 as for survivors at site 3 of previously released cohorts.	Yes	Yes	No	No	No
. .	.	.	.	.	.	.	.
.	.	.	.	.	.	.	.
.	.	.	.	.	.	.	.
TEST 2.Cj	$m_{vi,j+1}, ..., m_{vik}$ $i = 1, ..., j$	Parameters (ϕ, p) are the same for cohort j as for survivors at site j of previously released cohorts.	Yes	Yes	No	No	No
.	.	.	.	.	.	.	.
.	.	.	.	.	.	.	.
.	.	.	.	.	.	.	.
TEST 2.$Ck - 2$	$m_{vi,k-1}, m_{vik}$ $i = 1, ..., k - 2$	Parameters (ϕ, p) are the same for cohort $k - 2$ as for survivors at site $k - 1$ of previously released cohorts.	Yes	Yes	No	No	No

Notice that m_{12} was discarded, and that the row and column totals of this table were conditioned. To get TEST 2.$C3$, take the totals for columns 4 to k and compare them with recaptures from cohort 4:

$$
\begin{array}{cccc}
m_{14} + m_{24} & m_{15} + m_{25} & \cdots & m_{1k} + m_{2k} \\
m_{34} & m_{35} & \cdots & m_{3k}
\end{array}
$$

This summing of columns and adjoining of the next cohort continues until one uses cohort $k - 2$ (thereby getting TEST 2.$Ck - 2$). Note that for TEST 2.Ci, only recaptures downstream from dam i are used.

TEST 2 is comparing the proportion of counts in rows 1 and 2 across the columns of the contingency table. If these proportions do not differ significantly, then there is no statistical evidence that the underlying survival and capture probabilities differ for the two rows of counts.

The simulated control group data in Table 1.6 are here used for illustration (these are the m_{cij}):

Cohort i	$j = 2$	3	4	5	6
1	1,104	247	1,832	571	641
2		13	75	19	29
3			17	4	10
4				50	52
5					26

TEST 2.$C2$ is based on

$$
\begin{array}{cccc}
247 & 1,832 & 571 & 641 \\
13 & 75 & 19 & 29
\end{array}
$$

Column totals	260	1,907	590	670

Adjoin the cohort 3 recaptures to the above column totals (omitting the leftmost column) to get the table for TEST 2.$C3$ (note: "C" here denotes cohort, i.e., these tests are based on cohort data):

$$
\begin{array}{ccc}
1,907 & 590 & 670 \\
17 & 4 & 10
\end{array}
$$

Column totals	1,924	594	680

In this example, TEST 2.C4 is the final test that can be computed. It is based on the data

$$\begin{array}{|cc|} \hline 594 & 680 \\ 50 & 52 \\ \hline \end{array}$$

Thus, for the control data, we have

TEST	χ^2	df	P
2.C2	1.83	3	0.61
2.C3	2.47	2	0.32
2.C4	0.22	1	0.64
TEST 2	4.51	6	0.61

TEST 2 for the controls is the total of these three independent chi-square test statistics. None of these test statistics is significant here; this is expected because these data were generated under model $H_{1\phi}$. In a study with two or more groups, TEST 2 is computed for each group separately and the overall TEST 2 is obtained by summing the separate chi-squares and degrees of freedom over groups.

2.1.3.3. TEST 3. – TEST 3 is based on the subcohort information available in the full *m*-array. The data for the simulated treatment group example are shown in Table 1.3. Table 2.5 provides our recommendations for computing TEST 3. Basically, TEST 3 has a component for every cohort that has two or more subcohorts. In fish-turbine survival experiments, only cohorts 3 to k - 1 allow a TEST 3 component. In general Jolly-Seber studies, cohort 2 also has two subcohorts.

From Table 1.3, cohort 3, the contingency table of subcohort data on the fates of the releases at dam 3 is:

$$\begin{array}{cc} 224 & \begin{array}{|cccc|} \hline 19 & 7 & 5 & 193 \\ 1 & 0 & 0 & 10 \\ \hline \end{array} \\ 11 & \end{array}$$

Here, 224 fish were rereleased with capture history {101}. The other 11 had history {111}. Numbers of fish never recaptured were 193 and 10, respectively. As often happens, these data are sparse, and some pooling is necessary to enable a test. Because of this pooling, we recommend a routine splitting of these subcohort-fate contingency tables into two test components: TEST 3.*SRi* and TEST 3.*Smi*, i = 3, ..., k - 2 (capital *S* denotes subcohorts; *R* denotes that the test uses the *R, r* data; TEST 3.*Smi* is based on only the m_{ijh} data).

The previous table partitions into

31	193
1	10

for TEST 3.$SR3$

and into

19	7	5
1	0	0

for TEST 3.$Sm3$.

There are often insufficient data to carry out TEST 3.Smi (as is the case in the previous example), even if that table is further pooled into a simple 2×2 contingency table:

19	12
1	0

These 2×2 contingency tables are used in program RELEASE for TEST 3 components. Program RELEASE does this pooling automatically because the subcohort data are often sparse. The user can recompute these tests on the basis of less-pooled versions of these tables if that is warranted.

Table 2.5. – Explanation of TEST 3 components as we define them under the default pooling rules, and the (potential) computability of components. TEST 3 is computable only for the complete capture history protocol. Data are the subcohorts within released cohorts. Test components are often not computable if data are sparse.

TEST 3.SRi, $i = 3, ..., k - 1$.

Components are based on recaptures after time i. In RELEASE, the default test is computed from the 2×2 contingency table defined below; only data from subcohorts of releases at time i are used:

$h = \{10...01\}$, i.e., caught at dam i, but not at dams 2, ..., $i - 1$

r_{vih}	$R_{vih} - r_{vih}$
$r_{vi} - r_{vih}$	$(R_{vi} - r_{vi}) - (R_{vih} - r_{vih})$

The null hypothesis is that parameters (ϕ, p) for captures at times $i + 1$ to k are the same for all capture histories at release time i. There are $k - 3$ of these tables (in the fisheries context here where only the first release has newly marked fish). TEST 3 is not computable if $k < 4$.

TEST 3.Smi, $i = 3, ..., k - 2$.

Components are based on recaptures at time $i + 1$, given release at time i and subsequent recapture. In RELEASE, the default test is computed from the 2×2 contingency table defined below; only data from subcohorts of releases at time i are used; h is as above:

$m_{vi,i+1,h}$	$(r_{vih} - m_{vi,i+1,h})$
$m_{vi,i+1} - m_{vi,i+1,h}$	$(r_{vi} - m_{vi,i+1}) - (r_{vih} - m_{vi,i+1,h})$

The null hypothesis is the same as for TEST 3.SRi. There are $k - 4$ of these tables ($k \geq 5$).

Continuing with this example, the subcohort data for controls from Table 1.4 for cohorts 4 and 5 are

cohort 4		
48	49	1,678
1	2	68
1	1	14

cohort 5	
24	522
0	18
0	4
2	44
0	1
0	1

The 2×2 contingency tables for TEST 3 components are

TEST 3.SR4

97	1,678
5	82

TEST 3.SR5

24	522
2	68

TEST 3.Sm4

48	49
2	3

Note that TEST 3.Sm,k - 1 never exists. In general, there is more information in the 3.SRi series of components than in the 3.Smi series.

Results in this example for the control group are

TEST	χ^2	df	P
3.SR3	0.28	1	0.60
3.SR4	0.01	1	0.91
3.SR5	0.36	1	0.55
3.Sm3	1.25	1	0.26
3.Sm4	0.17	1	0.68
TEST 3	2.08	5	0.84

The overall goodness of fit test for the assumption of site-specific parameters, which are not subcohort dependent (i.e., the Jolly-Seber model), is the sum of TESTs 2 and 3:

TEST	χ^2	df	P
2	4.51	6	0.61
3	2.08	5	0.84
Total	6.59	11	0.83

Based on this goodness of fit testing for the control data, we would not reject the assumption of site-specific parameters (i.e., the Jolly-Seber model fits the control data).

2.1.4. Discussion

As a basic strategy, we recommend first computing the goodness of fit tests. If these tests reject the Jolly-Seber assumptions of site-specific parameters, one must consider using more general models than we present here (see the discussion in Section 1.4.4). This type of rejection is frequent in studies in which each release (by occasion or site) contains both new animals and previously marked animals. However, we do not consider such studies herein. When all initial releases are at site 1, there is a high likelihood (in our opinion) that the time-specific assumptions about parameters will be satisfied in a carefully conducted study where the rate of movement between dams is not affected by treatment, and there are no handling effects.

If, based on the results of TESTs 2 and 3, goodness of fit is satisfactory, one then proceeds to find an appropriate model to describe the results of the experiment. The first step in that search should be the computation of TEST 1 and an examination of its components. The set of models to be considered should then be determined by biological considerations. When treatment is "applied" at site 1, as in a fisheries turbine, screen, or bypass study, it is reasonable to consider the sequence of hypotheses presented here. The treatment effect is then expected either to wear off or to manifest itself over time. Thus, we believe that in this experimental setting, the time-ordering of parameters (ϕ_1, p_2, ϕ_3, etc.) is relevant in testing for treatment effect. Consequently, we recommend testing to determine if one of the hypotheses of Table 2.2 adequately describes the data. If none do, or if it is logical to investigate alternative hypotheses, one must resort to numerical optimization methods for further testing and estimation. Numerical methods would be required, for example, to analyze the data under a model wherein $\phi_{ci} \neq \phi_{ti}$ (a general effect on survival) but $p_{ci} = p_{ti}$ was assumed (no effects on capture probabilities). Program SURVIV (White 1983) handles this model. Program RELEASE produces output that is easily used as input to program SURVIV for analysis of these alternative scenarios.

2.2. First Capture Histories

2.2.1. Introduction

Under the first capture history protocol, the easiest of the protocols to understand and analyze, fish released at dam 1 are given a batch mark to distinguish treatment versus control groups. Fish in both groups are sampled at downstream dams 2, 3, ..., k and, upon first capture, are removed from the population.

The analysis theory for experiments where only one downstream sampling site is used (i.e., $k = 2$) dates back to Ricker (1945, 1948). His method is often referred to as the *relative recovery rate method* because the estimator of survival rate is the ratio of two "recovery" or recapture rates. Ricker (1958, 1975) extended the method to allow for k sampling occasions and the estimator was again of a similar form, after some pooling of the data across sampling sites. A more general theory was developed independently by Seber (1970) and Robson and Youngs (unpublished report, 1971) (also see Youngs and Robson 1975). This theory allowed greater generality in that marking could be done at n time periods (rather than just two), recovery could be done over k time periods ($k \geq n$), time periods could be unequal, and procedures were free of bias due to truncation. A full discussion of these ML methods can be found in Brownie et al. (1985). The methods of Ricker (1945, 1948), Seber (1970), and Robson and Youngs (unpublished report, 1971) are concerned with the estimation of survival rates based on marking of samples from the population at n time intervals, often once per year. For example, northern pintail ducks *Anas acuta* might be banded with unique band numbers each October for n years; therefore, the survival rate is the annual period between banding (e.g., 15 October of year 1 to 14 October of year 2). In the context here, the survival rate of interest relates not to the time between marking periods but rather to a treatment effect. The survival rate is the result of a treatment because the releases of the treatment and control groups are simultaneous, rather than a year apart. Finally, the probability of not being captured must be incorporated into these models, although the estimators of treatment survival remain the same. With this reinterpretation, the theory for the analysis and testing for the first capture history protocol already exists for model $H_{1\phi}$. We will use notation and terminology consistent with the rest of this monograph. Interested readers may want to refer to Brownie et al. (1985) for other applications and examples.

2.2.2. Model Structure and Expectations

Assuming that fish have independent fates and that all fish in the same treatment group have the same probabilities of being recaptured at downstream dams, the data on first captures are multinomial. If a marked fish is released, it can be captured and removed at dam 2, 3, ..., k, or "never." The model for this protocol is obtained by specifying the probabilities for each outcome as a function of the parameters ϕ_i and p_i. This corresponds to deriving the expected values of the elements in the reduced m-array, $E(m_{ij})$, for the two groups of marked fish. Some examples for the control group will illustrate the concept:

$$E(m_{c12}) = R_{c1}\phi_{c1}p_{c2} \; ;$$

$$E(m_{c13}) = R_{c1}\phi_{c1}q_{c2}\phi_{c2}p_{c3} \; ;$$

$$E(m_{c14}) = R_{c1}\phi_{c1}q_{c2}\phi_{c2}q_{c3}\phi_{c3}p_{c4} \; .$$

The first expression is the expected number of recaptures at dam 2 from the R_{c1} control fish released at dam 1. $E(m_{c12})$ equals the number of control fish released (R_{c1}), times the survival rate from dam 1 to dam 2 (ϕ_{c1}), times the probability of recapture at dam 2 (p_{c2}). The final expectation is read as the expected value of the m_{c14} equals the number of fish initially released (R_{c1}), times the survival probabilities for dams 1 to 2, 2 to 3, and 3 to 4 (ϕ_{c1}, ϕ_{c2}, ϕ_{c3}), times the probability of not being captured at dams 2 and 3 (q_{c2}, q_{c3}), times the probability of recapture at dam 4 (p_{c4}). The treatment fish have similar expectations, although parameters ϕ and p may differ from those in the control group:

$$E(m_{t12}) = R_{t1}\phi_{t1}p_{t2} \; ;$$

$$E(m_{t13}) = R_{t1}\phi_{t1}q_{t2}\phi_{t2}p_{t3} \; ;$$

$$E(m_{t14}) = R_{t1}\phi_{t1}q_{t2}\phi_{t2}q_{t3}\phi_{t3}p_{t4} \; .$$

The observed data are then functions of the dam-to-dam survival probabilities (ϕ_i), the recapture probabilities (p_i), and the probability of not being captured ($q_i = 1 - p_i$). In more complex protocols, the ϕ_i and p_i parameters can be estimated separately but are not individually estimable with the data collected under the first capture history protocol. Also, only limited tests of assumptions are possible under the first capture history protocol. Products of the other parameters can be estimated, but these are of little interest (e.g., $\phi_{v1}p_{v2}$, $\phi_{v1}q_{v2}\phi_{v2}p_{v3}$, and $\phi_{v1}q_{v2}\phi_{v2}\cdots\phi_{vk-1}p_{vk}$). For this reason, subsequent modeling is simplified if the following notation is used:

$$\pi_{tij} = \phi_{ti}q_{ti+1}\phi_{ti+1}q_{ti+2}\cdots\phi_{tj-1}p_{tj}$$

and

$$\pi_{cij} = \phi_{ci}q_{ci+1}\phi_{ci+1}q_{ci+2}\cdots\phi_{cj-1}p_{cj} \; .$$

The π_{ij} are called "cell probabilities." Under model $H_{1\phi}$, $\phi_{t1} = S\phi_{c1}$ and all other parameters (ϕ_i, p_i) are the same by treatment and control groups. Therefore, under model $H_{1\phi}$, $\pi_{tij} = S\pi_{cij}$.

Table 2.6 presents a summary of the data from the general numerical example and the corresponding notation, expectations, and summary statistics.

Table 2.6. – Example data, symbolic reduced m-arrays, expectations of the m-array, and sufficient statistics for the general numerical data under the first capture history protocol.

| Group | Releases R_{vi} | \multicolumn{6}{c}{Number recaptured and removed at dam j, m_{vij}} |
		$j = 2$	3	4	5	6	Total
t	30,000	1,029	238	1,669	549	590	4,075
c	29,000	1,104	247	1,832	571	641	4,395
Total		2,133	485	3,501	1,120	1,231	
t	R_{t1}	m_{t12}	m_{t13}	m_{t14}	m_{t15}	m_{t16}	r_{t1}
c	R_{c1}	m_{c12}	m_{c13}	m_{c14}	m_{c15}	m_{c16}	r_{c1}
Total		m_2	m_3	m_4	m_5	m_6	
t	R_{t1}	π_{t12}	π_{t13}	π_{t14}	π_{t15}	π_{t16}	$\sum_{j=2}^{6}\pi_{t1j}$
c	R_{c1}	π_{c12}	π_{c13}	$\pi_{c14}^{\,a}$	π_{c15}	π_{c16}	$\sum_{j=2}^{6}\pi_{c1j}$

[a] $\pi_{c14} = \phi_{c1}q_{c2}\phi_{c2}q_{c3}\phi_{c3}p_{c4}$.

2.2.3. Likelihood Function

The likelihood function is derived from the joint probability function of the data for both groups,

$$\Pr\{m_{v1j} \mid S, \underline{\phi}, \underline{p}, \underline{R}\} = \prod_{v=t}^{c}\left[\binom{R_{v1}}{m_{v12}\ m_{v13}\ \cdots\ m_{v1k}\ R_{v1}-r_{v1}}\right.$$

$$\left.\times \prod_{j=2}^{k}\left(\pi_{v1j}\right)^{m_{v1j}}\left(1-\lambda_{v1}\right)^{R_{v1}-r_{v1}}\right],$$

where v is a subscript to indicate the treatment (t) and control (c) groups, and $\lambda_{v1} = \sum_{j=2}^{k}\pi_{v1j}$.

Terms such as $\underline{\phi}$ indicate a vector of the dam-to-dam survival rates ($\underline{\phi} = \phi_1, \phi_2, ..., \phi_k$). The notation is formidable, but a simple example in which only two downstream dams are used ($k = 3$) is helpful:

	Treatment	Control
v	t	c
Releases	R_{t1}	R_{c1}
Recaptures	m_{t12} and m_{t13}	m_{c12} and m_{c13}
Never recaptured	$R_{t1} - r_{t1}$	$R_{c1} - r_{c1}$
Cell probabilities	$\pi_{t12} = \phi_{t1}p_{t2}$	$\pi_{c12} = \phi_{c1}p_{c2}$
	$\pi_{t13} = \phi_{t1}q_{t2}\phi_{t2}p_{t3}$	$\pi_{c13} = \phi_{c1}q_{c2}\phi_{c2}p_{c3}$
Pr{never recaptured}	$\lambda_{t1} = 1 - \sum_{j=2}^{3} \pi_{t1j}$	$\lambda_{c1} = 1 - \sum_{j=2}^{3} \pi_{c1j}$

An explanation of the probability function may be helpful. The joint probability function of the data for both groups is

$$\Pr\{m_{v1j} \mid S, \underline{\phi}, p, \underline{R}\}$$

and is read as "the probability of the reduced m-array, given the parameters S, ϕ_1, ϕ_2, p_2, p_3 and the known releases R_{t1} and R_{c1}." This probability function has two components: the first is composed of the product of two multinomial coefficients;

$$\binom{R_{t1}}{m_{t12}\ m_{t13}\ R_{t1} - r_{t1}} \binom{R_{c1}}{m_{c12}\ m_{c13}\ R_{c1} - r_{c1}} .$$

Alternatively, these coefficients can be expressed as ratios of factorial expressions,

$$\left(\frac{R_{t1}!}{m_{t12}!m_{t13}!(R_{t1} - r_{t1})!} \right) \left(\frac{R_{c1}!}{m_{c12}!\ m_{c13}!\ (R_{c1} - r_{c1})!} \right) .$$

These expressions include no unknown parameters and can, therefore, be ignored for purposes of parameter estimation. These expressions are part of the likelihood and are needed for deriving tests of various assumptions.

The second component of the probability function is important for deriving MLEs of the unknown parameters:

$$\prod_{v=t}^{c} \left(\prod_{j=2}^{3} [\pi_{v1j}]^{m_{v1j}} \right) \left(1 - \lambda_{v1}\right)^{R_{v1} - r_{v1}} .$$

Letting $v = t$ for treatment, we can write out the first half of this expression,

$$\left[\pi_{t12}\right]^{m_{t12}} \times \left[\pi_{t13}\right]^{m_{t13}} \times \left[1 - \lambda_{t1}\right]^{R_{t1} - r_{t1}} .$$

Letting $v = c$ for control, the second half is simply

$$\left[\pi_{c12}\right]^{m_{c12}} \times \left[\pi_{c13}\right]^{m_{c13}} \times \left[1 - \lambda_{c1}\right]^{R_{c1} - r_{c1}} .$$

These expressions can be compared with those developed for the die-tossing study in Section 1.2.1 with two differences. First, the cell probabilities π_{ij} are now functions of several parameters rather than being a simple probability (e.g., p_4 was the probability of getting a four on a die throw); and second, the final cell deals with the probability and number of fish never being recaptured, which is a possible outcome (but has no direct analogy with the throw of a die except, perhaps, if one did not tally the number of "sixes").

The likelihood function relevant for parameter estimation is

$$L\left(S, \underline{\phi}, \underline{p} \mid m_{vij}\right) = \prod_{v=t}^{c} \left[\prod_{j=2}^{3} \left(\pi_{v1j}\right)^{m_{v1j}} \right] \left(1 - \lambda_{v1}\right)^{R_{v1} - r_{v1}}$$

and the log-likelihood function is

$$\ln L\left(S, \underline{\phi}, \underline{p} \mid m_{vij}\right) = \sum_{v=t}^{c} \left[\left(\sum_{j=2}^{3} m_{v1j} \left[\ln(\pi_{v1j})\right] \right) + (R_{v1} - r_{v1}) \ln(1 - \lambda_{v1}) \right].$$

2.2.4. Estimable Parameters

As noted earlier, individual ϕ_{vi} and p_{vi} are not estimable from data collected under the first capture history protocol. However, under certain assumptions concerning the ϕ_{vi} and p_{vi}, treatment effects are estimable. In particular, if the treatment effect is direct, so that $\phi_{t1} = S\phi_{c1}$, $\phi_{ti} = \phi_{ci}$, $i = 2, ..., k - 1$, and $p_{ti} = p_{ci}$, $i = 2, ..., k$, the treatment survival rate $S = \phi_{t1}/\phi_{c1}$ is estimable. Referring to the sequence of models introduced in Chapter 2.1, we say that $S = \phi_{t1}/\phi_{c1}$ is estimable if the assumptions of model $H_{1\phi}$ are met. If the treatment effect persists to dam 2 (the first recapture site) and beyond, models more general than $H_{1\phi}$ are required and estimators of treatment effects may not be free of bias. We therefore discuss model $H_{1\phi}$ in some detail and present tests to be used to determine if the model assumptions are met.

Under model $H_{1\phi}$, all parameters ϕ_{vi} and p_{vi} are the same across treatment and control groups, except for ϕ_{t1} and ϕ_{c1}. Writing $\phi_{t1} = S\phi_{c1}$ shows that $\pi_{tij} = S\pi_{cij}$ for $j = 2, ..., k$, and $\lambda_{t1} = S\lambda_{c1}$. Making these substitutions simplifies the likelihood in Section 2.2.3 and enables the identification of a minimal sufficient statistic and the derivation of estimators.

2.2.5. Minimal Sufficient Statistics

A minimal sufficient statistic (MSS) is

$$\text{MSS} = \{r_{t1}, r_{c1}, m_2, m_3, ..., m_{k\text{-}1}\} ,$$

which is the two row totals and all the column totals, except the kth, of the reduced m-array. These summary statistics contain all the information relevant to optimal estimation of the parameters of the model under $H_{1\phi}$. The number of terms in the MSS dictates the maximum number of parameters that can be identified (estimated). In the present example, k "parameters" can be estimated,

$$\begin{array}{cccccc}
1 & 2 & 3 & 4 & \cdots & k \\
S & \phi_1 p_2 & \phi_1 q_2 \phi_2 p_3 & \phi_1 q_2 \phi_2 q_3 \phi_3 p_4 & \cdots & \phi_1 q_2 \phi_2 q_3 \cdots \phi_{k\text{-}1} p_k .
\end{array}$$

The previous "parameters" are the cell probabilities π_{1j}, except that the parameter S is separated and estimated uniquely.

2.2.6. Analysis

The MLE of S, when all the data from dams 2 through k are used, is

$$\hat{S} = \frac{r_{t1}/R_{t1}}{r_{c1}/R_{c1}}$$

$$= \frac{(m_{t12} + m_{t13} + \cdots + m_{t1k})/R_{t1}}{(m_{c12} + m_{c13} + \cdots + m_{c1k})/R_{c1}},$$

which is the total recapture rate for treatment fish (r_{t1}/R_{t1}) divided by the total recapture rate for control fish (r_{c1}/R_{c1}). Using the data on first captures from the general numerical example (Table 2.6),

$$\hat{S} = \frac{4,075/30,000}{4,395/29,000}$$

$$= \frac{0.1358333}{0.1515517}$$

$$= 0.896,$$

which, in this example, is close to the parameter value of 0.9.

MLEs of products of other parameters are

$$\widehat{\phi_1 q_2 \phi_2 q_3 \cdots \phi_{j-1} p_j} = \frac{r_{c1} m_j}{R_{c1}(r_{t1} + r_{c1})}.$$

These estimates maximize the likelihood function, given the data observed (m_{vij}). Other values are "less likely"; however, if a new sample was taken, then the ML estimates would take different values.

The sampling variance of the MLE of the treatment survival rate $\hat{S}$ under model $H_{1\phi}$ is

$$\hat{\mathrm{var}}(\hat{S}) = (\hat{S})^2 \left[\frac{1}{r_{t1}} - \frac{1}{R_{t1}} + \frac{1}{r_{c1}} - \frac{1}{R_{c1}} \right],$$

and the estimated standard error is

$$\hat{se}(\hat{S}) = \sqrt{\hat{var}(\hat{S})} \ .$$

The estimated sampling variance for the general numerical example is

$$\hat{var}(\hat{S}) = (0.896)^2 \left[\frac{1}{4,075} - \frac{1}{30,000} + \frac{1}{4,395} - \frac{1}{29,000} \right]$$

$$= (0.8028) \, (0.000212 + 0.000193)$$

$$= 0.000325 \ ;$$

$$\hat{se}(\hat{S}) = 0.0180 \ .$$

The estimator $\hat{S}$ has a high, positive sampling correlation with the estimator of its sampling variance, $corr[\hat{S}, \hat{var}(\hat{S})]$. This correlation can be seen by noting that the first term in the expression for the sampling variance is $(\hat{S}^2)$. Therefore, if $\hat{S}$ is too large, the estimated sampling variance will be too large, and similarly, if $\hat{S}$ is too small, the estimated sampling variance will also be too small. We computed estimates of this correlation for a few specific cases (see Monte Carlo studies, Part 5) and found them to be high (e.g., 0.89).

An approximate 95% confidence interval (CI) for S can be computed in the usual manner, assuming that the sample is reasonably large.

$$95\%CI = \hat{S} \pm 1.96 \, \hat{se}(\hat{S})$$

$$= 0.896 \pm 0.0354$$

$$= (0.861, 0.932) \ .$$

Alternatively, the coefficient of variation (cv) can be computed as a measure of precision,

$$\hat{cv}(\hat{S}) = \frac{\hat{se}(\hat{S})}{\hat{S}} \times 100$$

$$= 2.0\% .$$

Model $H_{1\phi}$ assumes the only effect of the treatment is to cause a direct mortality $(1 - S)$. This is a strong assumption (see Chapter 1.5).

2.2.7. Tests of Assumptions

The first capture history protocol allows only limited tests of underlying assumptions. Under model $H_{1\phi}$, an overall goodness of fit test is in the form of a $2 \times k - 1$ contingency table,

m_{t12}	m_{t13}	$\cdots$	m_{t1k}	$m_{t1.}$
m_{c12}	m_{c13}	$\cdots$	m_{c1k}	$m_{c1.}$
$m_{.12}$	$m_{.13}$	$\cdots$	$m_{.1k}$	$m_{.1}$

The test statistic is distributed as chi-square with $k - 2$ df under the null hypothesis, which states that the treatment and control groups have the same parameters except for ϕ_{t1} and ϕ_{c1}, thus,

$$\phi_{ti} = \phi_{ci} \quad \text{for all } i = 2, ..., k - 1 ,$$

and

$$p_{ti} = p_{ci} \quad \text{for all } i = 2, ..., k .$$

The alternative hypothesis for this general test is that model $H_{k-1,\phi}$ holds (all parameters ϕ_{ti} and p_{ci} differ by groups). This test is the sum of TESTS 1.$T2$, 1.$T3$, ..., 1.$Tk - 1$.

The contingency table for the general numerical example is

1,029	238	1,669	549	590	4,075
1,104	247	1,832	571	641	4,395
2,133	485	3,501	1,120	1,231	8,470

Computing the test statistic from the above table gives $\chi^2 = 3.2$, 4 df, with $P = 0.52$. Thus, we have no evidence to suspect the validity of the null hypothesis ($H_{1\phi}$ fits the data). We know that the null hypothesis is true in this case because the data were generated from this set of assumptions (cf. Table 1.1).

The goodness of fit test can be viewed in an alternative way that is often more intuitive. Most biologists think of a goodness of fit test as

$$\Sigma \frac{(\text{observed - expected})^2}{\text{expected}}.$$

The observed data under the first capture history protocol are the m_{t1j} and m_{c1j}. Their expected values, assuming $H_{1\phi}$ is true, can be estimated as

$$\hat{E}(m_{t1j}) = \overbrace{R_{t1}S\phi_1 q_2\phi_2 \cdots \phi_{j-1}p_j}$$

and

$$\hat{E}(m_{c1j}) = \overbrace{R_{c1}\phi_1 q_2\phi_2 \cdots \phi_{j-1}p_j}.$$

Therefore, an alternative, but equivalent test of the null hypothesis that $H_{1\phi}$ holds is

$$\chi^2 = \sum_{v=t}^{c} \sum_{j=2}^{k} \frac{\left[m_{v1j} - \hat{E}(m_{v1j})\right]^2}{\hat{E}(m_{v1j})}$$

with $k - 2$ df. The results are equivalent to the contingency table approach unless some pooling is necessary (in which case the contingency table approach should be used). Pooling is required if $\hat{E}(m_{v1j}) < 2$. Program RELEASE performs a thorough analysis of data under the first capture history protocol; example output is shown in Table 2.7.

Table 2.7. – The output of program RELEASE based on the example data given in Table 2.6. Note, most printers are unable to print subscripts, italics, or Greek letters; thus, for example, m_{ij} is shown as m(i, j) and ϕ is shown as phi.

```
                Observed Recaptures for Group 1
                        Treatment Group

     i   R(i)           m(i,j)              r(i)
                 j= 2   3    4    5    6
     1  30000  1029  238 1669  549  590  4075


    m(j)       1029  238 1669  549  590
    z(j)       3046 2808 1139  590    0


                Observed Recaptures for Group 2
                        Control Group

     i   R(i)           m(i,j)              r(i)
                 j= 2   3    4    5    6
     1  29000  1104  247 1832  571  641  4395


    m(j)       1104  247 1832  571  641
    z(j)       3291 3044 1212  641    0


                  Sums for the above Groups

    m.      0 2133  485 3501 1120 1231
    R.  59000    0    0    0    0
    z.      0 6337 5852 2351 1231
    r.   8470    0    0    0    0
```

```
+----------------------------------------------------------------+
|                                                                |
|         Maximum Likelihood Estimates under Model H'5Phi        |
|                                                                |
|        Ratio of Survival between Groups for Occasion 6.        |
|                                                                |
|                                    95% Confidence Intervals    |
|   Parameter     Estimate    Standard Error    Lower     Upper  |
|   ---------     --------------  --------------  --------------  -------------- |
|   S(1,2)        0.889756        0.050231      0.791303  0.988209 |
+----------------------------------------------------------------+
```

Table 2.7. – Continued.

```
TEST 1.T5: Test of p(5) and Phi(4) equal across groups,
assuming higher order parameters are equal across groups.

                  +------+------+
               O| 549  | 590  |1139
               E| 542.6| 596.4|
               C|   0.1|   0.1|
                  +------+------+
               O| 571  | 641  |1212
               E| 577.4| 634.6|
               C|   0.1|   0.1|
                  +------+------+
                  1120   1231   2351
         Chi-square=0.2786 (df=1) P=0.5976
```

```
+----------------------------------------------------------------+
|            Maximum Likelihood Estimates under Model H'4Phi      |
|                                                                |
|      Ratio of Survivals between Groups for Occasions 5 to 6.    |
|                                                                |
|                                      95% Confidence Intervals  |
|  Parameter     Estimate     Standard Error    Lower      Upper  |
|  ---------    ------------  ------------   ------------  ------------ |
|  S(1,2)       0.908443      0.036736       0.836442    0.980445 |
+----------------------------------------------------------------+
```

```
TEST 1.T4: Test of p(4) and Phi(3) equal across groups,
assuming higher order parameters are equal across groups.
                  +------+------+
               O|1669  |1139  |2808
               E|1679.9|1128.1|
               C|   0.1|   0.1|
                  +------+------+
               O|1832  |1212  |3044
               E|1821.1|1222.9|
               C|   0.1|   0.1|
                  +------+------+
                  3501   2351   5852
         Chi-square=0.3388 (df=1) P=0.5605
```

Table 2.7. – Continued.

```
+-------------------------------------------------------------------+
|            Maximum Likelihood Estimates under Model H'3Phi         |
|                                                                   |
|         Ratio of Survivals between Groups for Occasions 4 to 6.   |
|                                                                   |
|                                          95% Confidence Intervals |
|   Parameter      Estimate      Standard Error    Lower       Upper |
|   ---------     -------------  --------------  ------------- ------------- |
|   S(1,2)         0.891721        0.022147       0.848314    0.935129  |
+-------------------------------------------------------------------+
```

TEST 1.T3: Test of p(3) and Phi(2) equal across groups,
assuming higher order parameters are equal across groups.

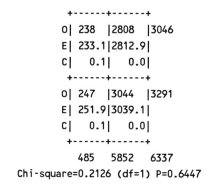

```
      +------+------+
     O| 238  |2808  |3046
     E| 233.1|2812.9|
     C|  0.1|  0.0|
      +------+------+
     O| 247  |3044  |3291
     E| 251.9|3039.1|
     C|  0.1|  0.0|
      +------+------+
        485   5852   6337
  Chi-square=0.2126 (df=1) P=0.6447
```

```
+-------------------------------------------------------------------+
|            Maximum Likelihood Estimates under Model H'2Phi         |
|                                                                   |
|         Ratio of Survivals between Groups for Occasions 3 to 6.   |
|                                                                   |
|                                          95% Confidence Intervals |
|   Parameter      Estimate      Standard Error    Lower       Upper |
|   ---------     -------------  --------------  ------------- ------------- |
|   S(1,2)         0.894703        0.021254       0.853044    0.936361  |
|                                                                   |
+-------------------------------------------------------------------+
```

Table 2.7. – Continued.

```
      TEST 1.T2: Test of p(2) and Phi(1) equal across groups,
      assuming higher order parameters are equal across groups.
                  +------+------+
                  O|1029  |3046  |4075
                  E|1026.2|3048.8|
                  C|  0.0|  0.0|
                  +------+------+
                  O|1104  |3291  |4395
                  E|1106.8|3288.2|
                  C|  0.0|  0.0|
                  +------+------+
                   2133   6337   8470
             Chi-square=0.0196 (df=1) P=0.8887
```

```
+------------------------------------------------------------------+
|            Maximum Likelihood Estimates under Model H1Phi         |
|                                                                  |
|       Ratio of Survivals between Groups for Occasions 2 to 6.    |
|                                                                  |
|                                    95% Confidence Intervals      |
|  Parameter      Estimate      Standard Error    Lower       Upper |
|  ---------    --------------  -------------- -------------- --------------|
|  S(1,2)        0.896284        0.018040       0.860925    0.931642 |
+------------------------------------------------------------------+
```

```
      TEST 1.R1: Test of Phi(1) equal across groups,
      assuming higher order parameters are equal across groups.
                  +------+------+
                  O| 4075 |25925 |30000
                  E| 4307.|25693.|
                  C| 12.5|  2.1|
                  +------+------+
                  O| 4395 |24605 |29000
                  E| 4163.|24837.|
                  C| 12.9|  2.2|
                  +------+------+
                   8470  50530  59000
             Chi-square=29.6316 (df=1) P=0.0000
```

Table 2.7. – Continued.

```
TEST 1:  Overall test of HO vs. H'5Phi
Chi-square=30.4812 (df=5) P=0.0000
TEST  1  is an omnibus test for a treatment effect(s),
i.e., significant differences between groups.  For the
complete capture history protocol and scheme A partial
capture history protocol, TEST 1 is an overall test of
equality of all survival and capture probabilities
among groups.
```

A second test examines the null hypothesis that $S = 1$ (no mortality due to the treatment). This test, termed TEST 1.R1, is based on a simple 2×2 contingency table:

	Recaptured	Not recaptured	
t	r_{t1}	$R_{t1} - r_{t1}$	R_{t1}
c	r_{c1}	$R_{c1} - r_{c1}$	R_{c1}
	$r_{.1}$	$R_1 - r_{.1}$	R_1

Using the data from the general numerical example, we obtain

	Recaptured	Not recaptured	
t	4,075	25,925	30,000
c	4,395	24,605	29,000
	8,470	50,530	59,000

which yields a χ^2 value of 29.6 with 1 df. The probability of a value this large, if the null hypothesis is true, is virtually zero. Therefore, we correctly conclude $S < 1$ as we know that $S = 0.9$ in this example (Table 1.2).

2.2.8. Extended Sequence of Models $H'_{2\phi}, H'_{3\phi}, ..., H'_{k-1,\phi}$

In this section we consider a sequence of hypotheses called models $H'_{2\phi}, H'_{3\phi}, ...,$ $H'_{k-1,\phi}$ and tests between these models under the first capture history protocol. Our discussion is brief because these models rest on assumptions about the recapture rates that may often be tenuous and because the estimators of treatment survival rates are special cases of the estimators under model $H_{1\phi}$. The estimators given in this section may also be useful as approximations to intractable models in certain cases (see Section 3.9.1). These models are mentioned in Part 5, but no other mention of them is made elsewhere in this work.

The sequence of models allows the treatment to affect survival probabilities beyond ϕ_{t1}. However, these models assume $p_{ti} = p_{ci}$ for all i. Thus, the treatment is assumed not to affect the recapture rates. The structure of these models is summarized in Table 2.8.

If model $H_{1\phi}$ is rejected by TEST 1.$T2$, the following MLE should be considered corresponding to model $H'_{2\phi}$.

$$\hat{S} = \frac{(r_{t1} - m_{t12})/R_{t1}}{(r_{c1} - m_{c12})/R_{c1}}$$

or, equivalently,

$$\hat{S} = \frac{(m_{t13} + m_{t14} + ... + m_{t1k})/R_{t1}}{(m_{c13} + m_{c14} + ... + m_{c1k})/R_{c1}} .$$

Table 2.8. – Cell probabilities π_{vij} for the models $H_{1\phi}$, $H'_{2\phi}$, and $H'_{3\phi}$ under the first capture history protocol ($k = 5$). Models under this protocol are based on the assumption $p_{ti} = p_{ci}$ for all i.

Model	v	$j = 2$	3	4	5
$H_{1\phi}$	t	$\phi_{t1}p_2$	$\phi_{t1}q_2\phi_2p_3$	$\phi_{t1}q_2\phi_2q_3\phi_3p_4$	$\phi_{t1}q_2\phi_2q_3\phi_3q_4\phi_4p_5$
	c	$\phi_{c1}p_2$	$\phi_{c1}q_2\phi_2p_3$	$\phi_{c1}q_2\phi_2q_3\phi_3p_4$	$\phi_{c1}q_2\phi_2q_3\phi_3q_4\phi_4p_5$
$H'_{2\phi}$	t	$\phi_{t1}p_2$	$\phi_{t1}q_2\phi_{t2}p_3$	$\phi_{t1}q_2\phi_{t2}q_3\phi_3p_4$	$\phi_{t1}q_2\phi_{t2}q_3\phi_3q_4\phi_4p_5$
	c	$\phi_{c1}p_2$	$\phi_{c1}q_2\phi_{c2}p_3$	$\phi_{c1}q_2\phi_{c2}q_3\phi_3p_4$	$\phi_{c1}q_2\phi_{c2}q_3\phi_3q_4\phi_4p_5$
$H'_{3\phi}$	t	$\phi_{t1}p_2$	$\phi_{t1}q_2\phi_{t2}p_3$	$\phi_{t1}q_2\phi_{t2}q_3\phi_{t3}p_4$	$\phi_{t1}q_2\phi_{t2}q_3\phi_{t3}q_4\phi_4p_5$
	c	$\phi_{c1}p_2$	$\phi_{c1}q_2\phi_{c2}p_3$	$\phi_{c1}q_2\phi_{c2}q_3\phi_{c3}p_4$	$\phi_{c1}q_2\phi_{c2}q_3\phi_{c3}q_4\phi_4p_5$

This estimator is similar to the estimator for model $H_{1\phi}$; however, the numbers in each group recaptured at dam 2 are deleted (i.e., the terms m_{t12} and m_{c12}). With these numbers deleted, the estimators of S, the sampling variance of $\hat{S}$, and the goodness of fit test have the same form as under model $H_{1\phi}$ (however, df $= k - 3$, instead of $k - 2$). The estimator $\hat{S}$ under model $H_{2\phi}$ actually estimates the quantity

$$S_1 \, S_2 \, q_{t2}/q_{c2} \,,$$

where

$$S_1 = \phi_{t1}/\phi_{c1}$$

and

$$S_2 = \phi_{t2}/\phi_{c2} \,.$$

Thus, the unbiased assessment of the treatment effect must assume $q_{t2} = q_{c2}$. This assumption is often poor, but under the first capture history protocol, the parameters p_{vi} (or q_{vi}) cannot be estimated.

A test of model $H_{1\phi}$ (the null hypothesis) versus $H'_{2\phi}$ (the alternative hypothesis) is computed from the 2×2 contingency table (TEST 1.$T2$)

m_{t12}	$m_{t13} + \cdots + m_{t1k}$
m_{c12}	$m_{c13} + \cdots + m_{c1k}$

which is distributed as a chi-square variable with 1 df. This 2×2 contingency table is obtainable from the $2 \times k - 1$ table for the overall goodness of fit test of model $H_{1\phi}$ by pooling, within rows, all of the columns 3 through k. Using data from the general numerical example, the following table is obtained,

1,029	3,046
1,104	3,291

yielding $\chi^2_1 = 0.0196$, $P = 0.89$, which supports the null hypothesis that $\phi_{t2} = \phi_{c2}$.

Estimators of treatment survival for models $H'_{3\phi}$, ..., $H'_{k-1,\phi}$ are similar in that the recapture data from dams 3, ..., $k - 1$ are deleted, respectively. Estimators of S and $\text{var}(\hat{S})$ are summarized in Table 2.9 for models $H_{1\phi}$, $H'_{2\phi}$, ..., $H'_{k-1,\phi}$. The sequence of tests corresponding to the models presented in Table 2.9 is given in Table 2.10. This sequence of models, tests, and estimators may often be useful, at least as an approximation where $p_{ti} \doteq p_{ci}$. Note, however, that no test of $p_{ti} = p_{ci}$ is possible based on data from the first capture history protocol. Program RELEASE provides all the relevant test statistics and estimates for this sequence of models (see Table 2.7); additional theory for these "peeled" models appears in Section 3.9.1.

Table 2.9. − Summary of the sequence of estimators available for data from the first capture history protocol. This sequence is similar to that discussed later for the complete capture history protocol.

Model	Data from dams	$\hat{S}$	$\hat{\text{var}}(\hat{S})$
H_0		1	0
$H_{1\phi}$	2, ..., k	$\dfrac{r_{t1}/R_{t1}}{r_{c1}/R_{c1}}$	$(\hat{S})^2\left[\dfrac{1}{r_{t1}} - \dfrac{1}{R_{t1}} + \dfrac{1}{r_{c1}} - \dfrac{1}{R_{c1}}\right]$
$H'_{2\phi}$	3, ..., k	$\dfrac{(r_{t1} - m_{t12})/R_{t1}}{(r_{c1} - m_{c12})/R_{c1}}$	$(\hat{S})^2\left[\dfrac{1}{r_{t1} - m_{t12}} - \dfrac{1}{R_{t1}} + \dfrac{1}{r_{c1} - m_{c12}} - \dfrac{1}{R_{c1}}\right]$
$H'_{3\phi}$	4, ..., k	$\dfrac{(r_{t1} - m_{t12} - m_{t13})/R_{t1}}{(r_{c1} - m_{c12} - m_{c13})/R_{c1}}$	$(\hat{S})^2\left[\dfrac{1}{r_{t1} - m_{t12} - m_{t13}} - \dfrac{1}{R_{t1}} + \dfrac{1}{r_{c1} - m_{c12} - m_{c13}} - \dfrac{1}{R_{c1}}\right]$
.	.	.	
.	.	.	
.	.	.	
$H'_{k-1,\phi}$	k	$\dfrac{m_{t1k}/R_{t1}}{m_{c1k}/R_{c1}}$	$(\hat{S})^2\left[\dfrac{1}{m_{t1k}} - \dfrac{1}{R_{t1}} + \dfrac{1}{m_{c1k}} - \dfrac{1}{R_{c1}}\right]$

Table 2.10. – Summary of between-model tests for the first capture history protocol. All tests are in the form of a 2×2 contingency table and are computed by program RELEASE.

Null hypothesis[a]	Alternative hypothesis	Test number[b]	Contingency table
H_0	$H_{1\phi}$	1.R1	$\begin{array}{ll} r_{t1} & R_{t1} - r_{t1} \\ r_{c1} & R_{c1} - r_{c1} \end{array}$
$H_{1\phi}$	$H'_{2\phi}$	1.T2	$\begin{array}{ll} m_{t12} & m_{t13} + ... + m_{t1k} \\ m_{c12} & m_{c13} + ... + m_{c1k} \end{array}$
$H'_{2\phi}$	$H'_{3\phi}$	1.T3	$\begin{array}{ll} m_{t13} & m_{t14} + ... + m_{t1k} \\ m_{c13} & m_{c14} + ... + m_{c1k} \end{array}$
. . .	. . .	. . .	. . .
$H'_{k-2,\phi}$	$H'_{k-1,\phi}$	1.Tk - 1	$\begin{array}{ll} m_{t1,k-1} & m_{t1k} \\ m_{c1,k-1} & m_{c1k} \end{array}$

[a] See Table 2.2.

[b] See Tables 2.1 and 2.3.

The sequence of alternative estimators in Table 2.10 is useful if the treatment affects survival beyond dam 2; however, the methods are only completely justified if there are equal recapture rates between groups. The alternative sequence of models can sometimes reduce bias in $\hat{S}$ substantially under the first capture history protocol, especially if the p_{vi} are small (see Chapter 3.9). The variance of $\hat{S}$ increases as more data are deleted from the analysis. For example, if we rejected model $H_{1\phi}$ and had to use model $H'_{2\phi}$ (i.e., deleted recaptures from dam 2 in the analysis), we would have computed $\hat{S} = 0.895$ (compared to $\hat{S} = 0.896$, the estimate based on model $H_{1\phi}$), but the precision would have been poorer ($\hat{se}(\hat{S}) = 0.0213$, rather than 0.0180). Other comparisons can be made from Table 2.7.

2.2.9. Relative Recovery Rate Method

The *relative recovery rate method* is mentioned because it represents a good analysis method for experiments as they have been conducted commonly in the past. The protocol involves first capture histories of batch-marked fish in two groups, as we have discussed. In this special case, however, fish are recaptured at only a single downstream dam (dam 2). Ricker (1945, 1948) gave the MLE of S as

$$\hat{S} = \frac{m_{t12} \, R_{c1}}{R_{t1} \, m_{c12}}$$

or, in our form,

$$\hat{S} = \frac{m_{t12}/R_{t1}}{m_{c12}/R_{c1}} \, .$$

The estimator of the sampling variance is also a special case of the theory we have just presented,

$$\hat{\text{var}}(\hat{S}) = (\hat{S})^2 \left[\frac{1}{m_{t12}} - \frac{1}{R_{t1}} + \frac{1}{m_{c12}} - \frac{1}{R_{c1}} \right] .$$

Although this procedure is an optimal estimation method for a given field design and certain (restrictive) assumptions, we do not generally recommend it. The data do not allow even minimal tests of assumptions, the assumption that $p_{t2} = p_{c2}$ in particular. Moreover, the approximate expected value of this $\hat{S}$ (under any model) is

$$E(\hat{S}) \doteq S \, \frac{p_{t2}}{p_{c2}};$$

thus, $\hat{S}$ is sensitive to the assumption that $p_{t2} = p_{c2}$. Additional discussion of absolute and relative recovery rates is found in Manly (1981).

2.2.10. Discussion

The first capture history protocol has several advantages. Only simple batch marks are required. Record keeping at dams 2, ..., k is simple, as recaptured fish are removed and not rereleased. Some tests of assumptions are possible, and estimation methods are developed and available. Although the various estimates and tests can be computed on a small calculator, we urge the use of program RELEASE for a thorough analysis of data.

A potential problem with the first capture history protocol arises because the theoretical variances (i.e., those derived from the likelihood function) may be underestimated due to a possible lack of independence among fish. Heterogeneity in large river systems yields data having more variability than the multinomial variation embedded in the model. This heterogeneity probably arises from a host of sources, but has almost no effect on the point estimators of treatment survival S. The solution to these issues relies on some form of replication that will enable computation of a proper empirical variance. This replication can be conducted in several potential ways, two of which we mention briefly here. (This subject is treated in more detail in Part 4.)

True replication represents one of two main approaches. Treatment and control fish would be allocated randomly to, say, 10 replicates. Fish in the various replicates would be handled, marked, held, and released together. The appropriate variance is the component due to variation in $\hat{S}$ among the 10 replicates.

Alternatively, quasi-replicates termed *lots* can be used. In this situation, the team conducting the experiment might release 10 lots, each consisting of 15,000 treatment and 15,000 control fish. The lots might be released over 10 nights. Here, the variance among the 10 estimates of treatment survival contains an additional component: the day-to-day variation. This component would include any known changes in experimental conditions (e.g., blade angle of turbine, river height behind the dam) as well as changes in unknown conditions (e.g., predation pressure). Lots, then, are not identical in terms of experimental conditions. Often, the lot-to-lot variance gives more useful information than if true replicates had been used. In general, the planning team can view the use of replicates or lots as alternatives, depending on the study objectives.

An estimate of the treatment survival rate could be made from the lots or replicates as a weighted or unweighted average of the individual estimates. In the weighted case,

$$\hat{S} = \frac{\sum_{i=1}^{10} w_i \hat{S}_i}{\sum_{i=1}^{10} w_i},$$

where $w_i = \left[\dfrac{1}{r_{t1}} - \dfrac{1}{R_{t1}} + \dfrac{1}{r_{c1}} - \dfrac{1}{R_{c1}}\right]^{-1}$ or a similar expression taken from Table 2.9. The sampling variance of $\hat{S}$ could then be computed empirically as

$$\hat{\text{var}}(\hat{S}) = \frac{\sum\limits_{i=1}^{10} w_i(\hat{S}_i - \hat{S})^2}{9 \sum\limits_{i=1}^{10} w_i}.$$

If such replication could be done carefully and with proper attention to all the field practicalities, an excellent experiment could be expected.

An alternative procedure would involve subsampling by time periods of the day at dams 2, ..., k. Consider releasing 150,000 treatment and 150,000 control fish with batch marks. The number recaptured and removed at each downstream dam would be tabulated by time period of the day (e.g., six 4-hour periods). If this subsampling could be done at each dam, six reduced m-arrays could be analyzed to provide six estimates of treatment survival. Each estimate would be a nearly independent estimate of S, and an average of the six estimates could be used to estimate the survival rate and an empirical variance. This procedure has advantages, but may not be feasible in all situations. However, our main point is that proper replication or subsampling should be built into the design of experiments involving the first capture history protocol (see Part 4).

Readers interested in further information on the analysis procedures for this general type of protocol are encouraged to study Seber (1970), Robson and Youngs (unpublished report, 1971), and Brownie et al. (1985:1-55, 170-175). However, an understanding of these studies requires the reinterpretation that S relates to a treatment survival rate rather than to a time-period survival rate. In addition, the q_i terms do not appear in the reports because the sampling, sport, or commercial exploitation of the population affects the entire population, not just the released, marked animals.

In many treatment-control survival experiments, it is informative to examine the number of losses on capture (d), by group, at each dam (this discussion relates to fish lost accidentally, rather than to deliberate removals). It seems reasonable that the losses on capture at each dam are proportional for treatment and control groups. This assumption can be tested by using a simple chi-square test. If d_{tj} and d_{cj} are the number of fish lost on capture at dam j for the treatment and control groups, respectively, the following $k - 1$ contingency tables can be formed:

d_{t1j}	$m_{t1j} - d_{t1j}$
d_{c1j}	$m_{c1j} - d_{c1j}$

$$j = 2, ..., k.$$

The total chi-square statistic has $k - 1$ df, as each 2×2 table has 1 df. A rejection of the null hypothesis as the result of this test may be evidence that the treatment has a delayed effect. Fish may be slightly injured, making them more susceptible to predation or other fates (lowered ϕ_{tj}) or more susceptible to capture (higher p_{tj}). Insight into these issues can be achieved by comparison of the pattern of observed and expected values in the contingency table (also see Part 3).

2.3. Unknown Capture Histories

2.3.1. Introduction

Under the unknown capture history protocol, fish are given a batch mark to distinguish between treatment and control groups released at dam 1. Fish in both groups are recaptured downstream at dams 2, 3, ..., k, and all fish are rereleased without further marking and without the investigators knowing their previous capture history. The data from an experiment conducted under this protocol are represented as

$$R_{t1} \quad m_{t2} \quad m_{t3} \quad \cdots \quad m_{tk}$$

$$R_{c1} \quad m_{c2} \quad m_{c3} \quad \cdots \quad m_{ck}.$$

Note that m_{vj} is the total number of fish of treatment group v captured at dam j. Referring back to Table 1.15, one sees that

$$m_{vj} = m_{v.j} = \sum_{i=1}^{j-1} m_{vij}.$$

Only the total number of fish captured at dam j is known for each treatment group because capture histories of marked fish are unknown. For example, it is not known how many of the recaptures at dam 3 were also recaptured at dam 2.

To illustrate data under this protocol, we use the data in Table 1.9 from the general numerical example

	Released at dam 1	Recaptures m_{tj} and m_{cj} by dam					Totals m_v.
		2	3	4	5	6	
t	30,000	1,029	249	1,762	616	691	4,347
c	29,000	1,104	260	1,924	644	758	4,690

The previous example shows that an additional statistic is needed:

$$m_{v.} = \sum_{j=2}^{k} m_{vj} .$$

For example,

$$m_{t.} = 4{,}347 \quad \text{and} \quad m_{c.} = 4{,}690 .$$

These totals are the basis of the estimate of S under this protocol.

This protocol has been used in many survival experiments conducted on the Columbia River in recent decades. Data collected under this protocol do not lead to an exact statistical analysis in the sense of the other three protocols, except in the special case where $k = 2$ (Ricker's *relative recovery rate method,* discussed in Sections 2.2.1 and 2.2.9). Although it has undesirable properties, the unknown capture history protocol may be a reasonable approach when the capture rates p_j are low and are not affected by treatment, and replicate lots enable estimates of precision.

2.3.2. Model Structure

The data under the unknown capture history protocol are not multinomial because a specific fish can be caught at more than one downstream dam. In fact, simple expressions for sampling models for these data cannot be derived. Consequently, exact theoretical methods cannot be developed for this protocol. In addition, losses on capture present further difficulties or require further assumptions. In the following material, we consider the case where the capture rates p_i are low (i.e., < 0.05), the number of capture sites (or times) is small (say, $k < 7$), and the number of fish released in each group is large.

We start with the special case of $k = 2$ to aid in understanding of this protocol. Only in this special case of the unknown capture history protocol are the capture histories known. The expectations are

$$E(m_{t2}) = E(m_{t12}) = R_{t1}\, \phi_{t1}\, p_{t2}$$

and

$$E(m_{c2}) = E(m_{c12}) = R_{c1}\, \phi_{c1}\, p_{c2} .$$

We make the assumption that $p_{t2} = p_{c2}$ and define the treatment survival rate as $S = \phi_{t1}/\phi_{c1}$.

Then the exact MLE of the treatment survival S is

$$\hat{S} = \frac{m_{t2}/R_{t1}}{m_{c2}/R_{c1}},$$

with estimated theoretical sampling variance

$$\hat{var}(\hat{S}) = (\hat{S})^2 \left[\frac{1}{m_{t2}} - \frac{1}{R_{t1}} + \frac{1}{m_{c2}} - \frac{1}{R_{c1}} \right].$$

Even with replication, we do not recommend this procedure; tests of the critical assumption that $p_{t2} = p_{c2}$ are not possible, making this a poor scientific design.

Finally, we note that the case of $k = 2$ is identical to the first capture history protocol with $k = 2$. (In fact, all protocols are the same when $k = 2$.) That equivalence does not hold for $k > 2$. However, we, of necessity, use some first capture history methods even with unknown capture history data.

In the case where $k > 2$ and there are no losses on capture, the expectation of the number of recaptures at dam j can be expressed as

$$E(m_{tj}) = R_{t1} \left(\prod_{i=1}^{j-1} \phi_{ti} \right) p_{tj}$$

and

$$E(m_{cj}) = R_{c1} \left(\prod_{i=1}^{j-1} \phi_{ci} \right) p_{cj}.$$

For example, for $k = 3$, the expectations for the control group are $E(m_{c2}) = R_{c1}\phi_{c1}p_{c2}$ and $E(m_{c3}) = R_{c1}\phi_{c1}\phi_{c2}p_{c3}$. In general, as long as there are no losses on capture, the expected number of captures at dam j is just R_{c1} times the probability of surviving until dam j multiplied by the (conditional) capture probability at dam j. Note that when there are no losses on capture, captures at intermediate dams 2 through $j - 1$ have no effect on the expected value of m_{vj} (extensions to the case of losses on capture are given in Section 2.3.5).

Some assumptions must be made in order to estimate a treatment effect. It suffices to assume that all of the ϕ_i and p_i are equal between treatment and control groups except ϕ_1 (i.e., $\phi_{t2} = \phi_{c2}, ..., \phi_{t,k-1} = \phi_{c,k-1}, p_{t2} = p_{c2}, ..., p_{tk} = p_{ck}$). This is model $H_{1\phi}$. We then define the treatment effect to be $S = \phi_{t1}/\phi_{c1}$. These assumptions mean that

$$\frac{E(m_{tj})}{R_{t1}} = S \frac{E(m_{cj})}{R_{c1}} , \quad j = 2, ..., k ,$$

and, by the method of moments, the estimator of S is

$$\hat{S} = \frac{\sum\limits_{j=2}^{k} m_{tj}/R_{t1}}{\sum\limits_{j=2}^{k} m_{cj}/R_{c1}} = \frac{m_{t.}/R_{t1}}{m_{c.}/R_{c1}} .$$

This estimator is similar to the MLE of S under the first capture history protocol for model $H_{1\phi}$.

For the first capture history protocol, the MLE is

$$\hat{S} = \frac{r_{t1}/R_{t1}}{r_{c1}/R_{c1}} .$$

The r_{t1} and r_{c1} do not include multiple counts of fish due to (unknown) multiple captures. Thus, one always has $r_{t1} \le m_{t.}$ and $r_{c1} \le m_{c.}$; however, the difference $m_{v.} - r_{v1}$ is small if capture probabilities are small. Contrary to what one might think, the extra counts reflected in $m_{c.}$ and $m_{t.}$ do not improve the precision of $\hat{S}$. If the p_i are low, the probability of a specific fish being captured more than once is small and then unknown capture history data are essentially removal data, just like those data under the first capture history protocol. In this case, the unknown capture history estimator is close to the fully efficient MLE of S for removal data.

An example will illustrate the effect of low capture probabilities. Assume that 30,000 fish are released; $k = 4, p_2 = 0.01, p_3 = 0.04$, and $p_4 = 0.02$, and survival rates are constant at 0.98 (i.e., $\phi_1 = \phi_2 = \phi_3 = 0.98$). Here we would expect only 39 of the 30,000 initially released fish to be caught twice. The expected number of fish caught at all three downstream dams is 0.2, less than one fish. In such cases, the data are similar to data under the first capture history protocol and the estimator can be considered approximately ML. Furthermore, the sampling variance is closely approximated by the theoretical sampling variance developed under the first capture history protocol, and the goodness of fit tests are similar because few fish are captured more than once.

As capture probabilities increase, the number of fish captured more than once increases, making the approximations noted above progressively poorer. However, provided $H_{1\phi}$ holds, the estimator

$$\hat{S} = \frac{m_{t\cdot}/R_{t1}}{m_{c\cdot}/R_{c1}}$$

remains appropriate. Although the estimator is not the MLE (because the likelihood is intractable), it appears to be the best estimator possible. The variance formula and goodness of fit tests developed for the first capture history protocol are not strictly justified, as capture probabilities or k, or both, increase, causing a substantial number of fish to be captured more than once. Alternative theoretical variance formulae are considered below. However, even those formulae are not totally satisfactory. The simple fact is that the first capture history protocol is superior to the unknown capture history protocol; we consider the unknown capture history protocol here only because many data have already been collected in this way.

The data for the general numerical example in Table 1.9, which can be used to illustrate the estimation of S, are reproduced here.

	Released at dam 1	\multicolumn{5}{c}{Recaptures m_{tj} and m_{cj} by dam}	
		2	3	4	5	Totals 6	$m_{v\cdot}$
t	30,000	1,029	249	1,762	616	691	4,347
c	29,000	1,104	260	1,924	644	758	4,690

Note that losses on capture are included in these counts and in the totals used to compute $\hat{S}$. The estimate of S is

$$\hat{S} = \frac{4,347/30,000}{4,690/29,000}$$

$$= 0.896.$$

From the first capture history protocol one has $r_{t1} = 4,075$ and $r_{c1} = 4,395$; thus, about 300 fish in each group (treatment and control) were captured more than once (about 1% of releases). When one conducts a study using the unknown capture history protocol, the rate of multiple captures will, of course, not be known.

If we treat the estimator in this example as if it were based on first capture history data, we have (from Chapter 2.2),

$$\hat{\text{var}}(\hat{S}) = (\hat{S})^2 \left[\frac{1}{m_{t.}} - \frac{1}{R_{t1}} + \frac{1}{m_{c.}} - \frac{1}{R_{c1}} \right]$$

$$= (0.896)^2 \left[\frac{1}{4,347} - \frac{1}{30,000} + \frac{1}{4,690} - \frac{1}{29,000} \right],$$

which gives $\hat{\text{se}}(\hat{S}) = 0.0174$. However, a slightly better formula for the sampling variance of $\hat{S}$ under the unknown capture history protocol, developed in Section 2.3.5, is used by RELEASE:

$$\hat{\text{var}}(\hat{S}) = (\hat{S})^2 \left\{ \frac{1}{m_{t.}} - \frac{1}{R_{t1}} \left[\sum_{j=2}^{k} \left(\frac{m_{tj}}{m_{t.}} \right)^2 \right] + \frac{1}{m_{c.}} - \frac{1}{R_{c1}} \left[\sum_{j=2}^{k} \left(\frac{m_{cj}}{m_{c.}} \right)^2 \right] \right\}.$$

Computed here, we obtain,

$$\hat{\text{var}}(\hat{S}) = (0.896)^2 \left[\frac{1}{4,347} - \frac{0.269}{30,000} + \frac{1}{4,690} - \frac{0.272}{29,000} \right],$$

or

$$\hat{\text{se}}(\hat{S}) = 0.0185.$$

This standard error is slightly larger than the one produced by treating these data as first capture history data. We expect, theoretically, that the unknown capture history protocol will produce results less precise than those under the first capture history protocol.

We recommend using empirical sampling variances with the unknown capture history protocol. For the estimation of these variances, we recommend a study design with at least five lots. The sampling variances are then computed empirically from the replicate lots. These ideas are developed in Part 4.

One is forced to use the methods appropriate for the first capture history protocol in testing the assumptions for this protocol. We do not repeat those tests here (see Chapter 2.2).

2.3.3. Estimable Parameters

The only estimable parameter of interest under this protocol is S, the treatment survival rate (we are assuming an acute treatment effect). Estimates of the products $\phi_{c1}\phi_2 \cdots \phi_{j-1}p_j$, $j = 2, ..., k$, can be made, assuming that the treatment and control groups are alike at, and after, dam 2 (hypothesis $H_{1\phi}$). These products are, however, not intrinsically of interest.

If losses on capture occur, the moment estimator of the treatment survival is valid if it is assumed that losses on capture are not affected by the treatment. An examination of the expectations for the m_{tj} and m_{cj} (presented in Section 2.3.5) illustrates this point. Also, this assumption can be tested by using the contingency table method given in Section 2.2.10.

The information on losses on capture for treatment and control groups is examined here to illustrate this procedure. Assuming model $H_{1\phi}$ (i.e., an acute treatment effect), the losses-on-capture data in Table 1.9 are summarized into the following contingency table as a basis for testing equality of loss rates over treatment and control groups.

	Dam				
	2	3	4	5	6
t	33	14	85	26	32
c	33	10	62	28	39

The chi-square value for this table is 4.1 with 4 df, $P < 0.48$. This value provides no evidence that the losses on capture have been affected by the treatment. In addition, there is no reason to suspect delayed mortality due to the treatment.

When program RELEASE is used to compute this chi-square test, it prints the observed and expected values along with the chi-square contribution, thus allowing the investigator to look for patterns among the observed and expected values (Table 2.11).

Table 2.11. – Observed and expected losses on capture and chi-square values for testing that losses on capture are not affected by treatment, for the general numerical example under the unknown capture history protocol.

Group		Dam				
		2	3	4	5	6
t	Observed(O)	33	14	85	26	32
	Expected(E)	34.6	12.6	77.2	28.3	37.3
	$(O-E)^2/E$	0.08	0.16	0.80	0.19	0.74
c	Observed(O)	33	10	62	28	39
	Expected(E)	31.4	11.4	69.8	25.7	33.7
	$(O-E)^2/E$	0.09	0.17	0.88	0.21	0.82

Here, no pattern is suggested and the chi-square value is about what is expected when the null hypothesis is true.

This way of examining losses on capture is valid under model $H_{1\phi}$ for any protocol when only an acute effect exists. In a test of equal loss rates for treatments and controls, which is valid under any hypothesis about the treatment effects, a series of 2×2 tables is used, one for each recovery dam. In this example, for dam 2, the table is

33	996	1,029
33	1,071	1,104

If we let d_{vj} = losses on capture for treatment group v at recapture dam j, then the general table under the unknown capture history protocol is

d_{tj}	$m_{tj} - d_{tj}$	m_{tj}
d_{cj}	$m_{cj} - d_{cj}$	m_{cj}

For dam 3 in this example, the general table is

14	235	249
10	250	260

Here, $\chi^2 = 0.89$ with 1 df.

In this example, there are five such 2×2 tables. The total chi-square (5 df) from these tables also provides an overall test of whether the rate of loss on capture is the same for treatments as for controls. That test statistic value is 7.68, and is not significant.

2.3.4. Discussion

The unknown capture history protocol has two operational advantages: only batch marks are needed, and fish do not need to be removed when caught. Schoenemon et al. (1961) presented examples where this protocol has been used. However, there are also serious disadvantages, the most serious of which is that nothing is known about the capture history of the marked fish; thus, a proper likelihood cannot be derived. Theoretically, the likelihood can be written, but it contains a large number of inestimable parameters. The estimator of S is a moment estimator (hence, of uncertain efficiency) whose theoretical sampling variance can only be approximated. Only limited testing of model assumptions is possible.

Ideally, this protocol might be considered after a conclusive study, in which unique marks are used, indicates that model $H_{1\phi}$ fits the data generated in a particular experimental setting, i.e., capture probabilities are equal for both treatment and control groups, and ϕ_2, ..., ϕ_{k-2} are equal for both groups. One might then consider further experiments using the shortcut unknown capture history protocol with proper replication. The poorest study design for conducting experiments is the use of the unknown capture history protocol without replication and with $k = 2$.

2.3.5. Theory for the Unknown Capture History Protocol

Material in this section is provided more for the sake of completeness than for its usefulness in most survival experiments.

In principle, one can write the probability model for the complete capture history case and then derive the likelihood for the unknown capture history case. In practice, however, this approach is difficult. The result is a convolution of different multinomial distributions that is difficult to write, let alone maximize.

We use moment techniques to derive an estimator and theoretical formulae. First we develop some theory for the recaptures m_2, ..., m_k from just one arbitrary released cohort of size R. Some notation used here:

π_j is the probability of loss on capture; in practice it suffices to treat this probability as the proportion of the m_j that is lost on capture,

$$
f_j = \begin{cases} \phi_1 p_2 , & j = 2 \\[2mm] \left[\displaystyle\prod_{i=2}^{j-1} \phi_{i-1}(1 - p_i \pi_i) \right] \phi_{j-1} p_j , & j = 3, ..., k . \end{cases}
$$

Then

$$E(m_j \mid R) = Rf_j, \quad j = 2, ..., k .$$

If there are no losses on capture, we put all $\pi_i = 0$, giving

$$f_j = \phi_1 \cdots \phi_{j-1}p_j .$$

The marginal distribution of m_j is binomial (R, f_j) under the assumptions that each fish represents an independent Bernoulli event. However, pairwise, the m_j and m_h are dependent:

$$\text{cov}(m_j, m_h) = R\left[p_j(1 - \pi_j) - f_j(1 - \pi_j p_j)\right] \frac{f_h}{1 - p_j\pi_j} , \quad j < h.$$

This covariance can be derived by considering a single fish. Define $x_j = 1$ if the fish is captured on occasion j, $x_j = 0$ otherwise. Then $E(x_j) = f_j$ and $\text{cov}(m_j, m_h) = R(E(x_j x_h) - f_j f_h)$. Next,

$$E(x_j x_h) = \text{Pr}(x_j = 1 \text{ and } x_h = 1)$$

$$= \text{Pr}\{x_j = 1\}\text{Pr}\{x_h = 1 \mid x_j = 1\}$$

$$= f_j(1 - \pi_j)\phi_j(1 - p_{j+1}\pi_{j+1}) \cdots \phi_{h-1}p_h$$

$$= \frac{p_j(1 - \pi_j)}{1 - p_j\pi_j}f_h, \quad j < h .$$

These results allow the derivation of $\text{var}(m.)$, $m. = \sum_{j=2}^{k} m_j$:

$$\text{var}(m.) = R\left[\sum_{j=2}^{k} f_j(1 - f_j)\right] + 2\sum_{j=2}^{k-1} \sum_{h=j+1}^{k} \text{cov}(m_j, m_h)$$

$$= R\left[\sum_{j=2}^{k} f_j(1 - f_j)\right] + 2R\left[\sum_{j=2}^{k-1} \frac{p_j(1 - \pi_j)}{1 - p_j\pi_j} \left(\sum_{h=j+1}^{k} f_h\right)\right]$$

$$- R\left[\left(\sum_{j=2}^{k} f_j\right)^2 - \sum_{j=2}^{k} (f_j)^2\right].$$

An alternative expression is

$$\text{var}(m.) = Rf.(1 - f.) + 2R\left[\sum_{j=2}^{k} \frac{p_j(1 - \pi_j)}{1 - p_j\pi_j} \left(\sum_{h=j+1}^{k} f_h\right)\right]$$

Here, $f. = \sum_{j=2}^{k} f_j$.

Note that if $\pi_2 = \cdots = \pi_k = 1$, the results apply to the first capture history case. At the other extreme, even if all $\pi_j = 0$, the theoretical variance of $m.$ is technically not estimable. In practice, this means that a biased theoretical estimator of $\text{var}(m.)$ must be used.

Consider point estimation of a treatment effect. Now a subscript is added for treatment or control to all parameters and statistics. Under $H_{1\phi}$, $f_{tj} = Sf_{cj}$, so

$$\frac{E(m_{t.})}{R_{t1}} = S\frac{E(m_{c.})}{R_{c1}}.$$

(Note that this requires $\pi_{tj} = \pi_{cj}$ for all j.) Under more general models, there are options for "peeling off" (discarding) data from upstream dams to obtain a better estimate of treatment effect not possible with the unknown capture history protocol. This procedure works like the one for first capture history data (see the discussion in Section 2.2.8).

The theoretical sampling variance of $\hat{S}$ is

$$\text{var}(\hat{S}) = (S)^2 \left[\frac{\text{var}(m_{t.})}{[E(m_{t.})]^2} + \frac{\text{var}(m_{c.})}{[E(m_{c.})]^2}\right].$$

One must select an approximation to $\text{var}(m.)$ to estimate this sampling variance. Both theory and some numerical work suggest to us that for low rates of loss on capture and low capture probabilities (as in typical turbine studies on the Columbia River), the better approximation is

$$\text{var}(m.) \doteq R\left[\sum_{j=2}^{k} f_j(1 - f_j)\right].$$

The f_j are estimable, $\hat{f}_j = m_j/R$, but the covariances are not estimable. If these covariances are negligible, an estimator of theoretical sampling variance is

$$\hat{\text{var}}(m_{v.}) = \sum_{j=2}^{k} m_{vj}(1 - \frac{m_{vj}}{R_{v1}}), \quad v = t, c .$$

(The alternative is $m_{v.}[1 - \frac{m_{v.}}{R_{v1}}].$) This approach produces

$$\hat{\text{var}}(\hat{S}) = (\hat{S})^2\left\{\frac{1}{m_{t.}} - \frac{1}{R_{t1}}\left[\sum_{j=2}^{k}\left(\frac{m_{tj}}{m_{t.}}\right)^2\right] + \frac{1}{m_{c.}} - \frac{1}{R_{c1}}\left[\sum_{j=2}^{k}\left(\frac{m_{cj}}{m_{c.}}\right)^2\right]\right\}.$$

This formula is used in program RELEASE. If there is sufficient empirical replication, we recommend using an empirical estimator of sampling variance.

The critical point is which approximation is the better for var($m.$). The following example is informative. Let $k = 6$, all $p_j = 0.03$, and all $\phi_j = 0.98$ (and no losses on capture). The exact result is then var($m.$) $= R(0.16649)$. Here $f. = 0.171236$, so

$$Rf.(1 - f.) = R(0.14192),$$

whereas

$$R\sum_{j=2}^{6} f_j(1 - f_j) = R(0.16311).$$

From the Cauchy-Schwartz inequality,

$$\left(\sum f_j\right)^2 \geq \sum\left(f_j\right)^2;$$

therefore, from the first expression for var($m.$), the second and third terms tend to cancel (hence the result in the example). In essence, the Cauchy-Schwartz inequality provides theoretical support for our choice of approximation to var($m.$).

2.4. Complete Capture Histories

2.4.1. Introduction

We here consider the experimental protocol whereby the experimenter can obtain the complete capture history of each marked fish, either by using a unique tag for each fish released or different batch marks at each dam. If we consider one group of fish (treatment or control), the basic model used to analyze these data is a special case of the Jolly-Seber model (Jolly 1965; Seber 1965, 1982:196). We follow only the marked animals and estimate survival and capture probabilities (Cormack 1964), whereas the general Jolly-Seber model also uses marked-to-unmarked ratios to estimate population sizes and numbers of new recruits. Literature on the Jolly-Seber model includes papers by Manly (1971a), Cormack (1973), Buckland (1980), Pollock (1981b), and Pollock and Mann (1983). Pollock and Mann (1983) and Hightower and Gilbert (1984) presented applications of the Jolly-Seber model in fisheries management. The Jolly-Seber approach must be extended in the present work because treatment and control fish potentially have different survival and capture probabilities. Many possible models are available, depending on the number of treatment and control parameters that are different or common (e.g., Table 2.2).

First we present the basic model structure for the case where all parameters are different for the two groups. Because this model is the core of our discussion, we present detailed descriptions of point estimators of parameters and their variances and covariances. We next consider the sequence of models obtained with the complete capture history protocol as we allow the number of parameters common to both treatment and control groups to decrease from all to none, briefly describe goodness of fit testing for this protocol, give a detailed hypothetical example using numbers to illustrate our methodology, and finally present some details of the specific theory for this protocol (complete details are in Part 3).

2.4.2. Model $H_{k-1,\phi}$

At the first site ($i = 1$), there is an initial release of marked fish of the treatment and control groups. At downstream sites ($i = 2, ..., k$), marked fish are recaptured. Typically, marked fish are released again, although some fish may be removed because they are wounded by capture or are needed for other research. The basic data are conveniently summarized initially as a capture history matrix (see Section 1.3.2.1).

Most analyses (except for the goodness of fit tests computed as components of TEST 3) can be performed on the reduced m-array summarization of the data represented in Table 2.12 (see Section 1.3.2.3), illustrated here for the case of $k = 4$ sampling times.

Table 2.12. – Data summary (as an m-array) for the complete capture history protocol ($k = 4$).

Release site	Releases R_{v1}	Number recaptured at dam j, m_{vij}			Total
		$j = 2$	3	4	
		Treatment group			
1	R_{t1}	m_{t12}	m_{t13}	m_{t14}	r_{t1}
2	R_{t2}		m_{t23}	m_{t24}	r_{t2}
3	R_{t3}			m_{t34}	r_{t3}
Totals		m_{t2}	m_{t3}	m_{t4}	
		Control group			
1	R_{c1}	m_{c12}	m_{c13}	m_{c14}	r_{c1}
2	R_{c2}		m_{c23}	m_{c24}	r_{c2}
3	R_{c3}			m_{c34}	r_{c3}
Totals		m_{c2}	m_{c3}	m_{c4}	

To illustrate the parameter structure, Table 2.13 shows the expected values of the number of captures – i.e., $E(m_{tij} \mid R_{ti})$ and $E(m_{cij} \mid R_{ci})$ – when all parameters may be different for the treatment and control fish.

Table 2.13. – Expected numbers of recaptures, $E(m_{tij})$ and $E(m_{dj})$, for the complete capture history protocol ($k = 4$) under the general model $H_{k-1,\phi}$.

Releases R_{v1}	Number recaptured at dam j, m_{vij}			Total
	$j = 2$	3	4	
	Treatment group			
R_{t1}	$R_{t1}\phi_{t1}p_{t2}$	$R_{t1}\phi_{t1}q_{t2}\phi_{t2}p_{t3}$	$R_{t1}\phi_{t1}q_{t2}\phi_{t2}q_{t3}\phi_{t3}p_{t4}$	$R_{t1}\lambda_{t1}$
R_{t2}		$R_{t2}\phi_{t2}p_{t3}$	$R_{t2}\phi_{t2}q_{t3}\phi_{t3}p_{t4}$	$R_{t2}\lambda_{t2}$
R_{t3}			$R_{t3}\phi_{t3}p_{t4}$	$R_{t3}\lambda_{t3}$
	Control group			
R_{c1}	$R_{c1}\phi_{c1}p_{c2}$	$R_{c1}\phi_{c1}q_{c2}\phi_{c2}p_{c3}$	$R_{c1}\phi_{c1}q_{c2}\phi_{c2}q_{c3}\phi_{c3}p_{c4}$	$R_{c1}\lambda_{c1}$
R_{c2}		$R_{c2}\phi_{c2}p_{c3}$	$R_{c2}\phi_{c2}q_{c3}\phi_{c3}p_{c4}$	$R_{c2}\lambda_{c2}$
R_{c3}			$R_{c3}\phi_{c3}p_{c4}$	$R_{c3}\lambda_{c3}$

Under the most general model structure $H_{k-1,\phi}$, we can apply the Jolly-Seber method to each group of fish (treatment or control) separately because we assume that every parameter is different for the two groups. Therefore, no information on treatment fish is obtained from control data or vice versa. The point estimators and their variances and covariances were given by Seber (1982:199). However, we use a different representation of these parameter estimators that leads to simpler formulae in the more complex models.

All point estimators depend on the minimal sufficient statistic

$$\text{MSS} = \{r_{t1}, r_{t2}, ..., r_{t,k-1}, m_{t2}, m_{t3}, ..., m_{t,k-1}, r_{c1}, r_{c2}, ..., r_{c,k-1}, m_{c2}, m_{c3}, ..., m_{c,k-1}\} \,.$$

Notice that the minimal sufficient statistic can be partitioned into two components, one for each group of fish, each component corresponding to the minimal sufficient statistic under the Jolly-Seber model for that single data set.

The parameter estimators under this model are

$$\hat{\phi}_{ti} = \frac{r_{ti}}{R_{ti}} \left[\frac{m_{t,i+1}}{T_{t,i+1}} + \frac{z_{t,i+1}R_{t,i+1}}{T_{t,i+1}r_{t,i+1}} \right], \quad i = 1, ..., k-2 \,;$$

$$\hat{\phi}_{ci} = \frac{r_{ci}}{R_{ci}} \left[\frac{m_{c,i+1}}{T_{c,i+1}} + \frac{z_{c,i+1}R_{c,i+1}}{T_{c,i+1}r_{c,i+1}} \right], \quad i = 1, ..., k-2 \,;$$

$$\widehat{\phi_{t,k-1}p_{tk}} = \frac{r_{t,k-1}}{R_{t,k-1}} \,;$$

$$\widehat{\phi_{c,k-1}p_{ck}} = \frac{r_{c,k-1}}{R_{c,k-1}} \,;$$

$$\hat{p}_{ti} = \frac{m_{ti}}{m_{ti} + z_{ti}R_{ti}/r_{ti}} \,, \quad i = 2, ..., k-1 \,; \text{ and}$$

$$\hat{p}_{ci} = \frac{m_{ci}}{m_{ci} + z_{ci}R_{ci}/r_{ci}} \,, \quad i = 2, ..., k-1 \,.$$

Recall that $T_{ti} = m_{ti} + z_{ti}$ and $T_{ci} = m_{ci} + z_{ci}$. Definitions of other terms are in both the Glossary and Section 1.4.2.

The theoretical variances for the treatment group are given as:

$$\hat{\text{var}}(\hat{\phi}_{ti}) = (\hat{\phi}_{ti})^2 \left[\frac{1}{r_{ti}} - \frac{1}{R_{ti}} + (\hat{q}_{t,i+1})^2 \left(\frac{1}{r_{t,i+1}} - \frac{1}{R_{t,i+1}} \right) \right.$$

$$\left. + (\hat{q}_{t,i+1})^2 \left(1 - \frac{r_{t,i+1}}{R_{t,i+1}} \right)^2 \frac{m_{t,i+1}}{z_{t,i+1} T_{t,i+1}} \right], \quad i = 1, ..., k - 2;$$

$$\hat{\text{var}}(\hat{p}_{ti}) = (\hat{p}_{ti} \hat{q}_{ti})^2 \left[\frac{1}{r_{ti}} - \frac{1}{R_{ti}} + \frac{1}{m_{ti}} + \frac{1}{z_{ti}} \right], \quad i = 2, ..., k - 1.$$

The survival effect $\hat{S}_i$ between dams i and $i + 1$ is estimated by

$$\hat{S}_i = \hat{\phi}_{ti} / \hat{\phi}_{ci} .$$

The estimated variance of $\hat{S}_i$ is

$$\hat{\text{var}}(\hat{S}_i) = (\hat{S}_i)^2 \left[\frac{\hat{\text{var}}(\hat{\phi}_{ti})}{\hat{\phi}_{ti}^2} + \frac{\hat{\text{var}}(\hat{\phi}_{ci})}{\hat{\phi}_{ci}^2} \right] .$$

Additional theory for variances and covariances of $\hat{S}$, under different models, is in Chapter 3.3.

Most of the possible covariances between the $2k - 3$ estimators (within a group) are zero; theoretical formulae for the non-zero covariances for the treatment group are:

$$\hat{\text{cov}}(\hat{\phi}_{t,i-1}, \hat{\phi}_{ti}) = -\hat{\phi}_{t,i-1} \hat{\phi}_{ti} \hat{q}_{ti} \left(\frac{1}{r_{ti}} - \frac{1}{R_{ti}} \right), \quad i = 2, ..., k - 2;$$

$$\hat{\text{cov}}(\hat{\phi}_{ti}, \hat{p}_{ti}) = \hat{\phi}_{ti} \hat{p}_{ti} \hat{q}_{ti} \left(\frac{1}{r_{ti}} - \frac{1}{R_{ti}} \right), \quad i = 2, ..., k - 2;$$

$$\hat{\text{cov}}(\hat{\phi}_{ti}, \hat{p}_{t,i+1}) = -\hat{\phi}_{ti} \hat{p}_{t,i+1} (\hat{q}_{t,i+1})^2 \left[\frac{1}{r_{t,i+1}} - \frac{1}{R_{t,i+1}} + \left(1 - \frac{r_{t,i+1}}{R_{t,i+1}} \right) \frac{1}{z_{t,i+1}} \right], \quad i = 1, ..., k - 3.$$

The variances and covariances for the control group estimators are of the same form; subscript t is replaced by subscript c. Notice that alternate survival estimators within each treatment group have a negative covariance. Because all parameters are distinct for the two groups in this model and the data are analyzed separately for each group, all treatment estimators are independent of all control estimators.

2.4.3. Model Sequence

The most general model $H_{k-1,\phi}$, discussed in Section 2.4.2, is often too general because treatment and control fish may differ only in a few of the initial survival and capture probabilities. In Chapter 2.1, we presented a sequence of models ranging from H_0 (no treatment effect on any parameters) to the most general, $H_{k-1,\phi}$. We reiterate the meaning of these hypotheses (models) here, ordered from the least general to the most general model.

H_0: $\phi_{t1} = \phi_{c1},\ p_{t2} = p_{c2},\ \phi_{t2} = \phi_{c2},\ p_{t3} = p_{c3}\ ,\ \cdots$
                    "all parameters the same for t and c"

$H_{1\phi}$: $\phi_{t1} \neq \phi_{c1},\ p_{t2} = p_{c2},\ \phi_{t2} = \phi_{c2},\ p_{t3} = p_{c3}\ ,\ \cdots$
                    "all parameters the same for t and c, except for ϕ_1"

H_{2p}: $\phi_{t1} \neq \phi_{c1},\ p_{t2} \neq p_{c2},\ \phi_{t2} = \phi_{c2},\ p_{t3} = p_{c3}\ ,\ \cdots$
                    "all parameters the same for t and c, except for ϕ_1, p_2"

$H_{2\phi}$: $\phi_{t1} \neq \phi_{c1},\ p_{t2} \neq p_{c2},\ \phi_{t2} \neq \phi_{c2},\ p_{t3} = p_{c3}\ ,\ \cdots$
                    "all parameters the same for t and c, except ϕ_1, p_2, and ϕ_2"

$H_{k-1,\phi}$: $\phi_{ti} \neq \phi_{ci}, i = 1, ..., k-1$ and $p_{ti} \neq p_{ci}, i = 2, ..., k$
                    "all parameters different for t and c"

In the following sections, we present more details on models H_0, $H_{1\phi}$, and H_{2p} giving, in particular, point estimators and variances and covariances.

2.4.4. Model H_0

Under model H_0, all the parameters for treatment and control groups are assumed to be common. Therefore, the minimal sufficient statistic is

$$\text{MSS} = \{r_{.1}, ..., r_{.k-1}, m_{.2}, ..., m_{.k-1}\},$$

which is the usual Jolly-Seber case, with all statistics pooled across groups. Recall that $r_{.i} = r_{ti} + r_{ci}$ and $m_{.i} = m_{ti} + m_{ci}$. Also, this results in $z_{.i} = z_{ti} + z_{ci}$ and $T_{.i} = T_{ti} + T_{ci}$.

The parameter estimators under model H_0 are structurally the same as those given for model $H_{k-1,\phi}$. We give these estimators below for comparison with results under model $H_{k-1,\phi}$:

$$\hat{\phi}_i = \frac{r_{.i}}{R_{.i}} \left[\frac{m_{.,i+1}}{T_{.,i+1}} + \frac{z_{.,i+1} R_{.,i+1}}{T_{.,i+1} r_{.,i+1}} \right], \quad i = 1, ..., k - 2 ;$$

$$\widehat{\phi_{k-1} p_k} = \frac{r_{.,k-1}}{R_{.,k-1}} ,$$

$$\hat{p}_i = \frac{m_{.i}}{m_{.i} + z_{.i} R_{.i}/r_{.i}} , \quad i = 2, ..., k - 1 .$$

The variances and covariances of the above are structurally identical to those given for the treatment group in Section 2.4.2; one just replaces the subscript t with a period "." (i.e., pool over t and c) throughout those variance-covariance formulae. For that reason, and because RELEASE computes these variances and covariances, we do not explicitly give their formulae under model H_0. (Note: all parameter estimators, variances, and covariances under all models for the complete capture history are given in Section 3.1.3.)

2.4.5. Model $H_{1\phi}$

Model $H_{1\phi}$ has all parameters common except the first survival rates ($\phi_{t1} \neq \phi_{c1}$). This model is reasonable if the treatment effect wears off completely by the second sampling time (i.e., is an acute effect).

This is an important model, so we present (for $k = 4$) the conditional expectations $E(m_{tij} | R_{ti})$ and $E(m_{cij} | R_{ci})$ in Table 2.14. Model $H_{1\phi}$ is closely related to models considered originally by Robson (1969) and Pollock (1975) for temporary trap response and to the age-dependent version of the Jolly-Seber model described by Pollock (1981b).

The minimal sufficient statistic under $H_{1\phi}$ is

$$\text{MSS} = \{ r_{t1}, r_{c1}, r_{.2}, ..., r_{.,k-1}, m_{.2}, ..., m_{.,k-1} \} .$$

Table 2.14. – Expected numbers of recaptures $E(m_{t1j} \mid R_{t1})$ and $E(m_{c1j} \mid R_{c1})$ for the complete capture history protocol ($k = 4$) model $H_{1\phi}$.

Releases	Number recaptured at dam j, $m_{\cdot ij}$			
$R_{\cdot i}$	$j = 2$	3	4	Total
	Treatment group			
R_{t1}	$R_{t1}\phi_{t1}p_2$	$R_{t1}\phi_{t1}q_2\phi_2 p_3$	$R_{t1}\phi_{t1}q_2\phi_2 q_3\phi_3 p_4$	$R_{t1}\lambda_{t1}$
R_{t2}		$R_{t2}\phi_2 p_3$	$R_{t2}\phi_2 q_3\phi_3 p_4$	$R_{t2}\lambda_2$
R_{t3}			$R_{t3}\phi_3 p_4$	$R_{t3}\lambda_3$
	Control group			
R_{c1}	$R_{c1}\phi_{c1}p_2$	$R_{c1}\phi_{c1}q_2\phi_2 p_3$	$R_{c1}\phi_{c1}q_2\phi_2 q_3\phi_3 p_4$	$R_{c1}\lambda_{c1}$
R_{c2}		$R_{c2}\phi_2 p_3$	$R_{c2}\phi_2 q_3\phi_3 p_4$	$R_{c2}\lambda_2$
R_{c3}			$R_{c3}\phi_3 p_4$	$R_{c3}\lambda_3$

The parameter estimators under model $H_{1\phi}$ are:

$$\hat{\phi}_{t1} = \frac{r_{t1}}{R_{t1}}\left[\frac{m_{\cdot 2}}{T_{\cdot 2}} + \frac{z_{\cdot 2}R_{\cdot 2}}{T_{\cdot 2}r_{\cdot 2}}\right];$$

$$\hat{\phi}_{c1} = \frac{r_{c1}}{r_{c1}}\left[\frac{m_{\cdot 2}}{T_{\cdot 2}} + \frac{z_{\cdot 2}R_{\cdot 2}}{T_{\cdot 2}r_{\cdot 2}}\right];$$

$$\hat{\phi}_i = \frac{r_{\cdot i}}{R_{\cdot i}}\left[\frac{m_{\cdot,i+1}}{T_{\cdot,i+1}} + \frac{z_{\cdot,i+1}R_{\cdot,i+1}}{T_{\cdot,i+1}r_{\cdot,i+1}}\right], \quad i = 2, ..., k-2;$$

$$\widehat{\phi_{k-1}p_k} = \frac{r_{\cdot,k-1}}{R_{\cdot,k-1}}; \text{ and}$$

$$\hat{p}_i = \frac{m_{\cdot i}}{m_{\cdot i} + z_{\cdot i}R_{\cdot i}/r_{\cdot i}}, \quad i = 2, ..., k-1.$$

Our recommended definition of the treatment effect (see Chapter 1.5) under model $H_{1\phi}$ is

$$S = \frac{\phi_{t1}}{\phi_{c1}} \; ;$$

hence, $\hat{S} = \dfrac{\hat{\phi}_{t1}}{\hat{\phi}_{c1}}$, which gives the simple result

$$\hat{S} = \frac{r_{t1}/R_{t1}}{r_{c1}/R_{c1}} \; .$$

The theoretical variance of $\hat{S}$ is

$$\hat{\text{var}}(\hat{S}) = (\hat{S})^2 \left[\frac{1}{r_{t1}} - \frac{1}{R_{t1}} + \frac{1}{r_{c1}} - \frac{1}{R_{c1}} \right].$$

The variances and covariances of the $\hat{\phi}$ and $\hat{p}$ are:

$$\hat{\text{var}}(\hat{\phi}_{t1}) = (\hat{\phi}_{t1})^2 \left[\frac{1}{r_{t1}} - \frac{1}{R_{t1}} + (\hat{q}_2)^2 \left(\frac{1}{r_{.2}} - \frac{1}{R_{.2}} \right) + (\hat{q}_2)^2 \left(1 - \frac{r_{.2}}{R_{.2}} \right)^2 \frac{m_{.2}}{z_{.2}T_{.2}} \right] ;$$

$\hat{\text{var}}(\hat{\phi}_{c1})$ is as above with subscript t replaced by subscript c;

$$\hat{\text{var}}(\hat{\phi}_i) = (\hat{\phi}_i)^2 \left[\frac{1}{r_{.i}} - \frac{1}{R_{.i}} + (\hat{q}_{i+1})^2 \left(\frac{1}{r_{.i+1}} - \frac{1}{R_{.i+1}} \right) \right.$$

$$\left. + (\hat{q}_{i+1})^2 \left(1 - \frac{r_{.i+1}}{R_{.i+1}} \right)^2 \left(\frac{m_{.i+1}}{z_{.i+1}T_{.i+1}} \right) \right], \quad i = 2, ..., k - 2 ;$$

$$\hat{\text{var}}(\hat{p}_i) = (\hat{p}_i\hat{q}_i)^2 \left[\frac{1}{r_{.i}} - \frac{1}{R_{.i}} + \frac{1}{m_{.i}} + \frac{1}{z_{.i}} \right], \quad i = 2, ..., k - 1 ;$$

$$\hat{\text{cov}}(\hat{\phi}_{t1}, \hat{\phi}_{c1}) = \hat{\phi}_{t1}\,\hat{\phi}_{c1}\,(\hat{q}_2)^2 \left[\frac{1}{r_{.2}} - \frac{1}{R_{.2}} + \left(1 - \frac{r_{.2}}{R_{.2}} \right)^2 \frac{m_{.2}}{z_{.2}T_{.2}} \right] ;$$

$$\hat{\text{cov}}(\hat{\phi}_{t1}, \hat{\phi}_2) = -\hat{\phi}_{t1}\,\hat{\phi}_2\,\hat{q}_2 \left(\frac{1}{r_{.2}} - \frac{1}{R_{.2}} \right) ;$$

$\hat{\text{cov}}(\hat{\phi}_{c1}, \hat{\phi}_2)$ is as above with subscript t replaced by subscript c;

$$\hat{\text{cov}}(\hat{\phi}_i, \hat{\phi}_{i+1}) = -\hat{\phi}_i\,\hat{\phi}_{i+1}\,\hat{q}_{i+1} \left(\frac{1}{r_{.,i+1}} - \frac{1}{R_{.,i+1}} \right), \quad i = 2, ..., k-3 ;$$

$$\hat{\text{cov}}(\hat{\phi}_{t1}, \hat{p}_2) = -\hat{\phi}_{t1}\,\hat{p}_2\,(\hat{q}_2)^2 \left(\frac{1}{r_{.2}} - \frac{1}{R_{.2}} + \frac{1 - \dfrac{r_{.2}}{R_{.2}}}{z_{.2}} \right) ;$$

$\hat{\text{cov}}(\hat{\phi}_{c1}, \hat{p}_2)$ is as above with subscript t replaced by subscript c;

$$\hat{\text{cov}}(\hat{\phi}_i, \hat{p}_i) = \hat{\phi}_i\,\hat{p}_i\,\hat{q}_i \left(\frac{1}{r_{.i}} - \frac{1}{R_{.i}} \right), \quad i = 2, ..., k-2; \text{ and}$$

$$\hat{\text{cov}}(\hat{\phi}_i, \hat{p}_{i+1}) = -\hat{\phi}_i\,\hat{p}_{i+1}\,(\hat{q}_{i+1})^2 \left(\frac{1}{r_{.,i+1}} - \frac{1}{R_{.,i+1}} + \frac{1 - \dfrac{r_{.,i+1}}{R_{.,i+1}}}{z_{.,i+1}} \right), \quad i = 2, ..., k-2 .$$

2.4.6. Model H_{2p}

In model H_{2p}, it is assumed that only ϕ_1 and p_2 are affected by the treatment. Hence, this model has all parameters common except the first survival rate ($\phi_{t1} \neq \phi_{c1}$) and the first capture probability ($p_{t2} \neq p_{c2}$). Again, it is informative to present the expected data values $E(m_{tij} \mid R_{ti})$ and $E(m_{cij} \mid R_{ci})$ as in Table 2.15. Model H_{2p} is closely related to a temporary trap response model originally presented by Pollock (1975).

Table 2.15. – Expected numbers of recaptures under model H_{2p} for the complete capture history protocol ($k = 4$).

Releases $R_{\text{·}i}$	Number recaptured at dam j, $m_{\text{·}ij}$			Total
	$j = 2$	3	4	
	Treatment group			
R_{t1}	$R_{t1}\phi_{t1}p_{t2}$	$R_{t1}\phi_{t1}q_{t2}\phi_2 p_3$	$R_{t1}\phi_{t1}q_{t2}\phi_2 q_3\phi_3 p_4$	$R_{t1}\lambda_{t1}$
R_{t2}		$R_{t2}\phi_2 p_3$	$R_{t2}\phi_2 q_3\phi_3 p_4$	$R_{t2}\lambda_2$
R_{t3}			$R_{t3}\phi_3 p_4$	$R_{t3}\lambda_3$
	Control group			
R_{c1}	$R_{c1}\phi_{c1}p_{c2}$	$R_{c1}\phi_{c1}q_{c2}\phi_2 p_3$	$R_{c1}\phi_{c1}q_{c2}\phi_2 q_3\phi_3 p_4$	$R_{c1}\lambda_{c1}$
R_{c2}		$R_{c2}\phi_2 p_3$	$R_{c2}\phi_2 q_3\phi_3 p_4$	$R_{c2}\lambda_2$
R_{c3}			$R_{c3}\phi_3 p_4$	$R_{c3}\lambda_3$

The minimal sufficient statistic under H_{2p} is given by

$$\text{MSS} = \{r_{t1}, r_{c1}, r_{.2}, ..., r_{.,k-1}, m_{t2}, m_{c2}, m_{.3}, ..., m_{.,k-1}\}.$$

The parameter estimators under model H_{2p} are:

$$\hat{\phi}_{t1} = \frac{r_{t1}}{R_{t1}} \left[\frac{m_{t2}}{T_{t2}} + \frac{z_{t2}R_{.2}}{T_{t2}r_{.2}} \right];$$

$$\hat{\phi}_{c1} = \frac{r_{c1}}{R_{c1}} \left[\frac{m_{c2}}{T_{c2}} + \frac{z_{c2}R_{.2}}{T_{c2}r_{.2}} \right];$$

$$\hat{\phi}_i = \frac{r_{.2}}{R_{.2}} \left[\frac{m_{.,i+1}}{T_{.,i+1}} + \frac{z_{.,i+1}R_{.,i+1}}{T_{.,i+1}r_{.,i+1}} \right], \quad i = 2, ..., k - 2;$$

$$\widehat{\phi_{k-1}p_k} = \frac{r_{.,k-1}}{R_{.,k-1}} \; ;$$

$$\hat{p}_{t2} = \frac{m_{t2}}{m_{t2} + z_{t2}R_{.2}/r_{.2}} \; ;$$

$$\hat{p}_{c2} = \frac{m_{c2}}{m_{c2} + z_{c2}R_{.2}/r_{.2}} \; ; \text{ and}$$

$$\hat{p}_i = \frac{m_{.i}}{m_{.i} + z_{.i}R_{.i}/r_{.i}} \; , \quad i = 3, ..., k - 1.$$

The effect of treatment on survival from dam 1 to dam 2 is estimated by

$$\hat{S} = \frac{\hat{\phi}_{t1}}{\hat{\phi}_{c1}}$$

(this ratio does not simplify under model H_{2p}). The difference between $\hat{p}_{t2}$ and $\hat{p}_{g2}$ also represents a treatment effect, but not one of major interest. The estimated variance of S is

$$\hat{\text{var}}(\hat{S}) = (\hat{S})^2 \left\{ \left[\frac{1}{r_{t1}} - \frac{1}{R_{t1}} + \frac{1}{r_{c1}} - \frac{1}{R_{c1}} \right] \right.$$

$$+ (\hat{p}_{t2} - \hat{p}_{c2})^2 \left[\frac{1}{r_{.2}} - \frac{1}{R_{.2}} \right]$$

$$\left. + \frac{(1 - \hat{\lambda}_2)^2}{\hat{\lambda}_2} \left[\frac{\hat{p}_{t2}\hat{q}_{t2}}{T_{t2}} + \frac{\hat{p}_{c2}\hat{q}_{c2}}{T_{c2}} \right] \right\},$$

where the $\hat{p}_{t2}$ and $\hat{p}_{c2}$ are given above and $\hat{\lambda}_2 = r_{.2}/R_{.2}$. Compare this formula for $\hat{\text{var}}(\hat{S})$ under model H_{2p} to the $\hat{\text{var}}(\hat{S})$ under model $H_{1\phi}$. The first large term of the above is the $\hat{\text{var}}(\hat{S})$ under model $H_{1\phi}$. The additional terms in the above reflect loss of precision in $\hat{S}$ when one uses model H_{2p} (actually that loss of precision is not great).

The variance formulae do not show us the bias that $\hat{S}$ will have if model H_{2p} is true but $H_{1\phi}$ is used. If model $H_{1\phi}$ is true, $\hat{S}$ is essentially unbiased. However, if model H_{2p} is true and one uses model $H_{1\phi}$ as the basis of one's estimator of S, we have, approximately,

$$E(\hat{S}) = S \, \frac{p_{t2} + q_{t2}\lambda_2}{p_{c2} + q_{c2}\lambda_2} \, .$$

Using these formulae, one can evaluate bias and precision of $\hat{S}$ if model H_{2p} is true but model $H_{1\phi}$ is used for data analysis.

The variances and covariances of the above estimators of the ϕ and p are:

$$\hat{\mathrm{var}}(\hat{\phi}_{t1}) = (\hat{\phi}_{t1})^2 \left[\frac{1}{r_{t1}} - \frac{1}{R_{t1}} + (\hat{q}_{t2})^2 \left(\frac{1}{r_{.2}} - \frac{1}{R_{.2}} \right) + (\hat{q}_{t2})^2 \left(1 - \frac{r_{.2}}{R_{.2}} \right)^2 \frac{m_{t2}}{z_{t2} T_{t2}} \right] ;$$

$\hat{\mathrm{var}}(\hat{\phi}_{c1})$ is as above with subscript t replaced by subscript c;

$$\hat{\mathrm{var}}(\hat{\phi}_i) = (\hat{\phi}_i)^2 \left[\frac{1}{r_{.i}} - \frac{1}{R_{.i}} + (\hat{q}_{i+1})^2 \left(\frac{1}{r_{.,i+1}} - \frac{1}{R_{.,i+1}} \right) \right.$$

$$\left. + (\hat{q}_{i+1})^2 \left(1 - \frac{r_{.,i+1}}{R_{.,i+1}} \right)^2 \frac{m_{.,i+1}}{z_{.,i+1} T_{.,i+1}} \right] , \qquad i = 2, ..., k - 2 ;$$

$$\hat{\mathrm{var}}(\hat{p}_{t2}) = (\hat{\phi}_{t2} \hat{q}_{t2})^2 \left[\frac{1}{r_{.2}} - \frac{1}{R_{.2}} + \frac{1}{m_{t2}} + \frac{1}{z_{t2}} \right] ;$$

$\hat{\mathrm{var}}(\hat{p}_{c2})$ is as above with subscript t replaced by subscript c;

$$\hat{\mathrm{var}}(\hat{p}_i) = (\hat{p}_i \hat{q}_i)^2 \left[\frac{1}{r_{.i}} - \frac{1}{R_{.i}} + \frac{1}{m_{.i}} + \frac{1}{z_{.i}} \right] , \qquad i = 3, ..., k - 1 ;$$

$$\hat{\mathrm{cov}}(\hat{\phi}_{t1}, \hat{\phi}_{c1}) = \hat{\phi}_{t1} \hat{q}_{t2} \hat{\phi}_{c1} \hat{q}_{c2} \left[\frac{1}{r_{.2}} - \frac{1}{R_{.2}} \right] ;$$

$$\hat{cov}(\hat{\phi}_{t1}, \hat{\phi}_2) = -\hat{\phi}_{t1}\hat{\phi}_2\hat{q}_{t2}\left[\frac{1}{r_{.2}} - \frac{1}{R_{.2}}\right] ;$$

$\hat{cov}(\hat{\phi}_{c1}, \hat{\phi}_2)$ is as above with subscript t replaced by subscript c ;

$$\hat{cov}(\hat{\phi}_i, \hat{\phi}_{i+1}) = -\hat{\phi}_i\hat{\phi}_{i+1}\hat{q}_{i+1}\left[\frac{1}{r_{.i+1}} - \frac{1}{R_{.i+1}}\right] , \quad i = 2, ..., k-3 ;$$

$$\hat{cov}(\hat{\phi}_{t1}, \hat{\phi}_{t2}) = -\hat{\phi}_{t1}\hat{p}_{t2}(\hat{q}_{t2})^2\left[\frac{1}{r_{.2}} - \frac{1}{R_{.2}} + \frac{1 - \frac{r_{.2}}{R_{.2}}}{z_{t2}}\right] ;$$

$\hat{cov}(\hat{\phi}_{c1}, \hat{p}_{c2})$ is as above with subscript t replaced by subscript c ;

$$\hat{cov}(\hat{\phi}_{t1}, \hat{p}_{c2}) = -\hat{\phi}_{t1}\hat{p}_{c2}\hat{q}_{t2}\hat{q}_{c2}\left[\frac{1}{r_{.2}} - \frac{1}{R_{.2}}\right] ;$$

$$\hat{cov}(\hat{\phi}_{c1}, \hat{p}_{t2}) = -\hat{\phi}_{c1}\hat{p}_{t2}\hat{q}_{c2}\hat{q}_{t2}\left[\frac{1}{r_{.2}} - \frac{1}{R_{.2}}\right] ;$$

$$\hat{cov}(\hat{\phi}_2, \hat{p}_{t2}) = \hat{\phi}_2\hat{p}_{t2}\hat{q}_{t2}\left[\frac{1}{r_{.2}} - \frac{1}{R_{.2}}\right] ;$$

$\hat{cov}(\hat{\phi}_2, \hat{p}_{c2})$ is as above with subscript t replaced by subscript c;

$$\hat{cov}(\hat{\phi}_i, \hat{p}_i) = \hat{\phi}_i\hat{p}_i\hat{q}_i\left[\frac{1}{r_{.i}} - \frac{1}{R_{.i}}\right] , \quad i = 3, ..., k-2 ; \text{ and}$$

$$\hat{\text{cov}}(\hat{\phi}_i, \hat{p}_{i+1}) = -\hat{\phi}_i \hat{p}_{i+1} (\hat{q}_{i+1})^2 \left[\frac{1}{r_{.,i+1}} - \frac{1}{R_{.,i+1}} + \frac{1 - \dfrac{r_{.,i+1}}{R_{.,i+1}}}{z_{.,i+1}} \right] \quad i = 3, ..., k - 2.$$

2.4.7. Comments on Models $H_{2\phi}$ to $H_{k-1,\phi}$

The remaining models in the sequence, i.e., $H_{2\phi}$ through $H_{k-1,\phi}$, are not discussed here in detail. For each of these models, explicit estimators of the parameters are given in Section 3.1.3. The estimators of ϕ_{t1} and ϕ_{c1}, hence, $S = \phi_{t1}/\phi_{c1}$ and $\text{var}(\hat{S})$ are identical for all models $H_{2\phi}$ through $H_{k-1,\phi}$ (general results for $H_{k-1,\phi}$ are given in Section 2.4.2). In particular, for $\hat{S} = \hat{\phi}_{t1}/\hat{\phi}_{c1}$ under any of these models,

$$\hat{\text{var}}(\hat{S}) = (\hat{S})^2 \left[\left[\frac{1}{r_{t1}} - \frac{1}{R_{t1}} + \frac{1}{r_{c1}} - \frac{1}{R_{c1}} \right] \right.$$

$$+ (\hat{q}_{t2})^2 \left[\frac{1}{r_{t2}} - \frac{1}{R_{t2}} \right] + (\hat{q}_{c2})^2 \left[\frac{1}{r_{c2}} - \frac{1}{R_{c2}} \right]$$

$$+ \left[\frac{(1 - \hat{\lambda}_{t2})^2}{\hat{\lambda}_{t2}} \frac{\hat{p}_{t2}\hat{q}_{t2}}{T_{t2}} + \frac{(1 - \hat{\lambda}_{c2})^2}{\hat{\lambda}_{c2}} \frac{\hat{p}_{c2}\hat{q}_{c2}}{T_{c2}} \right] \right],$$

where $\hat{\lambda}_{t2} = r_{t2}/R_{t2}$, $\hat{\lambda}_{c2} = r_{c2}/R_{c2}$. Compare this variance to $\text{var}(\hat{S})$ under models $H_{1\phi}$ and H_{2p}.

Program RELEASE computes results for these models and does the between-model tests. In fisheries or other experiments involving a treatment survival effect that is predominantly acute, models $H_{1\phi}$ and H_{2p} are by far the most useful models. If most new releases of fish (or other test animals) are at occasion 1 and capture probabilities are low, the only parameters estimable with good precision are ϕ_{t1}, ϕ_{c1}, p_{t2}, and p_{c2}, because the releases R_{ti} and R_{ci} at occasions $i = 2, ..., k - 1$ are so small relative to R_{t1} and R_{c1}. If these releases at occasion 2, ..., $k - 1$ are increased, other models in the sequence allow efficient parameter estimation.

With an acute treatment effect, the design having no new animals introduced after occasion 1 is effective. If the treatment effect is chronic and capture rates are not too high, this design is poor. With chronic effects, one needs efficient estimators of all the ϕ_{ti}, ϕ_{ci}, $i = 1, 2, ..., k - 2$; it is then important to have the full sequence of models. Alternative model sequences may then also be important. For example, one may want to have $p_{ti} = p_{ci}$, $i = 2, ..., k$ with only the ϕ_{ti} and ϕ_{ci} showing a possible effect. Such models do not have closed-form estimators;

rather, their analysis requires numerical methods (which can be done by using program SUR-VIV in conjunction with RELEASE).

2.4.8. On Alternative Forms of the Estimators

Much of the literature on the Jolly-Seber model presents the estimators of ϕ_i and p_i in a different form than we have used here (see, however, Brownie and Robson 1983). For example, one would usually see

$$\hat{\phi}_i = \frac{\hat{M}_{i+1}}{\hat{M}_i - m_i + R_i}$$

and

$$\hat{p}_i = \frac{m_i}{\hat{M}_i} \, ,$$

where

$$\hat{M}_i = m_i + \frac{z_i R_i}{r_i} \, .$$

This manner of presentation is tied to the heuristics of early capture-recapture developments wherein the emphasis was (initially) on estimating population size. That emphasis motivated concentration on the number of marked (and unmarked) animals still alive in the population at occasion i: the M_i. We could have followed this practice; however, theoretical derivations and expressions of formulae are simpler under the multinomial modeling approach. In particular, variances simplify greatly. Results are (or would be) the same under either approach. To illustrate this, substitute $\hat{M}_i$ and $\hat{M}_{i+1}$ into the above formula for $\hat{\phi}_i$ (the subtle part is knowing that $T_{i+1} = r_i + z_i$):

$$\hat{M}_i - m_i = \frac{z_i R_i}{r_i}$$

$$M_i - m_i + R_i = R_i + \frac{z_i R_i}{r_i}$$

$$= R_i \left(\frac{r_i + z_i}{r_i} \right)$$

$$= R_i \frac{T_{i+1}}{r_i} \; ;$$

hence,

$$\hat{\phi}_i = \frac{m_{i+1} + \dfrac{z_{i+1}R_{i+1}}{r_{i+1}}}{R_i \dfrac{T_{i+1}}{r_i}}$$

$$= \frac{r_i}{R_i} \left[\frac{m_{i+1}}{T_{i+1}} + \frac{z_{i+1}R_{i+1}}{T_{i+1}r_{i+1}} \right] .$$

Compare the form of the $\hat{\phi}_i$ above with that in any of the formulae for ϕ presented earlier in this chapter: it is the same.

2.4.9. Tests of Assumptions

We distinguish two types of assumption tests: (1) goodness of fit, separately by treatment group, to the Jolly-Seber model, and (2) tests among treatment groups to determine the extent and nature of the treatment effect. The latter tests may be thought of as tests made between models in an attempt to select the most appropriate model. We presented this testing material in detail in Chapter 2.1. Program RELEASE computes all the tests discussed in that chapter.

Each type of test involves a series of contingency tables. The goodness of fit testing, as we develop it here, involves only the subcohorts (based on capture history) at each release occasion. Under the complete capture history protocol, there is maximal information for goodness of fit testing. TESTS 2 and 3, taken together, constitute the goodness of fit testing under the complete capture history protocol. Details of these tests are given in Chapter 2.1.

TEST 1 and its subcomponents provide the test between models. Given that the goodness of fit testing confirms the Jolly-Seber assumptions (time-specific parameters, i.e., no behavioral effects), it is reasonable to use TEST 1 to select a best model. "Best" means the model with the fewest parameters that fits the data and is biologically reasonable (one can get good-fitting models that are not biologically reasonable). TEST 1 is not unique to the complete capture history protocol, and we have presented it in Chapter 2.1. The first few tests in the TEST 1 sequence are especially important in the context of the hydroelectric fisheries experiments.

2.4.9.1. TEST 1.R1. – The test of whether $\phi_{t1} = \phi_{c1}$, given all the other parameters are equal, is computed from the 2×2 table

r_{t1}	$R_{t1} - r_{t1}$
r_{c1}	$R_{c1} - r_{c1}$

The test computed from this table is the usual chi-square contingency table test. The alternative hypothesis is that $\phi_{t1} \neq \phi_{c1}$. TEST 1.R1 is equivalently testing that $S = 1$ versus $S \neq 1$ ($S = \phi_{t1}/\phi_{c1}$). Provided that the treatment effect is mostly a direct, acute effect, and that model $H_{1\phi}$ holds, TEST 1.R1 is one's best test for a significant treatment effect.

2.4.9.2. TEST 1.T2. – The next test in the sequence tests that model $H_{1\phi}$ holds versus the alternative model H_{2p}. TEST 1.T2 can also be considered as a determination of whether $p_{t2} = p_{c2}$, given $\phi_{t1} \neq \phi_{c1}$ but all other parameters are equal. The test is based on the 2×2 contingency table

m_{t2}	z_{t2}
m_{c2}	z_{c2}

It is labeled TEST 1.T2 because $m_{v2} + z_{v2} = T_{v2}$. If this test fails to reject and the composite results of TESTS 1.R2, 1.T3, ..., 1.Rk - 1 (the rest of the TEST 1 components) fail to reject, one is justified in concluding that model $H_{1\phi}$ is the appropriate model. If, however, TEST 1.T2 rejects model $H_{1\phi}$, one proceeds to a closer examination of the next model in the sequence, H_{2p}.

2.4.9.3. TEST 1.R2. – The test of whether $\phi_{t2} = \phi_{c2}$, given $\phi_{t1} \neq \phi_{c1}$ and $p_{t2} \neq p_{c2}$ but every other set of parameters is equal, is computed from the table

r_{t2}	$R_{t2} - r_{t2}$
r_{c2}	$R_{c2} - r_{c2}$

If this test does not reject (and the remaining components of TEST 1 do not reject), we conclude that model H_{2p} adequately describes the data. Thus, in this case, one has shown a treatment effect on both ϕ_1 and on p_2. This result is conceivable in fisheries experiments, although it has never been tested. Even if H_{2p} is the model selected, the best estimator of the treatment effect on survival is still $\hat{S} = \hat{\phi}_{t1}/\hat{\phi}_{c1}$; but now the estimators of ϕ_{t1} and ϕ_{c1} are those computed under model H_{2p}, not those from model $H_{1\phi}$.

2.4.10. Comprehensive Example

In Chapter 1.3 we introduced our general numerical (simulated) example data set. That example has $k = 6$ and the true model is $H_{1\phi}$; Table 1.2 gives the values of the parameters. For the complete capture history protocol, the data one will start from, for data analysis, will be either the capture history matrix (such as that shown in Table 1.1) or the set of full m-arrays (see Tables 1.3 and 1.4). For the analysis of these example data when RELEASE is used, the input form is the capture history matrix, as shown in Table 1.1; 22 pages of output are then generated. The first page of output (see Table 2.16) gives various data summaries. TEST 3 is then computed and summarized (Tables 2.17 and 2.18), followed by TEST 2 (Tables 2.19 and 2.20). The rest of the output consists of an analysis under each possible model and the corresponding between-model test components of TEST 1 (Tables 2.21-2.23). The first model presented is $H_{k-1,\phi}$, followed sequentially by models where more of the parameters have common values. Thus, model H_0 is the last model considered.

Not all 22 pages of output are presented here. The interested reader is encouraged to obtain RELEASE (which comes with these example data) and to run these data and other analyses as an integral part of learning the methods discussed in this monograph. The summary page (Table 2.16) gives the data as m-arrays, by group, and the summary statistics $R_., r_., m_.$, and $z_.$. Note also that RELEASE recognizes that all capture histories start with a one (1), i.e., no new fish were released after dam 1. Accordingly, adjustments to TEST 3 are made automatically. RELEASE will also handle Jolly-Seber data involving new releases as well as releases of previously marked animals at each occasion.

Table 2.17 shows all the components computable here for TEST 3 for the treatment group (group 1). This same set of tests is repeated for controls (group 2). The format is to print the test name, the corresponding table, and the test result. As part of the (usually) 2×2 tables, the data are shown as well as the expected cell values (under the null hypothesis) and, for each cell, the value of $(O - E)^2/E$, which is labeled as "C." This pattern is used by RELEASE for all chi-square contingency table tests.

All components of TEST 3 are summarized in Table 2.18. For example, the three separate chi-squares for TESTs 3.$SR3$, 3.$SR4$, and 3.$SR5$ for group 1 sum to 0.7845; this summation constitutes TEST 3.SR. None of the test components here lead to rejection of the (general) null hypothesis that recapture probabilities are independent of capture history at time of release. The overall result for TEST 3 is a chi-square value of 3.9387 with 10 df; this result is not statistically significant. Thus, based on the goodness of fit information for TEST 3, the Jolly-Seber model would not be rejected for these data.

Table 2.16. – Summary output from RELEASE for the general numerical example under the complete capture history protocol.

Observed Recaptures for Group 1
Treatment group

i	R(i)	m(i,j)					r(i)
		j = 2	3	4	5	6	
1	30000	1029	238	1669	549	590	4075
2	1000		11	73	17	27	128
3	235			20	7	5	32
4	1677				43	50	93
5	590					19	19
m(j)		1029	249	1762	616	691	
z(j)		3046	2925	1195	672	0	

Observed Recaptures for Group 2
Control group

i	R(i)	m(i,j)					r(i)
		j = 2	3	4	5	6	
1	29000	1104	247	1832	571	641	4395
2	1071		13	75	19	29	136
3	250			17	4	10	31
4	1862				50	52	102
5	616					26	26
m(j)		1104	260	1924	644	758	
z(j)		3291	3167	1274	732	0	

Sums for the above Groups

m.	0	2133	509	3686	1260	1449
z.	0	6337	6092	2469	1404	
R.	59000	2071	485	3539	1206	
r.	8470	264	63	195	45	

Data type is Complete Capture Histories.

All capture histories have a 1 for occasion 1,
so tests will ignore this initial release.

TEST 2 contributes additional, independent goodness of fit (to Jolly-Seber) information. These tests are based on the cohort data summarized in the m-array representation of the data.

Table 2.17. – Results of TEST 3 (goodness of fit) applied to group 1 (treatment) data for the complete capture history protocol data of the general numerical example.

```
          Goodness of fit test of seen before vs. not seen before
          against seen again vs. not seen again by capture occasions.

                          Test for Group 1
                          Treatment Group

          TEST 3.SR3: Animals captured on occasion 3
                      +------+------+
                    O|   1  |  10  |  11
                    E|   1.4|   9.6|
                    C|   0.1|   0.0|
                      +------+------+
                    O|  31  | 193  | 224
                    E|  30.6| 193.5|
                    C|   0.0|   0.0|
                      +------+------+
                         32    205    235
              Chi-square=0.2010 (df=1) P=0.6539
                   Fisher's Exact Test P=1.0000

 * *  WARNING  * *   One or more expected values were < 2.0.

          TEST 3.SR4: Animals captured on occasion 4
                      +------+------+
                    O|   5  |  84  |  89
                    E|   4.9|  84.1|
                    C|   0.0|   0.0|
                      +------+------+
                    O|  88  |1500  |1588
                    E|  88.1|1580.9|
                    C|   0.0|   0.0|
                      +------+------+
                         93   1584   1677
              Chi-square=0.0009 (df=1) P=0.9755
                   Fisher's Exact Test P=1.0000
```

Table 2.17. – Continued.

```
TEST 3.SR5: Animals captured on occasion 5
        +------+------+
     O|   1  |  63  |  64
     E|   2.1|  61.9|
     C|   0.5|   0.0|
        +------+------+
     O|  18  | 508  | 526
     E|  16.9| 509.1|
     C|   0.1|   0.0|
        +------+------+
         19    571    590
    Chi-square=0.6331 (df=1) P=0.4262
       Fisher's Exact Test P=0.5098
```

Cumulative result of TEST 3.SR over occasions for group 1
Chi-square= 0.8350 (df=3) P= 0.8411

Goodness of Fit Test of seen before versus not seen before
against when next seen again by capture occasions.

```
             Test for Group 1
             Treatment Group

TEST 3.Sm3: Animals captured on occasion 3
        +------+------+
     O|  19  |  12  |  31
     E|  19.4|  11.6|
     C|   0.0|   0.0|
        +------+------+
     O|   1  |   0  |   1
     E|   0.6|   0.4|
     C|   0.2|   0.4|
        +------+------+
         20     12     32
    Chi-square=0.6194 (df=1) P=0.4313
       Fisher's Exact Test P=0.1000
```

* * WARNING * *   One or more expected values were < 2.0.

Table 2.17. – Continued.

```
        TEST 3.Sm4: Animals captured on occasion 4
              +------+------+
           O|  40  |  48  |  88
           E|  40.7|  47.3|
           C|   0.0|   0.0|
              +------+------+
           O|   3  |   2  |   5
           E|   2.3|   2.7|
           C|   0.2|   0.2|
              +------+------+
                43     50     93
        Chi-square=0.4027 (df=1) P=0.5257
           Fisher's Exact Test P=0.6595

Cumulative result of TEST 3.Sm over occasions for group 1
Chi-square=1.0220 (df=2) P=0.5999
```

Table 2.18. – Summary of TEST 3 (goodness of fit) results for the complete capture history example data.

```
           Summary of TEST 3 (Goodness of fit) Results
```

Group 1	Component	Chi-square	df	P-level	Sufficient Data
1	3.SR3	0.2010	1	0.6539	No
1	3.SR4	0.0009	1	0.9755	Yes
1	3.SR5	0.6331	1	0.4262	Yes
Group 1	3.SR	0.8350	3	0.8411	
1	3.Sm3	0.6194	1	0.4313	No
1	3.Sm4	0.4027	1	0.5257	Yes
Group 1	3.Sm	1.0220	2	0.5999	
Group 1	TEST 3	1.8570	5	0.8686	
2	3.SR3	0.2798	1	0.5968	No
2	3.SR4	0.0128	1	0.9100	Yes
2	3.SR5	0.3633	1	0.5467	Yes

Table 2.18. – Continued.

Group 2	3.SR	0.6558	3	0.8835	
2	3.Sm3	1.2548	1	0.2626	No
2	3.Sm4	0.1712	1	0.6791	Yes
Group 2	3.Sm	1.4259	2	0.4902	
Group 2	TEST 3	2.0817	5	0.8377	
All Groups	TEST 3	3.9387	10	0.9501	

Table 2.19 presents results of TEST 2 for group 1. Each component of the overall test is presented (by group), followed by a summary table of results (see Table 2.20). The overall goodness of fit test statistic (to the Jolly-Seber model) is shown in Table 2.20: $\chi^2 = 11.10$ with 22 df; it is not significant. This nonsignificance provides the evidence that our general assumption about parameters being only time-specific is plausible; thus we can confidently proceed to select a model (i.e., evaluate the treatment effect).

Table 2.19. – Results of TEST 2 (goodness of fit) applied to group 1 (treatment) data for the complete capture history protocol data of the general numerical example.

```
        Goodness of fit test of recaptures partitioned by rows.


                        Test for Group 1
                        Treatment Group

            TEST 2.C2: Test of row 1 vs. row 2
                 +------+------+------+------+
              O| 238  |1669  | 549  | 590  |3046
              E| 239.0|1671.7| 543.2| 592.1|
              C|   0.0|   0.0|   0.1|   0.0|
                 +------+------+------+------+
              O|  11  |  73  |  17  |  27  | 128
              E|  10.0|  70.3|  22.8|  24.9|
              C|   0.1|   0.1|   1.5|   0.2|
                 +------+------+------+------+
                  249   1742   566    617   3174

            Chi-square=1.9445 (df=3) P= 0.5840
```

Table 2.19. – Continued.

```
TEST 2.C3: Test of rows 1-2 vs. row 3

        +------+------+------+
      O|1742  | 566  | 617  |2925
      E|1742.9| 566.8| 615.3|
      C|   0.0|   0.0|   0.0|
        +------+------+------+
      O|  20  |  7   |  5   | 32
      E|  19.1|   6.2|   6.7|
      C|   0.0|   0.1|   0.4|
        +------+------+------+
        1762    573    622   2957
   Chi-square= 0.6003 (df=2) P= 0.7407
```

```
TEST 2.C4: Test of rows 1-3 vs. row 4

        +------+------+
      O| 573  | 622  |1195
      E| 571.5| 623.5|
      C|   0.0|   0.0|
        +------+------+
      O|  43  |  50  | 93
      E|  44.5|  48.5|
      C|   0.0|   0.0|
        +------+------+
        616    672   1288
   Chi-square= 0.1015 (df=1) P= 0.7500
```

Table 2.20. – Summary of TEST 2 and overall goodness of fit results for the complete capture history example data.

```
              Summary of TEST 2 (Goodness of fit) Results
    Group  Component  Chi-square   df   P-level  Sufficient Data
    -----  ---------  ----------   ---  -------  ---------------
      1      2.C2        1.9445      3   0.5840       Yes
      1      2.C3        0.6003      2   0.7407       Yes
      1      2.C4        0.1015      1   0.7500       Yes
   Group 1 TEST 2        2.6463      6   0.8518
      2      2.C2        1.8265      3   0.6092       Yes
      2      2.C3        2.4691      2   0.2910       Yes
      2      2.C4        0.2175      1   0.6409       Yes
   Group 2 TEST 2        4.5131      6   0.6076
   All Groups TEST 2     7.1594     12   0.8469

        Goodness of Fit Results (TEST 2 + TEST 3) by Group
               Group  Chi-square   df   P-level
               -----  ----------   --   -------
                 1      4.5033      11   0.9528
                 2      6.5949      11   0.8309
               Total   11.0981     22   0.9733
```

Results for model $H_{5\phi}$ are shown in Table 2.21. In general, for any model, RELEASE presents the parameter estimates that differ by group, and then estimates of parameters that are the same for all groups. There are no parameters common to both groups for model $H_{k-1,\phi}$ ($H_{5\phi}$ in this case). In addition to the $\hat{\phi}$ and $\hat{p}$, the ratios $\hat{S}_j = \hat{\phi}_{tj}/\hat{\phi}_{cj}$ are shown along with these standard errors. For example, from Table 2.21, $\hat{S}_4$ is denoted as $S(1,2,PHI(4))$; thus, this $\hat{S}_4$ is the ratio $\hat{\phi}_{14}/\hat{\phi}_{24}$. From other places in the output we know that $v = 1$ corresponds to treatment and $v = 2$ corresponds to control. Note how the standard errors of $\hat{S}_2$ to $\hat{S}_4$ increase substantially over $\hat{se}(\hat{S}_1)$. The true S ($= S_1$) is 0.9; however, if separate Jolly-Seber models were used as the basis of the inference, one would conclude that there was no treatment effect on survival (e.g., the 95% CI on S under model $H_{5\phi}$ is 0.69 to 1.08).

RELEASE also prints out some of the sampling correlations between estimates. Within a treatment group, for example, Corr(Phi(1),Phi(2)) denotes the estimated sampling correlation of $\hat{\phi}_{v1}$ and $\hat{\phi}_{v2}$. From Table 2.21, this correlation is -0.443444 for the treatment group. Correlations are also given between pairs of values for $\hat{\phi}_{ti}$ and $\hat{\phi}_{ci}$; these correlations are relevant in obtaining variances and correlations of $\hat{S}_i$. Corr(1,2,Phi(1)) denotes the sampling correlation of $\hat{\phi}_{1i}$ and $\hat{\phi}_{2i}$; again we will know from the output which one (i.e., 1 or 2) is treatment and which is control. Under model $H_{k-1,\phi}$ all these correlations are zero.

Table 2.21. – Estimates of parameters under model $H_{5\phi}$ for the complete capture history protocol data of the general numerical example.

```
+-------------------------------------------------------------------------+
|            Maximum Likelihood Estimates under Model H5Phi                |
|                                       95% Confidence Intervals           |
|   Parameter      Estimate      Standard Error    Lower        Upper      |
|   ---------      --------      --------------   --------      ------      |
|                   Estimates for Group 1                                   |
|                     Treatment Group                                      |
|   Phi(1)         0.827529        0.066869       0.696467     0.958591     |
|   Phi(2)         0.876299        0.159697       0.563292     1.189305     |
|   Phi(3)         1.073454        0.203826       0.673955     1.472952     |
|   Phi(4)         0.924989        0.224379       0.485205     1.364772     |
|   p(2)           0.041449        0.003579       0.034435     0.048463     |
|   p(3)           0.011459        0.002006       0.007528     0.015390     |
|   p(4)           0.075588        0.007513       0.060863     0.090314     |
|   p(5)           0.028673        0.006475       0.015983     0.041364     |
|   Phi(5)p(6)     0.032203        0.007268       0.017958     0.046449     |
|   Corr(Phi(1),Phi(2))          -0.443444                                 |
|   Corr(Phi(2),Phi(3))          -0.771173                                 |
|   Corr(Phi(3),Phi(4))          -0.203837                                 |
|                   Estimates for Group 2                                   |
|                      Control Group                                       |
|   Phi(1)         0.931746        0.073081       0.788507     1.074984     |
|   Phi(2)         0.956006        0.176612       0.609846     1.302165     |
|   Phi(3)         0.976364        0.186592       0.610643     1.342085     |
|   Phi(4)         0.716070        0.150306       0.421470     1.010669     |
|   p(2)           0.040858        0.003423       0.034149     0.047566     |
|   p(3)           0.010077        0.001796       0.006557     0.013598     |
|   p(4)           0.076408        0.007256       0.062186     0.090629     |
|   p(5)           0.035804        0.006883       0.022313     0.049296     |
|   Phi(5)p(6)     0.042208        0.008101       0.026330     0.058086     |
|   Corr(Phi(1),Phi(2))          -0.424913                                 |
|   Corr(Phi(2),Phi(3))          -0.792323                                 |
|   Corr(Phi(3),Phi(4))          -0.213359                                 |
|                  Ratio of Survivals between Groups                       |
|                                       95% Confidence Intervals           |
|   Parameter      Estimate      Standard Error    Lower        Upper      |
|   ---------      --------      --------------   --------      ------      |
|   S(1,2,Phi(1))  0.888149        0.100016       0.692118     1.084181     |
|   Corr(1,2,Phi(1))             0.000000                                   |
|   S(1,2,Phi(2))  0.916625        0.237864       0.450411     1.382839     |
+-------------------------------------------------------------------------+
```

Table 2.21. – Continued.

```
+-------------------------------------------------------------------------+
|   Corr(1,2,Phi(2))              0.000000                                |
|   S(1,2,Phi(3))  1.099440       0.296190      0.518908      1.679972    |
|   Corr(1,2,Phi(3))              0.000000                                |
|   S(1,2,Phi(4))  1.291758       0.414375      0.479582      2.103934    |
|   Corr(1,2,Phi(4))              0.000000                                |
|                                                                         |
|   S(i,j,Phi(I)) equals treatment effect estimated as                    |
|     Phi(I) for group i / Phi(I) for group j.                            |
|   Corr(i,j,Phi(I)) equals estimated sampling correlation                |
|     between Phi(I) for group i and Phi(I) for group j.                  |
+-------------------------------------------------------------------------+
```

Table 2.22 shows the results for models H_{2p}, $H_{1\phi}$, and H_0 along with TEST 1 components 1.$R2$, 1.$T2$, and 1.$R1$. The same pattern of presenting models separated by the TEST 1 component that tests between them is used for the other models not illustrated here. At the end of the output regarding models, RELEASE gives a summary of TEST 1 (Table 2.23). The strategy for examining this output should be to confirm goodness of fit, then scan the summary of TEST 1 to see if one of the models in the sequence is acceptable (the most appropriate model might not be). From Table 2.23, only TEST 1.$R1$ leads to rejection. The null hypothesis rejected is that model H_0 fits the data. None of the other TEST 1 components (nor the sum of 1.$T2$ through 1.$R5$) reject. Consequently, the appropriate model for these data is judged to be $H_{1\phi}$. Given that decision, one can proceed to the results for model $H_{1\phi}$ (in Table 2.22).

Table 2.22. – Estimates of parameters for model H_{2p}, $H_{1\phi}$ and H_0 and some test components for the complete capture history protocol data of the general numerical example.

```
       TEST 1.R2: Test of Phi(2) equal across groups,
       assuming higher order parameters are equal across groups.
                    +------+------+
                 O| 128  | 872  |1000
                 E| 127.5| 872.5|
                 C|   0.0|   0.0|
                    +------+------+
                 O| 136  | 935  |1071
                 E| 136.5| 934.5|
                 C|   0.0|   0.0|
                    +------+------+
                    264    1807   2071
          Chi-square=0.0048 (df=1) P=0.9448
```

Table 2.22. – Continued.

```
+----------------------------------------------------------------------+
|              Maximum Likelihood Estimates under Model H2p             |
|                                                                      |
|                                            95% Confidence Intervals  |
|   Parameter      Estimate     Standard Error    Lower       Upper    |
|   ---------      ---------     --------------  ---------   ---------  |
|                     Estimates for Group 1                            |
|                        Treatment Group                              |
|   Phi(1)         0.830798      0.047782        0.737145    0.924452   |
|   p(2)           0.041286      0.002686        0.036021    0.046550   |
|   Corr(Phi(1),Phi(2))        -0.424661                               |
|                                                                      |
|                     Estimates for Group 2                            |
|                         Control Group                               |
|   Phi(1)         0.928307      0.053214        0.824008    1.032606   |
|   p(2)           0.041009      0.002642        0.035830    0.046188   |
|   Corr(Phi(1),Phi(2))        -0.426192                               |
|                                                                      |
|                   Estimates for Pooled Groups                        |
|   Phi(2)         0.915510      0.118772        0.682718    1.148303   |
|   Phi(3)         1.023456      0.137818        0.753334    1.293579   |
|   Phi(4)         0.804316      0.127598        0.554224    1.054407   |
|   p(3)           0.010737      0.001341        0.008108    0.013365   |
|   p(4)           0.076008      0.005219        0.065779    0.086236   |
|   p(5)           0.032401      0.004744        0.023103    0.041700   |
|   Phi(5)p(6)     0.037313      0.005458        0.026617    0.048010   |
|   Corr(Phi(2),Phi(3))        -0.782090                               |
|   Corr(Phi(3),Phi(4))        -0.209588                               |
|                   Ratio of Survivals between Groups                  |
|                                            95% Confidence Intervals  |
|   Parameter      Estimate     Standard Error    Lower       Upper    |
|   ---------      ---------     --------------  ---------   ---------  |
|   S(1,2,Phi(1))  0.894961      0.020341        0.855093    0.934829   |
|   Corr(1,2,Phi(1))            0.921665                               |
+----------------------------------------------------------------------+
```

Table 2.22. – Continued.

```
               TEST 1.T2: Test of p(2) equal across groups,
             assuming higher order parameters are equal across groups.
                        +------+------+
                      O|1029  |3046  |4075
                      E|1026.2|3048.8|
                      C|  0.0|  0.0|
                        +------+------+
                      O|1104  |3291  |4395
                      E|1106.8|3288.2|
                      C|  0.0|  0.0|
                        +------+------+
                        2133   6337   8470
                  Chi-square=0.0196 (df=1) P=0.8887
```

```
+-------------------------------------------------------------------------+
|                                                                         |
|            Maximum Likelihood Estimates under Model H1Phi               |
|                                                                         |
|                                          95% Confidence Intervals       |
|     Parameter       Estimate       Standard Error     Lower      Upper  |
|     ---------       --------       --------------     -----      -----  |
|                     Estimates for Group 1                               |
|                        Treatment Group                                  |
|  Phi(1)             0.831435        0.047607        0.738126   0.924745 |
|  Corr(Phi(1),Phi(2))               -0.426617                            |
|                     Estimates for Group 2                               |
|                         Control Group                                   |
|  Phi(1)             0.927648        0.052962        0.823843   1.031452 |
|  Corr(Phi(1),Phi(2))               -0.427860                            |
|                     Estimates for Pooled Groups                         |
|  Phi(2)             0.915510        0.118772        0.682718   1.148303 |
|  Phi(3)             1.023456        0.137818        0.753334   1.293579 |
|  Phi(4)             0.804316        0.127598        0.554224   1.054407 |
|  p(2)               0.041142        0.002474        0.036294   0.045990 |
|  p(3)               0.010737        0.001341        0.008108   0.013365 |
|  p(4)               0.076008        0.005219        0.065779   0.086236 |
|  p(5)               0.032401        0.004744        0.023103   0.041700 |
|  Phi(5)p(6)         0.037313        0.005458        0.026617   0.048010 |
|  Corr(Phi(2),Phi(3))               -0.782090                            |
|  Corr(Phi(3),Phi(4))               -0.209588                            |
```

Table 2.22. – Continued.

```
|                    Ratio of Survivals between Groups              |
|                                        95% Confidence Intervals   |
|    Parameter       Estimate    Standard Error    Lower      Upper  |
|    ---------       --------    --------------  ----------  --------- |
|    S(1,2,Phi(1))   0.896284      0.018040      0.860925   0.931642 |
|    Corr(1,2,Phi(1))              0.938042                          |
+------------------------------------------------------------------+
```

```
           TEST 1.R1: Test of Phi(1) equal across groups,
           assuming higher order parameters are equal across groups.
                    +------+------+
                  O| 4075 |25925 |30000
                  E| 4307.|25693.|
                  C| 12.5|   2.1|
                    +------+------+
                  O| 4395 |24605 |29000
                  E| 4163.|24837.|
                  C| 12.9|   2.2|
                    +------+------+
                    8470   50530   59000
           Chi-square=29.6316 (df=1) P=0.0000
```

```
+------------------------------------------------------------------+
|            Maximum Likelihood Estimates under Model HO            |
|                                        95% Confidence Intervals   |
|    Parameter     Estimate    Standard Error    Lower      Upper   |
|    ---------     --------    --------------  ----------  -------- |
|                     Estimates for Pooled Groups                  |
|    Phi(1)        0.878726      0.049456      0.781793   0.975660 |
|    Phi(2)        0.915510      0.118772      0.682718   1.148303 |
|    Phi(3)        1.023456      0.137818      0.753334   1.293579 |
|    Phi(4)        0.804316      0.127598      0.554224   1.054407 |
|    p(2)          0.041142      0.002474      0.036294   0.045990 |
|    p(3)          0.010737      0.001341      0.008108   0.013365 |
|    p(4)          0.076008      0.005219      0.065779   0.086236 |
|    p(5)          0.032401      0.004744      0.023103   0.041700 |
|    Phi(5)p(6)    0.037313      0.005458      0.026617   0.048010 |
|    Corr(Phi(1),Phi(2))        -0.434024                          |
|    Corr(Phi(2),Phi(3))        -0.782090                          |
|    Corr(Phi(3),Phi(4))        -0.209588                          |
+------------------------------------------------------------------+
```

Table 2.22. – Continued.

TEST 1: Overall test of HO vs. H5Phi
Chi-square=31.3078 (df=9) P=0.0003
TEST 1 is an omnibus test for a treatment effect(s),
i.e., significant differences between groups. For the
complete capture history protocol and scheme A partial
capture history protocol, TEST 1 is an overall test of
equality of all survival and capture probabilities
among groups.

Table 2.23. – Summary of TEST 1 (model selection) results for the data from the complete capture history example.

TEST	Chi-square	df	P
1.R5	0.84	1	0.360
1.T5	0.28	1	0.607
1.R4	0.01	1	0.930
1.T4	0.21	1	0.646
1.R3	0.16	1	0.690
1.T3	0.15	1	0.694
1.R2	0.01	1	0.945
1.T2	0.02	1	0.889
1.R1	29.63	1	0.001
TEST 1	31.3078	9	0.001

Because the data were simulated under model $H_{1\phi}$, we consider the model $H_{1\phi}$ output in Table 2.22 in some detail. The output for the other models is similar. Notice that treatment and control survival estimates for the first period are $\hat{\phi}_{t1} = 0.8314$ and $\hat{\phi}_{c1} = 0.9276$, which are the only estimates allowed to differ for the treatment and control groups under this model. The standard errors and confidence limits are also given for these estimates. The coefficients of variation are $0.0476/0.8314 = 0.06$ and $0.0530/0.9276 = 0.06$ for treatment and control groups, respectively. These coefficients of variation indicate that the estimates are relatively precise. The other survival estimates ($\hat{\phi}_{v2}$, $\hat{\phi}_{v3}$, $\hat{\phi}_{v4}$) are relatively less precise (coefficients of variation are about 0.12 to 0.14). The capture probability estimates are also presented; for example, $\hat{p}_2 = 0.0411$ ($\hat{se} = 0.00247$).

Perhaps the most important estimate presented is the treatment survival rate,

$$\hat{S} = \frac{\hat{\phi}_{t1}}{\hat{\phi}_{c1}} = \frac{0.8314}{0.9276}$$

$$= 0.896$$

(denoted S(1,2,Phi(1)), with $\hat{se}(\hat{S})$ = 0.01804. The 95% CI on S is 0.861 to 0.932. Recall that when model $H_{5\phi}$ is used, the standard error of the corresponding $\hat{S}$ is 0.10. The use of a parsimonious model has allowed us to say definitely that there is a treatment effect (either from TEST 1.R1 or the CI on $\hat{S}$).

Note again the meaning of some of the output: Corr(Phi(1),Phi(2)) is the sampling correlation of $\hat{\phi}_{v1}$ with either $\hat{\phi}_{v2}$, e.g., under model $H_{5\phi}$, or with $\hat{\phi}_2$, e.g., under models H_{2p} and $H_{1\phi}$ where ϕ_{v1} varies by group, but ϕ_2 is the same for both groups. For example, under model H_{2p} the sampling correlation of $\hat{\phi}_{t1}$ and $\hat{\phi}_2$ is -0.4247. Under H_{2p} the sampling correlation of $\hat{\phi}_3$ and $\hat{\phi}_4$ is -0.2096, this quantity being denoted by Corr(Phi(3),Phi(4)). Also of interest are the correlations of $\hat{\phi}_{ti}$ and $\hat{\phi}_{ci}$ for any i where these survivals are allowed to differ. In Table 2.22, t and c are indexed as 1 and 2, respectively. Under model H_{2p}, the correlation of $\hat{\phi}_{t1}$ and $\hat{\phi}_{c1}$ is denoted as Corr(1,2,Phi(1)) and equals 0.9217. Under model $H_{1\phi}$ the same correlation is 0.9380. It is largely this strong, positive correlation that makes $\hat{S} = \hat{\phi}_{t1}/\hat{\phi}_{c1}$ so precise under these two models (a standard error of around 0.02 as compared to se(S) = 0.1 when model $H_{5\phi}$ is used).

2.4.11. Likelihood Function for Models $H_{k-1,\phi}$, H_{2p}, $H_{1\phi}$

Our philosophy in writing this monograph is to present the theory along with the applied results. Moreover, it is important that all users have a basic understanding of the nature of the underlying theory. First, a sound theory must exist for survival experiments based on animal release-recapture, and second, the theory must be based on specific assumptions and subsequent probability models for the experimental data. Although the full mathematical details may extend beyond the training of some biologists, advanced training in quantitative methods is becoming increasingly common. Consequently, we include a section that gives the probability model formulae (likelihoods) for several models discussed in Chapter 2.4.

For a one-group Jolly-Seber study, the probability distribution of the number of fish recaptured, r_i, from those released, R_i, at occasion i is the binomial distribution

$$\Pr\{r_i \mid R_i\} = \binom{R_i}{r_i}(\lambda_i)^{\eta}(1-\lambda_i)^{R_i-\eta}, \quad i = 1, \ldots, k-1,$$

$$\lambda_i = E(r_i \mid R_i)/R_i \ [\text{or } \lambda_i = \phi_i(p_{i+1} + q_{i+1}\lambda_{i+1})].$$

Similarly, one can consider the (marginal) probability distribution of m_i given $T_i = m_i + z_i$; it also is binomial:

$$\Pr\{m_i \mid T_i\} = \binom{T_i}{m_i}(\tau_i)^{m_i}(1-\tau_i)^{T_i-m_i}, \quad i = 2, \ldots, k-1,$$

where $\tau_i = E(m_i \mid T_i)/T_i$, or $\tau_i = p_i/(p_i + q_i\lambda_i)$.

It has been proved (e.g., Brownie and Robson 1983) that the MSS (for estimating the ϕ and p) is representable as r_i given R_i, $i = 1, \ldots, k-1$ and m_i given T_i, $i = 2, \ldots, k-1$, and that this conditioning on R_i and T_i renders these binomial distributions conditionally independent. This means that for a one-group Jolly-Seber release-recapture study the probability distribution of the MSS is given as the products of $2k - 3$ independent binomial distributions:

$$\Pr\{\text{MSS}\} = \left[\prod_{i=1}^{k-1}\binom{R_i}{r_i}(\lambda_i)^{\eta}(1-\lambda_i)^{R_i-\eta}\right]\left[\prod_{i=2}^{k-1}\binom{T_i}{m_i}(\tau_i)^{m_i}(1-\tau_i)^{T_i-m_i}\right].$$

The above formula is the likelihood function for such a study; this probability distribution is the basis for ML inferences about survival rates from Jolly-Seber data.

For model $H_{k-1,\phi}$, no parameters are in common across the two experimental groups. As a consequence, it follows that the likelihood function for model $H_{k-1,\phi}$ can be written as

$$\Pr\{\text{MSS} \mid \text{model } H_{k-1,\phi}\} = \left[\prod_{i=1}^{k-1}\binom{R_{ti}}{r_{ti}}(\lambda_{ti})^{r_{ti}}(1-\lambda_{ti})^{R_{ti}-r_{ti}}\right]\left[\prod_{i=2}^{k-1}\binom{T_{ti}}{m_{ti}}(\tau_{ti})^{m_{ti}}(1-\tau_{ti})^{T_{ti}-m_{ti}}\right]$$
$$\times \left[\prod_{i=1}^{k-1}\binom{R_{ci}}{r_{ci}}(\lambda_{ci})^{r_{ci}}(1-\lambda_{ci})^{R_{ci}-r_{ci}}\right]\left[\prod_{i=2}^{k-1}\binom{T_{ci}}{m_{ci}}(\tau_{ci})^{m_{ci}}(1-\tau_{ci})^{T_{ci}-m_{ci}}\right].$$

As we proceed to more specialized models in the sequence considered here, terms in the above products collapse into single terms as we pool over various statistics.

The likelihood (i.e., probability distribution) for the MSS under model H_{2p} is

$$
\Pr\{\text{MSS} \mid \text{model } H_{2p}\} = \left[\binom{R_{t1}}{r_{t1}}(\lambda_{t1})^{r_{t1}}(1-\lambda_{t1})^{R_{t1}-r_{t1}}\right]\left[\binom{T_{t2}}{m_{t2}}(\tau_{t2})^{m_{t2}}(1-\tau_{t2})^{T_{t2}-m_{t2}}\right]
$$

$$
\times \left[\binom{R_{c1}}{r_{c1}}(\lambda_{c1})^{r_{c1}}(1-\lambda_{c1})^{R_{c1}-r_{c1}}\right]\left[\binom{T_{c2}}{m_{c2}}(\tau_{c2})^{m_{c2}}(1-\tau_{c2})^{T_{c2}-m_{c2}}\right]
$$

$$
\times \left[\prod_{i=2}^{k-1}\binom{R_{.i}}{r_{.i}}(\lambda_i)^{r_i}(1-\lambda_i)^{R_i-r_i}\right]\left[\prod_{i=3}^{k-1}\binom{T_{.i}}{m_{.i}}(\tau_i)^{m_i}(1-\tau_i)^{T_i-m_i}\right].
$$

Bear in mind that the identifiable parameters here are $\phi_{t1}, p_{t2}, \phi_{c1}, p_{c2}$, and ϕ_2, ..., ϕ_{k-2}, $(\phi_{k-1}p_k)$, p_3, ..., p_{k-1}. There are $2k - 1$ identifiable parameters and $2k - 1$ terms in the MSS. Basically, that is the reason one gets closed form estimators for this model. Finally, one must also know that $\lambda_{k-1} = (\phi_{k-1}p_k)$ and

$$
\lambda_i = \phi_i(p_{i+1} + q_{i+1}\lambda_{i+1}), \quad i = 2, ..., k - 2,
$$

$$
\tau_i = \frac{p_i}{p_i + q_i\lambda_i}, \quad i = 3, ..., k - 1,
$$

$$
\tau_{v2} = \frac{p_{v2}}{p_{v2} + q_{v2}\lambda_2}, \quad v = t, c,
$$

and

$$
\lambda_{v1} = \phi_{v1}(p_{v2} + q_{v2}\lambda_2), \quad v = t, c.
$$

Model $H_{1\phi}$ is developed from H_{2p} by making the added assumption that $p_{t2} = p_{c2}$. This results in $\tau_{t2} = \tau_{c2}$ so that the two binomials involving τ_{t2} and τ_{c2} collapse to a single binomial:

$$
\Pr\{\text{MSS} \mid \text{model } H_{1\phi}\} = \left[\binom{R_{t1}}{r_{t1}}(\lambda_{t1})^{r_{t1}}(1-\lambda_{t1})^{R_{t1}-r_{t1}}\right]\left[\binom{R_{c1}}{r_{c1}}(\lambda_{c1})^{r_{c1}}1-\lambda_{c1})^{R_{c1}-r_{c1}}\right]
$$

$$
\times \left[\prod_{i=2}^{k-1}\binom{R_{.i}}{r_{.i}}(\lambda_i)^{r_i}(1-\lambda_i)^{R_i-r_i}\right]\left[\prod_{i=2}^{k-1}\binom{T_{.i}}{m_{.i}}(\tau_i)^{m_i}(1-\tau_i)^{T_i-m_i}\right].
$$

Note that now $\lambda_{t1} = \phi_{t1}(p_2 + q_2\lambda_2)$, $\lambda_{c1} = \phi_{c1}(p_2 + q_2\lambda_2)$.

Finally, assuming also that $\phi_{t1} = \phi_{c1}$ (hence, assuming model H_0), then $\lambda_{t1} = \lambda_{c1}$ and the two terms in λ_{t1}, λ_{c1} above reduce to the single term

$$\binom{R_{.1}}{r_{.1}} (\lambda_1)^{r_{.1}} (1 - \lambda_1)^{R_{.1} - r_{.1}}$$

in $Pr\{MSS \mid model\ H_0\}$ (the terms in λ_2, ..., λ_{k-1} and τ_2, ..., τ_{k-1} from model $H_{1\phi}$ remain unchanged).

2.5. Partial Capture Histories

2.5.1. Introduction

The preceding chapters describe the analysis for data arising from two different marking strategies. The most easily implemented strategy (Chapters 2.2 and 2.3) involves use of a distinguishing batch mark at the initial release site. The second strategy (Chapter 2.4) involves use of distinct marks (or of a different batch mark at each recapture site) so that individual capture histories can be followed for each animal. We have shown that this second method provides more data and information but is not a feasible strategy in many situations. In order to present a compromise between these two extremes in terms of feasibility and information loss, we here describe two other experimental protocols, called schemes A and B, and the analysis for resulting data. Both of these protocols provide information concerning second, but not third or later recaptures; thus we refer to them as providing "partial capture histories."

In both schemes A and B, an initial release is assumed in which batch marks distinguish treatment and control groups. Both involve a second batch mark and removal. They differ in that under scheme A a second batch mark, specific to the recovery site, is applied to all first recaptures, whereas under scheme B only recaptures at dam 2 receive a second mark. Also, all fish recaptured for the second time are removed under scheme A, whereas all recaptures below dam 2 are removed under scheme B.

Before describing analyses for data generated by schemes A and B, we note that there are other ways to generate partial capture history information. For example, adding a third mark would provide information about third recaptures. Schemes A and B were chosen because, provided there is no effect on survival due to handling and marking, they appear to be the most practical ways to obtain information in addition to first recaptures. Also, in studies where capture probabilities are low, they result in little loss of information relative to unique marking. Neither scheme A nor scheme B should be used if the associated handling and marking are likely to affect survival.

Notation used in this chapter is the same as in Chapter 2.4, and the assumptions and parameters on which model structure is based are the same here as in Chapter 1.4.

2.5.2. Scheme A

2.5.2.1. Introduction and presentation of data. – Upon first recapture, a fish is given a second mark specific to the site of recapture. Upon second recapture, the fish is recorded and then removed from the study population. Thus, for each fish recaptured, the occasion of its last capture (release) is known, and the quantities m_{tij} and m_{cij}, $i = 1$, recapture data for scheme A is in Table 2.12.

This representation is illustrated by using data for the hypothetical example displayed in Table 2.24. Note that the first two rows of the data arrays for treatment and control groups are the same for scheme A as with unique marks (see Tables 1.5, 1.6, and 2.16). However, because fish are removed after the second recapture, releases and recoveries at dam 3 and below are fewer under scheme A. However, for this example where recapture rates are low, the differences are small.

Table 2.24. – Release-recapture data summarized as reduced m-array for the hypothetical example under scheme A protocol.

Release site	Releases R_{v1}	Number recaptured at dam j, m_{vij}					Totals, r_{ti} or r_{ci}
		$j = 2$	3	4	5	6	
Treatment group							
1	30,000	1,029	238	1,669	549	590	4,075
2	1,000		11	73	17	27	128
3	224			19	7	5	31
4	1,588				40	48	88
5	526					18	18
Totals m_{tj}		1,029	249	1,761	613	688	
Control group							
1	29,000	1,104	247	1,832	571	641	4,395
2	1,071		13	75	19	29	136
3	237			17	4	9	30
4	1,775				48	49	97
5	546					24	24
Totals m_{cj}		1,104	260	1,924	642	752	

2.5.2.2. Models H_0, $H_{1\phi}$, H_{2p}, $H_{2\phi}$, ..., $H_{k-1,\phi}$. – As in the case of complete capture histories (Chapter 2.4), we consider a series of increasingly general models, H_0, $H_{1\phi}$, H_{2p}, $H_{2\phi}$, ..., $H_{k-1,\phi}$, corresponding to increasingly general assumptions regarding the equality of survival and capture probabilities for treatment and control groups. The structure of each model is represented in terms of matrices of expected values corresponding to the release-recapture data matrices. For scheme A, model structures under H_0, $H_{1\phi}$, H_{2p}, $H_{2\phi}$, ..., $H_{k-1,\phi}$ are exactly as for the complete capture history data in Table 2.2. Statistical theory underlying estimation and testing is, therefore, the same.

Estimable parameters of interest are as in Chapter 2.4 for the series of models H_0, $H_{1\phi}$, H_{2p}, $H_{2\phi}$, ..., $H_{k-1,\phi}$. Formulae for estimators, variances, and covariances are also as in Chapter 2.4.

2.5.2.3. Testing between models. – To determine which model and estimators are appropriate for a given data set, we compare models in the sequence H_0, $H_{1\phi}$, H_{2p}, $H_{2\phi}$, ..., $H_{k-1,\phi}$. This comparison is done in a certain order, starting with the most general models and progressing to tests involving simpler models, as described in Chapter 2.4 for the unique mark or complete capture history data. Theory and formulae for contingency table chi-squares are exactly as in Chapter 2.4, but actual numbers of recaptures for cohorts released at dam 3 and below are generally smaller for data collected under scheme A.

2.5.2.4. Goodness of fit tests. – Under scheme A, removal of all second recaptures means that each m_{tij} or m_{cij} in a data matrix corresponds to a unique capture history. Thus, a finer partitioning of the data into subcohorts, as described in Chapter 2.1, is not possible under scheme A. Goodness of fit tests for the models in the sequence H_0, $H_{1\phi}$, H_{2p}, $H_{2\phi}$, ..., $H_{k-1,\phi}$ are therefore based on TEST 2, computed from the m_{tij}- and m_{cij}-arrays as described in Chapter 2.1. TEST 3 does not exist.

2.5.2.5. Comparing survival for treatment and control groups. – Of particular concern in these studies is the comparison of survival rates, for treatment and control groups, between the release and first recovery sites. The most appropriate test for making this comparison will depend on the true underlying model, which is not known. However, the tests between models and goodness of fit tests can be used to choose the model that seems most appropriate for a given data set. The estimates $\hat{\phi}_{t1}$ and $\hat{\phi}_{c1}$ and variances and covariances produced when this model is used are then the basis for making inferences about either the ratio ϕ_{t1}/ϕ_{c1} or the difference $\phi_{c1} - \phi_{t1}$.

As described in Chapter 1.5, if the treatment effect is direct, $1 - S = 1 - \phi_{t1}/\phi_{c1}$ measures treatment-related mortality, and tests or confidence intervals on S become of interest. If there is a strong, indirect treatment effect, then differences $\phi_{ci} - \phi_{ti}$ may also be of interest as measures of that treatment effect. With replicate lots (see Part 4), empirical variances for $\hat{S}$ or

$\hat{\phi}_{c1} - \hat{\phi}_{t1}$ can be obtained and used in constructing tests or confidence intervals for the corresponding parameters. When there is little or no replication, variances based on theoretical formulae must be used. Program RELEASE prints $\hat{S}_i = \hat{\phi}_{ti}/\hat{\phi}_{ci}$ and the corresponding standard error and 95% CI for each model and each period for which ϕ_{ti} and ϕ_{ci} are estimated separately. Validity of these confidence intervals for S produced by RELEASE depends on model assumptions being correct (so that theoretical variances are appropriate) and on sample sizes being large enough to ensure that the distribution of $\hat{S}$ is approximately normal.

Confidence intervals for the difference $\phi_{ci} - \phi_{ti}$ are not printed by RELEASE but can be constructed as

$$(\hat{\phi}_{ci} - \hat{\phi}_{ti}) \pm z_{\alpha}\text{se}(\hat{\phi}_{ci} - \hat{\phi}_{ti}),$$

where

$$\text{se}(\hat{\phi}_{ci} - \hat{\phi}_{ti}) = \sqrt{\text{var}(\hat{\phi}_{ci}) + \text{var}(\hat{\phi}_{ti}) - 2\text{cov}(\hat{\phi}_{ci}, \hat{\phi}_{ti})}$$

and z_{α} is the standard normal deviate chosen to give confidence level $(1 - \alpha)100\%$. The $\text{cov}(\hat{\phi}_{ci}, \hat{\phi}_{ti}) = \hat{\text{corr}}(\hat{\phi}_{ci}, \hat{\phi}_{ti})\hat{\text{se}}(\hat{\phi}_{ci})\hat{\text{se}}(\hat{\phi}_{ti})$, where the correlation between these two estimators is printed by RELEASE, and labeled as Corr(1,2,Phi(i)). Again, if variances and covariances produced by RELEASE are used to obtain $\text{se}(\hat{\phi}_{ci} - \hat{\phi}_{ti})$, the validity of the interval will depend on model assumptions being correct.

Sample output in Table 2.25 is used to illustrate construction and interpretation of these confidence intervals in Section 2.5.2.6.

2.5.2.6. Example. – Table 2.25 contains part of the computer printout for analysis of the data arising under scheme A for the hypothetical example. Comparison of Tables 2.25 and 2.21 shows the similarity between results for the scheme A and complete capture history protocols. As indicated before, this similarity is a result of little information being lost by failure to return second recaptures to the study population if recapture probabilities are low.

Table 2.25. – Some test summary and example output for the hypothetical sample collected under scheme A.

```
+---------------------------------------------------------------------+
|          Maximum Likelihood Estimates under Model H5Phi             |
|                                   95% Confidence Intervals          |
|   Parameter      Estimate     Standard Error    Lower       Upper   |
|   ---------      --------     --------------  --------    --------   |
|                     Estimates for Group 1                           |
|                       Treatment Group                              |
|   Phi(1)         0.827529       0.066869      0.696467    0.958591   |
|   Phi(2)         0.862386       0.158975      0.550796    1.173977   |
|   Phi(3)         1.092036       0.211044      0.678390    1.505681   |
|   Phi(4)         0.872132       0.216818      0.447169    1.297096   |
|   p(2)           0.041449       0.003579      0.034435    0.048463   |
|   p(3)           0.011644       0.002064      0.007599    0.015689   |
|   p(4)           0.075497       0.007690      0.060425    0.090570   |
|   p(5)           0.030359       0.007014      0.016611    0.044107   |
|   Phi(5)p(6)     0.034221       0.007927      0.018684    0.049757   |
|   Corr(Phi(1),Phi(2))         -0.438387                            |
|   Corr(Phi(2),Phi(3))         -0.771080                            |
|   Corr(Phi(3),Phi(4))         -0.206546                            |
|                     Estimates for Group 2                           |
|                        Control Group                               |
|   Phi(1)         0.931746       0.073081      0.788507    1.074984   |
|   Phi(2)         0.936700       0.175128      0.593448    1.279951   |
|   Phi(3)         0.998507       0.194106      0.618059    1.378955   |
|   Phi(4)         0.686250       0.149105      0.394003    0.978496   |
|   p(2)           0.040858       0.003423      0.034149    0.047566   |
|   p(3)           0.010285       0.001857      0.006646    0.013924   |
|   p(4)           0.076293       0.007408      0.061773    0.090813   |
|   p(5)           0.037317       0.007429      0.022756    0.051878   |
|   Phi(5)p(6)     0.043956       0.008773      0.026761    0.061151   |
|   Corr(Phi(1),Phi(2))         -0.419859                            |
|   Corr(Phi(2),Phi(3))         -0.792805                            |
|   Corr(Phi(3),Phi(4))         -0.213136                            |
|                 Ratio of Survivals between Groups                   |
|                                   95% Confidence Intervals          |
|   Parameter      Estimate     Standard Error    Lower       Upper   |
|   ---------      --------     --------------  --------    --------   |
|   S(1,2,Phi(1))  0.888149       0.100016      0.692118    1.084181   |
|   Corr(1,2,Phi(1))             0.000000                            |
|   S(1,2,Phi(2))  0.920665       0.241729      0.446875    1.394454   |
```

Table 2.25. – Continued.

```
| Corr(1,2,Phi(2))            0.000000                                        |
| S(1,2,Phi(3))  1.093669     0.299789      0.506081      1.681256           |
| Corr(1,2,Phi(3))            0.000000                                        |
| S(1,2,Phi(4))  1.270867     0.419606      0.448440      2.093295           |
| Corr(1,2,Phi(4))            0.000000                                        |
|                                                                            |
|  S(i,j,Phi(I)) equals treatment effect estimated as                        |
|     Phi(I) for group i / Phi(I) for group j.                               |
|  Corr(i,j,Phi(I)) equals estimated sampling correlation                    |
|     between Phi(I) for group i and Phi(I) for group j.                     |
+----------------------------------------------------------------------------+

+----------------------------------------------------------------------------+
|              Maximum Likelihood Estimates under Model H2p                   |
|                                              95% Confidence Intervals       |
|  Parameter      Estimate     Standard Error     Lower          Upper        |
|  ---------      --------     --------------  -------------   ------------    |
|                    Estimates for Group 1                                    |
|                      Treatment Group                                        |
|  Phi(1)        0.830798      0.047782        0.737145        0.924452       |
|  p(2)          0.041286      0.002686        0.036021        0.046550       |
|  Corr(Phi(1),Phi(2))        -0.419720                                       |
|                    Estimates for Group 2                                    |
|                      Control Group                                          |
|  Phi(1)        0.928307      0.053214        0.824008        1.032606       |
|  p(2)          0.041009      0.002642        0.035830        0.046188       |
|  Corr(Phi(1),Phi(2))        -0.421233                                       |
|                  Estimates for Pooled Groups                                |
|  Phi(2)        0.898918      0.117992        0.667654        1.130183       |
|  Phi(3)        1.044057      0.143045        0.763690        1.324425       |
|  Phi(4)        0.765901      0.125252        0.520387        1.011414       |
|  p(3)          0.010935      0.001383        0.008224        0.013646       |
|  p(4)          0.075902      0.005335        0.065446        0.086358       |
|  p(5)          0.033977      0.005926        0.023930        0.044023       |
|  Phi(5)p(6)    0.039179      0.005926        0.027564        0.050794       |
|  Corr(Phi(2),Phi(3))        -0.782301                                       |
|  Corr(Phi(3),Phi(4))        -0.210658                                       |
|                  Ratio of Survivals between Groups                          |
|                                              95% Confidence Intervals       |
|  Parameter      Estimate     Standard Error     Lower          Upper        |
|  ---------      --------     --------------  -------------   ------------    |
|  S(1,2,Phi(1))  0.894961     0.020341        0.0855093       0.934829       |
```

Table 2.25. – Continued.

```
| Corr(1,2,Phi(1))              0.921665                          |
+----------------------------------------------------------------+

+----------------------------------------------------------------+
|          Maximum Likelihood Estimates under Model H1Phi         |
|                                   95% Confidence Intervals      |
| Parameter      Estimate     Standard Error   Lower       Upper  |
| ---------      --------------  --------------  --------------  -------------- |
|                     Estimates for Group 1                       |
|                        Treatment Group                          |
| Phi(1)         0.831435       0.047607      0.738126    0.924745 |
| Corr(Phi(1),Phi(2))          -0.421653                          |
|                     Estimates for Group 2                       |
|                        Control Group                            |
| Phi(1)         0.927648       0.052962      0.823843    1.031452 |
| Corr(Phi(1),Phi(2))          -0.422881                          |
|                   Estimates for Pooled Groups                   |
| Phi(2)         0.898918       0.117992      0.667654    1.130183 |
| Phi(3)         1.044057       0.143045      0.763690    1.324425 |
| Phi(4)         0.765901       0.125262      0.520387    1.011414 |
| p(2)           0.041142       0.002474      0.036294    0.045990 |
| p(3)           0.010935       0.001383      0.008224    0.013646 |
| p(4)           0.075902       0.005335      0.065446    0.086358 |
| p(5)           0.033977       0.005126      0.023930    0.044023 |
| Phi(5)p(6)     0.039179       0.005926      0.027564    0.050794 |
| Corr(Phi(2),Phi(3))          -0.782301                          |
| Corr(Phi(3),Phi(4))          -0.210658                          |
|                 Ratio of Survivals between Groups               |
|                                   95% Confidence Intervals      |
| Parameter      Estimate     Standard Error   Lower       Upper  |
| ---------      --------------  --------------  --------------  -------------- |
| S(1,2,Phi(1)) 0.896284       0.018040      0.860925    0.931642 |
| Corr(1,2,Phi(1))             0.938042                           |
+----------------------------------------------------------------+

+----------------------------------------------------------------+
|          Maximum Likelihood Estimates under Model H0            |
|                                   95% Confidence Intervals      |
| Parameter      Estimate     Standard Error   Lower       Upper  |
| ---------      --------------  --------------  --------------  -------------- |
|                   Estimates for Pooled Groups                   |
| Phi(1)         0.878726       0.049456      0.781793    0.975660 |
| Phi(2)         0.898918       0.117992      0.667654    1.130183 |
```

Table 2.25. – Continued.

```
+--------------------------------------------------------------------------+
| Phi(3)              1.044057      0.143045      0.763690      1.324425    |
| Phi(4)              0.765901      0.125262      0.520387      1.011414    |
| p(2)                0.041142      0.002474      0.036294      0.045990    |
| p(3)                0.010935      0.002383      0.008224      0.013646    |
| p(4)                0.075902      0.005335      0.065446      0.086358    |
| p(5)                0.033977      0.005126      0.023930      0.044023    |
| Phi(5)p(6)          0.039179      0.005926      0.027564      0.050794    |
| Corr(Phi(1),Phi(2))              -0.428974                                |
| Corr(Phi(2),Phi(3))              -0.782301                                |
| Corr(Phi(3),Phi(4))              -0.210658                                |
+--------------------------------------------------------------------------+
```

```
              Summary of TEST 1 (Between Groups Test) Results
          Component    Chi-square    df    P-level   Sufficient Data
          ---------    ----------    ----  -------   --------------
          1.R5           0.6745       1     0.4115        Yes
          1.T5           0.2237       1     0.6363        Yes
          1.R4           0.0095       1     0.9223        Yes
          1.T4           0.2361       1     0.6270        Yes
          1.R3           0.1399       1     0.7084        Yes
          1.T3           0.1543       1     0.6944        Yes
          1.R2           0.0048       1     0.9448        Yes
          1.T2           0.0196       1     0.8887        Yes
          1.R1          29.6316       1     0.0000        Yes
          TEST 1        31.0940       9     0.0003
```

```
              Summary of TEST 2 (Goodness of fit) Results
        Group  Component  Chi-square   df   P-level  Sufficent Data
        -----  ---------  ----------   ---- -------  --------------
          1     2.C2        1.9445      3    0.5840       Yes
          1     2.C3        0.5400      2    0.7634       Yes
          1     2.C4        0.2045      1    0.6511       Yes
        Group 1 TEST 2      2.6890      6    0.8467
          2     2.C2        1.8265      3    0.6092       Yes
          2     2.C3        1.6054      2    0.4481       Yes
          2     2.C4        0.2885      1    0.5912       Yes
        Group 2 TEST 2      3.7203      6    0.7145
        All Groups TEST 2   6.4093     12    0.8941
```

Table 2.26. − Summary of estimates of various model parameters under model $H_{1\phi}$ for three protocols. The data from the general numerical example were used.

| | Complete capture history protocol | | Partial capture history protocol | | | |
| | | | Scheme A | | Scheme B | |
Parameters	Estimates	se	Estimates	se	Estimates	se
$\hat{\phi}_{t1}$	0.831	0.0476	0.831	0.0476	0.831	0.0476
$\hat{\phi}_{c1}$	0.928	0.0530	0.928	0.0530	0.928	0.0530
$\hat{\phi}_2$	0.916	0.1188	0.899	0.1180	Not estimable	
$\hat{\phi}_3$	1.023	0.1378	1.044	0.1430	Not estimable	

Note that for any specific model, data collected under these two protocols give the same values for $\hat{\phi}_{t1}$ and $\hat{\phi}_{c1}$, as illustrated below for model $H_{1\phi}$. Estimates of $\hat{\phi}_2$, $\hat{\phi}_3$, etc. are generally less precise with the scheme A data than under the complete capture history protocol. The difference in precision, based on estimated standard errors for model $H_{1\phi}$, is shown in Table 2.26 to be small for the hypothetical example.

Estimates under models $H_{2\phi}$, ..., H_{4p} are not included in Table 2.25 but are included in the output from RELEASE. For this example, tests between models with scheme A data and with the complete capture history data lead to the same conclusion. The test of H_0 versus $H_{1\phi}$ rejects H_0 ($\chi^2 = 29.63$ with 1 df, exactly as in Table 2.23; see TEST 1.R1). Tests comparing $H_{1\phi}$ with more general models, though not identical to those in Table 2.23, fail to be significant. Thus, $H_{1\phi}$ is the most appropriate model for these data, suggesting a treatment effect on survival that is negligible beyond dam 2. Examination of this treatment effect is carried out by using model $H_{1\phi}$ estimates $\hat{\phi}_{t1}$ and $\hat{\phi}_{c1}$. Results given below are the same as those derived from the complete capture history data. In particular, the model $H_{1\phi}$ estimate $\hat{S}$, denoted in RELEASE output as S(1,2,Phi(1)), is 0.896 with estimated $\hat{se} = 0.0180$. The 95% CI for S is 0.896 ± (1.96 × 0.0180), or 0.861 to 0.932.

Using model $H_{1\phi}$ estimates, $\hat{\phi}_{c1} - \hat{\phi}_{t1} = 0.9276 - 0.8314 = 0.0962$. The standard errors and correlation of $\hat{\phi}_{c1}$, $\hat{\phi}_{t1}$ are given in Table 2.25 under model $H_{1\phi}$. In particular, the correlation is 0.9380, hence, the covariance of $\hat{\phi}_{c1}$ and $\hat{\phi}_{t1}$ is cov($\hat{\phi}_{c1}$,$\hat{\phi}_{t1}$) = (0.9380)(0.05296)(0.04761) = 0.002365. The corresponding standard error of the difference is

$$\hat{se}(\hat{\phi}_{c1} - \hat{\phi}_{t1}) = \sqrt{(0.05296)^2 + (0.04761)^2 - 2(0.002365)}$$

$$= 0.0185 \, .$$

The 95% CI for the difference in treatment and control survival rates is $0.096 \pm (1.96 \times 0.0185)$. With 95% confidence, the survival rate in the control group exceeds that in the treatment group by between 0.060 and 0.132.

2.5.3. Scheme B

2.5.3.1. Introduction and presentation of data. – First recaptures at dam 2 (the first recapture site) are given a second mark and released, and all recaptures at dams 3 to k are removed from the study population. Thus, there are two releases for treatment and controls: R_{t1} and R_{c1} in the initial release, and R_{t2} and R_{c2} double-marked releases at dam 2. Hence, at sites 3 to k, first recaptures (m_{t1j}, m_{c1j}) can be distinguished from second recaptures (m_{t2j}, m_{c2j}) because of the double marking and removal. The release-recapture data can be represented symbolically as in Table 2.27.

For the hypothetical example, the data that would result from the use of scheme B are presented in Table 2.28. These data correspond to rows 1 and 2 of the reduced m-arrays for the complete capture history protocol (see Tables 1.5 and 1.6).

Table 2.27. – Symbolic representation of data for partial capture history, scheme B, protocol for $k = 5$ dams.

| Release site | Releases R_{vi} | \multicolumn{5}{c}{Numbers recaptured at dam j, m_{vij}} |
		$j = 2$	3	4	5	Total
\multicolumn{7}{c}{**Treatment group**}
1	R_{t1}	m_{t12}	m_{t13}	m_{t14}	m_{t15}	r_{t1}
2	R_{t2}		m_{t23}	m_{t24}	m_{t25}	r_{t2}
Total		m_{t2}	m_{t3}	m_{t4}	m_{t5}	
\multicolumn{7}{c}{**Control group**}
1	R_{c1}	m_{c12}	m_{c13}	m_{c14}	m_{c15}	r_{c1}
2	R_{c2}		m_{c23}	m_{c24}	m_{c25}	r_{c2}
Total		m_{c2}	m_{c3}	m_{c4}	m_{c5}	

Table 2.28. – Release-recapture data for the hypothetical example under the scheme B protocol.

Release site	Releases $R_{\mathbf{v}i}$	Number recaptured at dam j, $m_{\mathbf{v}ij}$					Totals, r_{ti} or r_{ci}
		$j = 2$	3	4	5	6	
				Treatment group			
1	30,000	1,029	238	1,669	549	590	4,075
2	1,000		11	73	17	27	128
Totals, m_{tj}		1,029	249	1,742	566	617	
				Control group			
1	29,000	1,104	247	1,832	571	641	4,395
2	1,071		13	75	19	29	136
Totals, m_{cj}		1,104	260	1,907	590	670	

2.5.3.2. Models. – Again, we may conceive of a series of increasingly general models to describe the data resulting from scheme B. However, because these data are more limited than those resulting from scheme A or unique marking (two releases compared to k - 1), there are fewer estimable parameters. The underlying statistical theory is presented in Section 2.5.6.

Model $H_{1\phi}$ assumes that survival may differ for treatment and control groups as far as, but not beyond, dam 2. All recapture probabilities are assumed to be the same for the two groups. The structure of $H_{1\phi}$ for scheme B data is represented in terms of matrices of expected numbers of recaptures in Table 2.29. Note that the structure of the first two rows in Table 2.14 is identical to those in Table 2.29. Estimable parameters of interest are ϕ_{t1}, ϕ_{c1},

Table 2.29. – Expected numbers of recaptures for model $H_{1\phi}$ and scheme B data, k = 5 dams.

Release site	Releases $R_{\mathbf{v}i}$	Number recaptured at dam j, $m_{\mathbf{v}ij}$			
		$j = 2$	3	4	5
			Treatment group, $E(m_{tij})$		
1	R_{t1}	$R_{t1}\phi_{t1}p_2$	$R_{t1}\phi_{t1}q_2\phi_2 p_3$	$R_{t1}\phi_{t1}q_2\phi_2 q_3\phi_3 p_4$	$R_{t1}\phi_{t1}q_2\phi_2 q_3\phi_3 q_4\phi_4 p_5$
2	R_{t2}		$R_{t2}\phi_2 p_3$	$R_{t2}\phi_2 q_3\phi_3 p_4$	$R_{t2}\phi_2 q_3\phi_3 q_4\phi_4 p_5$
			Control group, $E(m_{cij})$		
1	R_{c1}	$R_{c1}\phi_{c1}p_2$	$R_{c1}\phi_{c1}q_2\phi_2 p_3$	$R_{c1}\phi_{c1}q_2\phi_2 q_3\phi_3 p_4$	$R_{c1}\phi_{c1}q_2\phi_2 q_3\phi_3 q_4\phi_4 p_5$
2	R_{c2}		$R_{c2}\phi_2 p_3$	$R_{c2}\phi_2 q_3\phi_3 p_4$	$R_{c2}\phi_2 q_3\phi_3 q_4\phi_4 p_5$

and p_2. From the expectations in Table 2.29, separate estimation of ϕ_i and p_{i+1} for $i \geq 2$ appears impossible. Formulae for the estimators $\hat{\phi}_{t1}$, $\hat{\phi}_{c1}$, and $\hat{p}_2$, and variances and covariances are the same as for model $H_{1\phi}$ with complete capture history data (see Section 2.4.5.3). Numerical values of estimates $\hat{\phi}_{t1}$, $\hat{\phi}_{c1}$, and $\hat{p}_2$ for the hypothetical example will be the same when data are collected under the complete capture history, scheme A, or scheme B protocols, as noted in Section 2.5.2.6. To illustrate computation of $\hat{\phi}_{t1}$ for model $H_{1\phi}$, we use summary statistics from Tables 2.28 and 2.30 for the hypothetical example. Thus,

$$\hat{\phi}_{t1} = \frac{r_{t1}}{R_{t1}} \left[\frac{1}{m_{.2} + z_{.2}} \left(m_{.2} + \frac{z_{.2}R_{.2}}{r_{.2}} \right) \right]$$

$$= \frac{4,075}{30,000} \left[\frac{1}{8,470} \left(2,133 + \frac{6,337(2,071)}{264} \right) \right]$$

$$= 0.8314 \,,$$

which agrees with output for model $H_{1\phi}$ in Table 2.30.

Model H_{2p} assumes that ϕ_1 and p_2 are different for the treatment and control groups, but that other parameters are not. The model structure, represented in terms of expected numbers of recaptures, is determined from the first two rows of each matrix in Table 2.15. Estimable parameters of interest are ϕ_{t1}, ϕ_{c1}, p_{t2}, and p_{c2}. Formulae for estimators and covariances are as for model H_{2p} and complete capture history data (see Section 2.4.5.4). Again, numerical values of estimates for the hypothetical data will be the same under the three protocols (complete capture history, scheme A, and scheme B). Similarities can be seen by comparing computer outputs displayed in Tables 2.22, 2.25, and 2.30. Computation of $\hat{\phi}_{t1}$ and $\hat{p}_{t2}$ is illustrated below, based on data for the hypothetical example displayed in Tables 2.28 and 2.30.

$$\hat{\phi}_{t1} = \frac{r_{t1}}{R_{t1}} \left[\frac{1}{m_{t2} + z_{t2}} \left(m_{t2} + \frac{z_{t2}R_{.2}}{r_{.2}} \right) \right]$$

$$= \frac{4,075}{30,000} \left[\frac{1}{4,075} \left(1,029 + \frac{3,046\,(2,071)}{264} \right) \right]$$

$$= 0.8308 \,.$$

$$\hat{p}_{t2} = \frac{m_{t2}r_{.2}}{m_{t2}r_{.2} + z_{t2}R_{.2}}$$

$$= \frac{1,029\,(264)}{1,029\,(264) + 3,046\,(2,071)}$$

$$= 0.0413\,.$$

Models $H_{2\phi}, ..., H_{k-1,\phi}$ have assumptions as described in Section 2.4.5, but, for scheme B data, recaptures from only two releases are available. The estimable parameters of interest are ϕ_{t1}, ϕ_{c1}, p_{t2}, and p_{c2}, with estimators, variances, and covariances as given for model $H_{k-1,\phi}$ applied to complete capture history data (Section 2.4.4). The estimable parameter sets for models $H_{2\phi}, ..., H_{k-1,\phi}$ are all identical under scheme B. Again, computation of $\hat{\phi}_{t1}, \hat{p}_{t2}$ is illustrated by using data in Table 2.30.

$$\hat{\phi}_{t1} = \frac{r_{t1}}{R_{t1}} \left[\frac{1}{m_{t2} + z_{t2}} \left(m_{t2} + \frac{z_{t2}R_{t2}}{r_{t2}} \right) \right]$$

$$= \frac{4,075}{30,000} \left[\frac{1}{4,075} \left(1,029 + \frac{3,046\,(1,000)}{128} \right) \right]$$

$$= 0.8275\,.$$

$$\hat{p}_{t2} = \frac{m_{t2}r_{t2}}{m_{t2}r_{t2} + z_{t2}R_{t2}}$$

$$= \frac{1,029\,(128)}{(1,029)\,(128) + (3,046)\,(1,000)}$$

$$= 0.0414\,.$$

2.5.3.3. Testing between models. – In this section, a series of tests is presented to determine which model and estimators to use for a given data set. We cannot distinguish among all models in the series $H_{2\phi}$ to $H_{k-1,\phi}$, as only two releases are made for each group under scheme B. On the basis of statistical theory given in Section 2.5.3.7, the following sequence of tests is recommended.

Test (1), model $H_{2\phi}$ versus $H_{k-1,\phi}$, is based on a contingency chi-square test with $k - 3$ df computed from the contingency table

$$\begin{array}{|cccc|l} m_{t3} & m_{t4} & \cdots & m_{t,k} & T_{t3} \\ m_{c3} & m_{c4} & \cdots & m_{c,k} & T_{c3} \end{array}$$

This test is equivalent to an overall chi-square (with $k - 3$ df) obtained by summing individual 1-df chi-squares from the 2×2 tables

$$\begin{array}{|cc|} m_{ti} & z_{ti} \\ m_{ci} & z_{ci} \end{array}$$

where $i = 3, ..., k - 1$. These individual chi-squares are printed out by program RELEASE and are labeled TEST 1.$T3$, TEST 1.$T4$, ..., TEST1.$Tk - 1$. Sample values in these tables are generally smaller than in the analogous tables with scheme A or complete capture history data.

Test (2), model H_{2p} versus $H_{2\phi}$, involves a 1 df χ^2 statistic computed from the contingency table

$$\begin{array}{|cc|l} r_{t2} & R_{t2} - r_{t2} & R_{t2} \\ r_{c2} & R_{c2} - r_{c2} & R_{c2} \end{array}$$

It tests equality of ϕ_{t2} and ϕ_{c2}, assuming $\phi_{ti} = \phi_{ci}$, $i = 3, ..., k - 1$, and $p_{ti} = p_{ci}$, $i = 3, ..., k$. In output from RELEASE, this test is labeled TEST 1.$R2$.

Test (3), model $H_{1\phi}$ versus H_{2p}, involves a 1 df χ^2 statistic computed from the contingency table

$$\begin{array}{|cc|l} m_{t2} & z_{t2} & T_{t2} \\ m_{c2} & z_{c2} & T_{c2} \end{array}$$

It tests equality of p_{t2} and p_{c2}, assuming $\phi_{ti} = \phi_{ci}$, $i = 2, ..., k - 1$, and $p_{ti} = p_{ci}$, $i = 3, ..., k$. This test is labeled TEST 1.$T2$ in RELEASE.

Test (4), model H_0 versus $H_{1\phi}$, involves a 1 df χ^2 computed from the contingency table

r_{t1}	$R_{t1} - r_{t1}$	R_{t1}
r_{c1}	$R_{c1} - r_{c1}$	R_{c1}

It tests equality of ϕ_{t1} and ϕ_{c1}, assuming $\phi_{ti} = \phi_{ci}$, $i = 2, ..., k - 1$, and $p_{ti} = p_{ci}$, $i = 2, ..., k$ (see TEST 1.$R1$ in RELEASE). For the hypothetical example, one sees in Table 2.28 that this table is

4,075	25,925
4,395	24,605

yielding a χ^2 value of 29.63.

2.5.3.4. Goodness of fit tests. – Under scheme B, each entry in the data matrices corresponds to a single capture history; thus, there is no finer partitioning of these data (into subcohorts) on which to base tests of fit. Goodness of fit tests, based on the m-arrays m_{tij} and m_{cij}, are carried out as follows.

Test of Fit to $H_{k-1,\phi}$ involves an overall χ^2 statistic. To obtain this overall chi-square, one first computes χ^2 statistics χ^2_t and χ^2_c, each with $k - 3$ df from the respective contingency tables

m_{t13}	m_{t14}	$\cdots$	m_{t1k}
m_{t23}	m_{t24}	$\cdots$	m_{t2k}

m_{c13}	m_{c14}	$\cdots$	m_{c1k}
m_{c23}	m_{c24}	$\cdots$	m_{c2k}

These tests are labeled TEST 2.$C2$ in RELEASE. Then "χ^2 for fit to $H_{k-1,\phi}$" $= \chi^2_t + \chi^2_c$ with $k - 3 + k - 3 = 2(k - 3)$ df. A significantly large, overall χ^2 indicates that model $H_{k-1,\phi}$ is not appropriate.

Tests of fit to $H_{1\phi}$, H_{2p}, and $H_{2\phi}$ are obtained by combining χ^2 statistics for tests between models and for testing fit to $H_{k-1,\phi}$. An outline follows.

(1) χ^2 for fit to $H_{2\phi} = \chi^2$ for $H_{2\phi}$ versus $H_{k-1,\phi} + \chi^2$ for fit to $H_{k-1,\phi}$, with $k - 3 + 2(k - 3)$ $= 3(k - 3)$ df. (This χ^2 for fit to $H_{2\phi}$ is the sum of TEST 2.$C2$ for treatment and control groups plus TESTs 1.$T3$, 1.$T4$, ..., 1.Tk - 1).

(2) χ^2 for fit to $H_{2p} = \chi^2$ for H_{2p} versus $H_{2\phi}$ (TEST 1.$R2$) $+ \chi^2$ for fit to $H_{2\phi}$, with $1 + 3(k - 3) = 3k - 8$ df.

(3) χ^2 for fit to $H_{1\phi} = \chi^2$ for $H_{1\phi}$ versus H_{2p} (TEST 1.$T2$) $+ \chi^2$ for fit to H_{2p}, with $1 + 3k - 8 = 3k - 7$ df.

2.5.3.5. Comparing survival among treatment and control groups. – The comments in Section 2.5.2.5 apply here, except that with scheme B data inferences concerning the ratio ϕ_{ti}/ϕ_{ci} (or difference $\phi_{ci} - \phi_{ti}$) are only possible for period 1 ($i = 1$).

2.5.3.6. Example. – The analysis of scheme B data is illustrated by using output from program RELEASE for the hypothetical example. Part of the printout is displayed in Table 2.30.

Table 2.30. – Selected results for analyses of the hypothetical example, collected under scheme B protocol.

```
                Observed Recaptures for Group 1
                        Treatment Group
    i    R(i)            m(i,j)              r(i)
                 j= 2    3    4    5    6
    1   30000  1029   238 1669  549  590  4075
    2    1000          11   73   17   27   128

    m(j)        1029  249 1742  566  617
    z(j)        3046 2925 1183  617    0


                Observed Recaptures for Group 2
                        Control Group
    i    R(i)            m(i,j)              r(i)
                 j= 2    3    4    5    6
    1   29000  1104   247 1832  571  641  4395
    2    1071          13   75   19   29   136

    m(j)        1104  260 1907  590  670
    z(j)        3291 3167 1260  670    0


                  Sums for the above Groups
    m.         0 2133  509 3649 1156 1287
    R.     59000 2071    0    0    0
    z.         0 6337 6092 2443 1287
    r.      8470  264    0    0    0


Data type is scheme B capture histories.
```

Table 2.30. – Continued.

```
+-------------------------------------------------------------------------+
|                Maximum Likelihood Estimates under Model H2Phi            |
|                                           95% Confidence Intervals       |
|   Parameter      Estimate     Standard Error     Lower         Upper     |
|   ---------      --------------  --------------  --------------  -------------- |
|                      Estimates for Group 1                               |
|                         Treatment Group                                  |
|   Phi(1)         0.827529       0.066869         0.696467       0.958591  |
|   p(2)           0.041449       0.003579         0.034435       0.048463  |
|                      Estimates for Group 2                               |
|                         Control Group                                    |
|   Phi(1)         0.931746       0.073081         0.788507       1.074984  |
|   p(2)           0.040858       0.003423         0.034149       0.047566  |
|                 Ratio of Survivals between Groups                        |
|                                           95% Confidence Intervals       |
|   Parameter      Estimate     Standard Error     Lower         Upper     |
|   ---------      --------------  --------------  --------------  -------------- |
|   S(1,2,Phi(1))  0.888149       0.100016         0.692118       1.084181  |
|   Corr(1,2,Phi(1))              0.000000                                  |
+-------------------------------------------------------------------------+

+-------------------------------------------------------------------------+
|                Maximum Likelihood Estimates under Model H2p              |
|                                           95% Confidence Intervals       |
|   Parameter      Estimate     Standard Error     Lower         Upper     |
|   ---------      --------------  --------------  --------------  -------------- |
|                      Estimates for Group 1                               |
|                         Treatment Group                                  |
|   Phi(1)         0.830798       0.047782         0.737145       0.924452  |
|   p(2)           0.041286       0.002686         0.036021       0.046550  |
|                      Estimates for Group 2                               |
|                         Control Group                                    |
|   Phi(1)         0.928307       0.053214         0.824008       1.032606  |
|   p(2)           0.041009       0.002642         0.035830       0.046188  |
|                 Ratio of Survivals between Groups                        |
|                                           95% Confidence Intervals       |
|   Parameter      Estimate     Standard Error     Lower         Upper     |
|   ---------      --------------  --------------  --------------  -------------- |
|   S(1,2,Phi(1))  0.894961       0.020341         0.855093       0.934829  |
|   Corr(1,2,Phi(1))              0.921665                                  |
+-------------------------------------------------------------------------+
```

Table 2.30. – Continued.

```
+--------------------------------------------------------------------------+
|                                                                          |
|          Maximum Likelihood Estimates under Model H1Phi                   |
|                                                                          |
|                                               95% Confidence Intervals   |
|     Parameter      Estimate      Standard Error    Lower        Upper     |
|     ---------      --------------  --------------  --------------  -------------- |
|                      Estimates for Group 1                                |
|                        Treatment Group                                    |
|     Phi(1)         0.831435        0.047607       0.738126      0.924745   |
|                      Estimates for Group 2                                |
|                        Control Group                                      |
|     Phi(1)         0.927648        0.052962       0.823843      1.031452   |
|                      Estimates for Pooled Groups                          |
|     p(2)           0.041142        0.002474       0.036294      0.045990   |
|                                                                          |
|                  Ratio of Survivals between Groups                        |
|                                                                          |
|                                               95% Confidence Intervals   |
|     Parameter      Estimate      Standard Error    Lower        Upper     |
|     ---------      --------------  --------------  --------------  -------------- |
|     S(1,2,Phi(1))  0.896284        0.018040       0.860925      0.931642   |
|     Corr(1,2,Phi(1))               0.938042                                |
+--------------------------------------------------------------------------+


+--------------------------------------------------------------------------+
|                                                                          |
|                  Estimates under Model H0                                 |
|                                                                          |
|                                               95% Confidence Intervals   |
|     Parameter      Estimate      Standard Error    Lower        Upper     |
|     ---------      --------------  --------------  --------------  -------------- |
|                      Estimates for Pooled Groups                          |
|     Phi(1)         0.878726        0.049456       0.781793      0.975660   |
|     p(2)           0.041142        0.002474       0.036294      0.045990   |
|                                                                          |
+--------------------------------------------------------------------------+
```

Table 2.30. – Continued.

```
TEST 1.T5:  Test of p(5) equal across groups,
assuming higher order parameters are equal across groups.
              +------+------+
           O| 566  | 617  |1183
           E| 559.8| 623.2|
           C|   0.1|   0.1|
              +------+------+
           O| 590  | 670  |1260
           E| 596.2| 663.8|
           C|   0.1|   0.1|
              +------+------+
              1156   1287   2443
         Chi-square=0.2542 (df=1) P=0.6141

TEST 1.T4: Test of p(4) equal across groups,
assuming higher order parameters are equal across groups.
              +------+------+
           O|1742  |1183  |2925
           E|1752.0|1173.0|
           C|   0.1|   0.1|
              +------+------+
           O|1907  |1260  |3167
           E|1897.0|1270.0|
           C|   0.1|   0.1|
              +------+------+
              3649   2443   6092
        Chi-square=0.2751 (df=1) P=0.6000

TEST 1.T3: Test of p(3) equal across groups,
assuming higher order parameters are equal across groups.
              +------+------+
           O| 249  |2925  |3174
           E| 244.7|2929.3|
           C|   0.1|   0.0|
              +------+------+
           O| 260  |3167  |3427
           E| 264.3|3162.7|
           C|   0.1|   0.0|
              +------+------+
              509   6092   6601
        Chi-square=0.1543 (df=1) P=0.6944
```

Table 2.30. – Continued.

```
TEST 1.R2: Test of Phi(2) equal across groups,
assuming higher order parameters are equal across groups.
              +------+------+
          O| 128  | 872  |1000
          E| 127.5| 872.5|
          C|  0.0|  0.0|
           +------+------+
          O| 136  | 935  |1071
          E| 136.5| 934.5|
          C|  0.0|  0.0|
           +------+------+
              264   1807   2071
Chi-square=0.0048 (df=1) P=0.9448

TEST 1.T2: Test of p(2) equal across groups,
assuming higher order parameters are equal across groups.
              +------+------+
          O|1029  |3046  |4075
          E|1026.2|3048.8|
          C|  0.0|  0.0|
           +------+------+
          O|1104  |3291  |4395
          E|1106.8|3288.2|
          C|  0.0|  0.0|
           +------+------+
              2133   6337   8470
Chi-square=0.0196 (df=1) P=0.8887

TEST 1.R1: Test of Phi(1) equal across groups,
assuming higher order parameters are equal across groups.
              +------+------+
          O| 4075 |25925 |30000
          E| 4307.|25693.|
          C| 12.5|  2.1|
           +------+------+
          O| 4395 |24605 |29000
          E| 4163.|24837.|
          C| 12.9|  2.2|
           +------+------+
              8470  50530  59000
    Chi-square=29.6316 (df=1) P=0.0000
```

Table 2.30. – Continued.

```
          Goodness of fit test of recaptures partitioned by rows.

                          Test for Group 1
                          Treatment Group

              TEST 2.C2: Test of row 1 vs. row 2
                  +------+------+------+------+
                  O| 238  |1669  | 549  | 590  |3046
                  E| 239.0|1671.7| 543.2| 592.1|
                  C|   0.0|   0.0|   0.1|   0.0|
                  +------+------+------+------+
                  O|  11  |  73  |  17  |  27  |128
                  E|  10.0|  70.3|  22.8|  24.9|
                  C|   0.1|   0.1|   1.5|   0.2|
                  +------+------+------+------+
                    249    1742    566    617   3174
              Chi-square=1.9445 (df=3) P=0.5840


                          Test for Group 2
                          Control Group

              TEST 2.C2: Test of row 1 vs. row 2
                  +------+------+------+------+
                  O| 247  |1832  | 571  | 641  |3291
                  E| 249.7|1831.3| 566.6| 643.4|
                  C|   0.0|   0.0|   0.0|   0.0|
                  +------+------+------+------+
                  O|  13  |  75  |  19  |  29  | 136
                  E|  10.3|  75.7|  23.4|  26.6|
                  C|   0.7|   0.0|   0.8|   0.2|
                  +------+------+------+------+
                    260    1907    590    670   3427
              Chi-square=1.8265 (df=3) P=0.6092

          Cumulative result over both cohorts and groups
          Chi-square=3.7710 (df=6) P=0.7076
```

Under model $H_{1\phi}$, estimates of ϕ_{t1}, ϕ_{c1}, and p_2 are $\hat{\phi}_{t1} = 0.8314$, $\hat{\phi}_{c1} = 0.9276$, and $\hat{p}_2 = 0.0411$. Note that these values are identical to estimates produced with complete capture history and scheme A data (e.g., see Section 2.5.2.6). Similarly, corresponding standard errors are the same under these three protocols. In contrast, ϕ_2 is not estimable with scheme B data but is estimable under the other two protocols.

Estimates under H_{2p} are $\hat{\phi}_{t1} = 0.8308$, $\hat{\phi}_{c1} = 0.9283$, $\hat{p}_{t2} = 0.0413$, and $\hat{p}_{c2} = 0.0410$. Identical estimates for these same four parameters are obtained for data under scheme A and the complete capture history protocols. This similarity is a result of the estimation of ϕ_1 and p_2 depending on information relating to only the first two releases, and the three protocols are the same with respect to releases 1 and 2 and their subsequent recoveries. Thus, for examining a one-period effect on survival, scheme B is equivalent to the more complex scheme A and complete capture history protocols.

Estimates of ϕ_{t1}, ϕ_{c1}, p_{t2}, and p_{c2} are the same under $H_{2\phi}$ and other more general models in the sequence. Thus, only results for $H_{2\phi}$ are shown in Table 2.30. To determine which estimates or model to use for further inferences, we look at results for tests between specific models and goodness of fit tests. Tests involving models more general than $H_{2\phi}$ produce results under the scheme B protocol different from those for scheme A or the complete capture history data. These tests are labeled TEST 1.$T5$, TEST 1.$T4$, and TEST 1.$T3$ in Table 2.30. Note that not one of these tests yields a significantly large chi-square value, giving no reason to reject any of the models $H_{2\phi}$, ..., $H_{5\phi}$. Also note that under scheme B, data required for TEST 1.$R3$, TEST 1.$R4$, and TEST 1.$R5$ are not available because there are only two releases for each group (in contrast, see Table 2.25).

The next step is to determine if a model less general than $H_{2\phi}$ is adequate for these data. In Table 2.30, one sees that TEST 1.$R2$, which tests H_{2p} against the more general $H_{2\phi}$, yields $\chi^2 = 0.005$ with 1 df ($P = 0.94$), suggesting that $H_{2\phi}$ is unnecessarily general. Then, TEST 1.$T2$ for $H_{1\phi}$ against H_{2p} results in $\chi^2 = 0.02$ with 1 df ($P = 0.89$), suggesting that H_{2p} is also unnecessarily general. Finally, TEST 1.$R1$ for H_0 versus $H_{1\phi}$ yields $\chi^2 = 29.63$ with 1 df ($P = \,<0.001$), indicating that H_0 is rejected in favor of $H_{1\phi}$. Note that tests comparing H_0 versus $H_{1\phi}$, $H_{1\phi}$ versus H_{2p}, and H_{2p} versus $H_{2\phi}$ all produce identical results for data under the three protocols. Again, this similarity results from the use in these three tests of information relating to only the first two releases.

Results for goodness of fit tests appear last in Table 2.30. The test of fit to $H_{5\phi}$ is obtained by summing χ^2 values (and degrees of freedom) for TEST 2.$C2$ for treatment and control groups (i.e., groups 1 and 2 in the output). Summing the chi-square values gives a chi-square value of 3.771 with 6 df ($P = 0.71$).

χ^2 for fit to $H_{4\phi} = \chi^2$ for $H_{4\phi}$ versus $H_{5\phi}$ (TEST 1.$T5$) + χ^2 for fit to $H_{5\phi}$ (TEST 2) = $0.254 + 3.771 = 4.025$ with 7 df.

χ^2 for fit to $H_{3\phi} = \chi^2$ for $H_{3\phi}$ versus $H_{4\phi}$ (TEST 1.$T4$) + χ^2 for fit to $H_{4\phi} = 0.275 + 4.025 = 4.300$ with 8 df.

χ^2 for fit to $H_{2\phi} = \chi^2$ for $H_{2\phi}$ versus $H_{3\phi}$ (TEST 1.$T3$) + χ^2 for fit to $H_{3\phi} = 0.154 + 4.300 = 4.454$ with 9 df.

χ^2 for fit to H_{2p} = χ^2 for H_{2p} versus $H_{2\phi}$ (TEST 1.R2) + χ^2 for fit to $H_{2\phi}$ = .005 + 4.454 = 4.459 with 10 df.

χ^2 for fit to $H_{1\phi}$ = χ^2 for $H_{1\phi}$ versus H_{2p} (TEST 1.T2) + χ^2 for fit to H_{2p} = .020 + 4.459 = 4.479 with 11 df.

χ^2 for fit to H_0 = χ^2 for H_0 versus $H_{1\phi}$ (TEST 1.R1) + χ^2 for fit to $H_{1\phi}$ = 29.632 + 4.479 = 34.111 with 12 df.

Only the test of fit to H_0 produces a significantly large χ^2 (P = <0.001), confirming that model $H_{1\phi}$ is the appropriate model for these data.

The $H_{1\phi}$ estimates are used to make inferences about the treatment effect. (As explained previously, these estimates will be identical to inferences based on scheme A or complete capture history data for this particular example.) Thus, $\hat{S}$ = $\hat{\phi}_{t1}/\hat{\phi}_{c1}$ = 0.896. This result is labeled S(1,2,Phi(1)) in the output in Table 2.30. The 95% CI for S is seen to be 0.861 to 0.932.

2.5.3.7. Statistical theory. – Likelihoods used in deriving scheme B maximum likelihood estimators, tests between models, and goodness of fit tests are presented here for the more useful models in the sequence H_0, $H_{1\phi}$, H_{2p}, $H_{2\phi}$, ..., $H_{k-1,\phi}$.

A minimal sufficient statistic for model $H_{1\phi}$ is

$$\text{MSS} = \{r_{t1}, r_{c1}, m_{.2}, r_{.2}, ..., m_{.k-1}\}.$$

For k = 5, the likelihood under $H_{1\phi}$ is proportional to

$$
\Pr\{\text{MSS}\} = \begin{pmatrix} R_{t1} \\ r_{t1} \end{pmatrix} [\phi_{t1}(p_2 + q_2\lambda_2)]^{r_{t1}} [1 - \phi_{t1}(p_2 + q_2\lambda_2)]^{R_{t1} - r_{t1}}
$$

$$
\times \begin{pmatrix} R_{c1} \\ r_{c1} \end{pmatrix} [\phi_{c1}(p_2 + q_2\lambda_2)]^{r_{c1}} [1 - \phi_{c1}(p_2 + q_2\lambda_2)]^{R_{c1} - r_{c1}}
$$

$$
\times \begin{pmatrix} R_{.2} \\ r_{.2} \end{pmatrix} (\lambda_2)^{r_{.2}} (1 - \lambda_2)^{R_{.2} - r_{.2}}
$$

$$
\times \begin{pmatrix} r_{.1} \\ m_{.2} \end{pmatrix} \left(\frac{p_2}{p_2 + q_2\lambda_2} \right)^{m_{.2}} \left(\frac{q_2\lambda_2}{p_2 + q_2\lambda_2} \right)^{z_{.2}}
$$

$$
\times \begin{pmatrix} r_{.2} + z_{.2} \\ m_{.3} \, m_{.4} \, m_{.5} \end{pmatrix} \left(\frac{p_3}{p_3 + q_3\lambda_3} \right)^{m_{.3}} \left(\frac{q_3\phi_3 p_4}{p_3 + q_3\lambda_3} \right)^{m_{.4}} \left(\frac{q_3\phi_3 q_4\phi_4 p_5}{p_3 + q_3\lambda_3} \right)^{m_{.5}},
$$

where

$$\lambda_k = 0 \text{ and } \lambda_{i-1} = \phi_{i-1}(p_i + q_i\lambda_i) \quad i = 2, ..., k.$$

Also note that $r_{.1} = T_{.1}$ and $r_{.2} + z_{.2} = T_{.3}$.

A minimal sufficient statistic for model H_{2p} is

$$\text{MSS} = \{r_{t1}, r_{c1}, m_{t2}, m_{c2}, r_{.2}, m_{.3}, ..., m_{.k-1}\}.$$

For $k = 5$, the likelihood under H_{2p} is proportional to

$$\Pr\{\text{MSS}\} = \binom{R_{t1}}{r_{t1}} [\phi_{t1}(p_{t2} + q_{t2}\lambda_2)]^{r_{t1}} [1 - \phi_{t1}(p_{t2} + q_{t2}\lambda_2)]^{R_{t1} - r_{t1}}$$

$$\times \binom{R_{c1}}{r_{c1}} [\phi_{c1}(p_{c2} + q_{c2}\lambda_2)]^{r_{c1}} [1 - \phi_{c1}(p_{c2} + q_{c2}\lambda_2)]^{R_{c1} - r_{c1}}$$

$$\times \binom{R_{.2}}{r_{.2}} (\lambda_2)^{r_{.2}} (1 - \lambda_2)^{R_{.2} - r_{.2}}$$

$$\times \binom{r_{t1}}{m_{t2}} \left(\frac{p_{t2}}{p_{t2} + q_{t2}\lambda_2}\right)^{m_{t2}} \left(\frac{q_{t2}\lambda_2}{p_{t2} + q_{t2}\lambda_2}\right)^{z_{t2}}$$

$$\times \binom{r_{c1}}{m_{c2}} \left(\frac{p_{c2}}{p_{c2} + q_{c2}\lambda_2}\right)^{m_{c2}} \left(\frac{q_{c2}\lambda_2}{p_{c2} + q_{c2}\lambda_2}\right)^{z_{c2}}$$

$$\times \binom{r_{.2} + z_{.2}}{m_{.3}, m_{.4}, m_{.5}} \left(\frac{p_3}{p_3 + q_3\lambda_3}\right)^{m_{.3}} \left(\frac{q_3\phi_3 p_4}{p_3 + q_3\lambda_3}\right)^{m_{.4}} \left(\frac{q_3\phi_3 q_4\phi_4 p_5}{p_3 + q_3\lambda_3}\right)^{m_{.5}}.$$

A minimal sufficient statistic for model $H_{2\phi}$ is

$$\text{MSS} = \{r_{t1}, r_{c1}, m_{t2}, m_{c2}, r_{t2}, r_{c2}, m_{.3}, ..., m_{.k-1}\}.$$

For $k = 5$, the likelihood is proportional to

$$\Pr\{MSS\} = \prod_{i=1}^{2} \binom{R_{ti}}{r_{ti}} \lambda_{ti}^{r_{ti}} (1 - \lambda_{ti})^{R_{ti} - r_{ti}} \binom{R_{ci}}{r_{ci}} \lambda_{ci}^{r_{ci}} (1 - \lambda_{ci})^{R_{ci} - r_{ci}}$$

$$\times \binom{r_{t1}}{m_{t2}} \left(\frac{p_{t2}}{p_{t2} + q_{t2}\lambda_{t2}} \right)^{m_{t2}} \left(\frac{q_{t2}\lambda_{t2}}{p_{t2} + q_{t2}\lambda_{t2}} \right)^{z_{t2}}$$

$$\times \binom{r_{c1}}{m_{c2}} \left(\frac{p_{c2}}{p_{c2} + q_{c2}\lambda_{c2}} \right)^{m_{c2}} \left(\frac{q_{c2}\lambda_{c2}}{p_{c2} + q_{c2}\lambda_{c2}} \right)^{z_{c2}}$$

$$\times \binom{r_{.2} + z_{.2}}{m_{.3}\, m_{.4}\, m_{.5}} \left(\frac{p_3}{p_3 + q_3\lambda_3} \right)^{m_{.3}} \left(\frac{q_3\phi_3 p_4}{p_3 + q_3\lambda_3} \right)^{m_{.4}} \left(\frac{q_3\phi_3 q_4 \phi_4 p_5}{p_3 + q_3\lambda_3} \right)^{m_{.5}},$$

where

$$\lambda_{t1} = \phi_{t1}(p_{t2} + q_{t2}\lambda_{t2}),$$
$$\lambda_{t2} = \phi_{t2}(p_3 + q_3\lambda_3),$$
$$\lambda_{c1} = \phi_{c1}(p_{c2} + q_{c2}\lambda_{c2}),$$

and

$$\lambda_{c2} = \phi_{c2}(p_3 + q_3\lambda_3).$$

A minimal sufficient statistic for model $H_{k-1,\phi}$ is

$$MSS = \{r_{t1}, r_{c1}, r_{t2}, r_{c2}, m_{t2}, m_{c2}, ..., m_{t,k-1}, m_{c,k-1}\}.$$

For $k = 5$, the likelihood is proportional to

$$\Pr\{MSS\} = \prod_{v=t,c} \prod_{i=1}^{2} \binom{R_{vi}}{r_{vi}} \lambda_{vi}^{r_{vi}} (1 - \lambda_{vi})^{R_{vi} - r_{vi}}$$

$$\times \prod_{v=t,c} \left\{ \binom{r_{v1}}{m_{v2}} \left(\frac{p_{v2}}{p_{v2} + q_{v2}\lambda_{v2}} \right)^{m_{v2}} \left(\frac{q_{v2}\lambda_{v2}}{p_{v2} + q_{v2}\lambda_{v2}} \right)^{z_{v2}} \right.$$

$$\times \binom{r_{v2} + z_{v2}}{m_{v3}\, m_{v4}\, m_{v5}} \left(\frac{p_{v3}}{p_{v3} + q_{v3}\lambda_{v3}} \right)^{m_{v3}} \left(\frac{q_{v3}\phi_{v3} p_{v4}}{p_{v3} + q_{v3}\lambda_{v3}} \right)^{m_{v4}} \left(\frac{q_{v3}\phi_{v3} q_{v4}\phi_{v4} p_{v5}}{p_{v3} + q_{v3}\lambda_{v3}} \right)^{m_{v5}} \left. \right\}.$$

The following examples represent testing between models.

(1) H_0 versus $H_{1\phi}$ (TEST 1.R1) is based on

$$\Pr_{H_0}\{\text{MSS}_{H_{1\phi}} \mid \text{MSS}_{H_0}\} = \frac{\binom{R_{t1}}{r_{t1}}\binom{R_{c1}}{r_{c1}}}{\binom{R_{.1}}{r_{.1}}},$$

which tests equality of $\phi_{t1}(p_{t2} + q_{t2}\lambda_2)$ and $\phi_{c1}(p_{c2} + q_{c2}\lambda_{c2})$. If all $p_{vi} = p_i$, $i = 2, ..., k$ and all $\phi_{vi} = \phi_i$, $i = 2, ..., k - 1$, then the equality of ϕ_{t1} and ϕ_{c1} is being tested. Here MSS$_{H_0}$ = $\{r_{.1}, r_{.2}, m_{.2}, ..., m_{.k-1}\}$, a minimal sufficient statistic under H_0 for scheme B.

(2) $H_{1\phi}$ versus H_{2p} (TEST 1.T2) is based on

$$\Pr_{H_{1\phi}}\{\text{MSS}_{H_{2p}} \mid \text{MSS}_{H_{1\phi}}\} = \frac{\binom{T_{t2}}{m_{t2}}\binom{T_{c2}}{m_{c2}}}{\binom{T_{.2}}{m_{.2}}},$$

which tests equality of $\dfrac{p_{t2}}{p_{t2} + q_{t2}\lambda_2}$ and $\dfrac{p_{c2}}{p_{c2} + q_{c2}\lambda_{c2}}$. If $p_{vi} = p_i$, $i = 3, ..., k$ and $\phi_{vi} = \phi_i$, $i = 2, ..., k - 1$, then $p_{t2} = p_{c2}$ is being tested. Note that $T_{v2} = r_{v1}$.

(3) H_{2p} versus $H_{2\phi}$ (TEST 1.R2) is based on

$$\Pr_{H_{2p}}\{\text{MSS}_{H_{2\phi}} \mid \text{MSS}_{H_{2p}}\} = \frac{\binom{R_{t2}}{r_{t2}}\binom{R_{c2}}{r_{c2}}}{\binom{R_{.2}}{r_{.2}}},$$

which tests equality of $\phi_{t2}(p_{t3} + q_{t3}\lambda_3)$ and $\phi_{c2}(p_{c3} + q_{c3}\lambda_{c3})$. Again, equality of ϕ_{t2} and ϕ_{c2} is tested if $p_{vi} = p_i$, $i = 3, ..., k$ and $\phi_{vi} = \phi_i$, $i = 3, ..., k - 1$ is true.

(4) $H_{2\phi}$ versus $H_{k-1,\phi}$ (TESTs 1.T3 to 1.Tk - 1) involves pooling the remaining 1-df χ^2 tests to give a test based on

$$\text{Pr}_{H_{2\phi}}\{\text{MSS}_{H_{k-1,\phi}} \mid \text{MSS}_{H_{2\phi}}\} = \frac{\begin{pmatrix} r_{t2} + z_{t2} \\ m_{t3} \ \cdots \ m_{t,k-1} \end{pmatrix} \begin{pmatrix} r_{c2} + z_{c2} \\ m_{c3} \ \cdots \ m_{c,k-1} \end{pmatrix}}{\begin{pmatrix} r_{.2} + z_{.2} \\ m_{.3} \ \cdots \ m_{.k-1} \end{pmatrix}} \ .$$

This multiple hypergeometric can be factored into the following representation:

$$= \prod_{i=3}^{k-1} \frac{\begin{pmatrix} T_{ti} \\ m_{ti} \end{pmatrix} \begin{pmatrix} T_{ci} \\ m_{ci} \end{pmatrix}}{\begin{pmatrix} T_{.i} \\ m_{.i} \end{pmatrix}} \ .$$

The separate, simple hypergeometric distributions for i = 3 to k - 1 correspond to TEST 1.T3 through TEST 1.Tk - 1, respectively.

2.6. Summary of Models and Protocols

Several models do not exist under certain protocols, just as some tests do not exist, or cannot be computed, under certain protocols. Intensive information on available tests are presented in Tables 2.3 and 2.4. A summary of the model sequence, H_0, $H_{1\phi}$, ..., $H_{k-1,\phi}$, is given in Table 2.2. Finally, a summary of models that exist under each protocol is given for completeness.

| | Protocol | | | | |
Model	First CH	Unknown CH	Complete CH	Partial CH Scheme A	Scheme B
H_0	X	X	X	X	X
$H_{1\phi}$	X	X	X	X	X
H_{2p}			X	X	X
$H_{2\phi}$		X	X	X	
H_{3p}			X	X	
.			.	.	
.			.	.	
.			.	.	
$H_{k-1,\phi}$			X	X	X
$H'_{2\phi}$	X				
$H'_{3\phi}$	X				
.	.				
.	.				
.	.				
$H'_{k-1,\phi}$	X				

Part 3. Theory for Studies with Two or More Treatments

3.1. Theory for the Complete Capture History Protocol

As noted in the Reader's Guide (Chapter 1.1), most of Part 3 is intended for persons interested in the theory underlying the methods presented in this monograph. However, biologists cannot safely bypass Chapter 3.10.

3.1.1. Probability Distribution for One Data Set

The starting point for the theory for the complete capture history protocol is the probability distribution for a single data set. That distribution has been considered in the literature (for example, Brownie and Robson 1983; Pollock et al. 1985). Consequently, we do not give the derivations here.

We drop the index for group v in presenting results for a single data set. The complete data are represented as the known releases by subcohorts (subcohorts being determined here by capture histories) and the subsequent recaptures:

$$R_{ih}, i = 1, ..., k - 1,$$

and

$$m_{ijh}, j = i + 1, ..., k.$$

Capture history h depends on time of release and ranges over $h = 1, ..., H_i$. The exact set of capture histories being indexed is not relevant to expressing the general theory.

Given R_{ih}, the recaptures $m_{i,i+1,h}, ..., m_{ikh}$ have a multinomial distribution. By assumption, these distributions are independent over subcohorts within i and over cohorts $i = 1, ..., k - 1$. Let the various cell probabilities be π_{ijh}. Also, let $\lambda_{ih} = \sum_{j=i+1}^{k} \pi_{ijh}$ and $r_{ih} = \sum_{j=i+1}^{k} m_{ijh}$ as before. Thus,

$$E\left(\frac{r_{ih}}{R_{ih}}\right) = \lambda_{ih}.$$

174

Then symbolically,

$$\Pr\{\text{Data}\} = \prod_{i=1}^{k-1} \left[\prod_{h=1}^{H_i} \Pr\{m_{i,i+1,h}, ..., m_{ikh} \mid R_{ih}\} \right],$$

where

$$\Pr\{m_{i,i+1,h} \ \cdots \ m_{ikh} \mid R_{ih}\}$$

$$= \binom{R_{ih}}{m_{i,i+1,h} \ \cdots \ m_{ikh} \ R_{ih} - r_{ih}} \left[\prod_{j=i+1}^{k} (\pi_{ijh})^{m_{ijh}} \right] (1 - \lambda_{ih})^{R_{ih} - r_{ih}} .$$

One could consider models wherein the capture probabilities π_{ijh} are dependent on capture history; we do not do so here. Given $\pi_{ij} \equiv \pi_{ijh}$, then the totals $m_{ij} = m_{ij.}$ (and r_i) are a sufficient statistic (minimal sufficient if no particular structure is assumed for the π_{ij}). Thus, it is clear that, given R_i, the $m_{ij.}$ are multinomial. For convenience, we refer to the m_{ij} as the cohort recapture data (abbreviated here as cohorts), and write

$$\prod_{i=1}^{k-1} \Pr\{m_{i,i+1}, ..., m_{ik} \mid R_i\} = \Pr\{\text{cohorts} \mid \text{releases}\}$$

$$= \prod_{i=1}^{k-1} \binom{R_i}{m_{i,i+1} \ \cdots \ m_{ik} \ R_i - r_i} \left[\prod_{j=i+1}^{k} (\pi_{ij})^{m_{ij}} \right] (1 - \lambda_i)^{R_i - r_i} , \quad i = 1, ..., k - 1 .$$

We now can partition the full probability model:

$$\Pr\{\text{Data}\} = \Pr\{\text{subcohorts} \mid \text{cohorts}\} \ \Pr\{\text{cohorts} \mid \text{releases}\}.$$

The conditional distribution of the subcohorts (i.e., all the subcohort data m_{ijh}), given the cohorts, is a series of independent hypergeometric distributions:

Pr{subcohorts|cohorts}

$$= \prod_{i=1}^{k-1} \Pr\{m_{i,i+1,h} \cdots m_{ikh}, h = 1, ..., H_i \mid m_{i,i+1} \cdots m_{ik}\}$$

$$= \prod_{i=1}^{k-1} \frac{\prod_{h=1}^{H_i} \left(\begin{array}{c} R_{ih} \\ m_{i,i+1,h} \cdots m_{ikh}, R_{ih} - r_{ih} \end{array} \right)}{\left(\begin{array}{c} R_i \\ m_{i,i+1} \cdots m_{ik}, R_i - r_i \end{array} \right)} .$$

We then partition Pr{cohorts|releases} further. Given the classical Jolly-Seber model, which we assume, survival and capture probabilities depend only on the survival interval and recapture occasion, respectively. Hence,

$$\pi_{ij} = \begin{cases} \phi_i p_{i+1} , & j = i + 1 \\ (\phi_i q_{i+1}) \cdots (\phi_{j-2} q_{j-1})\phi_{j-1} p_j , & j > i + 1 \end{cases} .$$

The MSS may be taken as $r_1, ..., r_{k-1}, m_2, ..., m_{k-1}$. Its probability distribution is representable as $2k - 3$ conditionally independent binomial distributions:

$$r_i \mid R_i \sim \text{bin} (R_i, \lambda_i), \quad i = 1, ..., k - 1$$
$$m_i \mid T_i \sim \text{bin} (T_i, \tau_i), \quad i = 2, ..., k - 1 .$$

For completeness, we reiterate the definitions below:

$$T_2 = r_1 ;$$

$$T_{i+1} = T_i - m_i + r_i = z_i + r_i, \quad i = 1, ..., k ;$$

$$\lambda_i = \phi_i(p_{i+1} + q_{i+1}\lambda_{i+1}), \quad i = 1, ..., k - 1 ;$$

$$\lambda_k = 0 ;$$

$$\tau_i = \frac{p_i}{p_i + q_i\lambda_i}, \quad i = 2, ..., k - 1 .$$

The conditional distribution of the cohort data given the MSS has been considered by various authors. The earliest derivation appears to be that of Robson and Youngs (unpublished report, 1971). Symbolically we want

$$\Pr\{\text{cohorts}|\text{releases}\} = \Pr\{\text{cohorts}|\text{MSS}\}\, \Pr\{\text{MSS}|\text{releases}\}.$$

Some additional notation is needed. Let m^c_{ij} be the column sum of the m_{lj} for $l = 1, ..., i$:

$$m^c_{ij} = m_{1j} + m_{2j} + \cdots + m_{ij},$$

defined for $i = 1, ..., j - 1$, and $j = 2, ..., k$ (however, only the cases of $i = j - 2$ and $j - 1$ are needed). We note that $z_i = m^c_{i-1,i+1} + ... + m^c_{i-1,k}$, $T_{i+1} = m^c_{i,i+1} + ... + m^c_{ik}$, and $m^c_{i,i+1} = m_{i+1}$. Now

$$\Pr\{\text{cohorts} \mid \text{MSS} \} = \prod_{i=2}^{k-2} \frac{\begin{pmatrix} z_i \\ m^c_{i-1,i+1} \cdots m^c_{i-1,k} \end{pmatrix} \begin{pmatrix} r_i \\ m_{i,i+1} \cdots m_{ik} \end{pmatrix}}{\begin{pmatrix} T_{i+1} \\ m^c_{i,i+1} \cdots m^c_{ik} \end{pmatrix}}.$$

For completeness, the explicit expression for $\Pr\{\text{MSS}|\text{releases}\}$ is

$$\Pr\{\text{MSS} \mid \text{releases} \} = \left[\prod_{i=1}^{k-1} \binom{R_i}{r_i} (\lambda_i)^{r_i} (1-\lambda_i)^{R_i - r_i} \right] \left[\prod_{i=2}^{k-1} \binom{T_i}{m_i} (\tau_i)^{m_i} (1-\tau_i)^{T_i - m_i} \right].$$

Thus, we have presented here a partition, for one data set, of $\Pr\{\text{Data}\}$:

$$\Pr\{\text{Data}\} = \Pr\{\text{MSS}|\text{releases}\}\, \Pr\{\text{cohorts}|\text{MSS}\}\, \Pr\{\text{subcohorts}|\text{cohorts}\}$$
$$= (\text{component 1}) \times (\text{component 2}) \times (\text{component 3}).$$

Only component 1 depends on the survival and capture probabilities and is used in deriving the MLEs. Components 2 and 3 are used for goodness of fit tests.

Derivations are easier if one simplifies the notation by defining

$$A_i = \frac{r_i}{R_i}, i = 1, ..., k - 1,$$

$$B_i = \frac{m_i}{T_i}, i = 2, ..., k - 1,$$

$A_k = 1$, and $B_k = 1$, and adopting the convention that ϕ_{k-1} means $(\phi_{k-1}p_k)$. The MLEs of λ_1, ..., λ_{k-1} and τ_2, ..., τ_{k-1} are the above A_i and B_i, respectively. The solutions for $\hat{\phi}_i$ and $\hat{p}_i$ are facilitated by writing

$$A_i = \hat{\phi}_i(\hat{p}_{i+1} + \hat{q}_{i+1}A_{i+1}),$$

$$B_{i+1} = \hat{p}_{i+1}/(\hat{p}_{i+1} + \hat{q}_{i+1}A_{i+1}),$$

hence, $A_i = \hat{\phi}_i \hat{p}_{i+1}/B_{i+1}$, and solving for

$$\hat{p}_{i+1} = \frac{B_{i+1}}{B_{i+1} + (1 - B_{i+1})/A_{i+1}}, \quad i = 1, ..., k-2.$$

Thus,

$$\hat{\phi}_i = A_i(B_{i+1} + (1 - B_{i+1})/A_{i+1}), \quad i = 1, ..., k-1.$$

The main advantage of these representations of $\hat{\phi}_i$ and $\hat{p}_i$ are that the A_i and B_i are all mutually independent and have known distributions, thereby making it relatively easy to derive variances and covariances of the MLEs. For example, if the delta method is used,

$$\hat{\mathrm{var}}(\hat{\phi}_i) = \left(\frac{\partial\hat{\phi}_i}{\partial A_i}\right)^2 \frac{A_i(1 - A_i)}{R_i} + \left(\frac{\partial\hat{\phi}_i}{\partial B_{i+1}}\right)^2 \frac{B_{i+1}(1 - B_{i+1})}{T_{i+1}}$$

$$+ \left(\frac{\partial\hat{\phi}_i}{\partial A_{i+1}}\right)^2 \frac{A_{i+1}(1 - A_{i+1})}{R_{i+1}}.$$

More detailed consideration of variances and covariances is deferred to Sections 3.1.2 and 3.1.3.

3.1.2. Theory under the Sequence of Models

We outline here the probability theory and inference methods under the sequence of models H_0, $H_{1\phi}$, ..., $H_{k-1,\phi}$ for the complete capture history protocol. We begin with component 1 of the probability distribution $\Pr\{MSS|\text{releases}\}$; and re-introduce the group index v.

Under the most general hypothesis $H_{k-1,\phi}$, of all parameters differing by treatment, the MSS is

$$\text{MSS} = \{\text{MSS}_v, v = 1, ..., V\}$$

or

$$\{r_{v1}, ..., r_{v,k-1}, m_{v2}, ..., m_{v,k-1}, v = 1, ..., V\}.$$

The basic estimable parameters are $\phi_{v1}, ..., \phi_{v,k-2}, (\phi_{v,k-1}p_{vk}), p_{v2}, ..., p_{v,k-1}, v = 1, ..., V$. Each MSS_v is independently and binomially (bin) distributed as in the previous section:

$$r_{vi} \sim \text{bin}(R_{vi}, \lambda_{vi}), \quad i = 1, ..., k - 1,$$
$$m_{vi} \sim \text{bin}(T_{vi}, \tau_{vi}), \quad i = 2, ..., k - 1.$$

At the other extreme we have H_0: all parameters are the same over treatments. Therefore all $\lambda_{vi} \equiv \lambda_i$ and $\tau_{vi} \equiv \tau_i$. Thus, the MSS under H_0 is simply the sums $r_{.i}, i = 1, ..., k - 1$ and $m_{.i}, i = 2, ..., k - 1$, with probability distribution

$$r_{.i} \sim \text{bin}(R_{.i}, \lambda_i), \quad i = 1, ..., k - 1,$$
$$m_{.i} \sim \text{bin}(T_{.i}, \tau_i), \quad i = 2, ..., k - 1.$$

The theory under Section 3.1.1 applies to obtaining MLEs of the now common parameters.

We can next derive a test of H_0 versus the alternative H_A of $H_{k-1,\phi}$, all parameters may differ by treatments. Let MSS_{H_0} and MSS_{H_A} be the relevant minimal sufficient statistics under null and alternative hypotheses. We want

$$\text{Pr}_{H_0}\{\text{MSS}_{H_A} \mid \text{MSS}_{H_0}\} = \frac{\text{Pr}_{H_0}\left\{\text{MSS}_{H_A}\right\}}{\text{Pr}_{H_0}\left\{\text{MSS}_{H_0}\right\}}.$$

This distribution is a product of $2k - 3$ hypergeometric distributions. For ease of reference to the sequence of hypotheses, we write this distribution in the following order:

$$
\left[\frac{\prod\limits_{v=1}^{V}\binom{R_{v1}}{r_{v1}}}{\binom{R_{.1}}{r_{.1}}}\right] \prod_{i=2}^{k-1}\left[\frac{\prod\limits_{v=1}^{V}\binom{T_{vi}}{m_{vi}}}{\binom{T_{.i}}{m_{.i}}}\right]\left[\frac{\prod\limits_{v=1}^{V}\binom{R_{vi}}{r_{vi}}}{\binom{R_{.i}}{r_{.i}}}\right]. \tag{3.1}
$$

Let the terms (distributions) here be labeled $1.R1$, $1.T2$, $1.R2$, ..., $1.T_{k-1}$, $1.R_{k-1}$ ($2k - 3$ of these distributions). These terms produce the corresponding components of TEST 1. In this ordering, terms are aligned with the sequence of alternative hypotheses (models)

$$
\begin{array}{ll}
H_{1\phi} & (1.R1) \\
H_{2p} & (1.T2) \\
H_{2\phi} & (1.R2) \\
\quad \cdot & \\
\quad \cdot & \\
\quad \cdot & \\
H_{k-1,p} & (1.Tk - 1) \\
H_{k-1,\phi} & (1.Rk - 1).
\end{array}
$$

Consideration of the MSS under intermediate hypotheses remains. Although the "book-keeping" of this process can be confusing, the concept of what occurs is straightforward. The parameters have a natural ordering in time or space. The corresponding sequence of hypotheses produces a series of nested models allowing closed-form tests and estimators. (This sequence of nested models is not unique; this matter is discussed below.) For a given hypothesis such as $H_{2\phi}$, all lower-order parameters are allowed to be different over v: ϕ_{v1}, p_{v2}, and ϕ_{v2}. All higher-order parameters are the same over v: $p_{.3}$, $\phi_{.3}$, ..., $p_{.k-1}$, $(\phi_{.k-1}p_{.k})$, which translates into

$$
\lambda_{v1}, \ \tau_{v2}, \ \lambda_{v2}
$$

being different by treatment group but

$$
\tau_{.3}, \lambda_{.3}, ..., \tau_{.k-1}, \lambda_{.k-1}
$$

being the same over v. The above results allow an easy determination of the relevant MSS under $H_{2\phi}$:

$$
r_{vi} \sim \text{bin}\,(R_{vi}, \lambda_{vi}), \qquad i = 1, 2,
$$

$$
m_{v2} \sim \text{bin}\,(T_{v2}, \tau_{v2}), \quad \text{and}
$$

$$r_{.i} \sim \text{bin } (R_{.i}, \lambda_{.i}), \qquad i = 3, ..., k - 1,$$

$$m_{.i} \sim \text{bin } (T_{.i}, \tau_{.i}), \qquad i = 3, ..., k - 1.$$

The minimal sufficient statistics, point estimators, and variances and covariances are easily given if one adopts a few conventions. Specifically, let the treatment group index v range over the set $\{1, ..., v, "."\}$ where $v = "."$ denotes pooling over all groups. Thus, in the above expression the MSS is representable as

$$r_{v1}, r_{v2}, r_{.3}, ..., r_{.k-1}$$
$$m_{v2}, m_{.3}, ..., m_{.k-1},$$

for $v = 1, ..., V$ or just $r_{vi}, i = 1, ..., k - 1$ and $m_{vi}, i = 2, ..., k - 1$ with $v = .$ for $i = 3, ..., k - 1$. The complete specification of all MSSs, point estimators, and variances and covariances is given in Section 3.1.3.

The probability distribution represented by formula (3.1) is unique; however, the association (interpretation) of intermediate models (between H_0 and $H_{k-1,\phi}$) with terms of this distribution is not unique. A variety of nested models can be created that all give rise to the same sequence of MSSs, and thus to formula (3.1). The biology must dictate the sequence of models one considers. Moreover, there are models (and sequences) that do not produce an MSS of closed form that corresponds to that of any MSS in the sequence $H_0, H_{1\phi}, ..., H_{k-1,\phi}$. In those cases, closed-form results do not exist. Alternative sequences that will lead to closed-form results include $H_{1\phi}, H_{2\phi}, H_{3\phi}, ..., H_{k-1,\phi}$ (i.e., ignore the intermediate cases in H_{ip}) or $H_0, H_{2p}, H_{3p}, ..., H_{k-1,p}$. In the case of $v > 2$, there are subcases within each $H_{i\phi}$ or H_{ip}. Only the extremes have been formulated here: either all groups or no groups were pooled at a given stage. For example, under $H_{1\phi}$ with general V, the parameters of interest are $\phi_{11}, \phi_{21}, ..., \phi_{V1}$. The extremes are $\phi_{v1} = \phi_1$, all v or all ϕ_{v1} are different. However, closed-form results (as for estimators and tests) also exist under any simple subsetting hypothesis such as $\phi_{11} = \phi_{21} = \phi_{31} = \phi_{a1}, \phi_{41} = \cdots = \phi_{v1} = \phi_{b1}$ and $\phi_{a1} \neq \phi_{b1}$. We do not consider such an alternative nor do we consider expanded sequences of nested models in this general discussion of theory.

We now briefly consider the methodology for obtaining estimators and variances and covariances. Under any of these hypotheses (i.e., models), the following statement is true. If we let l = the number of estimable parameters, the MSS has l components representable in the form

$$y_i \sim \text{bin } [Y_i, \delta_i(\underline{\theta})], i = 1, ..., l.$$

All y_i are mutually independent. The parameters of natural interest are $\underline{\theta}' = (\theta_1, ..., \theta_l)$ and the $\delta_1, ..., \delta_l$ are a one to one transformation of $\theta_1, ..., \theta_l$. The MLEs of the δ_i are

$$\hat{\delta}_i = \hat{\delta}_i(\underline{\hat{\theta}}) = \frac{y_i}{Y_i}, \quad i = 1, \dots, l.$$

These l equations can be solved uniquely for the MLE $\underline{\hat{\theta}}$ (see, e.g., Davidson and Solomon 1974). The resulting $\hat{\theta}_i$ are explicit functions of the ratios $\bar{a}_j = y_j/Y_j$; for example,

$$\hat{\theta}_i = g_i(a_1, \dots, a_l), \quad i = 1, \dots, l.$$

Note that $E(a_j) = \delta_j$. Asymptotic theoretical variances (if the delta method or the equivalent ML theory approach is used) are

$$\text{var}(\hat{\theta}_i) = \sum_{j=1}^{l} \left(\frac{\partial g_i}{\partial a_j} \right)^2 \frac{\delta_j(1 - \delta_j)}{Y_j}.$$

Covariances are

$$\text{cov}(\hat{\theta}_i, \hat{\theta}_n) = \sum_{j=1}^{l} \left(\frac{\partial g_i}{\partial a_j} \right) \left(\frac{\partial g_n}{\partial a_j} \right) \frac{\delta_j(1 - \delta_j)}{Y_j}.$$

In the above expressions, partial derivatives are evaluated at $E(a_j) = \delta_j$. It is clear that if $\hat{\theta}_i$ and $\hat{\theta}_n$ have no a_j terms in common, then $\text{cov}(\hat{\theta}_i, \hat{\theta}_n) = 0$. In fact, in this case, $\hat{\theta}_i$ and $\hat{\theta}_n$ are independent.

In the capture models of this monograph, the g_i take only two forms. Thus, it is convenient to define the factors

$$G_{ij} = \frac{\partial g_i}{\partial a_j} \sqrt{\frac{\delta_j(1 - \delta_j)}{Y_j}}$$

and get $\text{var}(\hat{\theta}_i) = \sum_{j=1}^{l} (G_{ij})^2$, $\text{cov}(\hat{\theta}_i, \hat{\theta}_n) = \sum_{j=1}^{l} (G_{ij}G_{nj})$. The results in Section 3.1.3 were obtained in this manner.

For the sequence of models considered here, the estimators are all of the forms

$$\hat{\phi}_{vi} = A_{vi} \left[B_{v,i+1} + (1 - B_{v,i+1})/A_{v,i+1} \right], \quad i = 1, ..., k - 1,$$

$$\hat{p}_{vi} = B_{vi} \Big/ \left[B_{vi} + (1 - B_{vi})/A_{vi} \right], \quad i = 2, ..., k - 1,$$

$$v \in \{1, ..., V, .\}.$$

Here, $A_{vi} = r_{vi}/R_{vi}$ and $B_{vi} = m_{vi}/T_{vi}$, with $v = .$, meaning $A_{.i} = r_{.i}/R_{.i}$ and $B_{.i} = m_{.i}/T_{.i}$.

More explicit notation is used here for the G-functions, for example

$$G(A_{vi} \mid \hat{\phi}_{vi}) = \left(\frac{\partial \hat{\phi}_{vi}}{\partial A_{vi}} \right) \sqrt{\frac{A_{vi}(1 - A_{vi})}{R_{vi}}}.$$

For the B_{vi}, more than one representation of G is available. These G-functions (evaluated at data values) are given in Table 3.1. To obtain $\hat{\text{var}}(\hat{p}_{vi})$, for example, one has

$$\hat{\text{var}}(\hat{p}_{vi}) = [G(A_{vi} \mid \hat{p}_{vi})]^2 + [G(B_{vi} \mid \hat{p}_{vi})]^2$$

$$= (\hat{p}_{vi} \hat{q}_{vi})^2 \left[\frac{1}{r_{vi}} - \frac{1}{R_{vi}} + \frac{1}{m_{vi}} + \frac{1}{z_{vi}} \right], \quad i = 2, ..., k - 1.$$

To obtain theoretical variances and covariances, one substitutes parameters for the estimators and expected values for statistics.

Table 3.1. – Factors for generating variance and covariance formulae for the $\hat{\phi}_{vi}$ and $\hat{p}_{vi}$.

For $\hat{\phi}_{vi}$		For $\hat{p}_{vi}$	
Variable	$G(\text{variable} \mid \hat{\phi}_{vi})$	Variable	$G(\text{variable} \mid \hat{p}_{vi})$
A_{vi}	$\hat{\phi}_{vi}\sqrt{\dfrac{1}{r_{vi}} - \dfrac{1}{R_{vi}}},$ $i = 1, ..., k-1$	A_{vi}	$\hat{p}_{vi}\hat{q}_{vi}\sqrt{\dfrac{1}{r_{vi}} - \dfrac{1}{R_{vi}}},$ $i = 2, ..., k-1$
$A_{v,i+1}$	$-\hat{\phi}_{vi}\hat{q}_{v,i+1}\sqrt{\dfrac{1}{r_{v,i+1}} - \dfrac{1}{R_{v,i+1}}},$ $i = 1, ..., k-2$	B_{vi}	$\hat{p}_{vi}\hat{q}_{vi}\sqrt{\dfrac{1}{m_{vi}} + \dfrac{1}{z_{vi}}},$ $\equiv \hat{p}_{vi}\hat{q}_{vi}\sqrt{\dfrac{T_{vi}}{m_{vi}\,z_{vi}}},$ $i = 1, ..., k-1$
$B_{v,i+1}$	$-\hat{\phi}_{vi}\hat{q}_{v,i+1}(1 - A_{v,i+1})\sqrt{\dfrac{m_{v,i+1}}{z_{v,i+1}\,T_{v,i+1}}},$ $i = 1, ..., k-2$		all other $G(. \mid \hat{p}_{vi}) = 0$
all other $G(. \mid \hat{\phi}_{vi}) = 0$			

The general formula for a variance or covariance of arbitrary parameters θ_1 and θ_2 is

$$\hat{\text{cov}}(\hat{\theta}_1, \hat{\theta}_2) = \sum_{j=1}^{l} G(\text{variable } j \mid \hat{\theta}_1)\, G(\text{variable } j \mid \hat{\theta}_2).$$

The terms in this summation are zero except for variables in common to both parameter estimators. If there are no variables in common, the covariance is zero. As an example, consider $\hat{\text{cov}}(\hat{\phi}_{vi}, \hat{p}_{vi})$. Only A_{vi} is in common here; hence,

$$\hat{\text{cov}}(\hat{\phi}_{vi}, \hat{p}_{vi}) = \phi_{vi}\hat{p}_{vi}\hat{q}_{vi}\left(\frac{1}{r_{vi}} - \frac{1}{R_{vi}}\right), \quad i = 1, ..., k-1$$

(bear in mind that $\phi_{v,k-1}$ really means $\phi_{v,k-1}\, p_{vk}$).

The final step in the process is to interpret v against the model being considered. The next section presents all point estimators and variances and covariances under all models, given the complete capture history protocol.

3.1.3. Parameter Estimators, Variances, and Covariances

We here succinctly present formulae for all estimable parameters and their associated variances and covariances, under all models, for the complete capture history protocol. Results here apply also to partial capture history protocol scheme A and (with appropriate interpretation) to scheme B and first capture history protocol data. To achieve this generality, we use an abbreviated notation and some conventions. The index for treatment v ranges over the augmented set $\{1, ..., V, .\}$. The case of $v = $ "." represents a special type of "pooling" of statistics and parameters. The chain of models considered remains H_0, $H_{1\phi}$, H_{2p}, ..., $H_{k-1,p}$, and $H_{k-1,\phi}$. The most general model is $H_{k-1,\phi}$, for which one must adopt the convention that the estimator denoted $\hat{\phi}_{v,k-1}$ really estimates the product $(\phi_{v,k-1})(p_{vk})$. Given this convention about $H_{k-1,\phi}$, the key to these simplified representations is (1) separate treatment of the two subsequences $H_{j\phi}$, $j = 1, ..., k - 1$ and H_{jp}, $j = 2, ..., k - 1$, and (2) implicit use of the pooling rule to define the MSS and the parameters that vary by group v for any model in the sequence.

3.1.3.1. Pooling rule. – Under the most general model $H_{k-1,\phi}$, the MSS may be taken as r_{vi} given R_{vi}, $i = 1, ..., k - 1$ and m_{vi} given $T_{vi} = m_{vi} + z_{vi}$, $i = 2, ..., k - 1$. For all these quantities, v ranges over $1, ..., V$. The MSS for any submodel involves some pooling of these statistics over treatment classes $v = 1, ..., V$. We use the following notation (for any arbitrary i):

$$r_{.i} = \sum_{v=1}^{V} r_{vi} ;$$

$$R_{.i} = \sum_{v=1}^{V} R_{vi} ;$$

$$m_{.i} = \sum_{v=1}^{V} m_{vi} ;$$

$$z_{.i} = \sum_{v=1}^{V} z_{vi} ;$$

$$T_{\cdot i} = m_{\cdot i} + z_{\cdot i} = \sum_{v=1}^{V} (m_{vi} + z_{vi}) = \sum_{v=1}^{V} T_{vi} \, .$$

Next we define some ratios:

$$A_{vi} = \frac{r_{vi}}{R_{vi}}, \quad i = 1, ..., k - 1 \, ,$$

$$B_{vi} = \frac{m_{vi}}{T_{vi}}, \quad i = 2, ..., k - 1 \, ,$$

with $B_{vk} = 1$ and $A_{vk} = 1$ by definition. Pooled versions of these ratios are denoted by $A_{\cdot i}$ and $B_{\cdot i}$ and are defined as

$$A_{\cdot i} = \frac{r_{\cdot i}}{R_{\cdot i}} \quad \text{and} \quad B_{\cdot i} = \frac{m_{\cdot i}}{T_{\cdot i}} \, .$$

Similar notation regarding pooling applies to parameters, but with a different meaning: ϕ_{vi} and p_{vi} denote that survival, or capture probability, differs over the treatments whereas $\phi_{\cdot i}$ and $p_{\cdot i}$ means these parameters do not differ by treatment. Thus, the notation $\phi_{\cdot i}$ is equivalent to ϕ_i and means $\phi_{1i} = \phi_{2i} = \cdots = \phi_{k-1,i} = \phi_i$. Similarly, $p_{\cdot i}$ means $p_{vi} = p_i$, for all treatments $v = 1, ..., V$.

If these conventions about the parameters are used, the models can be defined in terms of pooling. Under $H_{j\phi}$, the parameters are $\phi_{v1}, ..., \phi_{vj}, \phi_{\cdot j+1}, ..., \phi_{\cdot k-1}$ and $p_{v2}, ..., p_{vj}, p_{\cdot j+1}, ..., p_{\cdot k-1}$. Under H_{jp}, the parameters are $\phi_{v1}, ..., \phi_{v,j-1}, \phi_{\cdot j}, ..., \phi_{\cdot k-1}$ and $p_{v2}, ..., p_{vj}, p_{\cdot j+1}, ..., p_{\cdot k-1}$. Note that H_{1p} is equivalent to H_0. Table 3.2 summarizes this information about model parameters and gives formulae for the number of estimable parameters in each model.

Under the most general model $H_{k-1,\phi}$, there is no pooling of parameters or of the summary statistics. Under the other extreme of H_0, all the parameters and MSS are pooled over v. The pooling rule for the relevant statistics under the sequence of models is given in Table 3.3.

Table 3.2. – Definition of the models in terms of a pooling rule for estimable parameters; also given are formulae for the numbers of estimable parameters by model. Note that here H_0 is equivalent to H_{1p} and that $\phi_{v,k-1}$ means, by convention, the product $(\phi_{v,k-1}p_{vk})$.

Model $H_{j\phi}$, $j = 1, ..., k - 1$:

separate by treatment class	number of parameters
$\phi_{v1}, ..., \phi_{vj}$	Vj
$p_{v2}, ..., p_{vj}$	$V(j - 1)$

pooled by treatment class	
$\phi_{j+1}, ..., \phi_{k-1}$	$k - 1 - j$
$p_{j+1}, ..., p_{k-1}$	$k - 1 - j$

Total estimable parameters = $V(2j - 1) + 2(k - j - 1)$.

Model H_{jp} , $j = 1, ..., k - 1$:

separate by treatment class	number of parameters
$\phi_{v1}, ..., \phi_{v,j-1}$	$V(j - 1)$
$p_{v2}, ..., p_{vj}$	$V(j - 1)$

pooled by treatment class	
$\phi_j, ..., \phi_{k-1}$	$k - j$
$p_{j+1}, ..., p_{k-1}$	$k - j - 1$

Total estimable parameters = $2V(j - 1) + 2(k - j) - 1$.

Table 3.3. – Definition of the pooling rule for statistics used in parameter estimators, variances, and covariances under the sequence of models H_0 ($= H_{1p}$), $H_{1\phi}$ to $H_{k-1,\phi}$.

Model $H_{j\phi}$, $j = 1, ..., k - 1$:

    statistics separate by treatment class:

        r_{vi}, R_{vi} and hence A_{vi} , $i = 1, ..., j$

        m_{vi}, z_{vi} and hence B_{vi} , $i = 2, ..., j$

    statistics pooled over treatment classes:

        r_i, R_i and hence A_i , $i = j + 1, ..., k - 1$

        m_i, z_i and hence B_i , $i = j + 1, ..., k - 1$

Model H_{jp} , $j = 1, ..., k - 1$:

    statistics separate by treatment class:

        r_{vi}, R_{vi} and hence A_{vi} , $i = 1, ..., j - 1$

        m_{vi}, z_{vi} and hence B_{vi} , $i = 2, ..., j$

    statistics pooled over treatment classes:

        r_i, R_i and hence A_i , $i = j, ..., k - 1$

        m_i, z_i and hence B_i , $i = j + 1, ..., k - 1$

3.1.3.2. Parameter estimators and their variances. – For every model in the sequence H_0 ($= H_{1p}$) to $H_{k-1,\phi}$, the parameter estimators have the same form:

$$\hat{\phi}_{vi} = A_{vi}(B_{v,i+1} + (1 - B_{v,i+1})/A_{v,i+1}), \quad i = 1, ..., k - 1,$$

$$\hat{p}_{vi} = \frac{B_{vi}}{B_{vi} + (1 - B_{vi})/A_{vi}}, \quad i = 2, ..., k - 1,$$

for $v \, \varepsilon \, \{1, ..., V, .\}$. Under any model, the MLEs are obtained by applying the pooling rules and conventions for that model. One would not want to compute the previous estimators by hand. The value of this representation for the MLEs is the subsequent ease of programming them (as into program RELEASE), and also the investigation of their theoretical properties.

Sampling variances follow:

$$\hat{\text{var}}(\hat{\phi}_{vi}) = (\hat{\phi}_{vi})^2 \left[\left(\frac{1}{r_{vi}} - \frac{1}{R_{vi}} \right) + (\hat{q}_{v,i+1})^2 \left(\frac{1}{r_{v,i+1}} - \frac{1}{R_{v,i+1}} \right) \right.$$

$$\left. + (\hat{p}_{v,i+1}\hat{q}_{v,i+1}) \frac{(1 - A_{v,i+1})^2}{A_{v,i+1}T_{v,i+1}} \right], \quad i = 1, ..., k - 1, \quad v \, \varepsilon \, \{1, ..., V, .\};$$

$$\hat{\text{var}}(\hat{p}_{vi}) = (\hat{p}_{vi}\hat{q}_{vi})^2 \left[\frac{1}{r_{vi}} - \frac{1}{R_{vi}} + \frac{1}{m_{vi}} + \frac{1}{z_{vi}} \right], \quad i = 2, ..., k - 1, \quad v \, \varepsilon \, \{1, ..., V, .\}.$$

If either m_{vi} or z_{vi} is 0 with poor data, then $\hat{p}_{vi} = 0$ or 1 and $\hat{\text{var}}(\hat{p}_{vi}) = 0$.

3.1.3.3. Covariances under model $H_{j\phi}$. – The subsequence of model $H_{j\phi}$ is defined for $j = 1, ..., k - 1$. Most possible covariances are zero. The formulae for the nonzero covariances are fairly simple; however, some are not defined for all values of j. Nonetheless, we give the formulae below in only their most general terms. Their interpretation thus requires that one use the pooling rules of Tables 3.2 and 3.3, and ignore impossible covariances; in all cases $v, v' \varepsilon \{1, ..., V, .\}$.

$$\hat{\text{cov}}(\hat{\phi}_{vi}, \hat{\phi}_{v,i+1}) = -\hat{\phi}_{vi}\hat{\phi}_{v,i+1}\hat{q}_{v,i+1} \left(\frac{1}{r_{v,i+1}} - \frac{1}{R_{v,i+1}} \right), \quad i = 1, ..., k - 2.$$

For $j = 1, ..., k - 2$, the number of these covariances is $Vj + k - j - 2$; when $j = k - 1$, the number is $V(k - 2)$. Next,

$$\hat{\text{cov}}(\hat{\phi}_{vj}, \hat{\phi}_{v'j}) = \hat{\phi}_{vj}\hat{\phi}_{v'j}\,(\hat{q}_{j+1})^2 \left[\left(\frac{1}{r_{.,j+1}} - \frac{1}{R_{.,j+1}}\right) + \left(1 - \frac{r_{.,j+1}}{R_{.,j+1}}\right)^2 \frac{m_{.,j+1}}{z_{.,j+1}T_{.,j+1}}\right],$$

for $j \le k$-2 and $v \ne v'$ for $z_{j+1} > 0$. If $z_{j+1} = 0$ (but $m_{.j+1} > 0$), clearly $\hat{\text{cov}}(\hat{\phi}_{vj}, \hat{\phi}_{v'j}) = 0$. There are $V(V-1)2$ of these covariances for $j = 1, ..., k-2$ (for $j = k-1$ we have $H_{k-1,\phi}$ and these covariances are all zero).

The nonzero covariances between $\hat{\phi}$ and $\hat{p}$ are:

$$\hat{\text{cov}}(\hat{\phi}_{vi}, \hat{p}_{vi}) = \hat{\phi}_{vi}\hat{p}_{vi}\hat{q}_{vi}\left(\frac{1}{r_{vi}} - \frac{1}{R_{vi}}\right), \quad i = 2, ..., k-1.$$

There are $V(j-1) + k - j - 1$ covariances here, for $j = 1, ..., k-1$. Finally,

$$\hat{\text{cov}}(\hat{\phi}_{vi}, \hat{p}_{v,i+1}) = -\hat{\phi}_{vi}\hat{p}_{v,i+1}(\hat{q}_{v,i+1})^2 \left[\left(\frac{1}{r_{v,i+1}} - \frac{1}{R_{v,i+1}}\right)\right.$$

$$\left. + \left(1 - \frac{r_{v,i+1}}{R_{v,i+1}}\right)\left(\frac{1}{z_{v,i+1}}\right)\right], \quad i = 1, ..., k-2.$$

If $z_{v,i+1} = 0$, then $\hat{\text{cov}}(\hat{\phi}_{vi}, \hat{p}_{v,i+1}) = 0$. The number of covariances here is $Vj + k - j - 2$ for $j = 1, ..., k-2$ and $V(k-2)$ for $j = k-1$.

From the above expression, we find that the total number of nonzero covariances to be computed under model $H_{j\phi}$ is

$$3(Vj + k - j - 2) + \frac{(V-1)(V-2)}{2}, \quad \text{for } j = 1, ..., k-2,$$

and

$$3V(k-2), \quad \text{for } j = k-1.$$

3.1.3.4. Covariances under models H_{jp} and H_0. – Formulae for all nonzero covariances under model H_{jp}, $j = 2, ..., k-1$ follow. Also, the special case of model H_0, where no parameters differ by group index v, is covered by the formal model H_{1p}, i.e., H_{jp} with $j = 1$. Interpretation of these formulae requires that one use the pooling rules of Tables 3.2 and 3.3 and ignore impossible covariances. In all examples, $v, v' \varepsilon \{1, ..., V, .\}$. There are $V(j-1)+k-j-1$

of the covariances below:

$$\hat{\text{cov}}(\hat{\phi}_{vi}, \hat{\phi}_{v,i+1}) = -\hat{\phi}_{vi}\hat{\phi}_{v,i+1}\hat{q}_{v,i+1}\left[\frac{1}{r_{v,i+1}} - \frac{1}{R_{v,i+1}}\right], \quad i = 1, ..., k-2.$$

Next,

$$\hat{\text{cov}}(\hat{\phi}_{v,j-1}, \hat{\phi}_{v',j-1}) = (\hat{\phi}_{v,j-1}\hat{\phi}_{v',j-1}\hat{q}_{vj}\hat{q}_{v'j})\left[\frac{1}{r_{.j}} - \frac{1}{R_{.j}}\right], \text{ all } v \neq v'$$

(v or $v' = .$ does not occur here); for $j = 2$ to $k-1$, there are $V(V-1)2$ of the above covariances. There are no such covariances for $j = 1$.

Under H_{jp}, there are some nonzero covariances among some p:

$$\hat{\text{cov}}(\hat{p}_{vj}, \hat{p}_{v'j}) = (\hat{p}_{vj}\hat{p}_{v'j}\hat{q}_{vj}\hat{q}_{v'j})\left[\frac{1}{r_{.j}} - \frac{1}{R_{.j}}\right], \text{ all } v \neq v'$$

(but not v or v'). For $j = 2$ to $k-1$, there are $V(V-1)2$ covariances (they do not exist for $j = 1$).

Next, we have the covariances between $\hat{\phi}$ and $\hat{p}$:

$$\hat{\text{cov}}(\hat{\phi}_{vi}, \hat{p}_{vi}) = (\hat{\phi}_{vi}\hat{p}_{vi}\hat{q}_{vi})\left[\frac{1}{r_{vi}} - \frac{1}{R_{vi}}\right], \quad i = 2, ..., k-1.$$

There are $V(j-1) + k - j - 1$ covariances here for $j = 1, ..., k-1$. Finally,

$$\hat{\text{cov}}(\hat{\phi}_{vi}, \hat{p}_{v,i+1}) = -\hat{\phi}_{vi}\hat{p}_{v,i+1}(\hat{q}_{v,i+1})^2\left[\left[\frac{1}{r_{v,i+1}} - \frac{1}{R_{v,i+1}}\right]\right.$$

$$\left. + \left(1 - \frac{r_{v,i+1}}{R_{v,i+1}}\right)\left(\frac{1}{z_{v,i+1}}\right)\right], \quad i = 1, ..., k-2;$$

if $z_{v,i+1} = 0$, then $\hat{\text{cov}}(\hat{\phi}_{vi}, \hat{p}_{v,i+1}) = 0$. There are $V(j-1) + k - j - 1$ of these covariances, $j = 1, ..., k-1$.

Under H_0, a total of $3k - 2$ nonzero covariances can be computed. For H_{jp}, $j = 2, ...,$ $k - 1$, the number of covariances to be computed is $3(V(j - 1) + k - j - 1) + V(V - 1)$.

3.1.4. Goodness of Fit Tests

If (as we assume) the Jolly-Seber model holds separately for each group, then $H_{k-1,\phi}$ or some less general model will fit the data. For each group, the goodness of fit test statistic is the sum of the TEST 2 and TEST 3 statistics. The information in the subcohorts conditional on the cohorts is used in TEST 3 and that contained in the cohorts is used in TEST 2. The overall goodness of fit test statistic is the sum of these statistics for all groups. Hence, it suffices to give the theory for goodness of fit testing for just one group (no "v" index is used).

3.1.4.1. TEST 3. – TEST 3 is based on the probability distribution of the subcohorts given the cohorts. From Section 3.1.1, that distribution is the product of, in general, $k - 1$ multiple hypergeometric probability distributions:

$$\prod_{i=1}^{k-1} \frac{\prod_{h=1}^{H_i} \begin{pmatrix} R_{ih} \\ m_{i,i+1,h} \cdots m_{ikh} \ R_{ih} - r_{ih} \end{pmatrix}}{\begin{pmatrix} R_i \\ m_{i,i+1} \cdots m_{ik} \ R_i - r_i \end{pmatrix}}.$$

In the case when no new (i.e., not previously released) fish enter the study after $i = 1$, then both $H_1 = 1$ and $H_2 = 1$; hence, there are $k - 3$ distributions to consider. We consider only such studies here.

In principle, for occasion i, the corresponding hypergeometric distribution corresponds to a $(k + 1 - i) \times H_i$ contingency table. For this table, one computes a chi-square test of homogeneity, thereby testing H_0: $\pi_{ijh} = \pi_{ij}$, $j = i+1, ..., k$ for all $h = 1, ..., H_i$. However, because the data are usually too sparse to support use of the full chi-square, some pooling is needed to justify the chi-square approximation. A knowledgeable user would have no difficulty in pooling contingency table cells based on the marginals of the table. We built some fixed pooling rules into RELEASE, following essentially the same logic used by Pollock et al. (1985).

The goodness of fit test component based on all subcohorts within cohort i is labeled TEST 3.Si. It nominally has $(H_i - 1)(k - i)$ df. As actually computed, the first part of this test is based on partitioning the corresponding distribution into two (multiplicative) components:

$$\frac{\prod_{h=1}^{H_i} \binom{R_{ih}}{r_{ih}}}{\binom{R_i}{r_i}},$$

which leads to TEST 3.SRi nominally as a $2 \times H_i$ contingency table; and

$$\frac{\prod_{h=1}^{H_i} \binom{r_{ih}}{m_{i,i+1,h} \cdots m_{ikh}}}{\binom{r_i}{m_{i,i+1} \cdots m_{ik}}},$$

which leads to TEST 3.Smi nominally as a $(k - i) \times H_i$ contingency table. The bulk of the data (i.e., information for testing) ends up in the first component, i.e., TEST 3.SRi, which tests H_0: $\lambda_{ih} = \lambda_i$, $h = 1, ..., H_i$. Because most of the r_{ih} will be small (note, however, that all $R_{ih} \geq 1$), pooling over capture histories may be needed. When capture probabilities are small, one r_{ih} will dominate the others; specifically, the r_{ih} for individuals released at time 1 and not caught again until occasion i (i.e., $h = \{10 \cdots 01\}$). If that capture history is denoted here as h', the full distribution underlying TEST 3.SRi further partitions as

$$\left[\frac{\binom{R_{ih'}}{r_{ih'}} \binom{R_i - R_{ih'}}{r_i - r_{ih'}}}{\binom{R_i}{r_i}} \right] \left[\frac{\prod_{h \neq h'} \binom{R_{ih}}{r_{ih}}}{\binom{R_i - R_{ih'}}{r_i - r_{ih'}}} \right].$$

The first component corresponds to a 2×2 table representing a maximal pooling of the full TEST 3.SRi table. Program RELEASE automatically pools down to the 2×2 table and computes TEST 3.SRi from it for most data sets. This strategy is usually good. The user can always obtain the full TEST 3.Si table and compute the test based on less pooling if that is warranted.

This pooled version of TEST 3.SRi tests

$$H_0: \lambda_{ih'} = \left[\sum_{h \neq h'} R_{ih} \lambda_{ih} \right] \bigg/ \left[\sum_{h \neq h'} R_{ih} \right].$$

An advantage of a 2×2 table is that the corresponding test can be made one-sided. One might test against

$$H_A: \lambda_{ih'} < \left[\sum_{h \neq h'} R_{ih} \lambda_{ih} \right] \Big/ \left[\sum_{h \neq h'} R_{ih} \right].$$

TEST 3.*Smi*, as routinely computed by program RELEASE, is also a predetermined pooling into a 2×2 table of what is nominally a $(k - i) \times H_i$ contingency table. The null hypothesis underlying that full table is

$$H_0: \frac{\pi_{ijh}}{\lambda_{ih}} = \frac{\pi_{ij}}{\lambda_i}, j = i + 1, ..., k \text{ for all } h = 1, ..., H_i.$$

The collapsed table from which TEST 3.*Smi* is usually computed by RELEASE is derived from the hypergeometric distribution

$$\frac{\begin{pmatrix} r_{ih'} \\ m_{i,i+1,h'} \end{pmatrix} \begin{pmatrix} r_i - r_{ih'} \\ r_{ih'} - m_{i,i+1,h'} \end{pmatrix}}{\begin{pmatrix} r_i \\ r_{ih'} \end{pmatrix}}.$$

The remaining information, if any, that could bear on TEST 3.*Smi* is not used by RELEASE. The actual null hypothesis tested by TEST 3.*Smi* is

$$H_0: \frac{\pi_{i,i+1,h'}}{\lambda_{ih'}} = \left[\sum_{h \neq h'} \frac{r_{ih} \pi_{i,i+1,h}}{\lambda_{ih}} \right] \Big/ \left[\sum_{h \neq h'} r_{ih} \right].$$

3.1.4.2. TEST 2. – There is also goodness of fit information in the cohort data given the Jolly-Seber MSS. The corresponding residual distribution has no unique representation; a convenient form was derived by Robson and Youngs (unpublished report, 1971); (see also Brownie and Robson 1983). TEST 2 is based on $k - 3$ separate contingency tables (hence, $k \geq 4$ is required for TEST 2 to exist for release-recapture data). Each component test, TEST 2.*Ci*, $i = 2, ..., k - 2$, derives from the conditionally independent multiple hypergeometric distribution indexed by i in Pr{cohorts|MSS} =

$$\prod_{i=2}^{k-2} \frac{\left(m^c_{i-1,i+1} \cdots m^c_{i-1,k}\right)^{z_i} \left(m_{i,i+1} \cdots m_{ik}\right)^{r_i}}{\left(m^c_{i,i+1} \cdots m^c_{ik}\right)^{T_{i+1}}} .$$

Thus, TEST 2.Ci is computed from a $2 \times (k - i)$ contingency table. Program RELEASE pools as needed, according to the rule of requiring all expected cell values to exceed two. Pooling of the m_{ij} and m^c_{ij} starts from $j = k$ and hence proceeds backwards from the sparser data.

We use π_{ij}, where $E\left(m_{ij} \mid R_i\right) = R_i \pi_{ij}$, $j = i + 1, ..., k$, to denote the null hypothesis most easily. Then, for TEST 2.Ci, the null hypothesis before any pooling is

$$H_0: \frac{\pi_{ij}}{\sum\limits_{j=i+1}^{k} \pi_{ij}} = \frac{\sum\limits_{n=1}^{i-1} R_n \pi_{nj}}{\sum\limits_{j=i+1}^{k} \sum\limits_{n=1}^{i-1} R_n \pi_{nj}}, \quad j = i + 1, ..., k .$$

(This null hypothesis is true under the Jolly-Seber model.)

As pointed out in Robson and Youngs (unpublished report, 1971), greater power can sometimes be gained by partitioning each TEST 2.Ci, especially into a 2×2 table on $j = i + 1$ versus pooling over $j = i + 2, ..., k$. We recommend this partition of TEST 2.C.

3.1.4.3. Comment on uniqueness. – Because TEST 2 has been in use for many years, something is known about it. In particular, it has fair to good power against many likely alternatives (such as age effects or behavioral effects to capture). Less is known about the power of TEST 3; however, it seems to be low (see Pollock et al. 1985), especially if the data are sparse. Conceptually, the goodness of fit testing arising from the sum of the chi-square TEST 2 and TEST 3 results is unique. However, this goodness of fit test must be computed as the sum of many components. These components constitute a partition of the overall goodness of fit test. There is no unique way to do this partitioning. There are even alternatives to the major split that we have called TEST 2 and TEST 3 (see, for example, Pollock et al. 1985). In principle, if one knows of a specific alternative hypothesis to Jolly-Seber, a partition of the full goodness of fit test can be found to split out an optimal subcomponent test against that alternative. The situation is analogous to 1 df contrasts in analysis of variance.

3.1.4.4. Comment on optimality. – The tests we present here have some desirable properties. This is true of all of TESTs 1, 2, and 3 despite the lack of uniqueness in their partitioned computational form. These tests are "similar tests" (see Lehmann 1959). This statistical property is highly desirable; here it just means these tests have the intended α-levels (given the assumptions) regardless of the true unknown parameters. Thus, in testing, for example, $\lambda_{c1} = \lambda_{t1} = \lambda_1$ (which TEST 1.R1 does), the significance level of the test is not dependent on the unknown value of λ_1 or on any other unknown parameters if the null hypothesis is true. All these tests also have maximum power. The optimality properties of these tests, under the theoretical models used here, assures us that no better tests can be found.

3.1.5. Tests Between Models (TEST 1)

The test between H_0: no treatment effects (i.e., model H_0) and H_A: model $H_{k-1,\phi}$ is based on the probability distribution of the MSS under H_A given the MSS under H_0 when H_0 is true. That distribution, given in Section 3.1.2, can be written as the product of $2k - 3$ hypergeometric distributions:

$$\left[\frac{\prod_{v=1}^{V} \binom{R_{v1}}{r_{v1}}}{\binom{R_{.1}}{r_{.1}}} \right] \prod_{i=2}^{k-1} \left[\frac{\prod_{v=1}^{V} \binom{T_{vi}}{m_{vi}}}{\binom{T_{.i}}{m_{.i}}} \right] \left[\frac{\prod_{v=1}^{V} \binom{R_{vi}}{r_{vi}}}{\binom{R_{.i}}{r_{.i}}} \right].$$

Thus, TEST 1 is conveniently computed as the sum of $2k - 3$ independent chi-squares, each from a $2 \times V$ contingency table. This representation of TEST 1 is valid without putting any interpretation on each test component. With data from an experiment where the treatment is applied at time 1, the sequence of models we gave in Table 2.2 is reasonable to consider. Each component of TEST 1 then has a clear interpretation in this sequence of models (see Table 2.3). Note, however, that when different alternatives intermediate between models H_0 and $H_{k-1,\phi}$ are considered, these individual test components may have no interpretive value. Rather, one must then go to numerical methods for model fitting and testing (by way of likelihood ratio tests).

TEST 1.Ri, $i = 1, ..., k - 1$ is associated with the distribution

$$\frac{\prod_{v=1}^{V} \binom{R_{vi}}{r_{vi}}}{\binom{R_{.i}}{r_{.i}}}.$$

The null hypothesis tested is that model H_{ip} holds (interpret H_{1p} as simply model H_0) versus the alternative that model $H_{i\phi}$ is true. Expressed in terms of parameters, the actual test is of

$$H_0: \lambda_{vi} = \lambda_i, v = 1, ..., V.$$

With specific null and alternative hypotheses such as these, it is possible that neither hypothesis is true. What happens then is not predictable; it can easily happen that H_0 is not rejected, not because the null model holds, but rather because the alternative model is not appreciably better than the null model.

TEST 1.Ti, $i = 2, ..., k - 1$ is associated with the distribution

$$\frac{\prod_{v=1}^{V} \binom{T_{vi}}{m_{vi}}}{\binom{T_{.i}}{m_{.i}}}.$$

The null hypothesis tested is that model $H_{i-1,\phi}$ holds versus the alternative that model H_{ip} is true. Expressed in terms of parameters we actually test

$$H_0: \tau_{vi} = \tau_i, v = 1, ..., V.$$

The powers of these tests can be found, given that one knows the R_{vi} or the T_{vi} and the hypothesized parameters λ_{vi} and τ_{vi}. In practice, the R_{vi}, for $i > 1$, and T_{vi} are not known before a study. (Chapter 3.6 defines a way to handle this situation.) To compute asymptotic power, one first needs the noncentrality parameter, and then either a table of the noncentral chi-square distribution (see Owen 1962) or a way to compute that distribution (PC-SAS and SAS version 5 have the noncentral chi-square distribution as a built-in function; SAS programs are produced by SAS, Incorporated, Cary, North Carolina). For example, the noncentrality parameter for TEST 1.Ri (summations on n are over $n = 1, ..., V$) is

$$\sum_{v=1}^{V} \frac{\left(R_{.i}\right)^2 \left[R_{vi}\lambda_{vi} - R_{vi} \frac{\left(\sum R_{ni}\lambda_{ni}\right)}{R_{.i}}\right]^2}{R_{vi}\left(\sum R_{ni}\lambda_{ni}\right)\left(\sum R_{ni}(1 - \lambda_{ni})\right)}.$$

The point here is that the power of these tests can be studied analytically; Monte Carlo methods are not required to get information on power, especially at a level of resolution useful for study design (e.g., it suffices to know if power will be large, such as >0.9, versus small, such as <0.5). For study design in fisheries-turbine experiments, the first test that should be examined is TEST 1.$R1$. Computing the power of that test under model $H_{1\phi}$ will give useful guidance on sample size (similar to results obtained by looking at $\mathrm{se}(\hat{S})$ under model $H_{1\phi}$). In the case of only a treatment and control group, any of these tests can be used as one-sided tests, and, correspondingly, one-sided powers can be computed.

3.2. Modifications for Other Protocols

3.2.1. Scheme A, Partial Capture Histories

Essentially no modifications are needed to apply all the theory from the complete capture history protocol to scheme A. Scheme A entails initial batch marks. Upon recapture after first release, a second distinguishing mark is applied which is unique to capture site or time. Thus, the second recaptures (i.e., recaptures after second release) can be distinguished and removed from the study. Under scheme A, most potential capture histories do not exist. However, there are releases R_i at every site, $i = 1, ..., k - 1$. Also, for every R_i, there are recaptures, m_{ij}, at all $j = i + 1, ..., k$. Thus, m-array data exist that are identical in structure to the m-arrays under the complete capture history protocol. The first two cohorts are, in fact, identical to the data under complete capture histories. The recapture counts for cohorts 3, ..., $k - 1$ are slightly smaller than under the complete capture history protocol because releases at occasions $i = 3, ..., k$ all have a single capture history, for example:

Occasion i	h
3	{101}
4	{1001}
5	{10001}

Consequently, all releases R_i at occasion i are from recaptures m_{1i} of fish initially released at occasion 1.

Under the Jolly-Seber assumptions of occasion-specific parameters ($\phi_1, ..., \phi_{k-1}, p_2, ..., p_k$), all the theory for TESTS 1 and 2 applies unchanged. All models in the sequence $H_0, H_{1\phi}, ..., H_{k-1,\phi}$ can be used. Estimation formulae are unchanged. The only modification is that TEST 3 cannot be computed (if new animals were being introduced into the study at each release occasion as per Jolly-Seber capture-recapture, then TEST 3 could be computed).

3.2.2. Scheme B, Partial Capture Histories

Only cohorts 1 and 2 exist under scheme B; however, recaptures exist for all occasions $i = 2, ..., k$. Thus, the m-array is simply

$$\{1\} \quad R_1 \qquad m_{12}, m_{13}, ..., m_{1k}$$

$$\{11\} \quad R_2 \ m_{23}, ..., m_{2k}$$

TEST 3 cannot be computed under scheme B. TEST 2 reduces to the single component TEST 2.$C2$. A modified form of TEST 1 can be computed.

There are k estimable parameters, including ϕ_1 and p_2, whereas $\phi_2, ..., \phi_{k-1}, p_3, ..., p_k$ are not separately estimable. It is convenient to take the estimable parameters as $\phi_1, p_2, \lambda_2, \tau_3, ..., \tau_{k-1}$. These are equivalent to $\lambda_1, \lambda_2, \tau_2, \tau_3, ..., \tau_{k-1}$, which is in contrast to the complete capture history or scheme A protocol where one can also estimate $\lambda_3, ..., \lambda_{k-1}$ from r_i / R_i, $i = 3, ...,$ $k - 1$. An MSS is

$$r_1 \mid R_1 \sim \text{bin}(R_1, \lambda_1)$$

$$r_2 \mid R_2 \sim \text{bin}(R_2, \lambda_2)$$

$$m_2 \mid T_2 \sim \text{bin}(T_2, \tau_2)$$

$$m_i \mid T_i \sim \text{bin}(T_i, \tau_i), \quad i = 3, ..., k - 1.$$

The first three components are exactly what one gets by pooling all recaptures, within each cohort, for occasions $j = 3, ..., k$. Thus, if one takes the data as

$$
\begin{array}{llll}
R_1 & m_{12} & z_2 \\
R_2 & & r_2
\end{array}
$$

and sets $k = 3$, all the theory for the complete capture history with $k = 3$ applies. This collapsed representation of the data allows one to get point estimates, variances, tests, etc. on ϕ_1, p_2, and $\phi_2 p_3 = \lambda_2$. (It is not necessary to do this collapsing; it is done here only for its heuristic value in understanding the theory.)

With multiple data sets, one can use models H_0, $H_{1\phi}$, and H_{2p}. The more general models are not useful because the corresponding ϕ_i and p_i are not estimable. If model $H_{2\phi}$ is the true case, the ratio $S_2 = \phi_{t2}/\phi_{c2} = \lambda_{t2}/\lambda_{c2}$ is estimable. However, a complete series of tests does not exist to support strongly the choice of $H_{2\phi}$.

All of the TEST 1.$R3$, ..., 1.$Rk - 1$ components drop out of TEST 1. The remaining components are computed exactly as under the complete capture history protocol. The statistics $m_3, ..., m_{k-1}$ and $T_3, ..., T_{k-1}$ have exactly the same meaning here as under the complete capture history protocol. The exact null hypothesis for TEST 1 components is

TEST	H_0
1.R1	$\lambda_{v1} = \lambda_1, v = 1, ..., V$
1.R2	$\lambda_{v2} = \lambda_2, v = 1, ..., V$
1.Ti	$\tau_{vi} = \tau_i, v = 1, ..., V, i = 3, ..., k - 1$

This hypothesis is the same as for these test components under complete capture histories. The problems that arise here are a result of the absence of the components for TEST $1.Ri, i = 3, ..., k - 1$. Thus, under scheme B, certain deviations from the null hypothesis of TEST 1 cannot be detected. This inability to detect some deviations from the null hypothesis relates to the nonidentifiability of parameters. In principle, one could construct some sets of these parameters (for one or more groups, v), which do not fit Jolly-Seber or which have treatment effects beyond model H_{2p}; yet one cannot detect these cases by testing.

If one views these components of TEST 1 as corresponding to a nested sequence of models, then the alternative to TEST 1.T3 is 1.T.4, not 1.R.3 as under complete capture histories. For 1.T4 the alternative is 1.T.5 and so forth. Hence, one cannot distinguish models H_{ip} from $H_{i\phi}$. For example, if TEST 1.T3 rejected model H_{3p} and all of TESTS 1.T4 to 1.Tk - 1 did not reject (and goodness of fit was acceptable), one still would not know if the "correct" model was $H_{3\phi}$ or H_{4p} (the matter is then, of course, somewhat academic, as one cannot estimate ϕ_{v3}).

3.2.3. First Capture Histories

The MSS for a single data set is

$$r_1 \mid R_1 \sim \text{bin} (R_1, \lambda_1)$$

$$m_j \mid T_j \sim \text{bin} (T_j, \tau_j), j = 2, ..., k - 1.$$

The above MSS is a subset of the MSS under scheme B, which is itself a subset of the MSS under complete capture histories. The meanings of the m_i and T_i are the same; their exact definitions change as compared with complete capture history: $m_j = m_{1j}, j = 2, ..., k - 1$ and $T_j = m_{1j} + \cdots + m_{1k}$. There is insufficient information to unravel any separate ϕ or p parameters (none of them are estimable). Under $H_{1\phi}$, $S = (\phi_{t1}/\phi_{c1}) = (\lambda_{t1}/\lambda_{c1})$ is estimable. The variance of $\hat{S}$ is the same under model $H_{1\phi}$ for first capture histories as under any of scheme A, B, or complete capture history protocols when $H_{1\phi}$ is true.

No components of TESTs 2 or 3 can be computed. For TEST 1, components 1.R1 and 1.Ti, $i = 2, ..., k - 1$ exist. TEST 1.R1 tests the null hypothesis that $\lambda_{v1} = \lambda_1$ for all $v = 1, ..., V$. TEST 1.Ti tests the null hypothesis that $\tau_{vi} = \tau_i$ for all $v = 1, ..., V$. As under scheme B, these tests cannot detect certain alternatives because of the nonidentifiability of the individual parameters. Under the first capture history protocol, one hopes that model $H_{1\phi}$ holds, in which case TEST 1.R1 should reject H_0 and all of TESTS 1.T2, ..., 1.Tk - 1 should not reject. In a general sense the sum of the test statistics for these 1.Ti series is a goodness of fit test to the overall model $H_{1\phi}$.

The identifiability problem is eliminated when the capture probabilities are not affected by the treatment; then $p_{1i} = p_{2i} = ... = p_{vi}$ for all $i = 1, ..., k$. The sequence of models under the first (or unknown) capture history protocol then simplifies to $H_{1\phi}, H'_{2\phi}, ..., H'_{k-1,\phi}$. The parameters of model $H'_{i\phi}$, for $i = 2$ to $k - 1$, are

$$\phi_{v1}, ..., \phi_{vi}, \quad v = 1, ..., V,$$

$$\phi_{i+1}, ..., \phi_{k-1},$$

and

$$p_2, ..., p_k .$$

Given this restrictive *assumption* about the capture probabilities, the sum of the chi-squares of TEST 1.Ti through TEST 1.Tk - 1 provides a test of the null hypothesis that $\phi_{vj} = \phi_j$ for $v = 1, ..., V$ and $j = i, ..., k - 1$.

3.2.4. Some Extensions

3.2.4.1. Relationship to temporal banding studies. – The theory for the first capture history protocol can be directly applied to certain types of experiments based on banded birds. In particular, the sequence of models described as $H_{1\phi}, H'_{2\phi}, H'_{3\phi}, ..., H'_{k-1,\phi}$ are applicable. Brownie et al. (1985) gave extensive background on the analysis of banding data. There are very close links and similarities between band recovery and recapture theory. Both methods are studying survival processes. It is mainly the resampling process that differs between the two types of studies. This difference translates into a different parameterization for expected values of the m_{vij}, which are either recaptures or band recoveries.

Let a banding experiment involve preseason release of treatment and control groups ($V = 2$). Treatment might be forced ingestion of lead pellets (see, for example, Deuel 1985). Then m_{vij} are the band recoveries in year j after banding. There are recoveries in year 1 (direct recoveries), as well as in years $j = 2, ..., k$. The model structure, the $E(m_{vij})/R_{v1}$, for treatment and controls is

| | Proportion of bands recovered in year j | | | | |
Banded	1	2	3	$\cdots$	k
R_{t1}	f_{t1}	$\phi_{t1}f_{t2}$	$\phi_{t1}\phi_{t2}f_{t3}$	$\cdots$	$\phi_{t1}\cdots\phi_{t,k-1}f_{tk}$
R_{c1}	f_{c1}	$\phi_{c1}f_{c2}$	$\phi_{c1}\phi_{c2}f_{c3}$	$\cdots$	$\phi_{c1}\cdots\phi_{c,k-1}f_{ck}$

The f_{vj} is a recovery rate; ϕ_{vj} is survival rate from year j to $j + 1$.

Treatment might affect the direct recovery rates f_{v1}. This can be tested with a 2×2 table:

$$
\boxed{\begin{array}{ll} m_{t1} & R_{t1} - m_{t1} \\ m_{c1} & R_{c1} - m_{c1} \end{array}}
$$

Then, dropping the first year (direct) recoveries, one has data analogous to recapture data under the first capture history protocol. In particular, assuming no treatment effect on recovery rates for $j < 1$ (hence, $f_{vj} = f_j$) and an acute effect, so ϕ_{t1} and ϕ_{c1} differ, but $\phi_{tj} = \phi_{cj} = \phi_j$ for $j > 2$, gives exactly the general structure of model $H_{1\phi}$ for first capture history recapture data. In particular, we can then define the treatment effect as $S = \phi_{t1}/\phi_{c1}$ and we have

$$
\frac{E(m_{tj})}{R_{t1}} = S \, \frac{E(m_{cj})}{R_{c1}} \, , \quad j = 2, ..., k \, .
$$

The m_{vj} are multinomial random variables and the two released groups (cohorts) are independent. Therefore, all the theory for the first capture history model $H_{1\phi}$ is directly applicable. Moreover, that theory extends to goodness of fit testing and exploring the sequence of models $H_{1\phi}, H'_{2\phi}, ..., H'_{k-1,\phi}$.

In banding studies, long time periods are involved; recoveries accrue over years and may be obtained from a spatially unrestricted area. In fisheries studies regarding the effect of a turbine or bypass, the temporal component is limited, and recaptures accrue at known spatial points. However, in both cases we are dealing with resampling cohorts of marked animals exposed to a survival process with possibly a treatment structure imposed on the released cohorts. A common general statistical theory underlies such release-resampling studies of survival processes.

3.2.4.2. Deeper insights. – A unified theory can be given for capture-recapture, release-resampling, bird-banding, and some related types of studies. Such a theory is given by Burnham (unpublished report, 1987); we give here a central feature of this unification (see also Brownie et al. 1985).

Let R marked animals be released as a cohort, at time 1, and then resampled at or after specific subsequent times. The resample counts are m_2, m_3, ..., m_k. We require only that the animals survive until time j, $j = 2$, ..., k, to be counted. Then, for some time interval at, or after, j and before $j + 1$, a sampling process occurs to make counts of survivors at time j. Let β_j = the probability of surviving from time j to $j + 1$, given the animal is alive at time j. Let α_j = the probability of being sampled (counted) in the jth sampling interval given the animal was alive at time j. Then the general model structure is

$$E(m_j) = \begin{cases} R\alpha_1, & j = 1 \\ R\beta_1 \cdots \beta_{j-1}\alpha_j, & j > 1 \end{cases}.$$

This is also the structure of banding data (with $\alpha_j = f_j$ and $\beta_j = \phi_j$). Band recoveries may occur continuously during a large part of time interval j to $j + 1$.

The model structure for release-recapture with $k + 1$ occasions is

$$E(m_j) = \begin{cases} R(\phi_1 p_2), & j = 2 \\ R(\phi_1 q_2) \cdots (\phi_{j-2}q_{j-1})(\phi_{j-1}p_j), & j > 2 \end{cases}.$$

A standardized structure occurs if we define

$$\alpha_{j-1} = \phi_{j-1}p_j, \quad j = 2, ..., k + 1, \text{ and}$$

$$\beta_{j-1} = \phi_{j-1}q_j, \quad j = 2, ..., k + 1.$$

With this definition, we have also shifted the indexing so that now we can write

$$E(m_{j+1}) = \begin{cases} R\alpha_1, & j = 1 \\ R\beta_1 \cdots \beta_{j-1}\alpha_j, & j = 2, ..., k \end{cases}.$$

Thus, with a shift of indexing, the standardized model structure is the same for banding data as release-recapture data. Moreover, in either case, the cohorts are multinomial data. Consequently, all underlying theory based on the standardized parameters and indexing is identical for capture-recapture and banding data under the assumptions of time-specific parameters. More general assumptions about parameters are possible and the equivalance of the two processes still holds.

For capture-recapture, β_j is survival in the released cohort; ϕ_{j-1} represents physical survival, and q_j represents not being captured. Once an animal is captured, it is removed from that cohort (of its last release) at risk of capture. Conversely, $\phi_{j-1}p_j$ represents a sampling rate conditional on being alive in the release cohort at time $j - 1$. Typically in capture-recapture, the resampling occurs at the end of the period $j - 1$ to j, rather than spread out over the interval, as in band recovery.

As far as abstract statistical theory is concerned, the only difference between capture-recapture, as regards survival estimation, and bird-banding is the interpretation of the standardized parameter presentations:

Standardized parameter	Banding	Capture-recapture
cohort sampling rate	$\alpha_j = f_j$	$\alpha_{j-1} = \phi_{j-1}p_j$
cohort survival rate	$\beta_{j-1} = \phi_j$	$\beta_{j-1} = \phi_{j-1}q_j$
	$j = 1, ..., k$	$j = 2, ..., k + 1$

(the range k is arbitrary, so shifting the indexing is trivial).

One can take capture-recapture data, as an m-array, analyze it with program ESTIMATE, and get Jolly-Seber MLEs as, for example,

$$\hat{\phi}_1 = \hat{\alpha}_1 + \hat{\beta}_1$$

(in Brownie et al. 1985 and ESTIMATE, the notation used is $\hat{f}_1$ for $\hat{\alpha}_1$ and $\hat{S}_1$ for $\hat{\beta}_1$).

3.3. Variances and Covariances of $\hat{S}$

3.3.1. Some Variance Formulae

If a general treatment effect is defined as

$$\hat{S}_i(v, v') = \frac{\hat{\phi}_{vi}}{\hat{\phi}_{v'i}}, i = 1, ..., k - 2, v \neq v',$$

the theoretical asymptotic variance of $\hat{S}_i$ is

$$\text{var}(\hat{S}_i) = (S_i)^2 \left\{ [\text{cv}(\hat{\phi}_{vi})]^2 + [\text{cv}(\hat{\phi}_{v'i})]^2 - 2\frac{\text{cov}(\hat{\phi}_{vi}, \hat{\phi}_{v'i})}{\phi_{vi}\,\phi_{v'i}} \right\}.$$

Of special interest to us is the case of models $H_{1\phi}$, H_{2p}, and $H_{2\phi}$ for complete capture histories or partial capture history scheme A (the formula below can also apply for partial capture history scheme B). For simplicity, we use t and c rather than v and v' and give $\text{cv}(\hat{S})$ rather than $\text{var}(\hat{S})$. Under model $H_{1\phi}$:

$$[\text{cv}_1(\hat{S})]^2 = \frac{1}{E(r_{t1})} - \frac{1}{R_{t1}} + \frac{1}{E(r_{c1})} - \frac{1}{R_{c1}}.$$

Under model H_{2p}:

$$[\text{cv}_2(\hat{S})]^2 = [\text{cv}_1(\hat{S})]^2 + (p_{t2} - p_{c2})^2 \left[\frac{1}{E(r_{.2})} - \frac{1}{E(R_{.2})} \right]$$

$$+ \frac{(1 - \lambda_2)^2}{\lambda_2} \left[\frac{p_{t2}\,q_{t2}}{E(T_{t2})} + \frac{p_{c2}\,q_{c2}}{E(T_{c2})} \right].$$

Under model $H_{2\phi}$:

$$[\text{cv}_3(\hat{S})]^2 = [\text{cv}_1(\hat{S})]^2 + \sum_{v=c}^{t} \left[\frac{p_{v2}q_{v2}\,(1 - \lambda_{v2})^2}{\lambda_{v2}\,E(T_{v2})} \right]$$

$$+ \sum_{v=c}^{t} (q_{v2})^2 \left[\frac{1}{E(r_{v2})} - \frac{1}{E(R_{v2})} \right].$$

An interesting way to use these specific results is to look at efficiency. Say, for example, that model $H_{1\phi}$ is true but either H_{2p} or $H_{2\phi}$ is considered to gain greater robustness (after all, it is not known that $H_{1\phi}$ is true with real data). Evaluation of these coefficients of variation when $H_{1\phi}$ is true yields $[\text{cv}_1(\hat{S})]^2$ as above, but for models H_{2p} and $H_{2\phi}$ (cv_2 and cv_3, respectively):

$$[cv_2(\hat{S})]^2 = [cv_1(\hat{S})]^2 + \frac{(1-\lambda_2)^2 p_2 q_2}{\lambda_2} \left[\frac{1}{E(r_{t1})} + \frac{1}{E(r_{c1})} \right],$$

$$[cv_3(\hat{S})]^2 = [cv_2(\hat{S})]^2 + (q_2)^2 \left[\frac{1}{E(r_{t2})} - \frac{1}{E(R_{t2})} + \frac{1}{E(r_{c2})} - \frac{1}{E(R_{c2})} \right].$$

From these formulae it becomes clear that the efficiency (regarding $\hat{S}$) when model H_{2p} rather than $H_{1\phi}$ is used (if $H_{1\phi}$ is true) is high, 80 to 90%. However, there is a large loss of efficiency in going to model $H_{2\phi}$; that efficiency, relative to model $H_{1\phi}$, is about 20 to 30%.

3.3.2. Covariances

In this section we index treatments as v, $v1$, $v2$, etc., and thus,

$$S_i(v, v1) = \frac{\phi_{vi}}{\phi_{v1i}}.$$

Of special interest to us are covariances under model $H_{1\phi}$ ($V > 2$) wherein

$$\hat{S}_1(v, v1) = \frac{r_{v,1} / R_{v,1}}{r_{v1,1} / R_{v1,1}};$$

$$\hat{S}_1(v2, v3) = \frac{r_{v2,1} / R_{v2,1}}{r_{v3,1} / R_{v3,1}}.$$

If it is assumed that all v, $v1$, $v2$, and $v3$ are distinct treatments, then $\text{cov}[\hat{S}_1(v, v1), \hat{S}_1(v2, v3)] = 0$. The only nontrivial cases are when the two different $\hat{S}_1$ depend on only three treatment levels, i.e., v, $v1$, and $v2$. If v is made the treatment index in common, e.g., $\hat{S}_1(v, v1)$ and $\hat{S}_1(v, v2)$, only two different formulae arise. In case 1, v is in either both denominators or both numerators and the covariance is

$$\text{cov}[\hat{S}_1(v, v1), \hat{S}_1(v, v2)] = S_a S_b \left[\frac{1}{E(r_{v,1})} - \frac{1}{R_{v,1}} \right];$$

where S_a and S_b represent the two different treatment effects. In case 2, v is in the numerator of one S_a and the denominator of the other S_b and the covariance is

$$\text{cov}[\hat{S}_1(v, v1), \hat{S}(v2, v)] = -S_a S_b \left[\frac{1}{E(r_{v,1})} - \frac{1}{R_{v,1}} \right].$$

In the completely general case,

$$\text{cov}[\hat{S}_i(v, v1), \hat{S}_j(v2, v3)] = (S_i S_j) \left[\frac{\text{cov}(\hat{\phi}_{vi}, \hat{\phi}_{v2j})}{\phi_{vi}\phi_{v2j}} - \frac{\text{cov}(\hat{\phi}_{vi}, \hat{\phi}_{v3j})}{\phi_{vi}\phi_{v3j}} \right.$$

$$\left. - \frac{\text{cov}(\hat{\phi}_{v1i}, \hat{\phi}_{v2j})}{\phi_{v1i}\phi_{v2j}} + \frac{\text{cov}(\hat{\phi}_{v1i}, \hat{\phi}_{v3j})}{\phi_{v1i}\phi_{v3j}} \right].$$

This covariance formula is needed to get variances of products. For example, one might have the product $\hat{S}_1\hat{S}_2$ as the estimate of the treatment effect, where

$$\hat{S}_1 = \hat{\phi}_{t1}/\hat{\phi}_{c1} ; \quad \hat{S}_2 = \hat{\phi}_{t2}/\hat{\phi}_{c2} .$$

Then

$$\text{var}(\hat{S}_1\hat{S}_2) = (S_1 S_2)^2 \left\{ [\text{cv}(\hat{S}_1)]^2 + [\text{cv}(\hat{S}_2)]^2 + 2 \frac{\text{cov}(\hat{S}_1, \hat{S}_2)}{S_1 S_2} \right\}.$$

This asymptotic variance formula can be extended to general products. However, such approximate variance (and covariance) formulae, and the assumption of approximate normality, are usually poor when applied to extended products such as $\hat{S} = \hat{S}_1 \cdots \hat{S}_j = (\hat{\phi}_{t1} \cdots \hat{\phi}_{tj})/(\hat{\phi}_{c1} \cdots \hat{\phi}_{cj})$. A superior procedure is to make inferences based on the log-transformation, $\ln(\hat{S})$. Section 3.5.1 gives general variance and covariance formulae related to $\ln(\hat{S})$.

3.4. Adjustments for Statistical Bias

Parameter estimators have some statistical bias even when the model used as a basis for analysis is true (Gilbert 1973). The survival rate estimator $\hat{\phi}$ is easily adjusted to be unbiased (assuming the model is true). The estimators of p and S can also be easily modified to reduce statistical bias.

There is an option in program RELEASE to print these bias-adjusted estimators. We do not dwell on statistical bias or its adjustment, however, because statistical bias is a trivial source of bias. The serious source of bias is "model" bias. By model biases, we mean biases which occur because the incorrect model is used. Statistical biases are smaller than one standard error of the parameter estimator; however, model biases can be large and thus serious if the wrong model is used. Our emphasis on model selection and tests of assumptions is designed to minimize model bias. Other significant bias sources are failures of assumptions resulting from tag loss, errors in data recording, and errors in knowing the exact numbers of animals released.

3.4.1. Survival Rate Estimators, $\hat{\phi}$

In all models, $\hat{\phi}$ is of the form

$$\hat{\phi}_{vi} = A_{vi}\left[B_{v,i+1} + (1 - B_{v,i+1})/A_{v,i+1}\right], \quad i = 1, ..., k - 1,$$

where

$$A_{vi} = r_{vi}/R_{vi} \text{ and } B_{vi} = m_{vi}/T_{vi}, \text{ and } v \, \varepsilon \, \{1, ..., V, . \}.$$

The bias-adjusted estimator of ϕ_{vi} is

$$\tilde{\phi}_{vi} = A_{vi}\left[B_{v,i+1} + (1 - B_{v,i+1})\middle/\left(\frac{r_{v,i+1} + 1}{R_{v,i+1} + 1}\right)\right].$$

The large sample variance of $\tilde{\phi}_{vi}$ is the same as $\hat{\phi}_{vi}$ (the MLE). The expected value of $\tilde{\phi}_{vi}$ is exactly (assuming the correct model)

$$E(\tilde{\phi}_{vi}) = \phi_{vi}\left[1 - q_{v,i+1}(1 - \lambda_{v,i+1})^{R_{v,i+1} + 1}\right].$$

Usually $\lambda_{v,i+1}$ and $R_{v,i+1}$ are jointly large enough to ensure that the bias in $\tilde{\phi}_{vi}$ is virtually zero (e.g., $\lambda_{v,i+1} \geq 0.05$ and $R_{v,i+1} \geq 99$ suffices).

3.4.2. Capture Probability Estimators, $\hat{p}$

The MLE of p_{vi} is always of the form

$$\hat{p}_{vi} = \frac{B_i}{B_i + (1 - B_i)/A_i}, \, i = 2, ..., k - 1.$$

The method that works to adjust the $\hat{\phi}_{vi}$ does not work for $\hat{p}_{vi}$.

Consider

$$\frac{1}{\hat{p}_{vi}} = 1 + \frac{1}{A_i}\left(\frac{1}{B_i} - 1\right).$$

Because A_i and B_i are independent, a good bias adjustment for $\dfrac{1}{\hat{p}_{vi}}$ is

$$\frac{1}{\tilde{p}_{vi}} = 1 + \left(\frac{R_{vi} + 1}{r_{vi} + 1}\right)\left(\frac{T_{vi} + 1}{m_{vi} + 1} - 1\right),$$

$$E\left(\frac{1}{\tilde{p}_{vi}}\right) = 1 + \frac{1}{\lambda_{vi}}\left[1 - (1 - \lambda_{vi})^{R_{vi} + 1}\right]\frac{1}{\tau_{vi}}\left\{\left[1 - (1 - \tau_{vi})^{T_{vi} + 1}\right] - 1\right\}.$$

Most situations will justify the following as a good approximation

$$E\left(\frac{1}{\tilde{p}_{vi}}\right) \doteq 1 + \frac{1}{\lambda_{vi}}\left(\frac{1}{\tau_{vi}} - 1\right) = \frac{1}{p_{vi}}.$$

A Taylor's series expansion now leads to

$$E(\tilde{p}_i) \doteq p_{vi}\left[1 + (cv(\tilde{p}_i))^2\right].$$

Thus, to a first order of approximation

$$E(\tilde{p}_{vi}) \doteq p_{vi} [1 + (cv(\hat{p}_i))^2],$$

and a bias-adjusted estimator of p_{vi} is

$$\overset{\approx}{p}_{vi} = \frac{\tilde{p}_{vi}}{1 + [cv(\hat{p}_i)]^2}.$$

3.4.3. Treatment Effect Estimators, $\hat{S}$

The general form of $\hat{S}_i$ is

$$\hat{S}_i = \frac{\hat{\phi}_{ti}}{\hat{\phi}_{ci}}, \quad i = 1, ..., k-2.$$

Here, t and c can be interpreted as any v, v'. One might consider using $\overset{\sim}{\phi}_{ti} / \overset{\sim}{\phi}_{ci}$ as a bias-adjusted estimator of S_i; however, this does not work. For example, under model $H_{1\phi}$, the complete capture history case, we have

$$\hat{S}_1 = \frac{r_{t1} / R_{t1}}{r_{c1} / R_{c1}} = \frac{\hat{\phi}_{t1}}{\hat{\phi}_{c1}} \equiv \frac{\overset{\sim}{\phi}_{t1}}{\overset{\sim}{\phi}_{c1}};$$

hence, bias-correcting the $\hat{\phi}_{v1}$ need have no effect on the bias of $\hat{S}_1$.

In the previous example, a bias-adjusted $\hat{S}_1 \equiv \hat{S}$ is

$$\tilde{S} = \frac{r_{t1}}{R_{t1}} / \frac{r_{c1} + 1}{R_{c1} + 1}.$$

For estimators of S under model $H_{1\phi}$, $\tilde{S}$ above is the appropriate bias-adjusted estimator.

For a completely general adjustment, we use a Taylor's series expansion to get the first order approximation

$$E(\hat{S}_i) \doteq S_i \left\{ 1 + [cv(\hat{\phi}_{ci})]^2 - S_i \frac{cov(\hat{\phi}_{ti}, \hat{\phi}_{ci})}{\hat{\phi}_{ti} \hat{\phi}_{ci}} \right\}.$$

Consequently, a generally valid bias-adjusted estimator of S_i is

$$\tilde{S}_i = \frac{\hat{S}_i}{1 + [\mathrm{cv}(\hat{\phi}_{ci})]^2 - \hat{S}_i \dfrac{\hat{\mathrm{cov}}(\hat{\phi}_{ti}, \hat{\phi}_{ci})}{\hat{\phi}_{ti} \hat{\phi}_{ci}}} .$$

3.5. Transformations of $\hat{S}$, $\hat{\phi}$, and $\hat{p}$

Asymptotically, MLEs such as $\hat{\phi}$, $\hat{S}$, and $\hat{p}$ are normally distributed. However, if the coefficients of variation of these parameter estimators are too large, the normal approximation is poor, especially for $\hat{S}$ and $\hat{\phi}$. Hypothesis testing and confidence intervals can be improved by using transformations that better approximate normality. Recommended transformations are the log-transform for $\hat{\phi}$ and $\hat{S}$ and the logistic (log-odds) transform for $\hat{p}$. These transformations are not routinely necessary; they make little difference if the cv of the parameter estimator in question is sufficiently small, say cv ≤ 0.1 .

3.5.1. Log-Transform for $\hat{\phi}$ and $\hat{S}$

The MLEs of ϕ and S invariably have variance formulae expressible as

$$\mathrm{var}(\hat{\phi}) = (\phi)^2 [\mathrm{cv}(\hat{\phi})]^2 ,$$

or

$$\mathrm{var}(\hat{S}) = (S)^2 [\mathrm{cv}(\hat{S})]^2 ,$$

where the corresponding coefficients of variation are relatively stable as $\hat{\phi}$ or $\hat{S}$ varies. In contrast, there is a high correlation between $\hat{\phi}$ and $\hat{\mathrm{var}}(\hat{\phi})$. The natural log-transformation greatly reduces this correlation. Asymptotically,

$$\hat{\mathrm{var}}[\ln(\hat{\phi})] = [\mathrm{cv}(\hat{\phi})]^2 ;$$

$$\hat{\mathrm{var}}[\ln(\hat{S})] = [\mathrm{cv}(\hat{S})]^2 .$$

Experience based in part on simulation results has shown that the distributions of $\ln(\hat{\phi})$ and $\ln(\hat{S})$ are more nearly normal, especially when the cv of $\hat{\phi}$ or $\hat{S}$ is large. As a useful rule of thumb, we suggest that cv is small at $\leq 10\%$, moderate near 20%, and large at $\geq 40\%$. The normal approximation for the distributions of $\hat{\phi}$ or $\hat{S}$ is poor when a cv of $\hat{\phi}$ or $\hat{S}$ is large. In fact, if a cv is large, the asymptotic variance formula itself is not good. However, if some random variable x is really log-normal, the exact variance of $\ln(x)$ is

$$\text{var}[\ln(x)] = \ln(1 + [\text{cv}(x)]^2).$$

Consequently, if the cv of some survival or treatment effect parameter estimator is not small, we recommend computing tests and confidence intervals based on the log-transform with

$$\hat{\text{var}}[\ln(\hat{\phi})] = \ln(1 + [\text{cv}(\hat{\phi})]^2), \text{ and}$$

$$\hat{\text{var}}[\ln(\hat{S})] = \ln(1 + [\text{cv}(\hat{S})]^2).$$

Manly (1984) gave a confidence interval procedure for ϕ that is specific to the Jolly-Seber model. The above method based on $\ln(\phi)$ is much simpler than Manly's method, yet performs almost as well (unpublished investigations of the authors).

Hypothesis tests of the type H_0: $\phi_{t1} = \phi_{c1}$ based on $\hat{\phi}_{t1} - \hat{\phi}_{c1}$ are less sensitive to the need for a transform. However, if one wants to test the equivalent hypothesis H_0: $S = 1$ based on $\hat{S}$, we recommend the log-transformation unless the $\text{cv}(\hat{S})$ is small. The corresponding log-based confidence intervals are also recommended. For example, for an approximate $(1 - \alpha)100\%$ CI, one computes lower and upper bounds, $\hat{S}_L$ and $\hat{S}_U$, as

$$\hat{S}_L = \hat{S}/C$$

and

$$\hat{S}_U = \hat{S}C,$$

where

$$C = \exp\left(z_{\alpha/2}\sqrt{\ln(1 + [\text{cv}(\hat{S})]^2)}\right).$$

This approach still does not solve the problem of $\hat{S}_U$ being possibly greater than one, but that problem cannot be solved until one constrains $\hat{S} \leq 1$. Moreover, in many experiments there will be no logical reason to constrain S either ≤ 1 or ≥ 1; thus, we have not pursued such a constraint here.

Asymptotic covariances are also simple for log-transformed $\hat{\phi}$ and $\hat{S}$:

$$\text{cov}[\ln(\hat{\phi}_t), \ln(\hat{\phi}_c)] = \frac{\text{cov}(\hat{\phi}_t, \hat{\phi}_c)}{\phi_t \phi_c} .$$

For inference purposes, we are assuming that $\hat{\phi}_t$ and $\hat{\phi}_c$ have a bivariate log-normal distribution. Then the exact relationship between these two covariances is

$$\text{cov}[\ln(\hat{\phi}_t), \ln(\hat{\phi}_c)] = \ln\left[1 + \frac{\text{cov}(\hat{\phi}_t, \hat{\phi}_c)}{\phi_t \phi_c}\right].$$

(This result is from Johnson and Kotz 1972:20.)

When one uses the log-transform, any $\hat{S}$ estimator of treatment effect becomes a linear function of $\hat{\phi}$-estimators. It is then easy to write the variance of $\ln(\hat{S})$ and the covariance between $\ln(\hat{S}_a)$ and $\ln(\hat{S}_b)$ for any pair of estimators $\hat{S}_a$ and $\hat{S}_b$. For example, if $\hat{S}_a = \hat{\phi}_{v1,i}/\hat{\phi}_{v2,i}$ and $\hat{S}_b = \hat{\phi}_{v3,j}/\hat{\phi}_{v4,j}$, then

$$\text{var}[\ln(\hat{S}_a)] = \ln\left(1 + [\text{cv}(\hat{\phi}_{v1,i})]^2\right) + \ln\left(1 + [\text{cv}(\hat{\phi}_{v2,i})]^2\right)$$

$$- 2\ln\left(1 + \frac{\text{cov}(\hat{\phi}_{v1,i}, \hat{\phi}_{v2,i})}{\phi_{v1,i} \phi_{v2,i}}\right).$$

Also,

$$\text{cov}[\ln(\hat{S}_a), \ln(\hat{S}_b)] = \ln\left(1 + \frac{\text{cov}(\hat{\phi}_{v1,i}, \hat{\phi}_{v3,j})}{\phi_{v1,i} \phi_{v3,j}}\right) - \ln\left(1 + \frac{\text{cov}(\hat{\phi}_{v1,i}, \hat{\phi}_{v4,j})}{\phi_{v1,i} \phi_{v4,j}}\right)$$

$$- \ln\left(1 + \frac{\text{cov}(\hat{\phi}_{v2,i}, \hat{\phi}_{v3,j})}{\phi_{v2,i} \phi_{v3,j}}\right) + \ln\left(1 + \frac{\text{cov}(\hat{\phi}_{v2,i}, \hat{\phi}_{v4,j})}{\phi_{v2,i} \phi_{v4,j}}\right).$$

A case that might arise is $\hat{S} = (\hat{\phi}_{t1} \hat{\phi}_{t2})/(\hat{\phi}_{c1} \hat{\phi}_{c2})$; using the above results and standard linear statistical theory it is easy to write $\text{var}[\ln(S)]$.

In general, we recommend the variance and covariance formulae based on treating the $\hat{\phi}$ as log-normal random variables. When coefficients of variation are small, the confidence intervals based on a log-transformation are almost identical to the asymptotic results. However, as coefficients of variation increase, the log-normal distribution for $\hat{\phi}$ provided a better approximation than the assumption of a normal distribution.

3.5.2. Log-Odds Transform for $\hat{p}$

The desirability of a transform on $\hat{p}$ is most noticeable when one computes a confidence interval $\hat{p}_L$ to $\hat{p}_U$ and finds $\hat{p}_L < 0$ or $\hat{p}_U > 1$. Because $\hat{p}$ will always be in $[0,1]$, we want a transformation that maps $[0,1]$ to $(-\infty, +\infty)$. Two commonly used transformations in this case are $\arcsin\sqrt{\hat{p}}$ and $\ln[\hat{p}/(1-\hat{p})]$, of which we recommend the latter (log-odds or logistic transform). The corresponding variance formula is

$$\text{var}\left[\ln[\hat{p}/(1-\hat{p})]\right] = \frac{\text{se}(\hat{p})}{p(1-p)} .$$

Treating the transformed variable as normally distributed leads to an approximate $(1-\alpha)$ 100% CI, as

$$\hat{p}_L = \frac{\hat{p}}{\hat{p} + (1-\hat{p})\,C}$$

and

$$\hat{p}_U = \frac{\hat{p}}{\hat{p} + (1-\hat{p})\,/C} ,$$

where

$$C = \exp\left(\frac{z_{\alpha/2}\text{se}(\hat{p})}{\hat{p}(1-\hat{p})}\right) .$$

3.6. Computing Theoretical Biases, Standard Errors, and Test Powers

There is a "quick and easy" numerical way to get a good idea of the bias of any estimator when the data do not fit the model. Assume that you postulate the parameters under model H_{2p} and want to know the biases that would occur in $\hat{\phi}_{t1}$ and $\hat{\phi}_{c1}$ (for example) if model $H_{1\phi}$ was used to analyze data arising from this specific case of model H_{2p}. Using the postulated values of ϕ_{v1} and p_{v2}, $v = 1, ..., V$ and $\phi_2, ..., \phi_{k-1}, p_3, ..., p_k$ for given k, and with specified R_{v1}, $v = 1, ..., V$, generate the expected values of m_{vij} and $R_{v2}, ..., R_{v,k-1}$, $v = 1, ..., V$. Next, analyze these expected data under $H_{1\phi}$ as if they were actual data (e.g., using an option called EXPECT in PROC SIMULATE of program RELEASE). The computed values of the $\hat{\phi}$, $\hat{p}$, and $\hat{S}$ estimators are good approximations to the expected values of the same estimators when the given model H_{2p} holds but $H_{1\phi}$ is used for the analysis.

In the procedure presented above, expected or known losses on capture could be allowed. Another refinement is to specify the releases R_{vi}, $i = 1, ..., k - 1$, $v = 1, ..., V$ at each release site, not just the first, and then generate $E(m_{vij} | R_{vi})$ rather than $E(m_{vij} | R_{v1})$.

The general procedure is strictly numerical but is "analytic," not Monte Carlo. One just completely specifies any given model and protocol and then generates expected data under that model and protocol. The model used to generate the expected data is the true model. The expected data are then analyzed, as if they were real data, under any alternative model for the same protocol. This analysis produces approximate expected values of the ML estimators under the analysis model used, given the true model used to generate the (expected) data. This procedure is suitable for determining if the bias associated with using the alternative model, rather than the true model, is small, medium, or large (e.g., $\leq 2.5\%$, about 10%, or $\geq 20\%$).

Further information accrues from this numerical procedure. The standard errors (or variances) produced are the theoretical standard errors. One could use them to compute a standardized bias:

$$\Delta = \frac{\text{bias}(\theta)}{\text{se}(\theta)}$$

(for any parameter θ). If $\hat{\theta}$ is assumed to be normally distributed, Cochran (1963:14) showed the effect of Δ on confidence interval coverage. Basically, if $\Delta \leq 0.5$, the effect is negligible (see Chapter 5.2). Of particular interest would be to analyze the expected data under the true model generating those "data," as this produces theoretical standard errors under the assumed model.

Information on the power of individual tests can also be extracted. When an analysis (model) is applied to expected values, $E(m_{vij} | R_{v1})$, any chi-square test statistic produced is really the noncentrality parameter of the corresponding noncentral chi-square power curve of that test. Table 3.4 gives some power values versus the noncentrality parameter for several degrees of freedom. (With current software like SAS, it is easy to compute any noncentral chi-square distribution.) For example, we could specify an instance of model $H_{1\phi}$, in terms of releases R_{t1} and R_{c1}, $k = 6$, and parameters $\phi_{t1}, \phi_{c1}, \phi_2, ..., \phi_{k-1}, p_2, ..., p_k$. One could then produce $E(m_{tij} | R_{t1})$ and $E(m_{cij} | R_{c1})$, $i = 1, ..., k - 1$, $j = i + 1, ..., k$ and analyze these as real data. TEST 1 (model H_0 versus $H_{4\phi}$) has 9 df; TEST 1.R1 (model H_0 versus $H_{1\phi}$) has 1 df. If the computed values of TEST 1 and its component 1.R1 are 15.0 (theoretically the noncentrality parameters of TESTs 1.T2 through 1.R5 are zero when model $H_{1\phi}$ is true), then, from Table 3.4, the power of TEST 1 is about 0.75 while the power of TEST 1.R1 is about 0.97.

If rounding (to integers) is done before "data" analysis, the biases, standard errors, and noncentrality parameters will be affected slightly. However, results will still be useful for judging when model bias is a problem. Similarly, one will be able to tell if power is poor, medium, or good. Attainment of the same level of precision regarding this information by Monte Carlo methods would probably require at least 1,000 replications of simulated data.

The validity of this theoretical evaluation of model bias, precision, and power depends on sample size being large. This procedure can give poor results if the R_{vi} are small. Monte Carlo methods are necessary to investigate small-sample properties of statistical procedures. Also, this numerical procedure does not aid in determining the properties of complex procedures such as model selection, which involves a sequence of steps. Finally, one cannot learn anything about the sampling distribution of estimators or statistics from this analytical procedure. Hence, there is still a need for Monte Carlo procedures (e.g., see Buckland 1984); however, simulation is not needed to determine asymptotic model bias, precision, or power.

Table 3.4. − Some powers for an α = 0.05-level chi-square test (i.e., under the null hypothesis that the test statistic has a central chi-square distribution) for selected df and a range of noncentrality parameter values.

Noncentrality parameter	df			Noncentrality parameter	df			
	1	2	5		10	20	30	40
0	0.05	0.05	0.05	0	0.05	0.05	0.05	0.05
1	0.17	0.13	0.10	2	0.12	0.10	0.09	0.08
2	0.29	0.23	0.16	4	0.21	0.16	0.13	0.12
3	0.41	0.32	0.22	6	0.32	0.23	0.19	0.17
4	0.52	0.42	0.29	8	0.43	0.31	0.26	0.22
5	0.61	0.50	0.36	10	0.54	0.40	0.33	0.28
6	0.69	0.58	0.43	12	0.64	0.49	0.40	0.35
7	0.75	0.66	0.50	14	0.72	0.57	0.48	0.41
8	0.81	0.72	0.56	16	0.79	0.65	0.55	0.48
9	0.85	0.77	0.62	18	0.85	0.72	0.62	0.55
10	0.89	0.82	0.68	20	0.89	0.78	0.68	0.61
11	0.91	0.85	0.73	22	0.92	0.82	0.74	0.67
12	0.93	0.88	0.77	24	0.95	0.87	0.79	0.72
13	0.95	0.91	0.81	26	0.96	0.90	0.83	0.77
14	0.96	0.93	0.84	28	0.98	0.92	0.87	0.81
15	0.97	0.94	0.87	30	0.98	0.94	0.90	0.84
16	0.98	0.96	0.89	32	0.99	0.96	0.92	0.88
17	0.98	0.97	0.91	34	0.99	0.97	0.94	0.90
18	0.99	0.97	0.93	36	1.00	0.98	0.95	0.92
19	0.99	0.98	0.94	38	1.00	0.99	0.97	0.94
20	0.99	0.99	0.95	40	1.00	0.99	0.97	0.95

The justification for this analytical methodology comes from large-sample and maximum likelihood theory as regards bias and standard error evaluation. This method of test power evaluation is justified by more recent work, for example, Moore (1984). This theory provides further ways to achieve computing efficiency. Asymptotic model bias is independent of the numbers of fish released, R_{v1} (note that this theory also applies to Jolly-Seber models with releases at each occasion $i = 1, ..., k - 1$). Thus, with model bias (if releases are not few), one only needs to do the computations for one set of release numbers.

Let the parameter θ represent ϕ or p. The variance of $\hat{\theta}$ is proportional to the reciprocal of the release numbers, R_{v1}. Let the theoretical standard errors be evaluated numerically (as above) based on releases R_{v1}, $v = 1, ..., V$. In this situation, one can denote the standard error of $\hat{\theta}$ as $se(\hat{\theta} \mid R_{v1})$. Then, if all releases are multipled to be a constant, C, (e.g., C = 0.1 or 100), the standard error under these alternate releases, all else being the same, is

$$se(\hat{\theta} \mid CR_{v1}) = \frac{se(\hat{\theta} \mid R_{v1})}{\sqrt{C}} .$$

Therefore, one could set all $R_{v1} = 100,000$, compute analytical results, and determine standard errors if releases were, for example, 1,000 by using the above relationship with C = 0.01 = 1,000/100,000. (The advantage of using $R_{v1} = 100,000$ is the minimization of rounding error when expected captures are rounded to integers.) Once $se(\hat{\theta})$ is known for any releases R_{v1}, it is essentially known for all releases.

Similar computing economics occur for evaluating test power. Let δ represent the non-centrality parameter of any test. The value of δ depends on the releases and other factors (i.e., the true model, the value of k, the ϕ_{vi}, and the p_{vi}). Denote the dependence of δ on release numbers by $\delta(R_{v1})$. Then if the release numbers are CR_{v1}, everything else being the same, one has

$$\delta(CR_{v1}) = C\delta(R_{v1}) .$$

For example, doubling the number of released fish doubles the noncentrality parameter. As a consequence of these analytical properties of $se(\hat{\theta} \mid R_{v1})$ and $\delta(R_{v1})$, it is easy to evaluate the effect of simply altering the numbers of releases with regards to standard errors and test power.

3.7. Testing Losses on Capture for a Treatment Effect

For each recapture datum m_{vij}, there corresponds d_{vij} losses on capture. For example, one might have $m_{t13} = 500$, $d_{t13} = 17$ and $m_{c13} = 561$, $d_{c13} = 21$; then, a 2×2 contingency table is used to test whether the loss rate is the same for treatments as for controls. In general, a $V \times 2$ contingency table is used for this testing for each $i = 1, ..., k - 1, j = i + 1, ..., k$. Losses on capture often are few or nil; such testing is then not needed.

Under our multinomial modeling approach, we obtain the conditional distributions

$$d_{vij} \mid m_{vij} \sim \mathrm{bin}(m_{vij}; \gamma_{vij})$$

independently for $v = 1, ..., V$ and all i, j. Under the hypothesis $H_0: \gamma_{vij} = \gamma_{ij}$, one has the distribution

$$\Pr\{d_{1ij}, ..., d_{vij} \mid H_0\} = \frac{\prod_{v=1}^{V} \binom{m_{vij}}{d_{vij}}}{\binom{m_{.ij}}{d_{.ij}}} .$$

If data are not too sparse, one can use the $V \times 2$ contingency table chi-square test of homogeneity. For sparse data, a useful ad hoc procedure is to pool some of the tables, say, over j. Computing and examining the ratios d_{vij}/m_{vij} could also be useful.

In the case of $V = 2$, one can conveniently examine the one-sided alternative H_A: a higher (or lower) loss on capture rate for treatment fish. An example is the use of the test statistic

$$z = \frac{\sum_{i=1}^{k-1} \sum_{j=i+1}^{k} \left[\left(d_{tij}/m_{tij}\right) - \left(d_{cij}/m_{cij}\right) \right]}{\sum_{i=1}^{k-1} \sum_{j=i+1}^{k} \sum_{v=c}^{t} \frac{1}{m_{vij}} \left(\frac{d_{vij}}{m_{vij}}\right) \left(1 - \frac{d_{vij}}{m_{vij}}\right)} ,$$

where z is approximately a standard normal variable under the null hypothesis. The point here is that one can test for a treatment effect of losses on capture. This testing reduces to a standard statistical problem of examining proportions; numerous statistical methods are available for this situation (see Fleiss 1981).

3.8. Handling Effects

One reason we use the Jolly-Seber model as the starting point for developing a general theory for each group is the nonidentifiability problems that arise with other more general models. The first generalization of the Jolly-Seber model that arises is to allow for a "release" or handling effect for fish recaptured then rereleased at dams 2, ..., k - 1. In particular, survival, ϕ_{vj}, after capture, handling, and release at dam j is likely to be affected. Such a handling effect is well known in the literature (see, for example, Manly 1971a; Brownie and Robson 1983; Arnason and Mills 1986). In general, just the capturing and handling may affect subsequent survival after release. In addition, there may be a capture and release effect in stud-ies at hydroelectric dams. If the fish are released below the dam (or even above the dam), they will probably experience different mortality stresses at that dam compared to fish passing the dam but not caught there. (This problem has implications for system-wide stu-dies.)

We can generalize the Jolly-Seber model by allowing such released fish at dam j to have survival rate ϕ'_j between dams j and $j+1$; after that, their survival rate is the same as that of other fish in the study (a one-period effect). It suffices to deal only with one treatment group here so we drop the subscript v. Now the parameters of the model are $\phi'_1, ..., \phi'_{k-1}, \phi_2, ..., \phi_{k-1}$ and $p_2, ..., p_k$. Note that we use ϕ'_1 here, not ϕ_1, for consistency of notation; we cannot define a handling effect at first release. When $\phi'_j \neq \phi_j$, $j = 2, ..., k - 1$, none of these parameters are identifiable. Moreover, none of our tests of hypotheses can detect such a handling effect. Thus, there is no point in considering such a model, even though it may be real. Considering more general models may be equally pointless unless either they entail getting additional infor-mation or parameters are identifiable. We here give the mathematical basis supporting this lack of identifiability.

Given the R_i, the $m_{i,i+1}, ..., m_{ik}, R_i - r_i$ are independent multinomials. The model is then (essentially) the structure we put on

$$\frac{E(m_{ij} \mid R_i)}{R_i} = \pi_{ij}.$$

For Jolly-Seber, a standardized representation is

$$\pi_{ij} = \begin{cases} \alpha_i, & j = i + 1 \\ \beta_i \cdots \beta_{j-2}\alpha_{j-1}, & j > i + 1 \end{cases},$$

for $i = 1, ..., k - 1$, $j = i + 1, ..., k$ with $\alpha_i = \phi_i p_{i+1}$ and $\beta_i = \phi_i q_{i+1}$. All that matters is the structure of these π_{ij}, i.e., for Jolly-Seber, they are time-specific only.

Under the one-period capture-handling and release-effects model superimposed on Jolly-Seber, we have the model structure as, for example, when $k = 5$

i	$k = 2$	3	4	5
1	$(\phi'_1 p_2)$	$(\phi'_1 q_2)(\phi_2 p_3)$	$(\phi'_1 q_2)(\phi_2 q_3)(\phi_3 p_4)$	$(\phi'_1 q_2)(\phi_2 q_3)(\phi_3 q_4)(\phi_4 p_5)$
2		$(\phi'_2 p_3)$	$(\phi'_2 q_3)(\phi_3 p_4)$	$(\phi'_2 q_3)(\phi_3 q_4)(\phi_4 p_5)$
3			$(\phi'_3 p_4)$	$(\phi'_3 q_4)(\phi_4 p_5)$
4				$(\phi'_4 p_5)$

The structure of these π_{ij} can be rearranged to arrive at the following standardized representation:

i	$k = 2$	3	4	5
1	α'_1	$\beta'_1\alpha'_2$	$\beta'_1\beta'_2\alpha'_3$	$\beta'_1\beta'_2\beta'_3\alpha'_4$
2		α'_2	$\beta'_2\alpha'_3$	$\beta'_2\beta'_3\alpha'_4$
3			α'_3	$\beta'_3\alpha'_4$
4				α'_4

Here,

$$\alpha'_i = \phi'_i p_{i+1}, \quad i = 1, ..., k - 1;$$

$$\beta'_i = (\phi'_i q_{i+1}\phi_{i+1} / \phi'_{i+1}), \quad i = 1, ..., k - 2.$$

This form is the same as Jolly-Seber. It therefore has the same MSS and cannot be distinguished from Jolly-Seber; i.e., we cannot test $H_0: \phi_i = \phi'_i$. Individual parameters are not estimable under this model (i.e., the ϕ'_i, ϕ_i, p_i). Intrinsically estimable are the α'_i and β'_i ($2k - 3$ parameters).

Only straightforward algebra is needed to derive these results. For example,

$$\pi_{13} = \phi'_1 q_2 \phi_2 p_3$$

$$= \phi'_1 q_2 \frac{\phi_2}{\phi'_2} \phi'_2 p_3$$

$$= \beta'_1 \alpha'_2 .$$

If one considers the large-sample expected values of the usual Jolly-Seber estimators of ϕ_i and p_i, one realizes that further algebraic manipulation is possible. We end up with the representation

$$\alpha'_i = \phi^*_i p^*_{i+1}, \quad i = 1, ..., k - 1;$$

$$\beta'_i = \phi^*_i q^*_{i+1}, \quad i = 1, ..., k - 2;$$

where

$$\phi^*_i = \phi'_i \left[p_{i+1} + q_{i+1} \frac{\phi_{i+1}}{\phi'_{i+1}} \right], \quad i = 1, ..., k - 1 ;$$

$$p^*_i = \frac{p_i}{p_i + q_i \dfrac{\phi_i}{\phi'_i}}, \quad i = 2, ..., k .$$

This shows that if we generalize the Jolly-Seber model to allow a first-period effect on survival rate after release on occasion j, then the model structure of the applicable π_{ij} is identical to

$$\pi_{ij} = \begin{cases} (\phi^*_i p^*_{i+1}), & j = i + 1 \\ (\phi^*_i q^*_{i+1}) \cdots (\phi^*_{i-2} q^*_{i-1})(\phi^*_{i-1} p^*_i), & j > i + 1 \end{cases},$$

with ϕ^*_i and p^*_i as given above. This structure is exactly time-specific, and thus is a Jolly-Seber model. We will not be able to detect a release and handling effect by any tests applied to the usual release-recapture data. However, the Jolly-Seber estimators are badly affected; their expected values are the above ϕ^*_i and p^*_i.

We note that, under $H_{1\phi}$, the estimator of $S = \phi_{t1}/\phi_{c1}$ is unaffected by this problem ($\phi_{c1} - \phi_{t1}$ *is* affected). However, under H_{2p}, $\hat{S}$ is affected; the expected value of $\hat{S}$ is then

$$E(\hat{S}) = S \frac{\left[p_{t2} + q_{t2} \dfrac{\phi_2}{\phi'_2} \right]}{\left[p_{c2} + q_{c2} \dfrac{\phi_2}{\phi'_2} \right]} .$$

When the capture probabilities are small, the bias in $\hat{S}$ is small. Under model $H_{2\phi}$, however, a handling effect such as the one considered here can seriously bias even $\hat{S}$. Further work on this problem, such as its affect on $\hat{N}$ in the Jolly-Seber model, was given by Arnason and Mills (1986).

3.9. Bias Reduction by Peeling for First Capture History and Unknown Capture History Protocols

In Chapters 2.2 and 2.3, we mentioned that, if model $H_{1\phi}$ does not fit the data, then $\hat{S}$, computed as if $H_{1\phi}$ were true, will be biased. Under these protocols, no separate ϕ or p

parameters are estimable for $H_{1\phi}$ (or for any more general models). For the other proto-cols, the strategy to reduce model bias is to seek a more general model by using some specific tests. A version of that strategy is applicable for these two protocols; however, it is less rigorous and less satisfactory. In the case of the first capture history protocol in particular, bias is not eliminated, it is only reduced. We next give equations for approximate bias evaluation relative to this peeling strategy.

Two concepts of bias must be distinguished: (1) statistical bias and (2) model bias. If θ is some estimator and the assumptions (i.e., model) underlying θ are true, we may still have $E(\theta) \neq \theta$; thus, θ is statistically biased. For example, even under $H_{1\phi}$,

$$\hat{S} = \frac{r_{t1}/R_{t1}}{r_{c1}/R_{c1}}$$

suffers some statistical bias (see Section 3.4.3). Much more severe bias is likely to occur if one's model is wrong. We take model bias to mean the value of $E(\theta) - \theta$ when the assumptions (i.e., models) are wrong. One can often adjust for statistical bias. We will consider model bias of various statistically bias-adjusted estimators under first capture history and unknown capture history protocols in Sections 3.9.1 and 3.9.2.

3.9.1. Model Bias and Peeling for the First Capture History Protocol

Under $H_{1\phi}$, we have

$$S = S_1 = \frac{r_{t1} / R_{t1}}{(r_{c1} + 1) / (R_{c1} + 1)}$$

as virtually unbiased. (Note: We will use a subscript on S in this section to denote degree of peeling.) As discussed in Section 2.2.8., one may do some tests and conclude that model $H_{1\phi}$ does not fit; thus, S suffers model bias. If $H_{2\phi}$ is not rejected, one recourse in reducing this model bias is to use

$$S_2 = \frac{(r_{t1} - m_{t12})/R_{t1}}{(r_{c1} - m_{c12} + 1) / (R_{c2} + 1)} \;.$$

In general, we could consider using

$$S_j = \frac{\left(\sum\limits_{n=j+1}^{k} m_{t1n}\right)/R_{t1}}{\left(\sum\limits_{n=j+1}^{k} m_{c1n} + 1\right)/(R_{c1} + 1)}, \quad i = 1, ..., k - 1.$$

The nearly exact expected value of S_j is

$$E(S_j) = \frac{\left(\sum_{n=j+1}^{k} \pi_{tin}\right)/R_{t1}}{\left(\sum_{n=j+1}^{k} \pi_{cin}\right)/R_{c1}} .$$

The expected value is irrespective of the true model assumptions about the ϕ_{vi} and p_{vi}. For example,

$$E(S) = E(S_1) = \frac{\lambda_{t1}}{\lambda_{t2}} = \frac{\phi_{t1}(p_{t2} + q_{t2}\lambda_{t2})}{\phi_{c1}(p_{c2} + q_{c2}\lambda_{c2})} ,$$

and

$$E(S_2) = \frac{\phi_{t1}q_{t2}\lambda_{t2}}{\phi_{c1}q_{c2}\lambda_{c2}} = \left(\frac{\phi_{t1}\phi_{t2}}{\phi_{c1}\phi_{c2}}\right)\left(\frac{q_{t2}}{q_{c2}}\right)\left(\frac{p_{t3} + q_{t3}\lambda_{t3}}{p_{c3} + q_{c3}\lambda_{c3}}\right) .$$

In general, if model $H_{j\phi}$ holds,

$$E(S_j) = S\left[\prod_{i=2}^{j+1} \frac{q_{ti}}{q_{ci}}\right], \quad j = 2, ..., k-1 .$$

Note that under model $H'_{j\phi}$, S_j is (essentially) unbiased because $H'_{j\phi}$ assumes that $p_{ti} = p_{ci}$ for all $i = 2, ..., k$.

Under model $H_{1\phi}$, $\widetilde{S}$ is unbiased. However, under any higher model, particularly H_{2p} or even $H_{2\phi}$, $\widetilde{S}$ suffers model bias. TEST 1.T2 tests $\tau_{t2} = \tau_{c2}$ ($\tau_{vi} = p_{vi}/(p_{vi} + q_{vi}\lambda_{vi})$). Because the null hypothesis is false if either $p_{t2} \neq p_{c2}$ or $\phi_{t2} \neq \phi_{c2}$, at best the alternative hypothesis is model $H_{2\phi}$ (not H_{2p}). However, we can evaluate theoretically $E(S_1)$ and $E(S_2)$ under model H_{2p}:

$$E(S_1) = S\left(\frac{p_{t2} + q_{t2}\lambda_2}{p_{c2} + q_{c2}\lambda_2}\right) ;$$

$$E(S_2) = S\frac{q_{t2}}{q_{c2}} .$$

If the capture probabilities are small, then approximately $E(S_1) \doteq S(p_{t2}/p_{c2})$ while $E(S_2) \doteq S$. More precise results can be obtained by computing numerical examples. For example, if H_{2p} held with $p_{t2} = 0.03$, $p_{c2} = 0.05$, and $\lambda_2 = 0.12$, then $E(S_1) = S(0.893)$, an 11% relative bias, whereas $E(S_2) = S(1.021)$, a 2% relative bias.

The simplest and perhaps most important alternative case is that H_{2p} might be true, not $H_{1\phi}$. One tests for this case (with first capture history data) by evaluating TEST 1.$T2$ and the sum of TESTS 1.$T3$ to 1.$Tk - 1$. If TEST 1.$T2$ rejects and the remaining tests do not, it is highly likely that S_1 will have substantial bias relative to its standard error. If the capture probabilities are known to be small, then we recommend peeling (discarding) m_{v12} because S_2 will be substantially less biased than S_1. (Note that matters are different with moderate or large capture probabilities; then, peeling with the above formulae could actually make bias worse.)

The following equation may provide an improved peeled estimator.

$$\widetilde{\widetilde{S}}_j = \frac{\left(\sum\limits_{n=j+1}^{k} m_{t1n}\right) \bigg/ \left(R_{t1} - \sum\limits_{n=2}^{j} m_{t1n}\right)}{\left[\left(\sum\limits_{n=j+1}^{k} m_{c1n}\right) + 1\right] \bigg/ \left(R_{c1} + 1 - \sum\limits_{n=2}^{j} m_{c1n}\right)}, \quad j = 2, ..., k-1.$$

The almost exact expectation of $\widetilde{\widetilde{S}}_j$ is

$$E\left(\widetilde{\widetilde{S}}_j\right) = \frac{\left(\sum\limits_{n=j+1}^{k} \pi_{t1n}\right) \bigg/ \left(1 - \sum\limits_{n=2}^{j} \pi_{t1n}\right)}{\left(\sum\limits_{n=j+1}^{k} \pi_{c1n}\right) \bigg/ \left(1 - \sum\limits_{n=2}^{j} \pi_{c1n}\right)}, \quad j = 2, ..., k-1.$$

In particular, under H_{2p},

$$E(S_2) = S\left(\frac{1 - p_{t2}}{1 - \phi_{t1}p_{t2}}\right) \bigg/ \left(\frac{1 - p_{c2}}{1 - \phi_{c1}p_{c2}}\right) ;$$

here $S = \phi_{t1}\phi_{t2}/(\phi_{c1}\phi_{c2})$ but this is the relevant treatment effect parameter. (If H_{2p} is true rather than $H_{2\phi}$, then $\phi_{t2} = \phi_{c2}$.) For small capture probabilities, the above formula for $E(S_2)$ is well approximated by

$$E(\overset{\approx}{S_2}) \doteq S\left(\frac{1 - p_{t2} + \phi_{t1}p_{t2}}{1 - p_{c2} + \phi_{c1}p_{c2}}\right) ,$$

which is closer to S than is $E(\overset{\sim}{S_2})$.

3.9.2. Model Bias and Peeling for the Unknown Capture History Protocol

We draw on notation and theory presented in Chapter 2.3 in general and Section 2.3.5 in particular to obtain results. Under $H_{1\phi}$ the appropriate estimator of S (adjusted for statistical bias) is

$$\tilde{S} = \overset{\sim}{S_1} = \frac{m_{t.}/R_{t1}}{(m_{c.} + 1)/(R_{c1} + 1)} .$$

Peeled estimators are

$$\overset{\sim}{S_j} = \frac{\left[\sum_{n=j+1}^{k} m_{tn}\right]/R_{t1}}{\left[(\sum_{n=j+1}^{k} m_{cn}) + 1\right]/(R_{c1} + 1)} , \quad j = 2, ..., k - 1 .$$

Here, m_{vj} is the number of fish captured at dam j and $m_{v.} = m_{v2} + \cdots + m_{vk}$.

By drawing on results presented in Section 2.3.5, one can develop a formula for $E(\overset{\sim}{S_j})$ in the general case of losses on capture. We present results here only for the case of no losses on capture; then

$$E(m_{vj}) = R_{v1}\phi_{v1} \cdots \phi_{v,j-1}p_{vj} , \quad j = 2, ..., k .$$

We define $f_{vj} = \phi_{v1} \cdots \phi_{v,j-1}p_{vj}$, $j = 2, \widetilde{} ..., k$ and thus write the approximate expectations of the $\overset{\sim}{S_j}$ as

$$E(\overset{\sim}{S_j}) = \frac{\sum_{n=j+1}^{k} f_{tn}}{\sum_{n=j+1}^{k} f_{cn}} , \quad j = 1, ..., k - 1 .$$

Under model $H_{j\phi}$ for this protocol,

$$E\left(\overset{\nu}{S}_j\right) = \frac{\phi_{t1} \cdots \phi_{tj}}{\phi_{c1} \cdots \phi_{cj}} = S \,.$$

Heuristically, it is as if dam $j + 1$ were actually the second dam and $H_{1\phi}$ was true.

One can evaluate the (approximate) bias to be expected in $\overset{\nu}{S}_1$ if, for example, H_{2p} is the true model:

$$E\left(\overset{\nu}{S}_1\right) = S\left(\frac{p_{t2} + Q}{p_{c2} + Q}\right) ;$$

$$Q = \phi_2 p_3 + \phi_2 \phi_3 p_4 + \cdots + \phi_2 \cdots \phi_{k-1} p_k \,.$$

For example, if $p_{t2} = 0.03$, $p_{c2} = 0.05$, $Q = 0.124$ (which would arise from $k = 6$, $\phi_2 = \phi_3 = \phi_4 = \phi_5 = 0.9$, and $p_3 = p_4 = p_5 = p_6 = 0.04$), and H_{2p} is true, then $E\left(\overset{\nu}{S}_1\right) = S(0.885)$.

Clearly, this approach can be used to assess model bias under any scenario one can specify; thus, it evaluates the effect of peeling on bias.

3.10. Synthetic Example of Multiple Treatments

We present here a simulated example of data having three treatment levels and a control; thus, there are $V = 4$ groups. The partial capture history scheme B protocol is used. Table 3.5 shows the values of the parameters used in generating the sample data. At release point (time) 1, three treatment groups and a control are released ($R_v = 1,000$ each group). These releases are followed by five recapture occasions. We envision batch marks being used, as per scheme B. These marks would distinguish fish by lot and treatment. At recapture time 2, another mark is applied to all recaptures and those fish are released. At times 3, 4, 5, and 6, all captured fish are removed. The full simulated example comprises 10 lots of the four groups. Here we present some key results for lot 1; in Part 4 we use results from all 10 lots to illustrate empirical replication in a complex design.

Model H_{2p} is the true underlying model; thus, the four ϕ_{v1} and the four p_{v2} differ by treatment. No other parameters depend on treatment, however. Of particular interest are the treatment effects. With $v = 4$, there are six possible combinations of $S_{v,v'} = \phi_{v1}/\phi_{v'1}$. We simplify matters by saying that the only meaningful effects evolve from comparisons of each treatment separately with the single control. Thus, treatment effects are S_1, S_2, and S_3 defined by ϕ_{v1}/ϕ_{c1}, $v = 1, 2, 3$, with notation $v = 1$ for t_1, $v = 2$ for t_2, $v = 3$ for t_3, and $v = 4$ for c.

Table 3.5. – Parameter values used in the simulation example of three treatment levels and a single control (four groups), partial capture history scheme B data with $k = 6$ release-recapture sites. This is model H_{2v}. Ten lots were generated. Releases at site 1 are $R_{v1} = 1,000$ for each group and lot.

Survival parameters, treatment effects	Capture parameters
$\phi_{11,1} = 0.81$, $S_1 = 0.90$	$p_{t1,2} = 0.1$
$\phi_{t2,1} = 0.675$, $S_2 = 0.75$	$p_{t2,2} = 0.1$
$\phi_{t3,1} = 0.63$, $S_3 = 0.70$	$p_{t3,2} = 0.1$
$\phi_{c,1} = 0.90$	$p_{c,2} = 0.2$

Common to all groups	Common to all groups
$\phi_2 = 0.85$	$p_3 = 0.2$
$\phi_3 = 0.80$	$p_4 = 0.2$
$\phi_4 = 0.70$	$p_5 = 0.2$
$\phi_5 = 0.85$	$p_6 = 0.2$

Table 3.6 shows what the input data look like in capture history matrix form. Note that, for most capture histories, the counts are shown as negative. For example, for $h = \{100010\}$, $X_{1h} = -38$, $X_{2h} = -31$, $X_{3h} = -29$, and $X_{4h} = -43$. At capture site 5, none of these fish were returned to the study. Fish were released only at sites 1 and 2. For example, the 10 fish for X_{1h}, $h = \{110100\}$ were released at site 1, recaptured and released at site 2, and recaptured at site 4 but not rereleased.

The reduced m-array representation of the data is constructed by RELEASE and is also shown in Table 3.6. Under partial capture history scheme B, there are no multiple subcohorts. Consequently, no components of TEST 3 exist.

TEST 2.$C2$ exists for each group. For example, for treatment group $v = 1$, TEST 2.$C2$ is computed from the 2×4 table

123	76	38	23
11	10	2	5

The results of this goodness of fit testing are given in Table 3.7. TEST 2.$C2$ for group 1 produces the chi-square value of 3.83 (3 df) and observed significance level $P = 0.280$. Summed over all four groups, we have the TEST 2 chi-square result of 12.36 (11 df), $P = 0.730$. Clearly, there is no reason to reject the basic Jolly-Seber model here (i.e., within each separate group, parameters are time-specific only).

Table 3.6. – The input capture history matrix, as printed by RELEASE, and the reduced m-array summaries of the data, by treatment group, for lot 1.

```
INPUT --- PROC CHMATRIX OCCASIONS=6 GROUPS=4 LOTS=10    ;

INPUT ---    GLABEL(1)=Treatment Group 1;
INPUT ---    GLABEL(2)=Treatment Group 2;
INPUT ---    GLABEL(3)=Treatment Group 3;
INPUT ---    GLABEL(4)=Control Group;

INPUT ---    LOT=1;
INPUT ---    100000    656    685    719    549;
INPUT ---    100010    -38    -31    -29    -43;
INPUT ---    101000   -123   -108   -100   -115;
INPUT ---    100100    -76    -80    -68    -78;
INPUT ---    110000     56     43     47    128;
INPUT ---    100001    -23    -27    -18    -25;
INPUT ---    110100    -10     -7     -3    -15;
INPUT ---    111000    -11    -10     -9    -27;
INPUT ---    110010     -2     -7     -5    -13;
INPUT ---    110001     -5     -2     -2     -7;


Number of capture histories read was    10



              Observed Recaptures for Group 1
                    Treatment Group 1


     i    R(i)           m(i,j)              r(i)
               j=  2    3    4    5    6
     1    1000     84  123   76   38   23   344
     2     84          11   10    2    5    28


     m(j)          84  134   86   40   28
     z(j)         260  154   68   28    0
```

Table 3.6. – Continued.

Observed Recaptures for Group 2
Treatment Group 2

i	R(i)			$m(i,j)$			r(i)
		j= 2	3	4	5	6	
1	1000	69	108	80	31	27	315
2	69		10	7	7	2	26
m(j)		69	118	87	38	29	
z(j)		246	154	67	29	0	

Observed Recaptures for Group 3
Treatment Group 3

i	R(i)			$m(i,j)$			r(i)
		j= 2	3	4	5	6	
1	1000	66	100	68	29	18	281
2	66		9	3	5	2	19
m(j)		66	109	71	34	20	
z(j)		215	125	54	20	0	

Observed Recaptures for Group 4
Control Group

i	R(i)			$m(i,j)$			r(i)
		j= 2	3	4	5	6	
1	1000	190	115	78	43	25	451
2	190		27	15	13	7	62
m(j)		190	142	93	56	32	
z(j)		261	181	88	32	0	

Sums for the above Groups

m.	0	409	503	337	168	109
z.	0	982	614	277	109	
R.	4000	409	0	0	0	
r.	1391	135	0	0	0	

Table 3.7. – Results of TEST 2, goodness of fit, for the simulated model H_{2p}, scheme B data for lot 1. Only TEST 2.C2 exists under scheme B.

```
                  Treatment Group 1
TEST 2.C2:  Test of row 1 vs. row 2
          +------+------+------+-----+
       O| 123  |  76  |  38  |  23  | 260
       E| 121.0|  77.6|  36.1|  25.3|
       C|   0.0|   0.0|   0.1|   0.2|
          +------+------+------+-----+
       O|  11  |  10  |   2  |   5  |  28
       E|  13.0|   8.4|   3.9|   2.7|
       C|   0.3|   0.3|   0.9|   1.9|
          +------+------+------+-----+
          134     86     40     28    288
       Chi-square=3.8329 (df=3) P=0.2801

                  Treatment Group 2
TEST 2.C2:  Test of row 1 vs. row 2
          +------+------+------+-----+
       O| 108  |  80  |  31  |  27  | 246
       E| 106.7|  78.7|  34.4|  26.2|
       C|   0.0|   0.0|   0.3|   0.0|
          +------+------+------+-----+
       O|  10  |   7  |   7  |   2  |  26
       E|  11.3|   8.3|   3.6|   2.8|
       C|   0.1|   0.2|   3.1|   0.2|
          +------+------+------+-----+
          118     87     38     29    272
       Chi-square=4.0808 (df=3) P=0.2529

                  Treatment Group 3
TEST 2.C2:  Test of row 1 vs. row 2
          +------+------+------+
       O| 100  |  68  |  47  | 215
       E| 100.1|  65.2|  49.6|
       C|   0.0|   0.1|   0.1|
          +------+------+------+
       O|   9  |   3  |   7  |  19
       E|   8.9|   5.8|   4.4|
       C|   0.0|   1.3|   1.6|
          +------+------+------+
          109     71     54    234
       Chi-square=3.1440 (df=2) P=0.2076
```

Table 3.7. – Continued.

```
                        Control Group
           TEST 2.C2:  Test of row 1 vs. row 2
                +------+------+------+------+
             O| 115  |  78  |  43  |  25  | 261
             E| 114.7|  75.1|  45.3|  25.9|
             C|   0.0|   0.1|   0.1|   0.0|
                +------+------+------+------+
             O|  27  |  15  |  13  |   7  |  62
             E|  27.3|  17.9|  10.7|   6.1|
             C|   0.0|   0.5|   0.5|   0.1|
                +------+------+------+------+
                 142     93     56     32    323
           Chi-square=1.2981 (df=3) P=0.7296
```

Group	Component	Summary of TEST 2 (Goodness of fit) Results			
		Chi-square	df	P-level	Sufficient Data
1	2.C2	3.8329	3	0.2801	Yes
2	2.C2	4.0808	3	0.2529	Yes
3	2.C2	3.1440	2	0.2076	Yes
4	2.C2	1.2981	3	0.7296	Yes
-	TEST 2	12.3558	11	0.3375	-

Next we look at the results of TEST 1, summarized in Table 3.8. Not all possible components of TEST 1 can be computed for scheme B data; only $1.R1$, $1.R2$, $1.T2$, $1.T3$, $1.T4$, and $1.T5$ components exist. Each component is (here) based on a 2×4 table of summary statistics. The full contingency table for TEST $1.T2$ is given in Table 3.8. The rows of that contingency table are m_{v2}, z_{v2} (which sum to T_{v2}) for $v = 1, 2, 3, 4$. The summary statistics m_{v2} and z_{v2} are given in Table 3.6. For example, $m_{v2} = 84$, $z_{v2} = 260$. The body of the contingency table for TEST $1.T2$ is thus easily found to be

	v	m	z
	1	84	260
	2	69	246
	3	66	215
(control)	4	190	261

Table 3.8. – Some results of TEST 1, model selection, for the simulated model H_{2p}, scheme B data for lot 1. Only TESTs 1.$R1$, 1.$R2$, 1.$T2$, 1.$T3$, 1.$T4$, and 1.$T5$ exist here.

```
TEST 1.T2:  Test of p(2) equal across groups,
assuming higher order parameters are equal across groups.
              +------+------+
            O|  84  | 260  | 344
            E| 101.1| 242.9|
            C|   2.9|   1.2|
              +------+------+
            O|  69  | 246  | 315
            E|  92.6| 222.4|
            C|   6.0|   2.5|
              +------+------+
            O|  66  | 215  | 281
            E|  82.6| 198.4|
            C|   3.3|   1.4|
              +------+------+
            O| 190  | 261  | 451
            E| 132.6: 318.4|
            C|  24.8|  10.3|
              +------+------+
               409    982   1391
        Chi-square=52.5708 (df=3) P=0.0000


TEST 1.R1:  Test of Phi(1) equal across groups,
assuming higher order parameters are equal across groups.
              +------+------+
            O| 344  | 656  |1000
            E| 347.7| 652.2|
            C|   0.0|   0.0|
              +------+------+
            O| 315  | 685  |1000
            E| 347.7| 652.2|
            C|   3.1|   1.6|
              +------+------+
            O| 281  | 719  |1000
            E| 347.7| 652.2|
            C|  30.7|  16.3|
              +------+------+
              1391   2609   4000
        Chi-square=71.4344 (df=3) P=0.0000
```

Table 3.8. – Continued.

```
           Summary of TEST 1 (Between Groups Test) Results
   Component  Chi-square   df   P-level  Sufficient Data
   ---------  ----------  ----  -------  ---------------
   1.T5         0.9793      3    0.8063       Yes
   1.T4         1.3006      3    0.7290       Yes
   1.T3         0.9354      3    0.8169       Yes
   1.R2         1.2292      3    0.7460       Yes
   1.T2        52.5708      3    0.0000       Yes
   1.R1        71.4344      3    0.0000       Yes
   TEST  1    128.4498     18    0.0000
```

The chi-square test statistic for TEST 1.$T2$ is 52.5708 (3 df); we reject the null hypothesis that model $H_{1\phi}$ fits these data. The result for TEST 1.$R1$ reinforces this conclusion. Further examination of the summary results in Table 3.8 show that TEST 1 components 1.$R2$ and 1.$T2$ through 1.$T5$ do not reject. The sum of the corresponding chi-squares is 4.4445 (12 df), which also supports the conclusion that model H_{2p} provides an appropriate model for these data.

Table 3.9 shows for lot 1 the parameter estimates under model H_{2p}. Under model H_{2p}, scheme B, the only estimable parameters of interest are ϕ_{v1} and p_{v2}, $v = 1, ..., V$. For treatment group 1, from Table 3.9, we have

$$\hat{\phi}_{11} = 0.872, \hat{se}(\hat{\phi}_{11}) = 0.069 \, ;$$

$$\hat{p}_{12} = 0.096, \hat{se}(\hat{p}_{12}) = 0.013 \, .$$

Also printed out are the asymptotic 95% confidence limits on the true parameter. For example, for ϕ_{11}, those limits are $0.872 \pm 1.96\,(0.069)$, or 0.736 to 1.007. The true value of ϕ_{11} is 0.81 and $p_{12} = 0.1$. For the control group ($v = 4$ here), we have

$$\hat{\phi}_{41} = 0.98, \hat{se}(\hat{\phi}_{41}) = 0.069 \, .$$

Table 3.9. – Output from program RELEASE for model H_{2p} for the simulated data: scheme B, $k = 6$, 4 groups, lot 1.

```
+-------------------------------------------------------------------------+
|              Maximum Likelihood Estimates under Model H2p               |
|                                         95% Confidence Intervals        |
|   Parameter      Estimate      Standard Error    Lower        Upper     |
|   ---------     ----------    --------------  -------------- ---------   |
|                     Estimates for Group 1                               |
|                        Treatment Group                                  |
|   Phi(1)         0.871704       0.069207       0.736057      1.007350    |
|   p(2)           0.096363       0.012532       0.071800      0.120926    |
|                     Estimates for Group 2                               |
|                         Control Group                                   |
|   Phi(1)         0.814289       0.066485       0.683978      0.944600    |
|   p(2)           0.084737       0.011894       0.061424      0.108049    |
|                     Estimates for Group 3                               |
|   Phi(1)         0.717370       0.060252       0.599277      0.835464    |
|   p(2)           0.092003       0.013146       0.066236      0.117770    |
|                     Estimates for Group 4                               |
|   Phi(1)         0.980733       0.068750       0.845983      1.115484    |
|   p(2)           0.193733       0.018519       0.157434      0.230031    |
|                                                                         |
|                  Ratio of Survivals between Groups                      |
|                                         95% Confidence Intervals        |
|   Parameter      Estimate      Standard Error    Lower        Upper     |
|   ---------     ----------    --------------  -------------- ---------   |
|   S(1,2,Phi(1)) 1.070509       0.073867       0.925730      1.215288     |
|   Corr(1,2,Phi(1))             0.633146                                  |
|   S(1,3,Phi(1)) 1.215138       0.087744       1.043159      1.387117     |
|   Corr(1,3,Phi(1))             0.610609                                  |
|   S(1,4,Phi(1)) 0.888828       0.056119       0.778835      0.998822     |
|   Corr(1,4,Phi(1))             0.649622                                  |
|   S(2,3,Phi(1)) 1.135102       0.083971       0.970519      1.299686     |
|   Corr(2,3,Phi(1))             0.601384                                  |
|   S(2,4,Phi(1)) 0.830286       0.054170       0.724113      0.936458     |
|   Corr(2,4,Phi(1))             0.639807                                  |
|   S(3,4,Phi(1)) 0.731463       0.050160       0.633150      0.829777     |
|   Corr(3,4,Phi(1))             0.617033                                  |
+-------------------------------------------------------------------------+
```

It is worth noting the formula and computation of these $\hat{\phi}_{v1}$ and $\hat{p}_{v2}$:

$$\hat{\phi}_{v1} = \frac{r_{v1}}{R_{v1}} \left[\frac{m_{v2}}{T_{v2}} + \frac{z_{v2}R_{.2}}{T_{v2}r_{.2}} \right] ;$$

$$\hat{p}_{v2} = \frac{m_{v2}}{m_{v2} + \dfrac{z_{v2}R_{.2}}{r_{.2}}} .$$

From Table 3.6, one finds the sums $r_{.2} = 135$ and $R_{.2} = 409$, and the control group,

$$r_{41} = 451 ;$$

$$R_{41} = 1{,}000 ;$$

$$m_{42} = 190 ;$$

$$z_{42} = 261 ;$$

(hence $T_{42} = 451$). Thus, for example,

$$\hat{p}_{42} = \frac{190}{190 + \dfrac{261 \times 409}{135}}$$

$$= 0.194 .$$

Finally, we get to the estimates of treatment effect on survival (also shown in Table 3.9). RELEASE automatically computes all such possible treatment effects, i.e.,

$$\hat{S}_{v,v'} = \frac{\hat{\phi}_{v1}}{\hat{\phi}_{v'1}} .$$

For example, $S(1, 4, \text{Phi}(1))$ denotes $\hat{S}_{1,4} = \hat{\phi}_{t1,1}/\hat{\phi}_{c1}$. One should examine only the effects that are meaningful. In this example,

$$\hat{S}_{14} = \hat{S}_1 = 0.889 \ (\text{se} = 0.056) \ ;$$

$$\hat{S}_{24} = \hat{S}_2 = 0.830 \ (\text{se} = 0.054) \ ;$$

$$\hat{S}_{34} = \hat{S}_3 = 0.731 \ (\text{se} = 0.050) \ .$$

Note the true values are $S_1 = 0.90$, $S_2 = 0.75$, and $S_3 = 0.70$. The approximate 95% CIs are also shown in Table 3.9 for each estimate of S_i. For example, for S_2, that interval is 0.724 to 0.936, which includes the true value even though $\hat{S}_2 = 0.830$.

Along with the ratios of $\hat{\phi}_{vi}$, RELEASE shows the estimated sampling correlations between the $\hat{\phi}_{vi}$ and $\hat{\phi}_{v'i}$ used in $\hat{S}_{v,v'} = \hat{\phi}_{vi}/\hat{\phi}_{v'i}$. These sampling correlations are labeled

$$\text{Corr}(v, v', \text{Phi}(i))$$

to denote they are for treatments v and v' for the survival rates between sites i and $i + 1$. For example, for $\hat{S}_1$, $\text{corr}(\hat{\phi}_{1,1}, \hat{\phi}_{4,1}) = 0.6496$. In Table 3.9, this correlation is denoted $\text{Corr}(1, 4, \text{Phi}(1))$.

Throughout this monograph we emphasize the importance of using the correct model. From the summary results of TEST 1 in Table 3.8, it is clear one should select model H_{2p}; TEST 1.$T2$ rejects model $H_{1\phi}$ as inadequate whereas the sum of TEST 1 components 1.$R2$, 1.$T3$, 1.$T4$, and 1.$T5$ do not reject, thereby corroborating model H_{2p} as a suitable choice. Tables 3.10 and 3.11 show the results under models $H_{1\phi}$ and $H_{2\phi}$, both of which are inappropriate here (keep in mind that, with real data, one does not know what the true model is). The estimators of S_1, S_2, and S_3 will be biased under model $H_{1\phi}$ because this model assumes no treatment effect on the capture probabilities p_{v2}. From Tables 3.9 and 3.10 we extract the following results regarding $\hat{S}$.

Parameter	True value	model $H_{1\phi}$		model H_{2p}	
		$\hat{S}$	$\hat{\text{se}}(\hat{S})$	$\hat{S}$	$\hat{\text{se}}(\hat{S})$
S_1	0.90	0.763	0.0426	0.889	0.0561
S_2	0.75	0.698	0.0407	0.830	0.0542
S_3	0.70	0.623	0.0383	0.731	0.0502

The estimators under the two models differ substantially. Also, under model $H_{1\phi}$, the 95% CIs for S_1 and S_3 do not cover the true values. Note, also, that the estimated standard errors of the estimates are larger under model H_{2p}.

Table 3.10. – Output from program RELEASE for model $H_{1\phi}$ for the simulated data: scheme B, $k = 6$, 4 groups, lot 1.

```
+-------------------------------------------------------------------------+
|          Maximum Likelihood Estimates under Model H1Phi                 |
|                                       95% Confidence Intervals          |
|     Parameter    Estimate    Standard Error      Lower        Upper     |
|     ---------    --------    --------------    --------------  --------- |
|                       Estimates for Group 1                             |
|                         Treatment Group 1                              |
|     Phi(1)       0.836901       0.063990       0.711480      0.962321   |
|                       Estimates for Group 2                             |
|                         Treatment Group 2                              |
|     Phi(1)       0.766348       0.059922       0.648902      0.883795   |
|                       Estimates for Group 3                             |
|                         Treatment Group 3                              |
|     Phi(1)       0.683631       0.055108       0.575620      0.791642   |
|                       Estimates for Group 4                             |
|                           Control Group                                |
|     Phi(1)       1.097216       0.078790       0.942787      1.251645   |
|                      Estimates for Pooled Groups                        |
|     p(2)         0.120859       0.009753       0.101743      0.139976   |
|                                                                         |
|                   Ratio of Survivals between Groups                     |
|                                       95% Confidence Intervals          |
|     Parameter    Estimate    Standard Error      Lower        Upper     |
|     ---------    --------    --------------    --------------  --------- |
|   S(1,2,Phi(1)) 1.092063       0.069769       0.955316      1.228811    |
|   Corr(1,2,Phi(1))             0.658898                                 |
|   S(1,3,Phi(1)) 1.224199       0.081808       1.063855      1.384543    |
|   Corr(1,3,Phi(1))             0.639127                                 |
|   S(1,4,Phi(1)) 0.762749       0.042634       0.679187      0.846312    |
|   Corr(1,4,Phi(1))             0.717458                                 |
|   S(2,3,Phi(1)) 1.120996       0.077124       0.969834      1.272159    |
|   Corr(2,3,Phi(1))             0.624982                                 |
|   S(2,4,Phi(1)) 0.698448       0.040678       0.618720      0.778176    |
|   Corr(2,4,Phi(1))             0.701579                                 |
|   S(3,4,Phi(1)) 0.623060       0.038287       0.548018      0.698102    |
|   Corr(3,4,Phi(1))             0.680527                                 |
+-------------------------------------------------------------------------+
```

Table 3.11. – Output from program RELEASE for model H_{2p} for the simulated data: scheme B, $k = 6$, 4 groups, lot 1.

```
+--------------------------------------------------------------------------+
|              Maximum Likelihood Estimates under Model H2Phi               |
|                                           95% Confidence Intervals        |
|    Parameter     Estimate    Standard Error    Lower        Upper         |
|    ---------     --------    --------------    ----------   ----------     |
|                       Estimates for Group 1                               |
|                         Treatment Group 1                                 |
|    Phi(1)        0.864000      0.127135       0.614816     1.113184        |
|    p(2)          0.097222      0.017457       0.063006     0.131439        |
|                       Estimates for Group 2                               |
|                         Treatment Group 2                                 |
|    Phi(1)        0.721846      0.107220       0.511694     0.931998        |
|    p(2)          0.095588      0.017828       0.060645     0.130531        |
|                       Estimates for Group 3                               |
|                         Treatment Group 3                                 |
|    Phi(1)        0.812842      0.151344       0.516208     1.109476        |
|    p(2)          0.081197      0.017856       0.046200     0.116193        |
|                       Estimates for Group 4                               |
|                           Control Group                                   |
|    Phi(1)        0.989839      0.092805       0.807942     1.171736        |
|    p(2)          0.191950      0.021914       0.149000     0.234901        |
|                     Ratio of Survivals between Groups                     |
|                                           95% Confidence Intervals        |
|    Parameter     Estimate    Standard Error    Lower        Upper         |
|    ---------     --------    --------------    ----------   ----------     |
|    S(1,2,Phi(1))  1.196931      0.250256       0.706429     1.687433       |
|    Corr(1,2,Phi(1))             0.000000                                   |
|    S(1,3,Phi(1))  1.062937      0.252253       0.568522     1.557352       |
|    Corr(1,3,Phi(1))             0.000000                                   |
|    S(1,4,Phi(1))  0.872869      0.152296       0.574368     1.171371       |
|    Corr(1,4,Phi(1))             0.000000                                   |
|    S(2,3,Phi(1))  0.888052      0.211517       0.473479     1.302625       |
|    Corr(2,3,Phi(1))             0.000000                                   |
|    S(2,4,Phi(1))  0.729256      0.128095       0.478190     0.980322       |
|    Corr(2,4,Phi(1))             0.000000                                   |
|    S(3,4,Phi(1))  0.821186      0.171188       0.485657     1.156715       |
|    Corr(3,4,Phi(1))             0.000000                                   |
+--------------------------------------------------------------------------+
```

Model $H_{2\phi}$ allows unbiased estimation of S_1, S_2, and S_3. However, because model $H_{2\phi}$ is more general than is needed here, the $\hat{S}_1$, $\hat{S}_2$, and $\hat{S}_3$ under that model have larger sampling variances than they have under model H_{2p}. If this loss in efficiency were slight, the best strategy under scheme B would be to use model $H_{2\phi}$. However, from Tables 3.9 and 3.11, we extract the following results regarding $\hat{S}$:

Parameter	True value	model H_{2p} $\hat{S}$	$\hat{se}(\hat{S})$	model $H_{2\phi}$ $\hat{S}$	$\hat{se}(\hat{S})$
S_1	0.90	0.889	0.0561	0.873	0.1523
S_2	0.75	0.830	0.0542	0.729	0.1281
S_3	0.70	0.731	0.0502	0.821	0.1712

The main point of the above is that the standard errors of the $\hat{S}$ are approximately tripled under model $H_{2\phi}$ as compared to the results under H_{2p}. This loss of efficiency is dramatic; one does not want to select model $H_{2\phi}$ under scheme B unless absolutely necessary.

Part 4. Importance of Replication

4.1. Introduction

The importance of replication and methods for the analysis of replicated experiments are covered in Part 4. The statistical estimation and testing theory for dealing with a single lot ("replicate") appears in Parts 2 and 3. Here, a variety of methods is given to extend the analysis methods to cover replicated experiments. This material is presented in a separate section of the monograph because of the importance of replication in experimental research.

4.1.1. Need for Replication and Multiple Lots

We now deal with issues of replication and multiple lots, statistical methods for combining results over lots, estimation of empirical variances, and some formulae for estimation of variance components. Repeatability, within measured statistical limits of precision, is fundamental for scientific credibility. When sampling variation is substantial, as in these fisheries experiments, there should be many repeated releases of treatment and control fish.

We define a lot to be the pairing of a batch of treatment fish and a batch of control fish released (almost) simultaneously. Prior to release, all the fish in a lot should be as similar as possible (in, for example, species, strain, age, and condition); they should have arisen from a common source, been handled, marked, and transported as a unit and assigned to treatment group randomly. A lot, so defined, is analogous to two paired experimental units in standard statistical terminology. Thus, we are here defining the experimental unit as a batch of fish to which there is a single application of one treatment condition (see Steel and Torrie 1980 for a general discussion of an experimental unit).

To demonstrate repeatability (and estimate precision), two sources of variation must be dealt with. First, there is the within-lot sampling variation, which manifests itself in var($\hat{S} \mid S$). This variation is reduced by increasing either the lot size or the recapture effort or both. Second, there is the possible statistical variation, from lot to lot, in S itself. The effect of this variation on the precision of $\overline{S}$ is reduced (and better estimated) only by having multiple lots.

Multiple lots are desirable because S may vary with environmental conditions. If so, a sample of those conditions should be observed. This sample of conditions can either be treated as a random sample, or a design can be imposed in terms of external variables that might affect S.

Multiple lots are also desirable to detect equipment failures or other methodological problems. For example, if nine of 10 lots all released under similar conditions produced estimates of S ranging from 0.83 to 0.94, but one of the 10 lots produced $\hat{S} = 0.5$, you can check to see if a methodological problem occurred (and they can occur). If that lot can be shown to be aberrant, it can be deleted. It is not wise to put all one's fish in a single lot.

Finally, some form of repeated experimentation, such as replicated experimental units, is needed to get empirical estimates of variance. It is not scientifically desirable to use unquestioningly a theoretical variance in environmental studies. Theoretical variance estimators often underestimate the amount of variance occurring in a study. This failure of theory can be attributed to the failure of one or more assumptions. Lack of independence of fish fates might inflate variances (failure of assumption 7), and thus cause the estimated theoretical variances to be too low. Parameter heterogeneity (failure of assumption 12) may result in increased variation. Finally, if one's choice of model is not correct, theoretical variances may not be reliable (assumption 9). With respect to assumptions 7 and 12, the bias of a parameter estimator is less affected by the assumption failures than is its theoretical variance.

4.1.2. Replication and Multiple Lots

4.1.2.1. Replication. – Replicated experimental units are needed in order to estimate residual (or pure) error. However, it is very difficult (if not impossible) to define replication unambiguously because it is really a concept about random selection of experimental units, and the relevant population of experimental units is elusive. Perhaps because of this difficulty, many texts on statistics do not define replication. Some texts, such as Steel and Torrie (1980:Chapter 6), define it so generally that replication is a generic term for almost any sort of repeated experimental unit. Such a general definition is useful; it allows discussion of different levels of replication that are associated with different sources of variation. We decided to use a narrow definition of replication despite some inherent difficulties with it.

We define replication to mean repeated, independent experimental units treated identically so that there are no known differences (which would affect response) between the units before their responses to the experiment are observed. Differences in the responses of n replicate units must then reflect only residual (unexplained) sampling variation. If one looks closely enough, however, there will *always* be identifiable differences among experimental units before a study. Thus, what constitutes replicate units is really a function of our level of ignorance about external variables that might affect the outcome for those experimental units.

It is difficult to achieve replication (as we have defined it) in fisheries survival experiments, especially for the purpose of estimating within-lot sampling variation. Replicate lots should be released at the same time, which often is not possible. If they have been held in separate holding facilities, such facilities may have had their own effects.

For two, or more, lots to be replicates, they must have the same underlying survival (ϕ) and capture (p) parameters. Thus, the same treatment effect S applies to all n replicates and the variation among $\hat{S}_1, ..., \hat{S}_n$ is strictly sampling variation. It follows that $\hat{S}_1, ..., \hat{S}_n$ are independent and identically distributed random variables if replication has been successful.

We would like to have replicate treatment-control releases as a basis for reliably estimating empirical sampling variances and variance components. Because true replication in these experiments is so difficult, theoretical sampling variances have often been used. This is not necessary; it is possible to obtain empirical variances without true replication. Moreover, it is more important to have multiple lots than to have true replicates. It suffices to have, for example, 10 treatment-control lots released one a day every 3 days. Such a design includes no true replication, but could include either sublots, some natural partitioning of the recapture data, or both. We discuss these approaches below.

4.1.2.2. Sublots. – A lot consists of many fish, often thousands, so potentially there is information on empirical variation from just a single lot. To exploit this potential, one must use multiple, if not unique, marks within a lot.

The optimal case, statistically, occurs when uniquely numbered tags are used. Then the releases in that lot can be partitioned randomly by tag number into, say, five or 10 sublots and parameter estimates from each sublot can be computed. A good approach with large lots would be to partition on the last digit of the number, thus, creating 10 sublots. From these, we get 10 estimates, $\hat{S}_1, ..., \hat{S}_{10}$. Because the releases were all from one lot, each $\hat{S}_i$ estimates the single parameter S. Therefore, the variation among these 10 $\hat{S}_i$ reflects only within-lot sampling variation.

It is necessary to assume the estimators $\hat{S}_1, ..., \hat{S}_n$, based on sublots, are independent. By assumption 7 (fish fates are independent), this is true. However, this assumption could fail. It is safer to assume lots are independent (assumption 8), but it is difficult to believe one can achieve true replicates of lots. There is a tradeoff here. We believe sublots will be the better approximation to (true) replication because then $S_i = S$ is very believable and independence of sublots seems reasonable to us if sublots are large (say 500 to 1,000 or more fish).

4.1.2.3. Multiple lots. – Typically, lots are released at different times, so they cannot be assumed to be replicates for the purpose of estimating the within-lot sampling variation. This is because, for the ith treatment-control release, the treatment effect S_i may differ from other lots. We must now consider how these potentially different S_i are related to one another in order to analyze the data. The simplest case is if we can treat the (unknown) $S_1, ..., S_n$ as a random sample from a distribution with average value $E(S)$ and var$(S) = \sigma^2$. The case $\sigma^2 = 0$ corresponds to all S_i being the same, which is what we would expect if the n lots were replicates.

The unknown S_i may be viewed as random variables if the multiple lots are released at random with respect to conditions (environmental and engineering) that affect S. In this case, we want to estimate the average, $\overline{S}$. Indeed, if we know the true $S_i, i = 1, ..., n$, we would use

$$\overline{S} = \frac{1}{n} \sum_{i=1}^{n} S_i$$

as our point estimator, and

$$\hat{se}(\overline{S}) = \left(\frac{\sum_{i=1}^{n}(S_i - \overline{S})^2}{n(n-1)} \right)^{1/2}.$$

The complication of having only an estimator $\hat{S}_i$, often subject to substantial within-lot sampling variation, is not difficult to deal with if the lots are random with respect to variations in the treatment effect S.

The more complex case is if the multiple lots are released as part of a "designed" study. They might be released at known river flows, or at predetermined turbine operating conditions. Other design factors can be fish size or releases at different turbines. These design factors potentially influence the S_i and we want to test for that influence and possibly incorporate it into a model. If the S_i were known and were statistically independent over lots, the analysis could be done as a standard analysis of variance, regression, or covariance. However, we only have estimates, $\hat{S}_i$, subject to possibly large sampling variances, $\text{var}(\hat{S}_i \mid S_i)$, relative to σ^2.

4.1.3. Empirical Variance Estimation without Replication

4.1.3.1. Quasi-likelihood theory. – Likelihood theory relies on a completely specified probability model. Given that model, one derives a theoretical variance of the ML estimators. Often, especially with count data, the variation in the data clearly exceeds the postulated theoretical variation. This is so even when the structure (expected values) of the model seems quite appropriate for the data. Consequently, the point estimators are still acceptable, but not their theoretical variances.

In a large class of problems, the ML estimators and their theoretical variances actually depend only on the expected values and the structure of the theoretical variances implicit in the probability model. That is, one does not actually need the likelihood to get the ML estimates. In these cases, which include all multinomial models, the ML estimators can be computed by iteratively reweighted least squares; this has been known for a long time (see Jennrich and Moore 1975; Green 1984). The term quasi-likelihood is due to Wedderburn (1974) and formally extends standard likelihood theory to allow for excess variation, and empirical estimation of an variance-inflation factor, c. Quasi-likelihood theory justifies the usual ML estimators as optimal point estimators of the parameters, even when there is excess variation (over-dispersion) in the data. Recent papers and references on theoretical properties of quasi-likelihood inference include Healy (1981), Williams (1982), Cox (1983), McCullagh (1983), McCullagh and Nelder (1983), McCullagh and Pregibon (1985), and Royall (1986). Other investigations have shown likelihood methods are robust in the face of certain failures of the assumed model (Cox 1961; Huber 1967; Kent 1982; Sprott 1982). Finally, there are numerous published instances of encountering and coping with over-dispersion in count data (e.g., Bartlett 1936; Fisher 1949; Armitage 1957; Finney 1971).

Getting replicate estimators $\hat{S}_1, ..., \hat{S}_n$ is one route to empirical sampling variances. The other approach, justified by quasi-likelihood theory, is analogous to using residuals from a fitted model. We give here the general idea for multinomial models. Let $n_1, ..., n_k$ be a multinomial with a sample size $n_. = n_1 + ... + n_k$ and cell probabilities $\pi_1(\theta), ..., \pi_k(\theta)$. Then the theoretical variance-covariance matrix is $\Sigma(\theta)$ with elements

$$\text{var}(n_i) = n_. \pi_i(1 - \pi_i), \quad i = 1, ..., k ;$$

$$\text{cov}(n_i, n_j) = -n_. \pi_i \pi_j, \quad i \neq j .$$

The quasi-likelihood approach uses the model as

$$
\begin{bmatrix} n_1 \\ . \\ . \\ . \\ n_k \end{bmatrix} = n_. \begin{bmatrix} \pi_1(\theta) \\ . \\ . \\ . \\ \pi_k(\theta) \end{bmatrix} + \underline{\varepsilon} ,
$$

where $\underline{\varepsilon}$ has variance-covariance matrix

$$c \, \Sigma(\theta) .$$

Here, c is an unknown variance-inflation factor (a parameter to be estimated) and θ is an "a"-dimensional vector of parameters. Using a generalized inverse of $\Sigma(\theta)$ and iteratively reweighted least squares, one finds the generalized least-squares estimator of θ, which is also the ML estimator when $c = 1$ (see McCullagh and Nelder 1983). Given this $\hat{\theta}$, one can compute the $\hat{\pi}_i = \pi_i(\hat{\theta})$ and $\hat{\Sigma} = \Sigma(\hat{\theta})$. The usual chi-square goodness of fit can be computed (it is analogous to a residual sum of squares), call it χ^2_{GOF}; this chi-square test statistic has $k - 1 - a$ df. The estimator of c is

$$\hat{c} = \frac{\chi^2_{GOF}}{k - 1 - a} .$$

Using this $\hat{c}$, we get an estimator of the actual (empirical) sampling variances, e.g.,

$$\hat{\text{var}}(n_i) = \hat{c} n_. \hat{\pi}_i(1 - \hat{\pi}_i) .$$

This quasi-likelihood method also leads to estimators of the variances and covariances of the $\theta_1, ..., \theta_a$ as

$$\hat{c}[\hat{v}ar\,(\theta_i)]$$

and

$$\hat{c}[\hat{c}ov\,(\theta_i, \theta_j)]\,,$$

where $\hat{v}ar\,(\theta_i)$ and $\hat{c}ov\,(\theta_i, \theta_j)$ are the likelihood-theory estimators. Because $\hat{c}$ is estimated based on $k - 1 - a$ df, the adjusted variances are also now based on $k - 1 - a$ df (for example, for purposes of setting confidence intervals).

Quasi-likelihood theory justifies using all the ML theory we present in this monograph and then, if overdispersion is a problem, estimating $\hat{c}$ by a method such as the one above and multiplying $\hat{c}$ times the theoretical likelihood estimators of variances and covariances of θ. In general, the variance-inflation method involves estimating c from some residual variation in the recapture data after a structural model has been selected.

4.1.3.2. Variance-inflation factor method. – In practice, there can be difficulties deciding on what structural model we should use. However, once that model is chosen, quasi-likelihood theory justifies the ML estimates and the practice of adjusting their variances and covariances with $\hat{c}$. For example, if we selected model $H_{1\phi}$ under the complete capture history protocol, then the goodness of fit statistic for this model is the sum of the chi-squares of TESTs 1.$T2$, 1.$R2$, ..., 1.Rk-1 and TESTs 2 and 3. Divide that total chi-square by its degrees of freedom to obtain $\hat{c}$. (An hypothesis test can be made to test whether c is significantly greater than one.) This sort of procedure has long been used in probit analysis (Finney 1971), and it is recommended by McCullagh and Pregibon (1985). It provides one approach for getting an empirical sampling variance-inflation adjustment with capture-recapture data when the design does not include lots or sublots. Exactly how to proceed depends on the design used.

The most restrictive design is to have only one lot and no sublots; hence, only a single batch mark is used for controls and a different single batch mark for treatment fish. No release-time replication of any sort is then available. However, the recapture process will usually lead to multiple counts of some type. These multiple counts can be used to assess the empirical variation in the experimental data. If there are multiple recapture sites, there then are at least $k - 1$ counts. In principle, some components of TEST 1 can be used as a basis for estimating the variance-inflation factor, c. For example, if we judged model $H_{1\phi}$ to be the correct model in a first capture history protocol, then we can pool the chi-squares of TEST 1 components 1.$T2$, 1.$T3$, ..., 1.Tk - 1 ($k - 3$ df) as a basis to estimate c. The problem with this is that there are too few degrees of freedom unless there are 10 or more sites or occasions.

A practical alternative arises when fish are recaptured in gatewells at large dams: put recapture effort at all gatewells and use the variation in the treatment-to-control ratios across gatewells, within a dam, to assess the degree to which variation conforms to theory. If there are 10 gatewells at a dam, we have a 2×10 contingency table of counts for that dam. This gives 9 df. When data are pooled over even two or three recapture dams, there will be enough degrees of freedom from large-scale studies to estimate c, and test $c = 1$. The estimate of c is of the form

$$\hat{c} = \frac{\text{pooled chi-square}}{\text{pooled df}}.$$

When theoretical variances such as $\hat{\text{var}}(\hat{S})$ are then modified to be $\hat{c}\hat{\text{var}}(\hat{S})$, these new, empirically adjusted, sampling variance estimates have the degrees of freedom involved in $\hat{c}$.

Because we judge it so likely that $c > 1$, we recommend seriously considering such an empirical adjustment to theoretical sampling variances if the pooled degrees of freedom exceed 10 and the pooled chi-square is significant at even the $P = 0.2$ level. With only a few (pooled) degrees of freedom available, say, less than five, one wants more stringent evidence of the need for such an adjustment, i.e., the "usual" 0.05 or even 0.01 significance level.

4.1.4. Example with Multiple Lots

4.1.4.1. Description of the study. – As part of a large study, Long et al. (1975) released 12 pairs of treatment-control lots of young coho salmon *Oncorhynchus kisutch* at Lower Monumental Dam on the Snake River, Idaho. The experiment was for the purpose of measuring survival of small salmonids passing through operating turbines with and without perforated bulkheads. Part of that study involved the release of four lots of young fish on each of 3 days (13, 17, and 21 April 1974). Test fish were released upstream, and control fish downstream, of the test structure. This was an unknown capture history protocol with recaptures made at Ice Harbor and McNary dams (in that order), hence, $k = 3$. Marking was by freeze branding; marks batch-identified each treatment and release date and time. Fish were marked at a common facility, transported to Lower Monumental Dam, and then randomly allocated (within each treatment group) to separate holding tanks for each of the four lots released that day. The four lots released each day are not true replicates because of the possibility of an equipment effect. However, we will refer to the lots released within a day as reps (not replicates but reps in the sense of repeating the basic experiment).

4.1.4.2. Example data. – In order to illustrate some analysis methods we have extracted, from Table 1 of Long et al. (1975), the data for turbine unit 2. On a given day, releases were made in the morning from about 0700 to 0900 hours, one lot after the other. It was later found there were equipment problems with the control batch of rep 3. The treatment batch of rep 3 could still be used; however, we are not doing a definitive reanalysis of these data. Rather, we chose to drop both treatment and controls for rep 3 on each day, and thus have nine paired releases to illustrate methods. Note that there is also strong evidence that reps 1 and 4 differed from rep 2, but there did not appear to be a day effect (Table 4.1).

Table 4.2 shows the data in CH-matrix form for input into program RELEASE. From the analyses produced, we extracted the results shown in Tables 4.1 and 4.3; note, however, the estimate of $\bar{S}$, based on the totals in Table 4.1, required a separate computation. For purposes of analysis by program RELEASE, day 1, rep 1 is considered lot 1. For this lot 1, there were 28,739 treatment fish released. Table 4.2 shows $m_{t2} = 1,014$ (captures at Ice Harbor Dam) and $m_{t3} = 766$ (captures at McNary Dam), so $m_{t.} = 1,780$, as shown in Table 4.1. The input number 26,959 (at $h = \{1..\}$) is the difference of 28,739 and 1,780.

The notation and methods used in the first part of the analysis here are from Chapter 2.3. In particular, for any treatment-control pair,

$$\hat{S} = \frac{m_{t.}/R_{t1}}{m_{c.}/R_{c1}} \, ,$$

and the theoretical $\hat{v}ar\,(\hat{S} \mid S)$ is that for the unknown capture history protocol.

Table 4.1. – Releases, R_{v1}, and total recaptures, $m_{v.}$, for nine lots from Table 1 of Long et al. (1975), plus the computed $\hat{S}$ and theoretical $\hat{s}e\,(\hat{S})$ based on the unknown capture history protocol and model $H_{1ϕ}$.

Lot	Day	Rep[a]	Treatment fish		Control fish		$\hat{S}$	Theoretical $\hat{s}e\,(\hat{S})$
			R_{t1}	$m_{t.}$	R_{c1}	$m_{c.}$		
1	1	1	28,739	1,780	13,724	970	0.876	0.0344
2	1	2	28,856	1,587	14,577	1,066	0.752	0.0293
3	1	4	28,558	1,722	14,590	1,006	0.875	0.0341
4	2	1	26,395	1,914	14,122	1,125	0.910	0.0335
5	2	2	23,710	1,336	14,121	1,229	0.647	0.0251
6	2	4	27,293	1,744	13,665	1,060	0.824	0.0315
7	3	1	31,929	2,270	15,100	1,161	0.925	0.0327
8	3	2	31,663	1,788	15,404	1,252	0.695	0.0251
9	3	4	30,951	2,128	14,856	1,173	0.871	0.0311
Total			258,094	16,269	130,159	10,042	0.817[b]	0.0102[b]

[a]Reps are repeated experiments but not true replicates. Rep 3 was not used due to equipment problems.
[b]These values were computed from the totals rather than being averages over the nine values.

Table 4.2. – Program RELEASE input for analysis of reps 1, 2, and 4, taken on 3 days for turbine unit 2, Lower Monumental Dam, as reported by Long et al. (1975).

```
proc title data from Table 1, Long et al. 1975, turbine unit 2;
proc chmatrix nodetail occasions=3, groups=2 lots=9;
/* group 1 is the treatment, group two is the control */
                lot 1 ;
                    11.         1014        548;
                    1.1          766        422;
                    1..        26959      12754;
                lot 2 ;
                    11.          969        606;
                    1.1          618        460;
                    1..        27269      13511;
                lot 3 ;
                    11.          966        578;
                    1.1          756        428;
                    1..        26836      13584;
                lot 4 ;
                    11.         1006        619;
                    1.1          908        506;
                    1..        24481      12997;
                lot 5 ;
                    11.          686        597;
                    1.1          650        632;
                    1..        22374      12892;
                lot 6 ;
                    11.          932        552;
                    1.1          812        508;
                    1..        25549      12605;
                lot 7 ;
                    11.         1198        643;
                    1.1         1072        518;
                    1..        29659      13939;
                lot 8 ;
                    11.          932        698;
                    1.1          856        554;
                    1..        29875      14152;
                lot 9 ;
                    11.         1162        651;
                    1.1          966        522;
                    1..        28823      13683;
                proc stop;
```

Table 4.3. – Results of model selection tests for the example data of Long et al. (1975); each individual test has 1 df; totals have 9 df.

			TEST 1.R1		TEST 1.T2	
Lot	Day	Rep	x^2	P	x^2	P
1	1	1	11.72	<0.001	0.06	0.812
2	1	2	55.52	<0.001	4.69	0.030
3	1	4	12.21	<0.001	0.48	0.490
4	2	1	6.78	0.009	1.73	0.189
5	2	2	131.85	<0.001	1.97	0.161
6	2	4	26.69	<0.001	0.49	0.483
7	3	1	5.08	0.024	2.10	0.147
8	3	2	105.56	<0.001	3.89	0.049
9	3	4	15.63	<0.001	0.24	0.622
Total			371.03	<0.001	15.64	0.075

4.1.4.3. Model selection. – It is natural to look first at the data summary and estimators of S under model $H_{1\phi}$, which we presented in Table 4.1. However, prior to using model $H_{1\phi}$, we must examine the available tests of assumptions. For the unknown capture history protocol, the only within-lots tests available are TESTs 1.R1 and 1.T2. First, look at the nine chi-square results and the pooled results for TEST 1.T2, which here is testing that, for each lot,

$$\frac{p_{t2}}{p_{t2} + \phi_{t2}p_{t3}} = \frac{p_{c2}}{p_{c2} + \phi_{c2}p_{c3}}$$

(assuming no losses on capture). These test results are (overall) consistent with this null hypothesis. Moreover, TEST 1.R1, by comparison, shows that the overwhelming effect certainly is on ϕ_1 (this judgment is made in terms of the ratio 371.032/15.644 = 23.717, which roughly will behave like an *F*-statistic with 9 and 9 df under the null hypothesis that direct and indirect effects are equal).

More can be done with these data and test results to investigate a rep effect or a day effect. Analysis of variance can be used on the nine $\hat{S}_i$. The chi-squares can be pooled by day or rep. We proceed, however, to use model $H_{1\phi}$ and illustrate estimation of $\overline{S}$ and $\text{se}(\hat{S})$.

4.1.4.4. Point estimation. – From model $H_{1\phi}$ we have nine estimates, $\hat{S}_1, ..., \hat{S}_9$; let the corresponding true treatment effects be S_i, $i = 1, ..., 9$. We assume that either all S_i are the same $(S_i \equiv S)$, or any variations in the S_i are random; hence, we treat the S_i as random variables with mean $E(S)$ and unknown variance σ^2. In either of these cases, $\overline{S} = E(\hat{S})$ is the parameter of interest and the recommended estimator of $\overline{S}$ is obtained by pooling over lots and analyzing the pooled data. The resultant $\overline{S}_{pooled}$ is almost identical to an optimally weighted average of the separate $\hat{S}_i$. It is superior to such an optimally weighted average in that the optimal weights depend on unknown parameters that would have to be estimated. In this example, given the above assumption about $S_1, ..., S_9$ (which may not be true; this is only an example of methods),

$$\overline{S}_{pooled} = \frac{16,269/258,094}{10,042/130,159} = 0.817.$$

From the pooled data, totals by recapture dam are

ν	Ice Harbor	McNary	m_ν
t	8,865	7,404	16,269
c	5,492	4,550	10,042

The estimate of $\hat{var}(\overline{S})$ for the unknown capture history protocol uses these sums by dam (see Chapter 2.3); we find the theoretical standard error for the $\overline{S}_{pooled}$ to be 0.0102.

The use of standard error of $\overline{S}_{pooled}$ is based on restrictive assumptions: (1) all $S_i \equiv S$, so there is no variation in treatment effect attributed to unknown (or known) variations in test conditions over reps and days, and (2) for a given lot the assumption of binomial variation is true. Both assumptions are likely to fail. In general, theoretical variances tend to underestimate the real sampling variance, so even if all $S_i = S$ (this is equivalent to assuming $\sigma^2 = 0$), the $\hat{se}(\hat{S}_i)$ are too low.

Because sample sizes of treatment and controls are about the same over the nine lots, we have reason to believe the nine true $var(\hat{S})$ are all about the same. It then follows that a simple average of the $\hat{S}_i$ is going to give about the same value as the pooled estimator, 0.817. We find

$$\overline{\hat{S}} = \frac{1}{9}\left[\sum_{i=1}^{9} \hat{S}_i\right] = 0.819.$$

The corresponding standard error for this average is computed (assuming independence among lots) from

$$\hat{\text{var}}\left(\frac{1}{9}\sum_{i=1}^{9}\hat{S}_i\right) = \frac{1}{9^2}\sum_{i=1}^{9}\hat{\text{var}}(\hat{S}_i),$$

or, here

$$\hat{\text{se}}\left(\frac{1}{9}\sum_{i=1}^{9}\hat{S}_i\right) = \frac{1}{9}\left(\sum_{i=1}^{9}[\hat{\text{se}}(\hat{S}_i)]^2\right)^{1/2}$$

$$= 0.0103.$$

Thus, for this example, pooling the nine lots and using the unknown capture history analysis gives virtually the same result as analyzing the unweighted means of the nine $\hat{S}_i$.

4.1.4.5. Variance estimation. – Either of the point estimates of $\overline{S}$ is reasonable; however, the theoretical standard error estimate of $\hat{\text{se}}(\hat{\overline{S}}) = 0.0103$ is not reliable and we recommend against it. A valid estimate of the variance that we should associate with $\hat{\overline{S}}$ in this example, under the assumption that the true $S_1, ..., S_9$ can themselves be considered a sample, is

$$\hat{\text{var}}(\hat{\overline{S}}) = \frac{\sum_{i=1}^{9}(\hat{S}_i - \hat{\overline{S}})^2}{(9)(8)}$$

$$= 0.0010844,$$

or $\hat{\text{se}}(\hat{\overline{S}}) = 0.0329$. The ratio of this empirical standard error (estimate) to the theoretical standard error (which assumes all $S_i \equiv S$) is

$$\frac{0.03293}{0.0102} = 3.228.$$

This empirical variance of $\hat{\overline{S}}$ is based on only 8 df; thus, one might want to test that this ratio is statistically significantly larger than one. A quick way to make this judgment is to treat $8(3.228)^2$ as a realization of a chi-square variable with 8 df. Symbolically, this test statistic is

$$\frac{[\text{empirical } \hat{v}\text{ar}(\hat{\overline{S}})] \ df}{[\text{theoretical } \hat{v}\text{ar}(\hat{\overline{S}})]},$$

where df is the degrees of freedom of the empirical estimator. Here, this test statistic has the value 83.4, which is highly significant ($P < 0.001$). We conclude that the theoretical standard error for $\overline{S}$ should not be used; we will, therefore, use the empirical $\hat{s}e(\hat{\overline{S}})$.

Given that the empirical $\hat{s}e(\hat{\overline{S}})$ is to be used, the 95% CI for $E(S)$ is based on the t-distribution for 8 df. From Table 6.7, the appropriate t-value in $\hat{\overline{S}} \pm t\hat{s}e(\hat{\overline{S}})$ is $t = 2.306$; hence, the 95% CI limits are 0.817 ± 0.076, or 0.741 to 0.893.

4.2. Empirical Variance Estimation

4.2.1. Estimation of the Variance-Inflation Factor

Here we consider a hypothetical example where practical constraints allowed only the release of 8,860 fish in one lot at dam 1. Only batch marks (one mark for treatment fish, one for control fish) were used and recaptured fish were removed at dams 2 and 3 ($k = 3$); thus, the first capture history protocol applied.

The biologists initially believed the treatment effect would be acute but quite severe at $S \sim 0.7$. From Part 6, the optimal number of treatment fish is $R_{t1} = 1.215 R_{c1}$. Thus, $R_{t1} = 4,860$ and $R_{c1} = 4,000$. Approximately 60% of the recapture effort was planned at dam 2, and the remaining effort at dam 3. From previous experience, biologists believed $p_{t2} = p_{c2} = 0.12$ and $p_{t3} = p_{c3} = 0.08$ could be achieved. This planning, based on model $H_{1\phi}$, resulted in careful consideration of all of the practical details. The resulting data for the single lot are

Group	R_{v1}	m_{v12}	m_{v13}	r_{v1}
t	4,860	346	146	492
c	4,000	413	166	579

With $k = 3$, TEST 1.$T2$ can be computed to test (approximately) $p_{t2} = p_{c2}$. In the example, the result of this test yields $\chi^2 = 0.13$, 1 df, $P = 0.72$. Thus, model $H_{1\phi}$ is supported. TEST 1.$R1$ tests $\phi_{t1} = \phi_{c1}$, and this is strongly rejected ($\chi^2 = 39.10$, 1 df, $P = <0.001$). Thus, a treatment effect on survival is shown.

The estimate of treatment survival under model $H_{1\phi}$ is 0.699 (se = 0.040). ($\hat{S}$ = 0.724, se = 0.081 under model H'_{2p}.) The model selected seems satisfactory and the point estimate also appears satisfactory. A valid criticism at this point is the measure of precision. The estimated theoretical standard error is based on multinomial sampling variation and may, indeed, be too low (i.e., the theoretical se may be underestimated). We have emphasized the importance of some form of replication so an empirical measure of precision can be obtained. Here, only one lot of fish was released; however, further analysis may yield insights into the adequacy of the variance estimate.

In the example, we find that the recapture data m_{v1j} were recorded for each gatewell in dams 2 and 3. These data are tabulated below, partitioned by dam and gatewell.

Gatewell	Dam 2		Dam 3	
	t	c	t	c
1	18	24	20	19
2	61	51	29	47
3	89	101	63	51
4	49	57	13	18
5	38	55	12	15
6	91	125	9	16
Total	346	413	146	166

These data can be used to estimate the variance-inflation factor c (as presented in Section 4.1.3). First, the two 2×6 contingency tables are analyzed by PROC CHISQ in program RELEASE.

Dam	χ^2	df	P
2	5.70	5	0.34
3	7.40	5	0.19
Total	13.10	10	0.22

The estimator of the variance-inflation factor c is $\hat{c} = \chi^2/\mathrm{df} = 13.10/10 = 1.31$ (from Section 4.1.3). Thus, $\hat{se}(\hat{S}) = \sqrt{1.31} \times$ the theoretical standard error; or $1.144 \times 0.040 = 0.046$. An approximate 95% CI for the example is

$$\hat{S} \pm t_{\alpha/2,10}\hat{se}(\hat{S})$$

or

$$0.699 \pm 2.228(0.046)$$

or

$$0.699 \pm 0.102 \,.$$

This interval compares with 0.699 ± 0.078 if the variance-inflation factor is not incorporated.

In summary, the recapture data m_{v1j} were partitioned by gatewell to allow a type of empirical variance to be computed using quasi-likelihood methods. Model $H_{1\phi}$ was selected, and the estimated treatment survival rate was 0.699 (se = 0.046). We believe the quasi-likelihood approach to variance estimation deserves full consideration. However, the use of replication or multiple lots is the superior procedure to be followed.

4.2.2. Replication Only

In the case of true replication, the underlying parameters (in particular S) are the same for each replicate and we infer that this is so from the design of the study. If parameters do not vary over replicates, this simplifies obtaining an optimal point estimate of S and an empirical variance estimator of $\hat{S}$. The closest we can come to replicates is the use of sublots based on different (or unique) within-lot marks.

For the purpose of discussion, we assume that the data have been thoroughly analyzed to determine a model, and that, on the basis of that model, $\hat{S}_1, ..., \hat{S}_n$ have been computed for the n replicates. By assumption, these estimated effects are independent. Also available are the corresponding estimated theoretical sampling variances $\hat{var}(\hat{S}_i \mid S_i)$. We make particular reference here to the simple estimator (valid under $H_{1\phi}$)

$$\hat{S}_i = \frac{r_{ti1}/R_{ti1}}{r_{ci1}/R_{ci1}} \,,$$

with sampling variance

$$\text{var}(\hat{S}_i \mid S_i) = c(S)^2 \left[\frac{1}{E(r_{ti1})} - \frac{1}{R_{ti1}} + \frac{1}{E(r_{ci1})} - \frac{1}{R_{ci1}} \right].$$

Here, r_{ti1} and r_{ci1} are the total recaptures (r_{t1} and r_{c1}) partitioned by sublot i. The partitioned releases at dam 1 are $R_{v11}, ..., R_{vm1}$; $v = t$ or c.

To get a best estimate of $\hat{S}$, pool the data over replicates and analyze the pooled data under the chosen model. In particular, if model $H_{1\phi}$ is used, the optimal estimator of S is

$$\hat{S} = \frac{r_{t1}/R_{t1}}{r_{c1}/R_{c1}}.$$

General statistical theory also tells us that the above pooled estimator is (asymptotically) equivalent to the optimal weighted average of the separate $\hat{S}_1, ..., \hat{S}_n$:

$$\hat{S} = \frac{\sum\limits_{i=1}^{n} w_i \hat{S}_i}{\sum\limits_{i=1}^{n} w_i},$$

where

$$w_i = \frac{1}{\text{var}(\hat{S}_i \mid S_i)}.$$

It is partly because these weights are not known, rather they have to be estimated, that we recommend pooling the replicates to get $\hat{S}$. The rest of the reason is that a nonlinear pooling is often superior to even the optimal linear weighted average.

The formula for the empirical variance of $\hat{S}$ is

$$\text{var}(\hat{S}) = \frac{\sum\limits_{i=1}^{n} w_i (\hat{S}_i - \hat{S})^2}{\left[\sum\limits_{i=1}^{n} w_i \right] (n - 1)}.$$

To compute an estimate, $\hat{\text{var}}(\hat{S})$, from this formula, we must know, or estimate, either the weights, or the relative weights,

$$\frac{w_i}{\sum\limits_{j=1}^{n} w_j} , \quad i = 1, ..., n .$$

Usually, one thinks of replicates as all having the same sample size. If that is true, then all R_{ti1} are the same, as are all R_{ci1}, and then (whether or not the $R_{ti1} = R_{ci1}$) all the weights are the same, $w_i = w$, so they drop out giving us the usual formula

$$\hat{\text{var}}(\hat{S}) = \frac{\sum\limits_{i=1}^{n} (\hat{S}_i - \hat{S})^2}{n(n-1)} .$$

We recommend equal sizes for all replicates because the relative weights are then known making empirical variance estimation easy.

In general, under model $H_{1\phi}$, the weight is given by

$$\frac{1}{w_i} = \frac{1}{R_{i1}} \left[\frac{1}{\gamma_i} \left(\frac{1}{S\lambda_{c1}} - 1 \right) + \frac{1}{1-\gamma_i} \left(\frac{1}{\lambda_{c1}} - 1 \right) \right] ,$$

where

$$R_{i1} = R_{ti1} + R_{ci1} ,$$

and

$$\gamma_i = \frac{R_{ti1}}{R_{i1}} .$$

If the release ratios are kept constant (e.g., at $R_{ti1} = R_{ci1}$), then all $\gamma_i = \gamma$ are the same and we can take the relative weights as $w_i = R_{i1}$. In this case, the formula for the empirical variance of $\hat{S}$ is

$$\hat{\text{var}}(\hat{S}) = \frac{\sum_{i=1}^{n} R_{i1}(\hat{S}_i - \hat{S})^2}{\left[\sum_{i=1}^{n} R_{i1}\right](n-1)} .$$

The optimal release ratios of treatment to control are the same for all replicates because the true parameters are the same over all n replicates. It should not arise, except by accident, that the ratios γ_i differ. Slight differences in the γ_i have little effect and it is then better to use the weight as $w_i = R_{i1}$ than to estimate w_i.

4.2.3 Random Multiple Lots Only

Replication, as above, is difficult to achieve in these fisheries experiments. The more likely design is multiple lots. We treat here the case where it is assumed that the $S_1, ..., S_n$ are a random sample, with $\overline{S} = \hat{E}(S)$ and population variance σ^2.

From general linear least-squares statistical theory, the optimal linear combination of the $\hat{S}_i$ is

$$\hat{\overline{S}} = \frac{\sum_{i=1}^{n} w_i \hat{S}_i}{\sum w_i} ,$$

where now

$$w_i = \frac{1}{\sigma^2 + \text{var}(\hat{S}_i \mid S_i)} .$$

Both σ^2 and the true sampling variance $\text{var}(\hat{S}_i \mid S_i)$ are unknown. The notation $\text{var}(\hat{S}_i)$ and $\text{var}(\hat{S}_i \mid S_i)$ mean the same thing; we merely wish to emphasize here the conditional nature of the within-lot sampling variation of $\hat{S}_i$. Note also that only the relative values of these weights need to be known to compute $\hat{\overline{S}}$.

The theoretical variance of $\hat{\bar{S}}$ is

$$\text{var}(\hat{\bar{S}}) = \frac{1}{\sum\limits_{i=1}^{n} w_i} \ .$$

This requires the absolute weights. Although $\text{var}(\hat{S}_i \mid S_i)$ is estimable if we assume $c = 1$, it is still necessary to know σ^2 to use the above formula.

An alternative, which leads to an empirical variance estimator, is

$$\text{var}(\hat{\bar{S}}) = \frac{\sum\limits_{i=1}^{n} w_i(\hat{S}_i - \hat{\bar{S}})^2}{\left[\sum\limits_{i=1}^{n} w_i\right](n-1)} \ .$$

When $\sigma^2 = 0$, the above reduces to the case of n replicates. Often, it will be better to take these weights, w_i, as equal rather than trying to estimate them (because the estimates are subject to uncertainty). Thus, a practical formula will often be the simple one of

$$\text{var}(\hat{\bar{S}}) = \frac{\sum\limits_{i=1}^{n} (\hat{S}_i - \hat{\bar{S}})^2}{n(n-1)} \ ,$$

with

$$\hat{\bar{S}} = \frac{1}{n} \sum\limits_{i=1}^{n} \hat{S}_i \ .$$

This simple formula is reasonable if the $\text{var}(\hat{S}_i \mid S_i)$ are all nearly equal, or if they are all small relative to σ^2 (for example, if σ^2 is an order of magnitude greater than any $\text{var}(\hat{S}_i \mid S_i)$). In theory, when the S_i vary, the $\text{var}(\hat{S}_i \mid S_i)$ will not be all equal. However, there is so much computational difficulty and statistical variation associated with estimating both σ^2 and $\text{var}(\hat{S}_i \mid S_i)$ that treating these weights as all equal will often give better results than estimating them.

With low sampling effort (so $\text{var}(\hat{S}_i \mid S_i)$ dominates σ^2), it suffices to use the approximation

$$w_i = \frac{1}{\text{var}(\hat{S}_i \mid S_i)} \; ;$$

that is, we treat the n lots as if they were replicates because most of the variation in the $\hat{S}_i$ is sampling variation. Now, again, only the relative values of the weights are needed (so the value of c is not needed). In this case we recommend the weights be estimated as

$$\hat{w}_i = \frac{1}{\hat{\text{var}}(\overline{\hat{S}} \mid S_i)} \; .$$

That is, replace $\hat{S}_i$ in $\hat{\text{var}}(\hat{S}_i \mid S_i)$ by $\overline{\hat{S}}$. For model $H_{1\phi}$, this corresponds to taking the relative weights as

$$\hat{w}_i = \left[\frac{1}{r_{ti1}} - \frac{1}{R_{ti1}} + \frac{1}{r_{ci1}} - \frac{1}{R_{ci1}} \right]^{-1} ,$$

then computing the weighted mean and empirical $\hat{\text{var}}(\overline{\hat{S}})$. In general, this procedure corresponds to using the weights as

$$\hat{w}_i = \left(\text{cv}(\hat{S}_i) \right)^{-2} ,$$

which we recommend if $\text{var}(\hat{S}_i \mid S_i)$ dominates σ^2.

If one is unwilling to settle for approximate relative weights, then σ^2 must be estimated. To estimate σ^2 requires a reliable (unbiased) estimate of the $\text{var}(\hat{S}_i \mid S_i)$, $i = 1, ..., n$ in order to separate σ^2 from sampling variation. Given such estimators, $\hat{\text{var}}(\hat{S}_i \mid S_i)$, the estimate of σ^2 requires iterative solution of a complicated equation. Because this is a matter of estimating variance components, we defer its discussion until Chapter 4.3.

4.2.4. Treatment Effect as a Relative Risk

Inference about the ratio of two proportions arises in many subject areas. In medical contexts, this problem is referred to as relative risk. There is an extensive literature on relative risk (Gart 1985). In our notation, the general statistical model assumed for relative risk is

$$r_{ti1} \mid R_{ti1} \sim \text{bin}(R_{ti1}, S_i \lambda_{ci1}) ,$$

$$r_{ci1} \mid R_{ci1} \sim \text{bin}(R_{ci1}, \lambda_{ci1}) ,$$

$i = 1, ..., n$. These n independent, paired data sets are replicates if $\lambda_{ci1} = \lambda_{c1}$ and $S_i = S$ for all $i = 1, ..., n$. We have dealt with this case. If the λ_{ci1} and S_i vary, then the MLE of S_i is

$$\hat{S}_i = \frac{r_{ti1}/R_{ti1}}{r_{ci1}/R_{ci1}} , \quad i = 1, ..., n .$$

We referred to this case as random multiple lots.

There is an intermediate case: all $S_i = S$ but the λ_{ci1} vary. Gart (1985) gives the ML solution for this intermediate case. The ML estimator of S is not closed-form; rather, it must be found by numerical iterative methods (program SURVIV can be used to do this computation). However, the pooled estimator has comparable efficiency:

$$\hat{S} = \frac{\sum_{i=1}^{n} r_{ti1}/\sum_{i=1}^{n} R_{ti1}}{\sum_{i=1}^{n} r_{ci1}/\sum_{i=1}^{n} R_{ci1}} .$$

In medical and pharmacological applications, the sample sizes R_{ti1} and R_{ci1} are often <100 (and often like the data of Stier and Kynard 1986); certainly such data are one to three orders of magnitude less than in many fisheries experiments. With such small sample sizes, it may be worth the effort to find the exact MLE. At small sample sizes, however, there is no guarantee that the MLE is optimal.

4.3. Estimation of Variance Components

4.3.1. Some Theory

Two conceptually distinct types of variation constitute the essence of "variance components": sampling variance and parameter variance across samples. These topics were introduced in Section 1.2.3. Let S_i represent the treatment effect for lot i, with n random lots in a study. Data analysis results in the estimates, $\hat{S}_i$, $i = 1, ..., n$. The uncertainty associated with $\hat{S}_i$ as an estimator of S_i is $\text{var}(\hat{S}_i \mid S_i)$, the sampling variance of $\hat{S}_i$. Usually we have denoted this sampling variance as $\text{var}(\hat{S}_i)$; the extended notation here is to emphasize the conditional nature of this sampling variance.

If one knows the values of $S_1, ..., S_n$, inference is simple:

$$\overline{S} = \frac{1}{n} \sum_{i=1}^{n} S_i \,,$$

(i.e., $\hat{E}(S) = \overline{S}$),

$$\hat{\sigma}^2 = \frac{1}{n} \sum_{i=1}^{n} (S_i - \overline{S})^2 \,,$$

and

$$\hat{\text{se}}(\overline{S}) = \frac{\hat{\sigma}}{\sqrt{n}} \,.$$

Unfortunately, the true S_i for lot i is never known. We have only estimators $\hat{S}_1, ..., \hat{S}_n$, each subject to a possibly different sampling variance. Within the context of the entire study, the total variation of $\hat{S}_i$ is

$$\text{var}(\hat{S}_i) = \sigma^2 + \text{var}(\hat{S}_i \mid S_i) \,.$$

Often, the sampling variance $\text{var}(\hat{S}_i \mid S_i)$ is larger than σ^2. However, $\text{var}(\hat{S}_i \mid S_i)$ depends on the size of lot i and recapture rates, whereas σ^2 is independent of the sample sizes and parameters that affect $\text{var}(\hat{S}_i \mid S_i)$; σ^2 depends on differences among lots with respect to fish characteristics and environmental factors (some controllable, some not). If, during a 1-month study, 10 lots are released, one every 3 days, then it is likely there will be differences in the parameters $S_1, ..., S_{10}$. The fact that fish in the 10th lot were larger and older at release than those in lot 1 could have an effect.

In Section 4.2.3, we discussed estimation of $E(S)$ in simple situations when we can avoid estimating σ^2. In particular, if all true (as opposed to estimated) sampling variances are the same then use

$$\hat{\bar{S}} = \frac{1}{n} \sum_{i=1}^{n} \hat{S}_i \, ,$$

with theoretical (total) variance

$$\text{var}(\hat{\bar{S}}) = \frac{\sigma^2 + E[\text{var}(\hat{S} \mid S)]}{n}$$

and the unbiased estimator

$$\hat{\text{var}}(\hat{\bar{S}}) = \frac{\sum_{i=1}^{n}(\hat{S}_i - \hat{\bar{S}})^2}{n(n-1)} \, .$$

Even though $\text{var}(\hat{\bar{S}})$ is the sum of two conceptually distinct components of variation, we can, in this simple case, estimate $\text{var}(\hat{\bar{S}})$ without having separate estimators of σ^2 and $E(\text{var}(\hat{S} \mid S))$. This is not always true. In more general situations, it becomes necessary to estimate σ^2 in the processes of computing $\hat{\bar{S}}$ and $\text{var}(\hat{\bar{S}})$. For this separation of variance components to be valid, one must first have a valid estimator of the sampling variance, $\text{var}(\hat{S}_i \mid S_i)$.

From the above, when we can assume the $\text{var}(\hat{S}_i \mid S_i)$ are all equal, then

$$\hat{\sigma}^2 = \frac{1}{n-1} \left[\sum_{i=1}^{n} (\hat{S}_i - \hat{\bar{S}})^2 \right] - \frac{1}{n} \left[\sum_{i=1}^{n} \hat{\text{var}}(\hat{S}_i \mid S_i) \right]. \tag{4.1}$$

This derives from

$$E[\hat{\text{var}}(\hat{\bar{S}})] = \frac{\sigma^2 + E[\text{var}(\hat{S} \mid S)]}{n}$$

and

$$\hat{E}[\text{var}(\hat{S} \mid S)] = \frac{1}{n} \sum_{i=1}^{n} \hat{\text{var}}(\hat{S}_i \mid S_i) \, .$$

Even when the sampling variances are not all equal, the above provides a (non-optimal) estimator of σ^2, which can be useful as a starting value for iterative solution of the better estimator below.

The general theory, as introduced in Section 4.2.3, is to use a weighted procedure, with weights equal to the reciprocals of the total variance of $\hat{S}_i$,

$$w_i = \frac{1}{\sigma^2 + \text{var}(\hat{S}_i \mid S_i)} \, ,$$

$$\hat{\bar{S}} = \frac{\sum_{i=1}^{n} w_i \hat{S}_i}{\sum_{i=1}^{n} w_i} \, ,$$

with theoretical variance

$$\text{var}(\hat{\bar{S}}) = \frac{1}{\sum_{i=1}^{n} w_i}$$

and empirical variance estimator

$$\hat{\text{var}}(\hat{\bar{S}}) = \frac{\sum_{i=1}^{n} w_i (\hat{S}_i - \hat{\bar{S}})^2}{\left[\sum_{i=1}^{n} w_i \right] (n - 1)} \, .$$

When the w_i are the true (unknown) weights, then

$$E[\hat{\text{var}}(\hat{\bar{S}})] = \text{var}(\hat{\bar{S}}) \, .$$

Therefore, if we have reliable estimators of sampling variance, we can solve the following equation for σ^2:

$$\frac{1}{n-1} \sum_{i=1}^{n} \hat{w}_i (\hat{S}_i - \hat{\bar{S}})^2 = 1 \, , \tag{4.2}$$

where $\bar{\hat{S}}$ is the weighted average

$$\bar{\hat{S}} = \frac{\sum\limits_{i=1}^{n} \hat{w}_i \, \hat{S}_i}{\sum\limits_{i=1}^{n} \hat{w}_i} \qquad (4.3)$$

and

$$\hat{w}_i = \frac{1}{\hat{\sigma}^2 + \hat{\text{var}}(\hat{S}_i \mid S_i)} \, . \qquad (4.4)$$

Because there is only one unknown here, $\hat{\sigma}^2$, numerical solution of this equation is straightforward. If the best estimator of each $\text{var}(\hat{S}_i \mid S_i)$ is the average

$$\hat{\text{var}} = \frac{1}{n} \sum\limits_{i=1}^{n} \hat{\text{var}}(\hat{S}_i \mid S_i), \qquad (4.5)$$

then the solution is the simple one, $\tilde{\sigma}^2$, given in equation (4.1).

A useful approximate test exists for the null hypothesis H_0: $\sigma^2 = 0$. Compute

$$\chi^2 = \frac{(n-1)\hat{\text{var}}(\bar{\hat{S}})}{\hat{\text{var}}(\bar{\hat{S}} \mid \sigma^2 = 0)} \, , \qquad (4.6)$$

where

$$\hat{\text{var}}(\bar{\hat{S}} \mid \sigma^2 = 0) = \frac{1}{\sum\limits_{i=1}^{n} \dfrac{1}{\hat{\text{var}}(\hat{S}_i \mid S_i)}} \, .$$

Under H_0: $\sigma^2 = 0$, χ^2 is distributed as chi-square with $n - 1$ df.

A confidence interval can be constructed for σ^2 by solving two modified versions of equation (4.2). Assume that we want a $(1 - \alpha)100\%$ CI, where $\alpha = \alpha_L + \alpha_U$ and L and U stand for lower and upper, respectively. Usually we will take $\alpha_L = \alpha_U$; hence, for a 95% CI, $\alpha_L = \alpha_U = 0.025$. One first looks up the percentile (critical) values for the central chi-square distribution corresponding to α_L and $1 - \alpha_U$, i.e., find $\chi^2_{n-1,\,\alpha_L}$ and $\chi^2_{n-1,1-\alpha_U}$. For example, for 10 df, $\chi^2_{10,0.025} = 3.25$ and $\chi^2_{10,0.975} = 20.5$. To find the upper limit, $\hat{\sigma}_U^2$, on σ^2, solve the equation (for $\sigma_U{}^2$)

$$\frac{1}{n-1} \sum_{i=1}^{n} \hat{w}_i \left(\hat{S}_i - \hat{\bar{S}} \right)^2 = \frac{\chi^2_{n-1,\,\alpha_L}}{n-1} , \tag{4.7}$$

where $\hat{\bar{S}}$ is the weighted average, as in equation (4.3), and the weights are as in equation (4.4). To find the lower limit, $\hat{\sigma}_L{}^2$, solve the equation (for $\sigma_L{}^2$)

$$\frac{1}{n-1} \sum_{i=1}^{n} \hat{w}_i \left(\hat{S}_i - \hat{\bar{S}} \right)^2 = \frac{\chi^2_{n-1,\,1-\alpha_U}}{n-1} . \tag{4.8}$$

If equation (4.8) does not have a positive solution for σ^2, then set $\hat{\sigma}_L{}^2 = 0.0$ and adjust to a one-sided $(1 - \alpha)100\%$ CI by redefining $\alpha_U = \alpha$.

Sometimes it suffices to have all $\hat{var}(\hat{S}_i \mid S_i)$ the same. Thus, one replaces each $\hat{var}(\hat{S}_i \mid S_i)$ by $\hat{var}$ of equation (4.5). Equation (4.1) is then the solution to equation (4.2). The confidence limits now also have explicit solutions:

$$\hat{\sigma}_L{}^2 = \frac{\sum_{i=1}^{n} \left(\hat{S}_i - \hat{\bar{S}} \right)^2}{\chi^2_{n-1,\,1-\alpha_U}} - \hat{var} \tag{4.9}$$

and

$$\hat{\sigma}_U{}^2 = \frac{\sum_{i=1}^{n} \left(\hat{S}_i - \hat{\bar{S}} \right)^2}{\chi^2_{n-1,\,\alpha_L}} - \hat{var} , \tag{4.10}$$

where, for these two equations,

$$\hat{\bar{S}} = \frac{1}{n} \sum_{i=1}^{n} \hat{S}_i .$$

The estimator of σ^2 obtained by equations (4.2)-(4.4) is not the MLE. The equations for the MLE are easily derived; they also require iterative solution in general. In the special case of all $var(S_i \mid S_i)$ being the same, the MLE exists in closed form; it is then given by equation

(4.1) *modified* to have n, not $n - 1$, in the denominator of the first term. When the number of lots is small, then the MLE of σ^2 is substantially biased. Of course, this bias can be substantially reduced by a simple adjustment to the likelihood equations. This bias-adjusted MLE would be acceptable for small n, and is preferred asymptotically as n gets large. However, n (lots) is unlikely to be large in these release-recapture experiments. Consequently, there is no compelling reason to use the MLE of σ^2 here. We would still use the MLE if we did not want confidence intervals on σ^2. Large-sample likelihood theory provides for likelihood intervals, but those intervals are not reliable for small sample sizes (n). Instead, we believe it is better, when n is small, to base a CI for σ^2 on the result that $\Sigma w_i(\hat{S}_i - \overline{S})^2$ has approximately a central chi-square distribution.

Using asymptotic theory, the relative efficiency of the chi-square based estimator to the MLE is

$$\left[1 + \frac{\sum_{i=1}^{n} (w_i - \overline{w})^2}{n (\overline{w})^2} \right]^{-1} ;$$

here

$$\overline{w} = \frac{1}{n} \sum_{i=1}^{n} w_i ,$$

$$w_i = \frac{1}{\sigma^2 + \text{var}(\hat{S}_i \mid S_i)} .$$

Notice that this is just $(1 + (\text{cv})^2)^{-1}$, cv being the coefficient of variation among the true $w_1, ..., w_n$. This relative efficiency is usually quite high; however, we again emphasize that our reason for recommending the moment estimator for small n is the more reliable confidence interval that can then be computed.

4.3.2. Simple Example

Section 1.2.2 introduced variance components and gave a numerical example. The parameter there is a proportion; the five true p_i are 0.13, 0.17, 0.16, 0.13, and 0.16; $\overline{p} = 0.015$; and the estimate of σ based directly on these p_i is $\widetilde{\sigma} = 0.0187$:

$$\widetilde{\sigma}^2 = \frac{1}{4} \sum_{i=1}^{5} (p_i - \overline{p})^2 .$$

In this example, the true sampling variances are the same for all 5 years. Consequently, the simple method works, equation (4.1):

$$\hat{\bar{p}} = \frac{1}{5} \sum_{i=1}^{5} \hat{p}_i$$

$$= 0.16$$

and

$$\hat{var}(\hat{\bar{p}}) = \frac{\sum_{i=1}^{5} (\hat{p}_i - \hat{\bar{p}})^2}{(5)(4)}$$

$$= 0.00034969 .$$

Also,

$$\hat{var}(\hat{\bar{p}} \mid \sigma^2 = 0) = \frac{1}{5^2} \sum_{i=1}^{n} \hat{var}(\hat{p}_i)$$

$$= 0.000300675 .$$

The estimate of σ^2 is thus

$$\hat{\sigma}^2 = 5 \left[\hat{var}(\hat{\bar{p}}) - \hat{var}(\hat{\bar{p}} \mid \sigma^2 = 0) \right]$$

$$= 0.00024508 ,$$

or, $\hat{\sigma} = 0.0157$.

Equations (4.9) and (4.10) can be used to compute the 95% CI on σ^2. Required quantities are

$$\hat{var} = \frac{1}{5} \sum_{i=1}^{n} \hat{var}(\hat{p}_i \mid p_i)$$

$$= 0.0015034 ,$$

$$\sum_{i=1}^{5} \left(\hat{p}_i - \hat{\bar{p}} \right)^2 = 0.0069938 \,,$$

$$\chi^2_{4, 0.025} = 0.484 \,,$$

$$\chi^2_{4, 0.975} = 11.1 \,.$$

Thus, we find

$$\hat{\sigma}_L^2 = \frac{0.0069938}{11.1} - 0.0015034$$

$$= -0.000873$$

and

$$\hat{\sigma}_U^2 = \frac{0.0069938}{0.484} - 0.0015034$$

$$= 0.01295 \,.$$

That the lower bound is negative shows we cannot be certain σ^2 is greater than zero here. It suffices to take the interval on σ as 0 to 0.114, with $\hat{\sigma} = 0.0157$.

The formal test of H_0: $\sigma^2 = 0$ is

$$\chi^2 = \frac{4 \, \hat{\text{var}}(\hat{\bar{p}})}{\hat{\text{var}}(\bar{p} \mid \sigma^2 = 0)}$$

$$= \frac{4 \, (0.00034969)}{0.000300675}$$

$$= 4.652$$

(P = 0.325). We cannot reject that σ^2 might be zero. The power of this test is low here because the number of years sampled is small (n = 5) and there is high within-year sampling variance relative to σ^2. The ratio of $\hat{\sigma}^2$ to the average var($\hat{p}_i \mid p_i$) is

$$\frac{0.00024508}{0.0015034} = 0.163 \, .$$

Thus, sampling variation far exceeds year-to-year variation in the true p_i. This makes it very difficult to detect changes in the p_i over time. Environmental studies commonly suffer from large sampling variation, making it difficult to detect effects of interest over space or time.

4.3.3. More Complex Example

We generated a large set of data under model $H_{1\phi}$ for six lots, to further illustrate inference about S with multiple random lots. Data for two groups (treatment and control) were available from six occasions (k = 6) and are summarized in Table 4.4. Ideally, we could imagine that these data were from uniquely marked releases; sublots would then be possible, each based on the last digit of the tag number. There would then be 10 tables, each similar to Table 4.4, and each with sample sizes about one-tenth of those now shown. Such replication would allow variances to be estimated empirically and additional tests would be possible to enable a full scrutiny of the results. We will ignore the possible sublots here and consider only the data set shown in Table 4.4.

Consider, for this illustration, that these data were collected on the Columbia River from releases over six biweekly periods. The objective of the experiment is to estimate the "total project" survival of salmon smolts for a particular dam (here called dam 1) and the pool upstream from the dam. Total project mortality then includes all deaths of fish in the pool and deaths associated with the spillways, various turbine units, deflecting barriers, screens, etc. Therefore, treatment fish are released at a point upstream from the pool and control fish are released at a later appropriate time just below dam 1 such that control and treatment fish begin migrating downstream at approximately the same time between dams 1 and 2. Perhaps the treatment fish in lot 1 were released above the pool on May 1 and 2 and their movements were monitored at dam 1. When they arrive at dam 1, the control fish are released, perhaps over a period of 3-8 days, depending on the continued arrival rate of the treatment fish.

Table 4.4. – Summary of synthetic data generated under model $H_{1\phi}$ of the first capture history protocol. Data were generated for six lots where the parameters are ϕ_{ti} = 0.95, i = 2, ..., 6; ϕ_{ci} = 0.95, i = 1, ..., 6; and ϕ_{t1} = 0.85, 0.80, 0.70, 0.65, 0.75, and 0.80 for lots 1, ..., 6, respectively; and p_{ti} = p_{ci} = 0.10, 0.17, 0.12, 0.08, 0.07, and 0.05 for lots 1, ..., 6, respectively.

| | | Releases | Number recaptured and removed at dam j, m_{tij} | | | | |
Lot	Group	R_{ti}	j = 2	3	4	5	6
1	t	20,000	1,752	1,445	1,256	1,013	918
	c	20,000	1,922	1,660	1,461	1,135	1,045
2	t	12,000	1,636	1,296	1,021	849	616
	c	12,000	2,014	1,549	1,198	936	786
3	t	27,000	2,302	1,936	1,591	1,241	1,117
	c	27,000	3,034	2,547	2,177	1,847	1,468
4	t	20,000	1,050	883	804	698	592
	c	13,000	986	874	734	670	555
5	t	14,000	682	617	573	506	440
	c	20,000	1,309	1,173	1,066	912	844
6	t	7,000	293	261	220	191	185
	c	7,000	307	288	277	252	197

If the six treatment releases are made at 2-week intervals, it is reasonable to think that the true treatment survival might vary over the course of the overall experiment. This variation among the parameters (σ^2) might be caused by flow and other variables affecting the river, as well as by dam variables such as head, spill, and wicket gate and turbine blade settings.

In this example, we know the true treatment effect (parameter) for each lot (S = 0.895, 0.842, 0.737, 0.684, 0.789, and 0.842 for lots 1 to 6, respectively). Consequently, the best possible estimates of $E(S)$ and σ are

$$\overline{S} = \frac{1}{6} \sum_{i=1}^{6} S_i = 0.798$$

and

$$\hat{\sigma}^2 = \frac{1}{5} \sum_{i=1}^{6} (S_i - \overline{S})^2 = 0.006016$$

or

$$\hat{\sigma} = 0.0776 \,.$$

From these results, we would have

$$\hat{se}(\hat{\overline{S}}) = \frac{0.0776}{\sqrt{6}} = 0.0317 \,,$$

and, using equations (4.9) and (4.10), with $\hat{var} \equiv 0$ (and $\chi^2_{5,0.025} = 0.831$, $\chi^2_{5,0.975} = 12.8$), a 95% CI on σ is 0.048 to 0.190. These results would arise only if all sampling variances $var(\hat{S}_i \mid S_i)$ were zero.

Using model $H_{1\phi}$ on the data for all six lots, we used RELEASE to compute $\hat{S}_i$ and $\hat{se}(\hat{S}_i \mid S_i)$. Those results are shown in Table 4.5.

Table 4.5. – Summary of total releases, estimates of treatment effects, and their standard errors under model $H_{1\phi}$ for the synthetic data in Table 4.4.

Lot i	R_1	$\hat{S}_i$	$\hat{se}(\hat{S}_i \mid S_i)$	True S_i
1	40,000	0.884	0.0123	0.895
2	24,000	0.836	0.0110	0.842
3	54,000	0.739	0.0087	0.737
4	33,000	0.685	0.0134	0.684
5	34,000	0.759	0.0156	0.789
6	14,000	0.871	0.0319	0.842
Unweighted average		0.796		0.798

The simplest way to compute an empirical estimate of $\text{var}(\hat{\bar{S}})$ from these six estimates of treatment survival is to use

$$\hat{\text{var}}(\hat{\bar{S}}) = \frac{\sum\limits_{i=1}^{6} (\hat{S}_i - \hat{\bar{S}})^2}{(5)(6)} = 0.0010635 ,$$

where

$$\hat{\bar{S}} = \frac{1}{6} \sum_{i=1}^{6} \hat{S}_i = 0.796 ;$$

hence,

$$\hat{\text{se}}(\hat{\bar{S}}) = 0.0326 .$$

Computing

$$\hat{\text{var}} = \frac{1}{6} \sum_{i=1}^{6} \hat{\text{var}}(\hat{S}_i \mid S_i)$$

$$= 0.00298$$

and using equation (4.1), the simple estimate of σ^2 is

$$\tilde{\sigma}^2 = (6)(0.0010635) - 0.000298$$

$$= 0.006083 ,$$

or $\tilde{\sigma} = 0.078$. Equations (4.9) and (4.10) lead to the 95% CI on σ as 0.050 to 0.196. Because the sampling variances are so small here, these results are almost the same as if the six true S_i were known.

Corresponding to these unweighted procedures, there is a simple version of the test of H_0: $\sigma^2 = 0$: use equation (4.6) with

$$\hat{\text{var}}(\hat{\bar{S}}) = \frac{1}{30} \sum_{i=1}^{6} \left(\hat{S}_i - \hat{\bar{S}} \right)^2 = 0.0010635 \,,$$

and

$$\hat{\text{var}}(\hat{\bar{S}} \mid \sigma^2 = 0) = \left(\frac{1}{6} \right)^2 \sum_{i=1}^{6} \hat{\text{var}}(\hat{S}_i \mid S_i)$$

$$= 0.0000496 \,.$$

Thus, the test statistic is

$$\chi^2 = \frac{5(.0010635)}{0.0000496}$$

$$= 107.1 \,,$$

which is highly significant. We conclude that there is substantial variation among the population parameters in addition to the sampling variation. Often, the estimation of σ^2 is as important as the separate point estimates of treatment effects.

The theoretically more efficient inference procedures require weighted analyses, as per equations (4.2), (4.3), (4.4), and (4.7) and (4.8), which themselves require iterative numerical solution. Solving the relevant equations, we find the weighted analysis gives

$$\hat{\sigma}^2 = 0.00638 \,;$$

$$\hat{\sigma} = 0.080 \,.$$

Then we can find the weighted results below:

$$\hat{\bar{S}} = 0.796 \,,$$

$$\hat{\text{var}}(\hat{\bar{S}}) = 0.0010304 \,,$$

and

$$\hat{v}ar(\hat{\overline{S}} \mid \sigma^2 = 0) = \frac{1}{\displaystyle\sum_{i=1}^{6} \frac{1}{\hat{v}ar(\hat{S}_i \mid S_i)}}$$

$$= 0.0000258 \,.$$

Hence, the weighted test of H_0: $\sigma^2 = 0$ is given by

$$\chi^2 = \frac{(5)(0.00103)}{0.0000258}$$

$$= 199.6 \,.$$

This weighted chi-square test statistic is much bigger than the unweighted one (of 107.1), but either one clearly rejects H_0: $\sigma^2 = 0$.

From the weighted analysis, $\hat{s}e(\hat{\overline{S}}) = 0.0321$ and a 95% CI on $E(S)$ is 0.796 ± (2.571)(0.0321) or 0.713 to 0.879. Also, from solving equations (4.7) and (4.8), we get the 95% CI on σ as 0.047 to 0.196 ($\hat{\sigma} = 0.080$). We see that there was no real advantage here to doing the weighted analysis. Unfortunately, that is not always true, and the only way to be sure is to do the weighted analysis.

To explore this example further, we generated another simulated six lots where the released numbers were one-tenth those shown in Table 4.4. Thus, for example, for lot 1, $R_{t1} = R_{c1} = 2,000$. All parameters were left unchanged. Thus, the only effect was to increase the within-lot sampling variances by a factor of 10. The results are shown in Table 4.6. It is fortuitous that the unweighted average of the $\hat{S}_i$ is so close to $\overline{S} = 0.798$. Note that the individual $\hat{S}_i$ are not as close to S_i now as in the original case (Table 4.5).

Table 4.6. – Summary of total releases and some results from the second simulated six lots under model H_{14}; the same parameters apply as for Table 4.4.

Lot i	R_1	$\hat{S}_i$	$\hat{se}(\hat{S}_i \mid S_i)$	True S_i
1	4,000	0.880	0.0391	0.895
2	2,400	0.774	0.0321	0.842
3	5,400	0.743	0.0273	0.737
4	3,300	0.677	0.0418	0.684
5	3,400	0.739	0.0476	0.789
6	1,400	0.984	0.1145	0.842
Unweighted average		0.800		0.798

Table 4.7 summarizes the various results (such as $\hat{\overline{S}}$, $\hat{\sigma}$), unweighted and weighted (and the case of all $\text{var}(\hat{S}_i \mid S_i) = 0$), computed based on Table 4.6. The main efficiency of the weighted analysis is to achieve smaller $\hat{se}(\hat{\overline{S}})$ and a more powerful test of the null hypothesis H_0: $\sigma^2 = 0$ (i.e., of H_0: $S_1 = S_2 = S_3 = S_4 = S_5 = S_6$). These results illustrate that if the true $\text{var}(\hat{S}_i \mid S_i)$ vary substantially, the weighted analysis should be used.

If we further reduced the release numbers, a point would be reached where the sampling variation would exceed σ^2 and the test of H_0: $\sigma^2 = 0$ would have low power. One could easily get data so poor that there would be no evidence that the treatment effects varied. A tradeoff faces us in environmental studies: having both multiple lots and yet sufficient within-lot sample sizes to allow demonstrating any important lot-to-lot variation in the treatment effect, or other parameters (see, for example, Eberhardt 1978; Armour et al. 1983).

Table 4.7. – Comparisons of weighted and unweighted results based on the Monte Carlo study results for $\hat{S}_i$ in Table 4.6; the values when all $\text{var}(\hat{S}_i \mid S_i) = 0$ are the best possible (hence, "true") values for these six lots.

Entity computed	If $\text{var}(\hat{S}_i \mid S_i) = 0$ (i.e., "truth")	Weighted analysis	Unweighted analysis
$\hat{\sigma}$	0.0776	0.0812	0.0959
$\hat{\overline{S}}$	0.798	0.780	0.800
$\hat{se}(\hat{\overline{S}})$	0.0317	0.0385	0.0458
$\hat{\sigma}_L$	0.048	0.028	0.039
$\hat{\sigma}_U$	0.190	0.261	0.269
χ^2	∞	30.1	18.5

4.4. Example with Four Groups and 10 Lots

In this chapter we will extend the synthetic example presented in Chapter 3.10. As before, we use data simulated under scheme B, $V = 4$ groups, $k = 6$ occasions, and $R_{v1} = 1,000$ fish released. Here, we extend the example with the inclusion of data for nine other lots. The parameters used are those in Table 3.5. Summaries of the m_{vij} arrays will not be given, but the data in Table 3.6 are representative. The data for each lot were generated under the same parameters. Therefore, there is no variance component issue because $\sigma^2 = 0$. Such data might arise from a large study using PIT tags and the lots correspond to the last digit of the tag numbers.

In this study, there are four groups. The first three are treatment groups ($v = 1, 2, 3$); each is then compared to the control group ($v = 4$). Thus, primary interest lies in the treatment effects S_{14}, S_{24}, and S_{34} (true values are 0.90, 0.75, and 0.70, respectively).

The results of various hypothesis tests are given in Table 4.8. The results of TEST 1.$R1$ convincingly show a strong treatment effect (i.e., $\phi_{t1} \neq \phi_{c1}$) for all 10 lots. If the test results for individual lots were less convincing, one might compute $\sum_{i=1}^{10} \chi^2_i = 897.5$, with 30 df. The results for TEST 1.$T2$ for each lot do not reject that $p_{t2} = p_{c2}$, which suggests model H_{2p} (which we know to be the correct model).

The results of TEST 1.$R2$ provide no evidence that ϕ_{t2} and ϕ_{c2} differ, tending to confirm that model H_{2p} is appropriate. The overall test for treatment effect (TEST 1) is highly significant. Although R_1 is only 1,000 individuals released, the model selection capability in this example is quite good because of reasonable recapture rates. We leave it to the reader to analyze this example with as few as, perhaps, 300 releases in each lot.

The 10 estimates of treatment effect are presented in Table 4.9. Within a lot, the estimates of S are somewhat variable; however, the mean of the 10 estimates is fairly precise for each of the three treatments. Because these 10 $\hat{S}_i$ are from replication with equal release numbers, the computing formulae used were

$$\hat{\bar{S}} = \frac{1}{10} \sum_{i=1}^{10} \hat{S}_i$$

and

$$\hat{se}(\hat{\bar{S}}) = \left[\frac{1}{90} \sum_{i=1}^{10} \left(\hat{S}_i - \hat{\bar{S}} \right)^2 \right]^{1/2} .$$

Table 4.8. – Summary of the results of modeling selection tests for the simulated data: scheme B, $k = 6$, four groups, 10 lots.

Lot	TEST 1.R1 H_0 vs. $H_{1\phi}$ (3 df)		TEST 1.T2 $H_{1\phi}$ vs. H_{2p} (3 df)		TEST 1.R2 H_{2p} vs. $H_{2\phi}$ (3 df)		TEST 1 H_0 vs. $H_{5\phi}$ (18 df)	
	χ^2	P	χ^2	P	χ^2	P	χ^2	P
1	71.4	<0.001	52.6	<0.001	1.2	0.75	128.4	<0.001
2	93.9	<0.001	12.0	<0.001	4.7	0.20	125.9	<0.001
3	86.0	<0.001	54.6	<0.001	1.6	0.66	148.1	<0.001
4	92.0	<0.001	35.2	<0.001	1.5	0.68	137.5	<0.001
5	91.9	<0.001	26.1	<0.001	1.3	0.73	131.0	<0.001
6	80.2	<0.001	28.8	<0.001	0.5	0.92	127.8	<0.001
7	104.6	<0.001	60.2	<0.001	1.7	0.63	175.3	<0.001
8	90.3	<0.001	58.5	<0.001	4.3	0.23	164.3	<0.001
9	87.6	<0.001	47.6	<0.001	2.8	0.43	150.3	<0.001
10	99.6	<0.001	39.7	<0.001	3.1	0.37	149.9	<0.001

Table 4.9. – Summary of the estimates of treatment survival rate, under analysis model H_{2p}, for the simulated data: scheme B, $k = 6$, four groups, 10 lots. True parameter values are shown at the bottom of table.

Lot	$\hat{S}_{14}$	$\hat{se}(\hat{S}_{14})$	$\hat{S}_{24}$	$\hat{se}(\hat{S}_{24})$	$\hat{S}_{34}$	$\hat{se}(\hat{S}_{34})$
1	0.8889	0.0561	0.8303	0.0542	0.7315	0.0502
2	0.8597	0.0512	0.6927	0.0453	0.6151	0.0422
3	0.8906	0.0554	0.7339	0.0498	0.7125	0.0489
4	0.9442	0.0563	0.7333	0.0484	0.6881	0.0468
5	0.8226	0.0487	0.6944	0.0441	0.6793	0.0438
6	0.8331	0.0511	0.7204	0.0471	0.7075	0.0466
7	0.9031	0.0531	0.7040	0.0465	0.6981	0.0458
8	0.8746	0.0530	0.7801	0.0500	0.6788	0.0460
9	0.8856	0.0537	0.7169	0.0473	0.6858	0.0461
10	0.9112	0.0536	0.6722	0.0577	0.7113	0.0469
$\hat{\bar{S}}$	0.8814	0.0362	0.7278	0.0465	0.6908	0.0315
S	0.90		0.75		0.70	

RELEASE uses these simple unweighted formulae to compute averages and standard errors over multiple lots. Often, these will not be the appropriate formulae. This summarization capability is in RELEASE primarily as part of the simulation options. Proper weighted averages, standard errors, and estimates of variance components for real data must be done separately by the investigator.

Part 5. Properties of Procedures

5.1. Introduction

We here assess the performance of the various statistical methods. Theory indicates that the desirable properties of each method become increasingly better as sample size increases. In these methods, sample size is not a single value; rather, it is related to the size of the releases (R_{vi}), the capture probabilities (p_{vi}), the number of sampling occasions (k), and (to a lesser degree) the survival probabilities (ϕ_{vi}). Furthermore, the methods perform best when the assumptions are fully met (see Manly 1970, 1971b).

Here we examine performance of estimators in terms of bias, precision, robustness, relative efficiency, and the effects of heterogeneity (terms to be defined later). The power of tests used in selecting the proper model and their nominal significance levels are also assessed. We use the Monte Carlo method and a method based on expectations in Part 5; however, some analytical results on power of certain tests are given in Part 3.

It is not possible to perform Monte Carlo studies on all, or even a significant fraction, of the cases of potential interest. A sequence of models has been developed under each of the four protocols. Each model has several estimators and associated tests. In each instance, k can reasonably range from two to at least six or eight; and we have seen studies where the numbers released vary from as few as 60 to as many as 100,000 individuals. Previous studies have had capture probabilities ranging from 0.01 to 0.8, whereas treatment survival rates have ranged from 0.3 to nearly 1.0. The parameter space suggested above is far too large for exhaustive Monte Carlo study (or even analytical-numerical investigation). Furthermore, we could not afford to tabulate these results, even if adequate computer time allowed the study of a large number of cases. Therefore, our approach here has been to tabulate the results of a few representative cases of potential interest.

Our approach in evaluating the statistical properties of various methods is twofold. First, a powerful Monte Carlo simulation procedure (PROC SIMULATE) is included in program RELEASE (see Part 9). Researchers are encouraged to use this procedure in both the design and analysis phases of their experiments. Second, we present the results of 48 Monte Carlo studies to give the reader an impression of the performance of various methods. This material focuses on experiments with two groups where the treatment effect is acute. The parameters for various simulated models are presented in Table 5.1. In all studies, $k = 5$, 1,000 replicate data sets were generated, and there were no unplanned losses on capture. These simulated data sets constitute the basis for much of the material presented in Part 5.

279

Table 5.1. – Summary of the parameters used in the Monte Carlo studies for four cases. Data were simulated under both the first and complete capture history protocols.

Case and parameters	True model[a]	Subpopulation[b]	ϕ_{ti} and ϕ_{ci}	p_{ti} and p_{ci}
Case A: $R_{t1} = R_{c1} = 5{,}000$				
Homogeneous	H_0		All 0.9	All 0.1
Homogeneous	$H_{1\phi}$		All 0.9, except $\phi_{t1} = 0.8$	All 0.1
Homogeneous	H_{2p}		All 0.9, except $\phi_{t1} = 0.8$	All 0.1, except $p_{t2} = 0.15$
Heterogeneous	H_0	1	All 0.95	All 0.15
		2	All 0.85	All 0.05
Heterogeneous	$H_{1\phi}$	1	All 0.95, except $\phi_{t1} = 0.85$	All 0.15
		2	All 0.85, except $\phi_{t1} = 0.75$	All 0.05
Heterogeneous	H_{2p}	1	All 0.95, except $\phi_{t1} = 0.85$	All 0.15, except $p_{t2} = 0.225$
		2	All 0.85, except $\phi_{t1} = 0.75$	All 0.05, except $p_{t2} = 0.075$

Case B: Same as case A, except $R_{t1} = R_{c1} = 1{,}000$
Case C: Same as case A, except $R_{t1} = R_{c1} = 200$
Case D: Same as case C, except all p_{ti} and p_{ci} are increased by 0.7

[a]In the heterogeneous cases, the parameter structure follows models H_0, $H_{1\phi}$, and H_{2p}; however, the assumption of independence is violated.

[b]Each subpopulation is of equal size, $R_{\tau i}/2$.

5.2. Estimator Bias

Bias in estimators of model parameters is undesirable. In this chapter we examine the statistical bias of MLEs under models for the first and complete capture history protocols for cases where the parameters are homogeneous. Bias is defined as

$$\text{bias} = E(\hat{\theta}) - \theta,$$

where θ is a particular parameter (e.g., S or ϕ). The exact value of θ is known in each of the Monte Carlo studies and the expected value can be estimated with good precision from the results of the Monte Carlo studies. The expected value is estimated as

$$\hat{E}(\theta) = \frac{1}{1,000} \sum_{i=1}^{1,000} \hat{\theta}_i,$$

where $\hat{\theta}_i$ is the estimate computed from the ith Monte Carlo trial. We used 1,000 replicate data sets for each Monte Carlo study to ensure that the expected values are estimated precisely.

Examination of the estimated expected values of the treatment survival probabilities in Tables 5.2 and 5.3 indicate that bias is negligible if the model assumptions are met. The bias is generally ≤ 0.004 if the numbers released were $\geq 1,000$. An exception is $\hat{S} = \hat{\phi}_{ti}/\hat{\phi}_{ci}$ when homogeneous first capture history data are generated under model H_{2p}. Here, the biases are -0.049 and -0.040 under $\hat{S}$ for model $H'_{2\phi}$ (Table 5.2). No estimator for model H_{2p} exists under the first capture history protocol, thus, model H'_{2p} is used as an approximation. Generally the estimator $\hat{S}$ performs similarly for both first and complete capture history protocols. When the true model is $H_{1\phi}$, the estimators of S are algebraically identical under the first and complete capture history protocols. However, estimated values of S under the first and complete capture history protocols in Table 5.2 (case A) under $H_{1\phi}$ are not identical because they are not based on exactly the same Monte Carlo data.

With only 200 releases in each group, bias in $\hat{S}$ is larger if the capture probability is low (Table 5.3, case C). However, the bias remains small (about 1%) if the assumptions of the model are realized. Comparison of bias in cases C and D in Table 5.3 shows the importance

Table 5.2. – Summary of estimated expected values and standard errors (computed empirically and theoretically) from Monte Carlo studies of complete and first capture history protocols for case A, $R_{\mathbf{v}1}$ = 5,000 and case B, $R_{\mathbf{v}1}$ = 1,000. The survival (ϕ_i) and capture (p_i) probabilities were allowed to be homogeneous or heterogeneous. Parameters used to simulate the data are given in Table 5.1.

True model	Capture history protocol	Parameter variation	$H_{1\phi}$ $\hat{E}(\hat{S})$	$\hat{se}(\hat{S})_e$	$\hat{se}(\hat{S})_t$	H_{2p} or $H'_{2\phi}$ $\hat{E}(\hat{S})^a$	$\hat{se}(\hat{S})_e$	$\hat{se}(\hat{S})_t$
			Case A					
H_0	Complete	Homogeneous	1.000	0.033	0.033	1.002	0.039	0.038
$(S = 1.0)$		Heterogeneity	1.001	0.030	0.032	1.001	0.034	0.036
$H_{1\phi}$	Complete	Homogeneous	0.889	0.031	0.030	0.888	0.037	0.035
$(S = 0.889)$		Heterogeneity	0.891	0.028	0.030	0.891	0.032	0.034
H_{2p}	Complete	Homogeneous	1.004	0.034	0.033	0.889	0.036	0.036
$(S = 0.889)$		Heterogeneity	0.996	0.030	0.032	0.890	0.032	0.033
H_0	First	Homogeneous	1.000	0.033	0.033	1.001	0.045	0.043
$(S = 1.0)$		Heterogeneity	1.000	0.030	0.032	1.000	0.039	0.042
$H_{1\phi}$	First	Homogeneous	0.890	0.030	0.030	0.891	0.040	0.039
$(S = 0.889)$		Heterogeneity	0.891	0.028	0.030	0.891	0.037	0.039
H_{2p}	First	Homogeneous	1.006	0.033	0.033	0.840	0.039	0.038
$(S = 0.889)$		Heterogeneity	0.997	0.030	0.032	0.825	0.034	0.037
			Case B					
H_0	Complete	Homogeneous	1.003	0.074	0.074	1.004	0.086	0.086
$(S = 1.0)$		Heterogeneity	1.004	0.066	0.073	1.003	0.074	0.082
$H_{1\phi}$	Complete	Homogeneous	0.893	0.068	0.068	0.889	0.078	0.079
$(S = 0.889)$		Heterogeneity	0.894	0.061	0.067	0.895	0.067	0.076
H_{2p}	Complete	Homogeneous	1.009	0.073	0.074	0.889	0.077	0.078
$(S = 0.889)$		Heterogeneity	0.999	0.066	0.072	0.895	0.066	0.075
H_0	First	Homogeneous	1.001	0.077	0.074	1.002	0.099	0.096
$(S = 1.0)$		Heterogeneity	1.009	0.069	0.073	1.006	0.069	0.073
$H_{1\phi}$	First	Homogeneous	0.892	0.068	0.068	0.898	0.087	0.089
$(S = 0.889)$		Heterogeneity	0.895	0.065	0.068	0.897	0.085	0.088
H_{2p}	First	Homogeneous	1.011	0.074	0.074	0.849	0.086	0.086
$(S = 0.889)$		Heterogeneity	0.998	0.069	0.072	0.826	0.080	0.083

[a]Estimates were computed under model H_{2p} for the complete capture history protocol and under model $H'_{2\phi}$ for the first capture history protocol.

Table 5.3. – Summary of estimated expected values and standard errors (computed empirically and theoretically) from Monte Carlo studies of complete and first capture history protocols for case C, $R_{\tau 1}$ = 200 and case D, $R_{\tau 1}$ = 200. The survival (ϕ_1) and capture (p_1) probabilities were allowed to be homogeneous of heterogeneous. Parameters used to simulate the data are given in Table 5.1.

True model	Capture History protocol	Parameter variation	Estimator performance under model					
			$H_{1\phi}$			H_{2p} or $H'_{2\phi}$		
			$\hat{E}(\hat{S})$	$se(\hat{S})_e$	$se(\hat{S})_t$	$\hat{E}(\hat{S})^a$	$se(\hat{S})_e$	$se(\hat{S})_t$
Case C								
H_0	Complete	Homogeneous	1.011	0.174	0.168	1.014	0.199	0.196
($S = 1.0$)		Heterogeneity	1.015	0.157	0.166	1.015	0.182	0.187
$H_{1\phi}$	Complete	Homogeneous	0.911	0.161	0.158	0.912	0.186	0.183
($S = 0.889$)		Heterogeneity	0.905	0.154	0.154	0.908	0.170	0.174
H_{2p}	Complete	Homogeneous	1.032	0.173	0.171	0.912	0.184	0.181
($S = 0.889$)		Heterogeneity	1.012	0.167	0.166	0.908	0.169	0.172
H_0	First	Homogeneous	1.016	0.171	0.169	1.034	0.231	0.225
($S = 1.0$)		Heterogeneity	1.006	0.154	0.164	1.022	0.216	0.219
$H_{1\phi}$	First	Homogeneous	0.896	0.158	0.155	0.905	0.209	0.204
($S = 0.889$)		Heterogeneity	0.908	0.148	0.155	0.918	0.201	0.204
H_{2p}	First	Homogeneous	1.024	0.170	0.170	0.870	0.200	0.199
($S = 0.889$)		Heterogeneity	1.005	0.157	0.164	0.836	0.183	0.190
Case D								
H_0	Complete	Homogeneous	1.000	0.038	0.038	1.000	0.039	0.038
($S = 1.0$)		Heterogeneity	1.001	0.037	0.038	1.000	0.037	0.038
$H_{1\phi}$	Complete	Homogeneous	0.889	0.041	0.041	0.889	0.042	0.041
($S = 0.889$)		Heterogeneity	0.890	0.040	0.041	0.890	0.040	0.042
H_{2p}	Complete	Homogeneous	0.895	0.041	0.041	0.889	0.041	0.041
($S = 0.889$)		Heterogeneity	0.894	0.040	0.041	0.888	0.040	0.041
H_0	First	Homogeneous	0.998	0.037	0.037	1.032	0.261	0.243
($S = 1.0$) ·		Heterogeneity	0.998	0.038	0.038	1.030	0.262	0.247
$H_{1\phi}$	First	Homogeneous	0.889	0.042	0.041	0.918	0.232	0.223
($S = 0.889$)		Heterogeneity	0.892	0.041	0.041	0.915	0.237	0.228
H_{2p}	First	Homogeneous	0.895	0.040	0.041	0.682	0.193	0.182
($S = 0.889$)		Heterogeneity	0.900	0.041	0.041	0.654	0.183	0.180

[a]Estimates were computed under model H_{2p} for the complete capture history protocol and under model $H'_{2\phi}$ for the first capture history protocol.

of a high capture probability if the numbers released are small. A general conclusion from the results in Tables 5.2 and 5.3 is that bias in $\hat{S}$ is probably acceptable in most instances if the model assumptions are satisfied. In addition, if no treatment effect occurs (model H_0) and one tries to estimate the treatment survival rate by using models $H_{1\phi}$ or H_{2p}, the estimate of S will be close to 1.00 on the average.

Although any bias is undesirable, it must be related to the standard error to assess more correctly its importance. The following table, adapted from Cochran (1963:14), shows the effect of the ratio bias/standard error on expected 95% CI coverage:

Bias/standard error	Expected coverage
0.02	0.95
0.04	0.95
0.06	0.95
0.08	0.95
0.10	0.95
0.20	0.95
0.40	0.93
0.60	0.91
0.80	0.87
1.00	0.83
1.50	0.68

As an example, consider the bias in $\hat{S}$ under case C, model $H'_{2\phi}$ for first capture history data for the constant-parameter case in Table 5.3, where the true model is H_{2p}. The bias is 0.870 - 0.889 = -0.019 and its average standard error is 0.200. Thus, the ratio of bias to standard error is 0.095; and we determine that a 95% CI would still have an expected coverage of about 95%.

The general conclusion is that bias in $\hat{S}$ is relatively small if the assumptions of a particular model are satisfied. An option (UNBIAS) in PROCs CHMATRIX, LMREAD, and SIMULATE of program RELEASE allows the computation of bias-adjusted estimators. However, all results in this chapter are for the unadjusted MLEs. Use of the UNBIAS option substantially reduces the already small statistical bias (see Chapter 3.4). Bias can be severe if a poor model, whose assumptions are not met, is used (e.g., case C, model $H_{1\phi}$ for first capture history data for the constant-parameter case in Table 5.3 where the true model is H_{2p}). Such model bias can be seen by examining Tables 5.2 and 5.3.

Approximations to the bias of an estimator can be computed using the EXPECT option in program RELEASE. Results can be obtained in a few seconds using this option, whereas an adequate Monte Carlo simulation can frequently take several hours. This subject is discussed briefly in Chapter 5.4 and more fully in Chapter 5.9

5.3. Measures of Precision

The sampling variance and its square root, the standard error, are measures of the precision of an estimator. True sampling variance can be estimated in different ways (e.g., empirically or by using theoretical formulae). The ML method assures us that the estimated variance or standard error based on theoretical formulae will have good properties as the sample size increases, if model assumptions hold. Here we assess the performance of the theoretical formulae for estimating sampling variance over a range of smaller sample sizes by first computing an empirical standard error of the treatment survival rate $\hat{se}(\hat{S})_e$ based on 1,000 replications from the Monte Carlo studies. Thus,

$$\hat{se}(\hat{S})_e = \left[\frac{1}{999} \sum_{i=1}^{1,000} (\hat{S}_i - \overline{S})^2\right]^{1/2},$$

where $\overline{S}$ is the average of the 1,000 estimates of S. This quantity is a measure of precision of the estimator of treatment survival rate under a particular model. In contrast, a theoretical estimate of the sampling variance and standard error is available, based on the model and ML theory (Section 1.2.1.2). The average of these,

$$\hat{se}(\hat{S})_t = \frac{1}{1,000} \sum_{i=1}^{1,000} \hat{se}(\hat{S}_i),$$

computed from the Monte Carlo studies, provides a basis for assessing average performance of the theoretical variance as a measure of precision.

Examination of the estimated standard errors in Tables 5.2 and 5.3 indicates that, on the average, the theoretical standard errors are satisfactory as a measure of estimator precision, even in case C and the heterogeneous populations, if the assumptions of the model are met.

5.4. Estimator Robustness

Estimator robustness relates to a large collection of issues. Many questions regarding the robustness of an estimator are specific to a particular study. In this chapter we present some general results that may be useful.

Experience with the general Jolly-Seber model and its extensions indicates that the survival rates (ϕ_i) are relatively well estimated, in terms of bias and precision, compared to the number of births and the population size. Estimates of population size or the estimated number of marked animals at a particular time may be seriously biased by failure of model assumptions but the corresponding estimate of survival is not often affected. Generally, the survival estimators (ϕ_{vi}) have good properties. Estimators of treatment survival rate (S) are ratios of the $\hat{\phi}_i$, and therefore might also be expected to have good statistical properties.

In general, if a model such as H_0 or $H_{1\phi}$ is the correct model, then estimators of S or the ϕ_i from other models in the sequence (e.g., H_{2p}, $H_{2\phi}$, H_{3p}) will be little biased; however, some precision will be lost. Problems with substantial bias occur when the true model is H_{2p}, $H_{2\phi}$, or a more general model in the sequence (e.g., $H_{3\phi}$), but the estimation is conducted under a more restrictive model such as $H_{1\phi}$. Cases A, B, and C in Tables 5.2 and 5.3 illustrate the situation where data sets were generated under model H_{2p} ($S = 0.889$) and estimates of treatment survival were made under model $H_{1\phi}$. The $\hat{E}(\hat{S})$ under model $H_{1\phi}$ for the homogeneous populations was about 1.00 to 1.030, a bias of 12 to 16%.

The above example indicates the problem of using an inappropriate model. The lack of estimator robustness forces additional attention on the tests for model selection. Finally, although estimators of treatment survival were biased by 12-16% in the example above, it must be noted that this bias was caused by the substantial inequality of capture probabilities (p_{t2} being 50% higher than p_{c2}). Thus, in this sense, $\hat{S}$ may be considered to be somewhat robust.

We have not attempted to present measures of robustness when mortality due to a treatment is chronic or indirect. These issues are left to the reader for specific studies. Clearly, potential bias exists and, in some cases, a better measure of treatment effect is $\hat{\phi}_{c1} - \hat{\phi}_{t1}$ (Section 2.5.2.5).

5.5. Heterogeneity

The models and estimation procedures presented in this monograph assume that all members of the population have homogeneous parameters at a given time and place. For example, all animals in the control group have the same probability of survival from dams 3 to 4, ϕ_{c3}. Alternatively, one could postulate that each animal has a unique parameter, i.e., $\theta_{(i)}$ for $i = 1, ..., N$ at a particular time and place. This situation is referred to as the heterogeneous case where the parameter θ itself has a distribution. This distribution is, of course, unknown to the investigator but the distribution has a conceptual mean and a variance. An example is an annual survival probability where individuals in the population vary in their innate ability to survive. The theory for model building to incorporate heterogeneity directly is quite complex and requires information that is rarely known (e.g., the form and variance of the distribution of θ_i).

We here present information on the performance of the models developed for the homogeneous case when they are used in the analysis of simulated data sets generated to incorporate heterogeneity in the parameters among animals. We generated data sets to allow heterogeneity in both the survival (ϕ_{vi}) and recapture (p_{vi}) parameters (Table 5.1), using program RELEASE. Use of this approach enables us to ask if the MLEs are robust (insensitive) to heterogeneity.

Recent studies (e.g., Nichols et al. 1982; Pollock and Raveling 1982; Vaupel and Yashin 1985) have shown that it is the variance among members of the population that is important, rather than the shape of the distribution. We included this information in the Monte Carlo studies by defining two subpopulations of equal size, each with different parameter values (see Table 5.1).

The estimators $\hat{S}$ are often less variable with heterogeneous data then with homogeneous data (see every comparison between the empirical variance estimates in cases A, B, and C, Tables 5.2 and 5.3). This result stems from the fact that the effective capture probability, with heterogeneity, exceeds the mean of the p_{vi}, $i = 2$, ..., k, for the two subpopulations (this is a manifestation of Jensen's inequality). As an example, under the complete capture history protocol, case A, the mean value of the $p_{vi} = 0.1$ for model $H_{1\phi}$ (Table 5.1); however, the effective (mean) capture probability is 0.13 under $H_{1\phi}$ (i.e., $\hat{p}_{v2} = \hat{p}_{v3} = 0.13$). Thus, the estimates under heterogeneity are less variable then the theoretical ML variance estimates would indicate. This result is important. In general, heterogeneity has little effect on the performance of the estimators of S or its standard error (Tables 5.2 and 5.3). We did not investigate the possibility of heterogeneity in the treatment effect itself. This might be caused if extreme heterogeneity existed in the marked releases in each group and each subpopulation. We suspect that bias in $\hat{S}$ could be expected in these extreme situations.

In the presence of heterogeneity, the parameters are weakly dependent upon previous capture histories. In addition, the assumption of independence is violated, but the effect on the statistical properties is often quite small. We tentatively conclude that a reasonable amount of heterogeneity in the survival and capture process will not seriously affect the performance of estimators of treatment survival, if the correct model is selected. This pattern is also generally true for the estimators of the ϕ_{vi} parameters.

5.6. Estimator Efficiency

An advantage in considering the sequence of models $H_{1\phi}$, H_{2p}, ..., $H_{k-1,\phi}$ under the complete capture history protocol is that assumptions about the equality of parameters across groups can be relaxed. Under model H_{2p}, one need not assume that treatment and control fish have the same capture probability on the second sampling occasion. Similarly, model H_{3p} also allows $p_{t3} \neq p_{c3}$ on the third sampling occasion. If $p_{t2} = p_{c2}$ and $p_{t3} = p_{c3}$ are incorrectly assumed (e.g., model $H_{1\phi}$), bias will result in $\hat{\phi}_{v1}$ and S. Thus, the choice among alternative models is important.

A disadvantage in selecting a model that allows relaxed assumptions is that the sampling variance of the estimators is larger than that for models entailing stronger assumptions. This loss in precision leads to a consideration of relative efficiency of estimators. The relative efficiency between two models is measured here by the ratio of their standard errors, with the convention that the model with the most assumptions (and, therefore, the smaller standard error) appears in the numerator. An example of the meaning of relative efficiency is the entry 0.79 in the first row in Table 5.4 under case A. The value 0.79 indicates that if model $H_{1\phi}$ is true, but one uses $\hat{S}$ under model H_{2p}, then the estimated standard error is $1/0.79 = 1.27$ times larger than it should be (under $H_{1\phi}$).

Some general conclusions can be drawn from the efficiency information in Tables 5.4-5.5. First, relative efficiency is similar for large or small numbers released (R_{v1} = 5,000 or 200, cases A and C, respectively). Second, if p_{vi} is nearly constant over sampling occasions, there is a substantial loss of efficiency when models with increasingly relaxed assumptions are considered. Third, the loss of efficiency is severe in models $H_{2\phi}$, H_{3p}, ..., $H_{k-1,\phi}$ compared to models $H_{1\phi}$ or H_{2p} for the complete capture history protocol. Consideration of the trade-off between bias and efficiency in the sequence of models, $H_{1\phi}$, H_{2p}, $H_{2\phi}$, ..., $H_{k-1,\phi}$ has implications in the design of experiments (Part 6).

Table 5.4. – Summary of relative efficiencies (the ratio of standard errors) for $\hat{S}$ under cases A and C (see Table 5.1). The Monte Carlo data were generated under model $H_{1\phi}$ for the first capture history protocol, assuming homogeneous parameters.

Model	Case A				Case C			
	$H_{1\phi}$	$H'_{2\phi}$	$H'_{3\phi}$	$H'_{4\phi}$	$H_{1\phi}$	$H'_{2\phi}$	$H'_{3\phi}$	$H'_{4\phi}$
$H_{1\phi}$	1	0.79	0.58	0.38	1	0.76	0.55	0.31
$H'_{2\phi}$		1	0.74	0.48		1	0.71	0.41
$H'_{3\phi}$			1	0.65			1	0.57
$H'_{4\phi}$				1				1

Table 5.5. – Summary of estimator efficiency (the ratio of standard errors) of $\hat{S}$ for cases A and C (see Table 5.1). The Monte Carlo data were generated under model $H_{1\phi}$ for the complete capture history protocol, assuming homogeneous parameters.

Model	Case A				Case C			
	$H_{1\phi}$	H_{2p}	$H_{2\phi}$	H_{3p}	$H_{1\phi}$	H_{2p}	$H_{2\phi}$	H_{3p}
$H_{1\phi}$	1	0.86	0.27	0.27	1	0.86	0.21	0.21
H_{2p}		1	0.32	0.32		1	0.24	0.24
$H_{2\phi}$			1	0.30			1	0.28
H_{3p}				1				1

5.7. Power of Tests

Statistical tests aid in the rejection of models that are poor for a particular data set. The Monte Carlo studies generally indicate that bias in the estimators is reasonably small if the correct model is used. In contrast, it is easy to show substantial bias if a model does not fit the data (e.g., an estimator $\hat{S}$ under $H_{1\phi}$ has poor properties if the data are from model H_{3p}). Therefore, it is important to assess the power of specific between-model tests. Power is defined as the probability of rejecting the null hypothesis.

If the null hypothesis is true, the power of the test should be equal to the significance level chosen (e.g., if $\alpha = 0.05$, then the power of the test should be 0.05). Table 5.6 provides summaries of the power of between-model tests for cases A to D, respectively. The first general conclusion is that heterogeneity has little effect on the performance of the between-model tests. This result is important as we believe heterogeneity is common in field studies of many biological populations. The power of the between-model tests is excellent for large samples (e.g, $R_t = R_c = 5,000$), as shown by the results for case A in Table 5.6. In releases of 1,000 animals per group (case B), the power drops to 0.31 for the test of H_0 versus $H_{1\phi}$ and the power is 0.79 for the test of $H_{1\phi}$ versus H_{2p} for both homogeneous and heterogeneous populations (Table 5.6).

In the worst example (case C, Table 5.6), the power of tests H_0 versus $H_{1\phi}$ and $H_{1\phi}$ versus H_{2p} decreases to 0.10 and 0.24, respectively, for both homogeneous and heterogeneous populations. With releases as small as 200 in each group and low capture probabilities, the power of between-model tests is poor. However, power for experiments with few animals released may be reasonable if the capture probabilities are high (case D, Table 5.6).

Interpretation of tests must be done with caution. For example, in case A the test of H_0 versus $H_{1\phi}$ has power of 0.05 when H_{2p} is the correct model. The power is poor because neither the null nor alternative hypothesis is true; however, there is a treatment effect. Other model parameters could have been chosen for model H_{2p} such that a treatment effect would have been much more easily detected (e.g., $p_{t2} = 0.05$). Thus, the results regarding power of tests must be interpreted with an understanding of the specific parameter values chosen. Knowledge of the approximate power of tests can increase the ability to interpret experimental results (e.g., Chapter 7.4).

The test for an overall treatment effect H_0 versus $H_{k-1,\phi}$ is powerful for data sets with large numbers of releases (e.g., case A) or where the capture probabilities are high (e.g., case D) for both first and complete capture history protocols (Table 5.7). The power for tests of overall treatment effect is poor for Cases B and C. The results in Table 5.7 show little difference in test power between homogeneous and heterogeneous parameters. These estimates of power are highly specific to the parameter values chosen and the magnitude of the treatment effect; thus, Table 5.7 gives only a rough impression of the power for some specific examples.

Table 5.6. – Estimated power of statistical tests at the 0.05 level of significance for cases A, B, C, and D of the complete capture history protocol. Parameters used to simulate the data are given in Table 5.1.

Test	Models tested[a]	True model					
		Homogeneous parameters			Heterogeneous parameters		
		H_0	$H_{1\phi}$	H_{2p}	H_0	$H_{1\phi}$	H_{2p}
Case A							
1.$R1$	H_0 versus $H_{1\phi}$	0.05	0.93	0.06	0.05	0.94	0.03
1.$T2$	$H_{1\phi}$ versus H_{2p}	0.05	0.05	1.00	0.04	0.05	1.00
1.$R2$	H_{2p} versus $H_{2\phi}$	0.04	0.05	0.05	0.05	0.05	0.04
1.$T3$	$H_{2\phi}$ versus H_{3p}	0.06	0.05	0.05	0.06	0.06	0.06
1.$R3$	H_{3p} versus $H_{3\phi}$	0.04	0.06	0.05	0.05	0.05	0.05
Case B							
1.$R1$	H_0 versus $H_{1\phi}$	0.06	0.31	0.05	0.03	0.31	0.29
1.$T2$	$H_{1\phi}$ versus H_{2p}	0.04	0.05	0.79	0.05	0.04	0.79
1.$R2$	H_{2p} versus $H_{2\phi}$	0.05	0.05	0.06	0.06	0.05	0.05
1.$T3$	$H_{2\phi}$ versus H_{3p}	0.05	0.05	0.05	0.06	0.04	0.04
1.$R3$	H_{3p} versus $H_{3\phi}$	0.05	0.06	0.06	0.05	0.05	0.05
Case C							
1.$R1$	H_0 versus $H_{1\phi}$	0.06	0.10	0.05	0.04	0.10	0.04
1.$T2$	$H_{1\phi}$ versus H_{2p}	0.05	0.05	0.24	0.06	0.06	0.24
1.$R2$	H_{2p} versus $H_{2\phi}$	0.05	0.04	0.05	0.04	0.05	0.04
1.$T3$	$H_{2\phi}$ versus H_{3p}	0.05	0.06	0.06	0.06	0.05	0.05
1.$R3$	H_{3p} versus $H_{3\phi}$	0.05	0.06	0.05	0.05	0.04	0.04
Case D							
1.$R1$	H_0 versus $H_{1\phi}$	0.05	0.75	0.71	0.05	0.74	0.71
1.$T2$	$H_{1\phi}$ versus H_{2p}	0.05	0.05	0.19	0.05	0.03	0.21
1.$R2$	H_{2p} versus $H_{2\phi}$	0.05	0.06	0.05	0.05	0.06	0.05
1.$T3$	$H_{2\phi}$ versus H_{3p}	0.05	0.06	0.06	0.06	0.05	0.05
1.$R3$	H_{3p} versus $H_{3\phi}$	0.05	0.04	0.04	0.05	0.04	0.04

[a]Null hypothesis versus the alternative hypothesis.

The ability of the statistical tests to select the correct model is largely dependent upon the number of fish released and the magnitude of the capture probabilities. For cases A and D, tests have high power when a treatment effect exists; therefore, the correct model is

Table 5.7. – Power of the test ($\alpha = 0.05$) for treatment effect H_0 versus $H_{4\phi}$ (TEST 1) for the Monte Carlo data simulated for homogeneous and heterogeneous populations. Parameters used to simulate the data are given in Table 5.1.

	True model					
	First capture history protocol			Complete capture history protocol		
Case	H_0	$H_{1\phi}$	H_{2p}	H_0	$H_{1\phi}$	H_{2p}
	Homogeneous populations					
A	0.06	0.80	1.00	0.05	0.71	1.00
B	0.05	0.19	0.52	0.05	0.16	0.46
C	0.06	0.08	0.12	0.04	0.06	0.12
D	0.05	0.52	0.60	0.06	0.43	0.48
	Heterogeneous populations					
A	0.03	0.79	1.00	0.04	0.70	1.00
B	0.05	0.18	0.60	0.05	0.14	0.45
C	0.05	0.06	0.12	0.04	0.05	0.12
D	0.06	0.52	0.60	0.04	0.40	0.47

selected (Table 5.8). Cases B and C were poor in that insufficient data were available to allow reliable model selection. Model selection appears poorer for the complete compared to the first capture history protocol (Table 5.8). Much of this is only due to the fact that more models are available under the complete capture history protocol, thus, the chance for error is greater.

Table 5.8. – Summary of the probability of selecting the correct model for the four Monte Carlo cases (see Table 5.1). Simulation results are based on 1,000 replications, $\alpha = 0.05$, for the homogeneous populations.

	True model					
	First capture history protocol			Complete capture history protocol		
Case	H_0	$H_{1\phi}$	H_{2p}	H_0	$H_{1\phi}$	H_{2p}
A	0.83	0.80	0.91	0.72	0.68	0.78
B	0.82	0.30	0.64	0.71	0.22	0.69
C	0.80	0.09	0.17	0.71	0.08	0.18
D	0.82	0.66	0.21	0.69	0.54	0.19

The analytic capabilities (EXPECT and SIMULATE) of program RELEASE should be used to assess the model selection and power of tests before field experiments are performed. The information in Table 5.8 provides only a glimpse of the performance of these statistical methods in selecting a good model, as these results are highly dependent on many factors. The comparable results for the heterogeneous cases were virtually identical with those for the homogeneous cases in Table 5.8.

5.8. Confidence Interval Coverage

Asymptotic theory assures that a 95% CI can be established as

$$\hat{S} \pm 1.96 \, \text{se}(\hat{S}) \, .$$

However, the actual or achieved coverage may be less than the nominal 95% level due to bias in $\hat{S}$, nonnormal sampling distribution of $\hat{S}$, a poor estimate of se($\hat{S}$), or sample sizes that are too "small" (not asymptotic). The Monte Carlo simulations (see Table 5.1) provide a means of assessing the coverage achieved.

Achieved coverage is summarized in Table 5.9 for cases A-D for the first and complete capture history protocols for both homogeneous and heterogeneous data. These results indicate that nominal coverage is achieved, even for the small numbers released in case C, if the model is correct. Little difference between homogeneous and heterogeneous parameters was found. Coverage is frequently less than the nominal level if an incorrect model is used (e.g., use of model $H'_{2\phi}$ for the first capture history protocol, when the true model is H_{2p}.

5.9. Analytical-Numerical Approximations

A method based on expectations, presented in Chapter 3.6, provides a useful alternative to Monte Carlo simulations. This method assumes a model, say $H_{1\phi}$, specific values for the model parameters (p_{vi} and ϕ_{vi}), and numbers released R_{v1}. This method can best be described as analytical-numerical. The numerical step involves the computation of the expected m_{vij}-array (i.e., $E[m_{vij} \mid R_{v1}]$). The computed expected values in the m_{vij}-array are then treated as "data." The analytic step involves the computation of estimates and test statistics using either the same model ($H_{1\phi}$) or another model (e.g., $H'_{2\phi}$). Thus, the method can be said to be based on expectations. Papers by Nelson et al. (1980) and Anderson and Burnham (1980) used this convenient approach in closely related contexts. The entire method can be easily done using the EXPECT option in PROC SIMULATE of program RELEASE. A typical run often takes about 11 seconds of microcomputer time, compared with, perhaps, 30-1,000 minutes for a Monte Carlo simulation run.

Table 5.9. – Summary of achieved confidence interval coverage (in %) on $\hat{S}$ for several estimators under the first and complete capture history protocols. Parameters used to simulate the data are given in Table 5.1.

Case	True model			
	First capture history protocol		Complete capture history protocol	
	$H_{1\phi}$	H_{2p}[a]	$H_{1\phi}$	H_{2p}
Homogeneous populations				
A	97	71	94	94
B	95	89	94	95
C	95	92	95	95
D	95	67	95	95
Heterogeneous populations				
A	97	58	96	96
B	97	86	97	97
C	96	90	96	95
D	95	63	95	95

[a]Coverage was assessed for $\hat{S}$ under model $H'_{2\phi}$ for the first capture history protocol.

The method can be used to obtain quick approximations of estimator bias and precision and to examine the power of certain tests. This method is quite useful and we recommend it. However, one would often want to refine insights with later Monte Carlo studies.

A comparison of results on estimator bias and precision is given in Table 5.10 for the Monte Carlo method and the method based on expectations. It is clear from the information in Table 5.10 that the quick method provides useful approximations in all cases. Computer runs required to prepare Table 5.10 took about 3 minutes of computer time, while the comparable runs for the Monte Carlo results took about 4,859 minutes (81 hours). Still, the Monte Carlo method has several distinct advantages. First, Monte Carlo studies can examine small-sample properties of estimators and test statistics, while the quick method is asymptotic. Second, the empirical sampling distribution can be studied only with Monte Carlo methods. Third, the numerical-analytical method cannot obtain the correct variances under conditions of heterogeneity. Finally, achieved confidence interval coverage can only be assessed by the Monte Carlo method.

Some results on the power of tests is given in Table 5.11, comparing the method based on expectations with the Monte Carlo method. Here, in particular, the quick method provides very useful results. The agreement between the two approaches is good. We recommend the use of EXPECT in program RELEASE for all but final, refined insights into issues regarding bias, precision, and test power.

Use of the option EXPECT provides chi-square statistics for a particular test. This chi-square value is a noncentrality parameter that can be used with its degrees of freedom and Table 3.4 to assess test power. Interpolation within Table 3.4 is usually satisfactory. Those wishing a copy of an expanded table can write the senior author.

Table 5.10. – Comparison of the Monte Carlo (MC) method with the method based on expectations (EXPECT) in estimating $E(\hat{S})$ and se$(\hat{S})$ for models $H_0, H_{1\phi}$, and H_{2p} for cases A and C for the complete and first capture history protocols.

| | | | Model $H_{1\phi}$ | | | | Model H_{2p} or $H'_{2\phi}$ | | | |
| | | | $\hat{E}(\hat{S})$ | | se$(\hat{S})$ | | $\hat{E}(\hat{S})$ | | se$(\hat{S})$ | |
Case	True model	Capture history	MC	EXPECT	MC[a]	EXPECT	MC	EXPECT	MC[a]	EXPECT
A	H_0	Complete	1.000	1.000	0.033	0.033	1.002	1.000	0.039	0.038
	$H_{1\phi}$	Complete	0.889	0.891	0.031	0.030	0.888	0.890	0.037	0.035
	H_{2p}	Complete	1.004	1.002	0.034	0.033	0.889	0.888	0.036	0.034
C	H_0	Complete	1.011	1.000	0.174	0.166	1.014	1.000	0.199	0.195
	$H_{1\phi}$	Complete	0.911	0.915	0.161	0.157	0.912	0.909	0.186	0.182
	H_{2p}	Complete	1.032	0.986	0.173	0.165	0.912	0.869	0.184	0.178
A	H_0	First	1.000	1.000	0.033	0.033	1.001	1.000	0.045	0.043
	$H_{1\phi}$	First	0.890	0.889	0.030	0.030	0.891	0.889	0.040	0.039
	H_{2p}	First	1.006	1.004	0.033	0.033	0.840	0.840	0.039	0.038
C	H_0	First	1.016	1.000	0.171	0.210	1.034	1.000	0.231	0.284
	$H_{1\phi}$	First	0.896	0.873	0.158	0.149	0.905	0.865	0.209	0.190
	H_{2p}	First	1.024	0.982	0.170	0.160	0.870	0.811	0.200	0.182

[a] se$(\hat{S})_e$ from case A, Table 5.2 and case C, Table 5.3.

Table 5.11. – Comparison of the Monte Carlo (MC) method with the method based on expectations (EXPECT) in estimating test power ($\alpha = 0.05$) for cases A and C for the complete and first capture history protocols.

Case	True model	Capture history	Test 1.R1 H_0 versus $H_{1\phi}$		Test 1 H_0 versus $H_{4\phi}$	
			MC[a]	EXPECT	MC[b]	EXPECT
A	$H_{1\phi}$	Complete	0.93	0.92	0.71	0.69
	H_{2p}	Complete	0.06	0.05	1.00	1.00
C	$H_{1\phi}$	Complete	0.10	0.07	0.06	0.06
	H_{2p}	Complete	0.05	0.05	0.12	0.10
A	$H_{1\phi}$	First	0.93	0.93	0.80	0.79
	H_{2p}	First	0.05	0.05	1.00	1.00
C	$H_{1\phi}$	First	0.10	0.11	0.08	0.08
	H_{2p}	First	0.04	0.05	0.12	0.14

[a]Partially from cases A and C, Table 5.6.

[b]From Table 5.7.

Part 6. Planning Experiments

6.1. Introduction

The careful design of survival experiments is important. The design must consider the assumptions (Section 1.4.4), the feasibility of different experimental protocols (Part 2), a set of statistical issues, and practical constraints. Our objective here is to provide a discussion of some of these general considerations. We make no attempt to cover field procedures because they are specific to each experiment and taxonomic group of interest. Before a more formal approach to the design of survival experiments can be given, we must have more experience with the analysis of real data. Until the methods presented here have been used, we can only provide a general discussion of some of the important issues, a mention of certain compromises, and a few "rules of thumb."

There is not much literature concentrating on design issues in release-recapture (see Manly 1977). Moreover, much of the existing literature on classical design issues for capture studies (Skalski 1985) is for simpler situations than we consider here. As experimental design is usually approached, one aspect involves examining tradeoffs of sampling effort and costs, and optimal allocation of resources to achieve preselected goals of precision or test power (the other aspect of design involves principles of validity such as randomization and replication). Nonlinear programming (Hadley 1964, Mangasarian 1969) provides an optimal approach for evaluating some of the tradeoffs in experimental design. However, in general, we lack a priori knowledge as to which design variables are known versus unknown. For a particular study, the total budget, number of fish available, the recapture rates (p_i), number of sampling sites (k), and costs of marks, handling, and marking may be known approximately. The design may then focus on the number of lots to use, the allocation of the proportion of fish to R_{t1} and R_{c1}, and issues such as stratification by size and timing of releases. Nonlinear programming provides a class of methods for assessing such compromises; we recommend this approach for achieving a nearly optimal design, at least for large, expensive experiments.

6.1.1. Desirability of a Pilot Experiment

The conduct of a small pilot experiment is important as it may provide needed insight into a variety of design questions. Critical to such a preliminary experiment is $k \geq 3$, which allows the assumption $p_{t2} = p_{c2}$ to be assessed by TEST 1.$T2$. Other statistical tests and field experience will aid in preliminary model selection. Rough estimates of ϕ_{vi}, p_{vi}, and S will be available following a pilot experiment. These estimates are useful in design considerations covered in the following chapters. Ideally, the complete capture history protocol should be used in the preliminary study.

In addition to the statistical considerations, a pilot experiment will provide evidence concerning feasibility of the field aspects of the full-scale experiment. Cost and labor requirements can be better projected from the experience gained during the pilot experiment. Difficulties with marking, handling, transporting, recapturing, and rereleasing animals will become apparent. The need for stratification and other issues can be assessed in preparation for the main experiment. We strongly recommend that such a preliminary experiment be conducted as an integral part of the study design.

6.1.2. Review of Assumptions

The general assumptions that underly the statistical methods presented here are repeated from Section 1.4.4.

(1) The test fish used are representative of the population of fish about which one seeks treatment mortality information.

(2) Test conditions are representative of the conditions of interest.

(3) Treatment and control fish are biologically identical prior to release at dam 1. A strong version of assumption 3 is that initial handling, marking, and holding do not affect survival rate.

(4) The numbers of fish released, by lots, are known exactly.

(5) Marking (tagging) is accurate; there are no mark (tag) losses and no misread marks (tags).

(6) All releases and recaptures occur in brief time intervals and recaptured fish are released immediately.

Assumptions 7-8 relate to the stochastic component of the models.

(7) The fate of each individual fish, after any known release, is independent of the fate of any other fish.

(8) With multiple lots (or other replication), the data are statistically independent over lots.

Assumptions 9-12 relate to model structure.

(9) Statistical analysis of the data is based on the correct model.

(10) Treatment and control fish move downstream together.

(11) Captured fish that are rereleased have the same subsequent survival and capture rates as fish alive at that site which were not caught, i.e., capture and rerelease do not affect their subsequent survival or recapture.

(12) All fish (in the study) of an identifiable class (e.g., treatment or control, size, or replicate) have the same survival and capture probabilities; this is an assumption of parameter homogeneity.

The first two assumptions are fundamental; they are not statistical nor testable, rather they are biological judgments. If these assumptions are not valid, there is little point in proceeding. If the treatment effect S is the only objective, then a weaker version of assumption 1 suffices: the treatment effect must be the same for the test fish and the population of fish being investigated.

The investigator has considerable control over the validity of assumptions 3-6 (some additional insight into these matters is provided in Part 7). It is important to assign randomly fish to treatment groups and lots within any stratifications, such as by age or size. If several persons are handling and marking fish, then these persons should be randomly rotated (e.g., marker A should not mark all of the control fish while marker B marks all of the treatment fish). The handling and transport methods should be identical for all treatment groups. Often, it is appropriate to hold marked fish for a period of time prior to release. Deaths during the holding period can be recorded and their total subtracted from the total numbers marked such that R_{v1} accurately reflects the actual numbers released (assumption 4).

A study should be designed so that any ill effects of marking on survival are minimized, otherwise, survival estimates ($\hat{\phi}_{vi}$) will be biased negatively. If the marking effect is equal for treatment and control fish, comparisons may still be reasonable. However, such comparisons may be invalid if an interaction between the marking and treatment-induced mortality occurs. Thus, treatment fish would have higher mortalities relative to control fish than if no marking mortality occurred. If marking is known to affect survival, then protocols that require a second batch mark (partial capture history schemes A and B) should be avoided.

Minimization of mark loss is important when study is designed. Once again, however, inferences about a treatment effect will still be valid if treatment and control fish lose their marks at the same rate. Another possibility with larger fish or other animals might be to use a double-marking scheme so that one could adjust for mark loss (Seber 1982:94). Accurate marking is critical; marks should not become lost or unreadable, and should be accurately recorded. Again, the validity of the treatment survival rate estimator $\hat{S}$ rests on somewhat weaker assumptions than estimators of ϕ_{vi} (see Section 1.4.4).

Treatment effects (S) and environmental and sampling effects (ϕ, p) should not be confounded with time effects, which are possibly associated with the release and recapture of fish; this is the essence of assumption 6. A given lot of treatment fish should be released in as short a time interval as possible so that all fish experience identical passage conditions. It is also desired that all recaptures occur in a brief time interval. In some types of studies, this objective can be accomplished; however, the recapture process at a given site usually is spread over time. This component of assumption 6 then gets replaced by assumption 10. When recaptures do occur, those fish should be immediately released. The longer the time recaptured fish are held, the more there may be a capture effect. Thus, captured and uncaptured fish that pass that dam will have different subsequent survival and capture rates.

Assumptions (7) and (8) relate to independence among fish and lots, respectively. The investigator usually has little control over these issues. Fortunately, these are relatively minor assumptions that are probably met approximately in most cases. Moreover, failure of assumption (7) does not cause any bias in parameter estimation; it only causes the theoretical variance to be too low. By using empirical estimators of variance, we avoid the need for assumption (7).

Substantial bias may arise if an incorrect model is used in the analysis of data (assumption 9). For example, if the recapture rate at dam 2 differs between treatment and control groups (i.e., $p_{t2} \neq p_{c2}$), then model H_{2p} is appropriate if other parameters for downstream dams are the same for each group. The use of the estimator of treatment survival under model $H_{1\phi}$ will result in a biased estimate of the treatment survival rate S. The design should allow adequate replication and sample sizes such that statistical tests will have high power. Thus, correct model selection will be likely, and use of the correct model is critical to valid, efficient inferences.

Treatment and control fish should move downstream together (assumption 10). This assumption, as the previous one, is closely tied with model selection. Ideally, fish in all the groups move at similar rates. If differential movement occurs, a more complex model may be required (e.g., H_{4p} rather than $H_{1\phi}$). In the extreme case where fish in the different groups never move simultaneously past some point j, then valid estimation may not be possible, although testing for a treatment effect remains valid.

Sometimes the treatment and control groups might have the same parameters (p_j and ϕ_j), but some groups move ahead of the others. In this case, it is important to sample at each dam j for a sufficient period of time such that all groups are appropriately sampled. We have seen one instance where sampling was terminated after, say 3 weeks at dam j and it appeared that the control fish had all passed the dam, but only perhaps 90% of the treatment fish had passed the dam by the time sampling efforts were terminated. This type of situation must be avoided.

Recapture and rerelease of fish should not affect their subsequent survival or recapture rates (assumption 11). This assumption is important for many of the models proposed. TESTs 2 and 3 provide powerful assessments of this assumption. In particular, this assumption may fail commonly with young fish. In that case, the first capture history protocol should be considered. An interesting alternative is provided by the use of PIT tags whereby recapture and rerelease do not involve handling. Instead, the tag number and, therefore, group membership, are recorded automatically as the fish pass through special recorders in the bypass system of a large hydroelectric dam.

When recapture is at dams, the ability to meet assumption 11 may depend on where the captured fish are rereleased. If fish are released below the dam, they are not exposed to the same risks as fish that pass through the dam by some route and are not caught. If the fish are released above the dam, they will have experienced more risk than fish not caught. The captured fish could be released into some bypass structure, but even then they would tend to experience slightly different risks than fish not caught that will take a variety of routes through the dam (turbines, bypasses, spillways, fish ladders). Perhaps the best strategy is to release the fish directly into the bypass route that most fish are expected to use.

Assumption 12 relates to homogeneity of fish within a group. Again, the investigator can stratify the sample fish by age, sex, size, or other variable to limit the degree of heterogeneity. If homogeneity is slightly violated, few problems will result (see Part 5). The main effect will be that the theoretical estimates of sampling variances will be slightly altered. However, this problem tends to vanish if replication is done to allow empirical estimates of variances.

6.2. Selection of an Experimental Protocol

The investigator must consider the type of tag or mark to use and whether fish are to be removed or rereleased upon capture at dam j ($j > 1$). A summary of the experimental protocols is presented in Table 6.1 for review here. Some considerations for each protocol follow.

Table 6.1. – Summary of the important elements involved in the different experimental protocols.

Protocol	Marking scheme	Remove or rerelease	Number of recaptures
Complete capture history	Unique marks	Either[a]	Up to $k - 1$
Complete capture history	$k - 1$ batch marks	Either[a]	Up to $k - 1$
Partial capture history, scheme A	$k - 1$ batch marks	Remove after second recapture	2
Partial capture history, scheme B	2 batch marks	Remove at sites 3 - k	2
Unknown capture history	1 batch mark	Rerelease at sites 2 - k	Up to $k - 1$
First capture history	1 batch mark	Remove at sites 2 - k	1

[a]Some fish, but not all, can be intentionally removed. Enough fish must be rereleased so that some are recaptured in future samples.

6.2.1. Complete Capture History Protocol

Setting aside costs and other nonstatistical considerations, the ideal experiment would use the complete capture history protocol. Under this protocol, the survival (ϕ_{vi}) and recapture (p_{vi}) rates can be estimated and several critical hypotheses can be tested (TESTs 2 and 3).

These estimates and test results provide flexibility in the analysis of a treatment effect. In addition, internal replication can be achieved by post-stratifying the data based on the last digit of the tag number. This procedure permits the estimation of empirical sampling variances based on the 10 internal replicates (see Chapter 7.3 for an example).

If resampling does not involve handling animals, which could be avoided by the use of PIT tags on fish or resighting methods on terrestrial vertebrates, the complete capture history protocol seems ideal if the recapture rates are high. If the p_{vi} are low, few recaptures are made and little information is gained.

6.2.2. Partial Capture History Protocol

The partial capture history protocol offers many of the same advantages as the complete capture history protocol. An advantage is that batch marks, identifying only group membership, can be used. However, if handling adversely affects the subsequent survival or recapture rates, the partial capture history protocol should not be used.

The recapture rates must be high or few animals will be remarked and available for subsequent recapture. We believe this protocol will be quite valuable for terrestrial vertebrates, but may see limited application in fisheries investigations.

6.2.3. Unknown Capture History Protocol

The unknown capture history protocol may sometimes be considered when the recapture rates are relatively low and are known a priori to be unaffected by the treatment. Only the parameter $S = \phi_{t1}/\phi_{c1}$ can be estimated from data under this protocol. This protocol has been used in the past in fisheries investigations where the cost of fish for the study and of batch-marking have been fairly low and the recapture rates have been low. In general, we do not recommend this protocol, especially when $k = 2$.

6.2.4. First Capture History Protocol

The first capture history protocol is most appropriate if $H_{1\phi}$ is the true model; i.e., there is a direct, acute treatment effect. Only batch marks are required. Only the treatment survival rate is estimable and the method is increasingly precise as the p_{vi} increase. The estimator of S is identical to those of the complete and partial capture history protocols under model $H_{1\phi}$. As this protocol relies on removal data, it is appropriate (actually necessary) when a handling effect is present.

The extended sequence of models $H'_{2\phi}, H'_{3\phi}, ..., H'_{k-1,\phi}$ should be considered if the treatment is chronic and it is known that treatment does not affect the p_{vi}. We doubt that this series of models will be generally useful, except as approximations, as mentioned in Chapter 3.9.

6.3. Effort and Sample Size Considerations

6.3.1. Introduction

The question most often asked of statisticians during a study design is "How big a sample do I need?" This question is not easy to answer, even for simple studies. For the experiments considered here, the question should be rephrased, "How much effort will this study require to achieve a given level of precision for $\hat{S}$ and to have high power of the statistical tests used to evaluate the assumptions of the experiment?" The standard approach is to assume a model structure (which cannot be done with certainty), specify the desired $cv(\hat{S})$, specify all the parameters of the model, write down the formula for $var(\hat{S})$, and solve for sample size. For example, under model $H_{1\phi}$, the theoretical large-sample variance of $\hat{S}$ is

$$var(\hat{S}) = (S)^2 \left[\frac{1}{E(r_{t1})} - \frac{1}{R_{t1}} + \frac{1}{E(r_{c1})} - \frac{1}{R_{c1}} \right].$$

This formula can be rewritten as

$$[cv(\hat{S})]^2 = \frac{1}{R_{t1}} \left[\frac{1}{S\lambda_{c1}} - 1 \right] + \frac{1}{R_{c1}} \left[\frac{1}{\lambda_{c1}} - 1 \right]$$

where

$$\lambda_{c1} = E\left(\frac{r_{c1}}{R_{c1}} \right).$$

If the investigator (1) assumes the model structure of $H_{1\phi}$, (2) assumes the theoretical variance is appropriate, (3) assumes a value for S, such as 0.9, (4) assumes a value for λ_{c1}, such as 0.15, (5) assumes, for example, $R_{t1} = R_{c1} = R$ (so $2R$ total fish are released), and (6) specifies $cv(\hat{S})$, say as 0.05, then the required sample size R can be found. In this example, the relevant equation becomes

$$[cv(\hat{S})]^2 = \frac{1}{R} \left[\frac{1}{(0.9)(0.15)} - 1 \right] + \frac{1}{R} \left[\frac{1}{0.15} - 1 \right];$$

hence,

$$(0.05)^2 = \frac{12.074}{R} ,$$

or $R = 4{,}830$. A total of about 10,000 fish is required. However, this sample size is only as reliable as the assumptions used to compute it. If the model structure is reasonable but the theoretical variance is too low (compared to the actual variance) by a factor or two or more (a common situation), then R can be substantially wrong. Further consideration of absolute numbers of fish to release is in Section 6.3.6.

The sample size questions must be generalized here to be a series of questions about (1) how much total effort is needed and (2) how effort should be allocated proportionally to different aspects of the experiment. Quantities that are at least partially controllable are R_{t1}, R_{c1}, and recapture effort. It is much easier to consider optimal allocation of total effort than to try and determine what the total effort should be. Also, knowing the optimal relative allocation makes it easier to determine total effort. For example, the sample size question has two components: (1) what is the necessary total size, $R_{t1} + R_{c1}$, and (2) what is the optimal ratio of treatment to control releases, R_{t1} versus R_{c1}? We will first consider questions of allocation of effort, given some total effort, and then return to the question of determining total effort.

6.3.2. Relative Numbers of Releases

6.3.2.1. Two groups. – Given a total number of available fish, one of the easiest questions to address is the optimal relative numbers of treatment and control fish, R_{t1} and R_{c1}, respectively. In particular, for two groups, it will be nearly optimal to have equal numbers of fish released for both groups, i.e., $R_{t1} = R_{c1}$. We explore here the two-group case in some detail.

Under model $H_{1\phi}$, the variance of $\hat{S}$ may be taken as

$$\text{var}(\hat{S}) = c\,(S)^2 \left[\frac{1}{R_{t1}} \left(\frac{1}{S\lambda_{c1}} - 1 \right) + \frac{1}{R_{c1}} \left(\frac{1}{\lambda_{c1}} - 1 \right) \right].$$

Here, c is an unknown variance inflation factor that reflects the phenomenon often observed of excess variation (see Part 4). Letting the total $R_{.1} = R_{t1} + R_{c1}$ be fixed but arbitrary, we use calculus to find the optimal allocation ratio R_{t1}/R_{c1} to minimize $\text{var}(\hat{S})$. This minimization is facilitated by realizing the form of $\text{var}(\hat{S})$ is

$$\text{var}(\hat{S}) = \frac{A}{R_{t1}} + \frac{B}{R_{c1}} \, ,$$

where

$$A = c(S)^2 \left[\frac{1}{S\lambda_{c1}} - 1 \right],$$

and

$$B = c(S)^2 \left[\frac{1}{\lambda_{c1}} - 1 \right].$$

Using $R_{c1} = R_{.1} - R_{t1}$, write the above as

$$\text{var}(\hat{S}) = \frac{1}{R_{.1}} \left[\frac{A}{\gamma} + \frac{B}{1 - \gamma} \right],$$

where

$$\gamma = \frac{R_{t1}}{R_{.1}}, \qquad 0 < \gamma < 1.$$

Taking the derivative of $\text{var}(\hat{S})$ with respect to γ, gives

$$\frac{\partial \text{var}(\hat{S})}{\partial \gamma} = \frac{1}{R_{.1}} \left[\frac{-A}{\gamma^2} + \frac{B}{(1 - \gamma)^2} \right].$$

Setting this derivative equal to zero and solving it yields the value of γ that gives the minimum $\text{var}(\hat{S})$ for any fixed $R_{.1}$:

$$\gamma = \frac{1}{1 + (B/A)^{1/2}} \, .$$

Translating this general result back into terms of the original variables gives

$$\frac{R_{t1}}{R_{.1}} = \left[1 + \left(\frac{1 - \lambda_{c1}}{\frac{1}{S} - \lambda_{c1}} \right)^{1/2} \right]^{-1} .$$
(6.1)

From (6.1) we find the optimal ratio of R_{t1}/R_{c1}:

$$\frac{R_{t1}}{R_{c1}} = \left(\frac{\frac{1}{S} - \lambda_{c1}}{1 - \lambda_{c1}} \right)^{1/2} .$$
(6.2)

From (6.2) it is clear that under optimal allocation of release numbers, we have $R_{t1} \geq R_{c1}$; they are equal if and only if $S = 1$.

Formulae (6.1) and (6.2) give the optimal ratio of treatment to total, or to control, releases (respectively) when $V = 2$ and model $H_{1\phi}$ is assumed. One interesting feature of this result is that the variance inflation factor, c, drops out. Thus, the actual magnitude of $\text{var}(\hat{S})$ does not influence the optimal allocations of fish to treatment and control groups. Rather, optimal allocation depends only on the true value of S and the probability of recapturing a fish that is alive below dam 1 (λ_{c1}).

Table 6.2 shows the value of the optimal ratio of treatment to control fish, R_{t1}/R_{c1}, for a range of values of S and λ_{c1}. For example, when $S = 0.9$ and $\lambda_{c1} = 0.20$, we have

$$\frac{R_{t1}}{R_{c1}} = \left(\frac{0.9611}{0.8500} \right)^{1/2}$$

$$= 1.063 .$$

Table 6.2. – Values of the optimal ratio R_{t1}/R_{c1}, for minimizing var($\hat{S}$) under model $H_{1\phi}$, for a range of values of S and λ_{c1} (based on formula 6.2).

			λ_{c1}		
S	0.10	0.15	0.20	0.25	0.30
0.95	1.029	1.030	1.032	1.034	1.037
0.90	1.060	1.063	1.067	1.072	1.076
0.85	1.094	1.099	1.105	1.111	1.119
0.80	1.130	1.138	1.146	1.155	1.165
0.75	1.171	1.180	1.190	1.202	1.215
0.70	1.215	1.226	1.239	1.254	1.270
0.50	1.453	1.475	1.500	1.528	1.558

Thus, for every 100 control fish, one would release 106 treatment fish. We believe this is not practical in the field. Moreover, the optimality of this allocation only applies exactly under model $H_{1\phi}$ with $S = 0.9$ and $\lambda_{c1} = 0.15$. We do not know if model $H_{1\phi}$ is true; we do not know S or λ_{1c}. Thus, if S is large, say $S \geq 0.8$, we recommend equal release numbers R_{t1} and R_{c1}.

From Table 6.2 we see that optimal allocation to treatment and control groups depends mostly on the true value of S. (This result is typical in optimality theory: the optimal experiment requires knowing the exact parameter or parameters that one is trying to estimate.) Some release ratios other than 1:1 could be practical, for example, 2:1 ($R_{t1}/R_{c1} = 2.0$), 3:2 (1.500), 4:3 (1.333), or 5:4 (1.25). If, for example, S was believed to be about 0.5, one should use a ratio of 3:2 treatment to control fish.

A quick rule of thumb is that R_{t1}/R_{c1} should be approximately equal to $1 / \sqrt{S}$; thus, at $S = 2/3$, 5:4 is about optimal. However, even for $S = 0.667$, a 1:1 allocation results in a se($\hat{S}$) that is not much larger than what is achieved at optimal allocation. With $\gamma = R_{t1}/R_{.1}$, the variance of $\hat{S}$ as a function of γ is

$$\text{var}(\hat{S}) = \frac{c(S)^2}{R_{.1}} \left[\frac{1}{\gamma} \left(\frac{1}{S\lambda_{c1}} - 1 \right) + \frac{1}{1-\gamma} \left(\frac{1}{\lambda_{c1}} - 1 \right) \right].$$

Using this formula, we computed the results below for $S = 0.667$ and $\lambda_{c1} = 0.20$:

γ	R_{t1}/R_{c1}	var($\hat{S}$)/[optimal var($\hat{S}$)]
0.500	1.000	1.015
0.560	1.275	1.000
0.600	1.500	1.006
0.670	2.000	1.051

The unknowns c and $R_{.1}$ drop out of the ratio

$$\frac{\text{var}(\hat{S})}{\text{optimal var}(\hat{S})}.$$

In this example, the optimal ratio is nearly 5:4, yet using 1:1 or even 2:1 results in only a trivial loss in precision.

The conclusion is that a release ratio of 1:1 is safe; we recommend it unless one knows S is <0.4. If $S < 0.4$, then use a release ratio of 2:1 for $R_{t1}:R_{c1}$.

6.3.2.2. The case of more than two groups. – With three or more groups the problems of allocation of release numbers to R_{v1}, $v = 1, ..., V$ are more difficult. The problems are not primarily of mathematical difficulty, but rather of deciding on appropriate criteria to use as a basis for determining optimal allocation. There are now $V - 1$ independent treatment effects, whereas for $V = 2$ we dealt with only one treatment effect. One simple situation is to have one control and then compare each treatment release to that control. For this purpose, we let the "last" group, V, be the control group (i.e., $R_{c1} = R_{V1}$) and define the vth treatment effect as

$$S_v = \frac{\phi_{v1}}{\phi_{c1}}, \quad v = 1, ..., V - 1.$$

The second situation that we will consider here corresponds to a series of releases at different locations along the river, with release 1 being upriver from release 2, which is upriver from release 3, and so forth. Treatment effects of interest are then

$$S_v = \frac{\phi_{v1}}{\phi_{v+1,1}}, \quad v = 1, ..., V - 1.$$

This situation corresponds (roughly) to a system-wide study.

Now there are $V - 1$ sampling variances, var($\hat{S}_v$), as well as covariances among these $\hat{S}_v$, and we have to specify an optimality criterion; the possibilities are endless, so we consider here only minimizing the sum of the $V - 1$ variances. It is also easy to deal with a weighted sum, if some treatment effects are deemed more important than others. In general, one could use numerical optimization (i.e., nonlinear programming) for more complex objective functions.

For the first situation, $S_v = \phi_{v1}/\phi_{c1}$ and, under model $H_{1\phi}$,

$$\mathrm{var}(\hat{S}_v) = \frac{A_v}{R_{v1}} + \frac{B_v}{R_{c1}}, \qquad v = 1, ..., V$$

with

$$A_v = c(S_v)^2 \left[\frac{1}{S_v \lambda_{c1}} - 1 \right],$$

and

$$B_v = c(S_v)^2 \left[\frac{1}{\lambda_{c1}} - 1 \right].$$

Subject to $R_{.1} = R_{11} + R_{21} + \cdots + R_{V1}$ being fixed, we want to minimize

$$\sum_{v=1}^{V-1} \mathrm{var}(\hat{S}_v)$$

in terms of the allocation ratios

$$\gamma_v = \frac{R_{v1}}{R_{.1}}, \qquad v = 1, ..., V.$$

An alternative representation for the solution is in terms of the ratios

$$\frac{\gamma_v}{\gamma_V} = \frac{R_{v1}}{R_{c1}}, \qquad v = 1, ..., V - 1.$$

The objective function to be minimized is now

$$f(\gamma_1, ..., \gamma_{V-1}) = \sum_{j=1}^{V-1} \frac{1}{R_{.1}} \left(\frac{A_j}{\gamma_j} + \frac{B_j}{\gamma_V} \right),$$

where

$$\gamma_V = 1 - \sum_{j=1}^{V-1} \gamma_j .$$

Take the $V - 1$ partial derivatives of $f(\gamma_1, ..., \gamma_{V-1})$, with respect to the γ_v, to obtain the equations to be solved:

$$\frac{1}{R_{.1}} \left[\frac{-A_v}{(\gamma_v)^2} + \sum_{j=1}^{V-1} \frac{B_j}{(\gamma_V)^2} \right] = 0 , \quad v = 1, ..., V .$$

The solution for γ_v / γ_V is obvious; thus, we get

$$\frac{R_{v1}}{R_{c1}} = \left(\frac{A_v}{\sum_{j=1}^{V-1} B_j} \right)^{1/2} , \quad v = 1, ..., V - 1 .$$

A little more algebra yields

$$R_{c1} = R_{.1} \left[1 + \sum_{v=1}^{V-1} \left(\frac{A_v}{\sum_{j=1}^{V-1} B_j} \right)^{1/2} \right]^{-1} .$$

Thus, we can compute R_{c1} given $R_{.1}$, then get the $R_{11}, ..., R_{V-1,1}$.

It is important to remember that this is the solution to optimal allocation for given $S_v = \phi_{v1}/\phi_{c1}$, $v = 1, ..., V - 1$ under model $H_{1\phi}$, and for just one simple optimality criterion. The unknown constant c will drop out of these ratios. However, we are still left with

$$\frac{R_{v1}}{R_{c1}} = \frac{S_v}{\left(\sum_{j=1}^{V-1} (S_j)^2 \right)^{1/2}} \left(\frac{\frac{1}{S_v} - \lambda_{c1}}{1 - \lambda_{c1}} \right)^{1/2} , \quad v = 1, ..., V - 1 .$$

A useful approximation to this solution, provided λ_{c1} is not too large (say, $\lambda_{c1} \leq 0.3$), is

$$\frac{R_{v1}}{R_{c1}} = \left(\frac{S_v}{\sum\limits_{j=1}^{V-1}(S_j)^2} \right)^{1/2} .$$

If the S_v do not vary too much (i.e., all S_v are in the range 0.6 to 0.9), then a suitable allocation would be to have the ratio R_{v1}/R_{c1} constant over $v = 1, ..., V - 1$. As with the case of $V = 2$ groups, the variance of $\hat{S}_v$ will be only weakly dependent on the allocation, so little loss in precision is seen with allocations that are only approximately optimal. This gives us the useful approximations

$$\frac{R_{v1}}{R_{c1}} = \frac{1}{\sqrt{V-1}} ;$$

$$R_{c1} = R_{.1} \left[1 + \sqrt{V-1} \right]^{-1} .$$

Thus, if one had four groups, a good starting allocation would be

$$R_{v1} = (0.577)R_{c1} ;$$

$$R_{c1} = (0.366)R_{.1} .$$

For practical purposes, we take this as

$$R_{v1} = \frac{2}{9} R_{.1} , \quad v = 1, 2, 3;$$

$$R_{c1} = \frac{R_{.1}}{3} .$$

For example, if $R_{.1}$ was taken as 90,000 fish, then we get

$$R_{c1} = 30,000 ;$$

$$R_{v1} = 20,000 , \quad v = 1, 2, 3 .$$

One conclusion here is that, with one control group and multiple treatments, optimal allocation requires proportionally more fish in the control group than in the treatment groups.

Now we consider the situation where treatment group $(v + 1)$ is the control for group v; thus,

$$S_v = \frac{\phi_{v1}}{\phi_{v+1,1}}, \quad v = 1, ..., V - 1.$$

This could, of course, be just an alternative way of defining the treatment effect from an experiment where each ϕ_{v1}/ϕ_{V1} is also of interest. The two formulations will, however, give different optimal allocation results. Now

$$\text{var}(\hat{S}_v) = (S_v)^2 \left[\frac{A_v}{R_{v1}} + \frac{A_{v+1}}{R_{v+1,1}} \right], \quad v = 1, ..., V - 1,$$

and

$$A_v = c \left[\frac{1}{\lambda_{v1}} - 1 \right], \quad v = 1, ..., V - 1.$$

We take as our objective the minimizing of

$$\sum \text{var}(\hat{S}_v) = \frac{1}{R_{.1}} \sum_{j=1}^{V-1} (S_v)^2 \left[\frac{A_j}{\gamma_j} + \frac{A_{j+1}}{\gamma_{j+1}} \right],$$

where, as before,

$$\gamma_j = \frac{R_{j1}}{R_{.1}}, \quad j = 1, ..., V - 1;$$

$$\gamma_V = 1 - \gamma_1 - \cdots - \gamma_{V-1}.$$

Now take the $V - 1$ partial derivatives of the above $\Sigma \text{var}(\hat{S}_v)$ with respect to $\gamma_1, ..., \gamma_{V-1}$ to get the equations

$$(S_1)^2 \frac{A_1}{(\gamma_1)^2} = (S_{V-1})^2 \frac{A_V}{(\gamma_V)^2} ;$$

$$\left[(S_{j-1})^2 + (S_j)^2\right] \frac{A_j}{(\gamma_j)^2} = (S_{V-1})^2 \frac{A_V}{(\gamma_V)^2} , \quad j = 2, ..., V - 1.$$

The algebra and solution are easier if we use symbols S_0 and S_V and define them to be $S_0 = 0$, $S_V = 0$. We now define

$$Q_j = \left\{ \left[\frac{(S_{j-1})^2 + (S_j)^2}{(S_{V-1})^2} \right] \left[\frac{A_j}{A_V} \right] \right\}^{1/2} , \quad j = 1, ..., V .$$

Note that $Q_V = 1$. The optimal release proportions are

$$\gamma_j = \frac{Q_j}{\sum\limits_{j=1}^{V} Q_j} , \quad j = 1, ..., V .$$

This result is for model $H_{1\phi}$ with the objective function being to minimize the sum of the $\text{var}(\hat{S}_v)$. When there is more than one treatment ($V > 2$), there are many possible optimality criteria. We cannot investigate them all here; however, for a given study, with $V > 2$, extensive analytical and numerical investigations of optimal release ratios could be done.

The optimal γ_j for this case and problem formulation depend on V parameters, $S_1, ...,$ S_{V-1} and λ_{v1}, because $\lambda_{v1} = S_v \cdots S_{V-1}\lambda_{V1}$. The relative ratios, $Q_1, ..., Q_{V-1}$, depend weakly on λ_{V1} but strongly on the treatment effects $S_1, ..., S_{V-1}$. The more treatment groups there are, the more sensitive Q_v appears to be to variations in the S_v. Consequently, a simple rule of thumb for nearly optimal allocation does not seem possible here. As a starting point to think about these results, note that when all $S_v = 1$, $v = 1, ..., V - 1$, then $Q_1 = 1$, $Q_{V-1} = 1$, and $Q_v = \sqrt{2}$, $v = 2, ..., V - 2$. One then finds the ratios γ_v from the normalized Q_v. Finally, we give the Q_v below for the case of $V = 4$, $\lambda_{V1} = 0.16$, and $S_1 = S_2 = S_3 = S$ for several values of S:

S	Q_1	Q_2	Q_3	Q_4
1	1	1.4	1.4	1
0.9	1.2	1.6	1.5	1
0.8	1.5	1.8	1.6	1
0.7	1.8	2.1	1.7	1

6.3.2.3. Comments. – The results on relative allocations to treatment groups were derived assuming model $H_{1\phi}$. They will hold reasonably well even under model H_{2p} because the variance of S is similar under these two models. If some other model holds, then one should explore allocations under that model. Analytical results are only easy to get under model $H_{1\phi}$. For more complex models, numerical procedures are recommended; the EXPECT option in program RELEASE can be used to explore alternative designs and models. The more difficult problem in complex, multiparameter situations is to specify a meaningful criterion to be optimized. Finally, the optimal solution will depend on the unknown parameters. Consequently, simple approximations may be more useful than exact results.

6.3.3. Relative Recapture Effort

Once it has been decided how many recapture sites to use; one needs to consider how to allocate recapture effort across sites 2 to k. There may not be any choices here due to practical constraints. If recapture is at dams, and one expends maximal effort at each dam, there are no choices to be made. Hence, we address here the case where some tradeoffs are possible about how much recapture effort is allocated to the $k - 1$ recapture sites (or occasions in the general Jolly-Seber model). Effort will be represented by the capture probabilities, $p_2, ..., p_k$.

With no constraints operating, the optimum is to put all $p_i = 1$. However, resources are always limited, so assume the general constraint

$$C = \sum_{j=2}^{k} c_i p_i ,$$

where C is fixed. Here, c_i can be thought of as cost-per-unit effort at site i. A useful case to consider will be all c_i equal; then we are just saying that total capture effort is fixed. Let model $H_{1\phi}$ be true, and assume one wants to minimize var($\hat{S}$). The mathematics get complex. However, it turns out to have at least one simple solution; if the costs at dam 2 are not too large, the variance of $\hat{S}$ is minimized by putting all the recapture effort at dam 2. The problem with this solution (which assumes $H_{1\phi}$ is true) is that one cannot test any hypothesis about the extent of the treatment effect on the equality of, for example, p_{t2} and p_{c2}. In fact, minimization of var($\hat{S}$) is a poor criterion for allocating effort to recapture sites.

An appropriate criterion for allocation of effort to recapture sites is to achieve high power of model selection tests, especially TEST 1.$T2$, which tests model $H_{1\phi}$ versus H_{2p} (nominally it tests $p_{t2} = p_{c2}$). The power of this test can be investigated numerically using the EXPECT option of program RELEASE (see Section 6.3.7).

We considered the reverse problem of minimizing cost given a fixed variance of $\hat{S}$. The problem is not analytically solvable in a sufficiently simple form to give useful results. This allocation problem (to minimize costs) could be solved numerically. It is probably not worth doing, given all the other more critical facets of the design problem.

The general principle that emerges here is that recapture site 2 is an important site; if at all possible, it should get more recapture effort than the others. Thus, for example, if $k = 5$, one should not aim for $p_2 = p_3 = p_4 = p_5$. Rather, have $p_2 > p_3, p_4$, and p_5. Substantial numbers of releases are important at site 2 in order to get good power of hypothesis tests. This is especially true if the treatment effect is mostly acute so that $H_{1\phi}$ or H_{2p} are likely the appropriate models.

A reasonable allocation of recapture effort over occasions $j = 2$ to k is

$$\frac{p_2}{p_.} = \frac{\sqrt{k-1}}{\sqrt{k-1} + k - 2} ;$$

and

$$\frac{p_j}{p_.} = \frac{1}{\sqrt{k-1} + k - 2} , \quad j \geq 3 .$$

Here $p_. = p_2 + p_3 + \cdots + p_k$. The ratios $p_j/p_.$ are relative capture rates; one can think of them as also indexing relative recapture effort at each site. With some rounding, the above formulae produce the following relative efforts:

j	$k = 3$	$k = 4$	$k = 5$	$k = 6$
2	60%	50%	40%	36%
3	40%	25%	20%	16%
4		25%	20%	16%
5			20%	16%
6				16%

In any study where allocation of recapture effort to sites is a critical feature, numerical studies must be done to find a good allocation scheme.

In the extreme case, think of allowing some p_i to be zero. This consideration raises the question of how many recapture sites to use; $k = 3$ is a minimum in order to test the crucial hypothesis of $p_{t2} = p_{c2}$. If all effort could be concentrated at two recapture sites, appropriately located, $k = 3$ would be excellent when the effect is mostly acute and the only releases at site 2 are recaptures made there. If capture probabilities (i.e., effort) are unavoidably low at any site, then increase the number of sampling sites.

6.3.4. Relative Allocation of Effort to Releases and Recaptures

There is a tradeoff between number of animals released versus total effort expended to recapture them. If it is easy (inexpensive) to release large numbers but difficult (expensive) to recapture them, then release thousands or tens of thousands and settle for low recapture rates. However, as recapture probabilities increase, release fewer individuals and still achieve the same precision of $\hat{S}$ with some test powers. If it is difficult to release large numbers of animals but easy to recapture them, then a good study should also be possible. When both options are difficult, then evaluate carefully any possible tradeoff between numbers released versus recapture efforts.

First we give an example of the relationship between release numbers and recapture rates. Under model $H_{1\phi}$, with $R_{t1} = R_{c1}$, the theoretical ($c = 1$) coefficient of variation of $\hat{S}$ is

$$[\text{cv}(\hat{S})]^2 = \frac{1}{R_{.1}} \left[\frac{1}{\lambda_{c1}} \left(\frac{1}{S} + 1 \right) - 2 \right].$$

For illustrative purposes, let $\text{cv}(\hat{S}) = 0.025$ and $S = 0.8$. The following pairs of values will then all produce a cv of 0.025:

λ_{c1}	$R_{.1}$
0.01	356,800
0.05	68,800
0.10	32,800
0.15	20,800
0.20	14,800
0.40	5,800
0.80	1,300
1.00	400

These pairs of points lie along the hyperbola described by

$$R_{.1} = \frac{3{,}600}{\lambda_{c1}} - 3{,}200 \, .$$

In general, there is an inverse relationship between sampling effort (capture probabilities) and release numbers.

The above example illustrates that it is highly desirable to avoid low recapture rates; inordinate numbers of animals ($R_{.1} = R_{t1} + R_{c1}$) are needed at low capture probabilities. Also note that a given proportional increase in λ_{c1} corresponds to a greater proportional decrease in $R_{.1}$, especially at high capture rates. When λ_{c1} increases $5 \times$ from 0.01 to 0.05, $R_{.1}$ decrease $5.19 \times$. Some cases of λ_{c1} doubling and the corresponding proportional decreases of $R_{.1}$ follow:

Change in λ_{c1}		Proportional decrease in $R_{.1}$
from	to	
0.05	0.1	2.097
0.1	0.2	2.216
0.2	0.4	2.552
0.4	0.8	4.462

Thus, in the tradeoff between increasing capture probabilities and increasing release numbers, the preferred strategy should be to increase capture probabilities and allow a corresponding decrease in $R_{.1}$. At the least, we recommend that first consideration be given to doing all that is possible to achieve high capture probabilities before adopting the "brute-force" approach of releasing as many animals as possible at site 1.

If the cost of releasing fish and recapturing them is known, then fix the precision of $\hat{S}$ and find the values of $R_{.1}$ and λ_{c1} that give minimum cost. What typically happens is that the recapture effort gets set in advance and then R_{t1} and R_{c1} are chosen to achieve the desired precision. We considered this approach but decided useful formulae could not be given without a specific context. Just the matter of cost functions themselves cannot be dealt with satisfactorily in the abstract (see Skalski 1985). Given a specific study, however, it is possible, in principle, to optimize over tradeoffs such as numbers released versus recapture effort.

Finally, we note a particular area where these ideas would be useful to pursue: the tradeoffs associated with using high technology marks, such as PIT or radio tags (Stier and Kynard 1986), versus batch marks. We would not be surprised to achieve a doubling or tripling of recapture rates with PIT tags and even greater corresponding reduction in releases. This reduction in release numbers needed might make the use of PIT tags not only feasible but quite attractive.

6.3.5. Numbers of Releases

Determining absolutes, such as the total number of fish to release, $R_{.1}$, is paradoxically both the simplest and hardest aspect of the problem. It is mathematically simple, but the results depend critically on many unknowns and cannot easily be made reliable. Consider that model $H_{1\phi}$ holds and our primary objective is to estimate S with good precision. Then, from the formula for $\mathrm{var}(\hat{S})$, the "solution" is

$$R_{.1} = \frac{2c}{[\mathrm{cv}(\hat{S})]^2} \left[\left(\frac{1}{S} + 1 \right) \frac{1}{\lambda_{c1}} - 2 \right]. \tag{6.3}$$

This is predicated on using $R_{t1} = R_{c1}$, which is certainly appropriate if $S \geq 0.8$. The general formula, based on using the optimal ratio of $\gamma = R_{t1}/R_{.1}$, is

$$R_{.1} = \frac{c}{[\mathrm{cv}(\hat{S})]^2} \left[\frac{1}{\gamma} \left(\frac{1}{S\lambda_{c1}} - 1 \right) + \left(\frac{1}{1-\gamma} \right) \left(\frac{1}{\lambda_{c1}} - 1 \right) \right]. \tag{6.4}$$

The determination of $R_{.1}$ is actually the final consideration. First, determine relative quantities like optimal γ and allocation of effort to sites, as well as number of recapture sites, and optimize λ_{c1}. As the last step, plug these quantities into equation (6.4), along with the target $\mathrm{cv}(\hat{S})$ and the value of c. $R_{.1}$ depends critically on λ_{c1} and c, neither of which, especially c, are well known. The survival rate S is often known well enough that $R_{.1}$ does not critically depend on it (e.g., if one believes $0.8 < S < 1$, just take $S = 0.9$). Finally, the number of released fish needed also depends on the true model (and protocol). For models $H_{1\phi}$ and H_{2p}, equation (6.4) can be used. For model $H_{2\phi}$, substantially more releases are needed.

As an example, let $S = 0.9$, $\lambda_{c1} = 0.2$, and our target $\mathrm{cv}(\hat{S}) = 0.02$. This corresponds to an approximate 95% CI of about 0.86 to 0.94 on S. Using $R_{t1} = R_{c1}$, then from equation (6.3)

$$R_{.1} = c \frac{17.1111}{[\mathrm{cv}(\hat{S})]^2}$$

$$= c \, 42,778 \, .$$

If binomial (or multinomial) variation would hold, then $c = 1$ would be used. However, experience has shown that empirical variances often exceed theoretical variances, especially for count data, even when the model structure is reasonable. It is common, especially in ecological and environmental sampling, to find that empirical standard errors are double the theoretical errors (this corresponds to $c = 4$). Unfortunately, it is quite possible to have this variance inflation be as large as $c = 9$. In a carefully controlled study, it can be hoped to have $c \leq 4$. Therefore, in the previous example, the use of $c = 1$, hence, $R_{.1} = 43,000$, is likely to fail to achieve $cv(\hat{S}) = 0.02$. A more realistic sample size is $R_{.1} = 4(42,778) = 171,112$; rounded off, $R_{.1} = 170,000$ and $R_{t1} = R_{c1} = 85,000$.

Despite the uncertainties involved, it is still better to go through planning procedures such as the above, rather than just guess at a sample size. This procedure can be used to explore the relative sensitivity of results to the different factors. What if $cv(\hat{S}) = 0.03$ were acceptable? Then

$$R_{.1} = c\ 19,012\ ,$$

which clearly allows a big decrease in sample size. In general, halving the target $cv(\hat{S})$ requires quadrupling the sample size.

If we continue with $cv(\hat{S}) = 0.02$, but explore sensitivity to λ_{c1} and S, we have the results below:

S	λ_{c1}	$R_{.1}/c$
0.95	0.25	31,053
0.90	0.25	32,222
0.85	0.25	33,529
0.95	0.20	41,316
0.90	0.20	42,778
0.85	0.20	44,412
0.95	0.15	58,421
0.90	0.15	60,370
0.85	0.15	62,549

Clearly, λ_{c1} or, more precisely, capture probabilities, are a critical factor in selection of sample size.

Often the practical and financial constraints are such that the design consists of using the largest affordable sample size. Then these calculations should be reversed to compute precision, given $R_{.1}$, using

$$[cv(\hat{S})]^2 = c\ \frac{2}{R_{.1}} \left[\left(\frac{1}{S} + 1 \right) \frac{1}{\lambda_{c1}} - 2 \right].$$

The above is still assuming model $H_{1\phi}$. If the budget would allow only $R_{.1} = 50,000$, then we have (for $S = 0.9$, $\lambda_{c1} = 0.2$)

$$[cv(\hat{S})]^2 = c \, \frac{2}{50,000} \left[\left(\frac{1}{.9} + 1 \right) \left(\frac{1}{.2} - 2 \right) \right]$$

$$= c \, (0.0003422) \, ,$$

or

$$cv(\hat{S}) = \sqrt{c} \, (0.0185).$$

We see that 50,000 is acceptable (i.e., $cv(\hat{S}) \sim 0.02$) only if the theoretical variances hold (i.e., $c = 1$). Realistically, one should allow $c = 4$; thus, $cv(\hat{S})$ is more likely to be ≥ 0.037; hence, a sample size of 50,000 is likely to cause a lower precision for $\hat{S}$ than desired.

An additional complication occurs when the design uses multiple lots (which it should) and the investigator gets $var(\hat{S})$ empirically. Then confidence intervals are based on only a few degrees of freedom, and, hence, are wider than intervals based on theoretical variances (even after inflation by c).

These types of precision and sample size calculations can be done assuming a model other than $H_{1\phi}$. It is then easiest to use the EXPECT option of PROC SIMULATE in program RELEASE to compute theoretical standard errors. Note that no variance inflation factor is used by RELEASE; users have to either accept the theory, $c = 1$, or make the simple modification by hand.

6.3.6. Numerical Evaluation of Some Design Features: an Example

The type of tradeoffs and total effort considerations in previous sections of this chapter can be investigated numerically using the EXPECT option of PROC SIMULATE in program RELEASE. Chapter 3.6 gives background details. Also, EXPECT has been used in Part 5. Consequently, rather than again explain EXPECT per se, we give here an example of its use. We encourage the user to enter the information in Tables 6.3-6.6 into RELEASE on their computer system and obtain the full output (none of which we give here). Such outputs will aid in understanding the material and in making comparisons. Let $k = 6$ and assume model $H_{1\phi}$ holds with $\phi_{t1} = 0.72$, $\phi_{c1} = 0.85$, $\phi_3 = \phi_4 = \phi_5 = 0.9$, $p_2 = 0.05$, $p_3 = 0.02$, $p_4 = 0.07$, $p_5 = 0.05$, and $p_6 = 0.09$. We use $R_{t1} = R_{c1}$ and, for convenience, set these to 50,000. Table 6.3 shows the inputs to RELEASE for this run. Note that treatment effect is $S = 0.847$, and the complete capture history protocol is used.

From the output, we find that the noncentrality parameter of the test for a treatment effect (TEST 1) is $\delta = 127.34$, with 9 df. Thus, from Table 3.4, the power of this test is one. Also, the theoretical standard error of $\hat{S}$ is $se(\hat{S}) = 0.0125$ (cv = 0.015). If $c = 4$, then the actual $se(\hat{S})$ would be $2 \times 0.0125 = 0.025$, which is probably acceptable. So one knows that in a carefully done study, if these are about the correct ϕ and p parameters, results will be reasonable with $R_{t1} = R_{c1} = 50,000$ if model $H_{1\phi}$ holds.

Table 6.3. – Inputs to program RELEASE to generate information on theoretical standard errors and test powers for the parameter values shown; the complete capture history protocols is used.

```
proc title example of using EXPECT to help in study design, model H1phi;
proc simulate expect occasions=6 groups=2;
phi(1)=.72 .85;
phi(2)=.9;
phi(3)=.9;
phi(4)=.9;
phi(5)=.9;
p(2)=.05;
p(3)=.02;
p(4)=.07;
p(5)=.05;
p(6)=.09;
R=50000 50000;
```

We now vary the conditions and see what happens. Table 6.4 shows the inputs if we assume model H_{2p} holds with $p_{t2} = 0.03$ and $p_{c2} = 0.05$, rather than model $H_{1\phi}$. So now there is a treatment effect on capture probabilities at dam 2. Using the output of RELEASE, we find out a number of things. The test for a treatment effect (TEST 1) still has power of one. In fact, component TEST 1.R1 still has power of one, and we find TEST 1.T2 also has power of one. This tests for $p_{t2} = p_{c2}$ in this case because there is no treatment effect on any parameters that apply downriver from dam 2. If the parameters in Table 6.4 were the true parameters of a study, the data analysis would, with high probability, select model H_{2p} as the appropriate model.

Under model H_{2p}, $\hat{S}$ is unbiased and has theoretical se($\hat{S}$) = 0.0140. Although the se($\hat{S}$) has increased, it is only a moderate increase (over se($\hat{S}$) = 0.0125 if $H_{1\phi}$ were true). However, we can look at what would happen if model H_{2p} were true and we used model $H_{1\phi}$ for data analysis. Then we find $E(\hat{S}) = 0.775$ with se($\hat{S}$) = 0.0117. Using the (wrong) model $H_{1\phi}$, we would be seriously misled: $\hat{S}$ would have a bias of only -0.072; however, the ratio of absolute bias to theoretical se($\hat{S}$) would be 6.2. From this, we infer the 95% CI would almost never cover the true value of S. We conclude that we really should use a protocol that allows us to test $p_{t2} = p_{c2}$; this provides protection against a possible treatment effect on p_2.

Table 6.4. – Inputs to program RELEASE when the setup of Table 6.3 (model $H_{1\phi}$) is changed to model H_{2p}.

```
proc title example of using EXPECT to help in study design, model H2p;
proc simulate expect occasions=6 groups=2;
phi(1)=.72 .85;
phi(2)=.9;
phi(3)=.9;
phi(4)=.9;
phi(5)=.9;
p(2)=.03 .05;
p(3)=.02;
p(4)=.07;
p(5)=.05;
p(6)=.09;
R=50000 50000;
```

We go one step further and ask what happens if there is slight treatment effect on ϕ_2. Table 6.5 shows the inputs to RELEASE after we modify model H_{2p} of Table 6.4 to allow ϕ_{t2} to be 0.86 and ϕ_{c2} to remain at 0.9. We find that model H_{2p} is still chosen; the power of the test of $\phi_{t2} = \phi_{c2}$ (TEST 1.R2) is only 0.07. However, under model H_{2p}, $E(\hat{S}) = 0.811$, so it is biased, and has theoretical $se(\hat{S}) = 0.0136$.

If model $H_{2\phi}$ is used as the basis of estimates in this case, results are imprecise because now the parameter estimators depend on the number of releases at dam 2, which are in the low thousands ($E(R_{t2}) = 1{,}079$, $E(R_{c2}) = 2{,}125$). Under model $H_{2\phi}$, we can estimate the treatment effects, the true values of which are

$$S_1 = \frac{\phi_{t1}}{\phi_{c1}} = 0.847$$

and

$$S_2 = \frac{\phi_{t2}}{\phi_{c2}} = 0.956.$$

Table 6.5. – Inputs to program RELEASE when the setup of Table 6.4 (model H_{2p}) is changed to model $H_{2\phi}$.

```
proc title example of using EXPECT to help in study design, model H2phi;
proc simulate expect occasions=6 groups=2;
phi(1)=.72 .85;
phi(2)=.86 .9;
phi(3)=.9;
phi(4)=.9;
phi(5)=.9;
p(2)=.03 .05;
p(3)=.02;
p(4)=.07;
p(5)=.05;
p(6)=.09;
R=50000 50000;
```

Theoretical results under model $H_{2\phi}$ are

$$E(\hat{S}_1) = 0.845, \quad \text{se}(\hat{S}_1) = 0.0729 ;$$

$$E(\hat{S}_2) = 0.958, \quad \text{se}(\hat{S}_2) = 0.0842 .$$

The large $\text{se}(\hat{S}_2)$ under model $H_{2\phi}$ shows why the test of $\phi_{t2} = \phi_{c2}$ has poor power. Estimates of S_1 and S_2 under model $H_{2\phi}$ are unbiased, but have large standard errors. In contrast, $\hat{S}_1$ under model H_{2p} is biased (-0.037), but has a much smaller standard error (0.0136 versus 0.0729). Thus, the use of estimates under H_{2p} is a reasonable compromise.

Given this situation, can we alter the design to protect ourselves against poor precision if there is a treatment effect on ϕ_2? Increasing the number of fish released will not be cost-effective. It would take $R_{v1} = 2,200,000$ under this model $H_{2\phi}$ to achieve a test power of 0.9 for testing $\phi_{t2} = \phi_{c2}$. This conclusion is based on knowing that the noncentrality parameter δ is 0.236 for $R_{v1} = 50,000$, and δ depends directly on the number of releases. That is, to double δ, one must double the releases. To get 90% power with a 1-df chi-square test, we must have (approximately) $\delta = 10.5$. Therefore, to achieve this 90% power by "brute force," we must increase the releases by a factor of 10.5/0.236, or roughly 44. Thus, we would need $R_{v1} = 44(50,000)$.

We can try altering the design, if it is possible to do the following. Table 6.6 shows inputs for a new design based on the same survival rates and release numbers as in Table 6.5. We dropped site 6, and put that effort, plus a little more, into site 2. Thus, $p_{t2} = 0.09$ and $p_{c2} = 0.15$. The results include the following:

$$E(R_{t2}) = 3{,}241 \, ,$$

$$E(R_{c2}) = 6{,}375 \, ,$$

and, under analysis model $H_{2\phi}$,

$$E(\hat{S}_1) = 0.846, \quad \text{se}(\hat{S}_1) = 0.0507$$

and

$$E(\hat{S}_2) = 0.957, \quad \text{se}(\hat{S}_2) = 0.0608 \, ,$$

while, under analysis model H_{2p},

$$E(\hat{S}_1) = 0.814, \quad \text{se}(\hat{S}_1) = 0.0163 \, .$$

Table 6.6. – Inputs to program RELEASE for an alternative design to that in Table 6.5.

```
proc title example of using EXPECT to help in study design, model H2Phi;
proc simulate expect occasions=5 groups=2;
phi(1)=.72 .85;
phi(2)=.86 .9;
phi(3)=.9;
phi(4)=.9;
p(2)=.09 .15;
p(3)=.02;
p(4)=.07;
p(5)=.05;
R=50000 50000;
```

Also, the power of TEST 1.$R2$, which here tests $\phi_{t2} = \phi_{c2}$, is now 0.11. Although we tripled p_{t2} and p_{c2}, there is little increase of power for this test, or improved precision of $\hat{S}_1$ (or $\hat{S}_2$) under model $H_{2\phi}$. This new design does not solve our problem. In fact, we probably cannot solve the problem of detecting that model $H_{2\phi}$ holds if it is the true model. This conclusion is both surprising and disturbing.

Similar "what-if" investigations should prove useful when study designs are contemplated.

6.4. Multiple Lots

6.4.1. Introduction

Multiple lots may be released simply at random (see Chapter 4.3), or as part of a larger design wherein different measured or preset conditions underly the release of each lot. If n multiple treatment-control lots are released at n different times, we let $S_1, ..., S_n$ stand for the true treatment effects at these times. In principle, there are explanatory variables $x = x_1, ..., x_a$ that exist so we could write $S_i = f(x) + \varepsilon_i$ (ε being unexplained residual variation). Then a design can be imposed on the multiple released lots in terms of the identified variables $x_1, ..., x_a$. If no such explanatory variables are used in the analysis, or even recorded, we are then treating the S_i as identically distributed random variables. This includes the possibility that $S_i = S$, which means, by definition, that these lots are replicates as regards the treatment effect.

6.4.2. Replication

A study with one treatment and one control is a poor one, even if batch sizes are $R_{t1} = R_{c1} = 100,000$. A point estimate of S can be computed, but only a theoretical variance estimator is possible unless uniquely numbered marks are used. It is much better, with 200,000 fish, to use 10 paired treatment-control lots, each of size 10,000. These might then be released on 10 consecutive days, either at a standardized time or under standardized (or prescribed) conditions. Replication of paired treatment-control lots also allows one to sample a wider range of conditions or times.

Because the theoretical variance often underestimates true variance, the best approach is to take n replicates of the treatment and control fish lots and estimate the variance empirically. Suppose that we obtain estimates

$$\hat{S}_1, \hat{S}_2, ..., \hat{S}_n$$

from equally sized replicates. Then an approximate $(1 - \alpha)$ percent confidence interval for $E(S)$ is given by

$$\overline{\hat{S}} \pm t_{\alpha/2,n-1} \, \hat{se}(\overline{\hat{S}}) \, ,$$

where

$$\overline{\hat{S}} = \sum_{i=1}^{n} \hat{S}_i/n \, ,$$

$$\hat{se}(\overline{\hat{S}}) = \frac{\hat{\sigma}}{\sqrt{n}} \, ,$$

and

$$\hat{\sigma}^2 = \sum_{i=1}^{n} (\hat{S}_i - \overline{\hat{S}})^2/(n - 1) \, .$$

The value $t_{\alpha/2,n-1}$ is the appropriate value from the Student's t-table with $n - 1$ df (Table 6.7).

If we assume that the total number of treatment and control fish is fixed, then the important question is how many replicates should be taken. Also, taking replication will probably cost more money than only releasing one batch each of treatment and control fish because the replicates would have to have different batch marks, unless each fish has a unique mark. The variance σ^2 will not be affected by the number of replicates; thus, the only consideration is how $t_{\alpha/2,n-1}$ changes as n increases. Consideration of a Student's t-table (Table 6.7) shows that this quantity decreases from 12.706 to 1.96 as n goes from two to infinity (if we use $1 - \alpha = 0.95$ or a 95% CI). Cost considerations aside, it is better to take a large number of replicates. Notice, however, that the t value has decreased to 2.262 when $n = 10$ and to 2.093 when $n = 20$. Therefore, from a practical viewpoint, it is probably adequate to have about 10 replicate samples. We advise no less than six replicates.

Table 6.7. – Critical values of Student's *t*-test for various levels of confidence (1 - α).

df	0.90	1 - α 0.95	0.99
1	6.314	12.706	63.657
2	2.920	4.303	9.924
3	2.353	3.183	5.841
4	2.132	2.776	4.604
5	2.015	2.571	4.032
6	1.943	2.447	3.707
7	1.895	2.365	3.499
8	1.860	2.306	3.355
9	1.833	2.262	3.250
10	1.812	2.228	3.169
11	1.796	2.201	3.106
12	1.782	2.179	3.055
13	1.771	2.160	3.012
14	1.761	2.145	2.977
15	1.753	2.131	2.947
20	1.725	2.086	2.845
30	1.697	2.042	2.750
∞	1.645	1.960	2.576

6.4.3. Use of More Complex Designs

The simplest study has only one treatment factor, hence, one effect S. It is unrealistic to ignore the effect of varying environmental and engineering conditions that can affect S. One could release batch fish in lots at different (known) flow rates. Fish size could be included as a design factor. If a dam had, say, five presumably identical turbines, it would be better statistically to release 10,000 fish through each turbine than 50,000 fish through only one turbine.

The inclusion of several known factors in a design with multiple lots is highly desirable, and we recommend it. However, it does not seem possible to make specific suggestions on how to incorporate such additional factors into the design. Each situation requires detailed evaluation (general theoretical developments are given by Grizzle et al. 1969; McCullagh and Nelder 1983). The key point is that more information can be gained out of multiple, smaller lots in a properly designed study than is possible with fewer but larger lots that do not account for the many factors that can influence the experimental outcome. This is a general principle in the design of experiments.

6.5. Coping with External Variables

6.5.1. Introduction

Thus far, we have concentrated on technical issues in the design of fish survival experiments. There are many nontechnical and nonstatistical matters to keep in mind, including fundamental design principles. Numerous texts exist on experimental design (e.g., Cox 1958) that discuss issues such as selection of experimental units, randomization, blocking, avoidance of confounding variables, use of covariates, and so forth. Most of these references are oriented toward settings where the investigator has a great deal more control over matters than exists in environmental impact studies. Some useful references oriented to statistical aspects of environmental studies include Eberhardt (1976), Green (1979), Armour et al. (1983), Hurlbert (1984), and Stewart-Oaten et al. (1986). We will mention only a few general concerns that this literature covers in more detail (see, in particular, Green 1979).

Two overall design principles are to use multiple experimental units and to not confound variables of interest (treatments here) with external variables (such as time, location, equipment, personnel). Much of the science of study design and conduct has to do with eliminating the influence of external variables by blocking, stratifying, randomizing treatments to units, recording covariates so their influence can be adjusted out in the analysis of the data, standardizing equipment and conditions, and careful training of personnel.

6.5.2. Stratification

It is important to consider stratifying the fish by any recognizable variable that might affect the parameters ϕ, p, and S. The most important variable is probably fish size, as measured, for example, by length; others are age, sex, strain, and so forth. The purpose of stratification is twofold. First, fish in a lot should be homogeneous in their response parameters. Homogeneity reduces extraneous sources of variation. Second, we want to identify factors that might influence treatment effects. If treatment effect varies by size (over the range of size of interest), we want to know this. We make size a design factor by releasing two or more size classes.

We recommend three size classes if stratification on size is used. Further, we recommend eliminating extremes of size, which provides further control of outliers and should reduce excess variation in the resultant data (i.e., helps achieve c near 1). Within each size stratum, there are V treatment groups of fish; fish are to be assigned randomly to treatment groups within strata.

6.5.3. Blocking

Given that there are, say, 10 lots each of treatment and control fish, it is best (statistically) to release lots as pairs with a day or two between releases. It is not good to release all 10 lots at once, as there is no advantage to pairing in this case. With paired treatment-control lots released over a span of time, the generality of the inference also improves.

6.5.4. Randomization and Balance

Random selection of experimental units and allocation of treatments is a fundamental principle for valid inferences. However, what can be randomized in these studies is constrained. Primarily, one should randomly assign fish to treatments. Randomization is often used to avoid confounding; so is balancing variables. For example, if there are two people marking fish, half of each lot should be marked by each person. Such a procedure avoids the possibility of confounding a person-effect with treatment effects. If the first person marked all the treatment fish and the second person marked all the control fish, marking and treatment effects are confounded and cannot be separated. There are many field details, such as this one, that are important in a study.

6.5.5. Timing of Recapture Effort

It takes days or even weeks for all the experimental fish to move past any downstream dam (or capture site). It is therefore critical that sampling at a recapture site begin before any of the fish arrive there and continues until all the study fish have passed that point. If treatment and control fish move together, the concern about the timing of sampling effort is less critical. The only way to know the temporal distribution of the fish passing a capture site is to extend one's effort until they have all passed. If recapture effort had been stopped at a site when 100% of control survivors had passed, but only 90% of treatment survivors had passed, important bias could result in $\hat{S}$.

There is much concern expressed in the literature about the temporal movement distributions of fish. Capture probabilities could change rapidly at a site as flow and other conditions change. This concern is not a problem if movements are independent of treatment status. If treatment and control movements differ, the analyses presented here are still valid if the time-averaged recapture probabilities at the site are the same for treatment and control fish passing that site.

6.5.6. Use of Sublots

All the fish in a lot must have a distinguishing batch mark as a minimum level of marking. From a statistical-information point of view, it is far better to give each fish a uniquely coded tag. The use of unique tags allows one to partition the lot into sublots (as well as use more protocols); these sublots provide a useful approximation to true replication, thereby allowing empirical estimation of (within-lot) sampling variance. When unique marks are not possible, a compromise is possible: use more than one distinct batch mark for each lot. Even having only two distinct batch marks in each lot allows a basis for estimating sampling variation if multiple lots are used. Because of the additional information that can be gained by having sublots, we recommend use of two or more (rather than one) distinct batch marks, even within a lot.

6.5.7. Partitioning Recaptures by Site

Under the complete capture history protocol, it is possible to partition both the releases and recaptures based on the last digit of the tag number. Such partitioning is not possible under the other sampling protocols. However, the recaptures m_{vij} can be partitioned within a site or occasion in some cases. In many fisheries studies, the fish are recaptured in gatewells within each dam. Recording the number of fish in each gatewell is simple. These partitioned data are useful in variance estimation using the quasi-likelihood methods given in Section 4.1.3. The number of partitions should be moderately large, say six or more.

6.5.8. Attention to Detail and Quality Control

Numerous steps and details are involved in any study involving thousands of fish. There are many ways for biases to arise in the handling, transporting, and releasing of fish, as well as in reading and recording of data from recaptures. It is beyond our scope or expertise to deal with these matters here. These sorts of details do not get published in the refereed literature, but there are numerous study reports that provide details on field considerations (e.g., Olson and Kaczynski, unpublished report, 1980; Heinle and Olson, unpublished report, 1981; Ruggles and Collins, unpublished report, 1981).

6.6. Refining the Design by Simulation

Many issues concerning the design of a survival experiment can be addressed by numerical methods, either Monte Carlo simulations or the EXPECT option of PROC SIMULATE in RELEASE. Program RELEASE provides a powerful simulator useful in answering questions about the finer points of experimental design. Most experiments are conducted under resource limitations; these limitations impose compromises in the design.

Once a preliminary design has been reached, the power of the proposed experiment is of concern. What is the probability of finding a treatment effect of size Δ, if it exists? This question concerns the power of the test of H_0 versus $H_{1\phi}$ or H_0 versus $H_{k-1,\phi}$. The use of simulation to approximate the power of such tests is straightforward with program RELEASE. Also, analytical approaches are sketched in Chapter 3.6 and are implementable with RELEASE.

The power of the above tests may be particularly important if the treatment survival rate is near one (i.e., little treatment effect). An example might be an experiment to estimate fish survival over a spillway at a hydroelectric dam. For a reasonable number of fish released (R_{1t} and R_{1c}), the ability to detect a significant treatment effect may be quite low (e.g., if $S = 0.98$ the power might be only 0.12). Low power should result in either the redesign of the proposed experiment or the decision not to conduct the experiment.

In some experiments, the confidence interval width and expected coverage are of particular concern. Often, these concerns relate to the treatment survival rate S, but the ϕ_{vi} may also be of interest. Monte Carlo simulation might be used to assess a proposed design by providing an estimate of the expected confidence interval widths and achieved confidence interval coverage. The shape and parameters of the sampling distribution of the estimator can be analyzed by specifying options within the SIMULATE procedure in program RELEASE. The sampling distribution of the ϕ_{vi} and S estimators are only normal in large samples; RELEASE provides means to study these distributions for particular sample sizes and parameter values. Results of Monte Carlo simulations also provide a basis for the parametric bootstrap method of establishing confidence intervals (Buckland 1984).

Simulation can be done to explore experimental designs where replicate lots are used (as we recommend strongly). Simulated data can be used to study the possible estimation of variance components, model selection, and interval estimation.

Heterogeneity, a violation of assumption 12, can be simulated to investigate its effect on the power of tests, bias of estimators, and interval estimation. RELEASE allows heterogeneity to be simulated in various ways (see Part 9), and heterogeneity can be hypothesized for the ϕ_{vi}, p_{vi}, or both.

Proper experimental design must consider the tests used in selection of an appropriate model. If a chronic treatment effect is suspected, simulation can be done to explore a model such as $H_{3\phi}$. Such simulation would allow examination of the power of tests and estimator bias if an incorrect model is used. The EXPECT option of PROC SIMULATE can be used to facilitate the scrutiny of a particular experimental design with little computer time.

In all cases, we urge investigators to use program RELEASE in fine tuning the design of experiments. The assessment of a tentative design is made easy if the interactive version of RELEASE is used.

Part 7. Application of Theory

7.1. Introduction

Several examples of real data taken from various experiments in the literature are analyzed here to give insight and understanding into the statistical theory and the interpretation of experimental results. The examples here relate to studies where recaptures are made over time (days, weeks, or years), whereas Parts 1 and 2 dealt mostly with recaptures recorded spatially at a sequence of downstream dams. The duality between temporal and spatial sampling was noted in Section 1.1.2. Examination of this material should provide the reader experience with program RELEASE and a better perspective of the extent of this class of experiments beyond the fisheries emphasis provided in Parts 1 and 2. Lastly, several subtle points are made; and we mention some extended approaches.

The material presented here is not a critical reanalysis; our results are not in conflict with the original work of the investigators. We refer the reader to the original publications for biological conclusions. We can only briefly describe the more important features of these experiments. Again, we encourage the reader to consult the original sources for detailed information on methods and results.

We urge meticulous care in the processing of data before analysis by the statistical methods presented here. Errors in data entry are always a concern. Computer scatter plots of the m_{tij} versus m_{cij} often reveal mistakes that can be corrected or outliers that are cause for concern. Generally we recommend that the data be recorded and entered into program RELEASE in the form of a capture history matrix because hand summarization of the data into an m_{ij} matrix is error prone and does not allow full testing of model assumptions.

Many more-advanced models can be considered for well-designed studies supported by adequate sample sizes and replication. We urge the reader to become acquainted with the capabilities of program SURVIV (White 1983). Program RELEASE will prepare an input file for program SURVIV. Modification of this input file allows estimation with more complex models.

A series of contingency tables can be made to check for homogeneity and to suggest subsets to be pooled in the final analysis. We refer the reader to Olson and Kaczynski (unpublished report, 1980) for an example of the extensive testing that should be done before a final analysis is attempted. As the investigator explores the experimental data, thought should be given to what assumptions seem reasonable. Are chronic effects of the treatment likely? Has the recapture effort across sampling occasions been nearly constant? (If so, perhaps all the recapture rates can be modeled as a constant.) Is the treatment likely to affect the recapture rates? These considerations are important in modeling the data, selecting an appropriate model, and interpreting the output of program RELEASE.

7.2. Lead-Dosing Experiments on Mallards

Bellrose (1959) conducted a series of experiments in the early 1950s to estimate the mortality caused by ingestion of lead shot by mallards *Anas platyrhynchos*. He used a sequence of treatments with one, two, and four lead pellets, each with a separate control (zero pellets). The experiments consisted of trapping and banding mallards during late fall and winter; every other duck was a treatment bird and the others were controls. Treatment birds were dosed with lead pellets and immediately released with control birds. The data came from recoveries of birds shot during annual sport-hunting seasons and, therefore, represent the first capture history protocol (see Table 7.1). The underlying parameterization is not exactly the same as that described in Chapter 2.2, as band recoveries during the year of banding were ignored in this example.

Estimates of treatment effect are made by using each treatment group versus its control group, assuming that $H_{1\phi}$ is the correct model. Here, it seems biologically reasonable to consider $H_{1\phi}$ as it corresponds to the direct effect

$$\phi_{t1} = S\phi_{c1}$$

and

Table 7.1. – Summary of Bellrose's (1959) data on lead-dosed mallards. The data represent recoveries shot by sport hunters and fall under the first capture history protocol.

Experiment number	Banding year	Age at banding	Number pellets	Number banded	Number recovered in year[a]		
					2	3	4
1	1949	Adult	1	559	52	36	22
			0	560	56	44	24
2	1950	Adult	2	277	12	9	4
			0	278	44	22	7
3	1951	Adult	4	284	13	7	2
			0	396	30	16	7
4	1950	Young	2	115	14	10	4
			0	111	12	12	2
5	1951	Young	4	220	14	8	2
			0	207	28	14	8

[a]Numbers in this table were provided by F. C. Bellrose and differ slightly from those in Bellrose (1959).

$$\lambda_{t1} = S\lambda_{c1} .$$

Alternatively, if the harvest rate of dosed mallards were to increase and the annual survival rate to decrease, one would have

$$p_{ti} > p_{ci}$$

and

$$\phi_{ti} < \phi_{ci} ,$$

and these conditions might result in $\lambda_{t1} \sim \lambda_{c1}$. If these conditions occur, the treatment effect, H_0 versus $H_{1\phi}$, would be difficult to detect.

If all the experiments for adults (or young) had been conducted the same year, all the data from the control groups could have been pooled for increased statistical efficiency. Estimates of treatment effect are given in Table 7.2. These estimates appear to show that lead pellets decreased survival. The tests of the null hypothesis of no treatment effect ($S = 1$) were rejected, except in experiment 4. A crude test of the null hypothesis can be computed by pooling the data for all the treatment groups versus all the control groups. Pooling all recoveries over the 3 years and five experiments results in the 2×2 table

t	209	1,246
c	326	1,226

which results in a chi-square value of 22.64, 1 df, $P = <0.001$, providing strong evidence of a treatment effect. This test is recommended to provide the investigator insight into the experimental results and to give background familiarity with the data.

Further insight is provided by examining the 2×2 contingency table for each treatment level (one, two, or four pellets) versus its control (zero pellets). Data are pooled over age for two- and four-pellet treatments as an example. In each treatment, the form of the table is from TEST 1.$R1$.

r_{t1}	$R_{t1} - r_{t1}$
r_{c1}	$R_{c1} - r_{c1}$

Table 7.2. – Summary of results of the survival experiments conducted by Bellrose (1959).

Experiment number	Dose	Survival $\hat{S}$	$se(\hat{S})$	H_0 versus $H'_{3\phi}$		$H_{1\phi}$ versus $H'_{3\phi}$	
				χ^2 (3 df)	P	χ^2 (2 df)	P
1	1	0.889	0.1036	1.23	0.747	0.20	0.906
2	2	0.344	0.0741	29.69	<0.001	1.35	0.509
3	4	0.579	0.1397	5.61	0.132	0.24	0.880
4	2	1.039	0.2470	0.95	0.812	0.93	0.629
5	4	0.452	0.1033	13.95	0.003	0.89	0.640

The contingency tables and test statistics are available through program RELEASE:

Dose	v	Contingency table		χ^2	df	P (one-tailed)
1	t	110	449			
	c	124	436	1.03	1	0.155
2	t	53	339			
	c	99	290	17.73	1	<0.001
4	t	46	458			
	c	103	500	14.91	1	<0.001

From this summary, it seems clear that a treatment effect is indicated; however, the treatment effect may be on survival or recapture rates, or both.

Estimates of S may be biased if $H_{1\phi}$ is not the correct model. This condition may result when the effect of the treatment is chronic rather than acute. The sum of TESTs 1.Ti represents a goodness of fit test to model $H_{1\phi}$, and these test results (Table 7.2) fail to provide evidence of chronic effects. These goodness of fit tests have low power in this example due to the small values of the m_{v3} and m_{v4} (see Table 7.1). If chronic effects of the treatment are reflected in ϕ_{t2}, ϕ_{t3}, p_{t2}, p_{t3}, or p_{t4}, then $\hat{S} = \hat{\phi}_{t1}/\hat{\phi}_{c1}$ under model $H_{1\phi}$ may be a poor measure of the magnitude of the treatment effect.

In experiments such as Bellrose's where a sequence of treatments was involved, one might consider estimating a function relating treatment survival to the number of pellets. We would then expect survival to decrease as the number of lead pellets increases. A generalized logistic model (Cox 1970) is often useful in modeling survival data (see discussion in Part 8).

The information above indicated a significant treatment effect, but not necessarily a direct, acute effect, $S = \phi_{t1}/\phi_{c1}$. Thus, it is reasonable to consider $S \doteq \lambda_{t1}/\lambda_{c1}$, where

$$\lambda_{v1} = E(\frac{r_{v1}}{R_{v1}}).$$

This formulation ignores the fact that a few birds were recovered during and shortly after initial banding and release. We modeled treatment effect as a function of dosage ($D = 1, 2, 4$) and age ($A = 0, 1$), ignoring year effects, as

$$E(\hat{S}) = \left[1 + e^{-[a_1 + a_2(D) + a_3(A)]}\right]^{-1}.$$

We estimated the parameters a_i, using the ML approach suggested by Jennrich and Moore (1975) as implemented in program BMDPLR (Dixon 1983). In this example $\hat{a}_1$, $\hat{a}_2$, and $\hat{a}_3$ are 2.23, -0.57, and -0.28, respectively. The respectively estimated standard errors are 0.15, 0.05, and 0.07. For a preliminary analysis, the variables can be transformed and run with a linear regression program such as

$$\ln\left[\frac{\hat{S}_i}{1 - \hat{S}_i}\right] = a_1 + a_2(D_i) + a_3(A_i).$$

We do not recommend this analysis as a final procedure, but merely as one that enables quick insight into the uses of this general modeling approach. Although both dose and age are significant in this logistic model, the model is crude because the data are too sparse to support much modeling (temporal effects are ignored as there are only five treatments involving two age-classes). We use this logistic analysis only as an example of what can be done when sequences of treatments are used.

Finally, we point out that the five treatment survival estimates in Bellrose's studies were independent (i.e., each treatment had a paired control). In other studies, several treatments may have used a common control. The S_i will then have sampling correlations that lead to a weighted analysis where the weighting matrix is not diagonal.

7.3. Lead-Dosing Study of Northern Pintails

Deuel (1985) reported on a study that measured indirect mortality from ingested lead shot in northern pintails *Anas acuta*. The ducks were caught in baited traps at seven areas in California in the winter months in early 1979. Birds were banded with aluminum leg bands, and every other bird received a treatment consisting of two #5 lead shot pellets put directly into the crops through a plastic tube inserted into the esophagus. Otherwise, all birds were handled alike and released. In subsequent hunting seasons, some of the banded birds taken by hunters were reported to the Bird Banding Office of the U.S. Fish and Wildlife Service.

We use the data from five of Deuel's (1985) areas for male pintails to illustrate the methodology presented in this monograph (relatively fewer females were banded and released, and three of the areas were poorly represented by banding, even for males). The data we use (Table 7.3) fall under the first capture history protocol. The numbers and the capture probability are both fairly small (e.g., $\hat{p}_2 \sim 0.04$).

Data collected under the first capture history protocol do not permit intensive tests of model assumptions, nor are the capture and survival rates separately estimable. The only estimable parameter of concern is S, the treatment effect. Estimates of this parameter under model $H_{1\phi}$ and results of TEST 1, the test for a treatment effect, are provided Table 7.4 for each of the five areas and the pooled data. There is no evidence of a significant treatment effect for any of the five areas (Table 7.4). A pooled test statistic, computed by summing the five chi-squared values and their degrees of freedom, yields $\chi^2 = 17.9$, 20 df, and $P = 0.60$. Thus, these data fit model H_0 quite well.

Table 7.3. – Summary of the experimental lead dosing study of male northern pintails banded in California in 1979 (from Deuel 1985). These data fall under the first capture history protocol.

Banding area	Group	Number released	$j = 2$	3	4	5	6	Total
			\multicolumn{5}{c}{Number recovered in year j}	
Mendota	t	930	27	29	12	9	8	85
	c	932	41	16	12	9	8	86
S. Grasslands	t	759	31	16	6	12	7	72
	c	759	28	16	8	9	8	69
Yolo Bypass	t	558	17	15	8	9	1	50
	c	562	20	8	4	7	4	43
Gray Lodge	t	1,354	45	26	13	20	10	114
	c	1,334	43	30	19	24	11	127
Delevan/	t	712	23	17	5	7	7	59
Colusa	c	783	19	14	6	11	7	57
Pooled	t	4,313	143	103	44	57	33	380
	c	4,370	151	84	49	60	38	382

Table 7.4. – Estimates of treatment survival under model $H_{1\phi}$ and the results of TEST 1 for treatment effect for the lead dosing study of male northern pintails banded in California in 1979 (from Deuel 1985).

Banding area	Estimated survival $\hat{S}$	Standard error $\hat{se}(\hat{S})$	Test of H_0 versus $H'_{5\phi}$		
			χ^2	df	P
Mendota	0.990	0.1444	6.67	5	0.246
S. Grasslands	1.043	0.1674	0.94	5	0.967
Yolo Bypass	1.171	0.2333	5.90	5	0.316
Gray Lodge	0.884	0.1089	2.17	5	0.825
Delevan/ Colusa	1.138	0.2030	2.15	5	0.828
Pooled data	1.008	0.0697	2.85	5	0.722

Further extending this example, we note that the five estimates of treatment survival computed under model $H_{1\phi}$ are all near 1.0, considering the size of their standard errors. The estimate of 1.008 for treatment survival computed by pooling the data over the five areas indicates a lack of treatment effect due to dosing with two lead shot pellets. Alternatively, TEST 1.R1 of the null hypothesis that $S = 1$ (H_0 versus $H_{1\phi}$) can be made for each area, and the results of the individual TEST 1.R1 can then be pooled for an overall test:

Area	χ^2	df	P
1	0.00	1	0.948
2	0.07	1	0.791
3	0.63	1	0.427
4	1.00	1	0.318
5	0.53	1	0.467
Total	2.23	5	0.816

Again, any indication of mortality due to the lead treatment appears to be lacking. Additional details on this study were given by Deuel (1985). Although his approach differed from that presented here, his conclusions were similar. Readers are encouraged to analyze these data by using program RELEASE to gain additional insights and familiarity with the various models and tests.

Deuel's (1985) data can be used to illustrate several other technical issues because the experiment was replicated over five areas. First we discuss estimates of treatment survival over the entire experiment. In view of the replicated nature of the study, the individual estimates of S_i (by area i) and their standard errors, and the results of testing the null hypothesis that $S = 1$, it is logical to pool the raw data and proceed to estimate S. This method yields an estimate of 1.008, with a theoretical $\hat{se}(\hat{S}) = 0.0697$. Under the null hypothesis, this outcome is satisfactory. However, the estimated standard error may be somewhat poor unless the

$se(\hat{S}_i)$ is equal for all i.

Alternatively, a simple average of the five estimates gives 1.046, with an empirical $\hat{se}(\hat{S})$ = 0.0517. It can be argued that this procedure is poor because some of the estimates have larger standard errors than others (observed range = 0.109 to 0.233), suggesting that some estimates should be given more weight (and therefore requiring a weighted average). If we assume all five estimates are of the same parameter, statistical theory states that the proper, optimal weight (w) is $var(\hat{S})^{-1}$, i.e., the inverse of the true sampling variance. We can estimate these weights as

$$w_i = \left\{ (\hat{S}_i^2) \left[\frac{1}{r_{t1}} - \frac{1}{R_{t1}} + \frac{1}{r_{c1}} - \frac{1}{R_{c1}} \right] \right\}^{-1}$$

and

$$\overline{S}_{wt} = \frac{\sum w_i \hat{S}_i}{\sum w_i}$$

$$= 0.989 \text{ or } 99\%.$$

This procedure is flawed because the estimate of S_i and its estimated sampling variance are positively correlated. The result causes estimates that are too low to have an estimated sampling variance that is too low and vice versa. Thus, low estimates receive a weight that is too large, which causes estimates of the weighted average to be biased low. The reason for the estimate being related to its own variance estimate can be seen by noting that the variance estimator contains the term $(\hat{S}_i)^2$ (see equation above).

A reasonable alternative is to weight the individual estimates by the final term of $\hat{var}(\hat{S}_i)$, which is a measure of "sample size." Actually, this final term is the (large-sample) variance of $\ln(\hat{S})$ (see Part 3). Here the weights are defined as

$$w_i = \left[\frac{1}{r_{t1}} - \frac{1}{R_{t1}} + \frac{1}{r_{c1}} - \frac{1}{R_{c1}} \right]^{-1},$$

and the weighted mean is computed as

$$\overline{S_{ut}} = \frac{\sum w_i \hat{S}_i}{\sum w_i} .$$

When the pintail data are used, the weights are 47.1, 38.3, 25.2, 66.0, and 31.4. This procedure yields a weighted mean of 1.015, close to the value obtained by pooling the data. Corresponding to the estimator of the weighted mean is an empirical estimator of its sampling variance,

$$\text{var}(\overline{S_{ut}}) = \frac{\sum_{i=1}^{5} w_i (\hat{S}_i - \overline{S_{ut}})^2}{\left(\sum_{i=1}^{5} w_i\right)(5 - 1)} .$$

For the pintail data, $\hat{\text{var}}(\overline{S_{ut}}) = 0.00272$, or $\hat{\text{se}}(\overline{S_{ut}}) = 0.0522$.

Another subject of concern is the degree to which theoretical sampling variances from the model reflect the amount of variation in the experiment. Using the pintail data, we can compare the sampling variance based on the model with the variance computed empirically. The comparison below is based on the unweighted mean but the extension to weighted means is straightforward.

Maximum likelihood theory provides the five estimates, $\hat{S}_i$, and their associated sampling variances, $\hat{\text{var}}(\hat{S}_i)$. If we take

$$\overline{S} = \frac{1}{5} \sum_{i=1}^{5} (\hat{S}_i) ,$$

then the ML estimator of the sampling variance of this average is estimated by

$$\hat{\text{var}}(\overline{S}) = \left(\frac{1}{5}\right)^2 \sum_{i=1}^{5} \hat{\text{var}}(\hat{S}_i) ,$$

because the five data sets are independent. The $\hat{\text{se}}(\overline{S}) = [\hat{\text{var}}(\overline{S})]^{1/2} = 0.079$.

Alternatively, an empirical variance of $\overline{S}$ could be computed as

$$\hat{\mathrm{var}}(\overline{S}) = \frac{1}{5(4)} \sum_{i=1}^{5} (\hat{S}_i - \overline{S})^2 .$$

Then, $\hat{\mathrm{se}}(\overline{S}) = [\hat{\mathrm{var}}(\overline{S})]^{1/2} = 0.052$, which is in reasonable agreement with the theoretical (model-based) estimate of 0.079. However, one could question whether the theoretical variance (or standard error) is too large. A useful guideline here is to compute

$$\frac{(n-1) \; (\text{empirical variance } of \; \overline{S})}{(\text{theoretical variance } of \; \overline{S})} ,$$

which is asymptotically distributed as χ^2 with $n - 1$ df, where n is the number of survival rates being averaged. This procedure tests the null hypothesis that the theoretical variance and the empirical variance are equal. Thus,

$$\frac{(5-1) \; (0.052)^2}{(0.079)^2} = 1.73 .$$

However, a value of 1.73 for a chi-square variable with 4 df is not unusual ($P = 0.785$) and provides no evidence for rejecting the null hypothesis. Usually, one is more concerned over the possibility that the empirical variance is larger than the theoretical (i.e., model-based) variance.

One possibility is that the true treatment survival varies among the five areas. This variation leads to a variance component we call σ_a^2, in contrast to the sampling variance associated with each estimate. (Statisticians would write this latter term as $\mathrm{var}[\hat{S}_i \mid S_i]$ to indicate that it is only sampling variation.) In this example, three estimates were >1.0; but the true rates cannot, of course, exceed 1.0, unless one naively believes that lead enhances survival in biological organisms. Nevertheless, a method of separating the variance components is illustrated. Variance component estimation can be difficult; here we use a procedure given by Anderson and Burnham (1976):

$$\hat{\sigma}_a^2 = \frac{1}{n-1} \sum_{i=1}^{n} (\hat{S}_i - \overline{S})^2 - \frac{1}{n} \left[\sum_{i=1}^{n} \hat{\text{var}}(\hat{S}_i \mid S_i) \right],$$

where $\hat{\sigma}_a^2$ is the estimator of the area-to-area population variance in S_i. The estimator of σ_a^2 is similar for the weighted approach

$$\hat{\sigma}_a^2 = \frac{1}{n-1} \frac{\sum_{i=1}^{n} w_i (\hat{S}_i - \overline{S}_{wt})^2}{\left(\sum_{i=1}^{n} w_i \right)} - \frac{1}{n} \left[\sum_{i=1}^{n} \hat{\text{var}}(\hat{S}_i \mid S_i) \right].$$

In this example, $\hat{\sigma}_a^2 = -0.01777$ (if weighting is used, this estimate is similar at -0.0176). Variance is a positive quantity; however, an estimate can be negative. Here the estimate is close to zero and we could conclude that we were unable to attribute any significant variation to an area-to-area component. This conclusion is logical given the proximity of the areas and the nature of the treatment and sampling program.

The pintail data can be separated into 10 replicates based on the last digit of the band number. Separation of data allows another assessment of the precision of the estimate of survival pooled over the five areas. These replicates can be considered as true replicates and are summarized in Table 7.5. The individual estimates of treatment survival (Table 7.6) yielded an unweighted average of 1.024. The standard error of this simple average can be computed in two ways. First the model-based estimates of the sampling variance of each of the 10 estimates can be used as

$$\hat{\text{var}}(\overline{S}) = \left(\frac{1}{10} \right)^2 \left[\sum_{i=0}^{9} \text{var}(\hat{S}_i) \right] = 0.0053$$

and

$$\hat{\text{se}}(\overline{S}) = \sqrt{\hat{\text{var}}(\overline{S})} = 0.0729.$$

Second, the sampling variance of the mean can be computed empirically from the 10 independent estimates as

$$\hat{var}(\overline{S}) = \frac{1}{10(9)} \sum_{i=0}^{9} (S_i - \overline{S})^2 = 0.0063$$

and

$$\hat{se}(\overline{S}) = \sqrt{\hat{var}(\overline{S})} = 0.0794 .$$

These estimates of precision are in close agreement with each other (0.073 versus 0.079) and to the comparable estimate of 0.079 based on the theoretical variance and the empirical estimates computed for the five areas (0.052).

Table 7.5. – Summary of the experimental lead dosing study of male northern pintails banded in California in 1979 (Deuel 1985). The data are pooled over the five areas and segregated into 10 replicates, based on the last digit of their band number; R_{t1} = 431 and R_{c1} = 437 in each replicate.

Replicate number	Group	Number recovered in year j					Total
		$j = 2$	3	4	5	6	
0	t	18	14	2	10	4	48
	c	13	9	1	6	3	32
1	t	13	5	4	7	1	30
	c	19	5	5	8	4	41
2	t	11	11	6	3	0	31
	c	15	7	9	7	4	42
3	t	12	12	9	6	6	45
	c	14	10	6	7	2	39
4	t	17	12	6	7	4	46
	c	18	9	4	5	6	42
5	t	9	9	2	5	3	28
	c	15	7	6	7	1	36
6	t	17	11	4	7	1	40
	c	18	7	8	5	5	43
7	t	16	10	3	3	5	37
	c	9	9	5	4	5	32
8	t	11	10	4	4	5	34
	c	12	11	4	9	4	40
9	t	19	9	4	5	4	41
	c	18	10	1	2	4	35

Table 7.6. – Estimates of treatment survival and associated statistics under $H_{1\phi}$ for the pintail dosing experiment (Table 7.5). Replicates are derived by partitioning the data on the basis of the last digit in the band number.

Replicate	Estimated survival $\hat{S}$	Standard error $\hat{se}(\hat{S})$	Null hypothesis $S = 1$[a] χ^2	df	P
0	1.521	0.3314	3.95	5	0.557
1	0.742	0.1710	3.14	5	0.678
2	0.748	0.1698	8.45	5	0.133
3	1.170	0.2433	3.20	5	0.670
4	1.110	0.2247	1.68	5	0.891
5	0.789	0.1914	5.10	5	0.404
6	0.943	0.1970	5.27	5	0.383
7	1.172	0.2716	2.78	5	0.734
8	0.862	0.1923	2.13	5	0.830
9	1.188	0.2612	3.42	5	0.636
Mean or total	1.025		39.12	50	0.867

[a]TEST 1.

7.4. Pesticide Dosing of Starlings

Stromborg et al. (in press) studied postfledgling survival of European starlings *Sturnus vulgaris* deliberately exposed to an organophosphate pesticide. This novel study of the effect of a pesticide under field conditions represents another example of other types of experiments that fall under the general methodology developed here. In the starling experiment, relatively small numbers of birds were released ($R_{t1} = 60$; $R_{c1} = 61$), but capture probabilities were high ($\bar{p} = 0.78$). Inasmuch as the recaptures were resightings of uniquely marked birds, the experiment falls under what we have termed the complete capture history protocol (see Nichols et al. 1981; Sandland and Kirkwood 1981; Buckland et al. 1983; and Clobert et al. 1985 for similar studies, but without treatments). The study was conducted on about 2,000 hectares of the Patuxent Wildlife Research Center near Laurel, Maryland.

During summer 1984, investigators set out nest boxes to attract starlings. Boxes were checked frequently during the nesting period to determine the date of hatching. All nestlings were banded 16 days after hatching, and half the birds, chosen at random, were given an oral dosage of organophosphate pesticide mixed in corn oil. Control birds were given pure corn oil under similar conditions. Two days later, the surviving birds were tagged with individually numbered wing tags (dead birds were tallied as "direct" mortality). The tags were made of orange or red vinyl-like material, cut in a pear shape and measuring approximately 35×40 mm. Letters or numerals about 20 mm high were painted on each tag with flat black paint. Tagged birds were sighted and their tag numbers were recorded over six sampling periods. (Further details are given by Stromborg et al., in press.)

Data from the study are presented in Table 7.7, taken directly from the output of program RELEASE in the form of a reduced m-array and its associated summary statistics. Stromborg et al. (in press) failed to find any significant treatment effect, and our analysis is in agreement with their results. Results for TEST 1 are summarized in the series of 2×2 contingency tables given in Table 7.8. Pooling of the chi-square values and their degrees of freedom results in an overall test of the null hypothesis of equality for all survival and capture probabilities between the treatment and control groups. This procedure yields $\chi^2 = 8.26$, 9 df, and $P = 0.508$; thus, there is no reason to suspect the validity of the null hypothesis. Either the pesticide had no effect on the survival rate of fledged starlings or the effects were too small to be detected in this limited experiment.

The estimated treatment survival under model $H_{1\phi}$ is 0.906 (standard error, 0.1036), which is not significantly different from 1.0 (in agreement with results of TEST 1.R1). If $S < 1$, a larger experiment is needed to provide a suitable measure of the treatment effect. Alternatively, a higher dose level or sequence of doses might be effective with the same sample sizes.

If the treatment affected survival throughout the experiment, a comparison of the average survival rates of the two groups would provide an indication of the extent of that effect. However, averaging the $\hat{\phi}_i$ over the four estimates available yielded 0.862 and 0.880 for treatment and control birds, respectively. Again, no indication of treatment-related mortality is shown. Readers are encouraged to run the data in Table 7.7 through program RELEASE and interpret the full output.

Table 7.7. – Data under the complete capture history protocol for survival studies of marked starlings dosed with pesticide by Stromborg et al. (in press).

i	R_{ti} or R_{ci}	Recaptures, m_{tij}					r_{ti} or r_{ci}
		$j = 2$	3	4	5	6	
			Treatment group				
1	60	24	6	9	2	0	41
2	24		22	1	0	0	23
3	28			24	0	0	24
4	34				30	0	30
5	32					21	21
m_{tj}		24	28	34	32	21	
z_{tj}		17	12	2	0	0	
			Control group				
1	61	22	13	9	2	0	46
2	22		18	1	0	0	19
3	31			30	0	0	30
4	40				33	1	34
5	35					28	28
m_{cj}		22	31	40	35	29	
z_{cj}		24	12	2	1	0	

Table 7.8. – A series of 2×2 contingency tables and associated information related to the null hypothesis that survival and capture (sighting) probabilities are equal for treatment and control groups of starlings.

Test 1 component	Contingency table		χ^2	df	P
1.R5	21	11			
	28	7	1.76	1	0.185
1.T5	32	0			
	35	1	0.90	1	0.342
1.R4	30	4			
	34	6	0.16	1	0.685
1.T4	34	2			
	40	2	0.03	1	0.874
1.R3	24	4			
	30	1	2.32	1	0.128
1.T3	28	12			
	31	12	0.04	1	0.834
1.R2	23	1			
	19	3	1.30	1	0.255
1.T2	24	17			
	22	24	1.00	1	0.318
1.R1	41	19			
	46	15	0.75	1	0.387
TEST 1			8.26	9	0.508

We used program RELEASE to simulate 1,000 replications of this study to investigate the performance of the statistical theory for several experiments similar to the starling study. The results of these studies are used to illustrate a number of points and to allow additional insight into the effect of a pesticide on young starlings. In general, we took the estimates of parameters computed from the starling study as parameters for the simulations. Thus, $\phi_2 = 0.94$, $\phi_3 = 0.92$, $\phi_4 = 0.87$, $\phi_5 = 0.87$ and $p_2 = 0.5$, $p_3 = 0.7$, $p_4 = 0.95$, $p_5 = p_6 = 0.98$ for both groups. We chose $\phi_{t1} = 0.71$ and $\phi_{c1} = 0.79$, giving $S = 0.899$. The true model was then $H_{1\phi}$ and data sets were generated under this model. The total number released in each group was studied at 60, 100, 200, and 400 individuals.

The statistical procedures performed well on the average, for all sample sizes studied (Table 7.9). In addition, the empirical variance of the 1,000 estimates is in close agreement with the average variance derived from the model and the ML method. The above results indicate that the asymptotic theory does well when small numbers of animals are released if the recapture rates are high. We recommend that simulations such as this one be performed before a study is conducted and during the analysis of experimental data. Simulations conducted during the design phase of an experiment allow appraisal of precision and sample size (e.g., note how precision increases in the final column of Table 7.9 as sample size increases). Also, the power of various tests can be evaluated. The standard error of $\hat{S}$ is relatively large when sample sizes are small.

Alternatively, the use of the option EXPECT in program RELEASE will provide very reliable insight into the properties of estimators and tests. The theory for this is given in Chapter 3.6. The use of the EXPECT option produces results in a few seconds of computer time whereas simulation times may often exceed 3 hours.

Table 7.9. – Monte Carlo results for four parameters and four sample sizes for experiments similar to the study of the effect of a pesticide on starlings by Stromborg et al. (in press). One thousand replications were generated with $S = 0.899$ and estimates were made under model $H_{1\phi}$ (the true model).

Number released $R_{t1} = R_{c1}$	Parameter	Average of estimates[a]	Standard error
60	$p_2 = 0.5$	0.501	0.055
	$\phi_{t1} = 0.71$	0.708	0.063
	$\phi_{c1} = 0.79$	0.793	0.060
	$S = 0.899$	0.898	0.102
100	$p_2 = 0.5$	0.500	0.043
	$\phi_{t1} = 0.71$	0.712	0.049
	$\phi_{c1} = 0.79$	0.790	0.048
	$S = 0.899$	0.903	0.080
200	$p_2 = 0.5$	0.501	0.031
	$\phi_{t1} = 0.71$	0.710	0.035
	$\phi_{c1} = 0.79$	0.792	0.034
	$S = 0.899$	0.899	0.055
400	$p_2 = 0.5$	0.501	0.022
	$\phi_{t1} = 0.71$	0.709	0.025
	$\phi_{c1} = 0.79$	0.791	0.024
	$S = 0.899$	0.896	0.040

[a]An estimate of the expected value of the estimator.

Table 7.10. – Power of the test (TEST 1.R1) of model $H_{1\phi}$ versus H_0 for five significance levels and four sample sizes in Monte Carlo studies with parameters similar to those estimated from the starling data of Stromborg et al. (in press). Data were simulated under model $H_{1\phi}$ where the survival rates averaged 0.9 and the recapture rates averaged 0.8. The treatment survival $S = \phi_{t1}/\phi_{c1}$.

Treatment survival	Number released $R_{t1} = R_{c1}$	Significance level (α)				
		0.01	0.05	0.10	0.20	0.50
$S = 0.9$ (small effect)	60	0.05	0.17[a]	0.24	0.38	0.65
	100	0.09	0.22	0.33	0.45	0.72
	200	0.20	0.40	0.53	0.68	0.87
	400	0.47	0.70	0.80	0.89	0.97
$S = 0.8$ (larger effect)	60	0.22	0.44	0.58	0.72	0.88
	100	0.42	0.68	0.79	0.87	0.96
	200	0.80	0.93	0.96	0.99	1.0
	400	0.98	1.0	1.0	1.0	1.0

[a]Comparable estimates of test power using the theory given in Chapter 3.6 are 0.16, 0.24, 0.42, 0.70, 0.47, 0.68, 0.93, and 1.00, respectively, for this column.

Simulated results on the power of the test of $H_{1\phi}$ versus H_0 are shown in Table 7.10. The top half of the table relates to the simulations in Table 7.9. The rest of the table relates to a larger treatment effect, where $S = \phi_{t1}/\phi_{c1} = 0.63/0.79 = 0.797$. The power of finding a significant treatment effect, at the $\alpha = 0.05$ level of significance where $S = 0.9$, is only about 0.17 for the starling experiment. Power increases with sample size and the magnitude of the treatment effect. The ideal experiment would consist of a larger treatment effect (i.e., low S), large samples released, high capture probabilities, many sampling sites or occasions, adequate replication, and the use of unique marks. The use of ordered treatments also has advantages (see Section 8.2.1).

Data collected under the complete capture history protocol have the advantage that one can make many tests of model assumptions, select an appropriate estimator, and make proper estimates of parameters. As noted by Stromborg et al. (in press), the goodness of fit tests indicate a poor fit of the data to the model. This matter is potentially serious. Stromberg et al. (in press) simulated the lack of fit and concluded that, in their case, the results were little affected. In this example, no treatment effect could be shown; thus, model H_0 was selected. If a significant treatment effect were to exist, the investigator would have a choice of models: $H_{1\phi}$, H_{2p}, $H_{2\phi}$, H_{3p}, ..., $H_{k-1,\phi}$. In general, however, only models $H_{1\phi}$ and H_{2p} have relatively good precision unless the capture probabilities are high. For the starling data, the full output from program RELEASE shows good precision for all estimators under all models because the capture (sighting) probabilities are high. If capture probabilities are low (say < 0.1), then good precision for S can be expected only when at least $\phi_{tj} = \phi_{cj}$ for $j = 2, 3, ..., k$ and $p_{tj} = p_{cj}$ for $j = 3, 4, ..., k$. This same situation is also true for scheme A in the partial capture history protocol. Under scheme B one can test $\phi_{t1} = \phi_{c1}$ and $p_{t2} = p_{c2}$ and also test that the other parameters are the same by treatment and control group. With scheme B data, one can estimate the relevant ϕ_{t1} and ϕ_{c1} and the treatment survival rate S can be estimated under models $H_{1\phi}$ and H_{2p}; however, ϕ_{ti} for $i > 1$ cannot be estimated under any model.

7.5. Partitioning Lazuli Bunting Data

Allen W. Stokes banded Lazuli buntings *Passerina amoena* in his yard in Logan, Utah, during winters from 1974 to 1980. Recaptures were recorded each year for 7 consecutive years, and his data (personal communication), summarized as an m-array, are shown in Table 7.11. The result of the TEST 2 goodness of fit tests is summarized below:

TEST	χ^2	df	P
2.C2	1.74	1	0.187
2.C3	1.68	1	0.194
2.C4	0.32	1	0.571
2.C5	2.29	2	0.130
2.C6	0.21	1	0.643
Total	6.25	5	0.282

(with only an m-array such as in Table 7.11, only TEST 2 goodness of fit can be computed).

Table 7.11. – The m-array for Lazuli buntings banded during winters of 1974-1980 by Allen W. Stokes in Logan, Utah (personal communication).

i	R_i	Recaptures, $m_{i,j}$							r_i
		1974	1975	1976	1977	1978	1979	1980	
1	168	31	4	0	1	0	0	0	36
2	398		19	14	4	1	0	1	39
3	88			20	3	1	0	0	24
4	264				41	6	3	1	51
5	304					58	13	1	72
6	322						67	9	76
7	323							76	76
m_j		31	23	34	49	66	83	88	
z_j		5	21	11	13	19	12	0	

The above test results, taken from the output of program RELEASE, indicate a satisfactory fit of the Jolly-Seber model (model $H_{7\phi}$) to the data. The estimates of the recapture and survival rate parameters are given in Table 7.12. The average annual survival is 0.399. At this point, one might be satisfied with the model and proceed to make inferences about this banded population. A further analysis, however, raises many questions.

We will use these Lazuli bunting data to illustrate several testing, model-building, and model selection concepts. In particular, we use PROC SURVIV, an option in program RELEASE, to generate input code to program SURVIV for the bunting data. The input file is then analyzed with program SURVIV, which allows extended model building, testing, and estimation. In this example, we do not claim to reach a completely satisfactory endpoint; rather, these data are used to show a path that might be followed in the analysis of a set of real data where complications arise.

Table 7.12. – Estimates of annual survival (ϕ_i) and recapture (p_i) rates for the Lazuli bunting data under the Jolly-Seber model (model $H_{7\phi}$), output from program RELEASE.

```
+-------------------------------------------------------------------+
|                                                                   |
|           Maximum Likelihood Estimates under Model H7Phi          |
|                                                                   |
|                                      95% Confidence Intervals     |
|   Parameter    Estimate    Standard Error    Lower        Upper   |
|   ---------    --------    --------------    -----        -----   |
|                  Estimates for Group 1                            |
|   Phi(1)       .488248       .142347       .209248      .767248   |
|   Phi(2)       .222704       .049248       .126178      .319231   |
|   Phi(3)       .551159       .128118       .300047      .802270   |
|   Phi(4)       .323701       .054803       .216288      .431114   |
|   Phi(5)       .408204       .058924       .292714      .523695   |
|   Phi(6)       .332919       .044263       .246163      .419675   |
|   p(2)         .377931       .118809       .145065      .610797   |
|   p(3)         .230000       .061706       .109056      .350944   |
|   p(4)         .373868       .086373       .204577      .543159   |
|   p(5)         .471658       .081868       .311196      .632119   |
|   p(6)         .450512       .069064       .315146      .585878   |
|   p(7)         .619403       .076551       .469364      .769442   |
|   Phi(7)p(8)   .235294       .023602       .189034      .281554   |
|                                                                   |
+-------------------------------------------------------------------+
```

The full m-array is shown in Table 7.13 along with some associated statistics. TEST 3 can be made from these further partitions of the data. The results are summarized below in two components; first for TEST 3.Sm:

TEST	χ^2	df	P
3.$Sm2$	1.36	1	0.243
3.$Sm3$	1.64	1	0.200
3.$Sm4$	0.28	1	0.597
3.$Sm5$	6.68	1	0.010
3.$Sm6$	1.27	1	0.260
Subtotal	11.25	5	0.047

This component of TEST 3 shows some lack of fit but this is nearly all from release 5 (TEST 3.$Sm5$). The second major component of TEST 3 is a contingency table where columns are r_i and $R_i - r_i$ while rows are newly caught and released birds, and previously captured and released birds. The results of this test component (TEST 3.SRi) are summarized below:

TEST	χ^2	df	P
3.$SR3$	25.09	1	<0.001
3.$SR4$	13.43	1	<0.001
3.$SR5$	33.48	1	<0.001
3.$SR6$	10.14	1	0.006
3.$SR7$	24.58	1	<0.001
3.$SR8$	21.89	1	<0.001
Subtotal	128.62	6	<0.001

The sum of these two test components (TEST 3) is $\chi^2 = 139.87$, 11 df, $P < 0.001$ and indicates a serious lack of fit to the Jolly-Seber model. It is clear that the banded population consists of a mixture of birds that are probably never seen again after banding and birds that are commonly recaptured. The new, unbanded birds that enter the study population are different from those banded birds already in the marked study population. The birds that return and are recaptured fit the Jolly-Seber model fairly well. The data in Table 7.11 can be partitioned into two m-arrays: new captures and previous captures (Table 7.14). If we use the convention $v = 1$ for new birds to be released and $v = 2$ for previously banded birds already in the population at year j, we can compute the test H_0 versus $H_{7\phi}$ to examine the homogeneity of the two data sets. Note that $R_{21} = 0$: no releases on occasion 1 for group $v = 2$. This test can also be made using program RELEASE and results in $\chi^2 = 130.26$, 11 df, $P < 0.001$. This partitioning of the data can be done in other applications to test assumptions about males versus females, young versus adult, birds with versus without neck collars, etc. In each case, the relevant test is H_0 versus $H_{k-1,\phi}$.

Table 7.13. – The full m-array for the Lazuli bunting data. The total number of initial captures (r_i) and the number of birds never recaptured $(R_i - r_i)$ are also shown.

				Occasion						
1	2	3	4	5	6	7	8		r_i	$R_i - r_i$
168	31	4	0	1	0	0	0		36	132
{11}	31	7	4	0	0	0	0		11	20
{01}	367	12	10	4	1	0	1		28	339
(release 3)	{101}	4	1	0	1	0	0		2	2
	{111}	7	5	0	0	0	0		5	2
	{011}	12	6	0	0	0	0		6	6
	{001}	65	8	3	0	0	0		11	54
(release 4)		{1101}	4	4	0	0	0		4	0
		{0101}	10	3	1	0	0		4	6
		{1011}	1	1	0	0	0		1	0
		{1111}	5	3	0	0	0		3	2
		{0111}	6	1	1	0	0		2	4
		{0011}	8	4	1	0	0		5	3
		{0001}	230	25	3	3	1		32	198
(release 5)			{10001}	1	1	0	0		1	0
			{01001}	4	2	0	0		2	2
			{00101}	3	1	0	0		1	2
			{11011}	4	1	0	0		1	3
			{01011}	3	2	0	0		2	1
			{10111}	1	1	0	0		1	0
			{11111}	3	1	0	0		1	2
			{01111}	1	0	0	0		0	1
			{00111}	4	2	0	0		2	2
			{00011}	25	9	0	0		9	16
			{00001}	255	38	13	1		52	203
(release 6)				{010001}	1	0	0		0	1
				{101001}	1	0	0		0	1
				{010101}	1	0	0		0	1
				{011101}	1	1	0		1	0
				{001101}	1	1	0		1	0
				{000101}	3	0	1		1	2
				{100011}	1	0	0		0	1
				{010011}	2	0	0		0	2
				{001011}	1	0	0		0	1
				{110111}	1	1	0		1	0
				{010111}	2	1	0		1	1
				{101111}	1	0	0		0	1
				{111111}	1	1	0		1	0
				{001111}	2	1	1		2	0

Table 7.13 – Continued.

{000111}	9	6	0	6	3
{000011}	38	16	0	16	22
{000001}	256	39	7	46	210
{0001001}	3	0	0		3
{0000101}	13	1	1		12
{0111011}	1	0	0		1
{0011011}	1	0	0		1
{1101111}	1	1	1		0
{0101111}	1	1	1		0
{1111111}	1	1	1		0
{0011111}	1	1	1		0
{0001111}	6	2	2		4
{0000111}	16	11	11		5
{0000011}	39	12	12		27
{0000001}	240	46	46		194

(release 7)

Table 7.14. – Partitioned m-arrays for the Lazuli bunting data. The data for birds recaptured only once ($v = 1$) appear at the top, followed by birds recaptured after being rereleased ($V = 2$). The statistics m_j and z_j are also shown.

i	R_i	Recaptures, $m_{i,j}$							r_i
		$j = 2$	3	4	5	6	7	8	
1	168	31	4	0	1	0	0	0	36
2	367		12	10	4	1	0	1	28
3	65			8	3	0	0	0	11
4	230				25	3	3	1	32
5	255					38	13	1	52
6	256						39	7	46
7	240							46	46
m_j		31	16	18	33	42	55	56	
z_j		5	17	10	9	19	10	0	
2	31		7	4	0	0	0	0	11
3	23			12	0	1	0	0	13
4	34				16	3	0	0	19
5	49					20	0	0	20
6	66						28	2	30
7	83							30	30
m_j		0	7	16	16	24	28	32	
z_j		0	4	1	4	0	2	0	

With the two extracted data sets in Table 7.14, the following parameter estimates were computed using program RELEASE:

i	$v = 1$		$v = 2$	
	$\hat{\phi}_{1i}$	$\hat{p}_{1i}$	$\hat{\phi}_{2i}$	$\hat{p}_{2i}$
1	0.575			
2	0.270	0.321	0.454	
3	0.544	0.137	0.591	0.497
4	0.255	0.200	0.720	0.900
5	0.494	0.428	0.408	0.621
6	0.296	0.284	0.508	1.000
7		0.513		0.835
Average	0.406	0.314	0.536	0.771

Here, it appears that the average annual survival rates are somewhat similar ($\overline{\phi}_1 = 0.406$ versus $\overline{\phi}_2 = 0.536$) but the average capture rates are quite different ($\overline{p}_1 = 0.314$ versus $\overline{p}_2 = 0.771$). Although one might expect the estimated average survival for the pooled data (Table 7.12) to lie between 0.406 and 0.536, this is not the case (0.399). These results show the danger of using the Jolly-Seber model without careful review of the results from TEST 3, which can only be computed from the CH matrix or the full m-array.

The analysis of these data was extended using PROC SURVIV, an option in program RELEASE (see Part 9). The following summarizes the parameters and indexing for the bunting data.

Releases	$j =$	3	4	5	6	7	8
Group $V = 1$							
$R_{12}, ..., R_{17}$	ϕ_{12}		ϕ_{13}	ϕ_{14}	ϕ_{15}	ϕ_{16}	ϕ_{17}
		p_{13}	p_{14}	p_{15}	p_{16}	p_{17}	p_{18}
Group $V = 2$							
$R_{22}, ..., R_{27}$	ϕ_{22}		ϕ_{23}	ϕ_{24}	ϕ_{25}	ϕ_{26}	ϕ_{27}
		p_{23}	p_{24}	p_{25}	p_{26}	p_{27}	p_{28}

PROC SURVIV was used to generate a computer file for analysis by program SURVIV (White 1983). A listing of this file is shown in Table 7.15, which shows the code generated for the expectations of each observed m_{vij} value. Constraints were imposed to enable three models to be analyzed using program SURVIV:

model A: ϕ and p constant over years, but p differing between groups;

model B: ϕ constant and the same for both groups; p year-specific and differing between groups;

model C: ϕ year-specific but the same for both groups; p year-specific and differing between groups.

Thus, the unknown parameters of interest are

model A: ϕ
p_v, $v = 1, 2$;

model B: ϕ
p_{vj}, $v = 1, 2$ and $j = 3, ..., 8$;

model C: ϕ_j, $j = 2, ..., 6$
p_{vj}, $v = 1, 2$ and $j = 3, ..., 7$.

In addition, the products $(\phi_7 p_{v8})$ are estimable for model C.

The parameter estimates under model A were $\hat{\phi} = 0.447$ (se $= 0.0227$), $\hat{p}_1 = 0.252$ (se $= 0.0241$), and $\hat{p}_2 = 0.813$ (se $= 0.0563$). Again, these results indicate differing capture probabilities by group. However, this model does not fit the data ($\chi^2 = 63.4$, 19 df, $P < 0.001$). Considerable pooling was required with an associated loss of 20 df.

The survival rate estimate under model B was 0.418 (se $= 0.0217$). The capture rates for group 1 varied from 0.080 to 0.409 while the range for group 2 was 0.744 to 1.0. The fit of this model was also poor ($\chi^2 = 23.0$, 9 df, $P = 0.006$) in spite of some pooling over cells with small expected values (and, again, a loss of 20 df). Neither model A nor B seems useful in making inference from these data.

Table 7.15. − Listing of the input file to program SURVIV created by program RELEASE (see Part 9 for additional information) for the Lazuli bunting data.

INPUT --- proc title 'Al Stokes Bunting data;

INPUT --- proc model npar=24;
INPUT ---   cohort=367 /* Releases for group 1 on occasion 2 */;
INPUT ---   12:s(1)*s(7);
INPUT ---   10:s(1)*(1.-s(7))*s(2)*s(8);
INPUT ---   4:s(1)*(1.-s(7))*s(2)*(1.-s(8))*s(3)*s(9);
INPUT ---   1:s(1)*(1.-s(7))*s(2)*(1.-s(8))*s(3)*(1.-s(9))*s(4)*s(10);
INPUT ---   0:s(1)*(1.-s(7))*s(2)*(1.-s(8))*s(3)*(1.-s(9))*s(4)*(1.-s(10))*s(5)*s(11);
INPUT ---   1:s(1)*(1.-s(7))*s(2)*(1.-s(8))*s(3)*(1.-s(9))*s(4)*(1.-s(10))*s(5)*(1.-s(11))*s(6)*s(12);
INPUT ---   cohort=65 /* Releases for group 1 on occasion 3 */;
INPUT ---   8:s(2)*s(8);
INPUT ---   3:s(2)*(1.-s(8))*s(3)*s(9);
INPUT ---   0:s(2)*(1.-s(8))*s(3)*(1.-s(9))*s(4)*s(10);
INPUT ---   0:s(2)*(1.-s(8))*s(3)*(1.-s(9))*s(4)*(1.-s(10))*s(5)*s(11);
INPUT ---   0:s(2)*(1.-s(8))*s(3)*(1.-s(9))*s(4)*(1.-s(10))*s(5)*(1.-s(11))*s(6)*s(12);
INPUT ---   cohort=230 /* Releases for group 1 on occasion 4 */;
INPUT ---   25:s(3)*s(9);
INPUT ---   3:s(3)*(1.-s(9))*s(4)*s(10);
INPUT ---   3:s(3)*(1.-s(9))*s(4)*(1.-s(10))*s(5)*s(11);
INPUT ---   1:s(3)*(1.-s(9))*s(4)*(1.-s(10))*s(5)*(1.-s(11))*s(6)*s(12);
INPUT ---   cohort=255 /* Releases for group 1 on occasion 5 */;
INPUT ---   38:s(4)*s(10);
INPUT ---   13:s(4)*(1.-s(10))*s(5)*s(11);
INPUT ---   1:s(4)*(1.-s(10))*s(5)*(1.-s(11))*s(6)*s(12);
INPUT ---   cohort=256 /* Releases for group 1 on occasion 6 */;
INPUT ---   39:s(5)*s(11);
INPUT ---   7:s(5)*(1.-s(11))*s(6)*s(12);
INPUT ---   cohort=240 /* Releases for group 1 on occasion 7 */;
INPUT ---   46:s(6)*s(12);
INPUT ---   cohort=31 /* Releases for group 2 on occasion 2 */;
INPUT ---   7:s(13)*s(19);
INPUT ---   4:s(13)*(1.-s(19))*s(14)*s(20);
INPUT ---   0:s(13)*(1.-s(19))*s(14)*(1.-s(20))*s(15)*s(21);
INPUT ---   0:s(13)*(1.-s(19))*s(14)*(1.-s(20))*s(15)*(1.-s(21))*s(16)*s(22);
INPUT ---   0:s(13)*(1.-s(19))*s(14)*(1.-s(20))*s(15)*(1.-s(21))*s(16)*(1.-s(22))*s(17)*s(23);
INPUT ---   0:s(13)*(1.-s(19))*s(14)*(1.-s(20))*s(15)*(1.-s(21))*s(16)*(1.-s(22))*s(17)*(1.-s(23))*s(18)*s(24);
INPUT ---   cohort=23 /* Releases for group 2 on occasion 3 */;

Table 7.15 – Continued.

INPUT ---   12:s(14)*s(20);
INPUT ---   0:s(14)*(1.-s(20))*s(15)*s(21);
INPUT ---   1:s(14)*(1.-s(20))*s(15)*(1.-s(21))*s(16)*s(22);
INPUT ---   0:s(14)*(1.-s(20))*s(15)*(1.-s(21))*s(16)*(1.-s(22))*s(17)*s(23);
INPUT ---   0:s(14)*(1.-s(20))*s(15)*(1.-s(21))*s(16)*(1.-s(22))*s(17)*(1.-s(23))*s(18)*s(24);
INPUT ---   cohort=34 /* Releases for group 2 on occasion 4 */;
INPUT ---   16:s(15)*s(21);
INPUT ---   3:s(15)*(1.-s(21))*s(16)*s(22);
INPUT ---   0:s(15)*(1.-s(21))*s(16)*(1.-s(22))*s(17)*s(23);
INPUT ---   0:s(15)*(1.-s(21))*s(16)*(1.-s(22))*s(17)*(1.-s(23))*s(18)*s(24);
INPUT ---   cohort=49 /* Releases for group 2 on occasion 5 */;
INPUT ---   20:s(16)*s(22);
INPUT ---   0:s(16)*(1.-s(22))*s(17)*s(23);
INPUT ---   0:s(16)*(1.-s(22))*s(17)*(1.-s(23))*s(18)*s(24);
INPUT ---   cohort=66 /* Releases for group 2 on occasion 6 */;
INPUT ---   28:s(17)*s(23);
INPUT ---   2:s(17)*(1.-s(23))*s(18)*s(24);
INPUT ---   cohort=83 /* Releases for group 2 on occasion 7 */;
INPUT ---   30:s(18)*s(24);
INPUT ---   labels;
INPUT ---   s(1)=Phi(Group=1 Occasion=2);
INPUT ---   s(2)=Phi(Group=1 Occasion=3);
INPUT ---   s(3)=Phi(Group=1 Occasion=4);
INPUT ---   s(4)=Phi(Group=1 Occasion=5);
INPUT ---   s(5)=Phi(Group=1 Occasion=6);
INPUT ---   s(6)=Phi(Group=1 Occasion=7);
INPUT ---   s(7)=p(Group=1 Occasion=3);
INPUT ---   s(8)=p(Group=1 Occasion=4);
INPUT ---   s(9)=p(Group=1 Occasion=5);
INPUT ---   s(10)=p(Group=1 Occasion=6);
INPUT ---   s(11)=p(Group=1 Occasion=7);
INPUT ---   s(12)=p(Group=1 Occasion=8);
INPUT ---   s(13)=Phi(Group=2 Occasion=2);
INPUT ---   s(14)=Phi(Group=2 Occasion=3);
INPUT ---   s(15)=Phi(Group=2 Occasion=4);
INPUT ---   s(16)=Phi(Group=2 Occasion=5);
INPUT ---   s(17)=Phi(Group=2 Occasion=6);
INPUT ---   s(18)=Phi(Group=2 Occasion=7);
INPUT ---   s(19)=p(Group=2 Occasion=3);
INPUT ---   s(20)=p(Group=2 Occasion=4);

Table 7.15. – Continued.

INPUT ---	s(21)=p(Group=2 Occasion=5);
INPUT ---	s(22)=p(Group=2 Occasion=6);
INPUT ---	s(23)=p(Group=2 Occasion=7);
INPUT ---	s(24)=p(Group=2 Occasion=8);

The results for model C from program SURVIV are shown in Table 7.16. The average annual survival is estimated to be 0.421 (assumed to be the same for both groups). The goodness of fit statistics are shown in Table 7.17. Several expected values $E(m_{vij})$ are less than two and must be pooled to obtain a test statistic that is more nearly chi-square distributed (e.g., note cohort 8, cell 3 gives $\chi^2 = 14.97$ when one bird was observed while 0.059 was expected). Appropriate pooling results in $\chi^2 = 22.1$, 18 df, $P = 0.228$, indicating a good fit of model C to the data.

The log-likelihood values for models A, B, and C are -95.1064, -66.2558, and -65.2174, respectively. The results of log-likelihood tests between the three models are summarized below:

H_0	H_A	χ^2	df	P
model A	model B	57.70	10	<0.001
model A	model C	59.78	14	<0.001
model B	model C	2.08	4	0.721

These results, taken alone, support the use of either model B or C. The goodness of fit test tends to support only model C.

Ideally, one might want to simulate data similar to those under, at least, models B and C to further understand the performance of the various tests. Alternatively, one could take the parameter estimates $\hat{\phi}_j$ and $\hat{p}_{vj}$ as input into the EXPECT option in program RELEASE. The m_{vij} arrays could be computed and then PROC SURVIV would set up the proper input file for program SURVIV. This would allow bias and precision to be assessed approximately. In addition, the chi-square statistics could be used with Table 3.4 to obtain approximations to the power of tests. The combination of programs RELEASE and SURVIV offer the investigator some powerful analysis tools.

Table 7.16. – Estimates of model parameters for the Lazuli bunting data under model C. Parameters 1-5 and 13-17 are ϕ_j, $j = 2, ..., 6$; 7-12 are $\hat{p}_{1j}$, $j = 3, ..., 7$; and 19-23 are $\hat{p}_{2j}$, $j = 3, ..., 7$, respectively. Parameters 12 and 24 are $(\phi_7 p_{18})$ and $(\phi_7 p_{28})$, respectively. This output is from program SURVIV.

I	Parameter	S(I)	Standard Error	95% Confidence Interval Lower	Upper
1	1	0.32832895	0.71477979E-01	0.18823211	0.46845279
2	2	0.54410820	0.10040752	0.34730946	0.74090694
3	3	0.41158185	0.66609613E-01	0.28102701	0.54213670
4	4	0.41867222	0.51833132E-01	0.31707928	0.52026516
5	5	0.40113225	0.50680044E-01	0.30179936	0.50046514
6	-23	1.0000000	0.00000000E+00	1.0000000	1.0000000
7	7	0.10198075	0.35142248E-01	0.33101943E-01	0.17085956
8	8	0.19840528	0.53712540E-01	0.93128698E-01	0.30368186
9	9	0.27146268	0.57229006E-01	0.15929383	0.38363154
10	10	0.29674715	0.51903390E-01	0.19501650	0.39847779
11	11	0.40027946	0.64594367E-01	0.27367450	0.52688442
12	12	0.17369512	0.23052430E-01	0.12851235	0.21887788
13	1	0.32832895	0.71477979E-01	0.18823211	0.46842579
14	2	0.54410820	0.10040752	0.34730946	0.74090694
15	3	0.41158185	0.66609613E-01	0.28102701	0.54213670
16	4	0.41867222	0.51833132E-01	0.31707928	0.52026516
17	5	0.40113225	0.50680044E-01	0.30179936	0.50046514
18	-24	1.0000000	0.00000000E+00	1.0000000	1.0000000
19	14	0.53822731	0.18980953	0.16620062	0.91025400
20	15	0.89278880	0.12672562	0.64440658	1.1411710
21	16	0.74418196	0.15468978	0.44098998	1.0473739
22	17	1.0000000	0.36776340E-08	0.99999999	1.0000000
23	6	0.88363930	0.96052303E-01	0.69537679	1.0719018
24	13	0.36914358	0.52853778E-01	0.26555017	0.47273699

Table 7.17. – Goodness of fit statistics for the Lazuli bunting data under model C. This output is from program SURVIV.

Cohort	Cell	Observed	Expected	Chi-square	Note
1	1	12	12.288	0.007	0 < P < 1
1	2	10	11.682	0.242	0 < P < 1
1	3	4	5.273	0.307	0 < P < 1
1	4	1	1.758	0.327	0 < P < 1
1	5	0	0.669	0.669	0 < P < 1
1	6	1	0.174	3.918	0 < P < 1
1	7	339	335.156	0.044	0 < P < 1
2	1	8	7.017	0.138	0 < P < 1
2	2	3	3.168	0.009	0 < P < 1
2	3	0	1.056	1.056	0 < P < 1
2	4	0	0.402	0.402	0 < P < 1
2	5	0	0.105	0.105	0 < P < 1
2	6	54	53.253	0.010	0 < P < 1
3	1	25	25.698	0.019	0 < P < 1
3	2	3	8.568	3.619	0 < P < 1
3	3	3	3.260	0.021	0 < P < 1
3	4	1	0.848	0.027	0 < P < 1
3	5	198	191.625	0.212	0 < P < 1
4	1	38	31.681	1.260	0 < P < 1
4	2	13	12.055	0.074	0 < P < 1
4	3	1	3.137	1.456	0 < P < 1
4	4	203	208.126	0.126	0 < P < 1
5	1	39	41.105	0.108	0 < P < 1
5	2	7	10.697	1.278	0 < P < 1
5	3	210	204.198	0.165	0 < P < 1
6	1	46	41.687	0.446	0 < P < 1
6	2	194	198.313	0.094	0 < P < 1
7	1	7	5.478	0.423	0 < P < 1
7	2	4	2.283	1.291	0 < P < 1
7	3	0	0.084	0.084	0 < P < 1
7	4	0	0.012	0.012	0 < P < 1
7	5	0	0.000	0.000	0 < P < 1
7	6	0	0.000	0.000	0 < P < 1
7	7	20	23.143	0.427	0 < P < 1
8	1	12	11.173	0.061	0 < P < 1
8	2	0	0.411	0.411	0 < P < 1
8	3	1	0.059	14.967	0 < P < 1
8	4	0	0.000	0.000	0 < P < 1

Table 7.17. – Continued.

8	5	0	0.000	0.000	0 < P < 1
8	6	10	11.357	0.162	0 < P < 1
9	1	16	10.414	2.996	0 < P < 1
9	2	3	1.499	1.504	0 < P < 1
9	3	0	0.000	0.000	0 < P < 1
9	4	0	0.000	0.000	0 < P < 1
9	5	15	22.087	2.274	0 < P < 1
10	1	20	20.515	0.013	0 < P < 1
10	2	0	0.000	0.000	0 < P < 1
10	3	0	0.000	0.000	0 < P < 1
10	4	29	28.485	0.009	0 < P < 1
11	1	28	23.394	0.907	0 < P < 1
11	2	2	1.137	0.655	0 < P < 1
11	3	36	41.469	0.721	0 < P < 1
12	1	30	30.639	0.013	0 < P < 1
12	2	53	52.361	0.008	0 < P < 1

7.6 Changes in Group Membership – Desert Tortoise Data

Desert tortoises *Gopherus agassizii* that were uniquely marked were identified near Goffs in eastern San Bernardino County, California, in 1977 and 1980, and between 1983 and 1986 (Turner and Berry, unpublished report, 1986). Only the 1984-1986 data are analyzed in this example.

The purpose of the Goffs study was to estimate sex- and age-specific survival of tortoises for use in the construction of a life table for this species. Carapace lengths and live body masses were recorded for all tortoises registered. The sex of tortoises with carapace lengths less than 180 mm could not be ascertained with certainty, but the sex of all tortoises 180 mm and longer was recorded. Measured carapace lengths ranged from 40 to 325 mm. The size of tortoises affects their susceptibility to capture. Small tortoises are difficult to find and are underrepresented in samples (Berry and Turner 1986). Adult tortoises are conspicuous and have high probabilities of recapture. The size of tortoises also affects survival rates because smaller individuals are more vulnerable to predation by birds, coyotes *Canis latrans*, and kit foxes *Vulpes macrotis*.

Any attempt to estimate survival rates of tortoises should include body size as a variable, and a reasonable approach would be to subdivide the population into groups based on lengths of tortoises measured at time of first capture. Because of possible behavioral and social differences between adult males and females, it would also be desirable to include sex in the analysis. The Goffs data were divided into 11 groups:

Group number	Sex and size range
1	Males > 208 mm
2	Females > 208 mm
3	Males 180-208 mm
4	Females 180-208 mm
5	155-179 mm
6	140-154 mm
7	120-139 mm
8	100-119 mm
9	80-99 mm
10	60-79 mm
11	< 60 mm

The basic data consist of

$$
\begin{array}{ccc}
R_{v1} & m_{v12} & m_{v13} \\
R_{v2} & & m_{v23}
\end{array}
$$

for each of the 11 groups (v = 1, ..., 11) plus the average carapace length for each of the groups. The basic data allow estimation of ϕ_{v1}, p_{v2}, and $\phi_{v2}p_{v3}$, giving 33 parameters. We seek a parsimonious model using size to reduce 33 parameters by incorporating growth into the model.

The logistic model provides a reasonable approach to modeling capture and survival probabilities as a function of size. Thus, the survival rate for group 6 during 1984-1985 is expressed as

$$
\phi_1 = \frac{\beta_2}{1 + \exp{(-\beta_0 - \beta_1 145)}} \, ,
$$

where β_0 is the intercept of the curve, β_1 is the slope and β_2 is the asymptote (≤ 1). The value 145 is the mean carapace length of group 6 tortoises captured in 1984. For group 5, the survival rate for 1984-1985 is

$$
\phi_1 = \frac{\beta_2}{1 + \exp{(-\beta_0 - \beta_1 171)}}
$$

because the mean carapace length of group 5 tortoises captured in 1984 was 171 mm. The parameters β_0, β_1, and β_2 are the same as for group 6 and all other groups from 1984 to 1985.

That is, these three parameters are common to all 11 groups because only the mean carapace length for each group is assumed to affect survival. Thus, the estimates of β_0, β_1, and β_2 reflect the environmental conditions of the 1984-85 interval, particularly rainfall. A different set of estimates for β_0, β_1, and β_2 could have been obtained for 1985-1986, and likewise for 1986-1987, had data been collected for all of these periods.

Some tortoises grew 50 mm over a 3-year period. Thus, a mechanism is required in the analysis that allows for the increase in size of tortoises through time – in effect, to allow tortoises to change their group membership. To provide the best estimate of the size of tortoises in 1985 that were in group v in 1984, the mean size of the recaptures in 1985 is calculated, and these values are used in the logistic functions. Further, size in 1985 is used in the logistic function for capture probability in 1985. Thus, for group 5 animals, the probability of recapture in 1985 is

$$p_2 = \frac{\gamma_2}{1 + \exp\left(-\gamma_0 - \gamma_1 184\right)}$$

where the mean carapace length of the tortoises classified as group 5 in 1984 is now 184 mm in 1985. Typically, animals in groups 3-11 increased in size over an interval, while the mature adults (groups 1-2) did not.

As with the models described earlier in this monograph, the final pair of parameters ϕ_2 and p_3 are not individually estimable, but the product of the pair can be estimated. Again, this product is treated as a logistic function with three parameters across all 11 groups.

To summarize, the basic model for group v consists of three parameters: ϕ_1, p_2, and the product $\phi_2 p_3$. Each of these three parameters is modeled as a three-parameter logistic function of size. Thus, a total of nine parameters (rather than 33) is estimated from the data, i.e., three logistic functions times three parameters per function.

The basic data for this model are given in Table 7.18. The recaptures are presented as an m_{ij} matrix because this input (Table 7.19) is needed by program SURVIV (White 1983). The second line in each entry is the mean carapace length for tortoises in the cohort. This mean is estimated from all tortoises starting the cohort, even though some of them may be represented in a new cohort because of a previous capture.

Two "tricks" are used to analyze the data with program SURVIV. First, the coding for a logistic function is complex. Rather than code each logistic function separately, a function call, RL, with three arguments is used: the index of the starting parameter for the triplet forming the logistic function, the index of the parameter specifying a correction for adult females (discussed later), and the carapace length used for calculating probability. Instead of separating these values with commas, percent signs (%) are used because SURVIV does not recognize % as a separator. After the compile run of SURVIV is completed, the EST.FOR file SURVIV generates is edited; the percent signs are converted to commas, and the code for the RL function is added. EST.FOR then is compiled and linked into SURVIV to complete the estimation process.

Table 7.18. – The *m*-array and mean carapace lengths (in parentheses) for desert tortoises captured at Goffs, California, 1984-1986. R_2 includes recaptures from the previous occasion.

Group	R_i	$m_{i,j}$	
		$j=2$	3
1	84	62	7
	(256)	(259)	(261)
	75		51
	(256)		(256)
2	67	57	4
	(222)	(223)	(223)
	71		56
	(222)		(222)
3	10	3	1
	(197)	(198)	(205)
	12		4
	(196)		(196)
4	18	11	4
	(195)	(204)	(204)
	18		12
	(196)		(196)
5	18	12	2
	(171)	(184)	(189)
	13		8
	(168)		(168)
6	11	3	3
	(145)	(161)	(167)
	12		6
	(147)		(147)
7	16	7	1
	(129)	(139)	(153)
	18		6
	(127)		(127)
8	19	10	1
	(107)	(117)	(123)
	27		5
	(109)		(109)
9	16	7	1
	(89)	(98)	(97)
	16		3
	(90)		(90)

Table 7.18. – Continued.

10	9	1	1
	(71)	(80)	(80)
	7		2
	(72)		(72)
11	13	2	1
	(49)	(58)	(64)
	10		0
	(52)		(52)

Table 7.19. – Input to program SURVIV for desert tortoise data.

```
proc title Analysis of tortoise, Section 8 only, sex differences,
84-86 only;
proc model npar=12
 /*rl(i,j,k) converted to
s(i+2)/(1.+exp(-s(i)-s(i+1)*dble(k)-s(j)*dble(k)) */;
 cohort=84 /* Group 1 Males > 208 mm captured 1984 */;
  62:rl(1%0%256)*rl(7%0%259);
   7:rl(1%0%256)*(1.-rl(7%0%259))*rl(4%0%261);
 cohort=67 /* Group 2 Females > 208 mm captured 1984 */;
  59:rl(1%10%222)*rl(7%11%223);
   4:rl(1%10%222)*(1.-rl(7%11%223))*rl(4%12%223);
 cohort=10 /* Group 3 Males 180-208 mm captured 1984 */;
   3:rl(1%0%197)*rl(7%0%198);
   1:rl(1%0%197)*(1.-rl(7%0%198))*rl(4%0%205);
 cohort=18 /* Group 4 Females 180-208 mm captured 1984 */;
  11:rl(1%10%195)*rl(7%11%204);
   4:rl(1%10%195)*(1.-rl(7%11%204))*rl(4%12%204);
 cohort=18 /* Group 5 155-179 mm captured 1984 */;
  12:rl(1%0%171)*rl(7%0%184);
   2:rl(1%0%171)*(1.-rl(7%0%184))*rl(4%0%189);
 cohort=11 /* Group 6 140-154 mm captured 1984 */;
   3:rl(1%0%145)*rl(7%0%161);
   3:rl(1%0%145)*(1.-rl(7%0%161))*rl(4%0%167);
 cohort=16 /* Group 7 120-139 mm captured 1984 */;
   7:rl(1%0%129)*rl(7%0%139);
```

Table 7.19. – Continued.

```
   1:rl(1%0%129)*(1.-rl(7%0%139))*rl(4%0%153);
cohort=19 /* Group 8 100-119 mm captured 1984 */;
  10:rl(1%0%107)*rl(7%0%117);
   1:rl(1%0%107)*(1.-rl(7%0%117))*rl(4%0%123);
cohort=16 /* Group 9 97-99 mm captured 1984 */;
   7:rl(1%0%89)*rl(7%0%98);
   1:rl(1%0%89)*(1.-rl(7%0%98))*rl(4%0%97);
cohort=9 /* Group 10 60-79 mm captured 1984 */;
   1:rl(1%0%71)*rl(7%0%80);
   1:rl(1%0%71)*(1.-rl(7%0%80))*rl(4%0%80);
cohort=13 /* Group 11 < 60 mm captured 1984 */;
   2:rl(1%0%49)*rl(7%0%58);
   1:rl(1%0%49)*(1.-rl(7%0%58))*rl(4%0%64);
cohort=75 /* Group 1 Males > 208 mm captured 1985 */;
  51:rl(4%0%256);
cohort=71 /* Group 2 Females > 208 mm captured 1985 */;
  56:rl(4%12%222);
cohort=12 /* Group 3 Males 180-208 mm captured 1985 */;
   4:rl(4%0%196);
cohort=18 /* Group 4 Females 180-208 mm captured 1985 */;
  12:rl(4%12%196);
cohort=13 /* Group 5 155-179 mm captured 1985 */;
   8:rl(4%0%168);
cohort=12 /* Group 6 140-154 mm captured 1985 */;
   6:rl(4%0%147);
cohort=18 /* Group 7 120-139 mm captured 1985 */;
   6:rl(4%0%127);
cohort=27 /* Group 8 100-119 mm captured 1985 */;
   5:rl(4%0%109);
cohort=16 /* Group 9 97-99 mm captured 1985 */;
   3:rl(4%0%90);
cohort=7 /* Group 10 60-79 mm captured 1985 */;
   2:rl(4%0%72);
cohort=10 /* Group 11 < 60 mm captured 1985 */;
   0:rl(4%0%52);
labels;
 s(1)=Intercept for 1984 survival function;
 s(2)=Slope for 1984 survival function;
 s(3)=Asymptote for 1984 survival function;
 s(4)=Intercept for 1986 survival and cap. prob. function;
 s(5)=Slope for 1986 survival and cap. prob. function;
```

Table 7.19. – Continued.

```
  s(6)=Asymptote for 1986 survival and cap. prob. function;
  s(7)=Intercept for 1985 capture probability function;
  s(8)=Slope for 1985 capture probability function;
  s(9)=Asymptote for 1985 capture probability function;
  s(10)=Adult female survival probability effect;
  s(11)=Adult female capture probability effect;
  s(12)=Adult female 1986 survival and capture probability
effect;
proc estimate novar nsig=5 name=asym_fix;
 initial; s(1)=0.8; s(2)=0.002; s(4)=0.8; s(5)=0.002;
        s(7)=-2.; s(8)=0.02;
 constraints; s(1)>-5.; s(1)<5.; s(2)>0.; s(2)<1.; s(3)=1.0;
  s(4)>-5.; s(4)<5.; s(5)>0.; s(5)<1.; s(6)=1.0;
  s(7)>-5.; s(7)<5.; s(8)>0.; s(8)<1.; s(9)=1.0;
  s(10)=0.0; s(11)=0.0; s(12)=0.0;
proc estimate novar nsig=5 maxfn=1200 name=phi_cons;
 initial; retain=asym_fix;
 constraints; s(1)>-5.; s(1)<5.; s(2)=0.; s(3)=1.0;
  s(4)>-5.; s(4)<5.; s(5)>0.; s(5)<1.; s(6)=1.0;
  s(7)>-5.; s(7)<5.; s(8)>0.; s(8)<1.; s(9)=1.0;
  s(10)=0.0; s(11)=0.0; s(12)=0.0;
proc estimate novar nsig=5 maxfn=1200 name=p_cons;
 initial; retain=asym_fix;
 constraints; s(1)>-5.; s(1)<5.; s(2)>0.; s(2)<1.; s(3)=1.0;
  s(4)>-5.; s(4)<5.; s(5)>0.; s(5)<1.; s(6)=1.0;
  s(7)>-5.; s(7)<5.; s(8)=0.; s(9)=1.0;
  s(10)=0.0; s(11)=0.0; s(12)=0.0;
proc estimate novar nsig=5 maxfn=1200 name=phi&p_cons;
 initial; retain=asym_fix;
 constraints; s(1)>-5.; s(1)<5.; s(2)=0.; s(3)=1.0;
  s(4)>-5.; s(4)<5.; s(5)=0.; s(6)=1.0;
  s(7)>-5.; s(7)<5.; s(8)=0.; s(9)=1.0;
  s(10)=0.0; s(11)=0.0; s(12)=0.0;
proc estimate novar nsig=5 maxfn=1200 name=sex_diff;
 initial; retain=asym_fix;
 constraints; s(1)>-5.; s(1)<5.; s(2)>0.; s(2)<1.; s(3)=1.0;
  s(4)>-5.; s(4)<5.; s(5)>0.; s(5)<1.; s(6)=1.0;
  s(7)>-5.; s(7)<5.; s(8)>0.; s(8)<1.; s(9)=1.0;
proc estimate novar nsig=5 maxfn=5000 name=asymptote;
 initial; retain=asym_fix;
  s(3)=0.95; s(6)=0.95; s(9)=0.95;
```

Table 7.19. – Continued.

```
constraints;
            s(1)>-5.; s(1)<5.;
            s(4)>-5.; s(4)<5.;
            s(7)>-5.; s(7)<5.;
            s(10)=0.; s(11)=0.; s(12)=0.;
proc estimate novar nsig=5 maxfn=5000 name=s&asymptot;
 initial; retain=asymptote;
 constraints;
            s(1)>-5.; s(1)<5.;
            s(4)>-5.; s(4)<5.;
            s(7)>-5.; s(7)<5.;
proc test;
proc stop;
```

Because of the complexity of the model developed above, a series of models is used to build up to the most complex model. First, estimates are made with program SURVIV for the model labeled ASYM_FIX: the model where the logistic functions for ϕ_1, p_2, and $\phi_2 p_3$ are individually estimated but the asymptotes of each logistic function (β_2, γ_2) are fixed at 1.0. This model only has six parameters; thus it provides a starting point for the estimation process. To test for the effect of growth on survival and capture probabilities, three additional models are included. The model PHI_CONS has $\beta_1 = 0$ for ϕ_1 to test if size affects survival; model P_CONS has $\gamma_1 = 0$ for p_2 to test if size affects capture probability; and PHI&P_CONS has the slope parameter set to zero for all three logistic functions to provide an overall test of the effects of size on survival and capture probabilities.

The final model in the sequence is labeled ASYMPTOTE: each of the three logistic functions in the model are assumed to have different parameter values and the asymptote of each logistic function is estimated rather than fixed at 1.0 (but constrained to <1). Goodness of fit results for this sequence of five models are

Model	Log-likelihood	df	P
ASYM_FIX	-70.086	27	0.009
PHI_CONS	-70.478	28	0.020
P_CONS	-75.667	28	<0.001
PHI&P_CONS	-121.125	30	<0.001
ASYMPTOTE	-67.371	24	0.014

None of the five models provided an adequate fit to the observed data as determined by the χ^2 goodness of fit test from program SURVIV. Although size was significantly related to capture probability ($P < 0.001$, likelihood ratio test of P_CONS versus ASYM_FIX), it was not significantly related to survival ($P = 0.376$, likelihood ratio test of PHI_CONS versus ASYM_FIX). Further, the likelihood ratio test of the general model ASYMPTOTE versus the simpler model ASYM_FIX was not significant ($P = 0.143$), suggesting that allowing the asymptote values of each of the logistic functions to deviate from 1 did not improve the fit of the model to the observed data. This result is consistent with the poor fit of the ASYMP-TOTE model as shown above.

Examination of the partitioned goodness of fit test in the output from program SURVIV showed a pattern in the lack of fit. group 2 (females $\geq$208 mm) generally contributed large chi-square values, usually with the observed captures exceeding the expected number of captures. This pattern also was visible for group 4 (females 180-208 mm). Further, males in groups 1 and 3 tended to show the opposite pattern – observed captures were generally less than the expected value, although the chi-square contribution from these groups was generally not significant.

These results suggested additional model building to account for sex of the mature tortoises (groups 1-4). Even though males and females might be the same size, behavioral differences might modify their capture and survival probabilities so that size alone would not explain the observed data. Thus, the logistic functions for groups 2 and 4 (females) were modified to include a fourth parameter for survival:

$$\phi_1 = \frac{\beta_2}{1 + \exp\left[-\beta_0 - \beta_1 \text{length} - \beta_3 \max(0, \text{length} - 180)\right]}.$$

The additional parameter β_3 allowed for differential behavior of mature females compared to other groups. Thus, β_3 is zero unless the cohort is in group 2 or 4. This modification added three parameters to the general model described previously because a parameter is needed for each of the three logistic functions.

The three additional parameters caused us to add two additional models to the sequence described above. SEX_DIFF allows for differences in sex, but continues to fix the asymptote value to 1.0 so that the effect of the three additional parameters can be tested against the ASYM_FIX model. The most general model, S&ASYMPTOT has 12 parameters, four for each of the three logistic functions. The goodness of fit results are now much improved:

Model	Log-likelihood	df	P
SEX_DIFF	-58.936	24	0.224
S&ASYMPTOT	-58.219	21	0.201

A summary of the pertinent likelihood ratio tests between models is:

H_0	H_A	χ^2	df	P
PHI_CONS	ASYM_FIX	0.78	1	0.376
P_CONS	ASYM_FIX	11.16	1	<0.001
PHI&P_CONS	ASYM_FIX	102.08	3	<0.001
ASYM_FIX	SEX_DIFF	22.30	3	<0.001
ASYM_FIX	ASYMPTOTE	5.43	3	0.143
ASYM_FIX	S&ASYMPTOT	23.73	6	<0.001
SEX_DIFF	S&ASYMPTOT	1.44	3	0.697
ASYMPTOTE	S&ASYMPTOT	18.30	3	<0.001

We conclude that model SEX_DIFF is the most parsimonious model that fits the observed data. The addition of asymptotes different from unity to the three logistic functions does not improve the fit of the model. The reduced model ASYM_FIX fits the data significantly more poorly than SEX_DIFF, demonstrating that the sex-specific parameters contribute significantly to the fit of the model. Likewise, a test of P_CONS versus ASYM_FIX demonstrates that p is significantly related to the size of the individual. Estimates of the parameters for the SEX_DIFF model are presented in Table 7.20, and plots of the ϕ and p functions are shown in Figure 7.1.

Table 7.20. – Estimates of model parameters for the program SURVIV model SEX_DIFF.

Parameter	Estimate	SE	95% CI
ϕ_1 Intercept	0.476	1.081	-1.643 to 2.595
ϕ_1 Slope	0.00490	0.00487	-0.00465 to 0.0145
ϕ_1 Asymptote	1.0		
p_2 Intercept	-1.405	0.668	-2.714 to 0.0965
p_2 Slope	0.0121	0.00241	0.00739 to 0.0169
p_2 Asymptote	1.0		
$\phi_2 p_3$ Intercept	-2.539	0.250	-3.029 to -2.049
$\phi_2 p_3$ Slope	0.0131	0.00117	0.0108 to 0.0154
$\phi_2 p_3$ Asymptote	1.0		
Adult Females			
ϕ_1 Effect	0.0381	0.0200	-0.00102 to 0.0773
p_2 Effect	0.0207	0.0125	-0.00373 to 0.0452
$\phi_2 p_3$ Effect	0.0238	0.00842	0.00733 to 0.0403

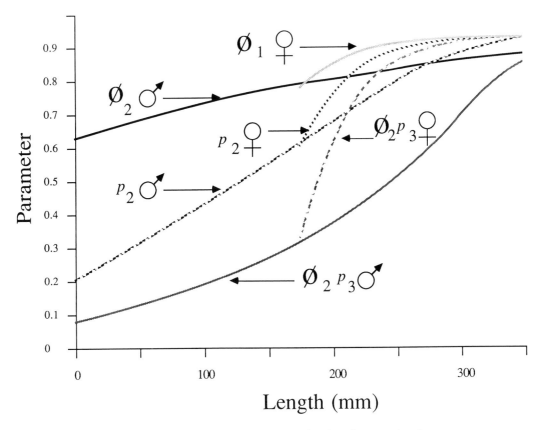

Figure 7.1. – Plots of ϕ_1, p_2, and $\phi_2 p_3$ as a function of carapace length.

Caution must be taken regarding the procedures used in the preceding analysis. The estimates of size for tortoises that were never recaptured may be biased because the probability of capture is related to size. Hence, the tortoises recaptured at a later occasion were probably larger, leading to size-biased sampling. However, because of the large number of groups used in the analysis, the effect of this size-biased effect is minimized. The smaller the size interval used to form a group, the smaller the effect of the size bias. However, adequate sample sizes must be maintained within each group to allow estimation of the group size, and to allow adequate sample sizes for program SURVIV to estimate the multinomial cells.

Part 8. Extensions and Other Comments on Methodology

8.1. Introduction

Many extensions and alternative approaches are possible for the class of experiments discussed in this monograph. Studies involving several groups allow further analysis and modeling to be conducted. In some studies, the treatments are ordered, again allowing extended analysis. We here discuss some general ideas for such extensions.

The statistical theory presented here has many similarities with the Jolly-Seber model for one group. Therefore, some existing methods have potential application to the extended treatment-control models we have examined. In Chapter 8.3, we consider designs for heterogeneous populations and age-specific treatment effects. Regression approaches have been used frequently in fisheries work for many decades and this approach is covered briefly under the first and unknown capture history protocols in Section 8.4.1. Finally, some experiments on small hydrodams have involved the release of dead fish as an integral part of the study. The theory for this unique case is covered in Section 8.4.2.

8.2. Studies with More Than Two Groups

Most of this monograph involves analysis of recapture data from two groups of marked animals corresponding to treatment and control groups. An exception is Part 3, which deals with the situation where there are more than two groups and which presents statistical theory and an example (Chapter 3.10). However, the methods in Part 3 do not consider specific relationships between groups corresponding, for example, to treatment with increasing levels of a toxin or to animals in different size-classes. In the present chapter, we concentrate on methods of analysis that are appropriate when more than two groups have a specific "treatment structure."

It is not possible to give a detailed account of all the variations likely to arise or of the most appropriate analyses (which require PROC SURVIV of program RELEASE). We instead discuss two general situations and indicate how to use some basic results from program RELEASE for further analysis. We consider first the case where groups correspond to ordered levels of a single factor and then groups corresponding to two factors, each at two or more levels.

8.2.1. Ordered Treatments

8.2.1.1. Direct modeling of treatment effect. – We assume here that the initial release consists of V groups of marked animals, where the labels $v = 1, 2, ..., V$ correspond to ordered treatment levels. For example, we may have $V = 3$ groups, where group 1 animals receive no treatment, and animals of groups 2 and 3 are dosed with lead at different levels.

Several difficulties are associated with determining an appropriate way to assess treatment effect. One concerns whether the effect is direct (acute) or indirect (see Chapter 1.5). If the effect is direct, it is reflected by a ratio of first-period survival rates; if it is chronic, the separation of treatment mortality from natural mortality is difficult (see Section 1.5.4), though the ratio (or difference) between treatment and control survival rates in some sense measures treatment-related mortality.

One way to study a dose-related treatment response is to build the relationship into the parameters of the model. Thus, assume that $D_1, ..., D_V$ represent increasing dose levels applied to groups $v = 1, ..., V$, respectively. A model often used in dose-response studies to relate survival and dose is the logistic model (Cox 1970). The simplest way to incorporate this model in the context of a release-recapture study is to relate total survival to dose, making no attempt to partition treatment-related and natural mortality (except for direct effect).

The survival rate parameters of a general model, allowing for a chronic dose-related treatment effect persisting throughout the study, are

$$\phi_{vi} = \frac{1}{1 + \exp(-a_i + b_i D_v)},$$

$v = 1, ..., V$ and $i = 1, ..., k - 2$. Thus, the $V(k - 2)$ survival rate parameters, ϕ, are effectively replaced by the $2(k - 2)$ parameters $a_1, b_1, ..., a_{k-2}, b_{k-2}$. The remaining parameters are

$$p_{vi}, i = 2, ..., k - 1, v = 1, ..., V, \text{ and}$$
$$\phi_{v,k-1} p_{v,k}, v = 1, ..., V.$$

This model uses a separate logistic structure for the survival of each group. Note that with this parameterization, if $b_i = 0$ for some i, then survival ϕ_{vi} is the same for all groups in period i. Thus, to test for a treatment effect on survival in period i, we test $b_i = 0$ against $b_i \neq 0$ or a one-sided alternative. The sequence of models $H_0, H_{1\phi}, H_{2\phi}, ..., H_{k-1,\phi}$ now has the following representation.

For model H_0, $b_1 = b_2 = \cdots = b_{k-2} = 0; p_{vi} = p_i, v = 1, ..., V, i = 2, ..., k - 1$;

$$\phi_{v,k-1} p_{vk} = \phi_{k-1} p_k, v = 1, ..., V.$$

For model $H_{1\phi}$, $b_1 \neq 0$, $b_2 = \cdots = b_{k-2} = 0$; $p_{vi} = p_i$, $v = 1, ..., V$, $i = 2, ..., k - 1$;

$$\phi_{v,k-1} \, p_{vk} = \phi_{k-1} \, p_k, \; v = 1, ..., V \, .$$

For model H_{2p}, $b_1 \neq 0$; $p_{v2} \neq p_{v'2}$, all v, v' in $1, ..., V$;

$$b_2 = \cdots = b_{k-2} = 0; p_{vi} = p_i, \; v = 1, ..., V, \quad i = 3, ..., k - 1;$$

$$\phi_{v,k-1} \, p_{vk} = \phi_{k-1} \, p_k, \quad v = 1, ..., V \, .$$

$$\vdots$$

For model $H_{k-1,\phi}$, $b_i \neq 0$, $i = 1, ..., k - 2$; $p_{vi} \neq p_{v'i}$, all v, v', $i = 2, ..., k - 1$;

$$\phi_{v,k-1} \, p_{vk} \neq \phi_{v',k-1} \, p_{v'k}, \text{ all } v, v' \, .$$

Unfortunately, estimation under the models $H_{1\phi}$, ..., $H_{k-1,\phi}$ requires a computer routine more general than program RELEASE. Testing between any two models in the sequence is carried out by means of likelihood ratio tests, which are also beyond the capabilities of program RELEASE. PROC SURVIV of program RELEASE is used to provide input to program SURVIV (White 1983) for the appropriate analyses. In some applications, it may be appropriate to model the capture probabilities (p_{vi}) as a logistic model based on effort or other variables. The above discussion applies largely to complete capture history (or scheme A) data because estimation with first capture histories is not possible under models more general than $H_{1\phi}$ (see Chapter 2.2).

If the treatment effect is entirely direct, and if group 1 is a control or zero-dose group (i.e., $D_1 = 0$), a parameterization that separates treatment-related and natural mortality is

$$\phi_{v1} = S_v \phi_{11} \, ,$$

where

$$S_v = \frac{1}{1 + \exp(-a + b \, D_v)} \, , \quad v = 2, ..., V \, ,$$

and

$$\phi_{vi} = \phi_i, \, i = 2, ..., k - 2; \, p_{vi} = p_i, \, i = 2, ..., k - 1; \, \phi_{v,k-1} \, p_{vk} = \phi_{k-1} \, p_k \, , \quad v = 1, ..., V \, .$$

Again, estimation is possible with first capture or complete capture history data but cannot be carried out for the above model by using program RELEASE. The test of no treatment effect, i.e., of $b = 0$, also needs a more general computer routine. Here again, the output of PROC SURVIV from program RELEASE can be modified for input to program SURVIV. Other programs for this type of modeling were discussed by North and Morgan (1979), White (1983), Conroy and Williams (1984), and Clobert et al. (1985).

8.2.1.2. Indirect modeling of treatment effect. – We now discuss alternative (and less satisfactory) procedures that can be applied to the output from program RELEASE. Tests carried out in RELEASE to compare models (see TEST 1, Chapter 2.1) provide some indication of how prolonged the treatment effect is. However, each component of TEST 1 tests the null hypothesis of homogeneity of some parameters across all groups against the general alternative that not all groups are the same. The tests are not designed to be sensitive to the types of alternatives expected with ordered groups, such as an ordering of group-specific survival rates. To achieve greater power or sensitivity, a test designed specifically for ordered alternatives (see Cochran 1954; Armitage 1955) can be applied to data in each of the $V \times 2$ contingency tables, which are printed out by program RELEASE as components of TEST 1.

Application of tests for ordered alternatives is illustrated here for TEST 1.$R1$, which is based on the $V \times 2$ contingency table with rows $(r_{v1}, R_{v1} - r_{v1})$, $v = 1, ..., V$ (see Section 2.1.2). When the row labels of this table correspond to increasing dose levels $D_1, ..., D_V$, an alternative to the null hypothesis of no treatment effect states that survival ϕ_{v1} is a decreasing function of dose D_v. For a direct treatment effect, this corresponds to stating that the probability of recapture (estimated by r_{v1}/R_{v1}) decreases as D_v increases. If the relation of ϕ_{v1} to D_v (or to scores Z_v related to D_v, e.g., $Z_v = \ln D_v$) is thought to be approximately linear, the Cochran-Armitage test for a linear trend in proportions is appropriate. In TEST 1.$R1$, the proportions of interest are the recapture probabilities $E(r_{v1})/R_{v1}$, $v = 1, ..., V$. Computational details were given by Cochran (1954), Armitage (1955), and Snedecor and Cochran (1980, Section 11.9). The test statistic is chi-square with 1 df, which is more sensitive to a trend in the proportions $E(r_{v1})/R_{v1}$ than is the nonspecific contingency chi-square with $V - 1$ degrees of freedom computed by TEST 1.$R1$.

The Cochran-Armitage test is most effective when the proportions $E(r_{v1})/R_{v1}$ are linearly related to doses D_v (or some appropriate transformation, Z_v, of D_v). An alternative approach may be needed when the relationship is not linear – e.g., when there is a threshold dose below which treatment has no effect. In this situation, a useful procedure is to partition the $V \times 2$ tables for TEST 1.$R1$ into a series of 2×2 tables, each yielding a chi-square with 1 df. One possible partitioning gives the series of tables

First table:

$$\begin{array}{|ll|} \hline r_{11} & R_{11} - r_{11} \\ r_{21} & R_{21} - r_{21} \\ \hline \end{array}$$

Second table:

$$
\boxed{
\begin{array}{ll}
r_{11} + r_{21} & R_{11} + R_{21} - r_{11} - r_{21} \\
r_{31} & R_{31} - r_{31}
\end{array}
}
$$

V - 1 table:

$$
\boxed{
\begin{array}{ll}
r_{11} + \cdots + r_{V-1,1} & R_{11} + \cdots + R_{V-1,1} - r_{11} - \cdots - r_{V-1,1} \\
r_{V1} & R_{V1} - r_{V1}
\end{array}
}
$$

These and other series of 2×2 tables can be used to combine the V groups into a smaller number of "classes" within each of which survival and recapture rates appear to be homogeneous. An example of such a series of tests is given in Chapter 7.6 for recapture data on tortoises. A useful discussion of partitioning chi-squares for a $V \times 2$ table was given by Cochran (1954, Section 6.1).

Tests that take into account the ordering of the V groups should be applied in a similar manner to the other components of TEST 1. These test results should then be used to select the most appropriate model in the sequence $H_0, H_{1\phi}, ..., H_{k-1,\phi}$. If group-specific survival estimates can be computed under the chosen model for the type of data available, these estimates would then be examined for dose-related trends.

Thus, with first capture history data, if model $H_{1\phi}$ fits and if group 1 at dose D_1 is a control, the period 1 survival rate ratios (relative to group 1), i.e., the S_v, $v = 2, ..., V$, can be examined for trends. Unfortunately, regression analysis (with a linear or nonlinear model such as the logistic model) to relate $\hat{\phi}_{v1}$ or $\hat{S}_v$ to D_v is not straightforward, because the usual regression assumptions concerning independent observations with common variance do not hold; the $\hat{S}_v$ are correlated and have different (not equal) sampling variances. We are not aware of any packaged routine that will straightforwardly perform the appropriate weighted regression analysis for the case where the error variance-covariance matrix (or the weighting matrix) is not diagonal. An additional problem is that these variances and covariances are unknown, and their estimates produced by program RELEASE may not be reasonably accurate unless sample sizes are large. Relating $\hat{\phi}_{v1}$ or $\hat{S}_v$ to D_v by regression analysis will be approximate and possibly crude. One such approach to a nonlinear regression of $\hat{\phi}_{v1}$ or $\hat{S}_v$ on D_v (e.g., with the logistic model) is to ignore covariances between estimates and carry out the weighted regression, weighting by the inverse of the estimated variance produced by RELEASE.

With complete capture history data, correlations among the $\hat{\phi}_{vi}$ can be avoided by using estimates from a sufficiently general model. Thus, $\hat{\phi}_{v1}$, $v = 1, ..., V$ are uncorrelated under $H_{2\phi}$ and more general models (see Part 3). However, using a general model can result in unnecessary loss of precision; thus, this approach is not satisfactory either.

8.2.2. Two Factors Each at Two or More Levels

Consider a release-recapture study where the releases of treatment and control groups consist of individuals in four size-classes, marked accordingly. We can regard this study as two-factor: $V = 8$ groups in a 2×4 classification with treatment at two levels and size-class at four levels. Other examples of studies with two factors each at several levels include treatment and control groups released at each of several locations (see Chapter 7.3), and several treatment levels applied to different sex or age-classes (see Chapter 7.2). In all these examples we can impose a definite structure upon the group labels $v = 1, ..., V$; this structure should not be ignored.

Analysis procedures are generalizations of those described for ordered treatments (Section 8.2.1), and again involve two different approaches. The first approach is to build the relationship between survival and treatment structure into the model parameters; the second approach is to obtain survival estimates, ignoring treatment structure and using program RELEASE, and then determine if in some way these estimates reflect the treatment structure. As noted in Section 8.2.1, the first method is beyond the capabilities of RELEASE, but is statistically sound; the second method is, at best, approximate.

Comments in Section 8.2.1 concerning direct and indirect effects and related models apply here also. Thus, a model that allows for a prolonged or chronic effect, for the study with treatment and control and four size-classes, has

$$\phi_{vi} = \frac{1}{1 + \exp\left(- a_i + b_i D_v + c_i X_v + d_i D_v X_v\right)}, \tag{8.2.1}$$

$$v = 1, ..., V,$$
$$i = 1, ..., k - 2,$$

where $D_v = 0$ or 1 for control and treatment, respectively, and X_v has four values corresponding to the midpoints of the four size-classes. More generally, D_v and X_v represent levels of two factors, one of which may be the dose of a toxin and the other a covariate such as size. A test of $b_i = c_i = d_i = 0$ is a test of the null hypothesis that survival in period i is not affected by either of the two factors. A test of $b_i = d_i = 0$ is a test of no effect on survival by factor 1 in period i.

The first type of analysis would estimate a_i, b_i, c_i, d_i using a model with ϕ_{vi} defined as in 8.2.1. Tests concerning b_i, c_i, and d_i would be likelihood ratio tests. The second type of analysis would use estimates $\hat{\phi}_{vi}$ and variances and covariances from RELEASE in a nonlinear weighted regression with $\phi_i = E(\hat{\phi}_{vi})$, as given by the equation above to obtain $\hat{a}_i, \hat{b}_i, \hat{c}_i$, and $\hat{d}_i$. Note that this second approach involves estimating a larger number of parameters than the first.

Examples of studies with two factors are given in Chapter 7.2. However, in both of these examples, only first capture histories are available; thus, unless the treatment effect is largely direct, it cannot be estimated satisfactorily. In each example, the data were partitioned into subsets, each containing a treatment and control group so that estimates $\hat{S}$ produced by RELEASE for different subsets were uncorrelated. The analyses used correspond to the second type of approach described here. However, there will be little difference between the two types of approaches for these examples because estimation with models more general than $H_{1\phi}$ is not possible and because the $\hat{S}_i$ are independent.

8.3. Testing for Treatment Effects in a General Capture-Recapture Setting

In this monograph we have concentrated on the situation where released, marked animals are recaptured. This allows estimation of survival and capture rates with primary emphasis on comparisons of survival rates between treatments. More generally, however, we may also obtain information on unmarked animals as part of the capture process. In these cases, we may also obtain estimates of population size and recruitment number for each period and test for effects on these abundance parameters.

A fisheries example might involve fish populations in small experimental ponds subject to different treatments (e.g., a control pond versus a pond subject to mild acidification). In some experiments, one pond may be used for each treatment; however, several ponds probably should be allocated to each treatment so that a valid estimate of experimental error can be obtained (see Part 4). Fish could be captured and marked as the study progressed so that survival rates, capture rates, population sizes, and recruitment numbers could be estimated. This chapter (i.e., estimation of population size) is not applicable when fish are migrating in a large river system.

As an illustration, suppose we have the situation described in Part 2 where there are two treatments with no replication. To begin with, let us assume that all the parameters are distinct so that we have

	Treatment group	Control group
Survival	$\phi_{t1}, ..., \phi_{t,k-1}$	$\phi_{c1}, ..., \phi_{c,k-1}$
Capture	$p_{t1}, ..., p_{tk}$	$p_{c1}, ..., p_{tk}$
Population size	$N_{t1}, ..., N_{tk}$	$N_{c1}, ..., N_{ck}$
Recruit. number	$B_{t1}, ..., B_{t,k-1}$	$B_{c1}, ..., B_{c,k-1}$.

When treatment is determined by the investigator, the N_{v1} will be known; and subsequent N_{vj} are just survivors from earlier releases. Moreover, in this situation, recruitment is known: B_{vj} are the known releases to treatment groups v, at time j, of previously unmarked animals. If unmarked animals are being caught and used in the study, there can be contexts in which N_{vj} and B_{vj} are of interest, especially if one defines being unmarked as a treatment category, or if population totals $N_{.j}$ and $B_{.j}$ are of interest. The alternative situation is that treatment is some naturally occurring distinction, such as strain (see Manly 1985). Then N_{vj} and B_{vj} are meaningful parameters to be estimated.

Recall from Chapter 2.4 that we can estimate ϕ_{ti}, ϕ_{ci} for $i = 1, 2, ..., k - 2$ and p_{ti}, p_{ci} for $i = 2, ..., k - 1$. A simple application of results for the general Jolly-Seber model (Seber 1982:200) provides estimates for population sizes

$$\hat{N}_{ti} = \frac{n_{ti}}{\hat{p}_{ti}} \text{ and }$$

$$\hat{N}_{ci} = \frac{n_{ci}}{\hat{p}_{ci}}, \text{ for } i = 2, 3, ..., k - 1,$$

and for recruitment numbers

$$\hat{B}_{ti} = \hat{N}_{t,i+1} - \hat{\phi}_{ti}(\hat{N}_{ti} - n_{ti} + R_{ti})$$

and

$$\hat{B}_{ci} = \hat{N}_{c,i+1} - \hat{\phi}_{ci}(\hat{N}_{ci} - n_{ci} + R_{ci}) \text{ for } 1 = 2, 3, ..., k - 2.$$

Note that $n_{ti} = m_{ti} + u_{ti}$ is the number of treatment animals captured in sample i, of which u_{ti} are unmarked and m_{ti} are marked. Also, R_{ti} is the number of the n_{ti} released at time i. There are similar definitions for n_{ci} and R_{ci}.

It is important to emphasize that the form of the estimators $\hat{N}_{ti}$, $\hat{N}_{ci}$, $\hat{B}_{ti}$, and $\hat{B}_{ci}$ remain unchanged for all the models in the sequence described in Chapter 2.4. All one needs to do is to use the appropriate $\hat{p}_{ti}$ and $\hat{\phi}_{ti}$ in the estimators (assuming such appropriate p_{ti} exist – see below). Testing between models involves only marked animals, so that all the model sequence tests in Chapter 2.4 still apply with few modifications (the u_{vi} effect TEST 3). Those modifications have been built into RELEASE.

It is possible to derive approximate variances and covariances for population size and recruitment number estimates for any of the models in Chapter 2.4; however, we do not present them here. On the basis of these variances and covariances, approximate normal test statistics could be used to test appropriate hypotheses.

Additional complications arise in estimating N. It is often difficult to interpret what population size means and to what area it applies. Given that we know what our reference population is, then a sample of unmarked animals must be taken along with the marked ones if population size is of interest. Moreover, we must know how the capture probability of unmarked animals relates to the p_{vi} for marked animals. If "treatment" really means strain (or some other naturally occurring distinction: for example, Manly 1985), then we have u_{vi} well defined at the time of capture and thus p_{vi} may apply equally to marked and unmarked animals of strain v. If treatment is imposed by the investigator, then, at the time of capture of $u_{\cdot i}$ unmarked animals, those animals are not distinguished by treatment. One then (randomly) allocates these animals to treatment groups. At that point, the u_{vi} are defined but the recapture probabilities at time i do not depend on the (subsequent) treatment status of these new captures.

If treatment is imposed by the investigator, then we can partition the population size $N_{\cdot i}$ into $V + 1$ classes by letting unmarked animals also be a "treatment" class; hence,

$$N_i = N_{ui} + \sum_{v=1}^{V} N_{vi} \, .$$

The N_{vi} are just the number of marked survivors, by treatment group; thus we actually have

$$N_i = N_{ui} + \sum_{v=1}^{V} M_{vi} \, ,$$

and hence

$$\hat{N}_i = \frac{u_i}{\hat{p}_{ui}} + \sum_{v=1}^{V} \frac{m_{vi}}{\hat{p}_{vi}} \, .$$

Capture probabilities of unmarked animals cannot be estimated except by knowing how they relate to capture probabilities for some segment of marked animals; that assumed relationship cannot be tested. The simplest case is that we find $p_{vi} = p_i$ acceptable and then also assume $p_{ui} = p_i$. Then

$$\hat{N}_i = \frac{n_{\cdot i}}{\hat{p}_i} \, ,$$

so we get an estimate of total population size. The partition of this $\hat{N}_i$ into treatment classes is entirely an artifact of allocating captured animals to treatments. As such, estimation (and testing) of the N_{ti}, N_{ci} is of almost no interest, and requires a restrictive model. We conclude that inference on population size and recruitment is only of interest when treatment is some naturally occurring distinction. Otherwise, the total emphasis is, properly, on survival effects of treatment.

8.3.1. Robust Designs that Allow for Heterogeneity and Trap Response

Here we assume that there are k distinct sampling periods in our study design and that the "treatment" is a naturally occurring distinction. These periods are far enough apart to make it essential that allowances be made for additions (births, immigrants, etc.) and deletions (deaths, emigrants, etc.) between the periods. The models used are based on the Jolly-Seber model for open populations. An alternative approach consists of a design and analysis that incorporates the better features of closed and open models (Lefebvre et al. 1982; Pollock 1982). The unequal catchability could involve inherent heterogeneity of capture probabilities between different animals and trap response, which involves increasing or decreasing probabilities of capture as a result of being marked.

Consider the following representation of a capture-recapture sampling experiment based on Pollock (1982) where there are k primary sampling periods (e.g., years), and within each of these, there are l secondary sampling periods that are close to each other in time (e.g., l consecutive days).

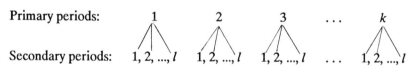

Primary periods: 1   2   3   ... k

Secondary periods: 1, 2, ..., l 1, 2, ..., l 1, 2, ..., l ...   1, 2, ..., l

If there are two treatments as before, the biologist will be interested in the population sizes for each of the primary sampling periods (N_{t1}, ..., N_{tk}, N_{c1}, ..., N_{ck}), assuming that the population is constant over the secondary sampling periods within a primary sampling period. Interest lies in survival probabilities (ϕ_{ti}, ϕ_{ci}, $i = 1$, ..., $k - 1$) and recruitment numbers (B_{ti}, B_{ci}, $i = 1$, ..., $k - 1$) between the primary sampling periods.

Assuming that the population is closed over the secondary sampling periods within a primary period, then two estimation procedures are possible. In the first procedure, all the secondary sampling periods within a primary period would be "pooled" (i.e., one would merely count the animals seen at least once in the primary period). These pooled samples would then be analyzed by the model described in the previous section. Heterogeneity and trap response can have a large effect on the estimators of population size (Cormack 1972; Carothers 1973). We suggest a modified procedure as follows.

(1)   Obtain population size estimators for (N_{ti}, N_{ci}, $i = 1$, ..., k) using closed population models that allow for unequal catchability (Otis et al. 1978; White et al. 1982) and are based only on the captures and recaptures within a primary sampling period.

(2)   Obtain survival rate estimators for (ϕ_{ti}, ϕ_{ci}, i = 1, ..., k - 2) using the "pooled" data and the Jolly-Seber model because survival rates are much less affected by unequal catchability.

(3)   Obtain recruitment number estimators using $\hat{B}_{ti} = \hat{N}_{t,i+1} - \hat{\phi}_{ti}(\hat{N}_{ti} - n_{ti} + R_{ti})$ as before; however, now the population size estimators are the "robust" versions described previously. Note that $\hat{B}_{ti}$ can be obtained for i = 1, ..., k - 2 and that a similar expression is available for $\hat{B}_{ci}$.

This strategy is not applicable when fish are moving downstream or when capture of unmarked animals is ignored.

8.3.2. Testing for Age-Specific Treatment Effects

Pollock (1981a) developed an extension of the Jolly-Seber model for populations with different identifiable age categories (see also Pollock and Mann 1983 for a fisheries example). He allowed the different identifiable age categories to have different survival and capture probabilities, and found explicit maximum likelihood estimators. The estimators take a form similar to those for the Jolly-Seber model. A computer program, JOLLYAGE, is available for these computations from the U.S. Fish and Wildlife Service, Patuxent Wildlife Research Center, Laurel, Maryland 20708, USA (see Brownie et al. 1986).

In our framework of comparing treatments, this model could be useful. It would be informative to examine possible interactions between treatment and age in terms of survival rates. In a toxicology study on birds, for example, young birds dosed with lead shot might be influenced either more or less than adult birds dosed with the same amount of lead shot.

8.4. Other Procedures

8.4.1. Regression Methods

Regression methods have been suggested as an approach to estimating treatment survival under the first and unknown capture history protocols. From the expected values for this protocol (Section 2.2.2), under $H_{1\phi}$, we have

$$E\left(m_{t1i}/R_{t1}\right) = S\, E(m_{c1i}/R_{c1}),$$

where i = 1, 2, ..., k, S = ϕ_{t1}/ϕ_{c1}. This relationship suggests the regression model

$$\frac{m_{t1i}}{R_{t1}} = b\frac{m_{c1i}}{R_{c1}} + \varepsilon_i \, ,$$

leading to the estimation of the slope term $b(= \hat{S})$ by least-squares methods.

The regression approach is poor relative to the ML approach because the main assumptions of simple linear regression are violated. The general problem falls under the title "errors in variables" in the literature (see Wald 1940 and Bartlett 1949 for early investigations of this problem). In the regression model above, the independent variable is not known without error, rather it is an estimated binomial proportion. This approach causes a bias in the estimator of the regression slope (Kendall and Stuart 1967; Snedecor and Cochran 1967; Johnston 1972). The effect of sampling variation in the independent variable is to diminish the estimated slope of the regression line. Thus, the least-squares estimator of the slope (= treatment survival rate) will be biased negatively.

The second problem is more serious in that a high correlation exists between the residuals and the values of the independent variable. Thus, the variance of the ε_i is not constant (see Draper and Smith 1981 for references on the analysis of residuals in regression). In addition, the ε_i are correlated with each other under multinomial sampling. This correlation produces an inconsistent estimator of the slope (Wonnacott and Wonnacott 1970; Neter and Wasserman 1974). Because consistency is perhaps the most fundamental property of an estimator, the lack of consistency in this application of regression makes the procedure undesirable (also see Johnston 1972:278).

The dependent variable is also an estimated binomial proportion and this affects var(ε_i). Thus, the variance in the dependent variable, given the independent variable, will not be constant over dams and violates the final assumption of regression analysis. Therefore, the estimator of the slope lacks the minimum variance property that is usually associated with least squares. A weighted regression might be an improvement if the weights were known, but the issues noted previously are more serious.

In summary, a simple linear regression analysis of the estimated recapture rates produces estimates of the treatment survival rate that are biased, lack the minimum variance property, and are not consistent. Consequently, we do not recommend this procedure; better estimation methods exist.

8.4.2. Release of Dead Fish

In this section we consider the case of a small low-head dam (Olson et al. 1985) where the survival of fish passing a turbine or a spillway is of interest. Conceptually, treatment and control fish are batch-marked and a sample of these fish is captured at a single site, usually close to the dam (e.g., 100 to 300 m downstream), with a single large net or several smaller nets. The intent is to catch only live fish – either control fish or fish that survived passage through the turbine. However, because the nets are so close to the dam, there is concern that some turbine-killed fish might also enter the net. Finally, because the nets are in place for a period of time, it is possible that some fish (either treatment or control) die in the net, and these fish cannot be distinguished from the treatment fish that entered the net dead.

Some authors have tried to separate these confounded data by releasing a number of dead fish (R_d) along with the treatment fish just above the dam (e.g., into the turbine intake or spillway). Of course, the R_t and R_d fish must be otherwise as identical as possible. The recaptures of these dead fish (r_d) are used in an effort to estimate treatment survival. We attempt to present a rationale for this type of experiment and provide an estimator of the treatment survival and its sampling variance. However, some restrictive assumptions are required and the ability to test the validity of these assumptions is largely lacking.

We denote the number of released treatment, control, and dead fish as R_t, R_c, and R_d, respectively, and the numbers of these fish recaptured at the single downstream sampling site as r_t, r_c, and r_d, respectively. However, we use the further subscripts l (live) and d (dead) to denote whether a fish, released alive, was alive or dead when it entered the net. For treatment fish, "alive" upon capture means that the fish was not seriously injured by the turbine, and thus, was not fated to die as a direct result of the turbine. The expectations of these five random variables are

$$E(r_{tl}) = R_t S \phi_{tl} p_{tl} ;$$

$$E(r_{td}) = R_t (1 - S) \phi_{td} p_{td} + R_t S (1 - \phi_t) p_{td} ;$$

$$E(r_{cl}) = R_c \phi_c p_{cl} ;$$

$$E(r_{cd}) = R_c (1 - \phi_c) p_{cd} ;$$

$$E(r_d) = R_d \phi_d p_d .$$

The parameters are conditional capture probabilities (given that a fish reaches the downstream site where the net is), $p_{tl}, p_{td}, p_{cl}, p_{cd}, p_d$; the treatment survival S; and survival probabilities from the tailrace to the site where the net is set, $\phi_t, \phi_c, \phi_{td}, \phi_d$. For fish released dead, ϕ_d is the probability that a carcass reaches the net, whereas ϕ_{td} is the probability that a carcass of a fish killed by the turbine reaches the net.

Although the above equations are not as general as they should be to be conceptually valid, they are already too general in the sense that several restrictive assumptions must be imposed to gain identification of the treatment survival rate S. We must assume that $\phi_{td} = \phi_d$ and that $p_{td} = p_d$; thus, dead fish have the same parameters, whether they were released dead or killed by the turbine. It is also necessary to assume that capture probabilities of live fish are the same for treatment and control fish: $p_{tl} = p_{cl} = p_l$.

Expressions for the expected number of treatment, control, and dead fish netted, given these added assumptions, are

$$E(r_t) = R_t[S\phi_t p_l + (1-S)\phi_d p_d + S(1-\phi_t)p_d] \; ;$$

$$E(r_c) = R_c[\phi_c p_l + (1-\phi_c)p_{cd}] \; ;$$

$$E(r_d) = R_d \phi_d p_d \; .$$

Only if $\phi_t = \phi_c = 1$ will these expressions simplify enough to render S estimable. Hence, we must further assume $\phi_t = \phi_c = 1$, which means no natural mortality between the tailrace and the net. This seems reasonable if the sampling nets are only 100 m downstream. The value of p_{cd} is irrelevant when $\phi_c = 1$. Only the product $\phi_d p_d$ is estimable, which is all that is needed. Hence, without loss of generality, one can set $\phi_d = 1$. The three expectations then become

$$E(r_t) = R_t[Sp_l + (1-S)p_d] \; ;$$

$$E(r_c) = R_c p_l \; ;$$

$$E(r_d) = R_d p_d \; .$$

The moment estimator of S is obtained by solving the above equations, which yield

$$\hat{S} = \frac{(r_t/R_t) - (r_d/R_d)}{(r_c/R_c) - (r_d/R_d)} \; .$$

For the binomial model, the estimator above is the MLE.

The sampling variance of $\hat{S}$ is estimated as

$$\hat{\mathrm{var}}(\hat{S}) = (\hat{S})^2 \left[\frac{\mathrm{var}(A)}{A^2} + \frac{\mathrm{var}(B)}{B^2} - 2\frac{\mathrm{cov}(A, B)}{AB} \right] ,$$

where $A = (r_t/R_t) - (r_d/R_d)$ and $B = (r_c/R_c) - (r_d/R_d)$. For the binomial model, the theoretical sampling variance of $\hat{S}$ is

$$\hat{\mathrm{var}}(\hat{S}) = (\hat{S})^2 \left[\left(\frac{r_t}{AR_t} \right)^2 \left(\frac{1}{r_t} - \frac{1}{R_t} \right) + \left(\frac{r_c}{BR_c} \right)^2 \left(\frac{1}{r_c} - \frac{1}{R_c} \right) \right.$$

$$\left. - 2 \frac{r_d(R_d - r_d)}{(R_d)^3} \left(\frac{1}{A} - \frac{1}{B} \right)^2 \right].$$

If $r_d = 0$ (i.e., no dead fish are recovered), these estimators simplify to those presented in Section 2.2.6.

Few analytical alternatives exist for this particular experiment. Clearly, some strong assumptions must be met for this method to be useful. The use of unique marks adds nothing to the analysis of such experiments. If this procedure is used, replication is needed.

Part 9. Comprehensive Computer Software

The computation of estimates and test statistics using the methods presented in this monograph often is difficult or, at best, tedious. Details on a computer software package are presented herein. Many options are discussed, and several examples are given. The program is easy to use on microcomputers, especially the interactive version.

9.1. Program Capabilities and Options

Program RELEASE is a general program that computes estimates of treatment effect $(\hat{S})$, survival $(\hat{\phi}_{vi})$, and capture $(\hat{p}_{vi})$ probabilities from release-recapture data for one or more groups under one of the four sampling protocols. The program reads a TITLE statement followed by the input of data either as a CH matrix (CHMATRIX) or a reduced m-array (LMREAD). These last two procedures (PROCs) allow a variety of options to be specified. Multiple analyses can be made, and PROC STOP terminates the execution. A semicolon is used as a delimiter at the end of each input statement. These four procedures are given in Table 9.1; more details appear in Table 9.2. The output of RELEASE provides parameter estimates, estimated standard errors, 95% CIs, and the tests given in Tables 2.1 to 2.4 for those appropriate models.

Other procedures (Table 9.1) allow data to be simulated and analyzed (SIMULATE), or contingency table data to be input and analyzed (CHISQ). PROC SIMULATE also has an option for exploring theoretical biases, precision, and test power. Finally, PROC SURVIV generates a data input file for analysis by program SURVIV (White 1983). Program SURVIV allows total flexibility in model building and analysis.

To improve the user's efficiency in using RELEASE, an interactive interface has been provided. The user is requested to select input from menus; this input is then translated into PROC statements and executed to produce the desired output. In addition, a log of the input is produced on an output file for later execution in batch mode. The interactive interface allows users unfamiliar with the program's input syntax to produce useful results.

Program RELEASE is available for IBM-PC microcomputers or equivalent compatibles running the DOS operating system. Microcomputers in this class with at least 512K of random access memory, a hard disk, and an 8087 math coprocessor (80287 for AT) can run RELEASE without alteration. Microcomputers lacking a hard disk can only run RELEASE with a smaller number of capture occasions and treatment groups. The program is written in FORTRAN 77 and is compiled with the Ryan-McFarland FORTRAN compiler.

Program RELEASE can be obtained without charge by writing to

> Dr. Gary C. White
> Department of Fishery and Wildlife Biology
> Colorado State University
> Fort Collins, Colorado 80523 USA.

Requests should include three double-density, double-sided 5.25-inch floppy disks that have been formatted on an IBM-PC compatible microcomputer or, preferably, a 1.2M, 5.25-inch floppy disk formatted on an AT-compatible machine. The FORTRAN 77 source code, executable module, and test data sets from this monograph will be returned.

Table 9.1. – Summary of procedures available in program RELEASE. All input can be either upper or lower case. Some procedures have numerous options.

PROC	Function
TITLE	Title to be used for a particular run.
CHMATRIX	Entry of data as a capture history matrix.
LMREAD	Entry of data as reduced m-arrays.
SIMULATE	Allows Monte Carlo data to be generated and analyzed; also allows some theoretical evaluations.
CHISQ	Allows entry and analysis of an $r \times c$ contingency chi-square table.
SURVIV	Generates input routine for program SURVIV.
STOP	Stops execution; end of job.

Table 9.2. – Detailed summary of command syntax for each of the procedures and their modifiers in program RELEASE. Modifiers enclosed in brackets ([ ]) indicate optional input. Program RELEASE allows comments enclosed between /* and */ symbols, and statements are delineated with semicolons; # means "number". Either upper or lower case characters may be used in the input.

/* COMMENTS can be enclosed in these symbols */
PROC TITLE Any title information to be printed at top of each page; titles
    may be changed later in a data file with a second PROC TITLE;
PROC CHMATRIX OCCASIONS=# of capture-recapture occasions
       GROUPS=# of groups
       [LOTS=# of replicate CH matrices to analyze (default is 1)];
       [UNBIAS (causes bias-corrected estimates of S and ϕ to be printed)]
       [SUMMARY | NODETAIL (either of these keywords reduces
       the amount of output to just a summary of the goodness
       of fit and model selection tests and only the
       $H_{k-1,\phi}, H_{2\phi}, H_{1\phi},$ and H_0 estimates)]
       [FULLM (causes the full m_{ij} array to be printed in the output when $k < 8$)];

/*   PROC CHMATRIX is the primary procedure to enter the capture-recapture histories for each animal. If GROUPS=2, treatment and control animals are entered in that order; if GROUPS>2, the treatment groups are entered, in order, followed by the control group. */

/*   OCCASIONS, GROUPS, and LOTS can be in any order on the PROC statement. Within LOTS, GROUPS must have the same order on the capture history statements. */
    [LOT [=] 1;] /* Only required if LOTS > 1 */

capture_history_1	#_captures_group_1	#_captures_group_2	...;
capture_history_2	#_captures_group_1	#_captures_group_2	...;
.	.	.	...;
.	.	.	...;
.	.	.	...;
capture_history_n	#_captures_group_1	#_captures_group_2	...;

/*   capture_history_i is the string of ones and zeros or dots (.) indicating the capture occasions on which the associated numbers of animals were captured for each group. A dot (.) indicates that the user does not know the capture history sequence (i.e., unknown capture histories), whereas zero (0) indicates that the animals were not captured at this occasion. The number of ones and zeros must match the OCCASIONS= parameter on the PROC statement. Likewise, the number of group entries must match the GROUPS= parameter on the PROC statement. */

Table 9.2. – Continued.

/*   #_captures_group_*i* is the number of animals in group *i* that had capture_history_*i*. A particular
capture_history can be repeated more than once, but the program will produce a warning to notify the user.
Animals lost on capture should be recorded as negative values (i.e., - 5 to indicate 5 animals were lost on capture) on a separate statement from the animals that were released again. Thus the statements, 10100 243 269
and 10100 - 24 - 27, tell the program that 243 treatment animals (group 1) and 269 control animals (group 2)
were captured and released on occasion 3, but 24 treatment and 27 control animals were lost on capture and
not rereleased on occasion 4. None of these animals had been captured on occasion 2, signified by the 0 in
the second position of the capture history string. */

[LOT [=] 2;] /* Required for LOTS > 1, otherwise not needed. */

capture_history_1	#_captures_group_1	#_captures_group_2	...;
capture_history_2	#_captures_group_1	#_captures_group_2	...;
.	.	.	...;
.	.	.	...;
.	.	.	...;
capture_history_n	#_captures_group_1	#_captures_group_2	...;

/*   The CH matrices for each lot, separated by the LOT subcommand, must continue up to the value specified
with the LOTS= parameter on the PROC statement. */

[GLABEL(1) = Identifying label for Group 1
        (default is "Treatment Group");]

        .
        .
        .

[GLABEL(#_groups) = Identifying label for last group
        (default is "Control Group");]

/*   The GLABEL statements may occur before the capture histories, if desired. GLABEL statements occur only
once regardless of the number of lots. */

Table 9.2. – Continued.

PROC LMREAD OCCASIONS=# of capture-recapture occasions

    GROUPS=# of treatment groups

    [LOTS=# of replicate m_{ij} matrices to analyze

    (default is 1)]

    [UNBIAS (causes bias-corrected estimates of S and

    ϕ to be printed)]

    [SUMMARY | NODETAIL (either of these keywords reduces

    the amount of output to just a summary of the goodness

    of fit model selection tests and only the $H_{k-1,\phi}$,

    $H_{2\phi}$, $H_{1\phi}$ and H_0 estimates)]

    [FCH | UCH | SCHEMEB | SCHEMEA (identifies that the

    m_{ij} matrix does not come from a complete capture

    history matrix. FCH or UCH require only the first row of

    m_{ij}, SCHEMEB requires the first two rows, and

    SCHEMEA requires the full m_{ij} matrix.)]

/*   PROC LMREAD is a second procedure for entering capture-recapture data. Not as much information for testing of assumptions is available with this data type as with PROC CHMATRIX; consequently, PROC CHMATRIX is preferred for most applications. The m_{ij} matrix (or matrices) for treatment animals must be entered first, followed by the matrix for control animals. */

[LOT [=] 1;] /* Only required for LOTS > 1 */

R_{t1}	R_{t2}	$\cdots$	R_{tk-1}	;
$m_{t1,2}$	$m_{t1,3}$	$\cdots$	$m_{t1,k}$	;
	$m_{t2,3}$	$\cdots$	$m_{t2,k}$	;
		$\cdot$		;
		$\cdot$		;
		$\cdot$		;
			$m_{tk-1,k}$	;

/*   The first row consists of the numbers of animals released for group 1 in LOT 1. The following k - 1 rows are the entries of the m_{ij} matrix for LOT 1, with rows of the matrix separated by semicolons. Each row after the second has one less entry than the previous row, and the last row has only one entry. */

Table 9.2. – Continued.

$$R_{c1} \qquad R_{c2} \qquad \cdots \qquad R_{ck-1} \qquad ;$$
$$m_{c1,2} \qquad m_{c1,3} \qquad \cdots \qquad m_{c1,k} \qquad ;$$
$$m_{2,3} \qquad \cdots \qquad m_{2,k} \qquad ;$$
$$\cdot \qquad\qquad ;$$
$$\cdot \qquad\qquad ;$$
$$\cdot \qquad\qquad ;$$
$$m_{ck-1,k} \qquad ;$$

/* The above entries are just the R_i vector and the m_{ij} matrix for group 2, LOT 1. This pattern continues for the number of GROUPS specified on the PROC LMREAD statement. */

[LOT [=] 2;] /* Required for LOTS > 1 */

$$R_1 \qquad R_2 \qquad \cdots \qquad R_{k-1} \qquad ;$$
$$m_{1,2} \qquad m_{1,3} \qquad \cdots \qquad m_{1,k} \qquad ;$$
$$m_{2,3} \qquad \cdots \qquad m_{2,k} \qquad ;$$
$$\cdot \qquad\qquad ;$$
$$\cdot \qquad\qquad ;$$
$$\cdot \qquad\qquad ;$$
$$m_{k-1,k} \qquad ;$$

/* The R_i and m_{ij} entries are continued for each group and each lot up to GROUPS= and LOTS= values from the PROC LMREAD statement. */

[GLABEL(1) = Identifying label for Group 1 (default is "Treatment Group");]

-
-
-

[GLABEL(#_groups) = Identifying label for last group (default is "Control Group");]

/* The GLABEL statements may occur before the capture data, if desired. */

PROC SIMULATE [NSIM = # of replications of each simulation (default is 5)]
    OCCASIONS=# of capture-recapture occasions
    [GROUPS=# of treatment groups, including the control group
    (default is 2)]
    [DETAIL (print details of each simulation,
    with default of only simulation summaries)]
    [SUMMARY (print a summary of each simulation with default
    of only simulation summaries)]
    [REMOVAL|FCH (causes first capture history only data to

Table 9.2. – Continued.

---

    be simulated; recaptures are removed from the population)]
[SCHEMEB (causes scheme B capture history data to be simulated]
[SCHEMEA (causes scheme A capture history data to be simulated]
[UCH (causes unknown capture history data to be simulated)]
[SEED = random number seed (default is 7654321)]
[SFILE = file name to receive estimates of $\hat{S}$ and
standard errors from simulated data for later analysis
(default is no data output)]
[PFILE = file name to receive estimates of $\hat{p}$ and
standard errors from simulated data for later analysis
(default is no data output)]
[PHIFILE = file name to receive estimates of $\hat{\phi}$ and
standard errors from simulated data for later analysis
(default is no data output)]
[UNBIAS (causes bias-corrected estimates of S and ϕ to be computed)]
[EXPECT (generates expected data values and computes estimates
and test statistics as described in Chapter 3.6);]

/*   FCH, SCHEMEB, SCHEMEA, and UCH options are mutually exclusive. If none of these options are specified, complete capture history data are simulated. */
[SUBPOPULATION [=] i [WEIGHT = weight];]

/*   The SUBPOPULATION statement is needed if more than one set of parameters is to be used to simulate subpopulations. The WEIGHT parameter specifies the relative weighting of each of the subpopulations so that a weighted mean over subpopulations for each parameter can be calculated to determine confidence interval coverage. */

    PHI(1)=survival_prob_group_1 [survival_prob_group_2 $\cdots$];
    PHI(2)=survival_prob_group_1 [survival_prob_group_2 $\cdots$];

      .
      .
      .

    PHI(k - 1)=survival_prob_group_1 [survival_prob_group_2 $\cdots$];

/*   Only k - 1 ϕ values are required, different ϕ_{si} values by group are optional. If only one value of ϕ_i is provided on a given line, this same value is used for the remaining groups. The parameter ϕ is a simple probability with a value in the interval 0,1. To simulate heterogeneity of survival rates, a beta probability density function can be specified as beta $(\alpha, \beta, \text{lower\_bound, upper\_bound})$, where the lower_bound must be $\leq$ upper_bound, and both are in the interval 0,1. Alternatively, subpopulations can be defined with different parameters to allow the study of heterogeneity. */

Table 9.2. – Continued.

P(2)=capture_prob_group_1 [capture_prob_group_2] $\cdots$;
P(3)=capture_prob_group_1 [capture_prob_group_2] $\cdots$;
.
.
.
P(k)=capture_prob_group_1 [capture_prob_group_2] $\cdots$;

/* Only k-1 p values are required; there may be different values for each group. If only one value is provided per line, the remaining groups use this same value. The parameter p is a simple probability with a value in the interval 0,1. To simulate heterogeneity of capture probabilities, a beta probability density function can be specified as beta (α, β, lower_bound, upper_bound), where the lower_bound must be $\leq$ upper_bound, and both are in the interval 0,1. */

R[(1)]=#_releases_group_1 [#_releases_group_2] $\cdots$;
[R(2)=#_releases_group_1 [#_releases_group_2] $\cdots$;]
.
.
.
[R(k - 1)=#_releases_group_1 [#_releases_group_2] $\cdots$;]

/* Only R(1) is required for each group, as new animals must be released only on occasion 1. If new animals are released only at time 1, R = is allowed, with the occasion defaulting to 1. For multiple releases, the release identifier must be included in the specification. If a value for only group 1 is provided, the remaining groups are assumed to have the same value. */

[SUBPOPULATION [2] [WEIGHT = weight];]

*/ The SUBPOPULATION statement is required if more than one set of parameters is to be used to simulate subpopulations. */

/* The entire set of PHI, P, and R specifications can be repeated for additional subpopulations. */

PROC CHISQ [POOL (causes pooling of cells to achieve larger expected values)];

$$
\begin{array}{cccc}
n_{1,1} & n_{1,2} & \cdots & n_{1,ncols}; \\
n_{2,1} & n_{2,2} & \cdots & n_{2,ncols}; \\
\cdot & \cdot & & \cdot \\
\cdot & \cdot & & \cdot \\
\cdot & \cdot & & \cdot \\
n_{nrows,1} & n_{nrows,2} & \cdots & n_{nrows,ncols};
\end{array}
$$

Table 9.2. – Continued.

/* The program prints the $r \times c$ contingency table, expected values, and standardized residual values. The POOL option only operates on cells with expected values less than 2. A total chi-square value is printed with the proper degrees of freedom and the significance level. For 2×2 tables with small expected values (<5), Fisher's exact test is also computed and printed. */

PROC SURVIV [CONSTRAIN (constrain estimates to 0,1 interval,
     default is unconstrained estimation)]
     [DETAIL (print details of RELEASE input estimates to SURVIV,
     with default of no output)]
     [SUMMARY (print summary of RELEASE input estimates to SURVIV,
     with default of no output)]
     [PARFILE = file name to receive SURVIVE input
     (default name is SURVIN)];

/* PROC SURVIV generates input to program SURVIV so that numerical maximum likelihood methods can be used to estimate parameters and test assumptions for models not provided in RELEASE. Either LMREAD or CHMATRIX must have been previously executed to provide a starting model. */

PROC STOP /* Stops execution. */;

9.1.1. Input of Information

Two general procedures are available to input the release and recapture data to program RELEASE. First, PROC CHMATRIX allows the CH matrix to be entered for each lot. The full input stream for the example used in Chapter 2.4 for the complete capture history protocol is shown in Table 9.3. Use of the CH matrix allows full testing of model assumptions for the complete capture history protocol. As a second input format, the reduced m-array can be read with PROC LMREAD, thus allowing the user to input a summary of the data. Table 9.4 provides an example of the LMREAD procedure for the same data as those used in Chapter 2.4 and Table 9.3. PROC LMREAD (or proc lmread, as either upper or lower case is permissible) does not allow TEST 3 to be computed for the complete capture history protocol. In general, most users will want to input their sample data by using PROC CHMATRIX because this method allows the most complete analysis.

At least one space is needed to separate the capture histories in the PROC CHMATRIX input from the numbers of animals with this particular history. Extra spaces can be added. Each command (usually a line) must end with a semicolon. The right-justified align-ment, as shown in Table 9.3, is recommended for ease in checking for errors. No special line continuation character is needed because the program is searching for a semicolon to indicate the end of a statement. Note that the numbers of animals lost on capture are coded as nega-tive values; this convention prevents the numbers of animals that are removed from being included with the numbers released. Each animal only appears in one row (i.e., capture his-tory). A minus sign indicates that the animal is not to be included in the new releases; it does not indicate that these animals should be subtracted from a previous frequency.

Two additional options are available for the LMREAD and CHMATRIX procedures. UNBIAS generates bias-corrected estimates of ϕ_i and S (Chapter 3.4) instead of MLEs. SUMMARY or its synonym, NODETAIL, reduces the amount of output produced. Only summaries of the goodness of fit and model selection tests are printed, and the estimates of only models $H_{k-1,\phi}$, H_{2p}, $H_{1\phi}$, and H_0 are printed.

Table 9.3. – Input to program RELEASE for the example from Chapter 2.4, when PROC CHMATRIX is used to enter the capture history for animals in each group. Capture frequencies for treatment animals are in the middle column and those for control animals in the last column.

```
proc title Example from Chapter 2.4;
proc chmatrix occasions=6 groups=2;
/* If GLABELs are not used, the final column
   is assumed to be the control group */
        100000          25925   24605;
        100001            563     605;
        100001            -27     -36;
        100010            508     522;
        100010            -23     -25;
        100011             17      23;
        100011             -1      -1;
        100100           1500    1678;
        100100            -81     -57;
        100101             45      48;
        100101             -3      -1;
        100110             37      44;
        100110             -2      -2;
        100111              1       2;
        101000            193     207;
        101000            -14     -10;
        101001              5       9;
        101010              7       4;
        101100             16      14;
```

Table 9.3. – Continued.

101100	-1	-1;
101101	1	1;
101110	1	1;
110000	872	935;
110000	-29	-33;
110001	26	28;
110001	-1	-1;
110010	16	18;
110010	-1	-1;
110100	67	68;
110100	-3	-4;
110101	1	2;
110110	2	1;
111000	10	12;
111001	0	1;
111100	1	0;

```
glabel (1) = Treatment group;
glabel (2) = Control group;
proc stop;
```

The GLABEL statements (Tables 9.3 and 9.4) demonstrate the default labels if identifying labels for each group are not specified by the user. If three or more groups are being analyzed, the default labels for treatment groups are "Treatment Group 1," "Treatment Group 2," etc.; the final group is still considered the control group. The control group should always be the last group because it will then be the denominator in the estimates of $\hat{S} = \hat{\phi}_{t1}/\hat{\phi}_{c1}$. GLABEL statements do not change the ordering of treatments in calculating $\hat{S}$. The GLABEL statements may either occur at the beginning or end of input for the CHMATRIX and LMREAD procedures. For clarity with the LMREAD procedure, the GLABEL statements can be immediately before the m_{ij} matrix entries, as shown in Table 9.4.

Four mutually exclusive parameters are also allowed for the LMREAD procedures:

FCH	indicates m_{ij} values are from a first capture history protocol;
UCH	indicates m_{ij} values are from an unknown capture history protocol;
SCHEMEB	indicates m_{ij} values are from scheme B of the partial capture history protocol; and
SCHEMEA	indicates m_{ij} values are from scheme A of the partial capture history protocol.

No option is needed if data are collected under a complete capture history protocol.

For first capture history and unknown capture history data, only the first row of the m_{ij} matrix is needed, as that is all that is observed. For SCHEMEB data, only the first two rows are needed. The method of entering SCHEMEA data is the same as that for complete capture history data.

The capture histories for PROC CHMATRIX are normally specified as a string of zeros and ones (no embedded blanks) to specify animals that are not (0) and are (1) captured. To specify unknown capture history data, zeros are replaced with dots (.) to indicate that the user does not know actual capture histories.

Table 9.4. – Input to program RELEASE for the example from Chapter 2.4 in which PROC LMREAD is used to enter the reduced m-array for each group. Data from the treatment group are entered first, followed by the data from the control group.

```
proc title Example from Chapter 2.4;
proc lmread occasions=6 groups=2;
/* Treatment group */
glabel(1)=Treatment group;

30000    1000     235    1677     590   ;
 1029     238    1669     549     590   ;
           11      73      17      27   ;
                   20       7       5   ;
                           43      50   ;
                                   19   ;

/* Control group */
glabel(2) = Control group;

29000    1071     250    1862     616   ;
 1104     247    1832     571     641   ;
           13      75      19      29   ;
                   17       4      10   ;
                           50      52   ;
                                   26   ;

proc stop;
```

PROC STOP is used to exit the program and is provided to stop execution in a data file when additional data follow but the user does not desire to run through the program. This feature allows data sets to be "saved" by moving them to the end of the input file, below the PROC STOP statement. PROC STOP allows the stacking of multiple data sets in an input file, but runs only the first data sets. PROC STOP is not required at the end of the input file; the end of a file will cause RELEASE to end execution.

9.1.2. Program Output

All input instructions read by program RELEASE are echoed in the output with the identifying INPUT--- to delineate them. The user should check this information carefully to be certain that the input is correct. PROC CHMATRIX provides a summary of the data in reduced m-arrays for each group. Again, careful checking is recommended at this point to guard against data entry errors. For $k < 8$, PROC CHMATRIX will print the full m-array if the FULLM option is specified.

Program RELEASE then computes the parameter estimates, standard errors, and confidence intervals for each appropriate model. All the within- and between-group test statistics are printed with the associated degrees of freedom and significance levels. Tests are labeled as in Tables 2.1-2.4. Examples of the output of RELEASE are shown throughout Part 2.

9.1.3. Monte Carlo Simulator

PROC SIMULATE can be used to generate Monte Carlo data for any of the four sampling protocols. Particular models within a specific protocol are specified by the user's assignment of appropriate parameter values. The details of SIMULATE are given in Table 9.2. Table 9.5 provides an example where 1,000 data sets are to be generated under model $H_{1\phi}$ of the complete capture history protocol, with 10,000 marked animals initially released in each group. In the example, $S = \phi_{t1}/\phi_{c1} = 0.8/0.9 = 0.889$. Because other parameters are equal across groups, only one numerical value is necessary for each line (e.g., $p(4) = 0.1$ would serve for both treatment and control groups). Program RELEASE provides a detailed summary of the Monte Carlo study, including estimated expected values of the estimators under various models, empirical estimates of sampling variance, and performance of various tests. In the example in Table 9.5, one could estimate the power of the test of model H_0 versus model $H_{1\phi}$, among other things. The results of a simple model selection algorithm are printed at the end of a simulation run. The algorithm selects a model when the P value for a test is less than the α level. Computer time for 1,000 repetitions with two groups would take several hours on an IBM-PC/AT.

Table 9.5. – Example input to program RELEASE to simulate an experiment where the only difference in survival between two groups of animals is in $\phi_{i1} \neq \phi_{c1}$. Model $H_{1\phi}$ is shown with 1,000 repetitions requested (i.e., nsim = 1000).

```
proc title Simulation of model H1PHI with complete capture history protocol;
proc simulate nsim=1000 occasions=5 groups=2 seed=4567655;
        phi(1)=0.8 0.9;
        phi(2)=0.9 0.9;
        phi(3)=0.9 0.9;
        phi(4)=0.9 0.9;
        p(2)=0.1 0.1;
        p(3)=0.1 0.1;
        p(4)=0.1 0.1;
        p(5)=0.1 0.1;
        R=10000 10000;
proc stop;
```

The DETAIL specification on PROC SIMULATE causes detailed output from each of the simulations. Thus, parameter estimates for each model and χ^2 goodness of fit tables are all printed. If the number of simulations performed is large, printed output will be large. Thus, DETAIL should only be used with NSIM $\leq$ 10. The SUMMARY specification causes a less detailed printout of each simulation. Only a summary of the χ^2 goodness of fit tables is printed. Likewise, only a summary of the tests for differences between groups is printed. Finally, estimates from only the most complex model $(H_{k-1,\phi})$ and the three simplest models $(H_{2p}, H_{1\phi},$ and $H_0)$ are printed. For data sets with a large number of occasions or a large number of groups, the SUMMARY option saves a great deal of space in the output. However, as with the DETAIL option, only a small number of simulations should be performed while this option is set.

The SIMULATE procedure also supports the UNBIAS parameter specification, allowing simulation of estimates that have been bias-corrected. The default is to provide MLEs, which are asymptotically unbiased but may exhibit small sample bias (Section 3.4).

Three parameters on PROC SIMULATE are used to name output files to receive the estimates and associated standard errors for each of the parameters estimated under each of the models. SFILE specifies a file to receive the estimates of S and $se(\hat{S})$, with PFILE and PHIFILE providing the same capabilities for p and ϕ, respectively. These files might be used as input to a statistical package to perform a more thorough analysis of the simulations than the summary printed by PROC SIMULATE (e.g., to examine the distribution of estimators such as $\hat{S}$). The columns of the file specified with the SFILE parameter are

Column	Information
1	iteration number (1,2, ..., NSIM)
2	model name
3	group number of numerator
4	group number of denominator
5	occasion
6	$\hat{S}$
7	$se(\hat{S})$

The columns of the files specified with the PFILE and PHIFILE parameters are

Column	Information
1	iteration number (1,2, ..., NSIM)
2	model name
3	group number
4	occasion
5	$\hat{p}$ or $\hat{\phi}$ depending on the file
6	$se(\hat{p})$ or $se(\hat{\phi})$ depending on the file

Values of estimates that were not identifiable were written to these files as missing values, signified by a single period (.).

A random number seed to simulate data with PROC SIMULATE is provided in the SEED = value specification. Generally the seed should be a 5- or 7-digit, odd random integer. Specifying the same seed for two PROC SIMULATEs generates identical data (on a given computer) if the same model and parameters are used.

A final option to SIMULATE, EXPECT, can be used to generate the expected values of the capture histories. These expected data values are then used to compute the various tests and estimators. A limitation of the EXPECT option is that the expected capture history frequencies are only precise to the nearest integer. Thus, rounding errors can be large. One approach to circumventing this limitation is to make the number of animals released large, i.e., R_{v1} large.

The subcommands for PROC SIMULATE specify the true parameter values to be simulated for ϕ, p, and the numbers of animals released, as shown in Table 9.2. Normally the parameters ϕ and p are simple probabilities. However, if a more realistic experiment is to be simulated, each animal can be given a unique value for ϕ_i and p_i by generating the value of ϕ or p from a beta probability density function. If BETA (α, β, lower_bound, upper_bound) is specified in place of a simple probability, the parameter is generated from a beta probability density function with parameters α and β and then scaled to the interval (lower_bound, upper_bound). Examples of the many possible shapes of the beta distribution for a range of αs and βs are shown in Figure 9.1. Note that only ϕ and p can be specified as beta random variables. The initial releases (R_{vi}) must be fixed, not random, variables.

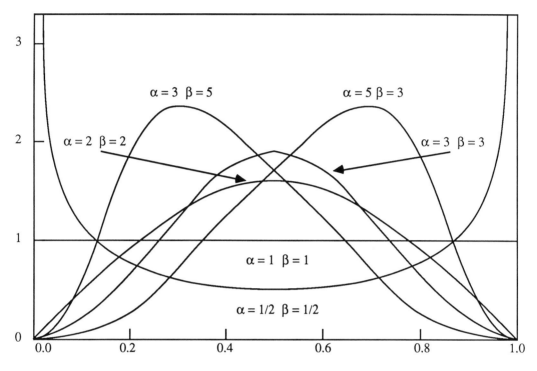

Figure 9.1. – Examples of the beta distribution for various values of α and β.

The beta probability density function allows one way to simulate the heterogeneity of population parameters. Only variability within a single population is assumed. Often, however, the biological population to be studied is thought to consist of two or more subpopulations. PROC SIMULATE allows such a multifaceted population to be simulated through the use of the SUBPOPULATION statement (as another way to simulate heterogeneity). Each SUBPOPULATION statement tells SIMULATE to set up another subpopulation with its own unique parameter values (which may include beta distributions).

The SUBPOPULATION statement also has the optional parameter WEIGHT, which may be specified to provide the weight of this particular subpopulation relative to the others being simulated. These weights are needed to calculate the average of each parameter over all subpopulations. For example, if subpopulation 1 is thought to occur one-half as often as subpopulation 2, the weights for 1 and 2 might be WEIGHT = 1 and WEIGHT = 2 or WEIGHT = 0.5 and WEIGHT = 1, both of which indicate that subpopulation 2 is to be weighted twice as heavily as subpopulation 1. If weights are not specified in the SUBPOPULATION statements, the default for each subpopulation is 1.0.

Normally, the weight of each subpopulation would be proportional to the R_i values. The average across subpopulations would then approximate the population mean. However, because the capture probabilities may vary by subpopulation, the R_i values may not always provide the relative weight of the subpopulation. The WEIGHT specification provides a completely general approach to providing the relative weights for each subpopulation, from which the true population parameter values are determined.

A second example is a Monte Carlo study of model H_{2p} under scheme B over four occasions with a treatment and control group (Table 9.6). The output of program RELEASE is shown in Table 9.7. Material in Part 5 was generated by using PROC SIMULATE.

Table 9.6. – Example input to program RELEASE that simulates an experiment under model H_{2p} when the scheme B sampling protocol is used.

```
proc title Simulation of H2p under schemeB;
proc simulate nsim=1000 occasions=4 groups=2 schemeB;
  phi(1)=0.56 0.8;
  phi(2)=0.8;
  phi(3)=0.7;
  p(2)=0.3 0.2;
  p(3)=0.2;
  p(4)=0.2;
  R=2000 2000;
  proc stop;
```

Table 9.7. – Output of program RELEASE for the input given in Table 9.6.

Simulation of H2p under schemeB

Simulation Results

Model	Group	Parameter	Mean	Standard Deviation	95% CI Lower	95% CI Upper	Cover	n
H2Phi	1	Phi(1)	0.565253	0.047447	0.562312	0.568193	0.947	1000
		SE Phi(1)	0.046768	0.007197	0.046322	0.047214		
		p(2)	0.299061	0.027234	0.297373	0.300749	0.952	1000
		SE p(2)	0.027368	0.001031	0.027304	0.027431		
	2	Phi(1)	0.806544	0.074056	0.801954	0.811134	0.946	1000
		SE Phi(1)	0.071395	0.011812	0.070663	0.072127		

Table 9.7. – Continued.

		p(2)	0.200008	0.020675	0.198726	0.201289	0.951	1000
		SE p(2)	0.019991	0.000888	0.019936	0.020046		
	All	S(1,2)	0.706586	0.086604	0.701218	0.711954	0.944	1000
		SE S(1,2)	0.085198	0.011021	0.084515	0.085881		
H2p	1	Phi(1)	0.562724	0.038212	0.560355	0.565092	0.943	1000
		SE Phi(1)	0.038045	0.003950	0.037800	0.038290		
		p(2)	0.299681	0.022966	0.298258	0.301105	0.954	1000
		SE p(2)	0.023620	0.001043	0.023556	0.023685		
	2	Phi(1)	0.804295	0.057696	0.800719	0.807871	0.941	1000
		SE Phi(1)	0.054673	0.006154	0.054291	0.055054		
		p(2)	0.199920	0.017275	0.198849	0.200990	0.938	1000
		SE p(2)	0.016648	0.000858	0.016595	0.016701		
	All	S(1,2)	0.701283	0.045117	0.698487	0.704080	0.946	1000
		SE S(1,2)	0.044108	0.002670	0.043943	0.044274		
H1Phi	1	Phi(1)	0.620578	0.041482	0.618007	0.623149	0.735	1000
		SE Phi(1)	0.041288	0.004313	0.041020	0.041555		
		p(2)	0.240779	0.016320	0.239768	0.241791	0.058	1000
		SE p(2)	0.016403	0.000456	0.016375	0.016431		
	2	Phi(1)	0.746440	0.050344	0.743320	0.749560	0.735	1000
		SE Phi(1)	0.047853	0.005220	0.047529	0.048176		
		p(2)	0.240779	0.016320	0.239768	0.241791	0.294	1000
		SE p(2)	0.016403	0.000456	0.016375	0.016431		
	All	S(1,2)	0.832419	0.040765	0.829892	0.834945	0.077	1000
		SE S(1,2)	0.041181	0.002024	0.041056	0.041307		
H0	1	Phi(1)	0.683509	0.042774	0.680858	0.686160	0.093	1000
		SE Phi(1)	0.041285	0.004661	0.040997	0.041574		
		p(2)	0.240779	0.016320	0.239768	0.241791	0.058	1000
		SE p(2)	0.016403	0.000456	0.016375	0.016431		
	2	Phi(1)	0.683509	0.042774	0.680858	0.686160	0.230	1000
		SE Phi(1)	0.041285	0.004661	0.040997	0.041574		
		p(2)	0.240779	0.016320	0.239768	0.241791	0.294	1000
		SE p(2)	0.016403	0.000456	0.016375	0.016431		

Table 9.7. – Continued.

Power of Tests

Test	<0.01	<0.05	<0.10	<0.20	<0.50
TEST 1.T3	0.016	0.063	0.115	0.223	0.534
TEST 1.R2	0.010	0.048	0.100	0.210	0.527
TEST 1.T2	0.976	0.993	0.997	0.998	1.000
TEST 1.R1	0.882	0.964	0.987	0.995	1.000
TEST 1	0.992	1.000	1.000	1.000	1.000

Model Selection Results

Type I Error Level for Individual Tests

Model	0.01	0.05	0.10	0.20	0.30
H3p	0.016	0.063	0.115	0.223	0.333
H2Phi	0.010	0.044	0.089	0.163	0.209
H2p	0.950	0.886	0.793	0.613	0.458
H1Phi	0.022	0.007	0.003	0.001	0.000
H0	0.002	0.000	0.000	0.000	0.000

The final example deals with the simulation of populations exhibiting heterogeneity. A beta distribution is used to mimic individual heterogeneity in survival or capture processes, or (as in Table 9.8) two subpopulations are used, each with different parameters but weighted equally because the default weights are 1.0 for each subpopulation. For example, for ϕ_{11}, treatment group 1 has values of 0.85 (200 animals) and 0.75 (200 animals), whereas treatment group 2 has values of 0.95 (200 animals) and 0.85 (200 animals). The Monte Carlo results in Part 5 for heterogeneity were generated by using the subpopulation approach.

Table 9.8. – Example input to program RELEASE to simulate an experiment under model $H_{1\phi}$ with heterogeneity between two subpopulations. Here, heterogeneity affects both the survival and capture probabilities.

```
proc title model H1PHI for complete capture history data;
proc simulate seed=1923949 nsim=1000 occasions=5 groups=2;
subpopulation 1;
     phi(1)=.85 .95;
     phi(2)=.95 .95;
     phi(3)=.95 .95;
     phi(4)=.95 .95;
     p(2)=.9;
     p(3)=.9;
     p(4)=.9;
     p(5)=.9;
     R=200 200;
subpopulation 2;
     phi(1)=.75 .85;
     phi(2)=.85 .85;
     phi(3)=.85 .85;
     phi(4)=.85 .85;
     p(2)=.7;
     p(3)=.7;
     p(4)=.7;
     p(5)=.7;
     R=200 200;
     proc stop;
```

9.2. Examples

In this section, we present two examples of the input stream for program RELEASE, using material given earlier. Table 9.9 provides the RELEASE input for the example in Chapter 2.5, and Table 9.10 provides the input for the starling example discussed in Chapter 7.4.

Table 9.9. – Input for the example given in Chapter 2.5 for the partial capture history protocol under scheme A. Input procedures for the CH matrix (top) and *m*-array (bottom) are illustrated. Output from program RELEASE can be seen in Chapter 2.5.

```
proc title Example from Chapter 2.5, scheme A, using CHMATRIX;
proc chmatrix occasions=6, groups=2;
/* Frequencies for the treatment group are entered first, following the
   capture histories */

     100000    25925    24605;
     100001      563      605;
     100001      -27      -36;
     100010      508      522;
     100010      -23      -25;
     100011      -18      -24;
     100100     1500     1678;
     100100      -81      -57;
     100101      -48      -49;
     100110      -40      -48;
     101000      193      207;
     101000      -14      -10;
     101001       -5       -9;
     101010       -7       -4;
     101100      -19      -17;
     110000      872      935;
     110000      -29      -33;
     110001      -27      -29;
     110010      -17      -19;
     110100      -73      -75;
     111000      -11      -13;

  proc stop;


  proc title Example from Chapter 2.5, scheme A, using LMREAD;
  proc lmread schemeA occasions=6 groups=2;

 30000    1000     224    1588     526;
  1029     238    1669     549     590;
            11      73      17      27;
                    19       7       5;
                            40      48;
                                    18;
```

Table 9.9. – Continued.

29000	1071	237	1775	546;
1104	247	1832	571	641;
	13	75	19	29;
		17	4	9;
			48	49;
				24;

```
proc stop;
```

Table 9.10. – Input stream for the starling data used in Chapter 7 (Stromborg et al., in press). The reduced *m*-array is read with PROC LMREAD; selected output is given in Chapter 7.4.

```
proc title Dosing study of starlings;
proc lmread occasions=6 groups=2;
```

```
    /* Treatment group */
```

60	24	28	34	32;
24	6	9	2	0;
	22	1	0	0;
		24	0	0;
			30	0;
				21;

```
    /* Control group */
```

61	22	31	40	35;
22	13	9	2	0;
	18	1	0	0;
		30	0	0;
			33	1;
				28;

```
proc stop;
```

9.3. Interface with Program SURVIV

PROC SURVIV is used to generate input to program SURVIV (White 1983) so that more general models can be used. Program SURVIV allows more flexibility in the construction of tests and estimates from the data; however, it also requires a better understanding of the statistical methods being used. Thus, we do not recommend program SURVIV for the casual user.

Either the CHMATRIX or LMREAD procedures must have been used to enter a set of capture-recapture data into program RELEASE. These data are then used by RELEASE to construct the input for SURVIV. The PARFILE parameter specifies the file for the SURVIV input, with the default being SURVIN.

An important option on the PROC SURVIV statement is CONSTRAIN, which sets up the SURVIV run with constrained parameter estimation of the ϕs and ps – i.e., the parameter estimates are constrained to the interval (0,1). The estimates of ϕ_{vi} computed by program RELEASE are not constrained, and occasionally exceed 1.0, meaning that the estimate is outside the range of admissible parameter values. The DETAIL and SUMMARY options specify that the output produced by the parameter process should be listed in the output file. DETAIL produces full output as would the LMREAD or CHMATRIX procedures. SUMMARY produces limited output corresponding to the SUMMARY option of LMREAD or CHMATRIX. The default is to produce no output from PROC SURVIV, the only item of interest being the input file to program SURVIV.

9.4. Executing RELEASE

Program RELEASE can be executed in two different modes: interactive and batch. Running RELEASE without additional parameters places the program in the interactive mode; all output scrolls across the screen and is not saved to a file. In the interactive mode, the user is queried for input from the screen. Numerous menus provide input to each of the procedures in Table 9.2. Based on the user's responses, RELEASE maintains a log of the input statements produced from the interactive session. This log is initially placed on the file RELEAS00.INP, but successive executions of RELEASE produce sequentially numbered files. Thus, if the file RELEAS00.INP already exists, the log file would be placed in RELEAS01.INP.

Output from program RELEASE can be saved to a file by using the O=filename parameter on the execution line. By specifying O=XYZ on the execution line, output from RELEASE is placed in file XYZ. Using the O parameter causes no output to be produced on the screen.

RELEASE is placed in batch mode by specifying I=filename on the execution line. The I parameter specifies an input file for the run, thus telling RELEASE to read this file rather than query the user for input. The command

RELEASE I=TEST.DAT O=TEST.OUT

specifies that the file TEST.DAT is to be read to obtain input, and output is to be placed in the file TEST.OUT. If an input file is not specified, RELEASE is put into the interactive mode. If an output file is specified, but no input file specified, the user is queried for input through the interactive mode, but output is saved to the output file and not printed on the screen. Typically, a user would use the interactive mode to build an input file through the log mechanism, verifying the output as it was scrolled across the screen. Once the appropriate commands are found to work, the log file created would be executed in batch mode to produce an output file for printing. An editor could be used to modify the log file, if necessary, before RELEASE is run in the batch mode to produce an output file.

Besides the I and O parameters on the execution line, two additional parameters can be specified. NOECHO causes the input lines to be omitted in the output. Although this option saves some paper when the output is printed, it is not advised because of the difficulty in locating errors in the input. LINES = # specifies the number of output lines to print per page; the default is LINES = 60.

9.5. Programming Details

Program RELEASE has about 8,000 lines of FORTRAN code in 78 subroutines. RELEASE is easy to use on a microcomputer. It can be modified for use on mainframe computers or microcomputers that are not IBM-compatible if a FORTRAN 77 compiler is available and the interactive interface is removed. Program RELEASE is provided on three 5.25-inch double-sided, double-density floppy disks. Five files are present on the first disk: RELEASE.EQE is the executable code in compressed form; RELEASE.DAT is example input, including many of the examples shown in this monograph; INSTALL.BAT installs RELEASE on a hard disk as RELEASE.EXE, and UNSQ.COM and SQPC.COM are public domain utilities to compress and uncompress files. The install command provided on the disk uses UNSQ.COM to uncompress RELEASE.EQE into RELEASE.EXE on the hard disk. RELEASE.EXE requires 425k of disk space, and is dimensioned for 15 capture occasions, 3 groups, and up to 512 different capture histories. The second disk contains the source code for RELEASE, and all but one of the necessary files to construct a new version of the code. The third disk contains a RMFORT-compatible library necessary to construct a new version of RELEASE and USERMAN.DOC, a printable copy of this part of the monograph plus updates to the documentation.

9.5.1. Source Code

The source code for program RELEASE is available to users as described above. For the IBM-PC, the code (consisting of 84 files) is distributed on a 360K diskette. The main program is in the file RELEASE.FOR. All subroutines are in the files *.F. Six files containing common blocks are INCLUDE files: HEADST (containing pagination headings), STATUS (containing I/O units and variables controlling input), MODELC (containing variables pertaining to data), ESTCOM (containing variables pertaining to estimates), SIMCOM (containing variables pertaining to simulations), and SCREEN (containing variables pertaining to the interactive interface). Each of these six files includes comments describing each of the variables in the associated common blocks. The file MAKEFILE is provided as input to MAKE.EXE (also supplied) to compile and link these routines. The file LINKREL.INP provides input to the LINK command. The Ryan-McFarland Fortran (or IBM Professional Fortran) compiler must be used to maintain compatibility with the object library provided.

Program RELEASE has been designed to be easy to change by experienced FORTRAN programmers. The most likely change will involve the dimension limitations for the numbers of treatment groups and capture occasions. These limits are set in common blocks through PARAMETER statements. The number of occasions is controlled by the parameter MAXOCC set in the INCLUDE file MODELC. Several other parameters that depend on MAXOCC are also set in MODELC, as described by comment statements. Likewise, the parameter MAXGRP is set on MODELC to define the maximum number of treatment groups. Again, additional parameters that depend on MAXGRP are described in comment statements. If MAXGRP or MAXOCC are changed in the file MODELC, all the routines that include this file must be recompiled. This may be done with the MAKE utility, which will generate a new RELEASE.EXE file. Many variables, including I/O unit numbers, are set in the main program. These defaults can be changed by recompiling RELEASE.FOR and relinking the code by using MAKE.

Summary

Statistical theory is presented to form the foundation for the analysis of survival experiments that rely on recapture or resighting data collected after the release of marked individuals. Survival experiments consist of at least one treatment and one control group, animals being marked to reflect group membership, with the purpose of comparing survival across treatment levels. Ideally, proper replication is included in the design of the survival experiment. Numerous alternative models are presented as a basis for robust analysis of the experimental results.

For completeness, an introduction to some basic statistical principles is included in the beginning material. This introduction is followed by development of theory specific to the type of data considered. Theory is provided for experiments where either batch or unique marks are used. The theory is based on a series of nested multinomial models (i.e., models H_0, $H_{1\phi}$, H_{2p}, $H_{2\phi}$, ..., $H_{k-1,\phi}$) for V groups, sampled over k occasions. Five experimental protocols are defined and maximum likelihood estimates of parameters are derived for each model in the sequence under each experimental protocol. Estimators of theoretical sampling variances and covariances are provided as measures of precision and coassociation, respectively, for all parameter estimators. Some empirical estimators of variances are also provided. An intensive battery of statistical tests of hypotheses are given to allow assessment of the validity of assumptions and to aid in model selection.

The importance of some form of replication is emphasized. Several analysis methods for multiple lots are given, including quasi-likelihood approaches. The design of experiments where marked animals are used is covered in some detail.

Material presented in several parts of the monograph is cast in terms of fish survival experiments in relation to hydroelectric dams. Although such experiments provide a convenient example, the theory and methods presented have potential application to many other taxonomic groups and experimental situations. The methodology presented provides a rigorous, comprehensive, and practical reference on the analysis of experiments involving recapture of marked animals. The emphasis is on general inference procedures: point and interval estimates and tests of hypotheses.

The methodology presented is relatively sophisticated and the computational requirements are large. Therefore, we provide comprehensive computer software (RELEASE) to allow a full analysis of experimental data collected under these protocols. RELEASE has a Monte Carlo simulation capability and several other options to allow an investigator to understand better the design and analysis methods for this large class of experiments. An interactive version of RELEASE is easy to use on currently available microcomputers.

The material is written for both biologists and statisticians in an effort to integrate theory and application. A team effort is needed for the effective conduct of large experiments. The design and analysis of large, complex survival experiments involving the replication of several treatments is now possible. Such experiments must involve expertise in several disciplines, and we recommend inclusion of a statistician on the team.

We believe a solid foundation is provided herein for making inference from survival experiments using marked animals. Many extensions and special cases can be developed and explored. Some new directions are given; however, we feel that more experience is needed with real data before major new developments are likely. The interaction between theory and practice under careful scrutiny of good biologists and statisticians (or other critical disciplines) will provide direction for further theory development.

References

Anderson, D. R., and K. P. Burnham. 1976. Population ecology of the mallard: VI. The effect of exploitation on survival. U.S. Fish and Wildlife Service Resource Publication 128.

Anderson, D. R., and K. P. Burnham. 1986. Effect of delayed reporting of band recoveries on survival estimates. Journal of Field Ornithology 51:244-247.

Armitage, P. 1955. Tests for linear trends in proportions and frequencies. Biometrics 11:375-386.

Armitage, P. 1957. Studies in the variability of pock counts. Journal of Hygiene, Cambridge University Press 55:564-581.

Armour, C., K. P. Burnham, and W. S. Platts. 1983. Field methods and statistical analyses for monitoring small salmonid streams. U.S. Fish and Wildlife Service FWS/OBS-83/33.

Arnason, A. N., and K. H. Mills. 1986. The detection of handling mortality and its effects on Jolly-Seber estimates for mark-recapture experiments. Canadian Journal of Fisheries and Aquatic Sciences 44.

Balser, J. P. 1984. Confidence interval estimation and tests for temporary outmigration in tag-recapture studies. Doctoral dissertation. Cornell University, Ithaca, New York.

Bartlett, M. S. 1936. Some notes on insecticide tests in the laboratory and in the field. Journal of the Royal Statistical Society, 1 of 3, Supplement, 185-194.

Bartlett, M. S. 1949. Fitting a straight line when both variables are subject to error. Biometrics 5:207-212.

Bellrose, F. C. 1959. Lead poisoning as a mortality factor in waterfowl populations. Illinois Natural History Survey Bulletin 27:235-288.

Berger, J. O., and R. L. Wolpert. 1984. The likelihood principle. Institute of Mathematical Statistics, Monograph Series 6, Hayward, California.

Berry, K. H., and F. B. Turner. 1986. Spring activities and habits of juvenile desert tortoises, *Gopherus agassizii*, in California. Copeia 1986:1010-1012.

Box, J. F. 1978. R. A. Fisher. The life of a scientist. John Wiley & Sons, New York.

Brownie, C., D. R. Anderson, K. P. Burnham, and D. S. Robson. 1978. Statistical inference from band recovery data – a handbook. U.S. Fish and Wildlife Service Resource Publication 131.

Brownie, C., D. R. Anderson, K. P. Burnham, and D. S. Robson. 1985. Statistical inference from band recovery data – a handbook, 2nd edition. U.S. Fish and Wildlife Service Resource Publication 156.

Brownie, C., J. E. Hines, and J. D. Nichols. 1986. Constant parameter capture-recapture models. Biometrics 42:561-574.

Brownie, C., and K. H. Pollock. 1985. Analysis of multiple capture-recapture data using band-recovery methods. Biometrics 41:411-420.

Brownie, C., and D. S. Robson. 1976. Models allowing for age-dependent survival rates for band-return data. Biometrics 32:305-323.

Brownie, C., and D. S. Robson. 1983. Estimation of time-specific survival rates from tag-resighting samples: a generalization of the Jolly-Seber model. Biometrics 39:437-453.

Buckland, S. T. 1980. A modified analysis of the Jolly-Seber capture-recapture model. Biometrics 36:419-435.

Buckland, S. T. 1984. Monte Carlo confidence intervals. Biometrics 40:811-817.

Buckland, S. T., I. Rowley, and D. A. Williams. 1983. Estimation of survival from repeated sightings of tagged galahs. Journal of Animal Ecology 52:563-573.

Carothers, A. D. 1971. An examination and extension of Leslie's test of equal catchability. Biometrics 27:615-630.

Carothers, A. D. 1973. The effects of unequal catchability on Jolly-Seber estimates. Biometrics 29:79-100.

Clobert, J., J. D. Lebreton, M. Clobert-Gillet, and H. Coquillart. 1985. The estimation of survival in bird populations by recapture or sightings of marked individuals. Pages 197-213 *in* B. J. T. Morgan and P. North, editors. Statistics in ornithology. Springer Verlag, Berlin, West Germany.

Cochran, W. G. 1954. Some methods for strengthening the common χ^2 tests. Biometrics 10:417-451.

Cochran, W. G. 1963. Sampling techniques, 2nd edition. John Wiley & Sons, New York.

Conroy, M. J., and B. K. Williams. 1984. Sensitivity of band reporting-rate estimates to violation of assumptions. The Journal of Wildlife Management 45:789-792.

Cormack, R. M. 1964. Estimates of survival from the sighting of marked animals. Biometrika 51:429-438.

Cormack, R. M. 1968. The statistics of capture-recapture methods. Oceanography and Marine Biology: an Annual Review 6:455-506.

Cormack, R. M. 1972. The logic of capture-recapture estimates. Biometrics 28:337-343.

Cormack, R. M. 1973. Common sense estimates from capture-recapture studies. Pages 225-234 *in* M. S. Bartlett and R. W. Hiorns, editors. The mathematical theory of the dynamics of biological populations. Academic Press, London.

Cormack, R. M. 1979. Models for capture-recapture. Pages 217-255 *in* R. M. Cormack, G. P. Patil, and D. S. Robson, editors. Statistical ecology, volume 5. Sampling biological populations. International Co-operative Publishing House, Fairland, Maryland.

Cormack, R. M. 1981. Loglinear models for capture-recapture experiments on open populations. Pages 217-235 *in* R. W. Hiorns and D. Cooke, editors. The mathematical theory of the dynamics of biological populations. Academic Press, London.

Cox, D. R. 1958. Planning of experiments. John Wiley & Sons, New York.

Cox, D. R. 1961. Tests of separate families of hypotheses. Proceedings Fourth Berkeley Symposium:105-123.

Cox, D. R. 1970. The analysis of binary data. Methuen, London.

Cox, D. R. 1983. Some remarks on overdispersion. Biometrika 70:269-274.

Cramer, F. K., and R. C. Oligher. 1964. Passing fish through hydraulic turbines. Transactions of the American Fisheries Society 93:243-250.

Crosbie, S. F., and B. F. J. Manly. 1985. A new approach for parsimonius modeling of capture-mark-recapture studies. Biometrics 41:385-398.

David, H. A., and M. L. Moeschberger. 1978. The theory of competing risks. Macmillan, New York.

Davidson, R. R., and D. L. Solomon. 1974. Moment-type estimation in the exponential family. Communications in Statistics 3:1101-1108.

Deuel, B. 1985. Experimental lead dosing of northern pintails in California. California Fish and Game 71:125-128.

Dixon, W. J. 1983. BMDP statistical software. University of California Press, Los Angeles.

Draper, N. R., and H. Smith. 1981. Applied regression analysis. John Wiley & Sons, New York.

Edwards, A. W. F. 1972. Likelihood. Cambridge University Press, London.

Finney, D. J. 1971. Probit analysis, 3rd edition. Cambridge University Press, Cambridge, England.

Fisher, R. A. 1922. On the mathematical foundation of theoretical statistics. Philosophical Transactions of the Royal Society of London, Series A: Mathematical and Physical Sciences 222:309-368.

Fisher, R. A. 1925. Theory of statistical estimation. Proceedings of the Cambridge Philosophical Society 22:700-725.

Fisher, R. A. 1949. A biological assay of tuberculins. Biometrics 5:300-316.

Fisher, R. A. 1956. Statistical methods and scientific inference. Hafner, New York.

Fisher, R. A. 1958. Statistical methods for research workers, 12th edition. Hafner, New York.

Fleiss, J. L. 1981. Statistical methods for rates proportions, 2nd edition. John Wiley & Sons, New York.

Fletcher, R. I. 1985. Risk analysis for fish diversion experiments: pumped intake systems. Transactions of the American Fisheries Society 114:652-694.

Gart, J. J. 1985. Approximate tests and interval estimation of the common relative risk in the combination of 2 x 2 tables. Biometrika 72(3):673-677.

Green, P. J. 1984. Iteratively reweighted least squares for maximum likelihood estimation, and some robust and resistant alternatives. Journal of the Royal Statistical Society, Series 8 46:149-192.

Green, R. H. 1979. Sampling design and statistical methods for environmental biologists. John Wiley & Sons, New York.

Grizzel, J. E., C. F. Starmer, and G. G. Koch. 1969. Analysis of categorial data by linear models. Biometrics 25:489-504.

Hacking, I. 1965. Logic of statistical inference. Cambridge University Press, London.

Hadley, G. 1964. Nonlinear and dynamic programming. Addison-Wesley, Reading, Massachusetts.

Hammersley, J. M. 1953. Capture-recapture analysis. Biometrika 40:265-278.

Healy, M. J. R. 1981. A source of assay heterogeneity. Biometrics 37:834-835.

Hightower, J., and R. J. Gilbert. 1984. Using the Jolly-Seber model to estimate population size, mortality, and recruitment for a reservoir fish population. Transactions of the American Fisheries Society 113:633-641.

Hogg, R. V., and A. T. Craig. 1970. Introduction to mathematical statistics, 3rd edition. Macmillan, New York.

Huber, P. J. 1967. The behavior of maximum likelihood estimates under nonstandard conditions. Proceedings Fifth Berkeley Symposium:221-233.

Hurlbert, S. H. 1984. Pseudoreplication and the design of ecological field experiments. Ecological Monographs 54:187-211.

Huzurbazar, V. S. 1976. Sufficient statistics: selected contributions. Marcel Dekker, New York.

Jennrich, R. I., and R. H. Moore. 1975. Maximum likelihood estimation by means of nonlinear least squares. Pages 57-65 in Proceedings of the statistical computing section, American Statistical Association, Washington, D.C.

Johnson, N. L., and S. Kotz. 1972. Distributions in statistics: continuous multivariate distributions. John Wiley & Sons, New York.

Johnston, J. 1972. Econometric methods, 2nd edition. McGraw-Hill, New York.

Jolly, G. M. 1965. Explicit estimates from capture-recapture data with both death and immigration-stochastic models. Biometrika 52:225-247.

Kalbfleisch, J. D., and R. L. Prentice. 1980. The statistical analysis of failure time data. John Wiley & Sons, New York.

Kale, B. K. 1962. On the solution of likelihood equations by iteration processes: the multiparametric case. Biometrika 49:479-486.

Kempthorne, O., and L. Folks. 1971. Probability, statistics, and data analysis. Iowa State University Press, Ames.

Kendall, M. G., and A. Stuart. 1967. The advanced theory of statistics. Hafner, New York.

Kent, J. T. 1982. Robust properties of likelihood ratio tests. Biometrika 69:19-27.

Lefebvre, L. W., D. L. Otis, and N. R. Holler. 1982. Comparison of open and closed models for cotton rat population estimates. Journal of Wildlife Management 56:156-163.

Lehmann, E. L. 1959. Testing statistical hypotheses. John Wiley & Sons, New York.

Lehmann, E. L. 1983. Theory of point estimation. John Wiley & Sons, New York.

Mangasarian, O. L. 1969. Nonlinear programming. McGraw-Hill, New York.

Manly, B. F. J. 1970. A simulation study of animal population estimation using the capture-recapture method. Journal of Applied Ecology 7:13-39.

Manly, B. F. J. 1971a. A simulation study of Jolly's method for analyzing capture-recapture data. Biometrics 27:415-424.

Manly, B. F. J. 1971b. Estimation of marking effect with capture-recapture sampling. Journal of Applied Ecology 8:181-189.

Manly, B. F. J. 1977. A note on the design of experiments to estimate survival and relative survival. Biometrical Journal 19:687-692.

Manly, B. F. J. 1981. Estimation of absolute and relative survival rates from the recoveries of dead animals. New Zealand Journal of Ecology 4:78-88.

Manly, B. F. J. 1984. Obtaining confidence limits on parameters of the Jolly-Seber model for capture-recapture data. Biometrics 40:749-758.

Manly, B. F. J. 1985. The statistics of natural selection on animal populations. Chapman and Hall, New York.

McCullagh, P., and J. A. Nelder. 1983. Generalized linear models. Chapman and Hall, London.

McCullagh, P., and D. Pregibon. 1985. Discussion comments on the paper by Diaconis and Efron. The Annals of Statistics 13:898-900.

Mood, A. M., and F. A. Graybill. 1963. Introduction to the theory of statistics, 2nd edition. McGraw-Hill, New York.

Mood, A. M., F. A. Graybill, and D. C. Boes. 1974. Introduction to the theory of statistics, 3rd edition. McGraw-Hill, New York.

Moore, D. S. 1984. Measures of lack of fit from tests of the chi-squared type. Journal of Statistical Planning and Inference 10:151-166.

Nelson, L. J., D. R. Anderson, and K. P. Burnham. 1980. The effect of band loss on estimates of annual survivals. Journal of Field Ornithology 51:30-38.

Neter, J., and W. Wasserman. 1974. Applied linear statistical models. Richard D. Irwin, Homewood, Illinois.

Nichols, J. D., J. E. Hines, and K. H. Pollock. 1984. Effects of permanent trap response in capture probability on Jolly-Seber capture-recapture model estimates. The Journal of Wildlife Management 48:289-294.

Nichols, J. D., B. R. Noon, S. L. Stokes, and J. E. Hines. 1981. Remarks on the use of mark-recapture methodology in estimating avian population size. Studies in Avian Biology 6:121-136.

Nichols, J. D., S. L. Stokes, J. E. Hines, and M. J. Conroy. 1982. Additional comments on the assumptions of homogeneous survival rates in modern bird banding estimation models. The Journal of Wildlife Management 46:953-962.

North, P. M., and B. J. T. Morgan. 1979. Modelling heron survival using weather data. Biometrics 35:667-681.

Olson, F. W., R. G. White, and R. H. Hamre, editors. 1985. Symposium on small hydropower and fisheries. American Fisheries Society, Bethesda, Maryland.

Ostle, B. 1963. Statistics in research. Iowa State University Press, Ames.

Otis, D. L., K. P. Burnham, G. C. White, and D. R. Anderson. 1978. Statistical inference from capture data on closed animal populations. Wildlife Monograph 62.

Owen, D. B. 1962. Handbook of statistical tables. Addison-Wesley, Reading, Massachusetts.

Pollock, K. H. 1975. A K-sample tag-recapture model allowing for unequal survival and catchability. Biometrika 62:577-583.

Pollock, K. H. 1981a. Capture-recapture models allowing for age-dependent survival and capture rates. Biometrics 37:521-529.

Pollock, K. H. 1981b. Capture-recapture models: a review of current methods, assumptions, and experimental design. Studies in Avian Biology 6:426-435.

Pollock, K. H. 1982. A capture-recapture design robust to unequal probability of capture. The Journal of Wildlife Management 46:752-757.

Pollock, K. H., J. E. Hines, and J. D. Nichols. 1985. Goodness-of-fit tests for open capture-recapture models. Biometrics 41:399-410.

Pollock, K. H., and R. H. K. Mann. 1983. Use of an age-dependent mark-recapture model in fisheries research. Canadian Journal of Fisheries and Aquatic Sciences 40:1449-1455.

Pollock, K. H., J. D. Nichols, C. Brownie, and J. E. Hines. (In prep.) Statistical inference for capture-recapture experiments.

Pollock, K. H., and D. G. Raveling. 1982. Assumptions of modern band-recovery models, with emphasis on heterogeneous survival rates. The Journal of Wildlife Management 46:88-98.

Popper, K. R. 1959. The logic of scientific discovery. Basic Books, Hutchinson, London.

Rao, C. R. 1973. Linear statistical inference and its applications. John Wiley & Sons, New York.

Ricker, W. E. 1945. Abundance, exploitation, and mortality of the fishes of two lakes. Investigations of Indiana Lakes and Streams 2:345-448.

Ricker, W. E. 1948. Methods of estimating vital statistics of fish populations. Indiana University Publications in Science Series 15.

Ricker, W. E. 1958. Handbook of computations of biological statistics of fish populations. Fisheries Research Board of Canada Bulletin 119.

Ricker, W. E. 1975. Computation and interpretation of biological statistics of fish populations. Fisheries Research Board of Canada Bulletin 191.

Robson, D. S. 1969. Mark-recapture methods of population estimation. Pages 120-140 in N. L. Johnson and H. Smith, Jr., editors. New developments in survey sampling. Wiley Interscience, New York.

Royall, R. M. 1986. Model robust confidence intervals using maximum likelihood estimators. International Statistical Review 54:221-226.

Sandland, R. L., and P. Kirkwood. 1981. Estimation of survival in marked populations with possibly dependent sighting probabilities. Biometrika 68:531-541.

Savage, L. J. 1962. The foundations of statistical inference. Methuen, London.

Schoenemon, D. E., R. Pressely, and C. O. Junge, Jr. 1961. Mortality of downstream migrant salmon at McNary Dam. Transactions of the American Fisheries Society 90:58-72.

Seber, G. A. F. 1962. The multi-sample single recapture census. Biometrika 49:339-350.

Seber, G. A. F. 1965. A note on the multiple-recapture census. Biometrika 52:249-259.

Seber, G. A. F. 1970. Estimating time-specific survival and reporting rates for adult birds from band returns. Biometrika 57:313-318.

Seber, G. A. F. 1982. The estimation of animal abundance and related parameters, 2nd edition. Macmillan, New York.

Seber, G. A. F. 1986. A review of estimating animal abundance. Biometrics 42:267-292.

Semple, J. R. 1979. Downstream facilities and turbine mortality evaluation, Atlantic salmon smolts at Malay Falls, Nova Scotia. Canadian Fisheries and Marine Service Manuscript Report 1541.

Skalski, J. R. 1985. Construction of cost functions for tag-recapture research. Wildlife Society Bulletin 13:273-283.

Snedecor, G. W., and W. G. Cochran. 1980. Statistical methods. Iowa State University Press, Ames.

Sprott, D. A. 1982. Robustness and maximum likelihood estimation. Communications in Statistics-Theory and Methods 11:2513-2529.

Steel, R. G. D., and J. H. Torrie. 1980. Principles and procedures of statistics: a biometrical approach, 2nd edition. McGraw-Hill, New York.

Stewart-Oaten, A., W. W. Murdoch, and K. R. Parker. 1986. Environmental impact assessment: "pseudoreplication" in time? Ecology 67:929-940.

Stier, D. J., and B. Kynard. 1986. Use of radio telemetry to determine the mortality of Atlantic salmon smolts passed through a 17-MW Kaplan Turbine at a low-head hydroelectric dam. Transactions of the American Fisheries Society 115:771-775.

Stokes, S. L. 1984. The Jolly-Seber method applied to age-stratified populations. The Journal of Wildlife Management 48:1053-1059. (Corrigendum: 1985. The Journal of Wildlife Management 49:282.)

Stromborg, K. L., C. E. Grue, J. D. Nichols, G. R. Hepp, J. E. Hines, and H. C. Borne. In press. Postfledging survival of nestling European starlings exposed to an organophosphate insecticide: a field experiment. Ecology.

Vaupel, J. W., and A. I. Yashin. 1985. Heterogeneity's ruses: some surprising effects of selection on population dynamics. American Statistician 39:176-185.

Wald, A. 1940. The fitting of straight lines if both variables are subject to error. Annals of Mathematical Statistics 11:284-300.

White, G. C. 1983. Numerical estimation of survival rates from band-recovery and biotelemetry data. The Journal of Wildlife Management 47:716-728.

White, G. C., D. R. Anderson, K. P. Burnham, and D. L. Otis. 1982. Capture-recapture and removal methods for sampling closed populations. Los Alamos National Laboratory, LA-8787-NERP, Los Alamos, New Mexico.

Wilks, S. S. 1962. Mathematical statistics. John Wiley & Sons, New York.

Williams, D. A. 1982. Extra-binomial variation in logistic linear models. Applied Statistics 31:144-148.

Wonnacott, R. J., and T. H. Wonnacott. 1970. Econometrics. John Wiley & Sons, New York.

Youngs, W. D., and D. S. Robson. 1975. Estimating survival rate from tag returns: model tests and sample size determination. Journal of the Fisheries Research Board of Canada 32:2365-2371.

Unpublished Reports

Anonymous. 1980. An evaluation of the effectiveness of water spilling for passage of juvenile salmon at Wanapum Dam. Report to Public Utility Districts of Grant, Douglas, and Chelan counties, Washington.

Burnham, K. P. 1987. A unified approach to animal release-resampling studies of survival processes and population estimation. North Carolina State University, Institute of Statistics, Mimeograph Series 1698, Raleigh.

Heinle, D. H., and F. W. Olson. 1981. Survival of juvenile coho salmon passing through the spillway at Rocky Reach Dam. Chelan County (Washington) Public Utility District, Report S13752.AO.

Long, C. W., F. J. Ossiander, T. E. Ruehle, and G. M. Matthews. 1975. Survival of coho salmon fingerlings passing through operating turbines with and without perforated bulkheads and of steelhead trout fingerlings passing through spillways with and without a flow deflector. Final report to U.S. Army Corps of Engineers from Northwest Fisheries Center, National Marine Fisheries Service, Seattle, Washington.

McKenzie, D., D. Carlile, and D. Weitkamp. 1984. 1983 Systems mortality study. Report to Public Utility Districts of Grant, Douglas, and Chelan counties, Washington.

McKenzie, D., D. Weitkamp, T. Schadt, D. Carlile, and D. Chapman. 1984. 1982 Systems mortality study. Report to Public Utility Districts of Grant, Douglas, and Chelan counties, Washington.

Olson, F. W. 1982. Rock Island Dam fingerling bypass evaluation. Chelan County (Washington) Public Utility District, Report S14734.AO.

Olson, F. W. 1983. Rock Island Dam fish bypass study. Chelan County (Washington) Public Utility District, Report S15931.AO.

Olson, F. W., and V. W. Kaczynski. 1980. Survival of downstream migrant coho salmon and steelhead trout through bulb turbines. Chelan County (Washington) Public Utility District, Report S12509.

Prentice, E. F., and D. L. Park. 1984. A study to determine the biological feasibility of a new fish tagging system. Annual report of research, Bonneville Power Administration, U.S. Department of Energy, Portland, Oregon and Coastal Zone and Estuarine Studies Division, Northwest and Alaska Fisheries Center, National Marine Fisheries Service, Seattle, Washington.

Prentice, E. F., C. W. Sims, and D. L. Park. 1985. A study to determine the biological feasibility of a new fish tagging system. Annual report of research, Bonneville Power Administration, U.S. Department of Energy, Portland, Oregon and Coastal Zone and Estuarine Studies Division, Northwest and Alaska Fisheries Center, National Marine Fisheries Service, National Oceanic and Atmospheric Administration, Seattle, Washington.

Robson, D. S., and W. D. Youngs. 1971. Statistical analysis of reported tag-recaptures in the harvest from an exploited population. Cornell University Biometrics Unit, BU-369-M, Ithaca, New York.

Turbak, S. C., D. R. Reichle, and C. R. Shriner. 1981. Analysis of environmental issues related to small scale hydroelectric development: fish mortality resulting from turbine passage. Oak Ridge National Laboratories, Environmental Science Division, Publication 1597, Oak Ridge, Tennessee.

Turner, F. B., and K. H. Berry. 1986. Population ecology of the desert tortoise at Goffs, California, in 1985. University of California Laboratory of Biomedical and Environmental Sciences, Report 12-1544, Los Angeles.

Acknowledgments

The research leading to this monograph and the substantial publication costs were supported by Public Utility District Number 1 of Chelan County, Wenatchee, Washington. We are grateful for the unique opportunity to explore this subject matter. In particular, we thank S. D. Smart and R. A. Nason of the Public Utility District for their assistance.

Comprehensive reviews of early drafts of the monograph were provided by S. T. Buckland and D. L. Otis. Review comments on various parts of the developing manuscript were received from W. J. Ebel, D. H. McKenzie, J. D. Nichols, P. J. Rago, C. Schwarz, J. R. Skalski, J. W. Wilson, and W. D. Youngs. We thank these individuals for their competent help.

A. N. Arnason, L. L. McDonald, and M. G. Southward provided the formal technical review for the American Fisheries Society. Their suggestions allowed the quality of the manuscript to be much improved. P. H. Eschmeyer made detailed editorial suggestions that improved the clarity and readability of the text. Our special thanks go to B. A. Knopf, who assisted in the preparation of the many drafts of the manuscript, provided editorial expertise, and produced the final camera-ready copy. Her efforts are most appreciated.

F. C. Bellrose, K. H. Berry, B. J. Deuel, J. D. Nichols, A. W. Stokes, and F. B. Turner allowed their data to be used as examples in Part 7. We thank them for this favor. We received technical help from many people. In particular, we acknowledge the assistance of S. P. Gloss, B. E. Kanard, and J. R. Skalski.

B. D. Hannu, B. A. Klein, M. M. Sessler, and P. J. Turner aided in the preparation of the manuscript and related correspondence. E. P. Bergersen allowed access to his computing system and E. A. Rexstad provided computer expertise.

Glossary

Throughout this monograph, we have tried to simplify our notation to the extent feasible by using a few basic symbols in conjunction with several levels of subscripts. An understanding of the general scheme should thus facilitate comprehension of all the specific notation used. The notation is consistent with any statistical modeling needs in capture-recapture and release-resampling of animals. It is often defined in the context of experiments with fish, turbines, dams, etc.; however, the reader will surely recognize more general applications.

Primary Symbols for Statistics

These symbols are subscripted to denote the following factors: treatment-control, release location, recapture location, and subcohort − i.e., capture history.

m, z	Numbers of recaptured fish with reference to a particular sampling site or occasion.
r	Total number of fish ever recaptured from a given release, R.
R	A known number of released fish.
T	A "block total" of the matrix of recaptures, $m + z$.

Primary Symbols for Parameters

The first three symbols are generally subscripted.

ϕ	A survival rate over some reach of river, conditional on fish being alive at the start of the reach.
p	A conditional probability of an animal being captured at a specified site (or on an occasion). This parameter is conditional on the fish arriving alive at that site.
q	$1 - p$, conditional probability of not being captured at a specified site.
S	Treatment effect between the point of release of treatment fish above a turbine at dam 1 and downstream dam 2. A common definition is $S = \phi_{t1}/\phi_{c1}$. If all the turbine mortality is direct and acute, mortality $= 1 - S$, and $S =$ the probability of a fish surviving turbine passage (or passage through a bypass system, spillway, etc.). In many applications, S is a probability, but this is not necessary in other applications.

Symbols Used as Subscripts

v A treatment level. In particular, $v = t$ or c is often used; for example R_{t1} is the number of treatment fish released at dam 1.

t, c Treatment and control fish, respectively, when only those two cohorts are released at dam 1; e.g., R_{t1} and R_{c1} or r_{t1} and r_{c1}.

i, j Release and recapture locations, respectively; $i < j$. For example, m_{cij}, where m_{cij} is the number of control fish first recaptured at location j from the numbers R_{ci} released at location i.

.   The dot notation replaces a subscript to denote summation (i.e., pooling) of a statistic over the range of values of that index (e.g., the total number of released fish, pooled over all treatment and control groups, is $R_{\cdot i} = \sum_{v} R_{vi}$). When used with a parameter, the dot notation means that the parameter does not depend on the subscript value. For example, $\phi_{\cdot 1}$ means $\phi_{c1} = \phi_{t1}$ ($= \phi_{\cdot 1} = \phi_1$); in this example, the v subscript would be dropped and ϕ_1 would be written to show that the parameters are equal.

h A capture history – for example, R_{cih} and m_{cijh} are components of R_{ci} and m_{cij}. This level of partitioning the data is used for testing of assumptions. Note that when one considers releases at site i having a capture history h, the h depends only on captures that have occurred (or not occurred) at sites 1 to i. We avoid using notation such as $h(i)$ by specifying that a capture history makes sense only with respect to releases at a specific capture site (or time) i.

Miscellaneous Symbols

k Number of sampling locations. In the current context, release site 1 is the hydroelectric dam at which turbine survival is to be estimated.

H A hypothesis of interest concerning survival and capture parameters. Specific sampling models for the data arise when one combines a hypothesis about parameters with a particular sampling protocol. Sampling models and hypotheses, such as $H_{1\phi}$, are not equivalent constructs.

Specific Notation

Meanings of the subscripts used here are explained in the previous section. The range of the subscript v includes "." (e.g., $v = t$, c, or "."). In general, $v = 1, ..., V$. Note: recapture always means the first recapture after a (known) release.

R_{vi} The number of fish of treatment group v released at dam i.

R_{vih} The number of fish of treatment group v released at dam i that have a particular capture history h at the time of release.

r_{vi} The number of specific fish ever recaptured from the R_{vi} fish released at dam i, treatment v ($r_{vi} = m_{vi,i+1} + \cdots + m_{vik}$).

r_{vih} The number of specific fish that had capture history h at the time of release at site i and were ever recaptured; these fish were part of the R_{vih} released at site i.

m_{vj} The total number of fish of treatment group v recaptured at dam j; $m_{vj} = m_{v1j} + m_{v2j} + \cdots + m_{v,j-1,j}$.

m_{vij} The number of fish of treatment group v recaptured at dam j from the cohort of R_{vi} fish released at dam i, $i < j$.

m_{vijh} The number of fish of treatment group v recaptured at dam j that had capture history h at the time they were released at dam i (as part of R_{vih}).

z_{vj} The total number of fish of treatment group v released before dam j, that were not recaptured at dam j but were recaptured after dam j; hence, fish recaptured at dams $j+1, ..., k$.

T_{vi} The total number of recaptures for treatment group v at all recapture sites i, $i + 1, ..., k$ from all releases upstream from site i; $T_{vi} = m_{vi} + z_{vi}$.

X_{vh} The number of fish of treatment group v having capture history h after occasion k. This symbol is used only with complete capture histories; hence, this notation provides a succinct record of the data.

M_{vj} The number (unknown) of marked fish from treatment group v that reach recapture dam j alive.

ϕ_{vi} The survival probability between release site i and recapture site $i + 1$ for fish in treatment group v. When the subscript v is present, it is assumed that this survival may depend on treatment group.

ϕ_i The survival probability between release and recapture site i and site $i + 1$ when this survival is the same for all treatment groups; hence, $\phi_i \equiv \phi_{\cdot i}$.

p_{vi} The capture probability at site i for fish in treatment group v that reach the site alive.

p_i The capture probability at site i when it is the same for all treatment groups, hence, $p_i \equiv p_{\cdot i}$.

λ_i The probability that a fish released at dam i will be recaptured; thus, $E(r_i \mid R_i) = R_i \lambda_i$.

$\lambda_i = \phi_i (p_{i+1} + q_{i+1}\lambda_{i+1}), \quad i = 1, ..., k - 1$
$\lambda_k \equiv 0$
$\lambda_i = E(r_i/R_i)$

τ_i The expected proportion of fish captured at dam i of those released prior and recaptured after dam i.

$$\tau_i = E(m_i/T_i)$$

Specific Terms

CH matrix   A presentation of the entire study results as a list of capture histories that occurred and the corresponding numbers of captures, by treatment group, having that capture history. The form for one line is $\{h\}$ X_{1h}, ..., X_{vh}. Losses on capture are denoted by having the X_{vh} signed negative, a convenient way to enter data for computer analysis.

full m-array   The representation of a complete data set for a given treatment group in terms of the releases R_{vih} and recaptures m_{vijh}; thus, releases and recaptures are shown for all subcohorts.

m-array   By convention, m-array means the "reduced" m-array; the data, for a given treatment, are summarized by cohort in terms of releases R_{vi} and recaptures m_{vij}.

cohort   A known number of fish all released at a given site, which may be defined further by treatment group.

subcohort   A subset of a cohort as defined, e.g., by capture history. Usually the survival and capture parameters are expected to be the same in all subcohorts of a cohort; the value of recognizing subcohorts is in testing this assumption.

lot   A batch of treatment and control fish that are all released at (almost) the same time and place, and that were processed together through the pre-release marking and holding activities. Typically, a lot is homogeneous prior to random assignment to treatment group.

sublot   Any identifiable fraction of a lot based on unique tagging information.

Mathematical Symbols

$\ln(\ )$ Natural logarithm (base 2.714).

!   Factorial (e.g., $5! = 5 \times 4 \times 3 \times 2 \times 1$).

Σ Summation operator; e.g., $\sum_{i=1}^{4} i = 1 + 2 + 3 + 4 = 10$.

Π Product operator; e.g., $\prod_{i=1}^{6} i = 1 \times 2 \times 3 \times 4 \times 5 \times 6 = 720$.

$\int$ Integral.

$\underline{x}$ Vector notation; i.e., $\underline{x}' = [x_1, x_2, ..., x_n]$.

~   Approximately equal to.

exp   Exponential, e.g., $\exp(a) = e^a$.

$\dfrac{\partial L}{\partial p_2}$ Partial derivative of the likelihood function with respect to the parameter p_2.

$\mathrm{bin}(n, \pi)$ Denotes the binomial probability distribution based on sample size n and probability parameter π.

$\binom{a}{b}$ Binomial coefficient $= \left(\dfrac{a!}{b!(a-b)!}\right)$; e.g., $\binom{10}{4} = \dfrac{10!}{4!6!} = 210$.

$\begin{pmatrix} a \\ b\ c\ d\ e \end{pmatrix}$ Multinomial coefficient $= \left(\dfrac{a!}{b!c!d!e!}\right)$; requires $b+c+d+e = a$.

Statistical Symbols

$\Pr\{\ \}$ Probability.

$\wedge$ A hat above a symbol denotes an estimate or estimator.

θ A generic parameter; used to denote some unspecified parameter (θ) or its estimator ($\hat{\theta}$), or a vector of parameters ($\underline{\theta}$).

$\overline{x}$ A bar over a symbol represents a sample mean.

$E(\hat{\theta})$ Expected value of the estimator $\hat{\theta}$.

$L(\ )$ Likelihood function.

$\ln L(\ )$ Log-likelihood function.

$I(\underline{\theta})$ Information matrix, i.e., matrix of expectations of the mixed partial derivatives of the log-likelihood with respect to the parameters.

π Cell probability; here a function of the survival and capture probabilities.

Measures of Variability and Covariability

σ^2 Population variance.

σ Population standard deviation; $\hat{\sigma}$ is an estimator of the population standard deviation.

$\mathrm{var}(\hat{\theta})$ Sampling variance of an estimator $\hat{\theta}$, often written as shorthand for $\mathrm{var}(\hat{\theta}\mid\theta)$, the sampling variance of $\hat{\theta}$, given the parameter θ.

$\mathrm{se}(\hat{\theta})$	Standard error of an estimator $\hat{\theta}$, $\mathrm{se}(\hat{\theta}) = \sqrt{\mathrm{var}\,(\hat{\theta})}$. Often only an estimator of this quantity is available, $\hat{\mathrm{se}}\,(\hat{\theta})$.
$\mathrm{se}(\hat{S})_t$	Theoretical (model-based) standard error of $\hat{S}$ (used only in Part 5).
$\mathrm{se}(\hat{S})_e$	Empirical standard error based on Monte Carlo replicates (used only in Part 5).
$\mathrm{cov}(\hat{\phi}, \hat{p})$	Sampling covariance between the estimators $\hat{\phi}$ and $\hat{p}$.
$\mathrm{corr}(\hat{\phi}, \hat{p})$	Sampling correlation between the estimators $\hat{\phi}$ and $\hat{p}$.
Σ	Matrix of sampling variances and covariances of estimators.
CI	Confidence interval.
$\mathrm{cv}(\hat{\theta})$	Coefficient of variation, often called "proportional standard error," but expressed as a percentage: $[100\,\mathrm{se}(\hat{\theta})] / \hat{\theta}$.

Hypotheses

H_0	The null hypothesis.
H_A	The alternative hypothesis.

Test Statistics and Related Values

t	A test statistic following Student's t distribution under the null hypothesis.
z	A test statistic distributed normally with $\mu = 0$ and $\sigma = 1$ under the null hypothesis.
χ_n^2	A test statistic distributed as chi-square with n degrees of freedom under the null hypothesis.
df	Degrees of freedom.

Less-Used Notation

d	The number of fish lost on capture; e.g., d_{cj} is the number of control fish lost on capture at dam j.
p	The probability of getting heads when flipping a coin, used in Chapter 1.2. This is not to be confused with capture probability, which appears with subscripts.
w_i	A weight. When normalized, the weights sum to 1.
$h_v(x)$	Instantaneous mortality rate, as a function of location, by treatment group $v = t$ or c (used only in Chapter 1.5).

$\Delta(x)$ Instantaneous treatment mortality effect, $\Delta(x) = h_t(x) - h_c(x)$ (used only in Chapter 1.5).

$\phi_v(0, d)$ Survival probability for fish in treatment group v from release point to downstream distance d (used only in Chapter 1.5).

$\phi_v(d_1, d_2)$ Survival probability for fish in treatment group v between distances d_1 and d_2 ($d_1 < d_2$); distances are measured from the most upstream release point (used only in Chapter 1.5).

$d*$ The point downstream from dam 1 after which treatment fish show no more residual treatment effect; hence, after point $d*$, treatments and controls have identical responses.   Mathematically, $\phi_c(d*, d) = \phi_t(d*, d)$ for   all $d \geq d*$,   and $\phi_t(d, d*) < \phi_c(d, d*)$ for all $d < d*$ (used only in Chapter 1.5).

Abbreviations

CCH   Complete capture history.

FCH   First capture history.

ML   Maximum likelihood.

MLE   Maximum likelihood estimator.

MSS   Minimal sufficient statistic.

NM   Natural mortality (used only in Chapter 1.5).

PCH   Partial capture history.

PIT   Passive integrated transponder, a new tag technology.

TM   Treatment mortality (used only in Chapter 1.5).

UCH   Unknown capture history.

Technical Terms

Accuracy   Freedom from error or defect: correctness; usually refers to numerical computations.

Bias   (Of an estimator): the difference between the "expected" value of an estimator and the true value of the parameter being estimated. Bias is a measure of how much the average estimate and the true parameter value differ. Bias = $E(\hat{\theta}) - \theta$, where θ is the parameter of interest.

Errors   Type I: rejection of a null hypothesis that is true.
           Type II: acceptance of a null hypothesis that is not true.

Estimate	The calculated value of an estimator, given a particular set of sample data, designated by a hat (^) over the symbol for the parameter being estimated.
Estimator	A function of sample data that is used to estimate some parameter. An estimator is a random variable and is also designated by a hat (^) over the symbol for the parameter.
Induction	Generalization from a single experiment to the inference class of all similar experiments. Reasoning from the particular to the general.
Power	The probability of rejecting a null hypothesis.
Precision	A property of an estimator related to the amount of variation among estimates from repeated samples.
Robustness	Insensitivity of an estimation or testing procedure to the breakdown of a specific assumption on which it is based.
Statistic	A function of the sample data.
Test statistic	A value, to be computed from the experimental data, that will determine the decision concerning a null hypothesis. The distribution of the test statistic is known if the null hypothesis is true.
Variance	Theoretical: a variance derived from the particular assumed model by using the ML method. All the models used here are based on the assumption of multinomial sampling variation.

Empirical: A variance that is based on some type of replication and is therefore free from specific probability distribution assumptions. If n lots are available, n point estimates of a parameter are available, $\hat{\theta}_1, \hat{\theta}_2, ..., \hat{\theta}_n$. The simplest empirical variance is then $\hat{var}\,(\hat{\theta}) = \dfrac{1}{n-1} \sum_{i=1}^{n} (\hat{\theta}_i - \bar{\hat{\theta}})^2$.

Index

Alpine swifts (*Apus melba*) viii
ASSUMPTIONS 51-55; 127; 297-299

BANDING viii; 3; 201
Batch mark 3; 37; 41
Beta probability density function 393
BIAS
  adjusted estimators 207-211; 222; 281-284
  concepts of 222
    model 207-208
    statistical 207
  definition 281
Binomial distribution 7-11
Bluegill (*Lepomis macrochirus*) 23
BMDPLR computer program, *see* STATISTICAL METHODOLOGY
Bunting, Lazuli (*Passerina amoena*) 348

CAPTURE
  losses on 27; 99; 217-218
  probability 10; 48
CAPTURE HISTORY
  complete 34-35; 39; 112-146; 173-174; 300-301
  first 37-38; 78-99; 173; 200; 221-222; 301
  partial 39-42; 146-173; 198; 301
  unknown 38; 100-111; 173; 221; 225; 301
Cochran-Armitage test 375
Competing risk theory 57-59
Confidence interval 85; 292

Desert tortoise (*Gopherus agassizi*) 361
DISTRIBUTIONS
  beta 401-402; 405
  binomial 143-144
  chi-square 17; 19; 197; 215-216; 264; 266
  joint probability (Pr) 6
  multinomial 6; 17; 49; 174